**Clergy of the Church of England 1835**

**Part Two: G to O**

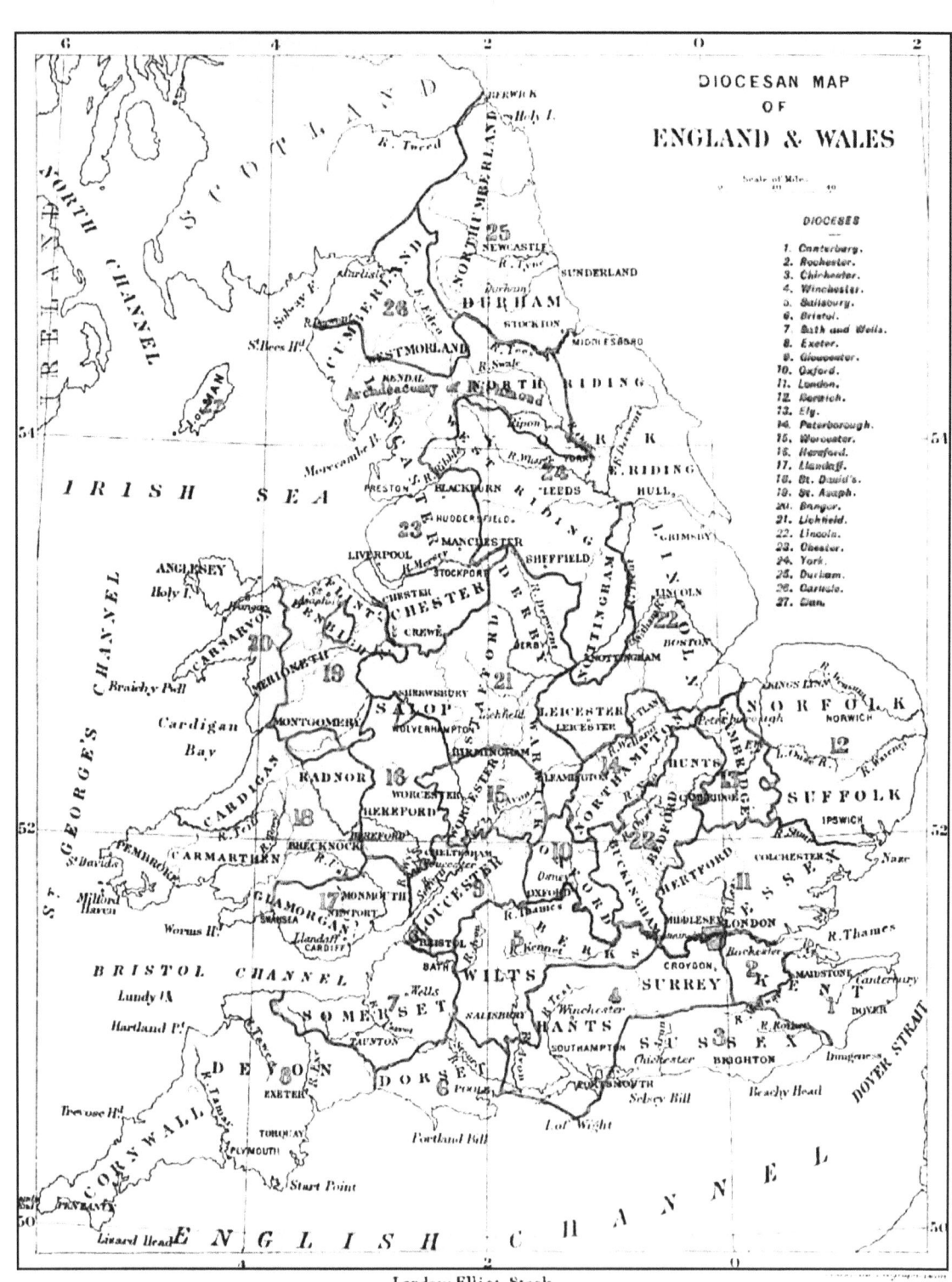

Map showing the Dioceses of England (and Wales) in 1835

# CLERGY OF THE CHURCH OF ENGLAND

## 1835

A Biographical Directory

Part Two: G to O

Compiled by Peter Bell

Published 2021 by Peter Bell

68 West Port, Edinburgh EH1 2LD

Scotland, UK

portsburghpress@gmail.com

0131-556-2198

ISBN (Part One):   978-1-871538-13-7

ISBN (Part Two):   978-1-871538-14-4

ISBN (Part Three): 978-1-871538-15-1

The right of Peter Bell to be identified as the compiler of this work has been asserted by him in accordance with the Copyrights, Designs & Patents Act 1988

Book production assistance by
Pixel Tweaks Publications
SELF PUBLISHING MADE SIMPLE
www.pixeltweakspublications.com

Cover: Walter Farquhar Hook
Public Domain image licensed under CC-PD-Mark

# FOREWORD

Ten years ago I purchased a copy of the massive Report of the Ecclesiastical Revenues Commission, published in May 1835, with its detailed statistical information of every parish in England and Wales for the three years ending 1833. Among that information was a column listing the holder of every benefice in England and Wales, albeit abbreviated (e.g. T. Jones). Having made a list of these names, I decided that a biographical directory could be made from it, one in which both the professional and the personal lives of each cleric could be combined to their mutual benefit, along the lines of Venn's Alumni Cantabrigienses. If I had known what I was letting myself in for, I would probably never have begun!

The resulting Directory has been made possible only because of the existence of the Clergy of the Church of England Database, 1540-1835, a vast online database (abbreviated here as CCEd, or C followed by each cleric's unique identifying number). Compiled locally by record offices throughout England and Wales (but only England here), and not yet complete, the resulting information varies depending on what records survive. Details usually include university degrees, exact dates of ordination, and exact dates of the curacies, benefices and other appointments held by each man until c.1835; although the great problem of what Wikipedia calls disambiguation - the mixing of two or more men of exactly the same name - remains unresolved in too many cases.

For further information it is necessary to turn to existing sources, both printed and electronic, some printed and familiar (such as the registers for Oxford and Cambridge Universities, at a time when eighty percent of the clergy were graduates of those two places), but also to a number of less familiar titles as listed here under Existing Published Sources with Biographical Material, in which some biographical work has already been done by others, usually in a specific diocese.

Regarding the online resources, especially Ancestry.co.uk, all of these must be used with great caution. If used last of all they can often provide additional or expanded personal information, especially (it would seem) of wives and children. Few men warrant a Wikipedia entry, although each man has been checked online for any relevant information whatsoever. Contradictions occur frequently, and these have been noted only if currently unresolvable. New online information appears regularly (and some, especially online links, disappear), reminding us that biographical information is always in a state of change and incompleteness. This is why this is essentially a work in progress, and a first draft which I hope people will feel free to correct and add to where necessary (using the email link below).

A very specific source which must be noted is in the University of Durham's Special Collections Library in Palace Green, namely the Hudleston Index, consisting of thousands of hand-written index cards covering the Northern Province only. I now realise that so much of the information here about the Northern clergy (recorded ten years ago) comes from that source alone.

Special mention must also be made of the two volumes of York Clergy Ordinations for 1750-1799 and 1800-1849 respectively, which include ordination details of every man ordained in the (large) Archdiocese of York between 1750 and 1849. This is a model which should be adopted by every diocese, and would enable the missing dates, places of birth, and parentage to be filled in.

Writing this book on and off over a decade has, rather strangely, involved only a few people, but each of them important. Professor Arthur Burns, the director of the CCEd project responsible for this period of the long Eighteenth Century, allowed me at an early stage to access unpublished CCEd material, for which I am most grateful. With Emeritus Professor Ted Royle of York University I learnt enormous amounts about the workings of the Church of England in this period, for which I am again extremely grateful. My sister Judith has rescued me from computer problems and losses, and has proofed the whole work. Finally, my dear MaryCatherine Burgess has endured ten years of clerical trivia and monologue (which probably makes her a not inconsiderable authority on the men here).

**Peter Bell**

# EDITORIAL METHOD & METHODOLOGY

The following model entry, accompanied by an interpretation, is rarely followed completely, as some vital information is invariably missing for most clergy. Many are anonymous, even after 200 years, and only persistent work (especially by a descendant) can produce fuller results.

> **HADEN** (Alexander Bunn) Bapt. Wednesbury, Staffs. 25/3/1783, | s. Rev. Alexander Bunn Haden, sen., and Mary Rotten. | St Edmund Hall, Oxford 1806, BA1810, dn10 (C&L), p11 (C&L), MA1813. | PC. Woore, Shropshire 1811-19 (res.), V. Brewood, Staffs. 1830 to death 16/8/1863, | leaving £1,000 | [C11358] | Married (1) Chetton, Shropshire 7/2/1826 Marianne Heptinstall (d.1850, 1st q.) (2) London 27/4/1859 Mary Ward (w). |

> **HADEN** (Alexander Bunn) Baptised Wednesbury, Staffordshire 25/3/1783, son of Reverend Alexander Bunn Haden, senior, and Mary Rotten. St. Edmund Hall, Oxford University 1806, Bachelor of Arts 1810, deacon 1810 (Coventry & Lichfield Diocese), priest 1811 (Coventry & Lichfield Diocese), Master of Arts 1813. Priest-in-Charge of Woore, Shropshire 1811-19 (resigned), Vicar of Brewood, Staffordshire 1830 to death 16/8/1863, leaving under £1,000 [Clergy of the Church of England Database 11358] Married (1) at Chetton, Shropshire 7/2/1826 Marianne Heptinstall (died 1850, 1st quarter) (2) in London 27/4/1859 Mary Ward (his widow). |

**Names**. In this example the father and son are identically named, an immediate cause of confusion. The father here was married twice, and this is his first wife. Mothers' names are often elusive, and often appear by their first name only, usually in the Census returns. The very many changes of surname are not normally noted here, although some doubled-barrelled names, and the many aristocratic titles, are usually cross-referenced. Future corrections should include a son's order in the male line (i.e. 2nd son). People with common surnames (not only Smith and Jones, but also Dixon, Carter, Wilkinson, &c.) when combined with identical forenames are a nightmare, and sometimes cannot be differentiated after 200 years.

**Birth and Baptism**. Not always differentiated in many original records, although attempted here. Baptism dates are recorded in the original ordination papers, and are given preference here if noted in CCEd. Saying that someone was, say, 60 at death in 1860, does not automatically make him born 1800, as birth and baptism dates could vary. Also the place of birth and/or baptism may not automatically be the parents' place of residence. Place names have been modernised wherever possible, though the original Report has some wild spellings and some joining of parishes which are not helpful in identifying them today.

**Schools** are not noted – something which should be rectified at a later date. Suffice it to say that the numbers at the 'Great Public Schools', especially Eton and Westminster, were high, especially among the clerical elite.

**University**. At this date, the vast majority of clergy were graduates of Oxford and (especially) Cambridge, as recorded in Foster and Venn respectively. Note that Foster gives the date of matriculation to the University; while Venn gives dates of admission to a particular college; matriculation at Cambridge was separate and is not noted here, but does account for children of 12 or 13 entering the university. Degrees did not have to be formally taken to make a man a university graduate, only matriculation. 'Ten Year Men' at Cambridge were extra-mural men, matriculating annually for 10 years, after which they could claim to be MA (Cantab.). Note that Foster described Doctors of Divinity as 'doctors', who are not Doctors of Medicine (who were MDs - as some were). Note also the number of men with legal degrees, or who were law students or actual lawyers of some sort before ordination. Non-graduates, known as literates (or 'literate persons'), were ordained at the discretion of the ordaining bishop.

**Ordination**. Deacons could only be ordained at the age of 23; priests at 24; and the vast proportion of men seem to have been ordained at this age, straight out of university. Bishops had to be 30 or more (and only George Murray, q.v., had a problem with this!).

**Careers**. Here I have followed a combination of CCEd and existing printed sources to ascertain the parishes in which a man was rector, vicar, or perpetual curate. (The Report also includes a number of 'miscellaneous' men who by rights should not really be there). Assistant or Stipendiary curacies are not noted (but are in CCEd), and information after 1835 (the cut-off date for CCEd) must be pieced together from all available sources, including early editions of The Clergy List (from 1840) and Crockford's (first useable edition 1860). The whereabouts of a man ordained and dying between 1835 to 1860 is the most difficult of all to track down.

**Date of death.** This is usually available, often from FreeBMD (Free Births, Marriages and Deaths) online; or alternatively that of burial, which is differentiated. Age at death is quoted when specifically given, and is not estimated from date of birth.

**Wealth at death.** This is available after January 1868 from the photographed printed records on Ancestry, and, as a printed legal document, is the most reliable of all documents. It gives all sums left at death as 'under' - which can be assumed here whenever a round figure is given. Many men did not leave a will at all; bishops can be found under their title, e.g. Samuel Winchester for Samuel Wilberforce, Bishop of Winchester.

**Marriage**. Marriages are included where known, and the absence of a wife here does not mean that a person was never married. Wives who had previously been married are designated Mrs., with their birth surname in brackets, whereas (w) – widow – indicates that a wife outlived her husband. Numbers of children vary with the original sources, which may or may not include those dying in infancy. Numbers of surviving children tend to be more reliable.

**References**. These are in square brackets. The CCEd is the unique reference number given to each individual in the Clergy of the Church of England Database 1540-1835, which is free to search. It can be assumed that Foster and Venn have been checked for every graduate clergyman - but the result, especially for a 'literate person', can be disappointing, or, in a few cases, almost non-existent.

**Notes**. Any miscellaneous information is included here, much of it trivial, but it may help to enliven what are often repetitive entries.

# LIST OF ABBREVIATIONS

| | |
|---|---|
| Abp. | Archbishop |
| b. | born |
| BA | Bachelor of Arts |
| BCL | Bachelor of Civil Law |
| BD | Bachelor of Divinity |
| Bapt. | baptised |
| Bp. | Bishop |
| C. | Curate |
| Cam. | Cambridge |
| CCEd/C | Clergy of the Church of England Database 1540-1835 |
| Chap. | Chaplain |
| d. | died |
| dau. | daughter |
| DCL | Doctor of Civil Law |
| DD | Doctor of Divinity |
| D.L. | Deputy Lieutenant [of a county] |
| Dom. Chap. | Domestic Chaplain |
| Don. Chap. | Donative Chaplain [of a church outside the jurisdiction of the diocesan bishop] |
| dn. | deacon |
| *d.s.p.* | died without issue (*decessit sine prole*) |
| ERC | Ecclesiastical Revenues Commission [Report, 1835] |
| FreeBMD | Free Births Marriages and Deaths [online resource] |
| G/S | Grammar School |
| HEIC | [Honourable] East India Company |
| H/M | headmaster |
| Hon. | The Honourable/honorary |
| J.P. | Justice of the Peace |
| Lect. | lecturer |
| LLD | Doctor of Laws |
| LNCP | Library of Nineteenth Century Photographs [Online resource with many clergy] |
| MA | Master of Arts |
| Min. | Minister |
| M.P. | Member of Parliament |
| non-res. | non-resident [only when specified] |
| NPC | National Probate Calendar [from Jan. 1858] |
| ODNB | Oxford Dictionary of National Biography |
| Ox. | Oxford |
| p. | priest |
| PC. | Perpetual Curate |
| pop. | population |
| Preb. | Prebendary |
| Prof. | professor |
| q. | quarter [of the year; from FreeBMD] |
| R. | Rector |
| (res.) | resigned (only when specified) |
| R.N. | Royal Navy |
| s. | son (of) |
| Sec. | Secretary |
| S/M | schoolmaster |
| *s.p.* | without issue (*sine prole*) |
| Univ. | university |
| V. | Vicar |
| (w) | widow, indicating that she outlived her husband (whereas Mrs. indicates that she was previously married). |

Entries will be found in Foster or Venn for all men at Oxford or Cambridge respectively unless otherwise specified.

| **OXFORD UNIVERSITY COLLEGES & HALLS** | **CAMBRIDGE UNIVERSITY COLLEGES & HALLS** |
|---|---|
| All Souls' | Christ's |
| Balliol | Clare |
| Brasenose | Corpus Christi |
| Christ Church | Downing |
| Corpus Christi | Emmanuel |
| Jesus | Gonville & Caius |
| Lincoln | Jesus |
| Magdalen College | King's |
| Magdalen Hall | Magdalene |
| Merton | Pembroke |
| New College | Peterhouse |
| New Inn Hall | Queens' |
| Oriel | Selwyn |
| Pembroke | Sidney Sussex |
| Queen's [The Queen's] | St Catharine's |
| St Catherine's | St John's |
| St Edmund Hall | Trinity College |
| St John's | Trinity Hall |
| St Mary Hall | |
| Trinity | |
| University | |
| Wadham | |
| Worcester | |

# BISHOPS OF THE CHURCH OF ENGLAND 1835

(appear in the text under their surname)

| | |
|---|---|
| Bath and Wells (B&W) | George Henry Law |
| Bristol (Bristol) | Robert Gray [as Bristol and Gloucester after 1836] |
| Canterbury (Cant.) | William Howley |
| Carlisle (Car.) | Hon. Hugh Percy |
| Chester (Chester) | John Bird Sumner |
| Chichester (Chich.) | Edward Maltby |
| Coventry & Lichfield (C&L) | Hon. Henry Ryder [as Lichfield after 1836] |
| Durham (Dur.) | William Van Mildert |
| Ely (Ely) | Bowyer Edward Sparke |
| Exeter (Ex.) | Henry Phillpotts |
| Gloucester (Glos.) | James Henry Monk [as Gloucester and Bristol after 1836] |
| Hereford (Heref.) | George Isaac Huntingford (to 1832) [Hon. Edward Gray from 1832, not included here] |
| Lincoln (Lin.) | John Kaye |
| London (London) | Charles James Blomfield |
| Norwich (Nor.) | Henry Bathurst |
| Oxford (Ox.) | Richard Bagot |
| Peterborough (Peterb.) | Herbert Marsh |
| Rochester (Roch.) | George Murray |
| Salisbury (Salis.) | Thomas Burgess |
| Sodor and Man (S&M) | William Ward |
| Winchester (Win.) | Charles Richard Sumner |
| Worcester (Wor.) | Robert James Carr |
| York (York) | Hon. Edward Venables-Vernon (then Harcourt) |

The four Welsh bishoprics (excluded from this survey) were:

| | |
|---|---|
| Bangor (Bangor) | Christopher Bethell |
| Llandaff (Llandaff) | Edward Copleston |
| St Asaph (St Asaph) | William Carey |
| St David's (St David's) | John Banks Jenkinson |

# EXISTING PUBLISHED SOURCES WITH BIOGRAPHICAL MATERIAL

| | |
|---|---|
| Al.Dub. | Alumni Dublinenses: a register of students, graduates … in the University of Dublin. Edited by G.D. Burtchaell and T.U. Sadleir. (1924). |
| ATV | Archbishop Thomson's Visitation Returns for the Diocese of York, 1865. Edited Edward Royle & Ruth M. Larsen. (York: Borthwick Institute for Archives, 2006). |
| Austin | The Church in Derbyshire in 1823-4: the parochial visitation of the Rev. Samuel Butler, Archdeacon of Derby, in the Diocese of Lichfield and Coventry. Edited M.R. Austin. (Derbyshire Archaeological Society, 1972). |
| Austin2 | 'A time of unhappy commotion': the Church of England and the people of central Nottinghamshire 1820-1870. (Chesterfield: Merton, 2010). |
| BBV | Bishop Bickersteth's Visitation Returns for the Archdeaconry of Craven, Diocese of Ripon, 1858. Edited Edward Royle. (York: Borthwick Institute for Archives, 2009). |
| Bennett1 | Lincolnshire parish clergy c.1214-1968: a biographical register. Part I: The Deaneries of Aslacoe and Aveland. Compiled by Nicholas Bennett (Lincoln Record Society, 2013). |
| Bennett2 | Lincolnshire parish clergy c.1214-1968: a biographical register. Part II: The Deaniers of Beltisloe and Bolingbroke. Compiled by Nicholas Bennett (Lincoln Record Society, 2016) And many more volumes to come! |
| Bertie | Scottish Episcopal Clergy 1689-2000. By David M. Bertie. (Edinburgh: T & T Clark, 2000). New edition in preparation. |
| Boase | Modern English Biography … of persons who have died between the years 1851-1900 … Compiled by Frederic Boase. (1908. Reprinted London: Cass, 1965). 6 volumes. |
| DEB | The Blackwell Dictionary of Evangelical Biography 1730-1860. Edited Donald M. Lewis. (Oxford, 1995). 2 volumes. |
| Fasti | Fasti Ecclesiae Anglicanae 1541-1857. By Joyce M. Horn [and others]. London, 1969-2014. 13 volumes. [Excludes the Welsh Dioceses] |
| Foster | Alumni Oxonienses: the Members of the University of Oxford, 1715-1886. Compiled by Joseph Foster. (1888-92. Reprinted Bristol: Thoemmes, 2000). 4 volumes. |
| Gelling | A history of the Manx Church (1698-1911). By John Gelling (Douglas, IoM: The Manx Heritage Foundation, 1998). |
| Hodson | Visitations of the Archdeaconry of Stafford 1829-1841. Edited David Robinson (HMSO for Historic Manuscripts Commission, 1980). |
| Kaye | Lincolnshire parish correspondence of John Kaye, Bishop of Lincoln, 1827-53. Edited R.W. Ambler. (Lincoln Record Society, 2006). |
| LFBI | Landed Families of Britain and Ireland. [The very beginnings of an extraordinary project by Ben Kingsley to link country houses and their owners – obviously including many clergy here. Only on letter 'B' at time of writing – unfortunately.] landedfamilies.blogspot.com/ |
| McClatchey | Oxfordshire clergy, 1777-1869 … By Diana McClatchey (Oxford, 1960). |

| | |
|---|---|
| Platt | The Diocese of Carlisle, 1814-1855: Chancellor Walter Fletcher's Diocesan Book, with additional material from Bishop Percy's notebooks … Edited by Jane Platt (Surtees Society, 2015). |
| Romilly | Romilly's Cambridge diary 1832-42. Edited J.P.T. Bury. (Cambridge, 1967). |
| Romilly2 | Romilly's Cambridge diary 1842-1847. Edited M.E. Bury & J.D. Pickles. (Cambridgeshire Records Society, 1994). |
| Romilly3 | Romilly's Cambridge diary 1848-1864. Edited M.E. Bury & J.D. Pickles. (Cambridgeshire Records Society, 2000). |
| Smart | Biographical Register of the University of St. Andrews 1747-1897. By Robert N. Smart. (St. Andrews University Library, 2004). |
| Snell | The Snell Exhibitions. From the University of Glasgow to Balliol College, Oxford. By W. Innes Addison. (Glasgow: James Maclehose, 1901). |
| Venn | Alumni Cantabrigienses … Part 2 from 1752 to 1900. Compiled by J.A. Venn (1922-54. Reprinted Bristol: Thoemmes, 2001). 6 volumes. |
| Wilberforce | The Diocese Books of Samuel Wilberforce, Bishop of Oxford 1845-1869. Edited Ronald and Margaret Pugh. (Oxfordshire and Berkshire Record Societies, 2008). |
| Wilberforce2 | The letter-books of Samuel Wilberforce, 1843-68. Transcribed and edited by R.K. Pugh. (Buckingham Record Society & Oxfordshire Record Society, 1970). |
| Wilberforce3 | Bishop Wilberforce's Visitation Returns for the Archdeaconry of Oxford in the year 1854 … Edited E.P. Baker. (Oxfordshire Record Society, 1954). |
| YCO | York Clergy Ordinations 1750-1799. Compiled by Debbie Usher (York: Borthwick Institute, 2002) [and] York Clergy Ordinations 1800-1849. Compiled by Sara Slinn (York: Borthwick Institute, 2001). [The latter has a most important Introduction.] |

**Clergy of the Church of England 1835**

**Part Two: G to O**

Parishes underlined (thus) are the ones held in plurality by one clergyman in the early 1830's

**GABERT (George Hilder Betterton)** Bapt. Marylebone, London 15/3/1797, s. Christopher Gabert and Sarah Claridge. Queens', Cambridge 1817, dn20 (Lin.), BA1821, p21 (London for Cant.), MA1826. PC. Claverley, Shropshire 1829 and PC. Bobbington, Shropire 1833 to death 10/6/1867, leaving £4,000 [C32135] Married (1) Marylebone, London 21/3/1814 Mary Wood (d.1849), w. issue (2) Chipperfield, Herts. 21/4/1853 Selina Elizabeth Jupp (w).

**GADSBY (Thomas)** From Beds. Corpus Christi, Cambridge 1777, BA1781, dn82 (Ely for Lin.), MA1784, p85 (Lin.). V. Wootton, Beds. 1785 to death (Bedford) 3/5/1840 aged 81 [C60786]

**GAGE (Thomas Wentworth)** From Binderton, Surrey, s. John Gage and Mary Milbanke. Christ Church, Oxford 1818 (aged 18), then Magdalene, Cambridge 1819, BA1824, dn24 (Lin.), p27 (Lin.), MA1827. PC. North Hykeham, Lincs. 1825 and V. Higham Ferrers, Northants. 1830 to death 19/3/1837 [C60789] Married Fareham, Hants. 17/2/1841 Lady Mary Elizabeth Douglas (dau. of 6th Marquess of Queensbury, *q.v.* LNCP) (w), 2s., 2 dau.

**GAISFORD (Charles)** Born Iford Manor, Wilts., s. John Gaisford and Elizabeth Bushell (a clergy dau.). Caius, Cambridge 1801, BA1805, dn05 (Salis. for Cant.), p06 (Cant.), MA1809. R. Chilton, Berks. 1808 to death 1/8/1857 [C22840] Brother, below.

**GAISFORD (Thomas)** Born Iford Manor, Wilts. 22/12/1779, s. John Gaisford and Elizabeth Bushell (a clergy dau.). Christ Church, Oxford 1797, Student [Fellow] 1800-16, BA 1801, MA1804, dn09 (Ox.). p10 (Ox.), BD and DD1831. Regius Professor of Greek, Oxford 1811-35. R. Westwell, Oxon. 1815-47 ('never comes near it'), Prebend of Fairwater in Llandaff Cathedral 1823-65, Prebend of Caddington Major in St Paul's Cathedral, London 1823-55, Canon of 2nd Prebend in Worcester Cathedral 1825-9, 4th Prebend 1829 then Prebend of 11th Canon in Durham Cathedral 1829-31 (res.), Dean of Christ Church Cathedral, Oxford 1831 to death 2/6/1855 [C3937 has wrong death date] Married (1) Oxford 11/5/1815 Helen Margaret Douglas (a clergy dau., d.1830), 5 ch (2) Dinder, Som. Jane Catharine Jenkyns (sister of the Master of Balliol). Brother, above. Photo. online. 'Very inefficient.' (Wilberforce). Good anecdotes at: -www.roger-pearse.com/weblog/2010/03/26/some-notes-on-thomas-gaisford/

**GALE (Henry Procter)** From Combe Florey, Som., s. Rev. John Gale (below?). Wadham, Oxford 1807 (aged 15), BA1812, dn15 (B&W), p16 (B&W). PC. Taunton St James, Som. 1824-41. Died 2/4/1843 [C41065] Married Cheltenham, Glos. 28/4/1819 Sophia Eyre (clergy dau.).

**GALE (John)** From Haydon, Somerset, s. Henry Procter Gale. Wadham, Oxford 1787 (aged 17), LLB1791, dn91 (B&W), p93 (B&W). R. Angersleigh, Som. 1794, R. Cheddon Fitzpaine, Som. 1796-1800, V. Old Cleeve, Som. 1803-1807, PC. Otterford, Som. 1810 and PC. Corfe, Som. 1831 to death 8/8/1842 [C41657] Son above? *J.P.* Somerset.

**GALE (Thomas Hinksman)** From Windsor, Berks., s. John Gale. Exeter, Oxford 1807 (aged 18), BA1810, dn11 (Glos. for Win.), p12 (Win.), MA1819. V. Milton Lilbourne, Wilts. 1812-46, V. Godmersham, Kent 1846 to death 19/1/1864, leaving £18,000 [C73759] Married Andover, Hants. 8/2/1813 Anne Elizabeth Poore, with issue.

**GAMBIER (Frederic)** Bapt. Shenley, Herts. 11/6/1797, s. Admiral Samuel Gambier (of Shenley Hall) and Jane Mathew. Merton, Oxford 1814, BA1818, then All Souls, Fellow 1818-39, dn21 (Ox.), MA1822, p23 (Ox.). V. Compton Valence, Dorset 1824-[38], R. Barford St Martin, Wilts. 1837-44. Died Dorking, Surrey 13/12/1870 aged 73, leaving £8,000 [C22842. DEB]

**GAMBIER (James Edward)** Born Aldermary, City of London 20/7/1759, s. William James Gambier (of Clerkenwell) and Mary Venn (a clergy dau.). Sidney, Cambridge 1779, BA1783, dn83 (Lin.), p84 (Lin.), MA1786. R. Langley, Kent 1789, R. St Mary le Strand, London 1813 to death. Dom. Chap. to 1st Baron Barham 1813. Died 12/5/1839 [C60858] Married 7/11/1782 Eleanor Bardwell (Beccles, Suffolk), with issue.

**GAMBLE (Henry)** Born Lurgan, Co. Armagh 9/6/1793, s. Rev. Henry Gamble and Anne Cutcliffe. Exeter, Oxford 1811, BA1815, dn16 (Chester for Ex.), p17 (Ex.). V. Launcells, Cornwall 1832 (w. Newport, Bishopstawton, Devon 1829), PC. Clifton, Ashbourne, Derbys. 1846 to death 31/1/1867 aged 73, leaving £1,000

[C143878] Married (1) Barnstaple, Devon 23/5/1816 Elizabeth Vere Law (d.1851), with issue (2) Hove, Sussex 3/11/1853 Mrs Caroline Fisgard (Downes) Tayspill [*sic* - FreeBMD confirms], with further issue.

**GAMLEN (Samuel [Punter])** Bapt. Corston, Som. 28/1/1783, s. William Gamlen and Elizabeth Vernon Fothergill. Wadham, Oxford 1801, then Balliol, BA1805, dn06 (London), p08 (Durham), MA1811. Minor Canon of Durham Cathedral 1810-34, V. Pittington, Durham 1810-15, V. Heighington w. Croxdale, Durham 1815-36, V. Bossall, Yorks. 1836-54, RD, V. Kirby Mallory, Leics. 1854 to death (unm.) 2/6/1855 aged 73 [C117947] Surrogate 1844.

**GANDY (Samuel Whitlock)** Bapt. Plymouth, Devon 12/1/1776, s. Rev. John Gandy. Eton/King's, Cambridge 1795, Fellow 1798-1817, dn99 (Win.), p99 (Cant.), BA1800, MA1803. S/M Eton College 1800-3; PC. East Stonehouse, Plymouth 1799-1826, V. Kingston-on-Thames w. Sheen, Surrey 1817 to death 24/12/1851 [C73762] Minor hymnologist.

**GAPE (Charles)** Bapt. St Albans, Herts. 5/8/1799, s. Rev. James Carpenter Gape (V. Redbourn, Herts.) and Elizabeth Vernon Fothergill. Peterhouse, Cambridge 1818, BA 1822, dn22 (Lin.), p23 (Lin.), MA1825. V. Sibsey, Lincs. 1826-71, V. Willoughton, Lincs. 1836-71, V. Hillington, Norfolk 1837-40. Died (Brondesbury, London) 24/2/1890, leaving £27,345-0s-9d. [C60864. Bennett2] Married St Alban's 29/9/1828 Mary Elizabeth Howard, w. clerical s. Charles Gape.

**GARBETT (James)** Bapt. Hereford 1775, s. Philip Garbett and Hannah Garston. Christ Church, Oxford 1792, BA1796, dn96 (Heref.), p98 (Heref.), MA1805. S/M Hereford Cathedral School 1803-7; R. Putley, Heref. 1799-1805 (res.), V. Weston Beggard, Heref. 1805-9, V. Yarkhill, Heref. 1809-10, V. Marden w. Amberley, Heref. 1810, Prebend of Hinton 1813-57 [and Minor Canon (Cormeilles) in Hereford Cathedral 1813-19], V. Hereford St John the Baptist 1819, V. Brinsop, Heref. 1831, V. Upton Bishop, Heref. 1839 to death 7/9/1857 [C105312] Married 1800 Charlotte Merrick, w. clerical s. James (Archdeacon of Chichester, *q.v.* ODNB).

**GARBETT (John)** From Hereford, s. Thomas and Mary Garbett. All Souls, Oxford 1814 (aged 23), dn17 (Lin.), BA1818, p18 (Lin.), MA1821. Min. 1823 then R. Birmingham St George 1830-51-, Hon. Canon of Worcester Cathedral, RD. Died Harborne, Staffs. 22/8/1858, leaving £4,000 [C11135] Married Sarah Powell before 1831, with issue.

**GARDINER (Frederick)** From Esher, Surrey, s. Rev. Edmund (*or* James) Gardiner and Elizabeth Barlow. Balliol, Oxford 1794 (aged 17), SCL1799, dn99 (Salis.), p00 (Salis.), MA 1806 (Lambeth). V. Wellow, Som. 1801, R. Combe Hay, Som. 1806 to death. Dom. Chap. to 3rd Baron Hawke 1806. Died 14/7/1857 [C3940] Married (1?) Birmingham 27/12/1810 Frances Ann Snow, w. issue. Brother two below?

**GARDINER (John)** From Beardley, Somerset, s. William Gardiner and Annabella Lucas. Queen's, Oxford 1778 (aged 21), then Wadham, dn80 (Ox. for B&W), p81 (Peterb. for C&L), BA1782, MA1796, BD & DD1796. V. Shirley, Derbys. 1781-1815, R. Brailsford w. Osmaston, Derbys. 1781-9, Min. Octagon Proprietary Chapel, Bath ('purchased for him by his father') 1796 to death 11 or 25/8/1838 [C11138] Married Bath 10/6/1791 Mary Gabbatt Speirs, with clerical son William. J.P. Somerset.

**GARDINER (Robert Barlow)** Born Yardley Hastings, Northants., s. Rev. James Gardiner and Elizabeth Barlow. Wadham, Oxford 1789 (aged 17), BA1793, dn94 (Lin. for Peterb.), p95 (Ox.), MA1798, Fellow 1819, etc. V. Wadhurst, Sussex 1818 to death 5/12/1845 [C29299] Wife Agnes, and issue. Brother Frederick, above?

**GARDNER (Christopher)** Born Blawith, Lancs. 1777, s. Christopher Gardner and Margaret Lancaster. [NiVoF] V. East Dean w. Friston, Sussex 1817 to death 26/8/1846 [C63530] Married Dorking, Surrey 1/7/1817 Jane Warneford.

**GARDNER, *born* PANTING (Lawrence)** Bapt. Wellington, Shropshire 11/6/1767, s. Rev. Stephen Panting and Josina Gardner (a clergy dau.). St John's, Cambridge 1784, BA1789, dn91 (C&L), MA1792, Fellow 1793-9, p94 (C&L), DD1815. R. Hope Bagot, Shropshire 1798-1817 (res.), PC. Clive, Shropshire 1810-44, R. Westbury (2nd Portion), Shropshire 1811-20 (res.), Min. Curzon Street Proprietary Chapel, Mayfair, London 1814-21, V. Condover, Shropshire 1816-26 (res.), R. Birmingham St Philip 1821-44,

3rd Canon Residentiary (w. Prebend of Sawley) and Treasurer of Lichfield Cathedral 1821 to death (Sansaw, Shropshire) 26/7/1844 [C11142. Venn under Panting] Married Wrockwardine, Shropshire 21/2/1799 Martha Pemberton. Inherited the Sansaw estates from his cousin 1801 and changed his name to Gardner.

**GARDNER (Thomas)** From Liverpool, s. Thomas Gardner (manufacturer). Queens', Cambridge 1827, BA1831, dn31 (Chester), p32 (Chester), MA1842. PC. (and patron) of Liverpool St Anne Stanley (o/w West Derby) 1831 to death (Southport, Lancs.) 19/5/1881 aged 80, leaving £4,643-16s-3d. [C168911. Probably LBSO] Married Walton on the Hill, Liverpool 23/9/1834 Margaret Hilton, of Jamaica (w), with clerical son. Surrogate 1844.

**GARNET (John)** Bapt. Kirkby Lonsdale, Westmorland. Usher at Queen Mary's School, Kirkby Lonsdale. Literate: dn97 (Chester), p02 (Chester). PC. Unsworth, Lancs. 1802-3 (res.), PC. Firbank, Kirkby Lonsdale 1808 to death 23/7/1843 aged 71 [C168914] Married Warton, Lancs. 10/12/1805 Elizabeth Clarkson (w), with issue.

**GARNIER (Thomas)** Born Wickham, Hants. 26/2/1776, s. George Charles Garnier and Margaret Miller (dau. of a baronet). Worcester, Oxford 1793, then All Souls, Fellow, BCL1800, DCL1850. V. Froyle, Hants. 1800, R. Hinton Parva, Wilts. 1807-08, R. Bishopstoke, Hants. 1807-68, R. North Waltham, Hants. 1819 (only), R. Brightwell, Berks. 1819-31 (res.), Canon of 10th Prebend in Winchester Cathedral 1831-40, Dean of Winchester 1840 to death 29/6/1873, leaving £40,000 [C73767 - death date is wrong. ODNB. Boase. LNCP] Married Bath 8/5/1805 Mary Parry (sister of the Arctic explorer), with clerical son Thomas (later Dean of Lincoln). Botanist and sanitary reformer. Photo. online.

**GARNSEY (Thomas Rock)** Bapt. West Hatch, Som. 27/12/1792, s. Robert Westcombe Garnsey and Anne Appleby. Literate: dn19 (Chester for London), p19 (London). Chap. in Sierra Leone 1819; PC. Dean Forest (or Forest of Dean) Christ Church, Glos. 1824 to death (North Curry, Som.) 1847 (1st q. as Roche) [C117952] Married Bristol 30/9/1819 Elizabeth Hare (who left £1,500 on her death in 1867), with clerical son.

**GARRATT (Thomas)** Born Baddesley Ensor, Warwicks. 22/2/1796, s. Thomas Garratt and Ann White. Christ's, Cambridge 1820, dn21 (Chester), p21 (Chester), MA1830 (a Ten Year Man). PC. Altcar, Lancs. 1822-6, PC. Talke (o/w Talk o' th' Hill), Staffs. 1831 and V. Audley, Staffs. 1833 to death (Holloway, London) 18/12/1841 aged 45 [C11147] Married (1) Kingsbury, Worcs. 20/7/1818 Ann Cooper (d.1820), w. child (2) Manchester 16/4/1823 Frances Dorothea White.

**GARRETT (John)** Born Broadhempston, Devon, s. William Garrett and Sarah Ellicott. Magdalen, Oxford 1812 (aged 23), then Peterhouse, Cambridge 1813, dn16 (Chester), p17 (Chester), BD1824. (Sinecure R. Dengie (Bacon's Portion), Essex 1821). Chaplain to 'Bethlehem Hospital and to House of Occupation, Southwark' 1833 to death (Eastbourne, Sussex) 5/7/1863. Will not traced [C73770] Married Surrey 27/6/1826 Louisa Robinson Wellington, with issue.

**GARTON (Joseph)** Bapt. Willoughby-on-the-Wolds, Notts. 7/6/1795, s. Thomas and Elizabeth Garton. Queens', Cambridge 1819, then St John's 1820, then back to Queens', BA 1824, dn25 (B&W), p25 (Ex.), MA1849. PC. Millbrook, Cornwall 1827, V. Towcester, Northants. 1840 to death 30/3/1855 [C41074] Married 1827 Mary Corrie Robertson, with clerical son Joseph Garton.

**GARVEY (Richard [Godfrey])** Born Dublin 18/1/1785, s. Capt. James William Garvey and Jane Little (a clergy dau). S/M Northampton Free G/S 1810. Literate: dn13 (Killaloe), p13 (Killaloe), MA1821 Lambeth. H/M Lincoln G/S 1820-8; R. Friesthorpe, Lincs. 1828-61, V. St Nicholas Newport, Lincs. 1828, V. Leicester St Nicholas w. St John the Baptist 1828, R. Lincoln St Mary Magdalen 1828-61, Senior Vicar Choral in Lincoln Cathedral 1828-61, Prebend of Milton Ecclesia 1845-61, R. Snarford, Lincs. 1858. Died 21/11/1861 aged 76, leaving £6,000 [C60888. Kaye] Married Bedford 2/1/1810 Lisa Maria Dew, 2 dau, 5s. (4 clerical). An ultra-Tory and High Churchman.

**GARWOOD (Edmund)** Bapt. Cawston, Norfolk 8/8/1756, s. William and Elizabeth Garwood. Magdalene, Cambridge 1775, BA 1779, dn79 (C&L for York), p80 (York), MA 1782, Fellow. V. Hessle, Yorks. 1799 to death (Elvington, Yorks.) 27/4/1837 aged 80

[C11152. YCO] Married Hull 19/5/1791 Dorothy Ramsey (Full Sutton Manor, Yorks.), with issue.

**GASKELL (Thomas)** Born New Mills, Derbys., s. of a farmer. Literate: dn86 (Chester), p88 (Chester). S/M Manchester G/S at some date; PC. Stretford, Manchester 1796, PC. Manchester Newton (Heath) All Saints, 1818 to death 20/6/1834 aged 71 (CCEd says 17/10/1834) [C168920] Married Manchester 25/4/1799 Ann Rigby, with issue.

**GATE (Joseph)** Bapt. Uldale, Cumberland 3/7/1786, s. Joseph Gate and Elizabeth Johnston. St. Bees adm. 1817, dn18 (Chester), p19 (Chester). PC. Bidston, Birkenhead, Cheshire 1819 to death 4/7/1851 [C168921] Married Uldale 18/3/1815 Mary Cape, w. issue.

**GATEHOUSE (Thomas)** Born North Cheriton, Som. 18/1/1789, s. Rev. Samuel and Sarah Gatehouse. Wadham, Oxford 1807, BA 1811, dn12 (B&W), p13 (Salis.). R. North Cheriton 1824-63, R. Blackford, Som. 1834 to death 1/7/1863, leaving £1,500 [C41076]

**GATENBY (John)** Born Husthwaite, Yorks. 27/2/1792, s. John Gatenby and Elizabeth Miller. Literate: dn16 (York), p17 (York). PC. Newton upon Ouse, Yorks. 1818 and V. Overton w. Shipton, Yorks. 1823 to death (unmarried) Scarborough, Yorks. 4/8/1854 [C131407. YCO]

**GATLIFF (John)** Bapt. Manchester 14/5/1763, s. James Gatliff and Mary Rogers. BNC, Oxford 1782, BA1785, dn88 (York), p92 (Chester), MA1789. R. Manchester St Mary 1804-42, PC. Manchester St James, Didsbury 1807-39, Clerk in Orders 1792 then Chap. 1798 then Fellow of Manchester Collegiate Church 1798-1839. Died Brinkworth Hall, Elvington, Yorks. 22/11/1842 aged 80 [C126587. YCO] Married Leeds 21/3/1788 Jane Conset, *s.p.*

**GAUNTLETT (Frederic(k))** Born Easton, Hants. 15/11/1788, s. Peter Gauntlett and Elizabeth Yalden. Wadham, Oxford 1807, BA 1810, dn11 (Win.), MA1813, p14 (B&W). S/M Hampton Lucy Free G/S, Worcs. 1819; PC. Bognor (Regis), Sussex 1822-34, R. Badgworth, Som. 1823-35, R. Fladbury, Som. 1834 to death 7/9/1863, leaving £8,000 [C41077] Married King's Bromley, Staffs. 18/12/1817 Elizabeth Sarah Melissa Matterley (w), with issue. Brother Henry, below.

**GAUNTLETT (Henry)** Born Market Lavington, Wilts. 15/3/1762, s. John Gauntlett and Elizabeth Wheeler. 'Was idle for some years'. Literate: dn86, p86 (Salis.). V. Olney, Bucks. 1815 to death 27/2/1834 [C73776. ODNB. DEB] Married Bristol 18/2/1800 Arabella Jenkinson Davies (Coychurch, Glamorgan), w. issue (incl. Henry John, organist and composer).

**GAUNTLETT (Henry)** Bapt. Winchester 6/6/1781, s. Peter Gauntlett and Elizabeth Yalden. Trinity, Oxford 1799, BA1802, dn03 (Win.), p05 (Win.), MA1806. R. Lainston, Hants. 1807-19 (res.), V. Cricklade St Sampson, Wilts. 1817-49, R. Longstock, Hants. 1819-28 (res.). Dom. Chap. to 4th Earl of Rosebery 1814. Died 16/3/1849 (CCEd is wrong here) [C60898] Married Terwick, Sussex 26/8/1806 Elizabeth Ann Ridge. Brother Frederick, above.

**GAUSSEN (Armytage)** Bapt. Marylebone, London 28/4/1791, s. Col. Samuel Robert William Gaussen, *M.P.*, and Elizabeth Bosanquet. Corpus Christi, Oxford 1810, BA1815, dn18 (London), p19 (London). R. Meesden, Herts. 1819 to death. Dom. Chap. to Hester Elizabeth, Baroness Selsey 1819. Died Royston, Herts. 15/7/1859, leaving £1,500. [C117959] Married Clifton, Bristol 16/6/1814 Sarah Elizabeth Sotheby (w), with issue.

**GAWTHROP (Thomas Holden)** Born Sedbergh, Yorks. 5/6/1768, s. Rev. William Gawthrop and Ann Holden. St John's, Cambridge 1786, BA1791, dn93 (Ex.), MA1794, BD1802, Fellow 1793-1817. R. Marston Moreteyne, Beds. 1815 to death 2/11/1836 [C60900] Married (1) Sedbergh 1816 Mary Gillett (d.1817) (2) Sedbergh 3/3/1818 Sarah Basford; with issue.

**GAY (William)** Bapt. City of London 26/3/1793, s. James and Susanna Gay. Corpus Christi, Cambridge 1819, dn23 (Nor.), BA1825, p26 (London), MA1826. R. Bidborough, Kent 1830 to death (Camberwell, London) 11/1846 aged 54 [C6733]

**GEARY (John)** Probably bapt. Worthen, Shropshire 27/2/1769, s. Edward Geary [*pleb*] (Westbury, Shropshire) and Agnes Lawrence. Christ Church, Oxford 1788, BA1792, dn92 (C&L), Chap. 1792-7, p93 (Ox.), MA1795. S/M

Dawddur, Montgomery 1796-1806, PC. Llandrinio (w. Trinity Chapel), Montgomery 1796-1825, Chap. of Donative of Uppington, Shropshire 1806. Died? [C11184]

**GEDGE (Joseph)** Born Bury St Edmunds, Suffolk 23/6/1799, s. Peter Gedge and Ann Johnson. Trinity, Cambridge 1815, then Jesus, BA1820, dn23 (Bristol for Lin.), MA1823, p23 (Llandaff for Lin.). V. Humberston, Lincs. 1823-44 (w. H/M Humberston Foundation School 1823-49), R. Ashby cum Fenby, Lincs, 1844-9, R. Bildeston, Suffolk 1849-79. Dom. Chap. to Earl Stanhope. Died Kelvedon, Essex 24/2/1893 aged 93, leaving £3,737-12s-0d. [C3943. Kaye] Married (1) Clee, Lincs. 12/10/1824 Harriet Thorold (d.1859), w. clerical s. Augustus (2) Clapham Park, Surrey 9/1/1862 Charlotte Frances Stokes, w. further issue. J.P.

**GEE (Robert)** From Yorkshire. Queens', Cambridge 1802, BA1807, dn09 (Nor.), then St Catharine's, Fellow, MA1810, p11 (London for Ely). R. Thornton in Craven, Yorks. 1813-32, PC. Tormohun w. Cockington, Devon 1830-61, R. Paignton, Devon (w. Preacher throughout the Diocese of Exeter) 1832 to death. Dom. Chap. to 2nd Baron Heathfield 1810; to 1st Earl of Kilmorley 1814. Died 11/5/1861 aged 75, leaving £557-19s-9d. (left unadministered). [C100017] Married Jane Mallock (w), w. issue. (incl. Rev. Walter Mallock Gee, founder of the militaristic Church Lads Brigade).

**GEE (Walter)** Born Cambridge 10/8/1784, s. Robert Gee (attorney). St John, Cambridge 1802, BA1806, dn07 (Lin. for Ely), then Sidney 1808, Fellow, p08 (Salis. for Ely), MA1809, BD 1816. R. Week St Mary, Corn-wall 1821-52, R. West Buckland >< Devon 1831-52, Archdeacon of East Cornwall 1842-5. Died (Week) 27/2/1852 from an infected scratch from his cat [C60903] Married Cambridge 23/8/1821 Sarah Gee [*thus*], with clerical sons Frederick, and Walter.

**GEE** see also under **JEE**

**GELDART (James)** Bapt. Masham, Yorks. 5/4/1760, s. Richard Geldart (Biggin Grange). Trinity, Cambridge 1778, BA1783, dn84 (York), p84 (York), MA1809, then Trinity Hall, LLD 1818. R.(and patron) Kirk Deighton, Yorks. 1795-1839 (succ. there by his son and grandson; living in Kirk Deighton Hall and Barnwell Abbey, Cambs.), PC. Aldfield w. Studley, Ripon, Yorks. 1799, Chap. of the Donative of Cambridge St Andrew the Less 1814. Died Kirk Deighton 12/11/1839 aged 79 [C108122. Boase. YCO] Married (1) Spofforth, Yorks. 12/5/1784 Sarah Williamson (d.1794), with two clerical sons, below (2) Camden, London 12/5/1796 Mary Ann Nicholas. J.P. West Riding 1818.

**GELDART (James William)** Born Swinnow Hall, Wetherby, Yorks. 15/2/1785, s. Rev. James Geldart (above) and Sarah Williamson. Trinity, Cambridge 1799, then Trinity Hall 1800, LLB1806, then St Catharine's 1808, Fellow 1808-20, dn09 (Ely), p09 (Ely), then back to Trinity Hall (Fellow, tutor and Vice-Master 1809-21), LLD1814. Regius Professor of Civil Law, Cambridge 1814. (succ. his father as) R. (and patron) of Kirk Deighton, Yorks. 1840 to death (Kirk Deighton Hall) 16/2/1876, leaving £30,000 [C100018. ODNB. Boase] Married (1) Midhurst, Sussex 14/7/1829 Mary Jane Wardroper (d.1830) (2) 4/8/1856 Mary Rachel Desborough, with issue (incl. son of same name in same place). Brother, below.

**GELDART (Richard John)** Bapt. Thorp Arch, Yorks. 16/6/1786, s. Rev. James Geldart (above) and Sarah Williamson. St Catharine's, Cambridge 1805, BA1809, dn09 (York), Fellow 1809, p10 (York), MA1812, DD1842. R. Little Billing, Northants. 1817 to (burial) 29/12/1871 aged 85, leaving £25,000 [C108124. YCO] Married Northampton 10/12/1818 Sarah Walker, with issue. Brother James William, above

**GELDART (Thomas)** [NiVoF] Literate: dn00 (Chester), p01 (Chester). S/M Dunchurch, Warwicks. 1811; PC. Rampside, Lancs. 1801-3 (res.), PC. Upper Shuckburgh, Warwicks. 1804 to death 2/3/1841, aged 65 [C11185]

**GELL (Philip)** Born Wirksworth, Derbys. 22/2/1783, s. Philip Gell and Elizabeth Wright. Trinity, Cambridge 1800, BA1806, dn06 (C&L), p07 (C&L), MA1808, BD1837. PC. Rocester, Staffs. 1812-20 (res.), PC. Derby St John the Evangelist 1829-46, RD 1837-46. Dom. Chap. to 5th Viscount Galway 1812. Died 7/1/1870, leaving £16,000 [C11186. Boase. DEB] Married (1) Ashbourne, Derbys. 1/5/1809 Ann Kerry (d.1834), w. issue (2) Matlock, Derbys. 17/1/1815 Elizabeth Dod, w. clerical sons Frederick (Bishop of Madras), and Joseph Philip Gell.

**GELL (Thomas)** Bapt. Edlaston, Derbys. 14/7/1769, s. Rev. Thomas Gell, sen. and Frances Fletcher. St John's, Cambridge 1787, BA1791, dn91 (C&L), p93 (C&L), MA1794. R. Boyleston, Derbys. 1808-34, R. Preston Bagot, Warwicks. 1826-31 (res.). Died 1/7/1834 (CCEd thus) [C11188. Austin] Married Ashbourne, Derbys. 8/12/1795 Frances Hogg, w. clerical s. Thomas Fletcher Gell.

**GELL** see also under **GILL**

**GELLING (Alexander)** Literate: dn09 (S&M), p11 (S&M). Chap. Ballure, IoM 1809-16, V. Arbory, IoM 1816 to death (Marown, IoM) 7/7/1859 aged 74. Will not traced [C7278. Gelling] Married Ramsay, IoM 11/6/1811 Ann Clucas (a clergy dau.), w. issue.

**GELLING (James)** Bapt. (Kirk) German, IoM 28/7/1771, s. James Gelling and Catherine Key. Literate: dn94 (S&M). V. German 1801 to sudden death (Peel, IoM) 8/7/1838 aged 67 [C7280. Gelling] Married 21/2/1794 Sophia LaMothe, 3s. (1 clerical), 3 dau.

**GELLING (John James)** Born Castletown, IoM 24/1/1791, s. John Gelling and Jane Tennant. Literate: dn19 (S&M), p22 (S&M), MA1842. PC. Grainsthorpe, Lincs. 1828-30 (res.), PC. St Katherine Cree, City of London 1829 to death Islington, London 12/8/1866, leaving £1,500 [C7281] Married Lambeth, Surrey 27/6/1837 Mrs Elizabeth Lowden

**GENESTE (Maximilian)** Born Douglas, IoM 16/9/1799, s. Lewis Geneste (of Huguenot extraction) and Catharine Callow. Queen's, Oxford 1820, dn23 (Salis.), BA1824, p25 (Lin. for Salis.), MA1827. (first) PC. West Cowes, IoW 1832 to death 27/7/1860, leaving £2,000 [C374781] Married 1825 Sarah Goodwin (Hatford, Berks., whose mother built the church for her son-in-law), and had issue.

**GEORGE (Charles)** Bapt. Enfield, Middx. 21/10/1781, s. Augustus George. St John's, Cambridge 1802, BA1806, dn08 (Ely), MA 1809, p13 (Bristol). R. Wicken Bonhunt (o/w Little Wicken), Essex 1814-56. Died Guildford, Surrey 16/5/1868, leaving £5,000 [C52631] Married (1) Cambridge 13/11/1806 Amelia Butcher, with issue (2) Mary Ann (w).

**GEORGE (John)** From ?Llantilo, Montgomery, s. James George. Jesus, Cambridge 1780 (aged 17), BA1784, dn86 (Ox.), MA1787, p88 (Heref.), BD1795. Chap. Aston Clinton, Bucks. 1799 and R. Grosmont, Montgomery 1803 to death 21/10/1847 [C3947]

**GEORGE (Patrick)** Born Rothes, Morayshire 13/6/1781 (but of Hutton, Berwickshire). Literate: dn07 (Durham), p08 (Durham). Minor Canon of Durham Cathedral 1810-34, V. Merrington, Durham 1812-22, V. Aycliffe, Durham 1821-31 (res.), PC. Durham St Margaret of Antioch 1831 to death. Bishop's Librarian, then first Librarian of Durham College/University 1832 to death 4/4/1834 (CCEd thus). [C130440] Married Elizabeth Hope, with issue.

**GEORGE (Richard)** Bapt. Feckenham, Warwicks. 9/8/1778, s. Richard George. Magdalen Hall, Oxford 1799, dn02 (Glos.), migrated to Trinity Hall, Cambridge 1806, p07 (Glos. for Wor.), LLB1807. S/M King's School, Worcester 1809-13; R. Worcester St Clement 1812-15 (res.), PC. Stoke Prior, Worcs. 1814-35, V. Wolverley, Worcs. 1835 to death 12/4/1838 [C121227]

**GEORGE (William)** From Usk, Monmouth, s. John George [*pleb*]. Jesus, Oxford 1774 (aged 19), dn77 (Ox. for Llandaff), BA1778, p79 (B&W), MA 1783. V. Western Zoyland, Som. 1780-1801, V. North Petherton, Som. 1801 to death 12/9/1835 [C29338]

**GERMAN, GERMON (Nicholas)** Born Moretonhampstead, Devon 23/2/1799, s. Nicholas German and Susannah Medland. Oriel, Oxford 1817, BA1821, dn22 (Chester), p23 (Chester), MA1825. S/M from 1822, then High Master Manchester Grammar School 1842-59; R. Manchester St Peter, Mosley Street 1825 to death (Edenbridge, Kent) 22/11/1882 aged 83, leaving £42,477-19s-3d. [C168924. Boase] Married Ashbourne, Derbys. 23/6/1827 Marianne Bellot, with issue. Surrogate.

**GERY, *later* WADE-GERY (Hugh Wade-)** Born Bushmead Priory, Beds. 8/1/1797, s. Rev. Hugh Wade and Hester Gery. Emmanuel, Cambridge 1815, BA1819, dn21 (Lin.), MA 1822, p22 (Lin.). R. (and patron) of Bolnhurst, Beds. 1828 to death, R. Thurning, Lincs. 1833. Died Llanfarifechan, Carnarvon 7/3/1874, leaving £5,000 [C77948 has wrong death date. Venn under Wade] Married (1) Newark on Trent, Notts. 17/7/1821 Sophia Josepha Sykes

(2) 2/7/1829 Ann Beckingham Milnes. Brother below.

**GERY,** *later* **WADE-GERY (Robert Wade-)** Born Bushmead Priory, Beds. 15/12/1802, s. Rev. Hugh Wade and Hester Gery. Emmanuel, Cambs. 1820, BA1823, dn25 (Lin.), p26 (Lin.), MA1827. R. (and patron) of Colmworth, Hunts. 1830-68. Died (West Malvern, Worcs.) 16/1/1892, leaving £3,519-19s-9d. [C60916. Venn under Wade] Married St Neots, Hunts. 14/6/1834 Harriet Day, with issue. Brother above.

**GEYT (Philip)** see under **LE GEYT**

**GIBBONS (John)** Born Westminster, London, s. Sir John Gibbons, 2nd Bart. (slave-owner and *M.P.*) and Martha Kenrick (a clergy dau.). Merton, Oxford 1771 (aged 17), BA1775, dn80 (Nor.), p80 (London), migrated to St John's, Cambridge 1786. Minor Canon of Westminster Abbey 1782-97, R. Collington, Heref. 1790 and R. Thornbury, Heref. 1790-1843, R. Brasted, Kent 1805 to death 1/5/1843 aged 90 [C113101] Married (1) Marylebone, London 23/1/1783 Rebecca Ashley (2) Whitby, Yorks. 10/101816 Mrs Margaret Hannah (Knowsley) Peters (a clergy dau.) (w).

**GIBBONS (John)** Born Swindon, Staffs. Clare, Cambridge 1786, BA1791, Fellow 1791-1800, p93 (C&L), MA1794. R. Harley, Shropshire 1805 to death 27/12/1858 aged 90, leaving £12,000 [C11192] Married Shrewsbury, Shropshire 12/5/1800 Helen Gordon Dana, w. issue.

**GIBBS (Joseph)** Born Exeter 22/7/1801, s. Anthony Gibbs and Dorothea Barnetta Hucks. Worcester, Oxford 1824, BA1828, dn28 (Peterb.), p29 (Chester), MA1842. PC. Clifton Hampden, Oxon. 1830 to death there 22/3/1864, leaving £20,000 [C29352] Married Llangattock, Breconshire 14/9/1801 Emily Vaughan, with issue. 'A very good man, everything in parish very satisfactory' (Wilberforce).

**GIBSON (Arthur)** Bapt. Crosby Ravensworth, Westmorland 10/1/1789, s. John and Ruth Gibson. Queen's, Oxford 1801, BA1804, MA 1808, dn08, p09, Fellow 1814-28. Min. Norwood St Luke, Surrey 1825, R. Chedworth, Glos. 1828 to death 7/8/1878, leaving £140,000 [C151110. Boase]

**GIBSON (Christopher Mends)** Bapt. Plymouth, Devon 22/2/1796 (a Presbyterian congregation), s. Archibald Burt Gibson and Ann Gibson [*thus*]. Jesus, Cambridge 1822, BA1828, dn28 (Ex.), p28 (Ex.). PC. Chacewater, Cornwall 1831-39, PC. Kenwyn, Cornwall 1832, V. Truro St Clement w. St Paul 1840-72. Buried 4/10/1872 aged 76, leaving £1,000 [C144420] Widow Ann, and clerical son.

**GIBSON (James)** Born Marylebone, London Nov. 1786, s. James and Elizabeth Gibson. Wadham, Oxford 1802, BA1806, dn08 (Lin.), p09 (Lin.), MA 1811, Fellow 1812-18. R. Worlington, Suffolk 1818 to death. Chap. to the Lock [venereal disease] Hospital 1818 to death 4/10/1850 [C60930. DEB] Married St James, Westminster, London 4/6/1819 Mary Elizabeth Phillips, w. clerical s. Henry Atkinson Gibson.

**GIBSON (John Edgar)** Born Ramsgate, Kent 20/10/1788, s. John Gibson (a lawyer) and Elizabeth Pars. St John's, Oxford 1806, BA 1810, dn12 (Lin. for Win.), MA1813, p13 (Salis.). R. Bermondsey, South London 1827 to death (Hastings, Kent) 29/6/1859 aged 70 leaving £20,000 [C60933] Married (1) Esher, Surrey 24/6/1822 Caroline Swann (Ufford Hall, Lincs., d.1826), w. issue (2) Bermondsey, Surrey 11/8/1829 Elizabeth Gaitskell (w), with further issue.

**GIBSON (Nicholas William)** Born Newcastle upon Tyne 21/6/1802 (nonconformist baptism), s. Nicholas Gibson and Susanna Cowing. Trinity, Cambridge 1819, BA1824, Chaplain, dn26 (Chester), p27 (Chester), MA 1827. PC. Manchester St Thomas Ardwick 1831-67, Senior Canon Residentiary Manchester Cathedral 1861 (and RD) to death Manchester (a widower) 18/6/1882 aged 79, leaving £15,007-10s-3d. Proctor in Convocation for Dean and Chapter of Manchester 1878-80 [C168937] Married Manchester 20/7/1829 Elizabeth Hodgkinson.

**GIBSON (Robert)** Born and bapt. Preston, Lancs. 13/4/1765, s. Rev. John Gibson and Anne Fulford. Trinity Hall, Cambridge 1790, dn93 (Lin. for York), p95 (London), LLB 1798. V. Newland, Glos. 1797-1803, PC. Caton w. Littledale, Lancaster 1803-40 (non-res.), R. Fyfield, Essex 1803-33 (res.). Dom. Chap. to 1st Baron Milford 1820. Died 30/3/1840 aged 74 [C60936. YCO] Married Little Burstead, Essex

7/12/1797 Charlotte Bullock (Shelly House, Essex), with issue.

**GIBSON (Robert)** From Quernmore Park, Lancaster, s. Charles Gibson. Pembroke, Cambridge 1812, BA1817, dn18 (Chester), p20 (Chester), MA1820. PC. Preston Holy Trinity, Lancs. 1820-4 [Venn attaches this parish to the man above], V. Bolton le Sands, Lancs. 1824 to death 16/5/1874 aged 78, leaving £4,000 [C168938] Married 2/7/1822 Ellen Smaley (Bagilt, Flintshire), with issue.

**GIBSON (Thomas)** Bapt. Orton, Cumberland 26/10/1784, s. of Robert (a yeoman farmer) and Jane Gibson. Literate: dn08 (Chester), p09 (Chester). V. Barton, Westmorland 1823 (and S/M) to death 16/1/1845 aged 60 [C5886. Platt] Married Orton 15/5/1813 Ann Bowness, with issue. Ran a school at Tirral Lodge.

**GIBSON (William)** From Westminster, London, s. Rev. Robert Gibson. Christ Church, Oxford 1768 (aged 16), then Queen's, BA1771, dn74 (London), MA1774, p75 (London). R. Gilston, Herts. 1774-1821 (res.), R. Wickham St Paul, Essex 1779, Chamberlainwood Prebend in St Paul's Cathedral 1781 to death Dom. Chap. to Bishop of Oxford, then of Hereford 1779. Died 25/11/1842 [C118303]

**GIFFARD (James)** Bapt. Cambridge 28/1/1770, s. William Giffard (of Quy Hall, Cambs.) and Elizabeth Bones. Trinity, Cambridge 1786, BA1791, dn92 (Lin.), MA1794, p97 ([Lin.]). Chap. R.N.; V. (and patron) of Wootton, Lincs. 1814 and V. Cabourne, Lincs. 1821 (and RD of Yarborough) to death 18/8/1849 [C60944. Kaye] Married 7/6/1808 Mrs Anne (Goodwin) Swan (widow of a Gainsborough banker), w. clerical son Frederick Walker Giffard.

**GILBANK (Thomas)** From York, s. Thomas Gilbank. Trinity, Cambridge 1768 (aged 17), BA1772, dn73 (London), p74 (London), Fellow 1774, MA1775, BD1792, Vice-Master 1793-7. PC. Burton Fleming (o/w North Burton), Yorks. 1777-1837, V. Bottisham, Cambs. 1788-1801, R. Dickleburgh, Norfolk 1796 to death 27/11/1837 aged 67 [C100020]

**GILBANKS (George)** Bapt. Bowness on Solway, Cumberland 21/9/1755, s. Rev. Joseph Gilbanks. Literate: dn77 (Car.), p80 (Car.). PC. Lanercost w. Kirkcambeck, Cumberland 1786-1845, PC. Farlam, Cumberland 1786-1840 and PC. Over Denton, Cumberland 1786 and R. Nether (or Upper) Denton, Cumberland 1792-4. Died Farlam 1/7/1845 [C5889. Platt] Married (1) Bampton, Cumberland 26/11/1774 Dorothy Bell (2) Lancaster 11/6/1787 Rebecca Calvert, with son Joseph, below. Brother, below.

**GILBANKS (John Clark)** Born Bowness on Solway, Cumberland 24/9/1759, s. Rev. Joseph Gilbanks. Literate: dn82 (Car.), p84 (Car.). PC. Haile (or Hayle), Cumberland 1783, PC. Culgaith, Kirkland, Cumberland (where 'the residents unsuccessfully attempted to block his appointment') 1791-1837 (and H/M Culgaith G/S 1799-1811), V. Aspatria, Cumberland 1815 to death (influenza) Feb. 1837 aged 77 [C5892. Platt] Married 1791 Mrs Mary Scaife, with clerical son. Brother, above.

**GILBANKS (Joseph)** Bapt. Lanercost, Cumberland 8/3/1788, s. Rev. George Gilbanks (above) and Rebecca Calvert. Literate: dn11 (Car.), p13 (Durham). R. Lamplugh, Cumberland 1817 to death 30/9/1853 aged 65 [C5893] Married Haltwhistle, Northumberland 7/6/1815 Jane Carrick, with clerical son.

**GILBERT (George)** From Kent. St John's, Cambridge 1813, then Corpus Christi 1815, BA 1819, dn20 (Peterb. for Lin.), MA1822, p22 (Lin.), incorporated at Oxford 1859. S/M Grantham G/S, Lincs. 1820-51; V. Syston, Lincs. 1830 (and Prebend of All Saints Thorngate in Lincoln Cathedral 1863) to death. Chap. to the Bishop of St. Helena 1862; to Bishop of Lincoln 1869. Died Grantham 12/12/1874, leaving £8,000 [C60945] Surrogate.

**GILBERT (John)** Bapt. Bradwell, Essex 1/2/1778, s. Henry Gilbert, Postwick Hall, Norfolk. Emmanuel, Cambridge 1796, BA1800, dn00 (Nor.), Fellow 1802, MA1803, p03 (Nor.). S/M Bungay School, Suffolk 1809-60; V. Ilketshall St Andrew, Suffolk 1809-60, R. Cantley, Norfolk 1812, V. Claxton, Norfolk 1838-60. Died 18/7/1862. Will not traced [C100021] Married 1812 Mary Anne Denny (Bergh Apton, Norfolk), with issue. Inherited The Manor House, Chedgrave, Norfolk from his uncle.

**GILBERT (John Pomeroy)** Bapt. Constantine, Cornwall 9/9/1778, s. Rev. Edmund Gilbert and Anne Garnett. Exeter, Oxford 1795, BA1800, dn01 (Ex.), p04 (Ex.), MA1806. V. St Wenn, Cornwall 1810-52 (but 'resides in

London'), Prebend of Exeter Cathedral 1815-53, V. Gwennap, Cornwall 1825 (only?). Died Barnstaple, Devon 29/9/1853 aged 75 [C144427] Married Ilfracombe, Devon 11/12/1807 Mary Storme (d.1829), with issue.

**GILBERT (Thomas)** Born Staffs. 17/12/1762, s. Thomas Gilbert, *M.P.* (Cotton Hall, Cotton, Staffs.) and Anne Philips. BNC, Oxford 1781, then St Mary Hall, BA1794, dn94 (C&L), p95 (C&L), MA1802. PC. Cockshutt, Shropshire 1795, PC. Cotton 1795. Died (unm.) and was buried Paris 21/6/1841 aged 78 [C11216]

**GILBY (Francis Duncan)** Born Yardley, Worcs. 30/12/1804, s. William (physician) and Eliza Gilby. Pembroke, Cambridge, 1822 then Clare 1824, BA1827, dn27 (Lin. for York), p29 (Bristol for York), MA1830. V. Eckington, Worcs. 1831-43, PC. Cheltenham St James, Glos. 1843-66, R. Whittington, Glos. 1866-71. Died there 26/11/1880, leaving £14,000 [C52637. YCO] Married Walcot, Bath 3/3/1831 Louisa Jane Capper, with issue.

**GILBY (William Robinson)** Bapt. Winterton, Lincs. 19/8/1787, s. Rev. John Gilby (R. Barmston, Yorks.). Trinity, Cambridge 1805, BA1809, Fellow 1811, MA1812, dn18 (Salis. for Bristol), p18 (Durham for Bristol). V. North Ferriby, Hull 1823, V. Beverley St Mary w. St Nicholas, Yorks. 1823-32. Died there 23/2/1848 aged 64 [C52638. Kaye] Married Clifton, Bristol Aug. 1820 Harriet Gilby [*thus*], w. issue. *F.R.A.S.* Mayor of Beverley 1835.

**GILDART (Frederick)** Bapt. City of London 8/4/1769, s. Richard Gildart and Mary Morland. Queen's, Oxford 1787, SCL, dn92 (Lin.), p95 (Lin.), BCL1797. R. Spridlington St Hilary, Lincs. 1822 (living at Norton Hall, Staffs.) to death (West Wickham, Cambs.) 23/4/1841 [C1845] Married Lamberhurst, Kent 4/10/1804 Anne Hussey (Scotney Castle, Kent). Inherited the estate of Norton Hall.

**GILL (Joseph)** Bapt. Doncaster, Yorks. 26/3/1756, s. Joseph Gill and Margaret Wharton. [In the army]. Clare, Cambridge 1784, dn87 (Peterb.), BA1788, p90 (Lin.), MA 1791. R. East Farndon, Northants. 1791-7, V. Exton, Rutland 1791-1812, V. Scraptoft, Leics. 1792 and R. Pickwell, Leics. 1812 to death. Dom. Chap. to 9th Earl of Thanet 1792-1812. Died 1/7/1849 aged 93 [C60951. Venn corrected]

Married Sandwich, Kent 9/3/1780 Harriet Jordan, with issue.

**GILL,** *born* **GELL (William)** Born 30/7/1797, s. Henry Gell (a Manx customs officer) and Marcia Corlett (a clergy dau.). Literate: dn20 (S&M), p24 (S&M). V. Malew, IoM 1830 to death. Diocesan Inspector of Schools 1850. Died 17/10/1871 aged 75. Will not traced [C8064. Gelling. [T.H. Gill], *The Rev. W. Gill: a sketch*. By One of his Sons (Castletown, IoM, 1871)] Married 7/9/1820 Anne Stowell, 9 ch. (including 3 clerical sons). 'A rigid disciplinarian ... he could not be persuaded to sit in an easy chair.' There are two good articles about him on the Web, with port. Surrogate 1847.

**GILL (William)** Born Thorganby, Yorks. 27/3/1802, s. of Richard (a tailor) and Hannah Gill. Literate: dn29 (Roch. for York), p30 (York). PC. Stannington, Ecclesfield, Yorks. 1830 to death 7/10/1879 aged 77, leaving £200 [C131414. YCO. *Memoir of the Rev. William Gill, Vicar of Stannington in the Parish of Ecclesfield*, edited A. Gatty (Sheffield, 1880)].

**GILL** see also under **GELL**

**GILLARD (John)** Born Brixham, Devon 24/9/1798, s. George and Mary Gillard. Oriel, Oxford 1816, BA1820, dn21 (Ex.), p24 (Ex.). R. Sydenham Damerel, Devon 1832 to death (Otterham, Cornwall) 8/2/1875, leaving £2,000 [C144429]

**GILLARD (Philip)** Bapt. Brixham, Devon 8/8/1783, s. Philip and Elizabeth Gillard. Sidney, Cambridge 1804, dn08 (Ex.), BA1809, p09 (Ex.). PC. Kingswear, Devon 1819-36. *Drowned* while bathing 2/8/1836 [C144430]

**GILLBEE (William)** Born Barby, Northants. 3/3/1795, s. Rev. Earle Gillbee and Ann Armitage. Worcester, Oxford 1813, BA1816, dn19 (Glos.), MA1819, p20 (Glos.). V. St Issey, Cornwall 1830, V. Gwennap, Cornwall 1844 to death 13/7/1856 aged 60 [C151116] Married (1) Redruth, Cornwall 29/9/1830 Barbara Molesworth (d.1835), w. clerical s. William Hender Gillbee (2) St Columb, Cornwall 1838 Anne Stephens, with further issue.

**GILLETT (Gabriel Edwards)** Born St Pancras, London 15/12/1798, s. Gabriel Gillett and Mary Ann Hodgson. Oriel, Oxford 1816,

BA1820, dn22 (London), MA1823, dn23 (London). R. Waltham on the Wolds, Leics. 1831-71. RD. Hon. Canon Peterborough Cathedral 1867 to death. Proctor in Convocation for Peterborough Diocese 1850. Died (Melton Mowbray, Leics.) 22/4/1871, leaving £90,000 [C60957. Kaye] Married Branston, Leics. 7/2/1826 Elizabeth Woodall, with issue. Online photo.

**GILLHAM (Thomas Wheeler)** Born Funtington, Sussex 1802, s. Thomas Wheeler Gillham and Harriet Creswall. Corpus Christi, Cambridge 1819, BA1823, dn25 (Chich), p25 (Chich.), MA1826. V. West Wittering, Sussex 1826, V. Liddington w. Caldecote, Rutland 1835-81. Lived at Guildford, Surrey. Died Worplesdon, Surrey 11/1/1887, leaving £3,525-15s-0d. [C60958] Married Lewes, Sussex 1/2/1831 Harriet Hurdis (w), w. clerical s. of same name.

**GILLY (William)** Born Hawkedon, Suffolk 17/12/1761, s. Rev. William Gilly and Mary Firmin. Caius, Cambridge 1780, BA1784, dn84 (Nor.), Fellow 1785-8, MA 1787, p88 (Nor.). R. Hawkedon 1788 and V. Wanstead, Essex 1812 to death 23/11/1837 [C113109 has wrong death date] Married Long Melford, Suffolk 23/4/1788 Anne Oliver, with clerical son, below.

**GILLY (William Stephen)** Born Hawkedon, Suffolk 28/1/1789, s. Rev. William Gilly (above) and Anne Oliver. Caius, Cambridge 1808, then St Catharine's 1808, BA1812, dn12 (B&W), p13 (London), MA1817, DD1833. R. North Fambridge, Essex 1817-32, Canon of 9th Prebend in Durham Cathedral 1826-55, PC. Durham St Margaret 1828-31, V. Norham, Northumberland 1831 to death. Dom. Chap. to 8th Earl of Lauderdale 1814. Died 10/9/1855 aged 67 [C41904. ODNB. Boase. DEB] Married 18/12/1825 Jane Charlotte Mary (dau. of Major Samuel Thomas Colberg, of Jersey), with issue. Concerned about the Protestants of the Vaudois; and in the peasantry of the Anglo-Scottish Border; his book *The peasantry of the Border: an appeal on their behalf* (1841) was reprinted (2001) with a biographical sketch.

**GILPIN (Bernard)** Born Whitehaven, Cumberland 20/10/1772, s. William Gilpin. Christ's, Cambridge 1790, BA1794, dn95 (Ely), MA 1797, p98 (Ely), Fellow 1806-33, Senior Greek Lecturer 1812-14. R. Wold Newton, Lincs. 1807-32, V. Burnham Westgate (o/w Norton) (2 Medieties) Norfolk 1832 to death (Aldburgh, Yorks.) 26/12/1848 [C100023]

**GILPIN (Bernard)** Born Pulverbach, Shropshire 26/1/1803, s. Rev. William Gilpin (below) and Elizabeth Farish. St John's, Cambridge 1821, then Queens' 1822, BA1825, dn26 (Lin.), p27 (Lin.), MA1828. R. Hertford St Andrew 1829-35 (when he resigned from the Church of England and ran a free church built by his followers). Died Pulverbach 10/1/1871, leaving £6,000 [C60959. Boase. R.B. Benson, *Memorials of the life and ministry of Bernard Gilpin. With a biography of his first wife Henrietta* (1874. port.)] Married (1) Layston, Herts. 3/2/1829 Henrietta Jeffreys (d.1841) (2) Avon Dassett, Warwicks. 13/4/1852 Jane Charlotte Guise.

**GILPIN (Martin)** Bapt. Barrow in Furness, Cumberland 13/9/1800, s. Major Martin Gilpin, *H.E.I.C.* St Bees adm. 1820, dn23 (Chester), p24 (Chester). PC. Stockport St Thomas, Cheshire 1825 to death (IoM, unmarried) 18/11/1839 [C168945]

**GILPIN (William)** Born Cheam, Surrey 8/4/1757, s. Rev. William Gilpin, sen. (*q.v.* ODNB) and Margaret Harrison. Queen's, Oxford 1773, BA1778, dn79 (Roch.), migrated to Magdalene, Cambridge, MA1782, p04 (Chester). S/M Cheam School; R. Norton-sub-Hamdon, Som. 1804-7, R. (Church) Pulverbach, Shropshire 1806 to death 29/2/1848 aged 91 [C1846] Married Boldre, Hants. 23/4/1783 Elizabeth Farish, with clerical son Bernard (above).

**GIMINGHAM (William)** Bapt. Norwich 7/3/1773, s. William (a wool stapler) and Hannah Gimingham. Caius, Cambridge 1790, BA1795, p00 (Ely), Fellow 1796-1820, MA1798. S/M The Perse School, Cambridge 1802-4; R. St Dionis Backchurch, City of London 1803-4, R. Bratton Fleming, Devon 1818, Prebend of Combe X in Wells Cathedral 1817 to death. Chap. to HRH Duke of Gloucester 1799. Died 2/3/1838 [C41906] Venn refers to his 'eccentric behaviour'.

**GIPPS (Henry)** Bapt. Canterbury 23/3/1786, s. George Gipps, *M.P.*, and Elizabeth Lawrence (a clergy dau.). St John's, Cambridge 1802, BA 1807 [Senior Wrangler], LLB1810, dn15 (Nor.), p15 (Glos.). V. Hereford St Peter w. St Owen 1824 to death 18/12/1832 [C105381] Married

Nonington, Kent 30/5/1812 Emma Maria Plumptree, with issue.

**GIPPS (Henry)** Bapt. Ringwould, Kent 24/09/1797, s. Rev. George Gipps and Susanna Bonnella Venn. Worcester, Oxford 1816, BA 1819, dn20 (Ox.), p22 (Ox.), MA1822, Fellow 1822-4. V. Corbridge, Northumberland 1829-53, Canon Residentiary (2nd Stall) of Carlisle Cathedral 1845 (w. Examining Chap. to the Bishop of Carlisle 1827-56) and V. Crosthwaite, Keswick, Cumberland 1855 to death (Carlisle) 10/12/1877 aged 80, leaving £18,000 [C3391] Married St James, Westminster 30/3/1824 Maria, dau. of Lt.-Gen. Bentham with issue. 'Hopeless and absentee'. Surrogate.

**GIRARDOT, *born* CHANCOURT (John Chancourt)** Bapt. Kelham, Notts. 18/9/1798, s. John Chancourt and Lydia Marianne Girardot. BNC, Oxford 1817, BA1821, dn21 (Lin.), p23 (Chester for York), MA1824. R. Screverton, Notts. 1824-78, V. Stanford on Soar, Notts. 1826-9 (res.), R. (and patron) of Car Colston, Notts. 1838 to death 23/10/1878 aged 80, leaving £25,000 [C131417. YCO. Austin2. M. Bray, *The Girardot family* (Upton upon Severn, 1996-8) has his port. on the cover of each volume] Married 1828 Sophia Georgiana Chaplin (a clergy dau.), with issue. 'A rich, sporting parson.'

**GIRDLESTONE (Charles)** Born City of London 6/3/1797, s. Samuel Rainbow Girdlestone (barrister) and Caroline Roberts Powell. Wadham, Oxford 1814, BA1818, then Balliol, Fellow 1818-26, dn20 (Ox.), MA1821, p21 (Ox.). R. Sedgley, Staffs. 1826-37, R. Alderley, Cheshire 1837-47, R. Kingswinford, Staffs. 1847-77. Died Weston-super-Mare, Som. ('in delicate health') 28/4/1881, leaving £1,692-9s-4d. [C11221. ODNB. Boase. DEB] Married 1826 Ann Elizabeth Morrell, with clerical sons Henry, and Robert Baker Girdlestone. Port. online. An enormous list of his publications in CR65 (incl. ones on sanitary reform). Brother below.

**GIRDLESTONE (Edward)** Born St Pancras, London 6/9/1805, s. of Samuel Rainbow Girdle-stone (barrister) and Caroline Roberts Powell. Balliol, Oxford 1822, BA1826, dn28 (Chester), MA1829, p30 (Chester). V. Deane, Bolton, Lancs. 1830-55, V. Farnworth, Bolton 1831, Canon Residentiary of Bristol Cathedral 1854-84, V. Bristol St Nicholas and St Leonard 1855-8, V. Wapley, Glos. 1858-62, R. Halberton, Devon 1862-72, V. Olveston, Glos. 1872 to death (Bristol) 4/12/1884 aged 78, leaving £2,271-9s-4d. [C168946. ODNB (and port.) paints an attractive picture. Boase] Married Deane 6/9/1832 Mary Ridgway, 4 dau., 7s. 'The [Devonshire] agricultural labourers' friend'. Brother above.

**GIRDLESTONE (Henry)** Born Wells-next-the-Sea, Norfolk 11/9/1785, s. Henry John Girdlestone and Ann Bolton. Trinity, Cambridge 1804, then St Catharine's 1807, dn08 (Nor.), BA1809, p12 (Nor.). R. Colton, Norfolk 1813-71, R. Landford, Wilts. 1833 to death Landford, Wilts. (a widower) 1/2/1871, leaving £4,000 [C92734] Married West Bradenham, Norfolk 27/12/1811 Elizabeth Ann Bolton, with issue.

**GIRDLESTONE (William Ewin)** Bapt. Norwich 1/11/1785, s. Rev. William Girdlestone (R. Kelling w. Salthouse, Norfolk) and Elizabeth Jessop Ewin. Caius, Cambridge 1803 [in army 1808-12] dn14 (Nor.), p14 (Nor.). (succ. his father as) R. Kelling w. Salthouse 1821 to death 3/12/1840 [C113114] Married Newington, London 9/2/1809 Mary Anne Spree, with issue.

**GISBORNE (James)** Bapt. Barton under Needwood, Staffs. 14/7/1792, s. Rev. Thomas Gisborne (Yoxall Lodge, Staffs.) and Mary Babington. Magdalene, Cambridge 1811, BA 1815, dn15 (Salis.), p16 (Salis.), MA1825. (succ. his father as) R. Barton under Needwood 1820-39, R. Croxall, Derbys. 1839 to death 1/2/1872 aged 79, leaving £35,000 [C11197. ODNB] Married Walcot, Bath 29/6/1841 Charlotte Trevelyan.

**GLADSTONE (John)** Born Liverpool 1/1/1803, s. Murray Gladstone and Susanna Finchett. BNC, Oxford 1820, BA1823, MA 1826, dn26 (Chester), p27 (Chester). PC. Bootle St Mary, Lancs. 1827-[46], R. Stoke upon Tern, Shropshire 1846 [income in CR65 £1,049] to death 20/5/1869 aged 66, leaving £450 [C168947] Married Edge Hill, Liverpool 12/5/1828 Mary Anne Wild, with clerical son.

**GLADWIN (Charles Thomas)** Born in the East Indies, s. Col. Charles Gladwin (Derbys.) and Thomasine Stanhope. Queens', Cambridge 1818, then Jesus 1818 (aged 33), dn20 (Lin.), p22 (Lin.), LLB1828, BCL1830. Chap. Liverpool St

Philip 1828, (joint) PC. Liverpool St Martin in the Fields 1830 (sole from 1834) to burial 11/3/1846 aged 61 [C60964] Married (1) Limerick, Ireland 1/5/1804 Barbara Ross-Lewin (2) Liverpool 4/11/1817 Mary Benson; with clerical son.

**GLAISTER (William)** Bapt. Camerton, Cumberland 6/2/1763, s. John Glaister and Elizabeth Fryer. Literate: dn89 (Chester), p90 (York for Chester). V. Kirkby Fleetham, Yorks. 1791 to death 3/3/1844 ('after a painful and protracted illness') [C132226. YCO] Married Kirby Fleetham 15/4/1794 Elizabeth Robinson, with clerical son.

**GLANVILLE (John)** Bapt. St Germans, Cornwall 29/4/1797, s. Francis Glanville and Elizabeth Fanshaw. Balliol, Oxford 1816, BA 1820, dn21 (Ex.), p22 (Ex.), MA1824. PC. St Germans 1822-[28], R. Jacobstow, Cornwall 1832 and V. Davidstow, Cornwall 1833 to death. Dom. Chap. to 2nd Earl of St Germans 1833. Died Jacobstow 15/8/1864 aged 66, leaving £2,000 [C136768]

**GLEADOW (Thomas Reader)** Bapt. Hull 19/9/1781, s. Thomas Gleadow (shipwright) and Anne Reader. Queens', Cambridge 1800, BA1804, dn04 (York), Fellow 1805, p05 (York), MA1807. H/M Walsall G/S 1811-24 (res.); R. Frodesley, Shropshire 1826 to death 1842 aged 62 [but not in BMD] [C11202. YCO] Married Doncaster, Yorks. 8/4/1807 Elizabeth Littlewood, with clerical son.

**GLEED (George)** Born Reading, Berks., s. Thomas Gleed and Jane Round. St John's, Oxford 1797 (aged 18), BA1801, dn03 (Ox.), p04 (Chester for Salis.), MA1806, BD1810, Fellow to 1831, etc. PC. Northmoor, Oxon. 1823-7, V. Chalfont St Peter, Bucks. 1830 to death 6/6/1863 leaving £16,000 [C29412. DEB]

**GLEIG (George Robert)** Born Stirling 30/4/1796, s. Rt. Rev. George Gleig (Bishop of Brechin in the Scottish Episcopal Church) and Janet Hamilton. Glasgow University 1809-12, Snell Exhibitioner to Balliol, Oxford 1811 [but left to join the army, fighting and being wounded in Spain, France and the United States], then Magdalen Hall, Oxford, BA1818, dn19 (Cant.), p20 (Peterb. for Cant.), MA1821. PC. Ash, Kent 1821-34, R. Ivychurch, Kent (and Preacher throughout the Diocese of Canterbury) 1822-79, Chap. to Chelsea [Army Pensioners'] Hospital, London 1834-46, Chaplain General to the Forces 1844-75 (and Inspector General of Military Schools 1846-75), Prebend of Willesden in St Paul's Cathedral, London 1848 to death (Stratfield Turgis, Hants.) 9/7/1888, leaving £1,629-5s-0d. [C111842. ODNB. Boase. Snell] Married Edinburgh 24/6/1819 [or Stirling 24/6/1818?] Sarah Cameron, of Kinlochbervie, with issue. Prolific writer on military subjects. 'A decided enemy to cant in every form'.

**GLENNIE (John David)** Born Dulwich, Surrey 20/1/1795, s. William Glennie and Mary Gardiner. Trinity, Cambridge 1814, BA1819, dn22 (Nor.), p22 (Lin. for Cant.), MA1823. PC. Sandgate Chapel, Folkestone, Kent 1822-35, Min. St Mary's [Proprietary] Chapel, Grosvenor Square, London 1835-66. Dom. Chap. to Earl of Darnley 1824-33; Secretary of the Clergy Orphans' Corporation 1841-61 and of S.P.C.K. 1842-68; Inspector of Schools 1857-60. Died London 4/11/1874, leaving £7,000. [C60968. Boase. LNCP] Married Camberwell, London 5/7/1873 Mary Maria Woodyear, with issue. Treasurer of the French Protestant Ecclesiastical Committee.

**GLOSSOP (Charles)** From Isleworth, Middx., probably s. Francis Glossop (merchant) and Ann Gapper. Corpus Christi, Cambridge 1805, re-adm. 1807, then Magdalene 1808, BA1811, p11 (Win. for Salis.). R. Rode (o/w Road) w. Wolverton, Som. 1812 to death 30/4/1874, leaving £30,000 [C41912] Brother below.

**GLOSSOP (Henry)** Born London 17/12/1780, s. Francis Glossop (merchant) and Ann Gapper. Pembroke, Cambridge 1799, then Corpus Christi 1802, BA1804, dn05 (London for Peterb.), p05 (London), MA1807. R. West Dean w. East Grinstead, Wilts. 1811-21, V. Isleworth, Middx. 1821-55, living latterly at Silver Hall there. Died 21/8/1869, leaving £7,000 [C92736] Married Marylebone, London 11/8/1814 Charlotte Newland (Westergate, Sussex), with issue. Brother above.

**GLOUCESTER (Bishop of)** see under **MONK, James Henry**

**GLOVER (George)** Bapt. Wigan, Lancs. 24/6/1777, s. of George Glover and Grace Ransom. BNC, Oxford 1797, BA1801, dn02 (Bangor), p02 (Bangor), MA1811. R. Water Stratford, Bucks. 1802-4 (res.), V. Finmere, Oxon. 1802-4, R. South Repps, Norfolk 1804-

62, V. Cromer, Norfolk 1807-31, V. Billingford, Norfolk 1818-21 (res.), Archdeacon of Sudbury 1823-62, PC. Bungay St Mary, Suffolk 1830, V. Gayton, Norfolk 1831 to death 4/5/1862. No will traced. [C157783] Described by E. Richardson (*Classical Victorians* ... (Cambridge, 2013)) as 'a fearsomely dedicated social climber' who was thrown out of the Royal Society for unpaid dues.

**GLOVER (John)** Born Creake, Norfolk, s. of Philip Glover (farmer, Sedgeford, Norfolk). Caius, Cambridge 1791 (aged 16), BA1796, dn97 (Nor.), p00 (Nor.). R. Stonham Parva, Suffolk 1803-16, V. Freiston w. Butterwick, Lincs. 1816 and R. Rand w. Fulnetby, Lincs. 1830 to death (Fulnetby) 28/12/1837 [C60972] Had issue.

**GLOVER (Robert [Merong])** Literate: dn94 (Lin.), p94 (Lin.). V. Wispington, Lincs. 1794 to death. Dom. Chap. to 1st Earl of Blessington 1814. Died 1838 aged 65 [C60974]

**GLOVER (William Lowder)** Born Bewdley, Worcs. 1784, s. John Glover. St Edmund Hall, Oxford 1804 (aged 20), then Queens', Cambridge 1805, dn09 (Ex.), BA1809, p09 (B&W), MA1812. C-in-C. Bedminster St Paul, Bristol 1820, R. Charmouth, Dorset 1826-33 (res.). Died Wells 7/11/1838 aged 54 [C41083] Married 19/1/1814 Rebecca Cooke.

**GLUBB (John Matthew)** Born Dartmouth, Devon 5/11/1791, s. Peter Goodman Glubb and Jane Matthew. Exeter, Oxford 1810, BA1814, dn14 (Ex.), p15 (Ex.), MA1822. PC. Dartmouth St Petrox, Cornwall (and S/M Dartmouth G/S) 1822, R. Shermanbury, Sussex 1836 (and RD 1855) to death. Diocesan Inspector of Schools 1855. Died 27/9/1871, leaving £2,000 [C144437] Married Little Petherick, Cornwall 10/7/1821 Mary Lyne (of Dartmouth), with issue. Surrogate.

**GLUBB (Peter)** Bapt. Bickton, Devon 10/12/1769, s. Rev. John Glubb and Dinah Warren. Exeter, Oxford 1787, BA1792, dn93 (C&L for Ex.), p94 (Ex.). R. Little Torrington, Devon 1803 and R. Clannaborough, Devon 1827 to death. Dom. Chap. to 1st Baron Rolle 1811; to Mary, Dowager Marchioness of Thomond 1812; to 3rd Earl of Mount Cashell 1827. Died 21/12/1852 [C11226] Wife Christian Mary, and issue. Kept a pack of foxhounds. *J.P.* Devon.

**GLYN (George Henry)** Bapt. Marylebone, London 2/2/1796, s. Thomas Clayton Glyn and Henrietta Elizabeth Sackville Hollingbury. Christ Church, Oxford 1814, BA1817, dn19 (Ox.), p20 (Chester for Cant.), MA1820. V. Henham, Essex 1824 to death (Brighton) 4/3/1847 [C118339] Married Marylebone 9/11/1826 Elizabeth Smith.

**GLYN (George Lewen, Sir, 4th Bart.)** Born Ewall, Surrey 20/8/1804, s. Sir George Glyn, 2nd Bart. and Catherine Powell. Christ Church, Oxford 1824, then St John's, Cambridge 1829, dn30 (Win.), p31 (Win.), BA1831. V. (and patron) of Ewell, Surrey 1831 to death. Lived latterly at St Leonards on Sea, Sussex. Dom. Chap. to Earl of Shaftesbury. Died 7/11/1885, leaving £21,583-16s-8d. [C73799. Boase] Married (1) 6/9/1838 Emily Jane Birch (of St Petersburg, she d. 1854), with issue (2) 5/5/1859 his cousin Henrietta Amelia Carr Glyn (w), with further issue. Succeeded to title 1840.

**GLYN (John Carr *some say* Carr John)** Born Westminster, London 1/7/1799, s. Sir Richard Carr Glyn, 1st Bart. (banker, *M.P.*, and Lord Mayor of London, *q.v.* ODNB) and Mary Elizabeth Plumptre. Christ Church, Oxford, Student [Fellow] 1818-25, BA1821, dn26 (Bristol), MA1827. R. Stanbridge, Beds. 1828, R. Little Hinton (Hinton Parva), Dorset 1830, R. Witchampton, Dorset 1830 to death. Dom. Chap. to Lord de Manley. Died 25/10/1896, leaving £76,244-12s-2d. [C52644. DEB] Married (1) Chelsea, London 21/6/1831 Augusta Granville (d.1837), with military issue (2) Bath 25/4/1839 Anna Cleather.

**GODBOLD (George Berry)** Born Bloomsbury, London 31/7/1785 (bapt. Medstead, Hants. 7/9/1802), s. Samuel (of Beccles, Suffolk) and Ann Godbold. Exeter, Oxford 1805, migrated to Emmanuel, Cambridge 1809, BA1810, dn10 (Win.), p11 (Win.), MA1813. R. (and patron) of Greatham, Hants. 1814 to death 25/4/1838 [C73800] Married St George's Hanover Square, London 5/1/1819 Elizabeth Ellen Clara Cooke.

**GODDARD (Charles)** Born Westminster, London 11/12/1769, s. Charles Goddard [though paternity disputed]. Christ Church, Oxford 1787. Protégé of the Grenville family. In Navy at Battle of Trafalgar; prisoner of war in France. Major civil servant. dn12 (Nor.), p13

(London), MA1821, BD & DD1821. Prebend of Louth in Lincoln Cathedral 1814-45, 'energetic' Archdeacon of Lincoln 1817 (3 years after ordination) -1845 (res.), Sub-Dean 1845, R. St. James Garlickhithe, City of London 1821-36 [Thomas in ERC], V. Bexley, Kent 1825-33 (res.), R. Ibstock, Leics. 1836 to death. Dom. Chap. to 1st Baron Grenville 1812; to Bishop of Rochester; to HRH Duke of Clarence/William 1V 1821-37. Died (unm.) 21/1/1845 [C60976. ODNB. Kaye]

**GODDARD (Edward)** Born Clyffe Pypard, Wilts. 10/5/1761, s. Rev. Edward Goddard, sen. and Joanna Reid. BNC, Oxford 1779, BA1783, dn84 (Salis.), p85 (Ox. for Salis.), MA1789. (succ. his father as) V. (and patron) of Clyffe Pypard 1791 (living at Clyffe House) to death 23/1/1839 [C29418] Married St Pancras, London 10/6/1802 Annica Susan Baynton, with clerical son.

**GODDARD (Edward Henry Emilius [William])** Born East Woodhay, Hants. 22/7/1792, s. Rev. William Goddard and Jennie Sloper. Sidney, Cambridge 1811, BA1815, MA 1818, incorporated at Oxford 1842. V. Pagham, Sussex 1823-50, V. Chidham, Sussex 1823-4, V. Sidlesham, Sussex 1823-49, V. Eartham, Sussex 1829 to death 1878 (3rd q.) aged 87. No will traced [C63554] Was married.

**GODDARD (Erasmus)** Bapt. Lingwood, Norfolk 8/10/1776, s. Rev. Thomas and Elizabeth Goddard. Corpus Christi, Cambridge 1795, BA1799, dn99 (Nor.), p16 (Chester for Nor.). PC. (and patron) of Lingwood 1816 to death 24/1/1844 [C113148]

**GODDARD (Richard)** Born Swindon, Wilts. 9/10/1787, s. Ambrose Goddard and Sarah M. Williams. St John's, Oxford 1803, BA1807, dn11 (Ox.), MA1811, p12 (Ox.), BD1816, Fellow 1817. R. Draycot Foliat, Wilts. 1817, V. Kemble, Wilts. 1826. Died Broadstone, Oxon. 25/8/1844 [C29420]

**GODDARD (William Stanley)** Born Stepney, London 9/10/1757, s. John (merchant) and Elizabeth Goddard. Merton, Oxford 1776, BA 1781, dn80 (Ox.), MA1783, BD and DD1795. Second Master 1784, then Headmaster of Winchester College 1795-1809 ('one of the best headmasters ever', counting Arnold among his reforming pupils); R. Bepton, Sussex 1785, Reculversland Prebend in St Paul's Cathedral, London 1814-45, R. Kingston, IoW 1819-27 (res.), Canon of Bedminster Secunda in Salisbury Cathedral 1829 and R. Wherwell, IoW 1835 to death. Dom. Chap. to Bishop of London/Archbishop of Canterbury 1814. Died (unmarried?) 10/10/1845, leaving £60,000 [C29421. ODNB]

**GODFREY (Daniel Race)** Born Bath, Som. 12/4/1787, s. Rev. Race Godfrey and Elizabeth Dewe. Queen's, Oxford 1807, BA1810, dn10 (B&W), MA1816, BD and DD1841. Principal of Grosvenor College, Bath ('for the sons of the gentry and nobility'); PC. White Colne, Essex 1817-33 (res.). Died (Stapleford Tawny, Essex) 28/5/1872, leaving £4,000 [C41084] Married Leigh Delamere, Wilts. 25/3/1812 Maria Ward. Confusion with clerical son of father's name.

**GODFREY (William)** From Bucks. Queens', Cambridge 1820, dn23 (Lin.), p23 (Lin.), BA 1824, MA1828. V. Ravenstone, Bucks. 1823, PC. Weston Underwood, Bucks. 1827-60, V. Studley, Warwicks. 1860 to death there 31/5/1872 aged 72, leaving £16,000 [C60991] Widow Jane.

**GODMOND (Samuel Francis)** Bapt. Ripon, Yorks. 15/2/1773, s. Rev. Isaac and Elizabeth Godmond. University, Oxford 1792, dn96 (York), BA1797, p97 (Ox.), MA1800. V. East Malling, Kent 1805 to death 23/9/1845 [C29423. YCO] Married City of London 30/7/1802 Anne Humphreys.

**GODWIN (William)** Born West Kirby, Cheshire, s. Roger Godwin. BNC, Oxford 1795 (aged 18), BA1799, dn01 (Chester), MA1802, p02 (Chester). R. Chester St Martin 1826 (and Minor Canon of Chester Cathedral 1828) to death 29/6/1842 aged 68 [C168952]

**GOE (Bartholomew)** Born Horncastle, Lincs. 24/8/1767, s. John Goe and Ann Meggitt. St Catharine's, Cambridge 1785, BA1790, dn90 (Lin.), p91 (Lin.), MA1822. V. Boston, Lincs. (and Preacher throughout the Diocese of Lincoln) 1817 to death (Huxham, Devon) 15/7/1838 [C60993] Married Boston 4/2/1796 Frances Flowers, with issue.

**GOFORTH (Francis)** Bapt. Bitchfield, Lincs. 2/3/1766, s. Richard Goforth and Ann Wilcox. Emmanuel, Cambridge 1795, BA1799, dn99 (Cant.), Fellow 1801, MA1802, p03 (Win. for Ely). V. Whitchurch Canonicorum w. Stanton St

Gabriel, Dorset (and Preacher throughout the Diocese of Bristol) 1805-39, Prebend of Haselbury in Wells Cathedral 1816 to death 17/2/1839 [C41917] Married Wells 6/4/1815 Susannah Wall. *J.P.* Somerset.

**GOGGS (Henry)** Born Whissonsett, Norfolk 30/8/1800 (bapt. 21/9/1817), s. Henry Goggs and Martha Buscall. Christ's, Cambridge 1819, BA1823, dn23 (Nor.), p24 (Nor.), MA1826. V. South Creake, Norfolk 1824 to sudden death there 2/1/1858 aged 58, leaving £4,000 [C113151] Married Stepney, London 21/4/1825 Mary Coley (w), with issue.

**GOLDESBROUGH (John)** Bapt. Bruton, Som. 17/7/1777, s. Rev. John Goldesbrough, sen. and Grace Mogg. Balliol, Oxford 1793, then Magdalen, Fellow BA1797, MA1799, dn00 (Ox.), p01 (Ox.), BD1809. R. Slimbridge, Glos. 1811 and PC. Redlynch, Som. 1813 to death (Bruton) 6/5/1846 [C29425] Wife Lydia Lowndes.

**GOLDFRAP (Frederick William)** Born Basseterre, St Kitts, West Indies, s. John George Goldfrap and Sarah Wharton. Literate: dn15 (London), p16 (Chester for Salis.). R. (and patron of) Clenchwarton, Norfolk 1817 to death 26/11/1838 aged 46 [C92742] Married 12/5/1817 Ann Stephans, with issue.

**GOLDING (Charles [William])** Bapt. Bury St Edmunds, Suffolk 11/9/1754, s. Thomas (a solicitor) and Martha Golding. Christ's, Cambridge 1772, BA1776, dn76 (Ely for Nor.). R. Crofton, Yorks. 1814-17, PC. Ruscombe, Berks. 1817-35, R. Stratford St Mary, Suffolk 1817-44. Died 4/9/1865. No will traced [C105827] clerical s. Henry (later Golding-Palmer), also at Stratford St Mary.

**GOLDING (Joseph)** From Wigton, Cumberland, s. Joseph Golding. Queen's, Oxford 1776 (aged 20), BA1780, dn83 (B&W), MA1784. V. Newbold Pacey, Warwicks. 1803 to death 16/1/1848 [C23899]

**GOLIGHTLY (Thomas)** Bapt. Liverpool 19/9/1781, s. Thomas Golightly. BNC, Oxford 1799, BA1803, MA1805, dn06 (Ox.), p07 (Ox.). R. Boddington, Northants. 1807 to death (Leamington, Warwicks.) 13/8/1867, leaving £9,000 [C29427] Clerical son.

**GOOCH (Charles John)** Born Layham, Suffolk 15/8/1803, s. Sir Thomas Sherlock Gooch, 5th Bart., *M.P.*, and Marianne Whittaker. Christ Church, Oxford 1821, BA1826, dn26 (Nor.), p27 (Nor.), MA1828. R. South Cove, Suffolk 1828 and R. Toppesfield, Essex 1828 [total income in CR65 £1,120] to death 25/6/1876, leaving £4,000 [C113155] Married Markshall, Essex 17/7/1832 Agatha Hanbury, with clerical son Philip Sherlock Gooch. Some say Thomas C.J.G.

**GOOCH (John Lewis)** Bapt. Saxlingham, Norfolk 19/11/1792, s. Ven. John Gooch (Archdeacon of Sudbury) and Barbara Sneyd. Christ Church, Oxford 1811, BA1814, dn15 (Nor.), p16 (B&W). R. Binegar (or Benager), Som. 1816 [blank in ERC] to death (Southampton) 19/7/1846 [C41086]

**GOOCH (Richard)** Bapt. Benacre, Suffolk 24/12/1781, s. Sir Thomas Gooch, 4th Bart. and Anna Maria Hayward. Christ Church, Oxford 1800, BA1804, dn06 (Nor.), p06 (Nor.). R. Frostenden, Suffolk 1806 and R. North Cove w. Willingham St Mary, Suffolk 1810 to death 22/3/1873 aged 91, leaving £2,000 [C113157]

**GOOCH (William)** Born Newcastle upon Tyne 18/9/1798, s. Col. William Gooch and Jane Bridget Wilson (dau. of a banker). Clare, Cambridge 1816, SCL, dn21 (Glos.), p22 (Glos.), LLB1823. R. Benacre, Suffolk 1823-76 (w. Easton Bavants after union in 1833), RD. V. Stainton in Cleveland, Yorks. 1833 [total income in CR65 £1,036] (and Prebend of Strensall in York Minster 1845) to death (London) 27/2/1876, leaving £1,000 [C41087] Married St George's Hanover Square, London 8/7/1822 Anne Jarrett (w) (of Jamaica), with issue.

**GOODACRE (William)** Bapt. Long Clawston, Leics. 29/6/1783, s. William Elsey Goodacre and Ruth Cobley. Literate: dn12 (York), p14 (York). Usher at Mansfield G/S 1813-39; PC. Mansfield Woodhouse, Notts. 1820-59, PC. Skegby, Yorks. 1820 and PC. Sutton in Ash, Yorks. 1820 to death 13/11/1859 aged 76, leaving £600 [C131418. YCO] Married Newark, Notts. 24/12/1811 Mary Wilkinson, at least 8 ch. Left a diary. W. Clay-Dove, 'Around the parish: memories of a 19th century Vicar of Sutton-in-Ash', *Nottinghamshire Historian*, No. 23 (1979).

**GOODALL (James Joseph)** Born Dinton Hall, Dinton, Bucks. 4/1/1800, s. Rev. William Goodall (below) and Rebecca Vanhattem. Pembroke, Oxford 1819, BA1823, dn24 (Ely), MA 1826, p26 (Lin.). V. Bromham w. Oakley annexed, Beds. 1827 (and RD) to death (Dinton Hall) 25/9/1886, leaving £4,553-17s-7d. [C61001] Married Gretton, Northants. 6/2/1824 Elizabeth Boon, with issue. *J.P.*

**GOODALL (Joseph)** Born Westminster, London 2/3/1760, s. Joseph and Mary Goodall. King's, Cambridge 1779, Fellow 1782-8, BA 1783, MA1786, dn87 (Lin.), p88 (London for Lin.), DD1798. S/M Eton College 1783-1801, H/M Eton College 1802-9, Provost of Eton 1809-40; R. Hedgerley, Bucks. 1787-97, R. Sessay, Yorks. 1797-8 (res.), V. Ellingham, Hants. 1804-8, Canon of Windsor 1808-40, R. Hitcham, Bucks. 1811-33, R. West Ilsley, Berks. 1827 to death 25/3/1840 [C61004. ODNB. Kaye] Married Eton 14/3/1788 Harriet Arabella Prior (dau. of a clerical master at Eton). 'Said to have possessed the virtues of the ideal headmaster of an English public school. An eminent scholar ... and scarcely less distinguished for the pure benevolence of his heart, his unbounded charity, and the liberal hospitality which he exercised in his high station', etc.; or alternatively: 'conservative in outlook and characterized as an insuperable obstacle to innovation'. Brother below.

**GOODALL (William)** Born Westminster, London 22/2/1757, s. Joseph and Mary Goodall. Christ's, Cambridge 1775, BA1780, dn80 (C&L for York), p81 (Lin.), MA1785. R. Marsham, Norfolk 1787 to death 19/3/1844 [C11234. YCO] Married Great Berkhampstead, Herts. 15/4/1788 Rebecca (dau. of Sir John Vanhattem), with clerical s. James Joseph (above). Brother above. *J.P.* Bucks.

**GOODCHILD (Thomas Oliver)** Born City of London 8/9/1800, s. Thomas and Sarah Goodchild. Exeter, Oxford 1819, BA1822, dn24, p25, MA1825. Chap. of Donative of South Malling, Sussex 1832, R. Hackney, London 1839 to death (Folkestone, Kent) 5/9/1877 aged 76, leaving £80,000 [C63557] Married Bloomsbury, London 4/9/1832 Ellen Perring, with issue. A sound Tory, noted for his 'hearty, sprightly manner'.

**GOODCHILD (William Thomas)** Born Christiansted, St Croix (now US Virgin Islands), West Indies 25/12/1777, s. Rev. Cecil Wray and Rebecca Goodchild. Literate: dn19 (Nor.), p21 (Nor.). V. East Tilbury, Essex 1832 to death 2/11/1844 [C113160] Married Westminster, London 18/5/1804 Elizabeth Ann Jeffries, with issue.

**GOODDAY (John William)** Bapt. Boughton, Northants. 16/1/1799, s. Rev. William Goodday (below) and Rebecca Tawke Frances Butcher. Queen's, Oxford 1818, BA1822, dn22 (London), p23 (London), MA1825. V. Falmer, Sussex 1832, R. Stanmer, Sussex 1832-[59]. Died 27/1/1868, leaving £600 [C63558]

**GOODDAY (William)** Born Strelly, Notts. 27/11/1773, s. Rev. William Goodday and Margaret Evetts. Queen's, Oxford 1792, BA 1796, dn96 (Peterb.), MA1798, p00 (Peterb.). V. Terling, Essex 1801 to death 7/8/1848 [C110235] Married 1797 Rebecca Tawke Frances Butcher, with clerical son, above.

**GOODDEN (George)** Born Bath 14/2/1803, s. Wyndham Goodden and Margaret Jeane. Jesus, Cambridge 1823, BA1827, dn27 (B&W), p28 (B&W), MA1836. R. North Barrow, Som. 1831 and PC. South Barrow 1836 to death (Gloucester, unmarried) 21/6/1870, leaving £6,000 [C41088] Brother below.

**GOODDEN (Wyndham Jeane)** Bapt. Bristol 26/7/1800, s. Wyndham Goodden and Margaret Jeane. Oriel, Oxford 1818, BA1822, dn23 (Bristol), p24 (Chester), MA1832. R. Nether Compton w. Over Compton, Dorset 1824 to death 18/4/1884, leaving £13,342-5s-8d. [C52650] Brother above.

**GOODE (Alexander)** From Westminster, London, s. Thomas Goode. Pembroke, Cambridge 1820 (aged 18), BA1824, dn25 (London), MA1826, p26 (London). V. Caverswell, Staffs. 1829 to death (Rome, where he lived) 20/12/1861, leaving £7,000 in England [C11235] Widow Anne Charlotte.

**GOODE (Ambrose)** Bapt. Cambridge 11/2/1770, s. Samuel Goode and Hannah Nicholson. Trinity, Cambridge 1788, BA1792, dn83 (Lin.), p94 (Lin.), MA1797. V. Waddingworth, Lincs. 1794 and V. Terrington St Clement w. St John, Norfolk 1803 to death 23/4/1843 aged 75 [C61005 and 113161] Married Ashley Puerorum, Lincs. 2/10/1794

Rachel Elmhirst, with issue. Son of same name followed him at Terrington.

**GOODENOUGH (John Joseph)** Born Boughton Pogis, Oxon. 1/1/17779, s. Rev. Edmund Goodenough and Ann Juliana Taunton. New, Oxford 1797, BA1801, dn01 (Salis.), Fellow, p03 (Salis.), MA1805, BD & DD1817. S/M Bristol G/S 1810, H/M 1812-43; R. Bow Brickhill, Bucks. 1820-40, R. Spernal, Warwicks. 1840-3, R. Broughton Pogis 1845 to death (Swindon) 22/4/1855 [C52652] Married (1) Marlborough, Wilts. 18/5/1807 Margaret Ward (d.1813) (2) Clifton, Bristol 7/7/1818 Isabella Newman, with issue. Brother William, below.

**GOODENOUGH (Joseph)** Born Frampton, Dorset 1801 (bapt.4/1/1813), s. Joseph Goodenough and Ann Jean Frowd. Balliol, Oxford 1818, dn23 (Chester), SCL, p24 (Chester). R. (and patron) of Godmanstone, Dorset and PC. Nether Cerne 1824 to death 24/7/1842 [C52651] Married Overmoigne, Dorset 9/4/1828 Mrs Margaret Jane (Maxwell) Birch.

**GOODENOUGH (Samuel James)** Born Ealing, Middx. 3/3/1774, s. Rt. Rev. Samuel Goodenough (Bishop of Carlisle) and Elizabeth Ford. Wadham, Oxford 1791, BA1795, p97 (Chester), p98 (Ox.), MA1802. R. Broughton Pogis, Oxon. 1798-1844, R. Hampton on Thames, Middx. 1803-44, Canon of 3rd Prebend in Carlisle Cathedral 1810 and R. Aikton, Cumberland 1844 to death 15/3/1858, leaving £600 [C3395. Platt] Married 14/12/1797 Anne Budden Prickett, with issue.

**GOODENOUGH (William)** Bapt. Broughton Pogis, Oxon. 24/1/1773, s. of Rev. Edmund Goodenough (V. Swindon, Wilts., and nephew of Bishop Goodenough) and Ann Juliana Taunton. Christ Church, Oxford 1790, BA1794, dn95 (Salis.), p97 (Peterb. for Salis.), MA1797. (succ. his uncle as Proprietor? of) Ealing Preparatory School; V. Warkworth, Northumberland 1818, R. Mareham le Fen, Lincs. 1818-54, Archdeacon of Carlisle 1827 (w. 2nd Prebend of Carlisle Cathedral 1826 and R. Great Salkeld appended 1827) to death (Mareham) 13/12/1854 aged 82 [C3396. Boase. Platt] Married Ealing, Middx. 1/6/1797 his cousin Mary Anne Goodenough (dau. of a Bishop of Carlisle), with issue. Brother John Joseph, above.

**GOODENOUGH (William Stephen)** Bapt. Winterbourne Stoke, Wilts. 19/9/1795, s. Stephen and Anne Goodenough. St John's, Oxford 1795, BA1798, dn99 (Glos.), p00 (Glos.), MA1801. R. (and patron) of Yate, Glos. 1801 to death 10/1/1843 [C151180] Married Iron Acton, Glos. 5/2/1816 Ann Mair, with issue.

**GOODMAN (John)** From Kemerton, Glos., s. Rev. Godfrey Goodman. [NiVoF] (succ. his father as) R. Kemerton 1832-[39] [blank in ERC]. Died? [C151182]

**GOODMAN (Maurice Hiller)** Born Easton Royal, Wilts. 27/8/1786, s. John Goodman and Mary Patient Stevens. BNC, Oxford 1804, BA 1808, dn09 (Salis.), MA1811. V. Bitton (o/w Kingswood), Glos. 1823, PC. East Kennett, Wilts. 1823 to death (Avebury, Wilts.) 24/1/1856 [C92746] Married Bath St Michael 27/4/1830 Mary Anne Pears, with issue.

**GOODRICH (Bartlet)** Bapt. Bristol 9/3/1790, s. John Goodrich and Dorothy Harwood. Oriel, Oxford 1808, then University, BA1812, MA 1815, dn16 (B&W), p16 (B&W). V. Great Saling, Essex 1816 (w. Sinecure R. Little Saling 1817), R. Hardmead, Bucks. 1817-55. In the Kensington House private asylum from 7/12/1854 to death 28/9/1855 [C41090] Married (1) Great Saling 17/5/1815 Mary Anne Goodrich (d.1821) (2) 16/11/1822 Mary Anne White, w. issue. Port. online.

**GOODWIN, *born* BONES (Charles)** Born Castle Hedingham, Essex, s. Rev. James Bones (V. Weedon Pinckney, Northants.) and Anne Goodwin. St John's, Cambridge 1791 & 1793, BA1796, dn98 (Lin. for Ely), MA1799, p99 (Ely). R. Hildersham, Cambs. 1806 to death 12/3/1847 aged 73 [C100028] Married (1) 1/9/1801 Eliza Naylor (a clergy dau.) (2) Chesterton, Cambs. 15/11/1803 Sarah Grainger, with issue.

**GOODWIN (Henry John)** Born ?Dalestoll, Notts. 21/11/1803, s. Francis Goodwin and Frances Gladwyn. Emmanuel, Cambridge 1823, BA1827, dn29 (C&L), p30 (C&L). PC. Morton, Derbys. 1830-41, not beneficed 1842-55, Inc. Okeover, Staffs. 1856. Lived at Hinchley Wood House, Mapleton, Derbys. Died Malvern, Worcs. 24/5/1863, leaving £1,500 [C11238] Married Morton, Derbys. 11/10/1832 Frances Eleanora Turbutt (w) (a clergy dau.).

**GOODYER, GOODYAR (George Dinely)** Probably bapt. Gloucester 17/8/1778, s. George Dinely Goodyar and Lucy Gregory. St John's, Cambridge 1807, [CCEd adds MA], dn09 (Car.), p10 (Car.). V. Tibshelf, Derbys. 1819, R. Otterden, Kent 1825 to death 27/9/1849 aged 72 [C5897] Married St Pancras, London 13/11/1805 Harriet Sanders, with issue.

**GORDEN (William)** see below under **GORDON**

**GORDON (George)** Bapt. Cambridge 7/12/1763, s. Ven. John Gordon (Archdeacon of Lincoln) and Mrs Anne (Dighton) Williams. St John's, Cambridge 1780, BA1784 [adm. Lincoln's Inn 1784] Fellow 1787, MA1787, dn88 (Ely), p88 (Lin.), BD1794, DD1810. R. Gumley, Leics. 1788-1807, Prebend and Precentor of Exeter Cathedral 1789-1809 (res.), R. Sedgebrook w. East Allington, Lincs. 1792-1845, R. West Deeping, Lincs. 1807-10 (res.), V. Horbling, Lincs. 1807-45 (non-res.), Canon of Lincoln Cathedral and Prebend of Decem Librarum in Lincoln Cathedral 1808-45, Dean of Exeter 1809-10, then Dean of Lincoln 1810-45, R. Whittington, Derbys. 1812-17, V. Orston w. Thoroton, Notts. 1818-21, (declined the Bishopric of Peterborough 1819), V. Hambledon, Rutland 1819-22. Chap. to Marquess of Bath 1792. Died 2/8/1845 aged 82. Will proved at £140,000 [C61021. Venn is confused. Bennett1 omits the last 2 charges. Kaye] Married Lincoln 11/8/1791 Sarah Tomlinson, with clerical sons George, Henry, and John below. 'Was distinguished all his life by a zealous and careful preservation of things as they were'.

**GORDON (George)** Bapt. Lincoln 29/7/1792, s. Very Rev. George Gordon (Dean of Lincoln, above) and Sarah Tomlinson. BNC, Oxford 1811, BA1814, dn15 (Lin.), p16 (Chester for C&L), MA1818. R. Fenny Bentley, Derbys. 1816-21, R. Whittington, Derbys. 1817, R. Muston, Leics. 1821 to death 15/6/1872, leaving £20,000. Dom. Chap. to Bishop of Gloucester / Bath & Wells [C11244 has several people here] Married Staunton, Notts. 28/6/1821 Elizabeth Katherine Staunton, w. clerical son John Gordon. Brothers Henry, and John, below.

**GORDON (George, Lord)** Born Aboyne Castle, Aberdeenshire 27/1/1794, s. George Gordon, 9th Marquess of Huntley and Catherine Anne Cope. Clare, Cambridge 1815, MA1817, dn18 (Lin.), p19 (Lin.). R. Chesterton, Hunts. 1819 and R. (and patron) of Haddon, Hunts. 1819 to death 25/9/1862, leaving £1,500 [C61022] Married Woodston, Hunts. 29/7/1851 Charlotte Anne Vaughan (w) (a military dau.). Full title: The Hon. and Rev. Lord George Gordon.

**GORDON (Henry)** Born Clifton, Bristol, s. John Gordon. Merton, Oxford 1813 (aged 18), BA1816, dn19 (Bangor for B&W), MA1819, p20 (Glos.). R. Bilsthorpe, Notts. 1822 and V. South Scarle w. Besthorpe and Girton, Notts. 1824 to death 6/1/1839 aged 44 [C135876]

**GORDON (Henry)** Bapt. Exeter Cathedral 19/12/1798, s. Very Rev. George Gordon, Dean of Exeter (above) and Sarah Tomlinson. Exeter, Oxford 1815, BA1819, MA1822, dn22 (Lin.), p23 (Lin.). R. Kirk Ireton, Glos. 1828, R. Edlaston, Derbys. 1830-54. Died Woodhall, Lincs. 6/5/1873, leaving £7,000 [C11245] Married (2?) Lincoln 28/4/1859 Mary Powell, with issue. Brothers George, and John, here.

**GORDON (John)** Born 20/10/1794, s. Very Rev. George Gordon, Dean of Exeter (above) and Sarah Tomlinson. St John's, Cambridge 1811, BA1815, MA1818, dn25 (Lin.), LLD. V. Bierton w. Broughton, Bucks. 1825-7, R. Carsington, Derbys. 1826-32, Prebend of Easton in Gordano in Wells Cathedral 1834, R. St Antholin w. St John the Baptist upon Walbrook, City of London 1826-35, V. Edwin-stowe w. Carburton, Notts. 1835 to death 8/5/1843 [C11247. Venn has dating errors] Had issue. Brothers George, and Henry, above.

**GORDON (Richard)** Born Gower, Glamorgan 1804. [MA but NiVoF] V. Elsfield, Oxon. 1832-77, RD, V. Marston, Oxon. 1849-72. Died 27/11/1877, leaving £2,000 [C29435] Married Ashchurch, Glos. 10/6/1832 Mary Frances Knight, with clerical son. Surrogate. A keen educationalist, as at: www.elsfield.net/history/elsfield-in-the-19th-century/the-reverend-gordon

**GORDON, GORDEN (William)** Bapt. Islip, Oxon. 21/4/1770, s. William Gordon [*pleb*]. All Souls, Oxford 1788, then Merton, BA1792, dn92 (Salis.), p94 (Ox.), MA1795. V. Duns Tew, Oxon. 1794-1834 (w. RD of Woodstock) [but interned 11 years in Verdun, France 1804-14 with the son of his patron (Sir Henry Dashwood, Bart.), and where he was responsible for the distribution of moneys from The (Lloyd's) Patriotic Fund], PC. Horsforth, Guisley, Yorks. 1823 (probably non-res.) to death. Dom. Chap. to 2nd Marquess of Ely 1814; to 5th Duke of Marlborough 1819. Died 9/5/1837 aged 66. [C29433 as Gorden] *J.P.* Oxon.

**GORDON (William)** Bapt. Hastings, Kent 28/10/1788, s. Rev. William Gordon. Trinity, Cambridge 1808, BA1812, dn12 (Roch.), p13 (Salis. for Roch.), MA1815. Priest-Vicar and Prebend of High Offley in Lincoln Cathedral 1819-29, V. West Bromwich Christ Church, Staffs. 1829-49 (and RD 1847-9). Died Lichfield 30/10/1857 [C11249] Married Bloomsbury, London 24/6/1816 Louisa Robinson Jervis, with issue.

**GORDON (William)** Bapt. Marylebone, London 21/11/1792, s. Charles and Mary Gordon. Exeter, Oxford 1813. BA1817, dn17 (B&W), p19 (B&W). R. Spaxton, Som. 1820-33, R. Newtimber, Sussex 1833 [C63564]. Died Charlinch, Som. 8/1/1879, leaving £25,000 [C41092]

**GORE (George)** Born Marylebone, London 1/1/1807, s. Rev. Charles Gore (Barrow Court, Barrow Gurney, Som.) and Harriet Little. Emmanuel, Cambridge 1824, BA1828, dn31 (Bristol for Llandaff), MA1831, p31 (Llandaff). R. Langstone, Monmouth 1831, R. Christon, Som. 1832-3, R. Newton St Lowe, Som. 1841 to death 22/5/1878, leaving £45,000 [C3954] Married Moreton in the Marsh, Glos. 1850 Susannah Hollier, with issue. Brother below.

**GORE (William Charles)** Bapt. Henbury, Glos. 2/7/1801, s. Rev. Charles Gore (Barrow Court, Barrow Gurney, Som.) and Harriet Little. Emmanuel, Cambridge 1818, BA1822, dn24 (Win.), MA1825, p25 (Win.). Chap. of Barrow Gurney 1829 to death (unm.) 17/2/1842 [C73967] Brother above.

**GOSLI (Arthur Judd)**  see under **CARRIGHAN**

**GOSLING (Edward)** Born Staining, London 9/10/1763, s. Sir Francis Gosling and Elizabeth Midwinter. Christ Church, Oxford 1782, then Pembroke, BA1786, MA1789, p91 (Nor. for Win.). R. Hawstead, Suffolk 1794 to death 21/5/1852 [C73968] Married Mary Ann Mills.

**GOSSET (Isaac)** Bapt. Marylebone, London 10/12/1782, s. Rev. Isaac Gosset (bibliographer, *q.v.* ODNB) and Catherine Hill. Exeter, Oxford 1800, BA1804, dn06 (London), MA 1807, p07 (Heref. for London), V. Datchet, Bucks. 1814-21, V. New Windsor, Berks. 1821 to death. 'Chap. to the Royal Household at Windsor under four sovereigns.' Died 11/2/1855 [C61027] Married London 21/4/1814 Dorothea Sophia Banks Lind, with clerical son Isaac Henry. Brother below.

**GOSSET (Thomas Stephen)** Born 1791, s. Rev. Isaac Gosset (bibliographer, *q.v.* ODNB) and Catherine Hill. Trinity, Cambridge 1808, BA 1812, Fellow 1813-47, MA1815, dn17 (B&W), p18 (Salis. for Bristol). V. Old Windsor, Berks. 1824-38. Died Regent's Park, London 22/7/1847 [C41093] Brother above.

**GOSTLING (John Whalley)** Bapt. Twickenham, Surrey 8/10/1787, s. George Gostling (a lawyer) and Lydia Newcombe. Trinity Hall, Cambridge 1804, BA1809, dn10 (Win.), p11 (Win.), MA1812. V. Egham, Surrey 1811 to death (Epsom, Surrey) 2/1/1838 [C73969] Had issue.

**GOULD (Charles Baring-)** Born Exeter 21/10/1807, s. William Baring (later Gould) and Diana Amelia Sabine. Trinity, Cambridge 1825, to Magdalene 1828, BA1831, dn31 (Ex.), p31 (Ex.). R. Lew Trenchard, Devon 1832 to death 12/2/1881, leaving under £800 [C14441] Married Lew Trenchard 23/7/1835 Mary Ann Tanner (w), with issue.

**GOULD (George)** Born Upwey, Weymouth, Dorset 16/1/1778, s. George Gould and Abigail Goodden. Wadham, Oxford 1796, BA1801, dn02 (Bristol), MA1802, p03 (Bristol). R. Fleet, Dorset 1802 to death (Fleet Manor). Died 29/4/1841 aged 62 [C52659] Married Upwey Catherine Barbara Jackson.

**GOULD (Henry)** From Bridgwater, Som., s. Richard Gould. Queen's, Oxford 1771 (aged 17), BA1775, dn77 (C&L), p78 (B&W), migrated to Trinity, Cambridge 1780, MA1780. R. East Chinnock, Som. 1780-90, V. East Pennard, Som. 1790, V. Butleigh, Som. 1790-1828, Prebend of Wedmore 1V 1795-1839 and Canon Residentiary 1805 in Wells Cathedral 1805-39, V. Pucklechurch w. Abson, Glos. 1827 to death. Chap. to HRH Duke of Cumberland 1780. Died 21/8/1839 [C11255]

**GOULD (John)** Born Milborne St Andrew, Dorset 1/9/1780, s. Nicholas Gould and Mary Stillman. Trinity, Oxford 1798, then Magdalen 1799-1808, BA1802 [adm. Lincoln's Inn 1804] dn05 (Ox.), MA1805, Fellow 1808-19, BD1814, p15 (Ox.). V. New Shoreham, Sussex 1815, R. Beaconsfield, Bucks. 1818 to death (a widower) 14/9/1866, leaving £4,000 [C29439] Married Calbourne, Hants. 10/9/1828 Mary Wellstead, with issue (including a daughter who managed his affairs, 'and tried to dispense with curates altogether' (Wilberforce3).

**GOULD (Robert Freke)** Born Milborne, Dorset 7/1/1755, s. Thomas Gould and Ann Freke. Wadham, Oxford 1773, dn78 (C&L for Bristol), p80 (C&L for Bristol), BCL1782. R. Luccombe (Luckham), Som. 1782 and V. Thorverton, Devon 1796 to death 4/11/1838 [Not in CCEd] Married Monksilver, Som. 1790 Ann Smith, with clerical son of same name.

**GOVETT (Robert)** Bapt. Tiverton, Devon 6/4/1789, s. John Govett. Sidney, Cambridge 1797, BA1801, dn03 (Win. for Ex.), Fellow, MA1804, p04 (Ex.). V. Staines (w. Laleham and Ashford), Middx. 1809 to death 7/10/1858, leaving £16,000 [C73972] Married Bristol 15/4/1812 Sarah Romaine, with clerical sons Decimus (Dean of Gibraltar), and Henry (Archdeacon of Taranaki, New Zealand).

**GOWER, *or* LEVESON-GOWER (Granville Leveson-)** Bapt. London 14/6/1787, s. Admiral Hon. John Leveson-Gower and Frances Boscawen. Trinity, Cambridge 1804, BA1808, dn11 (Nor.), p11 (Nor.), MA1812. R. Tatsfield, Surrey 1816-41, R. Titsey, Surrey 1818-41, Preacher throughout the Diocese of Exeter [*sic*] 1818. Dom. Chap. to 1st Earl of Falmouth 1818. Died (unm.) 28/9/1841 aged 54. [C73973]

**GOWER (Thomas Foote)** Born Chelmsford, Essex 8/1/1763, s. Rev. Foote Gower, sen. and Elizabeth Strutt. BNC, Oxford 1781, BA1785, dn88 (S&M), p88 (S&M). R. Snoreham, Essex 1810 ['church quite ruinous'], V. Great Totham, Essex 1835 to death (unmarried) 7/10/1849 [C7285] Excellent article at: https://totham1821.wordpress.com/2014/.../the-revd-thomas-foote-gower-1763-1849/

**GOWER (William)** [NiVoF] R. Littlehempston, Devon 1823 to death 4/4/1837 aged 77 [Not yet in CCEd] Devon Archives has papers relating to him.

**GRACE (Henry Thomas)** Born Risborough, Bucks. 9/2/1788, s. Thomas Grace. Pembroke, Cambridge 1807, BA1811, dn12 (London for Ely), p12 (Ely), MA1816, Fellow. R. Jevington, Sussex 1815 and R. Westham, Sussex 1821 (and RD) to death. Dom. Chap. to 2nd Viscount Hampden 1821. Died (Folkington, Sussex) 13/11/1871 aged 83 [total income £1,060 in CR65], leaving £14,000 [C63570 corrected].

**GRAHAM (Charles Clarke)** From Kensington, London, s. John Graham. Christ Church, Oxford 1796 (aged 18), BA1800, dn00 (London for Cant.), p01 (Roch. for Cant.), MA 1802. PC. Thanington, Kent 1801, V. Petham w. Waltham >< Kent 1808 to death. Dom. Chap. to 3rd Duke of Montrose 1810. Died 22/6/1837 [C1854]

**GRAHAM (Charles Ryves)** Bapt. Chelsea Army Pensioners' Hospital, London 9/5/1774, s. Richard Robert Graham and Anne Bowles. Oriel, Oxford 1793, BA1798, dn01 (Llandaff), p03 (Roch. for Cant.). V. Hayton w. Beilby, Yorks. 1814-57 and V. Kirkby Ireleth, Ulverston, Lancs. 1832 to death (Hayton) 24/10/1857, leaving under £100 [C1855] Wife Alice, with many children.

**GRAHAM (Henry Elliott)** Bapt. Colwall, Heref. 28/7/1793, s. Aaron Graham and Sarah Dawes. Oriel, Oxford 1812, then St Alban's Hall, BA1816, p17 (Salis.), LLB1821. V. Eltisley, Cambs. 1821-35, R. Ludgvan, Cornwall 1834 [blank in ERC] to death 29/8/1855 aged 62, leaving £3,000 (will left unadministered) [C3957] Married (1) Croxton, Cambs. 29/7/1819 Elizabeth Leeds (d.1844), with issue (2) St Pancras, London 26/8/1847 Louisa Graham Davenport, with further issue.

**GRAHAM (John)** Bapt. Setmurthy, Cumberland 19/11/1765, s. John Graham. Usher, St Peter's School, York 1787. Literate: dn88 (York), p90 (York), MA by 1822 (a Ten Year Man). R. York St Mary Bishophill Senior w. York St Saviour 1796 (and H/M Archbishop Holgate's School, York 1829) to death. Chap. to the York Asylum. Died 6/1/1844 aged 78 [C109071 corrected. YCO. DEB] Married York 6/1/1791 Dorothy Baines (a clergy dau.), with clerical son John Baines, below.

**GRAHAM (John)** Literate: dn03 (Car.), p03 (Car.). R. Bewcastle, Cumberland 1806 to death 23/11/1834 (CCEd thus) aged 66 [C3397. Platt] Married (1) before 1796 with issue (2) Bewcastle 8/7/1809 Jane Story, with further issue.

**GRAHAM (John)** St John's, Cambridge 1811, BA1815, dn15 (Peterb.), MA1818, p18 (Ely), BD1826, Fellow 1828-30 (res.). V. Comberton, Cambs. 1830-3 (res.), V. Swavesey, Cambs. 1833, R. Hinxton Cambs. 1833 to death 8/7/1862, leaving £4,000 [C109666] Married Claybooke, Leics. 28/5/1834 Frances Maria Gilson (w), and had issue.

**GRAHAM (John Baines)** Born Barwick in Elmet, Yorks. 6/11/1791, s. Rev. John Graham (three above) and Dorothy Baines. Queens', Cambridge 1809, BA1814, dn16 (York), p17 (Ex. for Ely), MA1817, Fellow 1817-22, then Queen's, Oxford 1829. S/M Hemsworth School, Yorks. 1832-37; V. York Holy Trinity, Micklegate 1822-60 [not C109071], V. Burnsall (1st Mediety), Yorks. 1832-8, V. Felkirk, Barnsley, Yorks. 1837 to death 9/3/1860, leaving £7,000 [C131423. YCO. DEB] Married Barton on Humber, Lincs. 14/7/1824 Louisa Thorley, with issue. An excellent web article which gives a good example of clerical intermarriage: https://mccollierheritage.wordpress.com/tag/rev-john-baines-graham/

**GRAHAM (William)** Born Wetheral, Cumberland 1768. Literate: dn96 (Car.), p97 (Peterb.). R. Wardley w. Belton, Rutland 1811 to death 2/2/1837 aged 70 [C5927] Married Mary Robinson, w. clerical s. John Graham (b.1890).

**GRAHAM (William)** Bapt. Netherby, Cumberland 29/6/1796, s. Sir James Graham, 1st Bart. and Lady Catherine Stewart (dau. of 7th Earl of Galloway). Christ Church, Oxford 1815, BA1819, dn24 (York for Car.), MA1824, p25 (B&W). PC. Allonby, Bromfield, Cumberland 1825-9, R. Arthuret, Cumberland 1829 and R. Kirkandrews on Esk, Cumberland 1829 to death (unm., in London) 28/7/1862 aged 66, leaving £3,000 [C5928. YCO. Platt]

**GRAINGER (John Cecil)** Born Marylebone, London 7/11/1801, s. Thomas Cecil Grainger (of Cuckfield, Sussex) and Euphemia Bannerman. Pembroke, Cambridge 1819, then Downing 1825, BA1827, dn27 (Salis.), p27 (Salis.). PC. Burcombe, Wilts. 1827-8, PC. Bramshaw, Wilts. 1828-35, V. Reading St Giles, Berks. 1834 to death (London) 6/5/1857 [C85931] Married Pitton w. Farley, Wilts. 23/12/1834 Margaret Bewicke Smart (of Trewhitt House, Northumberland), with clerical son of father's name.

**GRAINGER (Richard)** Bapt. Leeds, Yorks. 16/1/1781 (nonconformist chapel), s. Thomas Grainger and Martha Graham. Literate: dn13 (York), p14 (York). PC. Grimsargh, Preston, Lancs. 1823 to death 16/9/1849 aged 68 [C131424. YCO] Married Tong, Yorks. 25/6/1817 Mary Speight.

**GRANGE (Rochford Burrow)** Bapt. Bromley, Kent 28/9/1795, s. Rochfort Grange and Caroline Ann Burrow. Queen's, Oxford 1814, migrated to St. John's, Cambridge 1823, BA 1826, dn26 (London), p27 (Nor.). Curate Golcar, Huddersfield 1831. Moved to Tasmania 1840 and died in Australia Oct. 1855 [C113200] Wife Sarah, and child.

**GRANT (Francis Bazett)** Bapt. Farnborough, Hants. 12/9/1796, s. James Lewis/Ludovic Grant and Ann Bazett. Christ Church, Oxford 1813, Fellow 1813-31, BA1817, dn19, p20, MA 1822. V. Dartford, Kent 1830, R. Shelton, Staffs. 1845-64, V. Cullompton, Devon 1864 to death 14/8/1872, leaving £2,000 [C6721] Married Southwold, Suffolk 6/11/1821 Margaret Hay-Drummond (w) (a clergy dau.), with issue.

**GRANT (James Francis)** Bapt. Monymusk, Aberdeenshire 5/3/1766, s. Sir Archibald Grant, 3rd Bart. and Mary Callander. Hertford, Oxford 1785, no degree, dn89 (London for York), p96 (Bristol for York). Min. Merston (Marston), Sussex 1805 (R. 1815) and R. Wrabness, Essex 1809 to death 16/11/1837 [C52665. YCO] Married Oct. 1795 Anne Oughterstone (a clerical dau.), with naval son.

**GRANT (Johnson)** Born Edinburgh 1773, s. Gregory and Mary Grant. St John's, Oxford 1795, BA1799, dn99 (Chester), p00 (Chester), MA1805. Inc. Latchford St James, Cheshire 1805-7 (res.), R. Binbrook St Mary, Lincs. 1818-44, PC. Kentish Town Chapel, St Pancras, London 1822 to death 4/12/1844 [C61282. ODNB. Kaye] Married Marylebone, London 8/12/1818 Margaret Sherriff, and had issue. 'A zealous and hard-working clergyman.'

**GRANT (Robert)** Born Sheerness, Kent, s. Thomas Grant and Ann Sumpter Tassel. New, Oxford 1815 (aged 18), Fellow 1815-28, dn19 (Ox.), p20 (Ox.), BCL1823, Fellow of Winchester College 1828. V. Bradford Abbas, Dorset 1828-86 (w. RD and Prebend of Bedminster Secunda in Salisbury Cathedral 1845 to death. Dom. Chap. to 2nd Earl Manvers 1820. Died (Southsea, Hants.) 15/9/1887 aged 90, leaving £6,406-3s-0d. [C29454. Boase] Married Portsea, Hants. 19/8/1828 Frances Mary Barrett, with clerical son Edward Pierce Grant.

**GRANTHAM (George)** Bapt. Ashby cum Fenby, Lincs. 7/7/1781, s. Rev. John Grantham and Elizabeth Willan. Lincoln, Oxford 1797, then Magdalen 1798, BA1801, dn04 (Ox.), MA 1804, Senior Fellow 1809-40, BD1811, p13 (Ox.), etc. V. Waithe, Lincs. 1820 to death 'in College' 12/5/1840, 'his body being found lifeless in the park [grass] below his window,' 'having overbalanced as he opened his second floor window' [C29460] Brother below.

**GRANTHAM (Thomas)** Bapt. Ashby cum Fenby, Lincs. 13/5/1794, s. Rev. John Grantham and Elizabeth Willan. Chorister Magdalen, Oxford; matr. 1809, BA1813, Fellow 1813-31, MA1816, dn17 (Kildare), p18 (Ox.), BD1823, etc. R. Thorpe in the Glebe, Notts. 1823-9 (res.), R. Bramber cum Botolph's, Sussex 1830 to death. Dom. Chap. to Bishop of Killaloe w. Kilfenora, then of Kildare to 1846. Died 18/4/1864, leaving £20,000 [C29461] Widow Lucy. Brother above.

**GRAPE (Richard)** Born Stone, Worcs. 12/10/1777, s. Rev. William Grape. Worcester, Oxford 1795, BA1799, dn00 (Wor.), Fellow 1800-31, MA1802, p03 (Wor.) etc. R. Hindlip, Worcs. 1815, R. Hoggeston, Bucks. 1830 to death. Dom. Chap. to 2nd Earl of Mountnorris 1819. Died 9/7/1840 [C61288]

**GRAVES (Henry)** Bapt. Yarm, Yorks. 26/7/1803, s. Rev. John Graves and Mary Bedford Rayner. St Bees adm. 1825, dn26 (Durham for York), p28 (York). PC. High Worsall, Yorks. 1832 and R. Middleton St George, Durham 1837 to death (Yarm) 13/1/1865, leaving under £100 [C130453. YCO] Married 1833 Mary Clifford Rudd (w), with issue. Surrogate for NRY.

**GRAY (Charles)** Born 13/9/1799, s. Rt. Rev. Robert Gray (Prebend of Durham, later Bp of Bristol, *q.v.* ODNB) and Elizabeth Camplin. St John's, Cambridge 1819, BA1823, dn23 (Bristol for Durham), p23 (St Asaph), MA 1826, incorporated at Oxford 1834. Bury Prebend in Chichester Cathedral 1825-54, V. Godmanchester, Hunts. 1829 (with RD) to death. Chap. to his father as Bp of Bristol 1828-33; to Mayor of Bristol. Died 30/12/1854 aged 55 [C52666] Married 11/1/1848 Agnes Norris (Hughenden Manor, Bucks.), with issue. Brother Henry, below.

**GRAY (Edmund)** Born York 12/5/1789, s. William Gray (attorney) and Faith Hopwood. Queens', Cambridge 1814, dn17 (Lin.), p18 (Lin.), BA1819, MA1825. R. Kirby Misperton, Yorks. 1819-25 (res.), R. Kirbymoorside, Yorks. 1826-51, PC. St Thomas, Scarborough, Yorks. 1852-7. Died Foston, Yorks. 14/5/1867 aged 78, leaving £14,000 [C61292] Married 6/6/1822 Elizabeth Harvey, *s.p.* Brother William, below.

**GRAY (George Robert)** Born Dresden, Saxony, s. David Gray (former Chargé d'Affaires). Trinity, Cambridge 1818 (aged 18), then Caius 1821, BA1823, dn23 (Salis.), p24 (Ex.). V. Inkberrow, Worcs. 1830 [parish noted twice in ERC] to death 20/3/1883, leaving £4,670-3s-1d. [C92753] *J.P.* Warwicks. and Worcs.

**GRAY (Henry)** Born Bishopswearmouth, Co. Durham 19/4/1808, s. Rev. Robert Gray (Prebend of Durham, later Bishop of Bristol, below) and Elizabeth Camplin. Christ Church, Oxford 1816, BA1830, dn31 (Glos. for Bristol), p32 (Roch.), MA1834. V. Almondsbury, Glos. 1831 to death. Dom. Chap. to his father as Bishop of Bristol 1833-4. Died London 5/6/1864, leaving £8,000 [C52667] Married Clifton, Bristol 21/5/1835 Hon. Lady Emilie Caroline Pery (dau. of Lord Glentworth, and grand-daughter of 1st Earl of Limerick), with issue. Brother Charles, above.

**GRAY (Robert)** Born Cambridge, s. Robert Gray. Trinity, Cambridge 1777, BA1782, dn83 (Llandaff for Ely), p84 (Ely), MA1785. V. Sawston, Cambs. 1783, PC. 1783-5 (res.), R. Twinstead, Essex 1793 and R. Little Yeldham, Essex 1802 to death 2/12/1837 aged 77 [C3959]

**GRAY (Robert, Bishop of Bristol)** Born London 11/3/1762, s. Robert Gray (silversmith) and Ann Norman. St Mary Hall, Oxford [not in Foster?], BA1784, MA1787, BD1799, DD 1802.

Prebend of Chichester 1797, V. Faringdon, Berks. 1794-1800, V. Crayke, Yorks. 1800-5, 7th Prebend of Durham [income £1,700], (V. Bishopswearmouth, Durham 1805-27, Bishop of Bristol 1827 to death (Clifton, Bristol) 28/9//1834, aged 65 [C134662 and C52668 - ambiguous correlation. OBNB. G.M. Evans, 'Robert Gray, Bishop of Bristol', *Essays in Cathedral History*, ed. E. Ralph and J. Rogan (1991)] Married 7/11/1798 Elizabeth Camplin, many ch. (incl. Robert, Bishop of Cape Town and Metropolitan of Africa, and Henry, above). Underestimated: his concerns with working conditions (esp. in coal mines) while in Co. Durham led to his initiative resulting in the invention of Humphry Davy's miners' lamp. His Bristol palace was burnt-out in the 1832 Bristol reform riots (although he kept the Cathedral's services' going), but lost 6,000 books ('burnt *or stolen*') and his wine cellars [*sic*] were 'plundered'.

**GRAY (Robert)** Born St James, London 1/4/1787, s. Thomas and Mary Gray. Oriel, Oxford 1805, BA1809, dn13 (Durham), MA 1813, p14 (Durham). R. Sunderland (w. Sunderland St John's Chapel) 1819 to death (typhus) 11/2/1838 aged 48 [C130454] Married Bishopwearmouth, Co. Durham 14/2/1822 Mary Webster (aged 18), with issue.

**GRAY (William)** Born York 19/5/1785, s. of William Gray (attorney) and Faith Hopwood. Queens', Cambridge 1802, BA1807, dn08 (B&W), p09 (Ex.), MA1810. R. West Rounton, Yorks. 1812-21, PC. Cundall, Yorks. 1822, V. Brafferton, Yorks. 1822 (and Prebend of 2nd Stall w. Canon Residentiary in Ripon Collegiate Church 1828) to death 26/3/1863, leaving £1,500 [C42073] Married York 26/5/1814 Ann Elizabeth Howard, with clerical son. Brother Edmund, above.

**GRAY (William)** [NiVoF] S/M Plympton Free G/S, Devon 1830 ('dismissed'); PC. St Giles on the Heath, Devon 1830-[36]. Died? [C171630]

**GRAY (William)** Literate: dn13 (Chester), p14 (Chester). PC. Haslingden, Whalley, Lancs. 1815-47, PC. Glasson, Lancs. 1843. *Cut his throat with a razor in bed at 2.30pm 17/10/1847 aged 63* [C168960] Married Haslingden 18/9/1815 Letitia Dixon. *J.P.* Lancs. 1826.

**GRAYSON (Anthony)** Bapt. Whitehaven, Cumberland 22/10/1773, s. Thomas Grayson. Queen's, Oxford 1794, BA1797, dn00 (Ox.), p00 (Ox.), MA1801, Fellow to 1824, then St Edmund Hall, BD and DD1824, Principal of St Edmund Hall, Oxford (w. V. Bramley, Hants. appended) 1824 to death 6/9/1843 [C29579] Wife Catherine.

**GREAVES ([Alexander] Benjamin)** Probably born Hope, Derbys. 22/11/1750, s. Charles Greaves and Mary Barker. St Edmund Hall, Oxford 1775, dn75 (C&L), p77 (Heref.), then Trinity, Cambridge 1778 (a Ten Year Man). PC. Stony Middleton, Derbys. 1787 to death (Offerton Hall, Derbys.) 8/7/1834 aged 82 (CCEd says 18/12/1834) [C11268] Married 8/12/1785 Anne Green, with issue (inc. sons Caesar Augustus, and Agrippa Greaves).

**GREAVES (Richard)** Bapt. Merton, Surrey 26/5/1794, s. Charles Greaves and Anne Pierrepoint. Wadham, Oxford 1813, BA1816, dn17 (Chester), p18 (Chester), MA1820. V. Deddington, Oxon. 1822-37 (res.). A former Evangelical and friend of Newman, he moved into an 'inchoate mystical unorthodoxy' (and certainly left a theosophical library). Died Cheltenham, Glos. 28/3/1870, leaving £600 [C29581. DEB] Married Nether Worton, Oxon. 17/7/1817 Sophia Elizabeth Wilson (sister of Daniel Wilson, Bishop of Calcutta, who thought him 'very strange and sometimes not in his right mind'), with clerical sons Richard Wilson ('living in Boulogne'), and Joshua Greaves.

**GREAVES (Thomas Berkeley)** Bapt. Westoning, Beds. 10/11/1774, s. Rev. Thomas (R. Broughton Astley, Leics.) and Elizabeth Greaves. Emmanuel, Cambridge 1792, BA1797, Fellow 1799-1804, dn99 (Nor.), MA1800, p02 (Ely). V. King's Lynn All Saints (o/w South Lynn), Norfolk 1811 and V. Wiggenhall St Germans, Norfolk 1814 to death (Ranworth, Norfolk) 20/1/1850 [C1052] Married Marylebone, London 16/6/1804 Eleanor Humphreys, with clerical son Thomas William Greaves.

**GREEN, GREENE (Cecil James)** Probably born Selsey, Sussex 29/7/1803, s. Rev. Cornelius Greene and Frances Anne Piggott. Pembroke, Cambridge 1822, BA1827, MA1830, DD? V. Westhampnett, Chichester, Sussex 1829 to death 1849 (3rd q.) [C63588] Married Chichester 12/10/1830 Elizabeth Weguelin, with issue.

**GREEN (Charles, sen.)** Bapt. Buxhall, Suffolk 27/5/1773, s. Charles Green. Caius, Cambridge 1793, BA1797, dn97 (Nor.), p99 (Nor.). R.

Burgh Castle, Suffolk 1829 (with RD 1844 and Canon of Norwich Cathedral 1851) to death 9/8/1857 aged 83 [C113280] Son below.

**GREEN (Charles, jun.)** Born Haverscroft, Yorks. 18/2/1796, s. Charles Green, sen. (above). Trinity, Cambridge 1817, then Jesus 1819, BA1821, MA1824, Fellow 1824-34, p25 (Ely). R. Buxhall, Suffolk 1826-51-, R. Harleston, Suffolk 1826-51-. Died 9/9/1857 [C109669] Married Ackworth, Yorks. 4/9/1832 Elizabeth Maddison, with clerical son Charles Edward Maddison Green.

**GREEN (Cornelius)** Bapt. North Mundham, Sussex 14/10/1769, s. Rev. Richard and Margaret Green. Worcester, Oxford 1786, MA 1804. V. Rogate, Sussex 1815, R. East Preston, Sussex 1815, R. Terwick, Sussex 1820 to death. Dom. Chap. to 11th Earl of Kinnoull 1815. Died Terwick 2/6/1842 [C63589] Clerical son.

**GREEN (Edward)** From Burford, Shropshire, s. Rev. Jonathan Green. Pembroke, Oxford 1783 (aged 18), then New, BA1788, dn88 (Chester for Ox.), Fellow, p90 (Ox.), MA1791. PC. Ashford Bowdler, Shropshire 1792, R. Burford (2nd Portion, o/w Whitton) 1813 and R. Edvin Ralph, Heref. 1813 to death 26/6/1842 [C29582] Married Hope Bagot, Shropshire 25/5/1795 Martha Giles, with issue.

**GREEN (Henry)** Bapt. Upton Snodbury, Worcs. 11/5/1778, s. Rev. Henry Green, sen. Balliol, Oxford 1794, BA1798, MA1801, dn01 (Wor.), p02 (Wor.). V. Upton Snodbury 1802-41, V. Earl's Croome, Worcs. 1805-7, V. Bristol All Saints 1816 to death. Dom. Chap. to 2nd Baron Bayning 1814. Died 7/4/1841 [C155835] Had issue.

**GREEN (John)** Bapt. Greenwich, Kent 11/5/1758, s. Rev. John Green, sen. St John's, Oxford 1773, BA1777, dn80 (Ox. for Wor.), MA1782, p83 (Wor.), BD1786. V. Norton (o/w Newton Coleparte), Wilts. 1796 to death 14/4/1837 aged 78 [C29584]

**GREEN (John Cheale)** From Arundel, Sussex, s. William Green. Magdalene, Cambridge 1794, BA1798, dn00 (Ex. for Chich.), MA1801, p02 (Chich.). V. Littlehampton, Sussex 1802-23, V. Rustington, Sussex 1802 to death 6/5/1858, leaving £8,000 [C63593] Married Steyning, Sussex 30/12/1805 Miriam Pinfold, with issue.

**GREEN (Robert)** Bapt. South Shields, Durham 15/5/1789, s. Robert Green and Sarah Fairless. St John's, Cambridge 1807, BA1812, dn12 (Durham), p13 (Durham). V. Longhorsley, Northumberland 1823 to death (South Shields) 5/9/1877 aged 88, leaving £25,000 [C134170] Married Stannington Vale, Northumberland 16/5/1832 Isabella Agnes Hall, with clerical s. Thomas Robinson Green. Confusion with the man below.

**GREEN (Robert)** Born Westhoe, South Shields, Durham 24/3/1793, s. Thomas and Mary Green. Trinity, Cambridge 1810, BA1815, dn16 (St David's), p17 (Durham), MA 1818. PC. Newcastle upon Tyne All Saints 1817-46, PC. Whorlton, Durham 1822-27, Master of the Hospital [almshouses] of the Virgin Mary, Newcastle upon Tyne 1846-66. Dom. Chap. to 8th Viscount Arbuthnott 1847-54; to Countess of Strathmore 1855-66; Chap. to Trinity House, Newcastle at some date. Died 6/8/1868 aged 75. Will not traced [C130040] Married Norham, Northumberland 12/1/1819 Agnes Robinson (a clergy dau.), with issue. Surrogate. Confusion with the man above.

**GREEN (Thomas)** Born Steyning, Sussex 13/5/1788, s. Rev. Thomas Green and Ann Hanson. Christ Church, Oxford 1805, Student [Fellow] 1805-17, BA1809, dn11 (Ox.), MA 1811, p12 (Salis.). PC. Harkhurst, Sussex 1815-17, R. Badby w. Newnham, Northants. 1816 (and RD) to death 14/7/1871, leaving £25,000 [C29587] Married Harborne, Staffs. 21/7/1830 Mary Ann Stubbs, with issue.

**GREEN (Thomas Fordham)** Born Ware, Herts. 17/5/1796, s. John Green and Mary Anstee. Christ's, Cambridge 1813, BA1818, dn19 (Lin.), p20 (Lin.), MA1821. R. (and patron) of Graveley w. Chivesfield, Herts. 1820 [no church] to death 8/5/1869 (having had a stroke 4 years before), leaving £30,000 [C61332] Married Welwyn, Herts. 10/6/1834 Mary Peacock, with clerical son.

**GREEN (Valentine)** Bapt. Normanton-le-Heath, Leics. 16/4/1800, s. Valentine Green and Theodosia Frances Georgiana Mortimer. St John's, Cambridge 1817, BA1822, dn23 (Lin.), p24 (Lin.), MA1825. V. Plungar and Barkestone, Leics. 1826-31, R. Knipton, Leics. 1831-5, R. Birkin w. Haddlesey, Yorks. [income £1,050 in CR65] 1835 to death 2/12/1873, leaving £25,000 [C61337] Married (1) Chesterfield,

Derbys. 7/12/1830 Anne Barbara Vaughan (d.1837), w. issue (2) Montpelier, Glos. 5/3/1850 Sophia Lilly, w. clerical son.

**GREEN (William)** Bapt. Kirk Smeaton, Yorks. 26/2/1792, s. Thomas and Mary Green. Literate: dn15 (York), p16 (York). PC. Gateforth, Brayton, Yorks. 1825 and V. Muston, Scarborough, Yorks. 1834 to death (Filey, Yorks.) 2/5/1870 aged 78, leaving £12,000 [C136792. YCO. Not Joseph]

**GREENALL (George Hutton)** Bapt. Cranbrook, Kent 28/4/1774, s. Thomas Greenall. Christ's, Cambridge 1793, BA1797, dn97 (London), p99 (London), MA1801, Fellow 1802-24. PC. Otford, Kent 1822 and R. Moulton, Suffolk 1823 to death 1845 (2nd q.) [C63598]

**GREENALL (Richard)** Born Wilderspool, Cheshire 11/5/1806, s. of Edward Greenall (a brewer and banker) and Betty Pratt. BNC, Oxford 1824, BA1828, dn30 (Chester), p30 (Chester), MA1831. PC. (and patron) of Stretton, Cheshire 1831-67, PC. Witton, Cheshire 1833, RD of Frodsham 1839-67, Archdeacon of Chester 1866 to death (Northwich, Cheshire) 27/11/1867 aged 61, leaving £25,000. Proctor in Convocation for the Clergy of the Archdeaconry of Chester [C168978. Boase] Married Stretton 27/11/1855 Eliza Mary Lyon, with clerical son of the father's name.

**GREENE (Edward)** [NiVoF] V. Croft, Lincs. 1797-[1837]. Died 1848 (4th q.) [C61537. Foster has a possibility]

**GREENE (Henry Burnaby)** Born Southampton, Hants. 6/5/1795, s. Pitt Burnaby Greene and Joanna Tinling. Corpus Christi, Cambridge 1813, BA1818, dn18 (Salis.), p19 (Salis.), MA1822. R. Longparish (o/w Middleon), Hants. 1821 to death. Chap. to HRH Duke of Clarence 1819, Died 18/3/1884 aged 88, leaving £14,656-14s-9d. [C74011 as Barnaby]

**GREENE (William Henry)** From Ampthill, Beds. St John's, Cambridge 1820, BA1824, dn24 (Lin.), p25 (Lin.), MA1828. V. Felmersham w. PC. Packenham, Beds. 1825-7 (res.), R. Steppingley, Beds. 1830 to death (Bath) 23/3/1853 aged 53 [C61540] Married (2?) 25/4/1850 Susanna Vesina Spencer Hamilton Southcomb (a clergy dau.), 1 dau.

**GREENHILL (William)** From Watford, Herts., s. Thomas Greenhill. Trinity, Oxford 1789 (aged 17), BA1793, dn94 (London), MA 1796, p98 (Ox.), BD1806, Fellow to 1825. R. Farnham, Essex 1825 to death 2/2/1849 [C29660]

**GREENLY (John)** From Hereford, s. William Greenly. Christ Church, Oxford 1796 (aged 18), BA1800, dn00 (Salis.), p02 (Salis.), MA 1818. Chaplain R.N. [shrapnel wounds at Trafalgar, and a detailed account at: https://books.google.co.uk/books?isbn=1843838966]. Vicar Choral in Salisbury Cathedral 1812 (and Librarian 1825), V. Roydon, Essex 1818-30 (res.), PC. Salisbury St Thomas 1821 and R. Sharncote, Wilts. 1834 to death 1/12/1862 aged 85, leaving £600 [C85945] Married Hereford 1809 Mary Prosser, w. clerical son John Prosser Greenly.

**GREENWAY (William Whitmore)** Born Nuneaton, Warwicks. 3/3/1798, s. George Greenway and Jane Cox. Trinity Hall, Cambridge 1817, dn22 (Lin.), p22 (Lin.), LLB1825. V. Shackerstone, Leics. 1823-68, R. (and patron) of Newbold Verdon, Leics. 1823-68, RD, R. Hardwycke, Northants. 1836-66. Dom. Chap. to Earl of Strathmore. Died 28/5/1868 aged 70, leaving £1,500 [C61544] Married Twycross, Leics. 6/9/1824 Emma Mayo(u) (of Coleshill, Leics.). J.P. Leics. Cricketer.

**GREENWOOD (Edward)** Bapt. Dent, Sedbergh, Yorks. 15/8/1770, s. John and Isabel Greenwood. Literate: dn93 (York), p94 (York). PC. Stalling Busk, Yorks. 1795-[99], PC. Longsleddale, Westmorland 1797 to death 1845 (1st q.) [C109157. YCO]

**GREENWOOD (John)** Born Calne, Wilts. 22/1/1786, s. Rev. Thomas and Elizabeth Greenwood. Pembroke, Cambridge 1805, then Peterhouse 1808, BA1809, dn09 (Nor.), p09 (Nor.), MA1812, Fellow 1813-21, DD1834. S/M Christ's Hospital [School] 1816-27 then H/M 1827-36. Prof. of Classics and History at Royal Military College, Sandhurst 1813-15. V. Horley, Surrey 1827 (only), R. Colne Engaine, Essex 1827 to death 14/8/1865, leaving £3,000 [C109671. Boase] Married Wimborne Minster, Dorset 10/8/1819 Caroline Bowle (a clergy dau.), with issue. Brother below.

**GREENWOOD (Robert)** Bapt. Calne, Wilts. 14/7/1774, s. Rev. Thomas and Elizabeth

Greenwood, BNC, Oxford 1793, BA1797, dn97 (Bristol for Salis.), p98 (Salis.), MA1800. R. Colaton Raleigh, Devon 1809 to death 22/10/1843 [C52673] Brother above.

**GREENWOOD (William)** [NiVoF] V. Hose, Leics. 1801. Died Strathearn, Leics. 1837 aged 70 [C61548]

**GREENWOOD (William)** From Yorks. Corpus Christi, Cambridge 1814, BA1818, Fellow 1818-28, MA1821, dn21 (Ely), p22 (Ely). R. Thrapston, Northants. 1828 to death 18/2/1837 aged 48 [C109673] Married Claybrooke (Magna), Leics. 30/7/1828 Catherine Otter, with issue.

**GREETHAM (John Knight)** Bapt. Portsmouth, Hants. 6/8/1795, s. Moses Greetham and Mary Figg. Jesus, Cambridge 1817, dn18 (Nor.), p19 (Nor.), LLB1824. V. Kirdford, Sussex 1831-9, R. Sampford Brett, Som. 1839-65, Prebend of Wedmore in Wells Cathedral 1840 (and RD of Dunster) to death. Dom. Chap. to 2nd Viscount Hood 1820; and the Earl of Egremont 1841-9. Died 4/7/1865. No will traced [C63606]

**GREGG (James Henshaw)** Bapt. Southwark, Surrey 25/12/1802, s. James and Elizabeth Gregg. St John's, Cambridge 1822, BA1826, dn26 (B&W), p27 (B&W), MA1829. S/M Bridgwater Free G/S 1826; R. Stoke Lacy, Heref. -- [as sequestrator here in ERC] and V. Durleigh, Som. 1826. Probate granted 14/2/1835 [C41216]

**GREGG (Tresham Dames)** Born Dublin 11/8/1800, s. Hugh Gregg and Martha Dames. TCD1821, BA1826, dn28 (Ossory), p30 (York), MA1830, BD and DD1853. PC. Dewsbury St Peter, Earls Heaton, Yorks. 1830-3; in Dublin (where he was inhibited by the Archbishop but continued to rant in several private chapels). Died Dublin 28/10/1881 aged 82 [C131431. YCO. ODNB and port. Boase. Al.Dub.] Married Harrogate, Yorks. 21/12/1832 Sarah Pearson (w) (Pannel Hall, Knaresborough), with clerical son of the father's name. 'A wild sectarian', a virulent anti-Catholic controversialist - and a Christian bigot.

**GREGORY (Arthur William)** Bapt. Stivichall, Warwicks. 3/11/1799, s. Francis and Frances Gregory. Trinity, Oxford 1817, then St Alban Hall, BA1822, dn22 (Peterb.), p23 (Peterb.), MA1823. PC. Stivichall 1823, V. Corley, Warwicks. 1823 to death 11/12/1874, leaving £600 [C11289] Married Leamington, Warwicks. 29/10/1839 Louisa Georgina Russel.

**GREGORY (George)** Bapt. Down St Mary, Devon 23/4/1766, s. Robert Gregory. Oriel, Oxford 1784, BA1788, dn88 (Ex.), p90 (Ex.), MA1790. V. Dunsford, Devon 1792 to death 23/1/1839 [C144544] Married 1830 Frances Lambert, with issue.

**GREGORY (John)** From Canterbury, s. Rev. Francis Gregory. Lincoln, Oxford 1784 (aged 17), BA1787, dn89 (London), p90 (Ely), MA 1791. V. Preston, Kent 1792-1829 (res.), R. Elmstone, Kent 1792 to death. Dom. Chap. to 4th Earl Cornwallis 1792. Died 29/5/1839. [C118559]

**GRENSIDE (Christopher)** Bapt. City of London 30/7/1790, s. John Grenside and Sarah Spurgeon. Literate: dn14 (Nor.), p15 (Nor.). Preacher throughout the Diocese of Norwich 1814, R. Great Massingham, Norfolk 1816 to death 21/11/1871, leaving £25,000 [C113300] Married St Margaret's, Westminster, London 10/9/1817 Mary Bent, with clerical son.

**GRENSIDE (Ralph)** Bapt. Crathorne, Yorks. 11/10/1789, s. Rev. Ralph Grenside, sen. Peterhouse, Cambridge 1807, BA1811, dn16 (Nor.), p17 (Nor.). R. Crathorne 1827 and PC. Seamer, Stokesley, Yorks. 1827 to death (a widower) 2/3/1878 aged 88, leaving £300 [C113301] Married 1839 (3rd q.) Mary Ray, with issue. Confusing, as there were three generations of the same family holding this benefice for 110 years. Also an Oxford contemporary of the same name.

**GRENVILLE (George [Aldworth] Neville-, Hon.)** see under **NEVILLE, later NEVILLE-GRENVILLE**

**GRESLEY (William Nigel, Sir, 9th Bart.)** Born Nether Seale Hall, Seale, Leics. 25/3/1806, s. Rev. William Gresley and Louisa Jane Gresley. Christ Church, Oxford 1824, then St Mary Hall, BA1829, dn30 (Lin.), p30 (Lin.). R. Seale 1830 to death 3/9/1847. Succ. to title 1837 [C61563] Married 24/3/1831 Georgina Anne Reid, with clerical son.

**GRESWELL (William)** Born Denton, Manchester 10/7/1796, s. Rev. William Parr

Greswell (below) and Ann Yeardley. BNC, Oxford 1814, BA1818, then Balliol, Fellow 1818-38, MA1820, dn21 (Ox.), p22 (Ox.). (Sinecure R. Duloe, Cornwall 1830), R. Kilve, Som. 1837-76, V. Boyne Hill, Berks. at death 6/11/1876 aged 80, leaving £25,000 [C29671. Boase] Married Mary Ann Harrison, w. issue.

**GRESWELL (William Parr)** Born Tarvin, Cheshire 23/6/1765, s. John Greswell. Literate: dn89 (Chester), p90 (Chester). PC. Manchester St Lawrence, Denton 1791-1853 (where he also kept a school). Died 12/1/1854 [C168988. Boase] Married Manchester 30/8/1794 Anne Yeardley, 7s. (5 of whom distinguished themselves at Oxford, incl. the above). Photo. online.

**GRETTON (George Holdsworth Lowther)** Born Dartmouth, Devon 15/18/1782, s. Very Rev. George Gretton (Dean of Hereford) and Mary Clay. Trinity, Cambridge 1797, migrated to Oriel, Oxford, BA1802, MA1805, dn06 (Ex.), p13 (Heref.). V. Foy, Heref. 1815-17 (res.), V. Allensmore and V. Clehonger, Heref. 1822-33, V. Elmstone Hardwicke w. Uckington, Glos. 1829 to death 19/3/1833 (CCEd says 8/5/1833) [C105507] Married (1) Upton Bishop, Heref. 1812 Mary Donne (d.1814) (2) Clapham, Surrey 3/2/1816 Augusta Williams, w. issue. Brother below.

**GRETTON (Richard Henry)** Bapt. Southwell, Notts. 5/11/1785, s. Very Rev. George Gretton (Dean of Hereford) and Mary Clay. Trinity, Cambridge 1803, then Clare 1805, BA1808, MA 1812, dn19 (Heref.), p19 (C&L for Heref.). R. Nantwich, Cheshire 1819 to death 1/2/1846 [C105508] Married Nantwich 22/4/1822 Frances Bennion. Brother above.

**GRETTON (William Walthall)** Bapt. Hitcham, Bucks. 26/12/1787, s. George Gretton and Mary Sherwin. Clare, Cambridge 1805, BA1810, dn12 (Heref.), p13 (Heref.). V. Withington, Heref. 1816 to death 9/6/1857 aged 70 [C105510] Married Torquay, Devon 9/2/ 1825 Lucy Turner (from Ireland)

**GREVILLE (James)** Born Lorraine, France 27/6/1753, s. Fulke Greville, *M.P.*, and Frances Macartney. Pembroke, Cambridge 1772, then Trinity 1774, dn77 (Durham), p78 (Roch. for Durham), LLB1780. R. Stockton upon Tees, Co. Durham 1780-2, R. Wickham, Durham 1782-1816, R. Peasmore, Berks. 1816 to death (Bath) 23/1/1836 aged 84 [C1863]

**GREVILLE (Joshua)** Born St George's Hanover Square, London 16/7/1770, s. Caleb Greville and Esther Paterson. Trinity, Cambridge 1780, BA1794, dn95 (Bristol), p95 (Bristol), MA1797. Chap. Duston, Northants. 1811-51, R. Morborne, Hunts. 1827-31 (res.). Lived and did occasional duty at Weston Favel, Northants. 1820-41. Died 19/2/1851 [C52675] Married (1) Hackney, London 15/3/1800 Mary Donald (d.1817) (2) Kensington, London 8/7/1819 Sarah Senechel, w. issue.

**GRICE (John)** [probably] Literate: dn90 (Win. for Chester), p91 (Chester). PC. Drigg and Irton, Cumberland 1797 to death 1838 (3rd q.) [C136327] Married Irton 19/8/1811 Lucy Lutwidge (of Whitehaven), with issue.

**GRIER (Robert)** [NiVoF] PC. Walpole, Suffolk 1832-[40]. Dead by 1849 [C113303] Had issue.

**GRIESBACH (William Robert)** Bapt. New Windsor, Berks. 18/4/1802, s. Charles Frederick William Griesbach (a German musician) and Sarah Wigg. St Bees adm. 1824, dn26 (Durham for York), p26 (York), MA1836 (Lambeth). PC. Arkengarthdale, Yorks. 1827-29, V. Fridaythorpe, Yorks. 1829 and V. Millington, Yorks. 1836 to death 21/12/1861, leaving £600 [C130460. YCO] Married 1836 Hannah Singleton (w), with issue.

**GRIFFIES-WILLIAMS (Erasmus Henry Griffies-, Sir, 2nd Bart.)** see under **WILLIAMS**

**GRIFFIN (Edward, sen.)** Bapt. Dingley, Northants. 24/12/1751, s. Rev. Edward Griffin, sen. and Mary Boldero. Lincoln, Oxford 1769, BA1773, dn74 (Chester for Peterb.), p75 (Peterb.), then Trinity, Cambridge, MA1791. R. Hardwick, Northants. 1770-81 (res.), (succ. his father as) R. Dingley 1775 and R. Draughton, Northants. 1790 to death. Dom. Chap. to 2nd Earl Spencer 1790. Died 3/10/1840 [C110245. Foster differs] Married Cottingham, Yorks. 18/10/1784 Mary Burditt, with clerical son (two below). *J.P.* Leics. and Northants.

**GRIFFIN (Edward)** From Worcester, s. Edward Griffin. Trinity, Oxford 1773 (aged 18), BA1776, dn77 (Lin.), p78 (Lin.). R. Hulcott,

Bucks. 1779-90 (res.), R. Welham, Leics. 1787 [C61950], PC. Ipswich St Peter, Suffolk 1801 and R. Ipswich St Stephen, Suffolk 1815 to death 8/8/1833 (CCEd thus) [C113304]

**GRIFFIN (Edward, jun.)** Bapt. Dingley, Northants. 18/11/1786, s. Rev. Edward Griffin, sen. (above) and Mary Burditt. Lincoln, Oxford 1804, BA1808, dn10 (York), p11 (York). PC. Great Bowden, Leics. 1815-64, V. Weston by Welland w. Sutton Bassett, Northants. 1828, V. Wilbarston, Northants. 1831-64- R. Stoke Albany, Northants. 1831 to death 3/2/1870, leaving £3,000 [C110237. YCO] Married Weston by Welland 22/7/1818 Ann Fletcher, with clerical son of same name.

**GRIFFIN (John)** From Birmingham, s. John Griffin. Balliol, Oxford 1802 (aged 17), BA 1806, dn07 (C&L), p08 (Lin.). H/M Solihull G/S, Warwicks. 1816; R. Bradley, Hants. 1829-52 [Foster adds PC. Wield, Hants. to death]. Died 21/6/1852 [C11336] Wife Catherine, and issue.

**GRIFFINHOOFE (John George)** Bapt. Stoke Newington, Middx. 17/10/1770, s. Rev. Nicholas Griffinhoofe (R. Woodham Mortimer, Essex) and Elizabeth Philpott. Trinity, Oxford 1788, BA1792, dn93 (London), MA1795, p97 (Ox.), BD1804, etc. V. Catherington, Hants. 1805 to death (Arkesden, Essex) 16/2/1857 [C74020] Brother below.

**GRIFFINHOOFE (Thomas Sparkes)** Born Stoke Newington, Middx. 15/4/1780, s. Rev. Nicholas Griffinhoofe (R. Woodham Mortimer, Essex) and Elizabeth Philpott. Trinity, Oxford 1798, migrated to Pembroke, Cambridge 1804, dn04 (Win.), p04 (Win.), BA1805, MA1808. V. Mayland, Essex 1805-59, V. Arkesden, Essex 1811 to death. Chap. to HRH Duke of York and Albany 1811. Died Dover, Kent 22/2/1859, leaving £25,000 [C74021] Married Rodmarton, Glos. 2/12/1819 Harriet Hutchins, with clerical s. Thomas John. Brother above.

**GRIFFITH (Charles Tapp)** Born Elm, Frome, Som. 17/8/1789, s. Rev. John Griffith and Sarah Clavey. Wadham, Oxford 1806, BA 1810, dn12 (Salis.), Fellow, MA1813, p14, BD &DD1828. S/M Southampton Free G/S 1819 (res.), S/M Warminster G/S 1820-40; V. Southampton St Michael 1817-25, R. (and patron) of Elm 1825 (and RD of Frome 1845-64) to death 5/1/1866. Will not traced [C41219. Boase] Married Warminster 21/12/1812 Anne Bayly, with issue. Perhaps brothers Robert Clavey, and John Wickham Griffith, below? Online port.

**GRIFFITH (E.)** [NiVoF] R. Burmington Chapel, Wolford, Warwicks. 1816. Died? [Not traced in CCEd unless also a Prebend of St Davids?] Had issue.

**GRIFFITH (Henry Deer)** Born Newcastle upon Tyne 18/8/1784, s. Anthony Thomas Griffith and Sarah Deer. University, Oxford 1803, BA1807, dn07 (Durham), p08 (Durham), MA 1812. PC. Newcastle upon Tyne St Andrew 1811 to death 14/02/1834 aged 49 [C130461] Married Newcastle 27/6/1809 Maria Gardner, with issue.

**GRIFFITH (John)** Bapt. Bangor Cathedral 16/12/1789, s. Rev. Richard Griffith (V. Bangor). Trinity, Cambridge 1808, BA1812, then Emmanuel 1814, dn14 (Nor.), Fellow 1814, MA1815, p15 (Bristol), tutor 1817-28, BD1822, DD1831, incorporated at Oxford 1848. Chap. to Lord Amherst's Embassy to China 1816 (wrecked on St Helena on the return voyage and met Napoleon). R. Fulbourne All Saints, Cambs. 1827, Canon of 2nd Prebend in Rochester Cathedral 1827-72 (res.), PC. Stuntney, Camb. 1827, R. Llangynhafel, Denbigh 1830-1, V. Aylesford, Kent 1831-2, V. Boxley, Kent 1832-59, V. Thornton Curtis, Lincs. 1832-51, RD Sutton 1840, and of Shoreham 1850. Chap. to Lord Lyndhurst 1827. Died Cheltenham 29/5/1879, leaving £180,000 [C62619. Boase] Married Mary Elizabeth Barker (a clergy dau., of Hildersham Hall, Cambs.). 'Prosecuted his bankers for having unlawfully disposed of deeds, and obtained their transportation for 14 years.'

**GRIFFITH (John Wickham)** Born Warminster, Wilts. 27/1/1795, s. Rev. John Griffith and Sarah Clavey. Queen's, Oxford 1812, BA1816, dn18 (Salis.), Fellow 1819-30, MA1819, p20 (Ox.). R. Pertwood, Wilts. 1825 and R. Bishopstow, Wilts. 1846 to death 24/4/1859, leaving £340-7s-3d. [C29682] Married Walcot, Bath 14/10/1830 Maria Louisa Bayly, w. clerical s. Robert Charles Francis Griffith. Brothers (below), and Charles Tapp Griffith (above).

**GRIFFITH (Robert Clavey)** Born Frome, Somerset 20/6/1791, s. Rev. John Griffith and Sarah Clavey. Wadham, Oxford 1808, BA1813, dn14 (Ox.), MA1816, p16 (London), Fellow

1816-17. S/M Lord Weymouth's School, Warminster 1818; R. Corsley, Wilts. 1816-44, R. Fifield Bavant, Wilts. 1829. Died 4/11/1844 [C29685] Married Uppingham, Rutland 8/4/1823 Mary Elizabeth Adderley Hotchkin, w. issue. Perhaps brothers Charles Tapp, and John Wickham Griffith (above).

**GRIFFITH (Thomas)** Bapt. Islington, London 26/10/1797, s. of Thomas Griffith (saddler) and Katharine Coote. St John's, Cambridge 1818, dn21 (Nor. for Win.), BA1822, p22 (Nor. for Win.), MA1832. V. Guildford St Nicholas, Surrey 1823-6, V. Selmeston, Surrey 1827-33 (res.), R. Muckton, Lincs. 1828-32 (res.), V. St James (o/w Newchurch), Ryde, IoW 1829, Minister of Ram's Episcopal [Proprietary] Chapel, Homerton, Middx. ['*income uncertain*'] 1830-72, Prebend of Sneating in St Paul's Cathedral, London 1862-80. Lived latterly and died Clapton, London 24/8/1883, leaving £19,238-8s-0d. [C62623. Boase] Married Oswaldkirk, Yorks. 12/7/1821 Charlotte Comber, with issue.

**GRIFFITHS (Charles)** Born Bath 4/1/1800, s. Rev. William Griffiths and Amelia Warren Rogers. Exeter, Oxford 1818, BA1822, dn23 (Ex.), p24 (Ex.). R. Trentishoe, Devon 1823 to death 24/1/1859, leaving £300 [C144548]

**GRIFFITHS (John)** From Rodmill, Sussex, s. Rev. John Griffiths. Wadham, Oxford 1791 (aged 18), BA1794, dn95 (London for Salis.), then Queen's, MA1797, BD &DD1821. S/M King's School Rochester 1801-25 (res.); R. Hinxhill, Kent 1801, PC. Strood, Kent 1802-3, V. Rochester St Margaret, Kent 1803 to death 30/9/1832 (CCEd says 27/11/1832) [C1463]

**GRIFFITHS (Thomas)** Bapt. Bristol 3/3/1794, s. Thomas (medical doctor) and Martha Griffiths. Wadham, Oxford 1811, BA1815, Fellow 1819-38, MA1821, etc. PC. Oxford St Peter in the East 1832-4 (res.), R. Limington, Som. 1836 to death (Bristol) 31/3/1849 [C30017. DEB].

**GRIMSHAW, GRIMSHAWE ([Thomas] Shuttleworth)** Born Preston, Lancs. 4/5/1777, s. John Grimshaw and Penelope Shuttleworth. BNC, Oxford 1794, BA1798, MA1800. R. (and patron) of Burton Latimer, Northants. 1809-43 and V. Biddenham, Beds. 1809 to death. Dom. Chap. to 3rd Baron Montford 1809. Died 17/2/1850 [C110250] Married Bedford 1810 Charlotte Anne Libius, with issue.

**GRINFIELD (Thomas)** Born Bath, Somerset 27/9/1788, s. Rev. Thomas Grinfield, sen. (a Moravian Minister in Bristol) and Anna Joanna Foster Barham. Trinity, Cambridge 1807, BA 1812, dn13 (B&W), p13 (B&W for Bristol), MA1816. R. Shirland, Derbys. 1827 to death (Clifton, Bristol) 8/4/1870, leaving £16,000 [C11342. ODNB. Boase] Married Exeter 13/9/1813 his first cousin Mildred Foster Barham, with issue. Hymn-writer.

**GRISDALE (Lowther)** Bapt. Whitehaven, Cumberland 21/11/1790, s. Matthew Grisdale and Esther Fletcher. Literate: p14 (Chester). PC. Walmsley, Bolton, Lancs. 1821 (and H/M Bolton Free G/S) to death (unmarried) 12/5/1847 aged 57 [C168997]

**GRISENTHWAITE (John)** Bapt. Windermere, Westmorland 18/3/1792, s. William Grisenthwaite and Barbara Wilkinson. Literate: dn15 (Chester), p16 (Chester). PC. Kentmere, Kendal, Westmorland 1816 to death 8/12/1835 (CCEd thus) [C168998] Married Kendal 13/2/1830 Margaret Whinfield.

**GROOBY (James)** Bapt. Wootton, Warwicks. 7/7/1777, s. James and Elner Grooby. Worcester, Oxford 1800, BA1804, dn04 (C&L for Wor.), p05 (C&L for Wor.), MA1808. PC. Baunton, Glos. 1812-29 (res.), V. Swindon, Wilts. 1823 to death 6/3/1854 [C11344]

**GROOME (John Hindes)** Born Aldeburgh, Suffolk 16/6/1776, s. Robinson Groome (a mercer). Pembroke, Cambridge 1793, BA1798, dn98 (Nor.), Fellow, MA1801, p02 (Nor.). R. (and patron) of both Earl Soham w. Monk Soham >< Suffolk 1818 to death. Dom. Chap. to 1st Marquess of Salisbury 1810. Died Plomesgate, Suffolk 22/3/1845 aged 68 [C113318] Married Ipswich 24/3/1806 Mary Barham, with issue.

**GROSVENOR (Robert)** Bapt. Marylebone, London 30/6/1767, s. Thomas Grosvenor [of the ducal Westminster family] and Deborah Skynner. Christ Church, Oxford 1784, BA1788, dn92 (Ox.), p93 (Ox.), All Souls, MA and Fellow 1795-1842. V. Morden, Dorset 1793-1834, R. Almer w. Charlborough, Dorset 1798-1834, R. Elmley, Kent 1818. Dom. Chap. to 1st Viscount

Curzon 1819. Died 17/12/1842 aged 75 [C30024]

**GROVE (Charles)** Bapt. Salisbury 5/12/1792, s. Charles Grove (physician) and Elizabeth Acland. Jesus, Cambridge 1810, BA1815, dn15 (Salis.), p16 (Salis.), MA1819. R. Odstock, Wilts. 1817 (and RD1819 and Prebend of Minor Pars Altaris in Salisbury Cathedral 1828) to death 28/5/1868, leaving £60,000 [C92778]

**GROVE (Charles Henry)** Born Ferne, Wilts. 29/10/1794, s. Thomas and Elizabeth Grove. University, Oxford 1811, BA1815, dn17 (Salis.), p18 (Salis.), MA1826. R. Berwick St Leonard, Wilts. 1826-73. Died (Bournemouth, Dorset) 14/7/1878, leaving £35,000 [C74037. Foster as Henry Charles]

**GROVE (John Worrall)** Bapt. Chaddesley, Worcs. 20/6/1781, s. William and Mary Grove. St Edmund Hall, Oxford 1800, BA1804, dn05 (Nor.), p06 (Nor.), MA1819, BD & DD1828 (MD added to Will). R. Strensham, Worcs. 1807 to death (a widower) 30/5/1859, leaving £1,000 [C113317. Foster as H.C.] Married Norwich 12/12/1807 Ann Parker, w. issue.

**GROVE (Thomas)** From Honiley, Warwicks., s.William Grove. St Mary Hall, Oxford 1794 (aged 23), BA1800, MA1802. V. Mavesyn Ridware, Staffs. 1801 to death 1852 [C11349 has 2 men as one, and Foster has the death date as 1811]. Had issue.

**GROVE (William Frederick)** Born Melbury Abbas, Dorset, s. Rev. Hugh Grove (R. Kilmington, Som.) and Grace Snook. Oriel, Oxford 1788 (aged 18), then St Mary Hall BA1792, dn92 (London for Bristol), p94 (Bristol). R. Melbury Abbas 1794 to death 5/8/1847 aged 79, living at Zeals House, Mere, Wilts. [C52679] Married Pitcombe, Som. 25/1/1798 Jane Pouncett.

**GROVER (John Septimus)** Bapt. Hammersmith, Middx. 18/12/1766, s. Montague Grover and Letitia Moody. King's, Cambridge 1786, BA1791, dn97 (Lin.), MA1798, p98 (Nor.), Fellow 1789-99, Fellow of Eton College 1814 (Vice-Provost 1835-51). Tutor to son of Earl of Leicester; R. Helhoughton (o/w Raynham), Norfolk 1798-1821 (res.), R. Farnham Royal, Bucks. 1817 to death (London) 28/11/1852 aged 87 [C62700] Married Plumstead, Kent 28/11/1811 Harriet Ann Dickinson.

**GRUEBER (Arthur)** Bapt. Downpatrick, Co. Down 1/10/1792, s. Rev. Arthur Grueber, sen. and Louisa Ford. St Edmund Hall, Oxford 1826, BA1830, dn30 (Ex.), p31 (B&W for Ex.). V. Colebrooke, Devon 1831 to death 5/5/1848 [C144550] Married East Teignmouth, Devon 21/8./1828 Sarah Hentley Eaton, w. issue.

**GRUNDY (Samuel)** Literate: dn90 (Chester), p91 (Chester). PC. Chapel en le Frith, Derbys. 1792-1836, PC. Cauldon, Staffs. 1801-29 (res.). Died 21/12/1836 (CCEd thus) [C11352]

**GRYLLS (Henry)** Bapt. Helston, Cornwall 26/3/1794, s. Rev. Richard Gerveys Grylls (Chap. of Helston, Cornwall) and Charity Hill. Exeter, Oxford 1812, BA1816, dn17 (Chester for Ex.), p18 (Ex.), MA1821. V. St Neots, Cornwall 1820-62 to death. Dom. Chap. to Lord Vivian at some date. Died Helston 11/6/1862 aged 82 (of 'decline and atrophy, effusion of the brain'), leaving £9,000. [C144551. Boase] Married Holborn, London 30/12/1820 Ellen Mary Boulderson, with issue. Brothers, below.

**GRYLLS (John Couch)** Born Marhamchurch, Cornwall 20/9/1796, s. Rev. Richard Gerveys Grylls (Chap. of Helston, Cornwall) and Charity Hill. Jesus, Cambridge 1821, no degree, dn23 (Chester for York), p25 (Lin.), TCD1834 (as Gryll), MA1840 (Lambeth). PC. Saltash, Cornwall 1825 (and S/M Saltash G/S 1827). In Australia 1838-47. Died 22/4/1854 aged 57 [C62703. YCO. Al.Dub.] Married Stoke Damerel, Devon 19/12/1820 Sarah Richards, with issue. Brothers, above and below.

**GRYLLS (Richard Gerveys)** Born Helston, Cornwall 30/5/1785, s. Rev. Richard Gerveys Grylls, sen. (Chap. of Helston, Cornwall) and Charity Hill. Jesus, Cambridge 1803, SCL, dn09 (Ex.), BCL1809, p09 (Ex.). R. St Breock, Cornwall 1803, V. Breage w. Germoe, Cornwall 1809-52 (and Preacher throughout the Diocese of Exeter 1809), V. Luxulyan, Cornwall 1813 to death 4/11/1852 [C144553] Married St Austell, Cornwall 29/8/1816 Sophia Rashleigh, *s.p.* Brothers above and William, below.

**GRYLLS (Thomas)** Born Helston, Cornwall 19/11/1790, s. Thomas Grylls (attorney) and Mary Millet. Trinity, Cambridge 1809, BA 1813, dn13 (Bristol), p14 (B&W), MA1826. R. Cardynham, Cornwall 1814-45, Prebend of Exeter Cathedral 1833-45, proposed Dean of Exeter (for a few weeks only, blocked by Bishop

Phillpotts). Died Bodmin, Cornwall 26/2/1845 [C41224] Married Mawgan, Cornwall 4/1/1815 Sarah Willyams (of Carnanton), with clerical son.

**GRYLLS (William)** Born Helston, Cornwall 6/8/1786, s. Rev. Richard Gerveys Grylls and Charity Hill. Trinity, Cambridge 1804, BA1808, MA1812, dn19 (Ex.), p22 (Ex.). V. Crowan, Cornwall 1819-35, V. St Neot, Cornwall 1862? Died (unmarried) Exeter 6/11/1863 [C144554] Left his library of 14,000 volumes to Trinity College. Brothers, above.

**GUERIN (Joseph)** Bapt. Cirencester, Glos. 11/10/1765, s. Joseph Guerin. Trinity, Oxford 1784, BA1788, MA1790, p91 (Glos.). R. Norton Fitzwarren, Som. 1797 and R. West Bagborough, Som. 1798 to death. Dom. Chap. to 7th Lord Kinnaird 1798. Died 12/11/1863 aged 96. Will not traced [C42139] Married 3/9/1801 Maria Lucy Eliza Shuldham, with issue. *J.P., D.L.* Somerset.

**GUEST (Wilbraham Bootle)** Born Eccles, Lancs. 2/5/1795, s. Rev. Richard and Mary Guest. St Catherine's, Cambridge 1819, a Ten Year Man (BD1830), dn18 (Chester), p19 (Chester). PC. High Legh, Rostherne, Cheshire 1831 to death 10/7/1863, leaving £2,000 [C169006] Married Ashton-on-Mersey, Lancs. 28/12/1824 Ann Stelfox, w. clerical son George Wilbraham Guest.

**GUILFORD (Francis North, 6th Earl of)** see under **NORTH**

**GUILLEBAUD (Peter)** Born London 30/6/1773, s. Peter Guillebaud and Mary Anne Heureux. BNC, Oxford 1793, BA1797, MA 1799, then Trinity, Cambridge 1835. R. Nailsea, Som. 1811-34. Lived in Clifton, Bristol. Died (Clevedon, Som.) 1/3/1867 aged 93, leaving £120,000 [C144551] Married Eliza Ann Lea ('that flirt'), with clerical son Henry Lea Guillebaud.

**GUISE (Powell Colchester)** Born Highnam Court, Glos. 18/1/778, s. Sir John Guise, 1st Bart. and Elizabeth Wright. Christ Church, Oxford 1798, BA1802, dn03 (Glos.), p03 (Salis.), MA1804. R. Crayke, Yorks. 1805-35, V. Longney, Glos. 1818 and V. Elmore, Glos. 1835 to death (Crayke) 4/5/1835 (CCEd says 5/6/1835) aged 55 [C92782] Married 13/10/1808 Maria Clifford (formerly Winchcombe), of Frampton Court, Glos. Clerical sons George Clifford, and Frederick Charles Guise.

**GULLY (Samuel Thomas [Slade])** Bapt. Gorran, Cornwall 7/12/1788, s. William Slade Gulley and Jennifer Powne. Wadham, Oxford 1806, BA1811, MA1814, p14 (Ex.). R. Berrynarbor, Devon 1825 (and Preacher throughout the Diocese of Exeter 1830) to death on or about 27/5/1860, leaving £20,000 [C144557] Married Walcot, Bath 1/2/1835 Anne Slade Hunt Grubbe (w), with issue.

**GUNN (John)** Bapt. Irstead, Norfolk 9/10/1801, s. Rev. William Gunn (below) and Anne Mack. Exeter, Oxford 1819 [barrister at law] BA1824, MA1827, dn29 (Nor.), p29 (Peterb. for Nor.). (succ. his father as) R. Barton Turf w. Irstead >< Norfolk 1829-64-, RD of Waxham 1842. Chap. to HRH Duke of Sussex. Died Norwich 28/5/1890 aged 89. No will traced [C119252] Married (1) Harriet Turner (d.1869) (2) Norwich 23/4/1872 Eliza Moore.

**GUNN (William)** Born Guildford, Surrey 7/4/1750, s. Alexander Gunn (R. Irstead, Norfolk). Literate: dn74 (Nor.), p75 (Nor.) then Caius, Cambridge 1784 (a Ten Year Man, BD 1795), V. Hoveton St Peter w. V. Felmingham, Norfolk 1779-86, R. Sloley, Norfolk 1783-1841, V. Barton Turf w. Irstead >< 1786-1829, V. Gorleston w. Southdown and Weston, Suffolk 1832 to death (at his home Smallburgh Grange, Norfolk) 17/4/1841 [C113328, ODNB] Married 11/2/1789 Anne Mack, with clerical son John, above. *J.P.* Norfolk 1802, *D.L.* 'He made two long visits to Rome, where he procured access for study at the Vatican, and "so distinguished himself by his attention to Italian literature that he was admitted into the *Academia della Crusca* under the name of *Filistor*"' While in Rome on 4/4/1793 he conducted the morganatic marriage between HRH Augustus Frederick (later Duke of Sussex) and Lady Augusta Murray, and was examined later as to the legitimacy of their marriage and children. For an exhaustive survey of his life see: www.archives.norfolk.gov.uk/view/NCC099325

**GUNNING (George)** From Farmborough, Som., s. Rev. Peter Gunning. Merton, Oxford 1805 (aged 18), BA1809, MA1812. R. West Deeping, Lincs. 1822 (living at Bath, Som.) to death 26/12/1866, leaving £4,000 [C41226]

Married Newton St Cyres, Devon 14/12/1813 Louise Mary Quicke, w. issue.

**GUNNING (Henry John, Sir, 4th Bart. of Eltham).** Born 9/12/1797, s. George William Gunning, 2nd Bart. (Horton Hall, Northants.) and Hon. Elizabeth Bridgeman. Balliol, Oxford 1816, BA1820, dn21 (Peterb.), MA1822, p22 (Lin. for Peterb.). R. Knockin, Shropshire 1826, PC. Horton cum Piddington, Northants. 1826-33, R. Knockin, Shropshire 1826 (res.), R. Wigan All Saints, Lancs. 1833-64 (and RD) [net income £2,230 – coal mines under the parish]. Died Aldwincle, Northants. 30/6/1885 aged 87, leaving £1,988-17s-0d. [C62710. Boase]. Married (1) St George's Hanover Square, London 22/02/1827 Mary Catherine Cartwright, 1s. (2) Northants. 23/10/1879 Frances Rose, dau. of Rev. Hon. William Henry Spencer.

**GUNNING (Peter)** Born Langridge, Bath, s. Rev. Peter Gunning, sen. and Anne Randolph. Merton, Oxford 1796 (aged 18), BA1800, dn04 (Glos.), p04 (Ox.), MA1804. R. Bathwick, Som. 1805 and R. Newton St Loe, Som. 1820 to death. Chap. to HRH Duke of Kent 1817; Dom. Dom. Chap. to 1st Earl of Blessington 1820. Died 28/12/1840. [C30035] Married Bath Abbey 23/12/1805 Sarah Ann Phillott, with issue.

**GUNNISS (Friskney)** Bapt. Louth, Lincs. 19/1/1760, s. Friskney and Mildred Gunniss. St John's, Cambridge 1776, then Peterhouse, BA 1781, dn82 (Lin.), p84 (Lin.). R. Leasingham w. Roxholme, Lincs. 1784-1838, R. Knapwell, Cambs. 1786-1830, R. New Sleaford, Lincs. at death (Kentish Town, St Pancras, London) 9/11/1838 [C62712] Wife Susanna.

**GURDON (Philip)** Born London 18/6/1800, s. Theophilus Thornhaugh Gurdon and Anne Mellis. Trinity, Cambridge 1819, then Downing 1821, BA1823, dn24 (Nor.), p25 (Nor.), MA 1826, re-adm. Trinity 1827. R. Reymerston, Norfolk 1825-74, R. Southburgh, Suffolk 1829-74, R. Hackford, Norfolk 1829-32 (res.), R. Cranworth w. Letton, Norfolk 1832 [total income £1,191] to death (Cranworth) 1/8/1874, leaving £9,000 [C113335] Married Lyndhurst, Hants. 5/7/1832 Henrietta Laura Pulteney (Northerwood House, Herts.). J.P. Norfolk.

**GURDON, GURDEN (William)** Bapt. Towcester, Northants. 4/5/1792, s. William Gurdon and Elizabeth Shillingford. Lincoln, Oxford 1811, BA1814, dn15 (Nor.), p16 (Nor.). R. Westbury, Bucks. 1817-67. Died 1/12/1876, leaving £8,000 [C113332 - and other numbers?] Married Towcester 1/12/1817 Louisa Adams.

**GURNEY (John Phillips)** Bapt. Bletchley, Bucks. 22/1/1797, s. William Gurney and Mary Phillips. Queens', Cambridge 1819, dn22 (Ely for London), p22 (London), BA1823, MA1834. V. Great Canfield, Essex 1822 to death 8/3/1872, leaving under £450 [C109679, not Philip] Married Kennington, London 18/3/1834 Anne Langton (w), with issue.

**GURNEY (Samuel)** Bapt. Colan, Cornwall 10/10/1762, s. Rev. John Gurney and Arabella Harper. Wadham, Oxford 1781, BA1785, dn85 (Ex.), p87 (Ex.). V. St Erth, Devon 1800 to death. Dom. Chap. to 1st Baron de Dunstanville 1820. Died 15/6/1833 (CCEd thus) [C144562] Married 10/11/1784 Catherine Kneebone.

**GURNEY (Warwick Oben)** Bapt. Cuby w. Tregony, Cornwall 1/6/1780, s. Rev. Richard Gurney and Bridget Oben. Balliol, Oxford 1798, BA1802. dn02 (Ex.), p05 (Ex.). R. Billingsley, Shropshire 1821-3 (res.), R. Aston Botterell, Shropshire 1823. Probate granted 28/11/1849 [C105537] Married at Paul, Cornwall 22/4/1809 Grace Badcock, w. issue.

**GURNEY (William)** Bapt. Great Stanmore, Middx. 31/1/1768, s. Richard Gurney and Elizabeth Field. Clare, Cambridge 1784, BA 1791, dn93 (Bristol for Lin.), p94 (Lin.), then Sidney, MA1811. R. Ryhall w. V. Essendine, Rutland 1798-1807, Min. West Street Proprietary Chapel, St Giles in the Fields, London 1801-22, R. St Clement Danes, Strand, London (and Preacher throughout the Diocese of London) 1807 to death (Great Canfield, Essex) 23/1/1843 aged 76 [C52693] Married Cheshunt, Hants. 5/5/1791 Mary Phillips, w. clerical sons Thomas, and Henry Phillips Gurney.

**GUTCH (Robert)** Born Oxford 25/8/1777, s. Rev. John Gutch and Elizabeth Weller. Pembroke, Cambridge 1797, then Queens' 1799, BA1801, dn01 (Salis. for Win.), Fellow 1802, p02 (Win.), MA1804. R. Seagrave, Leics. 1809 (and RD) to death 8/10/1851 [C62758. ODNB] Married Marylebone, London 18/6/1810 Mary Anne James (of Oxford, a clergy dau.), w. issue.

**GUTHRIE (John)** Bapt. Newark-on-Trent, Notts. 8/9/1795, s. James and Mary Guthrie.

Trinity, Cambridge 1812, BA1817, dn20 (Chester for York), MA1820, p21 (York). R. Thorpe, Notts. 1827-33 (res.), V Calstone Wellington, Wilts. 1833-6, V. Hilmarton, Wilts. 1833-5, V. Calne, Wilts. 1835-65, PC. Cherhill, Wilts. 1835 (w. Prebend of Bedminster and Redcliffe in Salisbury Cathedral), Canon of Bristol 1858 to death. Dom. Chap. to Marquess of Lansdown 1824. Died 6/7/1865 aged 73, leaving £35,000 [C92785. YCO as Gutherie. Boase] Married Lodsworth, Sussex 21/10/1848 Mrs Caroline Beatty (Stanley) Dickson (w). First Chairman of the the Council of Clifton College, Bristol, where the Guthrie Chapel is called after him. Surrogate 1855.

**GUY (George)** From Chichester, s. Thomas Guy. St Mary Hall, Oxford 1781 (aged 20), BCL1788. V. Henfield, Sussex 1789, R. Chidham, Sussex 1800-4, R. West Stoke, Sussex 1804 to death 25/4/1849 [C63625]

**GUY (Thomas)** Bapt. Ravenstonedale, Westmorland 15/11/1789, s. John and Isabella Guy. Literate: dn13 (York), p14 (York). St Catharine's, Cambridge 1822 ('did not reside', so presumably a Ten Year Man). V. Howden, Yorks. 1825 to death 24/4/1862 aged 70, leaving £1,500 [C131438. YCO] Clerical son.

**GWATKIN (Richard)** Born Hereford 17/9/1791, s. Rev. Thomas Gwatkin and Jane Powle. St John's, Cambridge 1810, BA1814 (Senior Wrangler), Fellow 1814-23, MA1817, dn20 (Ely), p21 (Ely), Assistant Tutor 1822, then Tutor 1832. V. Barrow-upon-Soar, Leics. 1832-53. Living in Wellington, Som. 1851. Lived in, and died Torquay 14/10/1870 aged 79, leaving £30,000 [C62763] Married Barrow-upon-Soar 22/1/1838 Ann Middleton, w. clerical son Thomas.

**GWILLIM (John)** Bapt. Putley, Heref. 13/10/17782, s. Thomas Gwillim and Margaret Weight. Worcester, Oxford 1801, then All Souls, BA1805, dn05 (Lin.), p06 (Lin.), migrated to Trinity, Cambridge, MA1809. R. Bodenham, Heref. 1810, R. Bredenbury, Heref. 1810-59, R. Ingoldmells, Lincs. 1812 to death (London) 16/5/1859, leaving £14,000 [C62764]

**GWILT (Daniel)** Born Barton Mills, Suffolk, s. Rev. Robert Gwilt (Icklingham Hall, Icklingham, Suffolk) and Penelope Burridge. Caius, Cambridge 1796, BA1801, Fellow 1802, dn02 (Nor.), MA1804, p04 (Ely). S/M The Perse School, Cambridge 1806; R. (and patron) Icklingham St James and Icklingham All Saints 1820 to death 25/11/1856 [C100036], Married Widdington, Essex 20/8/1821 Mary Anne Birch. 'A zealous supporter of agricultural improvements'; 'an amusing clergyman, fond of shooting and riding'.

**GWYTHER (Henry)** Born Bristol 19/5/1794, s. Henry Gwyther and Mary Seager. St Edmund Hall, Cambridge 1817, migrated to Trinity, Cambridge 1817, BA1818, dn18 (C&L), p19 (Salis), MA1821. V. Yardley, Worcs. 1821 to death 17/9/1872, leaving £5,000 [C11316] Married (1) Pembroke 7/5/1812 Mrs Mary Philippa Artemesia (Child) Grant (d.1852) (2) Church Stretton, Shropshire 1863 (2nd q.) Fanny Fretwell; w. clerical stepson James Henry Alexander Philipps, and the 1st Baron Milford. 'During his incumbency the church pew-opener, at his bidding, burnt three barrowloads of parchments'.

**HACKER, *born* MARSHALL (Edward Marshall)** From Enstone, Oxon., s. Rev. Nicholas Marshall and Eleanor Coxwell. Worcester, Oxford 1792, BA1796, then Oriel, Fellow 1798, MA1799, dn99 (Ox.), p00 (Ox.). R. Iffley, Oxon. 1819-39, V. (and patron of) Sandford St Martin, Oxon. 1835 to death 31/1/1839 [C30045 as Marshall] Married (1) Oxford 21/6/1803 Priscilla Churchill (d.1804) (2) Oxford 29/11/1814 Mary Ann Burton, w. issue. Assumed surname of Hacker 'later in life', but this was dropped by his son.

**HADDOCK (Joseph)** Born Thorndon, Suffolk 13/8/1793, s. Joseph Haddock and Mary Cason. Pembroke, Cambridge 1818 (a Ten Year Man), dn19 (Nor.), p20 (Nor.). Chap. of the Donative of Ixworth Thorpe >< Suffolk 1824 [income £23] to death Flordon, Norfolk 8/11/1879, leaving under £300 [C113340] Married Great Yarmouth, Norfolk 11/7/1832 Theresa Casborne, and had issue.

**HADEN (Alexander Bunn)** Bapt. Wednesbury, Staffs. 25/3/21783, s. Rev. Alexander Bunn Haden, sen. and Mary Rotten. St Edmund Hall, Oxford 1806, BA1810, dn10 (C&L), p11 (C&L), MA1813. PC. Woore, Shropshire 1811-19 (res.), V. Brewood, Staffs. 1830 to death 16/8/1863, leaving £1,000 [C11358] Married (1) Chetton, Shropshire 7/2/1826 Marianne Heptinstall (d.1850, 1st q.) (2) London 27/4/1859 Mary Ward (w.)

**HADOW (James)** Born 30/1/1757, s. George Hadow (Prof. of Hebrew, St Andrews University) and Susan Scot. Glasgow University 1770, St Andrews University 1772, Snell Exhibitioner, Balliol, Oxford 1773-84, BA1777, dn79 (Ox.), MA1780, p81 (Lin.). V. Streatley, Beds. 1781 (w. V. Sundon, Beds. 1781-6) 1841. Dom. Chap. to 2nd Earl of Warwick 1780. Died 30/1/1847 aged 90 [C30163. Smart. Snell] Married Inveresk, Midlothian 25/1/1788 Sarah Wye, with clerical son below (and a further 40 living descendants).

**HADOW (William Thomas)** Born Streatley, Beds. 16/6/1798, s. Rev. James Hadow (above) and Sarah Wye. St John's, Cambridge 1814, then Trinity 1819, BA1821, dn21 (Lin.), p22 (Lin.), MA1824. R. Haseley, Warwicks. 1827 and V. Mickleton (w. Ebrington), Glos. 1834 to death 20/7/1865, leaving £4,000 [C62772] Married Elstree, Herts. 28/6/1825 Eleanor Ann Drinkwater, with clerical son.

**HAGGITT (D'Arcy)** Bapt. Scarborough, Yorks. 24/09/1794, s. Rev. George Haggitt (R. Rushton, Northants.) and Rosamund D'Arcy Preston. Peterhouse, Cambridge 1791, BA 1796, dn96 (Lin.), Fellow 1799, p99 (Durham), MA 1800. V. Branxton, Northumberland 1799-1835 (sequestrated and deprived), V. Pershore St Andrew, Worcs. 1825 to death. Dom. Chap. to Elizabeth, Countess Harcourt 1809. Died Bruges (thus still in debt?) 7/2/1850 [C62777] Married 11/11/1802 Mary Martin (of Hobart, Tasmania), with issue.

**HAGGITT (George John)** Bapt. Mileham, Norfolk 28/7/1790, s. Rev. George Haggitt and Penelope Higham. Christ's, Cambridge 1807, BA1811, dn13 (Ely), Fellow 1813-18, MA 1814, p14 (Ely), etc. V. Parham w. Hacheston, Suffolk 1818-47, Curate Bury St Edmunds St James, Suffolk 1818, R. Hawkedon, Suffolk 1838 to death 1/3/1847 aged 56 [C109680] Married Southampton, Hants. 28/10/1818 Harriet Porteus, with clerical son.

**HAGGITT (John)** From Ipswich, s. William Haggitt. Clare, Cambridge 1779, MA1783, Fellow 1785-1804, MA1786, dn89 (Ely), p90 (Ely), BD1796. V. Madingley, Cambs. 1796-1804, R. Addington, Bucks. 1804-[39] [Venn attributes this charge to the man above], R. Fen Ditton, Cambs. 1804 to death Jan. 1843 aged 81 [C62779]

**HAGGITT (John)** Born Scarborough, Yorks. 7/7/1768, s. Thomas (merchant) and Catherine Haggitt. Pembroke, Cambridge 1786, then Sidney 1787, Fellow, BA1791, dn91 (York), p92 (York), MA1794. S/M Dedham School, Essex 1798; V. Milton, Cambs. 1831. Died? [C86754. YCO] Married Islington, London Martha Godfrey. Brother below.

**HAGGITT (William)** Born Scarborough, Yorks. 10/11/1756, s. Thomas (merchant) and Catherine Haggitt. Trinity, Cambridge 1774, BA1778, dn79 (Ely), p80 (Ely), MA1781. PC. Bromley by Bow, Middx. 1783-1820, R. Armthorpe, Yorks. 1786-1801, R. Byfleet, Surrey 1801 to death (Chelsea Hospital) 19/3/1834 (CCEd thus) [C74654] Married Marylebone, London 6/4/1786 Sarah Chambers, with issue. Brother John above.

**HAIGH (William)** Bapt. Birstall, Yorks. 10/11/1760, s. John Haigh. Queens', Cambridge 1778, BA1783, dn83 (Llandaff for York), p85

(Durham), MA1786. V. Wooler, Northmberland 1805 to death 11/3/1836 aged 76 [C3976. YCO] Married Newcastle upon Tyne 16/5/1788 Frances Airey, with issue.

**HAILSTONE (John)** Born Hoxton, London 13/12/1759, s. John Hailstone (of the Bank of England) and Elizabeth Whitaker. St Catharine's, Cambridge 1778, then Trinity 1779, BA1782, Fellow 1783, MA1785, dn92 (Ely), p92 (Nor). Woodwardian Professor of Geology, Cambridge 1788-1818. V. Arrington, Cambs. 1796, V. Shudy Camps, Cambs. 1798-1818, V. Trumpington, Cambs. 1817 to death 9/6/1847 [C113343. ODNB] Married ('late in life') York 25/5/1818 Mary Telford, his wife predeceased him, 'and his 4 natural children must have belonged to his younger days'. *F.R.S.* (1801), etc

**HAKE (George)** Bapt. Enfield, Middx. 26/8/1783 (CCEd thus), s. Thomas Hake and Mary Keeling. St John's, Cambridge 1802, re-adm. 1810, no degree, dn11 (Nor.), p12 (C&L). PC. Rocester, Staffs. 1820-48, and V. Chilvers Coton, Warwicks. 1829-44, and V. Ellastone, Staffs. 1830 to death (Derby) 16/5/1848 aged 64 [C11366] Brother below.

**HAKE (Henry)** Born St Pancras, London 6/10/1803, s. Thomas Hake and Mary Keeling. [NiVoF] PC. Astley, Warwicks. 1832-44, V. Chilvers Coton, Warwicks. 1844-[59]. Died Warwick 1888 (4th q.) aged 85. No will traced [C11367] Married (1) 8/11/1831 Fanny Hill (d.1858) (2) 17/12/1862 Fanny Elizabeth Best, w. issue. Brother above.

**HALE (John)** Bapt. City of London 7/2/1772, s. Joseph Hale and Margaritta Pewtriss. Magdalen Hall, Oxford 1795, dn97 (Heref.), BA1800, MA1813. R. Holton cum Beckering. Lincs. 1802-43, R. Salmonby, Lincs. 1812-27, R. Buslingthorpe, Lincs. 1828 to death (Holton) 28/8/1843 [C62788] Married City of London 1/10/1799 Mary Margaret Ayscough, w. child.

**HALE (Richard)** Born Guisborough, Yorks. 10/10/1773, s. Gen. John Hale and Mary Chaloner. Peterhouse, Cambridge 1790, BA 1794, dn97 (Lin.), MA1797, p97 (Peterb.), then Trinity 1798. V. Great Sampford, Essex 1797-1801, V. Weston, Herts. 1798-1801, V. Harewood, Yorks. 1801 (with Dom. Chap. to 1st Earl of Harewood 1803) and R. Goldsborough 1803 to death 27/9/1854 aged 80 [C62789] Married Stainton Market, Lincs. 26/4/1825 Mary Anne Loft. Suspended for six months in Jan. 1849 For 'alleged irreverence and unseemly conduct in the pulpit … and for quarrelling, chiding and brawling in the parish church'.

**HALES,** *born* **DIXON (John Dixon)** Born Liverpool, s. John Dixon. Trinity, Cambridge 1822 (aged 22), BA1826, MA1828, dn28 (B&W), p29 (B&W). R. Charmouth, Dorset 1833-7, V. Richmond St John, Surrey 1837-79, RD of Kingston, Hon. Canon of Rochester Cathedral to death 11/1/1879 aged 79, leaving £12,000 [C41285] Married (1) Abbots Leigh, Som. 19/3/1832 Susanna Ann Bayly (d.1840) (2) Wraxall, Som. 15/7/1845 Charlotte Ann Kington, w. issue. Surrogate.

**HALES (Robert)** Bapt. King's Lynn, Norfolk 21/3/1778, s. Robert Hales and Ann Turner. Corpus Christi, Cambridge 1797, then St John's 1798, BA1801, dn01 (Nor.), MA1804, p05 (Nor.). V. Hemsby, Norfolk 1805-53, V. Herringswell, Suffolk 1811 and R. Hillington, Norfolk 1822 to death (unm.) 11/6/1853 [C113345]

**HALKE (James)** Born Faversham, Kent 26/4/1787, s. Rev. Richard Halke and Mary Thomas. Sidney, Cambridge 1803, BA1809, dn10 (Salis. for Cant.), p11 (Win. for Cant.), then Clare, Fellow, MA1812. PC. Queenborough, Kent 1811-14, V. Selling, Kent 1814-31, V. Weston by Welland w. Sutton Bassett, Northants. 1831 to death. Dom. Chap. to 3rd Baron Sondes 1818. Died Market Harborough, Leics. 20/12/1853 [C74657] Married (1) Sheppey, Kent 6/11/1811 Frances Swift (d.1815) (2) Canterbury Cathedral 23/10/1817 Mary Starr, with issue.

**HALL (Charles)** Bapt. Scorborough, Yorks. 5/8/1797, s. John and Margaret Hall. Trinity, Cambridge 1815, BA1820, dn21 (York), p22 (York), MA1823. R. (and patron) of Terrington, Yorks. 1823 and R. Routh, Yorks. 1827 to death. Dom. Chap. to 3rd Lord Macdonald 1827. Died Terrington 12/12/1864 aged 66 [total income, £1,124], leaving £40,000 [C131440. YCO. ATV] Had clerical son.

**HALL (Edward Moorhouse)** Born Skipton, Yorks. 2/8/1792, s. of David Hall (a surgeon) and Ann Bailey. Lincoln, Oxford 1813, BA 1816, dn16 (York), p17 (York), MA1819. V. Corringham, Lincs. 1827-31, PC. Idle, Yorks. 1830-57, PC. Rufforth, Ainsty of York 1835,

PC. West Fordington, Dorset 1849-50. Died Spondon, Derbys. 10/4/1880 aged 87, leaving £12,000 [C62798. YCO]. Married (1) Halifax, Yorks. 8/2/1820 Mary Anne Swainson (2) Sutton Coldfield, Warwicks. 15/2/1832 Mary Anne Smith (w).

**HALL (Francis)** Bapt. 4/10/1792, s. John Hall (a yeoman farmer) and Mary Marriott. Literate: dn20 (Chester for York), p21 (York). PC. Attercliffe cum Darnall, Yorks. 1821, PC. Greasbrough, Rotherham, Yorks. 1826 to death 25/2/1850 [C131441. YCO] Married Rotherham 23/12/1823 Ann Kirk, with issue.

**HALL (Francis Russell)** Born Manchester 17/5/1788, s. Rev. Samuel Hall and Elizabeth Russel. St John's, Cambridge 1806, BA1810, dn13 (Salis.), MA1813, p15 (Chester), Fellow 1815-26, BD1820, DD1839. R. Fulbourn St Vigoris, Cambs. 1826 (w. Fulbourn All Saints 1828) to death 18/11/1866, leaving £6,000 [C92787. ODNB. Boase] Married (1) Cambridge 13/5/1757 Elizabeth Dorothy Newby, w. issue (2) Clerkenwell, London 4/1/1853 Mary Annie West, w. issue. Composer.

**HALL (George)** [NiVoF] V. Tenbury, Worcs. 1827 and V. Rochford, Heref. to death. Dom. Chap. to Lord Brougham and Vaux. CCEd says died 27/6/1845 [C105560] Married Eliza Ellis.

**HALL (George William)** Bapt. Chelsea, London 8/4/1770, s. John Hall and Mary de Gilles [a French Huguenot]. Pembroke, Oxford 1788, BA1792, dn93 (Ox.), p94 (Ox.), MA1795, BD1808, DD1809. Master of Pembroke College, Oxford 1809-43. Vice-Chancellor of Oxford 1820-4. R. Taynton, Glos. 1810 (w. Canon of Gloucester Cathedral annexed 1820) to death 10/12/1845 [C30176] Married by 1811 Sarah Harriet Hall, with clerical sons William David Hall, and George Charles Hall.

**HALL (James)** Bapt. Hungerford, Berks. 6/1/1797, s. James and Margaret Hall. Wadham, Oxford 1813, BA1817, dn20 (Ely for Salis.), p20 (Salis.), MA1820. V. Great Bedwyn, Wilts. 1822-26 (and Dom. Chap. to his patron the Marquess of Ailesbury 1822), R. West Tanfield, Bedale, Yorks. 1826 to death 30/3/1873 aged 75, leaving £30,000 [C92788]

**HALL (John)** From Ross, Hereford, s. Thomas Hall. BNC, Oxford 1772 (aged 16), BA1775, dn77 (Heref.), p79 (Heref.). V. Chew Magna, Som. 1787 to death 20/4/1841 [C42164] Married (1) Brignall, Yorks. 14/8/1782 Sarah Blackburne (a clergy dau., d.1811), w. issue (2) Dundry, Som. 1/5/1817 Harriet Mary Ball.

**HALL (John)** Bapt. City of London 8/6/1781, s. William and Dorothy Hall. St Edmund Hall, Oxford 1809, dn11, p12, BA1813, MA1816, BD1823. R. Bristol St Werburgh 1832 and Hon. Canon of Bristol 1846 to death 3/8/1871, leaving £4,000 [C52761]

**HALL (John Cecil)** Born 1804, s. Very Rev. Charles Henry Hall (Dean of Christ Church Cathedral, Oxford) and Anna Maria Bridget Byng. Christ Church, Oxford 1820, Student [Fellow] 1820-31, dn26 (Cashel for Ox.), p27 (Ox.), BCL1829. R. Offham, Kent 1830-2, R. Great Cressingham w. Bodney, Norfolk 1832, Archdeacon of Man and R. (Kirk) Andreas 1839 to death there 8/2/1844 [C6734] Married Marylebone, London 21/7/1832 Frances Amelia (dau. of Col. the Hon. Wingfield Stratford, Addington, Kent), with issue. Note: the Abp of Cashel was also Prof. of Hebrew at Oxford.

**HALL (John Hancock)** Born Risley, Derbys. c.1769, s. Rev. John Hancock Hall, sen. Trinity Hall, Cambridge 1787, dn93 (London), LLB 1793, p00 (Chester). R. Risley cum Breaston, Derbys. 1811 and R. Keyworth, Notts. 1842 to death (Risley Hall, Derbys.) 2/4/1859 aged 90, leaving £5,000 [C11375] Married Derby 13/4/1795 Robert Mary Hayhurst, w. clerical s. Henry Banks Hall.

**HALL (John Robert)** From Bocking, Essex, s. Rev. Charles Hall and Elizabeth Carsan. Christ Church, Cambridge 1783 (aged 18), BA 1787, dn88 (Chester), p89 (Chester), MA1790. R. Batsford, Glos. 1807 (and Prebend of Exeter Cathedral 1802) to death 18/10/1841 [C30182] Married Hampstead, London 9/4/1807 Frances Longley, with clerical s., also John Robert.

**HALL (Robert)** From Lincoln. St John's, Cambridge 1803, dn08 (Lin.), LLB1809, p09 (Peterb. for Lin.). R. Westborough (1st Mediety w. Dry Doddington) 1809 (and 2nd Mediety 1809) Lincs. to death 2/6/1861, leaving £35,000 [C62812] Had issue.

**HALL (Samuel)** Born Manchester 1/5/1782, s. Rev. Samuel Hall, sen. and Elizabeth Russel [sic]. St John's, Cambridge 1800, BA1804, dn05

(Chester), p06 (Chester), Fellow 1806-15, MA 1807. PC. Billinge, Wigan, Lancs. 1813-33 (res. and left the CoE 1834). Latterly ran a Calvinist meeting house in Southport, 'but eventually returned to the church'. Died London 21/10/1858 aged 76, leaving £6,000 [C169035. DEB] Married Wigan 29/6/1814 Laura Matilda Kerr, of London, with issue. J.P. Lancs.

**HALL (Samuel)** Bapt. Macclesfield, Cheshire 29/9/1786, s. David Hall and Mary Huxley. BNC, Oxford 1806, BA1810, Fellow 1812-32, MA1812, dn13 (Ox.), p14 (Ox.), BD1820, etc. R. Middleton Cheney, Glos. 1831 to death. Chap. to HRH Duke of Clarence 1819. Died 25/5/1853 [C1873] Married Wakefield, Yorks. 3/9/1831 Anne Holdsworth, with issue. Port. online.

**HALL (William)** From Suffolk. Jesus, Cambridge 1823, then Peterhouse (aged 24) 1825, dn26 (Nor.), LLB 1829. R. Tuddenham, Suffolk 1829-52. Then unbeneficed. Died? [C21224. In *Clergy List* as William Brown Hall]

**HALL (William John)** From Middx., s. John Hall. Corpus Christi, Cambridge 1816, dn20 (London), BA1821, p21 (London), MA1824. 5th Minor Canon of St Paul's Cathedral, London 1826-61, V. Sandon, Herts. 1829-35, R. St Benet w. St Peter, City of London 1835-51, V. Tottenham, London 1851 to death. Priest-in-Ordinary 1829-61. Proprietor and editor of *The Christian Remembrancer*. Died 16/12/1861, leaving £7,000 [C62820. Boase] Wife Julia, 8 ch.

**HALLETT (Richard Southcott)** Born Axmouth, Devon 12/4/1788, s. Rev. Richard Southcott (Hothersall) Hallett and Sarah Cooke. Exeter, Oxford 1808, then Sidney, Cambridge 1811, SCL, dn12 (Ex.), p13 (Ex.). (succ. his father as) V. (and patron) of Axmouth 1814 and R. Rousdon (o/w St Pancras), Devon 1814 to death 1/1/1858 (Wokingham, Berks.) aged 69. Will not traced [C144568] Married Bath 1815 Jane Maria Shaw, with issue.

**HALLIDAY (Edmund Trowbridge)** Bapt. Teignmouth, Devon 3/6/1793, s. Rev. Edmund Trowbridge, sen. (living at Yard House, Chapel Cleeve, Som. where the family had been for 200 years) and Jane Halliday. Oriel, Oxford 1811, migrated to Christ's, Cambridge 1813, BA1816, dn16 (B&W), p17 (B&W). PC. Broomfield, Som. 1829 and PC. (and patron) of Wilton, Som. 1831 to death 1844 (4th q.) [C41289] Married Teignmouth 11/9/1790 Jane Hodgkinson.

**HALLIFAX (John Savile)** Probably bapt. Finsbury, London 22/6/1804, s. Thomas Hallifax and Anna Maria Stourton. Trinity, Oxford 1823, BA1827, dn28 (Nor.), p29 (Nor.), MA1830. V. Melton Mowbray, Leics. 1832, R. (and patron) of Groton, Suffolk 1837 to death (Edwardstone House, Suffolk) 6/3/1872 aged 67, leaving £9,000 [C63227] Married Bury St Edmunds, Suffolk 26/9/1832 Catherine Sarah Godfrey, with issue.

**HALLIFAX (Robert)** From Reading, Berks., s. Thomas Hallifax. Lincoln, Oxford 1776 (aged 16), then Magdalen 1780-2, BA1781, dn82 (Ox. for London), MA1783, p84 (Chester). V. Standish w. Hardwicke, Glos. 1785 to death (Wheatenhurst, Glos.) 13/9/1838 [C30185] Married St Martin in the Fields, London 1/5/1782 Sarah Sentence [*sic*], with issue. J.P. Gloucestershire.

**HALLIFAX (Robert Fitzwilliam)** Bapt., 5/7/1778, s. Rt. Rev. Samuel Hallifax (Bishop of St Asaph) and Catherine Cooke (dau. of a Dean of Ely). Trinity Hall, Cambridge 1795, BA1800, dn02 (Glos.), p02 (London), MA1803. R. Richard's Castle, Shropshire 1802-37, V. Caynham, Shropshire 1816-18, Registrar of Diocese of Gloucester. Died Batchcott Hall, Ludlow, Shropshire 16/7/1837 ('Visitation of God. Apoplexy') [C105559] Married Ashford Bowdler, Shropshire 29/7/1803 Eliza Bourke Ricketts (d.1814), 8 ch.
*powys.org/pl_tree/ps03/ps03_146.html*

**HALLIWELL (Henry)** From Burnley, Lancs., s. Rev. William Halliwell. BNC, Oxford 1773 (aged 17), BA1786, MA1789, dn90 (Ox.), p90 (Ox.), Fellow and Tutor, BD1803. PC. Arkholme, Lancs. 1800-1 (res.), R. Clayton w. Kemer, Som. 1803-35, Chap. Manchester Collegiate Church 1805. Died 15/2/1835 (CCEd says 2/5/1835) [C30186]

**HALLWARD (John)** Born Assington, Suffolk 14/5/1789, s. Rev. John Hallward, sen. and Mary Lambarde. Worcester, Oxford 1807, BA1811, dn12 (Nor.), p13 (Nor.), MA1814. R. Stanton on the Wolds, Notts. 1819-27, R. Easthorpe, Essex 1826, (succ. his father as) V. Assington 1826, R. Swepstone w. Snarestone, Leics. 1844 to death. Dom. Chap. to Bishop of Dromore, Elphin and Kilmore/Elphin and

Ardargh 1827. Died 6/6/1865, leaving £800 [C113361] Married Walcot, Bath 3/1/1820 Emily Jane Leslie, with clerical son. Brother below.

**HALLWARD (Nathaniel William)** Bapt. Assington, Suffolk 16/6/1797, s. Rev. John Hallward and Mary Lambarde. Worcester, Oxford 1814, BA1818, dn20 (Nor.), MA1820, p21 (Nor.). R. Milden, Suffolk 1827-82. Dom. Chap. to Viscount Lorton; British Chap. at Caen 1842-7. Died 21/10/1884 aged 87. No will traced [C113362] Married by 1828 Harriet Leslie, with issue. Brother above.

**HALSTED (Thomas)** Bapt. Thurlow, Suffolk 28/6/1806, s. Rev. Samuel Halsted and Decima Mitchell. Trinity Hall, Cambridge 1822, BA1828, dn29 (Nor.), p30 (Nor.), MA1831. (succ. his father as) R. Little Bradley, Suffolk 1831-8. Died Westley Waterless (Waterleys), Cambs. 6/8/1847 aged 42 [C113364] Another man of this name in this parish also.

**HALTON (Imanuel/Emanuel)** Born Wingfield Manor, South Wingfield, Derbys., s. Wingfield Halton and Ann Bateman. Trinity, Oxford 1803 (as Emmanuel, aged 17), migrated to Magdalene, Cambridge 1811 (aged 24), dn12 (C&L), BA1813, p13 (C&L). R. South Wingfield 1813 and Upper Langwith, Derbys. 1819 to death 9/5/1875 (as Immanuel) aged 89, leaving £3,000 [C11384] Married Askrigg, Yorks. 11/2/1801 Elizabeth Dinsdale, with issue.

**HALTON (John)** Probably literate: dn90 (Chester), p91 (Chester). V. Clapham, Yorks. 1803-37 and PC. Chester St Peter 1815 to death 18/1/1837 aged 72 [C169042] Married 1822 Margaret Taylor (d.1824).

**HALTON (Lancelot Miles)** Bapt. Mere, Wilts. 6/11/1800, s. Rev. Lancelot Greenthwaite and Harriet Halton. St John's, Cambridge 1820, BA1824, dn24 (Win.), p25 (Salis.). R. (and patron) of Woolhampton, Berks. 1827-59, R. Thruxton 1832 to death (Newbury, Berks.) 2/12/1873, leaving £7,000 [C74665] Married (1) Waterstock, Oxon. 30/2/1827 Eliza Penelope Louise Sclater (a clergy dau., d.1831), w. issue (2?) Westminster, London 1863 (2nd q.) Phoebe Briggs (w).

**HAMBLETON (John)** Born Wallingford, Berks. 1779, s. John Hambleton and Eliza Humfrey. St Edmund Hall, Oxford 1822, BA 1825, dn25 (London), p26 (London), MA1829. Min. Islington St John's, Holloway Road, London 1830 to death 22/10/1865, leaving £600 [C118765. Boase] Married (1) Westminster, London 16/4/1816 Elizabeth Lawrence (d.1833), w. issue (2) Islington 9/12/1834 Sophia Anglin Lawrence (w).

**HAMES (William)** Born Croydon, Surrey, s. John Hames. Emmanuel, Cambridge 1810, BA 1814, dn16 (Salis.). [Inherited Chagford House, Devon 1820 and so] R. Chagford 1821-52, R. Ham, Kent 1827 to death (Walmer, Kent) 8/8/1859, leaving £35,000 [C92790] Married Dawlish, Exeter 10/8/1824 Jemima Belinda Perkins (w) (a clergy dau.), with clerical son Heyter George Hames.

**HAMILTON (Andrew)** Literate: dn76 (Down), p77 (Down). R. Binstead, IoW 1797 (and R. St Helens, IoW 1814) to death 6/6/1833 (CCEd thus) [C74668]

**HAMILTON (Anthony)** Born 12/7/1778, s. Ven. Anthony Hamilton (Archdeacon of Colchester) and Anne Terrick. St John's, Cambridge 1796, BA1800, dn01 (London), p02 (London), MA1803. R. Loughton, Essex 1805-51, Prebend of Warminster in Wells Cathedral 1810-28, R. St Mary le Bow and St Pancras Soper Lane w. All Hallows Honey Lane, City of London 1820-51, Archdeacon of Taunton (w. Prebend of Milverton Prima in Wells Cathedral annexed) 1827-51, 1st Canon Residentiary (and Precentor) of Lichfield Cathedral 1831-50 (res.) (w. Prebends of Bishop's Itchington, and of Colwich annexed 1831-50). Chap. in Ordinary 1812-37. Died 10/9/1851 [C21643 Boase] Married St George's Hanover Square, London 13/7/1807 Charity Graeme, dau. Sir Walter Farquhar, 1st Bart., with issue (including Walter Kerr Hamilton, Bishop of Salisbury).

**HAMILTON (Henry Parr)** Born Midlothian 3/4/1794, s. Alexander Hamilton (Prof. of Midwifery at Edinburgh University, *q.v.* ODNB) and Katherine Reid. Trinity, Cambridge 1811, BA 1816, Resident Fellow 1818, dn19 (Chester for Bristol), p19 (Chester for Bristol), MA1819. R. Wath, Yorks. 1830-50, PC. Cambridge St Mary the Great 1833-44, RD 1847, Dean of Salisbury 1850 to death [income £1,000; contributed to the restoration of the cathedral]. Chap. to HRH Duke of Sussex 1831. Died 7/2/1880 aged 85, leaving £14,000 [C52774. ODNB. Boase] Married 31/10/1833 Eleanor Mason, Yorks. (w) with issue. *F.R.S.* (1828 as 'a gentleman well versed in mathematics'); *F.R.A.S.; F.R.G.S.* Much concerned with primary education, especially of girls.

**HAMILTON (James)** Born Tobago, West Indies 4/4/1784, s. John Hamilton (a Scot) and Mary Susannah Anna Wilson. Middle Temple 1800. St John's, Cambridge 1801, BA 1805, dn07 (Win.), MA1808, p08 (Win.). V. Warlingham w. Chelsham, Surrey 1821-9, V. Hackington, Kent 1823-40, V. Ardingly, Sussex 1826 [C63543], R. Stapleford Abbots, Essex 1829-40, R. Great Baddow, Essex 17/7/1840 to death. A Six Preacher of Canterbury 1828. Died 29/9/1840 (CCEd death date is wrong) [C74676. LBSO] Married Margaret Fuller (Ashdown House, Forest Row, Sussex), w. issue.

**HAMILTON (John Vesey)** Born Londonderry, Co. Donegal 24/11/1795, s. Rev. William Hamilton and Sarah Walker. Magdalen Hall, Oxford 1816, BA1818, p22 (Ex.), MA1824. V. Sandwich St Mary, Kent 1824, R. Little Chart, Kent 1838 to death (St Omer, France) 3/9/1870, leaving £300 [C144571] Married Walcot, Bath 16/6/1824 Frances Agnes Malone, with issue (inc. Admiral Sir Richard Vesey Hamilton).

**HAMILTON (Joseph Harriman)** Born Edinburgh 28/5/1800, s. James Hamilton (physician) and Isabella Harriman. Trinity, Cambridge 1817, BA1822, dn24 (Lin.), Chap. 1824, p25 (Ely), MA1829. V. Shepshed, Leics. 1831-48, PC. St Michael Chester Square, London 1848-71, Prebend of Chiswick in St Paul's Cathedral 1859-72, R. Frant, Sussex 1871-9, Canon Residentiary Rochester Cathedral 1872 to death 17/8/1881 aged 81, leaving £25,543-2s-6d. [C63238. Boase] Married Liverpool 17/5/1838 Anna Bold, with clerical son.

**HAMILTON, *born* WARD (Peploe William)** Born Chester 16/12/1781, s. Rev. Peploe Ward and Sarah Hamilton. Queens', Cambridge 1798, BA1803, MA1806. V. Winston, Suffolk 1818, PC. Guilden Sutton, Cheshire 1831 to death 24/3/1854 (Hoole Lodge, Chester) [C109878. Venn under Ward] Married Beaumaris, Anglesey 11/2/1821 Martha Panton, with issue.

**HAMILTON (William Jennings)** From Wallingford, Berks., s. Jeremiah Hamilton. Pembroke, Oxford 1821 (aged 17), BA1825, dn26 (Lin.), p27 (Lin.), MA1828. PC. Boxmoor, Hemel Hempstead, Herts. 1830, R. Nettleden, Bucks. 1834-57, V. Ivinghoe, Bucks. 1845 to death (unmarried) 28/2/1874 aged 70, leaving £10,000 [C63241]

**HAMLEY (Edward)** Bapt. St Columb Major, Cornwall 25/10/1764, s. Rev. Thomas and Mary Hamley. Literate: dn87 (Ox.), p88 (Chester for Ox.), then New, Oxford 1783, BCL1791, LLB. R. Cusop, Heref. 1804 and R. Stanton St John, Oxon. 1806 to death. Dom. Chap. to 5th Earl of Oxford and Mortimer 1814, Died 25/2/1835 (CCEd thus) [C30196] Clerical s. of same name in ODNB.

**HAMMERTON (William)** Bapt. Kirby Malhamdale, Yorks. 27/2/1763, s. Thomas Hammerton. Literate: dn90 (York), p93 (York). PC. Tong, Yorks. 1806 to burial 22/9/1834 aged 71 [C86837. YCO] Widow Ann, with issue.

**HAMMOND (Henry)** Born Basingstoke, Hants. 25/5/1765, s. Henry Hammond and Mercy Rempnant. Magdalen Hall, Oxford 1782, BA1786. PC. Horsell, Surrey 1800 to death (Windlesham, Surrey) 2/11/1840 [C118790 as Hamond]

**HAMMOND (James)** From London, s. Richard Hammond. Merton, Oxford 1806 (aged 17), BA1810, dn12 (Win.), p13 (Win.), MA1817. R. Hannington Kingsclere, Hunts. 1814-[37]. Died (Staunton, Glos.) 8/3/1871 aged 82, leaving £8,000 [C74679]

**HAMMOND (John)** Born Sneaton, Yorks. 20/3/1790, s. Rev. John Hammond, sen. Sidney, Cambridge 1812, dn15 (C&L for Win.), BA 1816, p16 (Lin.). R. Priston, Som. 1820 to death 13/8/1859, leaving £6,000 [C11390] Widow Harriet.

**HAMMOND (William Andrew)** From Philadephia, USA, s. George & Margaret Hammond. Christ Church, Oxford 1811 (aged 17), BA1816, dn19 (Chester for Salis.), MA 1819, p19 (Salis.). R. Kirby Laythorpe w. Asgarby >< Lincs. 1821-3, R. Whitchurch, Oxon. 1823-40 (res.). Dom. Chap. to 1st Marquess of Bristol 1820. Died Naples 29/11/1844 [C30220] Married Aston Rowant, Oxon. 1/1/1828 Maria Brown, with clerical son.

**HAMOND (Henry)** Bapt. Cheltenham, Glos. 16/4/1805, s. William Parker Hamond and

Mary Carr. St John's, Cambridge 1826, BA 1829, dn30 (London), p31 (London). R. Widford, Herts. 1831 to death 10/5/1877 aged 72, leaving £12,000 [C118790] Married High Ongar, Essex 13/9/1831 Sophia Edridge (a clergy dau.), with issue.

**HAMPDEN,** *later* **HOBART-HAMPTON (Augustus Edward, 6th Earl of Buckinghamshire)** see under **HOBART-**

**HAMPDEN (John)** [BA but NiVoF] R. Winterbourne Stickland, Dorset 1825-8 (res.), R. Hinton Martell, Dorset 1829-49. Probate granted 2/3/1849 [C52773/41298?]

**HANBURY (Arthur)** Born Edmonton, Middx. (registered as a Quaker) 18/5/1801, s. Osgood Hanbury (banker, Holfield Grange, Coggeshall, Essex) and Susannah Willett Barclay. Trinity, Cambridge 1818, BA1823, dn27 (Lin.), MA1828, p28 (Nor.). V. Bures St Mary, Suffolk 1828 to death (a widower) 2/3/1888, leaving £12,594-15s-3d. [C63250] Married Marylebone, London 13/8/1829 Janet/Jessie Scott, with clerical son also Arthur.

**HANBURY (George)** Bapt. Kelmarsh, Northants. 21/3/1786, s. William Hanbury and Charlotte Packe. Worcester, Oxford 1803, BA 1807, dn11 (Nor.), MA1811, p11 (Nor.). R. Kelmarsh 1812-62, Chap. of the Donative of West Acre, Norfolk 1823. Died London 4/2/1862, leaving £4,000 [C110265]

**HANBURY (Thomas)** Bapt. Church Langton, Leics. 31/3/1789, s. Rev. William Hanbury and Frances Payne. Emmanuel, Cambridge 1806, BA1811, dn12 (Ox.), p13 (Ox.), MA1817. V. Somerby, Leics. 1814-48, R. Burrough on the Hill, Leics. 1814 and R. Church Langton >< (and Preacher throughout the Diocese of Lincoln) 1817 to death. Chap. to HRH Duke of Sussex 1817. Died 7/11/1848 aged 58 [C11282] Married Cheltenham, Glos. 2/7/1818 Anne Sanders, with issue. Brother below.

**HANBURY (William)** Bapt. Church Langton, Leics. 5/7/1786, s. Rev. William Hanbury and Frances Payne. Christ Church, Oxon. 1802, BA 1806, dn08 (Lin.), MA1809, p09 (Ox.). R. Great Harborough (Harborough Magna), Warwicks. 1809-64-, R. Oxford St Ebbe 1809 to death. Chap. in Ordinary 1813. Died East Langton Leics. (a bachelor, 'without cure of souls')

11/2/1868, leaving £450 [C11394] Brother above.

**HAND (James Thomas)** Bapt. Wymondham, Norfolk 12/9/1756, s. Christopher Hand. Emmanuel, Cambridge 1770, BA1775, dn76 (Peterb.), MA1778, p78 (Nor.). R. (and patron) of Cheveley, Cambs. 1778-1831 [56 years], R. (and patron) of Ousden, Suffolk 1806 to death 3/12/1834 aged 81 (CCEd says 25/2/1835) [C110266] Married Cheveley 25/5/1779 Mary Folkes.

**HAND (John)** Born Stoke, Staffs. 12/6/1802, s. Enoch Hand (solicitor in Uttoxeter, Staffs.) and Mary Phillips. St Catharine's, Cambridge 1822, then Trinity Hall 1823, dn26 (C&L), LLB 1826, p28 (C&L). R. Handsworth, Sheffield 1830 to death. Dom. Chap. to 2nd Earl of Donoughmore. Died Cheltenham, Glos. (a widower) 9/9/1870 aged 68, leaving £5,000 [C11396. ATV] Married Uttoxeter 15/4/1830 Sarah Broughton, and issue.

**HAND (John Staples)** Bapt. New Windsor, Berks. 9/8/1756, s. Rev. John Hand and Mary Hand [*sic*]. King's, Cambridge 1774, Fellow 1777-99, BA1779, MA 1782, dn85 (Lin.), p89 (Car.). Private tutor at Eton College *c.*1781-8; Chap. of the Donative of Beaulieu, Hants. 1786, R. Dunton Waylett, Essex 1798-1834, R. Bulphan, Essex 1829-30 (res.). Dom. Chap. to 2nd Marquess of Donegal 1829. Died 11/6/1834 (CCEd says 28/11/1834). [C5952] Married Prittlewell, Essex 25/8/1802 Mary Vandersee, w. clerical s. Thomas, below.

**HAND (Thomas)** Bapt. Great Burstead, Essex 10/2/1806, s. Rev. John Staples Hand (above) and Mary Vandersee. Trinity, Oxford 1823, BA 1827, dn28 (London), p29 (London), MA1830. (succ. his father as) R. Bulphan, Essex 1830-47, R. Clones, Co. Monaghan 1847, R. Compton, Surrey at death 4/8/1874, leaving £25,000 [C118796] Married Compton 17/5/1831 Cassandra More Molyneux (Loseley Park, Surrey), with issue. Photo. online.

**HANDLEY (Charles Richard)** Born Newark on Trent, Notts. 6/9/1786, s. William and Ann Handley. Trinity, Cambridge 1804, BA1809, dn10 (York), p10 (York), MA1812. V. Herne Hill, Kent 1816-65, V. Sturry, Kent 1826-49, RD of Ospringe 1845-65. Dom. Chap. to 6th Baron Middleton 1826. Died 12/9/1873, leaving £14,000 [C86841. YCO] Married Canterbury

22/8/1816 Cassandra Hutchinson (Hatfield Old Hall, Herts.), and had issue.

**HANHAM (James, Sir, 7th Bart.)** Born Corfe Mullen, Dorset 10/3/1760, s. Rev. Sir James Hanham, 6th Bart. and Jane Phelips. Trinity, Oxford 1778, SCL, dn82 (Bristol), p84 (Bristol). 'Priest of the Collegiate Church of Wimborne', Dorset ---, R. Winterbourne Zelstone, Dorset 1800 to death 2/4/1849 aged 89 [C52798] Married (1) Lytchell Minster, Dorset 16/4/1793 Anne Pyke (d.1801), w. issue (2) Camden, London 14/12/1815 Eliza Dean Patey, with further issue.

**HANKINSON (Robert)** Born King's Lynn, Norfolk 2/10/1769, s. Thomas Hankinson (a cork cutter). Trinity, Cambridge 1791, BA1791, dn92 (Nor.), p93 (Nor.), MA1794. V. Walpole St Andrew, Norfolk [net income £1,259] 1808-63, PC. West Bilney, Norfolk 1817-33 (res.), PC. Pentney, Norfolk 1817, Hon. Canon of Norwich Cathedral 1845 to death 8/1/1863, leaving £30,000 [C113376] Married King's Lynn 18/7/1794 Ann Edwards, with 3 clerical sons.

**HANLEY (John)** From Masham, Yorks., s. Richard Hanley. Christ's, Cambridge 1775, BA1780, dn80 (Lin. for Chich.), Fellow 1792, MA1792. V. Bolney, Sussex 1793-5, Gates Prebend in Chichester Cathedral 1794-6 (res.), V. Ditchling, Sussex 1795, V. Amberley w. Houghton, Sussex 1795, R. Clipston, Northants. ('with all its parts') 1812. Died 16/2/1849 aged 82 [C63258] 'Noted for his hospitality and benevolence'.

**HANMER (George Edward)** Born Hanmer, Flintshire 28/8/1786, s. Sir Thomas Hanmer, 2nd Bart. and Margaret Kenyon. University, Oxford 1804, BA1807, dn09 (Ox.), MA1810, p10 (Ox.), LLB. R. Overstone, Northants. 1814 and R. Loddington, Northants. 1817 to death. Dom. Chap. to 2nd Baron Kenyon 1815. Died 3/8/1857 [C30345] Brother below.

**HANMER (John)** Born Hanmer, Flintshire 28/2/1784, s. Sir Thomas Hanmer, 2nd Bart. and Margaret Kenyon. BNC, Oxford 1801, BA1805, dn08 (York for Chester), MA1808, p08 (Chester). V. Hanmer (Chester Diocese, a family living) 1808-50, R. Aswarby, Lincs. 1814-30, V. Deeping St James, Lincs. 1823-30, V. Swarby, Lincs. 1823-30. Died Hanmer 4/10/1850 aged 66 [C63260. YCO] Married 19/9/1816 Catherine, dau. of Sir Thomas Whichcote, 5th Bart., with issue. Brother above.

**HANMER (Thomas Walden)** Bapt. Simpson, Bucks. 17/11/1780, s. Rev. Graham Hanmer, and Elizabeth Child. BNC, Oxford 1799, BA 1803, dn04 (Ox.), p04 (Ox.), MA1807. R. Acton, Suffolk 1806-8, R. Simpson (Sympson) 1807 [blank in ERC] and R. Little Missenden, Bucks. 1810 [blank in ERC] to death. Dom. Chap. to Mary, Baroness Suffield 1810. Died 7/1/1871, leaving under £50 [C30346]

**HANNAFORD (Richard Ash)** Born Totnes, Devon 8/8/1788, s. George Hannaford and Mary Ash. St John's, Cambridge 1807, dn11 (Salis.), BA1812, p14 (Peterb.). V. Irthlingborough, Northants. 1830 (and RD) to death 12/3/1865, leaving £6,000 [C92792] Married 13/10/1813 Mary Southwell (of Clopton, Northants.), with issue. Surrogate.

**HANSELL (Peter)** Born Reading, Berks. 23/8/1764, s. Peter and Maria Hansell. Chorister Magdalen, Oxford 1777-83; Magdalen College 1781, BA1785, p88 (Nor.). PC. Norwich St John de Sepulchre 1788, Minor Canon (and Precentor) of Norwich Cathedral 1786, V. Worstead, Norfolk 1811 to death 9/1/1841 aged 75, leaving £14,000 [C1054 has confusion with another man] Married (1) St Mary in the Marsh, Norfolk 1/9/1794 Rebecca Garland (d.1802), with issue (2) Norwich 7/9/1804 (Katharine) Mary Partridge, with further (and clerical) issue.

**HARBIN (Charles)** Bapt. Yeovil, Som. 28/3/1800, s. Rev. Robert Harbin and Mary Kellow. Wadham, Oxford 1818, BA1822, Fellow 1823-6, dn23 (Ox.), p24 (B&W), MA 1826. Chap. of the Donative of Hindon, Wilts, 1829, R. Wheathill, Som. 1831, R. Teston, Kent 1854 to death there 7/4/1875 aged 75, leaving £600 [C30347] Married Cossington, Som. 24/5/1826 Abigail Rose Warry (w).

**HARBIN (Edward)** From Hunton, Kent, s. Rev. John Harbin. Magdalen Hall, Oxford 1790 (aged 21), dn92 (Bristol), LLB1792, p93 (Bristol). V. Takeley, Essex 1804 to death 21/1/1837 [C52802]

**HARBIN (Edward)** Bapt. Sherborne, Dorset 21/10/1803, s. William Harbin and Rhoda Phelips. Wadham, Oxford 1820, BA1825, dn26 (B&W), p27 (B&W), MA1827, LLB1829. R.

Kingweston, Som. 1827 and R. East Lydford, Som. 1829 to death 5/10/1833 (CCEd says 26/10/1833) [C41303] Married Yeovil, Som. 13/9/1825 Jane Hooper, with issue.

**HARBIN (Wadham)** Born Langton Maltravers, Dorset c.1797, s. Rev. John Harbin. Wadham, Oxford 1812, BA1817, Fellow 1818-29, dn18 (Ox.), p20 (Ox.), MA 1820, etc. R. Esher, Surrey 1828 to death (unm.) (Yeovil, Som.) 9/1/1870 aged 73, leaving £1,000 [C30348]

**HARBUR (William)** Born Ipswich, Suffolk. Christ's, Cambridge 1815, BA1819, p22 (Chester). PC. Ipswich St Mary at the Quay 1830 [C113402] to death 5/3/1851 aged 54 [C11402]

**HARCOURT, *born* VENABLES-VERNON (Edward)** see under **VENABLES-VERNON**

**HARCOURT, *born* VERNON, *later* VERNON HARCOURT (William [Venables] Vernon)** see under **VERNON**

**HARDEN (Edmund)** Born Tottenham, Middx. 15/1/1796, s. Nathaniel Harden and Lydia Beach. Trinity, Cambridge 1813, BA1817, dn19 (Chester for Cant.), MA1820, p20 (Chester for Cant.). Curate Norwood All Saints, Middx. 1819, then PC 1845 to death 5/6/1856 [C123779 not Eedmund] Married (1) Hadley, Middx. 12/5/1820 Maria Blanckenhagen (from Amsterdam, d.1823) (2) City of London 28/8/1826 Frances Winkworth (d.1829), w. clerical s. Henry William (3) Lambeth, Surrey 28/8/1837 Martha Jane Tarbutt, w. further issue.

**HARDING (Henry)** Bapt. Hampton Lucy, Warwicks. 2/11/1794, s. William Harding and Harriet Sweadland. King's, Cambridge 1814, Fellow 1817-29, BA1818, dn18 (Nor.), p18 (Nor.), MA1824. H.E.I.C. Chap. at English Factory in Canton, China 1819. R. Aldridge, Staffs. 1829-49, Precentor of Lichfield Cathedral 1843 (and Prebend 1844-62), V. Stratford upon Avon, Warwicks. 1849-54, R. Stapleton, Shropshire 1854 to death (London) 25/11/1862 aged 68, leaving £4,000 [C11403] Married Monks Kirby, Warwicks. 11/10/1827 Hon. Emily Feilding (w) ('commonly called Lady Emily,' dau. of Viscount Feilding), with issue.

**HARDING (John)** From Bridgnorth, Shropshire, s. Rev. John Harding. Christ Church, Oxford 1780 (aged 16), BA1784, dn87 (Ox. for Heref.), MA1788, p90 (C&L). R. (and patron) of Hopesay, Shropshire 1804 to death 14/1/1836 [C11420]

**HARDING (John)** From Pilton, Devon, s. Robert Harding. Balliol, Oxford 1819 (aged 19), BA1822, dn24 (Lin. for Ex.), p24 (Ex.), MA 1825. R. (and patron) of Goodleigh, Devon 1831 (RD 1835) to death 22/5/1880 aged 81, leaving £8,000 [C63379] Married Upcott, Devon 1815 Charlotte Goldie.

**HARDING (John)** Born Shifnal, Shropshire 10/5/1803, s. Peter Harding and Thomasine Smith. Christ Church, Oxford 1821, BA1825, dn26 (Heref.), MA1828, p29 (Heref.). PC. Shrewsbury St George 1832 to death 15/7/1866, leaving £800 [C11421] Married Cleobury Mortimer, Shropshire 10/8/1848 Martha Compson (w).

**HARDING (John Limebear)** Born Ilfracombe, Devon 14/1/1784, s. Thomas Harding and Elizabeth Webber. Exeter, Oxford 1802, migrated to Emmanuel, Cambridge 1804, dn07 (Ex.), LLB1810, p11 (Ex.). R. Loxhore, Devon 1811-25, V. Monkleigh, Devon 1815-50 and R. Littleham, Devon 1828-43. Died Bideford, Devon 17/2/1850 aged 66 [C136931] Married Barnstaple, Devon 31/12/1811 Anna Squire, w. son of same name. 'For many years one of the most active magistrates of Devon'.

**HARDING (St John)** Born Kimbolton, Hunts. 10/10/1768, s. John Harding (surgeon). Sidney, Cambridge 1788, BA1792, dn92 (Lin.), MA1795. R. (and patron) of Margaret Roding >< Essex 1811 to death 1838 aged 69 [C63381]

**HARDING (William)** Bapt. Burton Dasset, Warwicks. 8/10/1765, s. Rev. William and Mary Harding, University, Oxford 1824, BA1828, dn28 (Peterb.), p29 (Peterb.), MA1831. V. (and patron) of Sulgrave, Northants. 1829 to death 27/3/1882, leaving £11,546-14s-0d. [C110273. Boase] Widow Ann?

**HARDING (William)** From Westminster, London, s. William Harding. Wadham, Oxford 1817 (aged 17), BA1822, dn23 (Ox.), p24 (Ox.), Fellow 1827-37, MA1827, etc. PC. Bubbenhall, Warwicks. 1828, V. Hockley, Essex 1837 to death 20/10/1845 [C11423] Had clerical son.

**HARDINGE (Charles, Sir, 2nd Bart.)** Born Hampton, Middx. 22/3/1780, s. Rev. Henry Hardinge and Frances Best. University, Oxford 1798, BA1801, dn03 (Roch.), p04 (Roch.), MA1804. R. Crowhurst, Sussex 1804 and R. Tonbridge, Kent 1809 [net income £1,100] to death. Dom. Chap. to 2nd Earl of Enniskillen 1809. Died Boundes Park, Tunbridge Wells, Kent 3/2/1864 aged 84, leaving £35,000. [C266. Boase. DEB] Married Marylebone, London 13/6/1816 Emily Bradford Callander, with clerical son. Succ. to title 1826.

**HARDWICKE (William)** Bapt. Wisbech, Cambs. 6/12/1777, s. Robert and Mary Hardwicke. Corpus Christ, Cambridge 1795, BA 1799, dn00 (Ely), p01 (Ely), MA1825. R. Outwell, Norfolk 1803-38, V. Lenton (o/w Lavington), Lincs. 1824-35 (res.). Dom. Chap. to Lord Gwydir 1820; to 22nd Baron Willoughby de Eresby 1823. '*Accidentally drowned*' in Outwell Canal 25/4/1838 [C63389] Married Bourne, Lincs. 25/9/1810 his cousin Mary Rawnsley, with issue.

**HARDY (Charles)** Bapt. Walberton, Sussex 1/10/1803, s. Rev. Robert Hardy (below?). Christ's, Cambridge 1822, dn26 (Chich.), BA 1826, p27 (Chich.). V. Hayling North and South, Herts. 1832-80. Died Hildenborough, Kent 9/8/1885 aged 82, leaving £3,480-17s-7d. [C63758] Married Keston, Kent 14/1/1845 Charlotte Martin, with clerical son John Hasler Hardy.

**HARDY (Robert)** From Middx. Emmanuel, Cambridge 1784, BA1788, dn89 (London), MA 1791, p92 (Nor.). V. East Marden. Sussex 1792-1802, V. Stoughton, Sussex 1792 and V. Walberton w. Yapton, Sussex 1802 to death 11/2/1843 aged 75 [C63761] Had clerical son (above?).

**HARDYMAN (William)** Bapt. King's Lynn, Norfolk 17/4/1766, s. William Hardyman and Anne Coe. Emmanuel, Cambridge 1781, Fellow 1783, BA1786, dn88 (Nor.), MA 1789, p90 (Ely), BD1796. R. North and South Luffenham, Rutland 1806 to death 23/4/1837 aged 71 [C100050] Married King's Lynn, Norfolk 22/12/1806 Molly Paget.

**HARE (Augustus William)** Born Rome 17/11/1792, s. Francis Hare-Naylor (of Hurstmonceux, Surrey) and Georgina Shipley (dau. of a Bishop of St Asaph's). New, Oxford 1810, Fellow 1812-29, BA1814, MA1818, Tutor 1818, dn25 (Heref.), p26 (Heref.). R. Alton Barnes, Wilts. 1829 to death (Rome, for health) 14/2/1834 (CCEd says 12/8/1834) [C92796. ODNB] Married Stoke upon Tern, Shropshire 2/6/1829 Maria Leycester (a clergy dau.). Brother Julius Charles, below. https://en.wikipedia.org/wiki/Augustus_William_Hare

**HARE (John)** Bapt. Findern, Derbys. 6/1/1788 (in a Presbyterian Chapel), s. of Isaac and Ann Hare. Christ Church, Oxford 1808, BA1812, dn12 (C&L), p13 (C&L). Chap. of the Donative of Newton Solney, Derbys. 1814-61. Died Repton, Derbys. 29/3/1864, leaving under £300 [C11427] Had issue.

**HARE (Julius Charles)** Born Valdagno, Italy 13/9/1795, s. Francis Hare-Naylor (of Hurstmonceux, Sussex) and Georgina Shipley (dau. of a Bishop of St Asaph). Trinity, Cambridge 1812 [adm. Lincoln's Inn 1816] BA1816, Fellow 1818, MA1819, etc., dn26 (B&W for Ely), p26 (Ely), Prebend in Chichester Cathedral 1851-55, R. Hurstmonceux 1832-55, Archdeacon of Lewes 1840 to death. Chaplain in Ordinary 1853-55. Died 23/1/1855 [C41310. ODNB. Boase] Married Reading, Berks. 12/11/1844 Jane Esther Maurice (sister of his friend Rev. F.D. Maurice). *s.p.* 'Was remarkable for vehemence, sympathy, unpunctuality and eccentricity generally', and for his knowledge of German literature (12,000 books in all). Brother Augustus William, above.

**HARE (Michael)** Probably bapt. Lincoln 24/10/1790, s. John (possibly of Irish extraction) and Mary Hare. Pembroke, Cambridge 1808, BA1812, MA1823. R. Ashby by Partney, Lincs. 1817-24, V. Liddington, Wilts. 1824 (and Sinecure R. 1830) to death 16/9/1843 [C63662] Married Broomfield, Ex. 24/4/1821 Anne Maria Brackenbury.

**HARFORD (Alfred)** Born Blaise Castle, Bristol 20/8/1792, s. of John Scandrett Harford (a banker) and Mary Gray. Christ's, Cambridge 1820, dn24 (Glos.), BA1824, MA 1830. V. Locking, Som. 1824 and R. Hutton, Som. 1825 to death 4/8/1856 aged 63 [C41312] Married 14/1/1851 Emily Taverner, with issue.

**HARGREAVES (James, sen.)** From Mill End, Newchurch in Rossendale, Lancs., s. Henry Hargreaves. BNC, Oxford 1778 (aged

19), BA 1782, dn84 (Bristol), MA1785, p86 (Chester). V. Shenstone, Staffs. 1800-35, R. Handsworth St Mary, Staffs. 1835 to death 20/6/1841 [C11429] Clerical son below.

**HARGREAVES (James, jun.)** Born Tamworth, Staffs., s. Rev. James Hargreaves, sen. (above, V. Shenstone, Staffs.). St John's, Cambridge 1817, BA1822, dn22 (Chester), p23 (Chester), MA1827. PC. (Lower) Stonnall, Shenstone 1823-35, R. (West) Tilbury, Essex 1847 to death 21/10/1871 aged 70, leaving £800 [C11407] Widow Jane. Confusion with father above.

**HARINGTON (Edward Charles)** Bapt. Douglas, IoM 6/11/1804, s. Rev. Edward Harington and Frances Boote [but not the same person as the two entries above]. Worcester, Oxford 1824, BA1828, dn28 (Ex.), p29 (Ex.), MA1833. PC. Exeter St David 1832-47, Prebend of Exeter Cathedral 1845, Chancellor 1847-80, Canon Residentiary 1856-80 (when he spent £15,000 on repairs to the Cathedral fabric). Died (unm.) 14/7/1881 aged 77, leaving £31,936-2s-5d. [C144576. ODNB. Boase]. 'Shy and considered somewhat eccentric, residing first with his sisters and then alone.'

**HARINGTON (James Eyre)** Born Salisbury 16/6/1774, s. Rev. John Harington and Rachel Hawes. Exeter, Oxford 1791, BA1795, dn96 (Salis.), MA1799, p99 (Ex. for Salis.). R. Thruxton, Hants. 1799-1801 (res.), R. Sapcote, Leics. 1810-15, R. Chalbury, Dorset 1815 to death. Dom. Chap. to 5th Duke of Dorset 1815. Died Sapcote 16/8/1836 [C52814] Married Holborn, London 12/12/1799 Margaret Moffat ('now in an unfortunate state of derangement'), w. issue. The first of three generations of rectors here.

**HARINGTON (John)** [NiVoF] PC. Guernsey St James [the English-speaking garrison church], Channel Islands 1830-[48]. Died? [Possibly C52816?]

**HARKER (George)** From (Sebergham?), Cumberland. Literate: dn08 (Chester), p10 (Car.), then St John's, Cambridge 1811 (a Ten Year Man), MA. (first) PC. Chatham St John, Kent 1820, then V. 1826-43, V. Rochester St Nicholas w. St Clement, Kent 1826-53. Chap. Maidstone Prison 1819-21. Lived latterly and died Clapham, Surrey 20/5/1862 aged 71, leaving under £200 [C5956]

**HARKNESS (Robert)** Born Ireland, s. William Harkness (a director of the Bank of Ireland) and Mary Price. St John, Cambridge 1819, BA1823, dn24 (Chester), p24 (Chester), MA1827. PC. Brampton, Som. 1824-36, V. Stowey, Som. 1824 and V. East Brent, Som. 1837 to death (Cheltenham, Glos.) 27/4/1839 [C11430] Married Marylebone, London 2/4/1823 Jane Waugh Law (dau. of a Bishop of Bath).

**HARNESS (William)** Born Wickham, Hants. 14/3/1790, s. John Harness (a medical doctor and also 'Commissioner of Transports') and Mary Dredge. St John's, Cambridge 1808, then Christ's 1809, BA1812, dn13 (Salis. for Win.), p14 (Ely for Win.), MA1816. Min. St Anne, Soho, London 1816, Min. St John, Downshire Hill [Proprietary] Chapel, London 1823-5, PC. St Peter's, Regent St., Camden, London (o/w Regent Sq. Chapel) 1826-44. Min. Brompton Proprietary Chapel, London 1844-7, R. Pilton, Northants. 1845-6, PC. Knightsbridge Holy Trinity, London 1846-8, (builder and first) V. Knightsbridge All Saints 1849-69, Prebend of St Paul's Cathedral 1866 to death. Dom. Chap. to Catherine, Countess de la Warre 1819. Clerical Registrar to the Privy Council 1841-69. *Killed* 11/11/1869 'by falling down a flight of steps at the Deanery, Battle' (probably unm.), leaving £6,000 [C76425. ODNB. Boase. A.G.L. L'Estrange, *The literary life of the Rev. William Harness* ... (1871)] Editor of Shakespeare, and friend of many literary figures. Lame.

**HARPER, HARPUR (Latimer)** Born Coton House, Nuneaton, Warwicks. 25/11/1800, s. Joseph Harper and Maria Cooper. Emmanuel, Cambridge 1819, BA1823, dn23 (Lin.), p24 (Lin.). R. Calcethorpe, Leics. 1825 and R. (and patron) of Cathorpe, Leics. [blank in ERC] 1825 to death (Burton Latimer, Northants.) 29/11/1872, leaving £3,000 [C63679. Venn as Harpur] Married 15/4/1827 Anne Ebdell (a clergy dau.), with clerical son.

**HARRIOTT (William)** Bapt. Clifton, Bristol 26/12/1791, s. William Harriott (of Metz, Lorraine) and Ann Pitter. Exeter, Oxford 1807, BA1811, dn13 (B&W for Win.), p14 (B&W for Win.), MA1814. V. Odiham, Hants. 1824 to death (Hartley Witney, Hants.) 11/6/1847 [C41313. LBSO] Married South Stoneham, Hants. 1/9/1818 Caroline Lucy Warre, with issue. Claimed slave compensation.

**HARRIS (Henry Berners Shelley)** Bapt. Turville, Bucks. 31/12/1800, s. Rev. Joseph Harris and Elizabeth Jane Caroline Shelley. Worcester, Oxford 1820, BA1824, dn24 (Peterb.), p25 (Peterb.). R. Leaden Roding >< Warwicks. 1832-44. Master of the Earl of Leycester's Hospital [almshouses], Warwick 1843 to death 14/9/1863, leaving £18,000 [C110279] Widow Louisa, and issue.

**HARRIS (Joseph)** Born Rochford Mount, Heref., s. Henry Harris. Balliol, Oxford 1787 (aged 19), BA1790, dn90 (Ox.), p91 (Ox.), MA 1795. V. Turville, Bucks. 1794-1812, R. Corby, Northants. 1812, R. Stonton Wyville, Leics. 1812-20 (res.), R. Deene, Northants. 1820 to death 30/5/1834 (CCEd thus) [C30405]

**HARRIS (Robert)** Born Clitheroe, Lancs. 20/2/1764 (s. of a 'goods carrier' or 'merchant'). Emmanuel, Cambridge 1783, then Sidney 1783, BA1787, MA1790, dn92 (Chester), p93 (Chester), BD1797, Fellow. H/M Preston G/S, Lancs. 1788-1835; V. Preston St George 1798-1862, V. Hoole, Lancs. 1805-11 (res.). Died Preston 6/1/1862 aged 97, leaving £50,000 [C169057. Boase] Married Preston 19/11/1801 Nancy Lodge (dau. of a solicitor), 2s. (both lawyers, whose £300,000 bequest [sic] became the Harris Charity), 1 dau. The Harris Charity website: *www.theharrischarity.co.uk* has details and a portrait.

**HARRISON (Bowyer)** Bapt. IoM 10/8/1792, s. Rev. David Harrison and Anne Woods. Literate: dn15 (S&M), p16 (S&M). Chap. Ballure, IoM 1816-18, V. Maughold, IoM 1818 to death 19/4/1871 aged 79, leaving £3,000 in England [C7286. Gelling] Married (1) Braddan, IoM 29/8/1826 Elinor Cosnahan (d.1828) (2) Liverpool 23/6/1832 Theodosia Rimmer, with clerical son.

**HARRISON (Edwin)** Bapt. Flixborough, Lincs. 10/5/1797, s. Rev. Jonathan Harrison and Elizabeth Foster. St Catharine's, Cambridge 1815, BA1819, dn20 (Lin.), p21 (Lin.), MA1823. V. Redbourne, Lincs. 1822 and V. Little Grimsby, Lincs. 1828 to death. Dom. Chap. to his patron the Duchess of St Albans. Died 18/1/1866 aged 68, leaving £3,000 [C63694] Married South Collingham, Notts. 5/10/1841 Mary Elizabeth Fletcher (w).

**HARRISON (Hamlet)** Bapt. Prescot, Lancs. 2/3/1764, s. Peter Harrison and Elizabeth Lord. BNC, Oxford 1783, BA1787, MA1789, dn90 (Ox.), p90 (Ox.), BD1808. H/M Brewood G/S, Staffs. 1793; PC. Shareshill, Staffs. 1793-1811, R. Stratford-le-Bow, London 1809, R. Pontesbury (1st & 2nd Portions) w. Cruckton, Shropshire 1809 to death 2/10/1843 [C30409] Married Liverpool 20/12/1827 Margaret Sutton.

**HARRISON (Henry)** Bapt. Diss, Norfolk 1/1/1797, s. Rev. Henry Harrison, sen. Jesus, Cambridge 1813, BA1818, dn20 (Nor.), p21 (Nor.), MA1821. (succ. his father as) R. (and patron) of Shimpling, Norfolk 1821 to burial 15/9/1849 aged 52 [C113447]

**HARRISON (Hezekiah Goodeve)** Born Faulkbourne, Essex, s. Rev. John Harrison and Ann Bernard. St John's, Cambridge 1776 (aged 16), BA1780, dn82 (Lin. for London), MA1783, p84 (Chester for London). R. Thorpe Morieux, Suffolk 1786-1824 (res.), R. Little Stambridge, Essex 1786 to death. Dom. Chap to 4th Earl Waldegrave 1796. Died 15/3/1840 [C63700] Married Semer, Suffolk 19/11/1793 Mary Cooke (a clergy dau.), with issue. J.P. Essex.

**HARRISON (James)** Bapt. Rothwell, Northumberland 13/9/1767, s. of Thomas Harrison (an excise officer). Literate: dn93 (Lin. for York), p95 (York). PC. Fylingdales, Yorks. 1800 to death 8/7/1854 aged 88 [C86874. YCO]

**HARRISON (James Harwood)** Born Brockhall, Northants. 1799, s. Rev. Henry Bagshaw Harrison and Sarah Harwood. Wadham, Oxford 1817, then Merton [Lincoln's Inn 1822] BA1823, MA1826, dn28 (Peterb.), p29 (Peterb.). (succ. his father as) R. (and patron) of Bugbrooke, Northants. 1831-59 (and was succ. there by his son of same name 1859). Died 7/2/1890, leaving £6,801-18s-3d. [C110276] Married (1) Walcot, Bath 24/1/1833 Gertrude Maria Rose (d.1840), 2 clerical sons (2) Weedon Lois, Northants. 25/9/1849 Charlotte Grant (3) St Neots, Cambs. 1864 (2nd q.) Charlotte Maule.

**HARRISON (John Butler)** Bapt. Southampton, Hants. 25/5/1790, s. John Butler Harrison and Elizabeth Matilda Austen (a second cousin of Jane Austen). Magdalen, Oxford 1807, BA1811, dn14 (Glos.), MA1814, p14 (Glos.), Fellow 1816-33, BD1821, etc. V. Evenley, Northants. 1832 to death (Brackley, Northants.) 31/5/1871 aged 81, leaving £20,000 [C92799] Married 1832 Mary Ann Hyde, with clerical s., also John Butler Harrison.

**HARRISON (John Edward)** Born Arbory, IoM 23/11/1783, s. Edward Harrison and Margaret Nelson. Literate: dn06 (S&M), p07 (S&M). V. Maughold, IoM 1814-18, V. Jurby, IoM 1818 to sudden death (unm.) 2/11/1858. Will not traced [C7288. Gelling] Manx folklorist.

**HARRISON (John Holden)** From Aston, Birmingham, s. John Harrison. Wadham, Oxford 1815 (aged 19), BA1819, MA1825. PC. Water Orton, Warwicks. 1831 to death (Erdington, Birmingham) 29/9/1862, leaving £1,500 [C11444]

**HARRISON (Joseph)** Bapt. Pontefract, Yorks. 3/9/1751, s. Rev. Joseph Harrison, sen. Literate: dn79 (York for Car.), p81 (Car.). V. Marske in Cleveland, Yorks. 1790 to death 23/8/1837 aged 86 [C135095. YCO]

**HARRISON (Matthew)** Bapt. Appleby St Lawrence, Westmorland 6/9/1792, s. John and Ann Harrison. Queen's, Oxford 1810, BA1814, Fellow 1815-33, MA1818, dn18 (Salis.), p19 (Salis.). R. Church Oakley, Hants. 1832 to death 1/1/1862, leaving £5,000 [C76439. Boase]

**HARRISON (Octavius Swale)** Bapt. Taunton, Som. 6/3/1806, s. Richardson Harrison and Mary Moore. Queen's, Oxford 1823 [Student Inner Temple 1824] BA1828, dn29 (B&W), MA1830, p30 (B&W). Chaplain R.N. 1831-41; R. Stawley, Som. 1831-42, R. Thorn Falcon, Som. 1842 to death 5/6/1881 aged 75, leaving £4,234-11s-11d. [C41316] Brother William Moore Harrison, below.

**HARRISON (Peter)** Literate: dn85 (Salis.), p94 (Salis.). PC. Winterbourne Earls, Wilts. 1797-[1851]. Died 1851 [C92801]

**HARRISON (Richard)** Bapt. Worcester 2/3/1778, s. Rev. Richard Harrison, sen. Pembroke, Oxford 1795, BA1800, dn01 (Wor.), p02 (C&L), MA1812. V. (and patron) of Crowle, Worcs. 1803 to death 24/6/1835 (CCEd says 19/9/1835) [C11447]

**HARRISON (Robert, sen.)** Literate: dn93 (Car.), p94 (Car.). Schoolmaster; PC. Temple Sowerby, Westmorland 1803 [C5962 as John] to death 19/6/1834 (CCEd thus) [C5967] Married Elizabeth Brownrigg before 1791, with son, also Robert (two below), with whom there is confusion.

**HARRISON (Robert)** Born Westminster, London, s. Thomas and Rachel Harrison (of Esher, Surrey). Trinity, Cambridge 1790 (aged 16) [adm. Lincoln's Inn 1791] BA1794, p08 (York). PC. (High) Blanchland, Northumberland 1827-48, V. Lastingham, Yorks. 1828 to death 28/11/1850 aged 77 [C130489. YCO]

**HARRISON (Robert, jun)** Bapt. Temple Sowerby, Westmorland 15/5/1791, s. Rev. Robert Harrison (two above) and Elizabeth Brownrigg. Literate: dn14 (York), p15 (York). PC. West Allen, Northumberland 1825, PC. Temple Sowerby 1845 to death 18/1/1863 aged 71, leaving £3,000 [C131467. Platt. YCO] Married (1) Allendale, Northumberland 21/7/1819 Rebecca Simpson (d.1828), with issue (2) Temple Sowerby 1830 Mrs Mary Wilkinson, with further issue; clerical son, also Robert, with confusion.

**HARRISON (Thomas)** Born Whitehaven, Cumberland, s. Thomas Harrison. Queen's, Oxford 1798 (aged 16), BA1802, dn05 (Glos.), MA1806, p06 (Salis.), Fellow 1814-21. V. Whitehaven Holy Trinity 1808 and R. Corney, Cumberland 1814 to death (Whitehaven) 19/10/1840 aged 57 [C92804] Married 1820 Mary Anne Bridget Benn (Hensingham House, Cumberland), with issue.

**HARRISON (Thomas Bernard)** Born Faulkbourne, Essex, s. Rev. John Harrison and Anne Bernard (a clergy dau.). St John's, Cambridge 1776 (aged 17), then Jesus 1776, BA 1780, dn81 (Lin. for London), p82 (Nor. for London), MA 1783. R. Little Bardfield, Essex 1782 to death 19/12/1844 [C63711]

**HARRISON (Thomas Thomas)** From Copford Hall, Colchester, Essex, s. John Haynes Harrison. St John's, Cambridge 1815, BA1820, dn20 (London), p21 (London), MA1825. R. Thorpe Morieux, Suffolk 1824 to death 27/1/1868 aged 70, leaving £12,000 [C113454] Married East Teignmouth, Devon 2/10/1827 Ann (w) (dau. of Rear-Admiral Nicholas Tomlinson), with issue.

**HARRISON (William)** Bapt. Croyden, Surrey 17/4/1768, s. Rev. John and Jane Harrison. Oriel, Oxford 1786, BA1790, p92 (C&L), MA 1799. V. Overton, Hants. 1796 (and Sinecure R. 1817), V. Fareham, Hants. 1811, 3rd Prebend of Winchester Cathedral 1820 (and Treasurer) to death. Dom. Chap. to 3rd Baron Rodney 1807.

Died 1/9/1846 [C11450] Married Alresford, Hants. 12/12/1801 Ann Elizabeth Nicolls, w. clerical s. William Dann Harrison, below.

**HARRISON (William)** Bapt. Walton-le-Dale, Preston, Lancs. 18/9/1770, s. Edward and Anne Harrison. BNC, Oxford 1790, dn94 (Chester), p94 (C&L), BA1797, MA1811, DD1813. PC. Leigh, Surrey 1793-1821, Chap. Southwark St Saviour, Surrey 1804 to death. Chap. to HRH Duke of Cambridge 1812. Died 10/10/1833 (CCEd thus) [C11451]

**HARRISON (William)** Born London, s. James Harrison. Christ Church, Oxford 1816 (aged 19), BA1820, Chap. 1820-3, dn20 (Lin.), p21 (Ox.), MA1823. V. Chester St Oswald 1827-80 (and S/M King's School, Chester 1823), Minor Canon Chester Cathedral 1839-73. Died Chester 11/2/1880 aged 83, leaving £800 [C33785. Boase] Was married, with issue. Ran a boarding school 1834. Surrogate.

**HARRISON (William)** Born Brockhall, Northants. 17/1/1800, s. Rev. Henry Bagshaw Harrison and Sarah Harwood. Christ Church, Oxford 1818, Student [Fellow] 1818-32, BA 1821, dn23 (Ox.), p26 (Ox.). Usher at Westminster School 1822-31; R. Warmington, Warwicks. 1831 to death 30/10/1877, leaving £3,000 [C11452] Widow Mary Ann, and issue. Doubtless related to the man below.

**HARRISON (William Bagshaw)** Born Daventry, Northants., s. Henry Bagshaw Harrison and Catherine Wyment. Merton, Oxford 1786 (aged 17), BA1790, dn91 (Peterb.), p94 (Cant. for Peterb.), MA1809. Minor Canon Rochester Cathedral 1801, V. Darenth, Kent 1801, V. Goudhurst, Kent 1801-49, R. Gayton le Marsh, Lincs. 1833. Died 28/1/1849 aged 80 [C1426] Married 1819 Charlotte Tonkin, with clerical son of father's name who succ. him at Goudhurst. Doubtless related to the man above.

**HARRISON (William Dann)** Born Overton, Hants. 27/9/1803, s. Rev. William Harrison (above) and Ann Elizabeth Nicolls. Worcester, Oxford 1822, BA1826, dn26 (B&W), p27, MA 1829. V. Keevil, Wilts. 1828-30, V. East Langdon, Kent 1830-4, V. Hartley Mauditt, Hants. 1833, V. Crondall, Hants. 1833-64-, V. South Stoneham, Hants. 1835-92, V. Naburn, Yorks. 1867-9, V. Stretton, Lincs. 1869 [total income £1,093 in CR65] Died 13/3/1892 aged 88, leaving £7,508-5s-2d. [C41317] Married Kingston, Surrey 17/4/1838 Mary Smith Roots.

**HARRISON (William Moore)** Born Taunton, Somerset 1793, s. Richardson Harrison and Mary Moore. Exeter, Oxford 1810, migrated to Peterhouse, Cambridge 1813, BA1816, dn17, p18 (Ex.), MA1819. R. (and patron) of Clayhanger, Devon 1818 to death 20/10/1866 aged 73, leaving £6,000 [C145009] Married St Pancras, London 13/3/1823 Elizabeth Dyne (w), with issue. Brother Octavius Swale Harrison, above.

**HART (Samuel)** Bapt. Crediton, Devon 28/5/1762, s. Rev. Samuel Hart, sen. Exeter, Oxford 1780, BA1784, dn84 (Ex.), p86 (Ex.), Fellow and Chap. 1786-1806, MA1786, BD 1798. V. Merton, Oxon. 1796-1806, V. Gwenapp, Cornwall 1805, V. Altarnon (o/w Altarnun), Cornwall 1806-42. Died 27/10/1846 [C145011] Married Holsworthy, Devon 12/5/1806 Anne Cory, s.p. J.P. Devon and Cornwall.

**HARTLEY (John)** Born Otley, Yorks. 11/10/1777, s. James Hartley. Trinity, Cambridge 1796, dn01 (Chester), BA1802, p02 (Chester). PC. Boroughbridge, Yorks. 1805 and PC. Dunsforth, Yorks. 1805 to death (Marton cum Grafton, Yorks.) 21/8/1854 aged 76 [C169094] Married Leeds 25/10/1807 Elizabeth Harrison (of Howick) (w), 9 ch. Note confusion with an Oxford man. Silhouette online.

**HARTLEY (Richard)** Born Bingley, Yorks. 5/9/1764, s. Rev. Richard Hartley, sen. and Ann Perkins. Christ's, Cambridge 1782, BA1787, dn89 (Roch. for York), p89 (Ely), MA1790, DD1805. V. Bingley 1797 (and H/M Bingley G/S 1791) to death 26/10/1836 aged 72 [C1878. YCO. DEB] Married (1) Bingley 22/3/1791 Charlotte Harvey (a clergy dau., d.1820) (2) Hipperholme, Yorks. 22/3/1821 his cousin Mary Hudson (a clergy dau.). 'An excellent classic, a hard reading man, and of irreproachable character'.

**HARTLEY (Richard)** Born Staveley, Westmorland 10/8/1783, s. Rev. James Hartley. Trinity, Cambridge 1801, then Clare 1803, BA 1806, dn06 (York), p07 (Car. for York), MA 1809. PC. Newcastle upon Tyne St Andrew 1808-25, R. (and patron) of Staveley 1820-47. Died there 6/9/1861, leaving £2,000 [C86911.

YCO] Married London 4/8/1810 Jane Bishop, with clerical sons.

**HARTLEY (Thomas)** Bapt. Millom, Cumberland 25/6/1806, s. of James Hartley (farmer) and Margaret Fisher. TCD1826, BA1830, dn30 (York), p31 (Chester), MA1833. PC. Lowick, Ulverston, Lancs. 1831-45, and PC. Blawith, Lancs. 1841-5, PC. Raskelf, Yorks. 1846 to death 27/3/1885 aged 78. Will not traced [C169095. Al.Dub. YCO. ATV] Married (1) before 1836 Ann Elizabeth Hand (d.1846), with issue (2) Bridlington, Yorks. 10/1/1848 Ann Elizabeth Howard, 1 ch.

**HARTLEY (Wilfred)** Born Egremont, Cumberland 19/1/1804, s. Thomas Hartley and his cousin Anne Hartley. Christ's, Cambridge 1823, BA1827, dn28 (Durham for York), p29 (Car.), MA1831. PC. Allonby, Cumberland 1829 to death (unmarried) 21/2/1850 aged 46 [C5974. YCO. Platt]

**HARTOPP (Samuel)** Bapt. Dalby, Leics. 3/11/1763, s. Edward William Hartopp (Little Dalby Hall) and Elizabeth Boothby. Trinity Hall, Cambridge 1781, LLB1798, dn87 (Peterb.), p87 (Peterb.). V. Little Dalby 1788 and R. Cold Overton, Leics. 1788 to death 2/1/1852 [C63728] Married Barnwell, Northants. 1/9/1783 Mary Pywell. Doubtless related to the man below.

**HARTOPP (William Evans)** Born Dalby, Leics. 30/10/1793, s. Edward Hartopp and Hon. Juliana Evans (dau. of Lord Carbery). Trinity, Cambridge 1811, BA1817, dn19 (Lin.), p20 (Lin.), MA1831. V. Thurnby w. Stoughton, Lincs. 1820-32, R. Great Kington, Dorset 1825-6, V. Harby, Leics. 1826 to death 2/10/1852 [C52825] Married (1) 28/10/1817 Eliza Georgiana Gubbins (Kilfrush, Co. Limerick, d.1848), with issue (2) Goadby Marwood, Leics. 2/10/1850 Eliza Manners (a clergy dau.). Doubtless related to the man above.

**HARVEY (Bridges)** Born Doddinghurst, Essex, s. Bridges Harvey and Dorothy Morley. Jesus, Cambridge 1799, dn03 (Win.), p04 (Win.), LLB1805. V. Yealmpton w. Revelstoke, Devon 1807-10, Chap. of the Donative of Alsager, Barthomley, Cheshire 1807-33, PC. Blackmore, Essex 1808-49, R. Doddinghurst 1813 (and RD) to death (Ongar, Essex) 10/2/1849 [C76426] Married St James, Westminster, London 11/11/1811 Jane Douglas, with clerical son, also Bridges Harvey.

**HARVEY (George Gayton)** Born Great Yarmouth, Norfolk 17/3/1802, s. James Harvey and Dorcas Catherine Clyde. St John's, Cambridge 1811, BA1826, dn27 (C&L for York), p27 (York). V. Horton, Staffs. 1831-40, PC. Winster, Derbys. 1840-6, V. Hailsham, Sussex 1846-72. Lived latterly at Hampstead, London and died there 29/4/1895 aged 73, leaving £1,000 [C11416. YCO. DEB] Married 12/9/1832 Sarah Frances Sheppard (Folkingham Place, Sussex) (w), w. clerical s. Francis Clyde Harvey.

**HARVEY (George Ludford)** Born London 1/10/1798, s. Sir Ludford Harvey (physician) and Lucy Skinner. BNC, Oxford 1816, migrated to Sidney, Cambridge 1817, dn21 (Glos.), BA 1822, p22 (Glos.), V. Diseworth, Leics. 1822-36, R. (and patron) of Yate, Glos. 1843 [income £1,017 in CR65] to death 28/6/1869 aged 72, leaving £10,000 [C63734] Married (1) Northampton 18/5/1837 Elinor Young (of Walton on Thames, d.1842), with issue (2) Bath 9/4/1844 Persis Scott Nichols (w), with further issue.

**HARVEY (Henry)** Born Hampstead, London 4/5/1792 (bapt. 10/8/1796). Christ Church, Oxford 1810, BA1814, dn18 (Cant.), p19 (Nor.), MA1822. V. Olveston, Glos. 1821-54, Canon of 3rd Prebend of Bristol Cathedral 1831-54, V. Bristol St Augustine the Less 1832. V. Bradford on Avon, Wilts. 1834. Chap. to HRH the Duke of Cambridge. Died 20/11/1854 [C52823] Married Bristol 24/10/1844 Elizabeth Hunt, with issue.

**HARVEY (John, *but bapt.* William)** Born Finningley, Notts. 21/1/1764, s. Rev. Edmund Harvey. Magdalene, Cambridge 1782, dn87 (Ely), LLB1789, p92 (Ely). (succ. his father as) R. Finningley 1824 to death 14/11/1835 at Wood's Hotel, London aged 70 ('after being brutally knocked down while standing in a public gateway in Tyler Street') [C63735]

**HARVEY (Richard, sen.)** From Wingham, Kent, s. Rev. Richard Harvey and Judith Matson. Corpus Christi, Cambridge 1784, dn89 (London for Cant.), LLB1790, p91 (Cant.). (succ. his father as) V. St Lawrence in Thanet, Ramsgate. Kent 1793 to death. Dom. Chap. to 1st Marquess Conyngham 1817. Died Bath

11/2/1836 aged 67 [C118828] Married 30/8/1794 Anne Wade (a clergy dau.), with clerical son below.

**HARVEY (Richard, jun.)** Bapt. Wingham, Kent 15/3/1798, s. Rev. Richard Harvey (above) and Anne Wade. Eton (where he was Shelley's fag). St Catharine's, Cambridge 1814, BA1818, dn21 (Nor.), MA1821, p22 (Nor.). V. Ramsgate, Kent 1827 (but did not accept?), R. Hornsey, Middx. 1829-80, Brownswood Prebend in St Paul's Cathedral, London 1843-58, Canon Residentiary in Gloucester Cathedral 1858 (and RD) to death. Chap. in Ordinary 1847-89; Chap. to Archbishop of York 1862-74. Died 27/6/1889 aged 91 (the day after his wife's death), leaving £5,359-16s-6d. [C113457. Boase] Married London 28/12/1830 Eliza(beth) Hankey, and clerical son.

**HARVEY (Thomas)** From Tonbridge, Kent, s. Thomas Harvey. Pembroke, Cambridge 1771. [adm. Middle Temple 1774] LLB1778, dn83 (Roch.), p85 (Roch.). R. (and patron) of Cowden, Kent 1785-1835, V. Pembury, Kent 1803-4. Died 30/10/1835 (CCEd thus) [C228] Clerical son of father's name in same place.

**HARWARD (John)** Bapt. Hartlebury, Worcs. 7/4/1760, s. Michael and Mary Harward. Worcester, Oxford 1778, BA1782, p84 (Ox.), MA1785. R. Icomb, Glos. 1792-1855, V. Denchworth, Berks. 1796-1823. Died 24/10/1855 [C30423] Brother Thomas, below.

**HARWARD (John)** From Portsea, Hants, s. William Harward. Trinity, Oxford 1801 (aged 17), BA1804, dn08 (Win.), MA1809, p09 (Win.). V. Stanton by Dale, Derbys. 1815-16 (res.), V. Wirksworth, Derbys. 1831-51, V. Whaplode, Lincs. 1851 to death. Dom. Chap. to 3rd Earl Stanhope 1812. Died 26/1/1859, leaving £3,000 [C11462] Widow Amelia.

**HARWARD (Thomas)** From Hartlebury, Worcs., s. Michael and Mary Harward. Worcester, Oxford 1793 (aged 17), BA1797, MA1800, Fellow to 1813. R. Dorsington, Glos. 1830 to death (Winterfold, Worcs.) 1/1/1856 aged 81 [C152281] Brother John, two above.

**HARWOOD (John)** From Dean, Southampton, s. John Harwood. Queen's, Oxford 1789 (aged 17), BA1793, dn94 (Salis.), MA 1797. R. Ewhurst, Hants. 1799-1846, V. Laverstoke, Hants. 1820-46, V. Sherborne St John, Hants. 1820 (and R. 1829) to death. Dom. Chap. to 1st Baron Dorchester. Died 20/12/1846 [C76455]

**HARWOOD (Thomas)** Born Shepperton, Middx. May 1767, s. Rev. Thomas Harwood, sen. University, Oxford 1784, dn87 (London), migrated to Emmanuel, Cambridge 1789, p89 (London), BD1811, DD1822. H/M Lichfield G/S 1791-1814; PC. Hammerwich, Staffs. 1800-42 (w. Burntwood, Staffs. 1831-42), R. Stawley, Som. 1814-19. Died 23/12/1842 [C11463. ODNB] Married Birmingham 7/1/1793 Maria Woodward, with issue. 'Strenuously supported Roman Catholic emancipation'. *F.S.A.*

**HASELL (Robert Pickford)** From Barrow, Somerset, s. William Hasell. Pembroke, Oxford 1813 (aged 20). R. Butcombe, Som. 1818. Probate granted 6/12/1836 [C41324] Married 1828 Charlotte Light.

**HASLEWOOD, HAZELWOOD (Boulby Thomas)** Born Aycliffe, Durham 30/1/1796, s. Rev. Dickens Haslewood and Elizabeth Boulby. Trinity, Cambridge 1813, then Peterhouse 1816, BA1818, dn19 (York for Durham), p20 (Ox.). PC. (Low) Ford (o/w South Hylton), Gateshead, Co. Durham 1821-31, V. Ribchester w. Stidd, Lancs. 1829 to death. Dom. Chap. to R.E. Egerton Warburton 1855. Died 28/5/1876 aged 80, leaving £5,000 [C130494. YCO as Bowlby] Married Bishopwearmouth 15/2/1822 Margaret Maude Ogden, w. clerical s. of same name as father.

**HASLEWOOD (George Hugh)** Bapt. Bridgnorth, Shropshire, 22/6/1769, s. Thomas Haslewood and Jane Davis. Pembroke, Oxford 1787, BA1791, dn91 (C&L), p95 (C&L). PC. Morvill w. Aston Eyre, Shropshire 1797, R. Quatford, Shropshire 1801-36, V. Leighton, Shropshire 1815-16 (res.). Died Aberystwyth, Cardigan 6 or 13/11/1839 [C11466] Married Bridgnorth 8/1/1792 Jane Pryce, w. issue. Brother below.

**HASLEWOOD (John Daniel)** Born Bridgnorth, Shropshire 26/3/1772, s. Thomas Haslewood and Jane Davis. St John's, Cambridge 1789, MA 1793, dn94 (C&L), MA1796, p96 (C&L). PC. Thurmaston, Leics. 1798-1821, PC. Leigh, Surrey 1821-3, V. Boughton Monchelsea, Kent 1823 to death 4/9/1857 aged 86 [C1425. CR65 as John David] Married 22/7/1806 Hannah Dixon (Barwell Court, Kingston), with clerical son. Brother above.

**HASLEWOOD**  see also under **HAZELWOOD**

**HASTED (Edward)** Bapt. Sutton at Hone, Kent 6/11/1760, s. Edward and Ann Hasted. Oriel, Oxford 1778, BA1781, dn84 (Cant. for Lin.), p85 (Lin.). V. Hollingbourne, Kent 1790 to death 1855 (3rd q.) [C63747]

**HASTED (Henry)** Born Bury St Edmunds, Suffolk, 17/9/1771, s. Roger Hasted (apothecary) and Elizabeth Craske. Christ's, Cambridge 1789, BA1793, dn94 (Nor.), Fellow 1795-1804, p95 (Nor.), MA1796. Curate Bury St Edmunds St Mary, Suffolk 1802, R. Ickworth w. Chedburgh, Suffolk 1803-32, R. (and patron) of Bradfield Combust, Suffolk 1808-32, R. Braiseworth, Suffolk 1812-52, R. Horningsheath (Great and Little) (o/w Horringer), Suffolk 1814 to death 26/11/1852 aged 81 [C113460. Boase] Married (1) Bury St Edmunds 30/10/1807 Mary Ann Ord (d.1810) (2) Jane Becher; with issue. *F.L.S.* (1810). *F.R.S.* (1812).

**HASTINGS (Henry James)** Born Martley, Worcs. 11/8/1798, s. Rev. James Hastings (below) and Elizabeth Paget. Trinity, Cambridge 1814, BA1819, dn20 (Wor.), p21 (Wor.), MA1822. R. Areley Kings >< Worcs. 1831-56, RD of Worcester West 1847, Hon. Canon of Worcester Cathedral 1848-75, (succ. his father as) R. (and patron) of Martley 1856 [income £1,100] to death 12/5/1875 [C121376. Boase] Married (1) Claines, Worcs. 19/12/ 1822 Theodosia Eleanor Parsons (Wirswall Hall, Cheshire, d.1823), w. son (2) Woodhouse, Huddersfield, Yorks. 28/3/1826 Elizabeth Whitacre, w. issue. *J.P.* Photo. online.

**HASTINGS (James)** From Westminster, London, s. James Hastings. Wadham, Oxford 1776 (aged 20), SCL, dn79 (Ox.), p82 (C&L). R. Martley, Worcs. 1796 to death 10/7/1856 aged 100 [C11469. Boase] Married Chipping Norton, Oxon. 22/2/1871 Elizabeth Paget, with son Henry James, above.

**HATCH (Charles)** Bapt. New Windsor, Bucks. 27/1/1796, s. Thomas Hatch (attorney) and Margaretta Eleanora Cliffe. King's, Cambridge 1815, Fellow 1818-40, dn19 (Ely), BA 1820, MA1823, p23 (Nor.), Bursar 1835-8. PC. Kersey w. Lindsey, Suffolk 1822-35, V. Fordingbridge, Hants. 1839 and R. Ibsley, Hants. 1840 to death 27/6/1878, leaving £5,000 [C109713] Surrogate. Brothers Henry, and Thomas, below.

**HATCH (George Avery)** Born New Windsor, Berks. 1757, s. George Hatch. Merton, Oxford 1775 (aged 18), BA1779, dn79 (Ox.), then Exeter, Fellow 1779-92, p81 (Ox.), MA1782. R. Weekley, Northants. 1786-91, R. St Matthew Friday Street w. St Peter Cheap, City of London 1791 to death 15/1/1837 [C31046] Married City of London 21/12/1796 Martha Emlyn. One of the founder members of the (R)SPCA.

**HATCH (Henry)** Bapt. New Windsor, Berks. 1/5/1793, s. Thomas Hatch (attorney) and Margaretta Eleanora Cliffe. King's, Cambridge 1812, Fellow 1815-21, BA1817, dn19 (Salis. for Win.), p20 (Glos. for Win.), MA 1821. R. Sutton, Surrey 1831-58. Died London (a widower) 23/11/1866, leaving under £200 [C76493. Venn corrected] Married Stratford Bow, London 4/4/1831 Hannah Hall, with issue. Brother Charles, above, and Thomas below.

**HATCH (Thomas)** Bapt. New Windsor, Berks. 30/10/1788, s. Thomas Hatch (attorney) and Margaretta Eleanora Cliffe. King's, Cambridge 1808, Fellow 1811-16, BA1813, dn14 (Salis. for Win.), p14 (London), MA1817. V. Walton on Thames, Surrey 1816 to death 25/6/1851 [C76504] Had issue. Brothers Charles, and Henry, above.

**HATCHARD (John)** Born London 26/6/1793, s. of the Piccadilly bookseller and publisher John Hatchard (*q.v.* ODNB) and Elizabeth Lambert. St Edmund Hall, Oxford 1812, migrated to Magdalene, Cambridge 1813, BA1816, dn16 (Nor.), p17 (C&L), MA1820. V. Plymouth St Andrew 1824 to death 1/12/1869 aged 76, leaving £16,000 [C11470] Married Brighton, Sussex 5/9/1816 Anne Alton, with clerical son. 'His practical piety during the visitations of cholera in 1832 and 1847 will be his best claim to the grateful recollection of all classes in Plymouth'.

**HATHERELL (James Williams)** Born Ewell, Surrey 25/11/1801, s. Abraham Hatherell and Anna Maria Williams. BNC, Oxford 1820, then St Alban Hall, BA1823, then BNC again, dn24 (C&L), MA1826, p26 (Wor.), BD & DD1841. R. Eastington, Glos. 1831-7, R. Charmouth, Devon 1839-43, V. Southampton St James West End 1843 to death (Lowestoft, Suffolk) 21/8/1876, leaving £3,000 [C11471] Married (1) Pershore, Glos. 9/1/1823 Anna Baker (d.1834), with issue (2) Woodchester, Glos. 1835 Eliza Cooke

Williams (d. Malta 1842) (3) Edinburgh 29/8/1842 Constantia Grey (w), of Bamburgh, Northumberland:
www.freshford.com/hatherell.htm

**HATHWAY (Robert)** From Hereford, s. Robert Hathway. BNC, Oxford 1783 (aged 16), BA1787, dn88 (Heref.), p91 (Heref.). R. Ballingham and Bolstone, Heref. 1801, R. Stretton Sugwas, Heref. 1810 to death 13/2/1846 [C105666. Venn corrected]

**HATT (Andrew)** From Greenwich, Kent, s. Andrew Hatt. Magdalen Hall, Oxford 1789 (aged 21), dn92 (C&L), BA1800, MA1800, BD & DD1823. R. Greenstead, Essex 1825 to death. Chap. to Hon. Artillery Company 1796 to death 23/4/1837 [C11472]

**HATTON (Daniel Heneage Finch-, Hon.)** Born Eastwell Park, Kent 1795, s. George Finch-Hatton, *M.P.*, and Lady Elizabeth Mary Murray (dau. of 2nd Earl of Mansfield). Christ's, Cambridge 1814, BA1818, dn18 (Cant.), p19 (Salis. for Cant.), MA1821. R. Great Weldon, Northants. 1819-64. Dom. Chap. to 3rd Duke of Montrose 1819; Chaplain in Ordinary 1823. Died Torquay, Devon 3/1/1866, leaving £45,000. [C93128] Married 15/12/1825 Lady Louisa Fulke Greville, with issue.

**HAUGHTON, HOUGHTON (John)** Born Co. Kerry 10/11/1802, s. Rev. John Haughton (PC. Middleton, Lancs.). Pembroke, Cambridge 1821 [President of the Union 1824] BA1826, dn27, p28 (Chester), MA1830. PC. Ainsworth (o/w Cockey [Moor]), Middleton, Lancs. 1828-36 (res. and joined the Catholic Apostolic Church). Died Kensington, London 28/1/1848 [but C93129 is mistaken here] Married Chester 1/7/1824 Harriet Sophia Ashworth, of Manchester.

**HAVERFIELD (Thomas Tunstall)** Bapt. Kew, Surrey 21/5/1787, s. John Haverfield and Elisabeth Tunstall. Corpus Christi, Oxford 1803 (aged 15), BA1807, MA1810, dn10 (Ox.), p11 (Ox.), Fellow 1812-27, BD1818. R. Godington, Oxon. 1826 to death. Chap. to HRH Duke of Sussex 1811. Died Barnes, Surrey 3/5/1866 aged 79, leaving under £100 [C21687] Married Kew, Surrey 30/3/1837 Caroline Sophia Bryant (w).

**HAVERGAL (William Henry)** Born High Wycombe, Bucks. 18/1/1793, s. William Havergal [*pleb*] and Mary Hopkins. St Edmund Hall, Oxford 1812, BA1816, dn16 (B&W), p17 (Glos.), MA1819. R. Astley, Worcs. 1829-42. R. Worcester St Nicholas 1845-60, Hon. Canon of Worcester Cathedral 1845, V. Snareshill, Worcs. 1860 to death (Leamington) 19/4/1870, leaving £18,000 [C41332. ODNB. Boase. *Records of the life of Rev. William H. Havergal, MA.*, by his dau. Jane Miriam Crane ([1882])] Married (1) East Grinstead, Sussex 2/5/1816 Jane Head (d.1848) (2) Gloucester 29/7/1851 Caroline Ann Cooke (a clergy dau.) (w). His dau. was the hymn-writer Frances Ridley Havergal, and he had a clerical son. He was himself a hymn-writer and composer:
https://en.wikipedia.org/wiki/William_Henry_Havergal.

**HAWES (Herbert)** Bapt. Salisbury 23/3/1765, s. Rev. John Hawes and Ann Hawkins. Oriel, Oxford 1782, BA1786, dn87 (Salis.), MA1789, p89 (Salis.), BD1800, DD1810. R. Mellis, Suffolk 1792 to death, R. Salisbury St Edmund 1802-37, Prebend of Wetherbury in Terra in Salisbury Cathedral 1812-30, then Grimston Prebend 1830 to death 17/1/1837 [C93130]

**HAWKER (Peter)** Bapt. Woodchester, Glos. 7/7/1773, s. Rev. Peter Hawker, sen. Pembroke, Oxford 1790, BA1794, dn95 (Glos.), MA1797, p98 (Glos.). R. Wootton, Kent 1808-9, R. Otterden, Kent 1808-11, (succ. his father as) R. Woodchester 1809 to death 26/3/1833 (CCEd says 11/4/1833) [C152762]

**HAWKINS (Charles)** Born London 16/8/1778, s. of Sir Charles Hawkins, 1st Bart. (Sergeant-Surgeon to George the Second and Third, of Kelston Hall, Som.) and Sarah Coxe. Trinity, Cambridge 1798, dn02 (B&W), LLB 1805, p06 (Ex.). R. Kelston 1806-32, R. Coaley, Glos. 1814-32, Prebend of Barnby in York Minster 1824-57 (and Canon Residentiary York Minster 1830-57), PC. Fangfoss, Yorks. 1831, V. Barmby (on the) Moor, Yorks. 1831, V. Pocklington, Yorks. 1832, V. Topcliffe w. Dalton, Yorks. 1834-[38], V. Stillingfleet, Yorks. 1838 to death 11/4/1857 [C41334] Married Harrow, Middx. 1/8/1807 Anne Augusta (dau. of Sir James Cockburn, 8th Bart., *M.P.*), with clerical son.

**HAWKINS (Charles Botterell)** Born Shrewsbury, Shropshire 7/7/1761, s. Rev. John Hawkins and Bridget Botterell. Worcester, Oxford 1777, BA1781, then All Souls, BCL

1784, dn88 (Chester for Ox.), p94 (Ox.). V. Lewknor, Oxon. 1794 until death 2/5/1835 aged 73 (CCEd thus) [C31054] Married Handsworth, Birmingham 30/9/1795 Maria Bratt, and had issue.

**HAWKINS (Edward)** Born Bath 27/2/1789, s. Rev. Edward Hawkins, sen. and Margaret Howes. St John's, Oxford 1807, BA1811, Tutor 1812, then Oriel, Fellow 1813-28, MA1814, dn15 (Ox.), p17 (Ox.), tutor 1819, BD & DD 1828. Provost of Oriel College, Oxford 1828-74. (first) Ireland Professor of the Exegesis of Holy Scripture, Oxford 1847-61. V. Oxford St Mary the Virgin 1823-8 (res.), R. Purleigh, Essex (annexed to the Provostship, with Prebend of 5th Canon of Rochester Cathedral 1828-8 (net income £1,141) 1828-8, V. Lamberhurst, Kent 1830-4 (res.). Retired to Rochester 1874, dying there 18/11/1882 aged 93, leaving £29,061-8s.8d. [C1428. ODNB. Boase. J.R. Burgon, *Lives of Twelve Good Men* (1886)] Married Cheltenham, Glos. 28/12/1828 Mary Ann Buckle (w),

**HAWKINS (James)** Bapt. Broughton, Oxon. 1/6/1755, s. Rev. William Hawkins and Blanch Griffiths. Magdalen, Oxford 1770, BA1774, MA1777, dn77 (Salis.), Fellow 1789-99, p80 (Ex. for Bristol), BD1791. R. Ducklington, Oxon. 1798-1836. Died 7/3/1846 [C31057] Wife Jane.

**HAWKINS (James Fendal)** Bapt. Dorchester, Dorset 4/1/1760. Trinity, Cambridge 1791, dn92 (Peterb. for Bristol), p92 (Glos. for Bristol), then Queens' 1795, Hon. DD1820 (Glasgow). R. Buckhorn Weston, Dorset 1792 to death. Probate granted 21/1/1837 [C52885] Married (1) Croydon, Surrey 27/8/1792 Frances Sharpe (2) Lancaster 7/9/1798 Grace Loxham. *F.L.S.*

**HAWKINS (John)** [BA, MA but NiVoF]. R. (and patron) of Ratlinghope, Heref. 1796 to death 5/3/1833 aged 72 [C171656]

**HAWKINS (William Hawkins)** From Abingdon, Berks. Pembroke, Oxford 1792 (aged 16), BA1797, MA1799, p99 (Ox.), BD1810. V. (Great) Faringdon w. Little Coxwell, Oxon. 1800, R. Oxford St Aldate 1810, S/M Cheltenham G/S 1817 to death 26/1/1849 [C31062] Married Charlton Kings, Glos. 11/12/1811 Mary Ann Newcombe, w. clerical s. William.

**HAWKS (William)** Born Gateshead, Co. Durham 22/1/1799, s. Sir Robert Shafto Hawks (a Newcastle solicitor, but others say s. of a woollen draper) and Anna Pembroek Akenhead. Trinity Hall, Cambridge 1819, SCL, dn24 (St David's for Durham), p24 (Durham), LLB 1826. V. Gateshead (Fell), Co. Durham 1824-40, PC. Saltash, Cornwall 1846 to death (Bath) 28/1/1870 aged 71, leaving £80,000 [C134172] Married Dec. 1825 Anna Elizabeth Crozer (dau. of a wine merchant, d.1839) (2) Plymouth 9/2/1843 Mary Mitchell; 15 ch. in all.

**HAWKSLEY (John Webster)** Bapt. Sheffield 12/2/1768, s. of John Hawksley (apothecary) and Mary Webster. St John's, Cambridge 1785, BA1789, dn90 (Ely for York), p92 (Ely), MA 1794. R. Knotting w. Souldrop, Beds. 1792-1856, V. Little Marlow, Essex 1803-21, V. Melchbourne, Beds. 1821, R. Turvey, Beds. 1827-56, R. Lower Gravenhurst, Beds. 1834-42. Dom. Chap. to 2nd Baron Southampton 1804; to Louisa, Baroness St John 1827. Died Redruth, Cornwall 27/4/1856 [C136938. YCO] Married Harworth, Notts. 26/4/1792 Rebecca Downes (a clergy dau.), with clerical son of father's name.

**HAWKSWORTH (John)** Born Mappleton, Derbys. 15/1/1795, s. John Hawksworth and Lydia Rains. TCD1803, BA1812, MA1816 [barrister 1819-29] dn30 (C&L), p31 (C&L). PC. Woore, Shropshire 1830-64. Died Wem, Shropshire 17/9/1876, leaving £4,000 [C18054. Al.Dub.] Married Alton, Staffs. 20/8/1827 Maria Smith, with issue.

**HAWLEY (John Toovey-)** From Hartley Witney, Hants., s. Henry Hawley. St John's, Oxford 1817 (aged 17), BA1822, dn24 (Salis.), p25 (Salis.), MA1826. R. Eversley, Hants. 1831-44. Died? [C76513] A womanising clergyman, he fled the country following 'an indiscretion of a most revolting nature': yateleylocalhistory.pbworks.com/w/page/9285956/HighwaymenSuspects

**HAWORTH (George)** Bapt. Newchurch-in-Rossendale, Lancs. 3/11/1782, s. George and Hannah Haworth. Literate: dn14 (Chester), p14 (Chester). PC. Goodshaw, Whalley, Lancs. 1814 to death 5/11/1836 aged 54 [C169111]

**HAWORTH, HOWORTH (Solomon)** Born Lower Darwen, Lancs. 1/2/1793, s. George and Phoebe Haworth. St Bees: dn22 (York), p24 (York). PC. Hipswell, Richmond, Yorks. 1831 to death 5/7/1837 aged 44 ('while on a visit to his mother') [C169114. YCO as Howorth]

**HAWTREY (Stephen Hurnard)** Bapt. Exeter 17/9/1779, s. Stephen Hawtrey (Recorder of Exeter) and Sarah Hurnard. King's, Cambridge 1799, Fellow 1802-13, BA1803, dn03 (Nor.), p03 (Nor.), MA1806. R. Broad Chalke, Wilts. ('where he resided and laboured assiduously') 1813 to death (Windsor, Berks.) 3/8/1858, leaving £800 [C93135] Married Kersey, Suffolk 28/12/13 Mary Ann Bennett.

**HAY (Edward)** Born Dukinfield, Cheshire 16/4/1800, s. Rev. William Robert Hay (below) and Mary Astle. Christ Church, Oxford 1817, Student [Fellow] 1817-31, BA1821, dn24 (Ox.), p25 (Ox.), MA1824. V. Broughton w. Elslack, Yorks. 1830 to death (Exeter) 30/7/1860 aged 60. Will not traced [C135881]

**HAY (Thomas, 'commonly called Lord Thomas Hay')** Born Yester House, East Lothian 25/8/1800 (the survivor of triplets), s. George, 7th Marquess of Tweeddale and Lady Hannah Charlotte Maitland. Trinity, Cambridge 1818, MA1823, dn25 (Lin.), p30 (Chich.). R. Rendleham, Suffolk 1830-74 (and RD). Died Nice, France 26/2/1890, leaving £7,587-6s-8d. [C63834] Married North Bersted, Sussex 29/8/1833 Harriet Kinloch (dau. of a baronet), with issue (all of whom predeceased him).

**HAY (William Robert)** Born Lisbon, Portugal 3/12/1761, s. Hon. Edward Hay (Ambassador to Portugal, and s. of 7th Earl of Kinnoull) and Mary Flower. Christ Church, Oxford 1776, BA1780, MA1783 [barrister, Inner Temple 1788; Stipendiary Magistrate for Salford 1802-23] dn97 (Win. for Chester), p98 (Chester). R. Ackworth, Yorks. 1802 (and Prebend of Dunnington in York Minster 1806-39) and V. Rochdale St Chad, Lancs. 1820 [income £1,730] to death. Dom. Chap. to 8th Earl of Haddington 1820. Died Ackworth 10/12/1839 aged 78 [C86938] Married Stockport 28/1/1793 Mrs Mary (Wagstaffe) Astle, with clerical son, above. Was one of the two clerical *J.P*'s at the 'Peterloo Massacre' of 16/8/1819; 'More a magistrate than a clergyman'; *D.L.*. His papers are in Chetham's Library, Manchester.

**HAYES (Charles)** Born Calcutta 13/11/1798. Queens', Cambridge 1824, then Trinity, BA 1828, dn28 (B&W), p29 (B&W). R. North Stoke, Som. 1830-57. Died (unmarried) 1861 (3rd q.). No will traced [C41344]

**HAYES, HAYS (William)** Bapt. Durham 8/7/1769, s. Rev. Thomas Hayes. Lincoln, Oxford 1786, BA1791, dn92 (C&L for Cant.), p96 (Durham). Minor Canon of Durham Cathedral 1792-1844, V. Monk Hesleden, Co. Durham 1806 to death 2/10/1859 aged 91, leaving £3,000 [C11479]

**HAYGARTH (George)** Bapt. Dent, Yorks, 4/3/1763, s. William Haygarth and Mary Burton. [NiVoF] PC. Wivesfield, Sussex 1806, V. Hooe, Sussex 1833. Died Cuckfield, Sussex 1840 (1st q.) [C63835] Married Lewes, Sussex 2/2/1815 Mary Kennard.

**HAYGARTH (John)** Born Chester 20/11/1787, s. Rev. John Haygarth, sen. and Sarah Vere Widdens. St John's, Cambridge 1803, BA1809, dn09 (Win. for Glos.), p10 (Glos.), MA1811. R. Upham w. Durley >< Hants. 1814 to death 26/10/1854 [C76519] Married Winchester 17/7/1810 Sophia Poulter, with issue.

**HAYGARTH (Richard)** Bapt. Casterton, Kirkby Lonsdale, Westmorland 29/12/1784, s. William and Sara Haygarth. Literate: dn08 (York), p09 (York). PC. Stapleford, Notts. 1815 to death (London) 16/12/1847 aged 63 [C86944. YCO] Widow Elizabeth.

**HAYLEY (John Burrell)** Born Kidderminster, Worcs. 3/12/1780, s. Rev. William and Sophia Hayley. Worcester, Oxford 1799 (aged 18), BA 1804, dn04 (C&L for Chich.). R. (and patron) of Brightling, Sussex 1805 to death 12/2/1850 [C11480 confuses father and son] Married (1) Wadhurst, Surrey 16/5/1808 Elizabeth Rosam (d.1846) with clerical son Thomas, and John Burrell Hayley, jun. (2) Marylebone, London 18/8/1848 Maria Georgina Pilkington, w. child.

**HAYNE (William Burgess)** Born Plympton, Devon 23/12/1793, s. Rev. William and Jane Hayne. Caius, Cambridge 1811, then Sidney 1813, BA1816, dn17 (Nor.), p18 (Nor.), MA 1819. V. Henlow, Beds.1823-44, V. Ashbourne, Derbys. 1844-51, Min. of the Episcopal [Proprietary] Chapel, Sydenham, Kent 1851 to death 30/1/1862, leaving £8,000 [C63083] Married Twickenham, Surrey 3/5/1823 Emma Eardley-Wilmot (w).

**HAYTHORNE (Joseph)** Bapt. Gloucester 11/5/1796, s. John Haythorne ('a merchant of Bristol') and Mary Taylor. Magdalen, Oxford

1814, then St Mary Hall, BA1820, dn21 (Bristol), p21 (Bristol), MA1822. V. Congresbury, Som. (and Preacher throughout the Diocese of Bath & Wells) 1824 to death 5/2/1867, leaving £600 [C41347]

**HAYTON (Amos)** Bapt. Torpenhow, Cumberland 15/1/1774, s. Amos Hayton Hayton (a yeoman farmer) and Ruth Longcake. St John's, Cambridge 1791, BA 1796, dn97 (London for York), Fellow 1799-1810, MA 1799, p00 (Nor.), BD1806. V. Brabourne w. Monk's Horton, Kent 1831-46. Died 9/1/1851 [C85854. YCO says Jesus, Cambridge] Married Workington, Cumberland 4/8/1810 Eleanor Beeby, with issue. Another man of same name.

**HAYTON (John)** Bapt. Bolton, Cumberland 28/2/1779, s. John and Ann Hayton. Literate: dn04 (York), p05 (York). 'For more than 30 years the respected and indefatigable curate of Sunderland', PC. Ryhope, Bishopwearmouth, Durham 1828 to death 29/1/1843 [C130497. YCO] Was married with clerical son.

**HAYTON (John)** Bapt. Orton, Westmorland 4/9/1798, s. of Thomas Hayton (a yeoman farmer) and Ann Cleasby. St Bees adm. 1821 (as Heyton), dn24 (York), p25 (York). PC. Arkengarthdale, Yorks. 1829 to death 6/3/1862, leaving £1,500 [C135882. YCO] Married Brompton, Northallerton, Yorks. 3/2/1830 Anne Peirson, with issue.

**HAYTON (Thomas)** From Wigton, Cumberland, s. John Hayton. Queen's, Oxford 1815 (aged 21), BA1818, dn18 (Lin.), p20 (Lin.). PC. Long Crendon, Bucks. 1821 and PC. Nether Winchendon, Bucks. 1833 to death 3/11/1887, leaving £544-1s-1d. [C240. Yates. J. Donald (ed.), *The letters of Thomas Hayton, Vicar of Long Crendon, Buckinghamshire, 1821-1887* (Aylesbury, 1979)] A radical, and a defender of the poor.

**[HAYWARD (A. F. Curtis.)** In CCEd noted as the R. of the Donative of Quedgeley, Glos. A problem - because not a man! This is the *patron* of the parish Mrs Albinia Frances Curtis Hayward (d.1860). It has not been possible to track the rector at this time].

**HAYWARD (George)** Bapt. Blandford Forum, Dorset 13/8/1773, s. Rev. George Hayward, sen. (V. Tewkesbury, Glos.). BNC, Oxford 1790, then Pembroke 1790, BA1794, dn94 (Glos.), p96 (Glos.), MA1796. V. Nympsfield, Glos. 1797-1833, V. Frocester, Glos. 1814 to death. Dom. Chap. to 1st Earl of Ducie 1809. Died 14/5/1837. [C152926] Married before 1797 Charlotte Elizabeth Nicholls, with issue. Above?

**HAZELWOOD (Samuel)** Probably bapt. Anwick, Lincs. 12/7/1800, s. William Hazelwood and Mary Robinson. St John's, Cambridge 1819, BA1824, dn24 (Lin.), p25 (Lin.). R. Brauncewell w. Dunsby and Anwick, Lincs. 1826 to death 18/3/1846 [C64097. Kaye]

**HAZELWOOD** see also under **HASLEWOOD**

**HEACOCK (William)** Bapt. Etwall, Derbys. 16/11/1767, s. of William Heacock and Millicent Smith. Worcester, Oxford 1788, BA 1792, dn92 (C&L), p93 (C&L). V. Barrow w. Twyford, Derbys. 1825, Chap. of the Donative of Foremark, Derbys. 1828, R. Newton Regis (o/w Newton-in-the-Thistles), Warwicks. 1834 to death (Etwall) 16/9/1863, leaving £450 [C11652]

**HEAD (Henry Erskine)** Bapt. Higham, Kent 26/3/1797, s. James Roper Head. St Mary Hall, Oxford 1821, dn24 (Salis.), BA1825, p25 (B&W), MA1828. PC. Broomfield, Som. 1825-9, R. Feniton, Devon 1828 to death. Chap. to HRH Duke of Cumberland, King of Hanover. Died Pimlico, London 'on or about' 17/5/1860, leaving £4,000. [C41353. Boase] Married Honiton, Devon 15/12/1823 Elizabeth Margaret Hood, with issue.

**HEAD (John, Sir, 7th Bart.)** Born 3/1/1773, s. Sir Edmund Head, 6th Bart. (of South Carolina) and Mary Raineau. Magdalen, Oxford 1793 [Student of Lincoln's Inn 1794] dn99 (London), p99 (London), BA1800, MA 1800. R. Rayleigh, Essex 1799-1838, PC. Egerton Chapel, Charing, Kent 1807-15 (res.). Died 4/1/1838 aged 65 [C118932] Married Marylebone, London 8/10/1801 Jane Walker, with issue.

**HEAD (William)** From Edmonton, Middx., s. Thomas Head. Trinity, Cambridge 1784 (aged 17), BA1789, dn89 (Ely for Peterb.), p89 (Peterb.), MA1792. Minor Canon of Peterborough Cathedral 1791-1833 (Precentor 1801), R. Northborough, Northants. 1806 to death 21/1/1833 aged 68 (CCEd says 2/4/1833) [C100051]

**HEADLAM (John)** Born Gilmonby Hall, Barnard Castle, Co. Durham 9/5/1769, s. Thomas Emerson Headlam and Jane Emerson. Lincoln, Oxford 1786, BA1790, MA1792, dn92 (Lin. for Chester), p93 (York for Chester). R. Wycliffe, Yorks. 1793-1854, Archdeacon of Richmond 1826 (of Craven from 1836) to 1854, Chancellor of Ripon Cathedral 1846 to death 4/5/1854 aged 85 [C64172. YCO. Boase] Married Easby, Richmond, Yorks. 10/6/1806 Maria Wilson Morley (a clergy dau., Easby House, Yorks.), with issue. J.P. Durham.

**HEALD (William Margetson)** Born Dewsbury, Yorks. 19/2/1767, s. of John Heald (a farmer and maltster). Studied medicine in Edinburgh and in London under John Hunter, and practiced in Wakefield. St Catharine's, Cambridge 1790, BA1794, dn94 (Ely), p98 (York), MA1798. V. Birstall, Yorks. 1801-36 (res. after a stroke). Died 11/1/1837 aged 70 [C85872. ODNB. YCO. DEB] Married York 31/12/1800 Harriet Greenwood, with clerical son of father's name. Port. online. Strong Bronte associations.

**HEAP (Henry)** Born Haslingden, Lancs. 12/4/1789, s. Henry Heap and Betty Wilkinson. Literate: dn12 (Salis. for Chester), p13 (Chester), then St John's, Cambridge 1814 (a Ten Year Man, BD1834 Lambeth). V. Bradford St Peter, Yorks. 1816 to death 17/1/1839 (his youngest dau. dying the same day) An incompetent timeserver [he was] 'a man of insufficient talent for the situation he holds, "very vain and jealous of popularity so that he always takes care to have a curate worse, if possible, than himself"'. Strong Bronte associations – he claimed the right to appoint Patrick Bronte [C93143] Married Haslingden 2/1/1810 Jane Rothwell, w. issue.

**HEATH (Charles)** Bapt. Monks Risborough, Bucks. 6/8/1789, s. Rev. George Heath and Mary Ann Keen. King's, Cambridge 1808, Fellow 1811-22, BA1812, MA1816, dn19 (St Asaph for Bristol), p19 (Chester for Bristol). R. of United Parishes of Gunton w. Hanworth w. Suffield, Norfolk 1828 (and RD 1845) to death. Dom. Chap. to Louisa, Countess of Mansfield 1819. Died 15/2/1864, leaving £5,000. [C52895] Married Lytchett Minister, Dorset 17/12/1822 Mary Anne Pointer (w), with clerical son.

**HEATH (George)** Born Hemblington, Norfolk 6/2/1801 (CCEd thus), s. William Heath and Ann Johnson. Corpus Christi, Cambridge 1826, BA1830, dn30 (Nor.), p31 (Nor.). Curate of Whetstone Chapel, Finchley, London 1832, V. Canewdon, Essex 1847 to death 2/12/1869, leaving £2,000 [C113472] Married East Dereham, Norfolk 22/6/1830 Frances Nelson Cooper with issue.

**HEATH (Robert)** Born Coventry, Warwicks. 26/2/1791 (bapt. 1/4/1806), s. Joseph and Ann Heath. St John's, Oxford 1810, BA1814, dn15 (Ox.), p15 (Ox.), MA1817. R. Saddington, Leics. 1829 to death. Chap. of London Orphan Asylum, Clapton, London. Died 10/5/1852. [C31135]

**HEATHCOTE (Charles John)** Born Brampton, Northants. 16/6/1796, s. Rev. Charles Thomas Heathcote and Dorothea Ward. Trinity, Cambridge 1812, BA1817, MA1820, dn22 (Chester for C&L), Chap. 1822-6, p24 (Ox.). Curate St Thomas Stamford Hill, Middx. 1827-61. Died Upper Clapham, Surrey 4/5/1874, leaving £4,000 [C11654] Married 21/8/1826 Anna Maria Isted Dodd (a clergy dau., Fordham, Essex).

**HEATHCOTE (Gilbert Wall)** Born Winchester 5/5/1806, s. Ven. Gilbert Heathcote (Archdeacon of Winchester) and Sophia Elizabeth Wall. New, Oxford 1824, Fellow 1824-38, dn29 (Heref.), SCL, p30 (Win.), BCL 1832, etc., MA1865; Fellow of Winchester College 1838. V. Hursley, Hants. 1830-5 (res.), V. Ash, Surrey 1839-83. Died Winchester 17/7/1893, leaving £19,939-11s-11d. [C76535] Married Clifton, Bristol 21/7/1841 Clara Rosalie Stonhouse Vigor.

**HEATHCOTE (Robert Boothby)** Born Conington Hall, Conington, Cambs. 13/5/1805, s. John Moyer Heathcote and Mary Anne Thornhill. St John's, Cambridge 1823, BA1827, p28 (Lin.), p29 (London). R. Chingford, Essex 1829 to death 10/9/1865. No will traced [C64199] Married (1) St Martin in the Fields, London 9/3/1837 Charlotte (dau. Admiral Sir Thomas Sotheby, she d.1845), with issue (2) St George's Hanover Square, London 10/10/1848 Elizabeth Bridget Wells (Holme Wood, Hunts.), with further issue.

**HEATHCOTE (Thomas Henry)** Born Walton on the Hill, Liverpool 23/12/1783, s. Rev. Henry Heathcote and Mary Ellen Statham. Clare, Cambridge 1809, BA 1813, p13 (Chester),

MA1816. Chap. Liverpool St James, Toxteth Park 1822-33, V. Leek, Staffs. 1822 (and RD) to death there. Dom. Chap. to Earl of Macclesfield. Died 10/9/1860, leaving £30,000 [C11658] Married (1) Liverpool 3/11/1818 Elizabeth Roughsedge (a clergy dau.) (2) Sefton, Liverpool 8/5/1847 Dorothea Tyson (w).

**HEBDON, HEBDEN (Jeffrey)** Bapt. Ravenstonedale, Westmorland 11/6/1794, s. Henry Hebden (a cordwainer) and Elizabeth Fothergill. Literate: dn17 (Chester), p19 (Chester). PC. Preston Patrick, Westmorland 1829 to death 28/1/1871 aged 76, leaving £600 [C105710] Married New Hutton, Kendal, Westmorland 13/2/1819 Betsy Moore Atkinson, with issue.

**HEBERDEN (Thomas)** Born Overbury, Worcs. 28/9/1754, s. William Heberden, *M.D.*, and Elizabeth Martin. St John's, Cambridge 1770, BA1774, Fellow 1775-80, MA1778, dn78 (Ex.), p78 (Ex.). Prebend of Brecklesham in Chichester Cathedral 1784-1843, Prebend and Canon Residentiary in Exeter Cathedral 1778-1843, R. Bridestow, Devon 1779-86, V. Bishopsnympton (o/w Nymet Bishop), Devon 1782-1843, Prebend of Cudworth in Wells Cathedral 1786 and R. Whimple, Devon 1786 to death. Dom. Chap. to Bishop of Exeter 1778. Died 17/10/1843 [C23689] Married (1) City of London 19/12/1784 Althea Hyde Wollaston (a clergy dau., d.17786), with issue (2) 21/4/1794 Mary, dau. Joseph Martin, *M.P.*, with clerical son two below. Port. online.

**HEBERDEN (William)** Born 8/1/1797, s. William Heberden (medical doctor, *q.v.* ODNB) and Elizabeth Catherine Miller. St John's, Cambridge 1813, BA1819, then Exeter, dn20 (Chester for Cant.) p21 (Salis. for Cant.), MA 1822. V. Great Bookham, Surrey 1821 (and RD of Leatherhead) to death 16/12/1879, leaving £16,000 [C76887] Married Marylebone, London 3/2/1824 Elvina Rainier Underwood, with clerical son John Heberden [C205636]

**HEBERDEN (William)** Bapt. Exeter 16/1/1804, s. Rev. Thomas Heberden (above) and Mary Martin. Oriel, Oxford 1821, BA1825, dn27 (B&W), Chap. 1828-30, p28 (Ex.), MA 1828. V. Broadhembury, Devon 1828-74. Died Marylebone, London 17/8/1890, leaving £140,037-19s-4d. [C41357] Married Exmouth, Devon 1/7/1835 Susannah Catherine Buller, with clerical son. Another identically named cleric with similar details, confused in Foster, CCEd and online.

**HEELIS (Edward)** Bapt. Appleby, Westmorland 25/4/1796, s. Rev. John Heelis and Jane Loraine. Queen's, Oxford 1815, migrated to Emmanuel, Cambridge 1816, BA1819, dn19 (Car.), p21 (Car.), MA1822. R. Dufton 1823-34 and (succ. his father as) R. Brougham, Westmorland 1823-34, R. Long Marton, Westmorland 1833-74. RD of Appleby *c.*1859-74, Hon. Canon of Carlisle 1867 to death. Dom. Chap. to 5th Earl of Tankerville 1823. Died Appleby 27/4/1880 aged 84, leaving £25,000 [C5984. Platt] Married Kirkby Stephen, Westmorland 5/9/1825 Anne Hopes, with clerical son John Heelis.

**HEIGHAM (Henry)** Born Peyton Hall, Boxford, Suffolk 21/1/1768, s. Pell Heigham (Bury St Edmunds, Suffolk) and Penelope Dashwood. Caius, Cambridge 1784, BA1789, Fellow 1789-90, dn90 (Ely), MA1792, p92 (Car. for Cant.). V. (and patron) of Hunston, Suffolk 1792-1834, R. Bradfield Combust, Suffolk 1830-2 (res.). Died London 29/12/1834 (CCEd says 7/4/1835). Married Bury St Edmunds, Suffolk 13/7/1790 Elizabeth Symonds (a naval dau., Hunston Hall, Hunston, Suffolk), with issue [C5987]

**HEIGHWAY (Richard)** From London, s. Richard Heighway. Balliol, Oxford 1782 (aged 18), BA1786, MA1789, dn89 (Lin.), p90 (Salis.). V. Ogbourne St Andrew, Wilts. 1790 to death 18/2/1847 [C64207]

**HELE, *born* SELBY (George Selby)** Bapt. Colmworth, Beds. 25/12/1801, s. Rev. Robert Hele Selby (below) and Felicia Elizabetha Horne (dau. of a Bishop of Norwich). Exeter, Oxford 1819, then Peterhouse, Cambridge 1821, dn23 (Salis.), BA1824, p25 (Chich.), MA1827. V. Grays Thurrock, Essex 1826-[37]. Lived at Bishopsteignton, Devon and died 28/4/1879, leaving £25,000 [C63849] Married (1) Preston, Sussex 29/7/1828 Sarah Stanford (d.1847), w. issue (2) Bishopsteignton 17/5/1849 Emily Wise (a clergy dau., Wenwell Court, Devon), w. further issue.

**HELE, *born* SELBY (Robert Hele Selby)** Born Marazion, Cornwall 25/6/1765, s. Robert Selby and Mary Hele. Exeter, Oxford 1783, BA 1788, MA1789. [sometime V. (and patron) of Grays Thurrock, Essex], R. Bolnhurst, Beds.

1803-6 (res.), R. Colmworth, Beds. 1804 (res.), R. (and patron) of Brede, Sussex 1821 to death (Hastings) 18/11/1839 [C63851] Married Westminster, London 18/5/1791 Felicia Elizabetha Horne (dau. of a Bishop of Norwich), with clerical son George Selby Hele, above. Assumed the surname of Hele.

**HELLICAR (Ames)** From Bristol, s. Joseph Hellicar and Henrietta Gresley. Trinity, Oxford 1817 (aged 20), BA1821, dn22 (Bristol), p23 (Bristol), MA1824. Minor Canon of Bristol Cathedral, V. Fivehead w. Swell, Som. 1832 to death 18/9/1839 [C41358] Married Clifton, Bristol 15/8/1833 Jane Steele, w. issue.

**HELPS (William, sen.)** Born Bristol 6/7/1772, s. William Helps. Wadham, Oxford 1790, BA1794, dn95 (Bristol), p98 (C&L). R. Hawton 1798 to death (Painswick, Glos.) 14/1/1848 [C11715] Married Bristol 19/8/1796 Elizabeth Rennie, with clerical son, below.

**HELPS (William, jun.)** Born Hawton, Notts. 17/12/1797, s. Rev. William Helps, sen. (above) and Elizabeth Rennie. St Bees adm. 1826, dn26 (York), p27 (York). V. Ratcliffe on Soar, Notts. 1830-35 (res.). Military chaplain on St Helena c.1864. Died St George's Hospital, Hyde Park, London 18/1/1874 aged 77, leaving £200 [C131481. YCO] Married St Bees, Cumberland 19/2/1826 Mary Hale, with issue.

**HELYAR (Henry)** From Coker Court, East Coker, Somerset, s. William Helyar. St Mary Hall, Oxford 1803 (aged 18), BA1807, dn09 (Salis.), MA1810, p10 (B&W), then Oriel, MA 1810. R. Pendomer, Som. 1810, R. Hardington Mandeville, Som. 1823. Died Combe Florey, Som. 16/7/1856, leaving £8,000 (left unadministered) [C41359] Married Combe Florey 8/7/1811 Maria Perring (w). Brother below?

**HELYAR (Hugh Welman)** Born East Knoyle, Wilts. 28/3/1793, s. William and Elizabeth Helyar. St John, Cambridge 1812, BA1816, dn17 (B&W), p18 (Bristol), MA1819. R. (and patron) of Sutton Bingham, Som. 1820 w. R. (and patron) of Beer Hackett, Dorset 1825 to death 25/6/1877, leaving £10,000 [C41360] Married Combe Florey, Som. 30/6/1826 Honoria Perring, with clerical s. Wyndham Hugh Helyar. J.P. Somerset. Brother above?

**HEMING (Samuel Bracebridge)** Born Caldecote, Warwicks., s. George Heming and Amicia Bracebridge (a clergy dau.). St John's, Cambridge 1789, BA1793, then Caius 1793 (aged 22), dn94 (C&L), Fellow 1795-8, MA 1796, p97 (C&L). R. (and patron) of Weddington, Warwicks. 1797-1834 (res.), R. Ravenstone, Derbys. 1799-1809 (res.), R. Newbold Verdon, Leics. 1816-23 (res.), R. (and patron) of Fenny Drayton, Leics. 1824 to death. Dom. Chap. to 1st Marquess of Hastings 1799-1824; and to Lord Rawdon 1816-22. Died 15/12/1856 aged 88 [C11661]

**HEMMING (George)** Born Teddington, Middx. 2/5/1798, s. Rev. Samuel Hemming and Elizabeth Baker. Merton, Oxford 1815, BA 1819, dn21 (Win. for Roch.), MA1822, p22 (Lin. for Roch.). R. (and patron) Thundersley, Essex 1822-80, R. (and patron) Little Parndon, Essex 1830 to death 27/10/1880, leaving £20,000 [C247] Married before 1825 Elizabeth Spence, with clerical son William Spence Hemming.

**HENDERSON (John)** Bapt. Wigton, Cumberland 17/5/1792, s. James Henderson (a bricklayer) and Anne Shannan. Literate: dn17 (Chester), p18 (Chester). PC. Colne, Lancs. 1821-76, Canon of Chester Cathedral. Died Colne 10/6/1879 aged 87, leaving £6,000 [C169132] Possibly married Workington, Cumberland 23/4/1816 Mary Sparke, with issue.

**HENDERSON (Thomas)** Bapt. Streatham, Surrey 11/9/1799, s. Thomas Henderson and Elizabeth Child. Christ Church, Oxford 1820, Student [Fellow] 1820-9, BA1824, dn25 (Ox.), MA1826, p26 (Ox.). V. Messing, Essex 1828-61, R. Colne Wakes >< Essex 1831-56, Chamberlainwood Prebend in St Paul's Cathedral, London 1842 to death. Dom. Chap. to 1st Earl of Verulam 1831. Died 4/8/1861, leaving £5,000 [C31150] Married Kelvedon, Essex 19/7/1832 Frances Dalton, and had issue. Photo. online.

**HENNIKER (Augustus Brydges, Sir, 3rd Bart.)** Born Eastbourne, Sussex 24/1/1795, s. Lt.-Gen. Sir Brydges Trecothick Henniker, 1st Bart. and Mary Press. Jesus, Cambridge 1815, then 1820, dn20 (B&W), p20 (B&W), SCL, MA1826. R. Great Thornham (Thornham Magna) w. Thornham Parva (Little Thornham), Suffolk 1820 to death 28/1/1849 aged 54. Lived at Newton Hall, Essex [C41362] Married (1) Marylebone, London 21/7/1821 Frances

Amelia Stewart, with issue (2) Middx. 14/2/1826 Elizabeth Minet Henniker-Major (dau. of 3rd Baron Henniker), w. further issue. Succ. to title 1825.

**HENSHAW (Robert Ibbetson Bazett)** Born Barking, Essex c.1797, s. Robert aand Anne Maria Harrington. Queen's, Oxford 1815, BA 1819, MA1822, dn22 (Chester for London), p23 (Lin.). V. Hungarton w. Twyford, Leics. 1823, R. Lydlinch (Lidlinch), Dorset 1845 to death (Bournemouth, Dorset) 14/8/1874, leaving £600 [C64238] Married Highgate, London 21/5/1835 Harriet Findlay, w. issue. Surrogate.

**HENSLOW (John Stevens)** Born Rochester, Kent 6/2/1796, s. John Prentice Henslow (solicitor) and Frances Hooper. St John's, Cambridge 1813, BA1818, MA1821, dn24 (Ely), p24 (Ely), incorporated at Oxford 1830. Professor of Mineralogy, Oxford 1822-7. Professor of Botany, Oxford 1825-61 (where his lectures became one of the main courses in the University). V. Cholsey (cum Moulsford), Berks. 1832-37, R. Hitcham, Suffolk 1837 to death 16/5/1861, leaving £25,000 [C94885. ODNB. Boase. L. Jenyns, *Memoir of the Rev. John Stevens Henslow, late Rector of Hitchin and Professor of Botany in the University of Cambridge* (1862 and photo.); S. Walters, *Darwin's mentor: John Stevens Henslow, 1796-1851* (Cambridge, 2009)] Married Paddington, London 16/12/1823 Harriet Jenyns (a clergy dau., of Bottisham, Cambs.), with clerical son. 'An exemplary parish priest, and worked hard for better conditions among the agricultural labourers in East Anglia. On more than one occasion took an active part in suppressing bribery at the Parliamentary elections at Cambridge'. etc.' Close friend and mentor of Charles Darwin.

**HENVILLE (Charles Brune)** Bapt. Rowner, Hants. 27/9/1781, s. Rev. James Henville and Susanna Kedder. New, Oxford 1797, BA1801, p10 (Glos.), Fellow to 1827, 'Perpetual V'. Sydling St Nicholas, Dorset 1815-19, R. Bedhampton, Hants. 1818-23, V. Portsmouth 1814-38, V. of Portsea St Mary, Hants. 1823-38. Died South Stoneham, Hants. 17/7/1849 [C52915] Married Warblington, Hants. 11/4/1844 Margaret Lind McArthur.

**HEPTINSTALL (Robert Henry)** Bapt. Astbury, Cheshire 12/9/1803, s. Rev. John and Alice Heptinstall. Exeter, Oxford 1822, BA 1826, dn27 (Chester), p29 (Chester). PC. United Chapelries of Capesthorne and Liddington, Cheshire 1829 to death (Douglas, IoM) 4/11/1866, leaving £600 [C169134] Widow Helen Maria.

**HEPWORTH (John)** Bapt. Batley, Yorkshire 31/7/1778, s. John Hepworth (a clothier) and Martha Burnley. Literate: dn04 (York), p05 (York). PC. Woodkirk (o/w West Ardsley), Yorks. 1808 to death 1846 aged 68 [C85907. YCO] Married (1) Batley 2/3/1801 Sarah Blackburn (2) Woodkirk 26/11/1815 Sarah Scatchard (Morley, Yorks.) 'Much beloved by his parishioners', etc.

**HEPWORTH (Robert)** Born Grafham, Hunts, s. Rev. John Hepworth. St Catharine's, Cambridge 1793, BA1797, dn97 (Ely), p99 (Ely), MA1800. V. Gamlingay, Cambs. 1802 to death 24/12/1845 aged 72 [C100056]

**HEPWORTH (Robert)** Born Long Preston, Yorks. 19/1/1800, s. Rev. Abraham Hepworth and Susannah Christian. St Edmund Hall, Oxford 1820, BA1823, dn23 (Glos.), p24 (Glos.). PC. Tredington, Glos. 1829-57. Died Cheltenham, Glos. 10/7/1877, leaving £10,000 [C153065] Married Bushey, Herts. 1/6/1828 Barbara Maria Platt, with issue.

**HERBERT (Edward)** Bapt. Upton on Severn, Worcs. 31/7/1795, s. Rev. Edward John and Mary Herbert. Oriel, Oxford 1813, BA1819, dn20 (Wor.), MA1822. R. Abberton, Worcs. 1820-34, R. Flyford Flavell, Worcs. 1822-34. Died? [C121383. Al.Dub.]

**HERBERT (William, Hon.)** Born London 12/1/1778, s. Henry, 1st Earl of Carnarvon and Lady Elizabeth Maria Wyndham. Christ Church, Oxford 1795, BA1798, then Merton, MA1802 [Whig *M.P.* for Hampshire 1806-7; for Cricklade 1811-12], BCL and DCL1808, dn14 (Ely for York), p14 (Heref. for York), BD1840, Hon. LLD. R. Spofforth, Yorks. [net income £1,538] 1814-40, Warden of Manchester Collegiate Church 1840 to death (London) 28/5/1847 aged 69 [C105729 with no details. YCO. LBSO. *Dictionary of Scientific Biography*, 6 (1972)] Married 17/5/1806 Hon. Letitia Dorothea Allen, dau. 5th Viscount Allen, 4 ch. 'An eminent botanist'. 'The International Bulb Society offers the Herbert Medal to persons advancing the knowledge of bulbous plants'.

**HEREFORD (Bishop of)** see under **HUNTINGFORD (George Isaac)**

**HERNE, *or* BUCKWORTH-HERNE (John Buckworth-)** Born 20/3/1766 (CCEd thus), s. of Sir Everard Buckworth, 5th Bart. and Ann Herne (natural dau. of Paston Herne, Haviland Hall, Norfolk). Literate, then Emmanuel, Cambridge 1784 (a Ten Year Man, BD), p91 (Nor.). R. Heydon, Essex 1792-1810 (res.), V. West Hendred, Berks. 1810 to death 1852 (1st q.) [C94891] Married (1) Marylebone, London 14/10/1786 Mary Annee (dau. Sir Charles Price) (2) Elizabeth; *s.p.*

**HERON (George)** Born Moore Hall, Runcorn, Cheshire 12/3/1805, s. Gen. Peter Heron, *M.P.*, and Catherine Hopwood. BNC, Oxford 1823, BA1826, dn28 (C&L), p29 (C&L), MA1829. PC. Whitworth, Rochdale, Lancs. 1829, PC. Carrington, Ashton on Mersey, Cheshire 1831-77 (living at Moore Hall), RD of East Frodsham 1870, Hon. Canon of Chester 1880. Dom. Chap. to Lady Grey of Groby. Died (unm.) Moore Hall 27/8/1894 aged 89, leaving £109,769-1s-3d. [C11722]

**HERRING (Thomas)** Bapt. Elmham, Norfolk 24/2/1783, s. Rev. Thomas and Elizabeth Herring. Trinity, Cambridge 1801, then Corpus Christi 1804, MA1805, dn06 (Nor.), p07 (Nor.), MA1808, Fellow 1809, BD1816. R. Great Braxted, Essex 1828 to death 30/9/1841 [C113491]

**HERRINGHAM (John Philip)** Born Ingatestone, Essex 30/1/1789, s. Rev. William Herringham (R. Chipping Ongar, Essex). Pembroke, Cambridge 1806, BA1810, dn12 (London), p13 (London), MA1816. R. (and patron) of Chadwell St Mary, Essex 1819-56, R. Borley, Essex 1819 to death. Dom. Chap. to 6th Earl Waldegrave 1819. Died 4/12/1861, leaving £9,000 [C119110] Married Little Waltham, Essex 9 or 13/12/1833 Susanna Jackson Bird (a clergy dau.), with clerical son William Walton Herringham.

**HERVEY (Arthur Charles, Lord, *later* Bishop of Bath and Wells)** Born 20/8/1808, s. 1st Marquess of Bristol and Elizabeth Albana Upton (dau. of 1st Lord Templetown). Trinity, Cambridge 1827, MA1820, dn32 (Nor.), p32 (Peterb. for Nor.), DD1870, Hon. DD Oxford 1885. R. Ickworth w. Chedburgh, Suffolk 1832-69, Archdeacon of Sudbury 1862-9, Bishop of Bath and Wells 1869 to death (Hackwood House, Basingstoke) 9/6/1894 ged 85, leaving £27,731-1s-6d. [C113492. ODNB. Boase. J.F.A. Hervey, *A memoir of Lord Arthur Hervey, Bishop of Bath and Wells* (PPC, 1896)] Married Marylebone, London 30/7/1839 Patience Singleton (of Haseley, IoW and Mell, Co. Louth), with 12 ch.(incl. Rev. John Frederick Arthur Hervey). A member of the Old Testament Revision Committee. A champion tennis player in his youth, he was a good classicist, and a good and tolerant bishop.

**HERVEY (Humphrey Archer)** Born Underbarrow, Westmorland 13/12/1768, s. Rev. Thomas and Ann Hervey. Literate: dn93 (Car.), p94 (Car.). V. Bridekirk, Cumberland 1794 (and S/M at Bridekirk 1796, then Broughton, then Dovenby Free G/S) to death 20/9/1843 aged 76 [C5992. Platt] Married Bridekirk 4/6/1795 Sarah Mawson, with issue.

**HESKETH (Charles)** Born 15/3/1804, s. Robert Hesketh (Rossall Hall, Fleetwood, Lancs.) and Maria Rawlinson. Trinity, Oxford 1822, BA1827, dn27 (Chester), p28 (Chester), MA1830. V. Poulton le Fylde, Lancs. 1828-35 (res.), PC. Bispham, Fleetwood 1831, R. (and patron) of North Meols, Southport 1835 (and RD) to death 15/7/1876 aged 72, leaving £16,000 [C169139] Married Derby 21/1/1828 Anna Maria Alice Saunders (w), with issue.

**HESKETH (Robert [Cuthbert])** Born Shrewsbury, Shropshire, s. Robert Hesketh and Margaret Thornes. Christ Church, Oxford 1792 (aged 18), BA1797, p99 (Bristol), MA1814. R. Acton Burnell, Shropshire 1813, R. St Dunstan's in the East, City of London 1817 to death. Dom. Chap. to Anne, Dowager Countess Townshend 1817. Died Epsom, Surrey 11/2/1837 [C11724] Married Holborn, London 16/8/1809 Emma Martha Daniell, with issue.

**HESKETH (William)** Born Warrington, Lancs. 13/5/1791, s. William, *R.N.*, and Margaret Hesketh, Liverpool. BNC, Oxford 1808, BA1812, MA1815, dn16 (Chester), p17 (Chester). PC. Toxteth Park St Michael, Liverpool 1822 to death (Southport, Lancs.) 11/10/1858, leaving £4,000 [C169140] Married Walton, Liverpool 19/4/1822 Lucy Hannah Satterthwaite (w), with issue.

**HESLOP (John)** Bapt. Wath upon Dearne, Yorks. 13/7/1790, s. Francis and Anne Heslop.

St Catharine's, Cambridge 1812, dn13 (York), p14 (York). R. Skelton cum Newby, Clapham, Yorks. 1828-46, R. Langton, Yorks. 1846 to death (Brantwood, Coniston, Lancs.) 23/6/1850 aged 59 [C131484. YCO says Literate] Married before 1817, with issue.

**HESLOP (Richard)** Bapt. Morland, Westmorland 6/11/1800, s. Richard Heslop (farmer) and Margaret Wilkinson. Literate: dn26 (York), p27 (York). PC. Slaley, Northumberland 1831-48, PC. Birch in Middleton, Lancs. 1834-6, PC. Ainsworth, Lancs. 1836-51, PC. Otterford, Somerset 1851-5, PC. St John the Evangelist, Sheffield 1855-64- (non-res., 'address unknown, except to the sexton'). Died West Derby, Liverpool 1879 (2nd q.) aged 78. Will not traced [C131485. YCO] Wife Jane Brown, and issue.

**HESLOP (William)** Born Ravensworth, Yorks. Literate: dn94 (Chester), p96 (Chester). PC. Forcett Chapel, Gilling, Yorks. 1800 and PC. Hutton Magna, Yorks. 1800 to death 23/2/1863 aged 92. Will not yet traced [C169141. Noted in Venn under his clerical s., also William] Wife Margaret.

**HESSE (Frederick Legrew)** Bapt. Bloomsbury, London 16/4/1803, s. Obadiah Legrew Hesse and Margaret Playford. Emmanuel, Cambridge 1821, then Trinity Hall 1822, LLB 1827 [adm. Middle Temple 1830] dn33 (Lin.), p34 (Lin.). R. Rowbarrow, Som. 1834 and PC. Puxton, Som. 1840 to death 2/10/1874, leaving £14,000 [C41367] Married Datchworth, Herts. 11/2/1834 Jane Broadley Green (w), with issue. Brother below.

**HESSE (James Legrew)** Bapt. Bloomsbury, London, s. Obadiah Legrew Hesse and Margaret Playford. Trinity, Oxford 1821 (aged 20), BA1825, p28 (Ely), MA1829. R. Rowbarrow, Som. 1829-34, R. Knebworth, Herts. 1830, R. Chiddingfold w. Haslemere, Surrey 1838 to death 17/9/1868, leaving £10,000 [C41369. CR65 says Legrew James] Married Datchworth, Herts. 6/5/1834 Susannah Green, with clerical son George John Hesse. Brother above.

**HETT (William)** Born Potter Hanworth, Lincs., s. Michael and Martha Hett. BNC, Oxford 1769, BA1773, migrated to Sidney, Cambridge 1777, dn74 (Lin.), p77 (Nor.). Priest-Vicar in Lincoln Cathedral 1782-1833, R. Mavis Enderby >< Lincs. 1782-1834 (non-res.), Prebend of Bedford Minor in Lincoln Cathedral 1786-1833, V. Dunholme w. Newport St John, Lincs. 1786-1833, R. Lincoln St Paul in the Bail 1787-1833, PC. Greetwell, Lincs. 1795-1833. V. Lincoln St Nicholas 1803-6, R. Thorpe on the Hill, Lincs. 1806-33. Dom. Chap. to Marquess of Stafford (later 1st Duke of Sutherland) 1806. Died 21/11/1833 aged 82 [C64258. Bennett2. Kaye] Married (1) Mary Hamilton (d.1792), with issue (2) City of London 23/7/1794 Catherine Crowder, with further issue.

**HETT (William)** Born Leeds 15/12/1792, s. William Hett and Elisabeth Henrietta Keir. Jesus, Cambridge 1812, dn17 (York), BA1818, p26 (York), MA1821. V. Elksley, Notts. 1828 to death 15/6/1838 aged 44 [C131486. YCO] Married York 31/12/1816 Frances Smith.

**HEWER (John)** Literate: dn93 (Car. for Win.), p95 (Car. for Win.). S/M Dalton G/S, Cumberland 1791; S/M Bassenthwaite, Cumberland 1795; R. Tunworth, Hants. 1808 to death (Chobham, Surrey) 17/2/1845 aged 74 [C5998] Wife Mary Potter.

**HEWES (James)** Literate: dn82 (York for Lin.), p83 (Lin.). R. Grove, Bucks. 1799. Died? [C64368. YCO]

**HEWETSON (John)** Born Kirkland, Cumberland 5/4/1770, s. of John (a farmer) and Sarah Hewetson. Literate: dn94 (York), p95 (York). PC. Byrness, Northumberland 1797 and PC. (Nether or Lower) Whitley, Northumberland 1813 to death (Byrness) 17/3/1841 aged 71 [C85955. YCO] Wife Elizabeth, with issue.

**HEWETT (Charles)** Born Dublin 18/11/1796, s. Gen. Sir George Hewett, 1st Bart. (C.-in-C. Ireland) and Julia Johnson. BNC, Oxford 1814, BA1818, dn19 (Bangor - in London), p21 (Ex.), MA 1822. Chap. of the Donative of Ansty, Wilts. 1834 [not in CCEd], PC. Swallowcliffe, Wilts. 1835. Lived in Birmingham and then Southampton. Died Folkestone, Kent 10/11/1871 aged 74, leaving £16,000 [C94894] Married Oxford 26/9/1837 Frances Sophia Cator, *s.p.*

**HEWETT (John Short)** Bapt. Bengal 23/8/1779, s. William Nathan Wright Hewett and Martha Tuting. Clare, Cambridge 1799, BA1803, dn03 (Ely), p04 (Nor.), Fellow 1805, MA1806, DD1824. V. Cromer, Norfolk 1804-7 (res.), PC. Sheringham, Norfolk 1811-13, R. Elmsett, Suffolk 1816-17 (res.), R. Rotherhithe,

Surrey 1817-35, R. Ewhurst, Sussex 1824 to death (Boulogne) 12/12/1834 (CCEd says 8/4/1835) [C63866] Married Brede, Sussex 19/2/1829 Mary Anne Selby-Hale, and had issue.

**HEWGILL, HUGILL (Francis)** Bapt. Great Smeaton, Yorks. 17/10/1781, s. Rev. Henry Hugill (Hornby Grange, Yorks.) and Antonia Willoughby. Trinity, Cambridge 1799 [adm. Inner Temple 1801] BA1803, MA1806, dn07 (Car. for York), p09 (Win.). R. Saundby, Notts. 1814-38, V. North Wheatley, Notts. 1819-38, R. Littleborough, Notts. 1820-38, R. Sturton le Steeple, Notts. 1820-36, R. Wollaton w. Cossall, Notts. 1838-46, R. Trowell, Notts. 1838 to death 19/1/1858 aged 75, leaving £6,000 [C76921. YCO] Married Alnwick, Northumberland 4/3/1851 Margaret Dawson. Brother, below.

**HEWGILL, HUGILL (James)** Bapt. Great Smeaton, Yorks. 4/6/1776, s. Rev. Henry Hugill (Hornby Grange, Yorks.) and Antonia Willoughby. Jesus, Cambridge 1794, dn01 (York), p01 (York), LLB1803. Curate Appleton Wiske, Yorks. 1804-47, (succ. his father as) R. Great Smeaton 1804 to death 25/11/1847 aged 71, leaving £6,000 [C85964. YCO] Married 1808 Margaret Close (Easby Hall, Hutton Bonville, Yorks.), with issue. Brother, above.

**HEWITT (Charles)** Bapt. Bacton, Norfolk 28/12/1753, s. Rev. Thomas (R. Ridlington, Norfolk) and Ann Hewitt. Caius, Cambridge 1770, BA1775, dn78 (London), MA1778, p79 (London), Fellow 1779-81. R. Colchester St James, Essex 1783-98, R. Pitsea, Essex 1797-1848 and R. East Grinstead, Essex 1797. Dom. Chap to 2nd Marquess of Bath 1797. Died 1851 (1st q.) [C66803] Married Cornhill, City of London 3/5/1781 Harriet Gibson.

**HEWITT (David)** Bapt. Bolton le Moors, Lancs. 21/7/1793, s. Pitt and Margaret Hewitt. Trinity, Cambridge 1812, BA1817, dn17 (Chester), p18 (Chester), MA1826. PC. Horwich, Lancs. 1826-51. Retired to Lytham (St Anne), Lancs., living with 3 unmarried sisters. Died Wrexham, Denbigh (unmarried) 20/11/1867, leaving £60,000 [C169145]

**HEWITT (George)** Born Norfolk. Queens', Cambridge 1777, BA1782, dn83 (Ely), Fellow 1783, MA1785, p85 (Peterb.), BD1793. PC. Stoke by Clare, Norfolk 1785-1807, V. Ickleton, Suffolk 1788-91, V. Witton, Norfolk 1791-1835, R. Cambridge St Botolph 1799-1834, R. Sandon, Essex 1834 to death 1846 [C100059] 'A scandalous old reprobate'.

**HEWITT (John)** Born Norfolk 10/5/1758. Corpus Christi, Cambridge 1780, BA1784, dn84 (Nor.), p84 (Nor.), Fellow 1796, MA1787, BD 1795. PC. Walcot and Ridlington, Norfolk 1784-1844, V. Grantchester, Cambs. 1806-50, R. Stoke near Clare, Suffolk 1807, R. Sandon, Essex 1834. Died 13/1/1850 aged 91 [C100060]

**HEWITT (Richard)** Born Burton upon Trent 20/5/1771, s. John Hewitt. BNC, Oxford 1792, BA1796, dn96 (Chester), p97 (Chester), MA 1799, BD and DD1824. PC. Little Lever (o/w Little Bolton), Bolton (le Moors), Lancs. 1799-1841, R. (and patron) of Westhorpe, Suffolk 1819 to death (widower, West Derby, Liverpool) 16/3/1852 aged 82 [C113498] Married Bolton 14/11/1799 Jane Kaye, with issue.

**HEWITT (William)** Literate: dn25 (St David's for Durham), p26 (Durham). PC. Ancroft, Berwick upon Tweed, Northumberland 1827 to death (unm.) 14/10/1866 aged 66, leaving £2,000 [C130504]

**HEWLETT (John)** Born Chetnole, Dorset 1762, s. Timothy Hewlett and Mary Highmore. Ordained as a Literate. Magdalene, Cambridge 1786 (a Ten Year Man, BD1796). Kept a school at Shackleford, Surrey; Morning Preacher at the Foundling Hospital, London from c.1802. R. Hilgay (o/w Hilgate), Norfolk 1819 [net income £1,291] to death. Chap. in Ordinary 1812. Died London 13/4/1844 aged 86 [C113501. ODNB as a biblical scholar is thin] Married (1) Hackney, London 12/8/1782 Elizabeth Hobson (d.1822), with issue (2) Holborn, London 4/8/1823 Caroline Price; all his children predeceased him.

**HEXT (Francis [John])** Born 10/4/1779 (bapt. Bodmin, Cornwall 3/4/1781), s. Francis John Hext and Margaret Lang. Exeter, Oxford 1797, BA1802, dn17 (Salis. for Nor.), p17 (Ely for Nor.). R. Helland, Cornwall 1817 to death (Bath) 27/1/1842 'from overexertion in the promotion of' the education of chimney sweep boys [C94897] Had issue. J.P., D.L. Cornwall; ERC says Francis G. Hext.

**HEXTALL (John)** Born Leicester 12/9/1792, s. Clay Hextall and Susannah Jane Brown. Literate: dn15 (York), p17 (York). PC. Mossley, Ashton under Lyne, Lancs. 1831 to death

17/6/1864, leaving £3,000 [C131488. YCO] Married Halifax, Yorks. 10/4/1817 Mary Knight, with issue.

**HEY (Samuel)** Bapt. Leeds 25/1/1781, s. William Hey and Alice Banks. Queens', Cambridge 1805, BA1809, dn09 (C&L), p10 (C&L), MA1812. V. Ockbrook, Derbys. 1816 to death (Belper, Derbys.) 14/8/1852 [C11670] Married York Minster 26/5/1810 Margaret Gray, with issue.

**HEYCOCK (Charles)** Born East Norton, Leics. 15/10/1794, s. John Heycock and Susannah Hippisley. St John's, Cambridge 1812, BA1816, dn17 (Lin.), p20 (Lin.), MA 1822. PC. Owston, Leics. 1827-57, R. Withcote, Leics. 1827-57, R. Pytchley, Northants. 1854 to death 25/1/1871, leaving £35,000 [C64382] Married Knipton, Leics. 26/7/1831 Catherine Bissill (Whissendine, Rutland), with issue.

**HEYNES (Thomas)** Born Chipping Norton, Oxon. 30/9/1758, s. Thomas Heynes [*pleb*]. Queen's, Oxford 1783, dn86 (Ox. for Wor.), BA1787, p87 (Wor.). Minor Canon of Worcester 1795 and V. Wolverley, Worcs. 1814 to death 2/12/1835 [C31172]

**HEYRICK,** *later* **HILL (Samuel)** Bapt. 6/3/1764, s. John Heyrick (Town Clerk of Leicester) and Mary Erpe. Trinity, Cambridge 1780, BA1785 [as Samuel Heyrick Hill], dn86 (Lin. for Ely), p86 (Ely), MA1788. R. Brampton Ash, Leics. 1790 (and Master of Leicester G/S 1799-1802), R. (East) Carlton, Northants. 1819-20 (res.). Dom. Chap. to 1st Earl of Lonsdale 1790-1840. Died 19/10/1840 [C64383] Married Leicester 9/6/1791 Catharine Ellis, w. issue.

**HEYSHAM (John)** Born Carlisle 9/1/1793, s. John Heysham, *M.D.* ('the demographer', *q.v.* ODNB) and Elizabeth Mary Coulthard. St. John's, Cambridge 1811, BA1815, dn16 ([Car.]), p17 (Car.), MA1818. Minor Canon Carlisle Cathedral 1816-46, PC. Hayton, Cumberland 1819-20, PC. Sebergham, Cumberland 1820-46, V. Lazonby, Cumberland 1846 to death (unm.) 12/2/1877 aged 85, leaving £4,000 [C3406. Platt] *J.P.* Cumberland; Hon. Sec. and Treasurer to Clergy Widows' and Orphans' Relief Society 1823-46. Surrogate 1827.

**HEYWOOD (George)** From Lymington, Hants., s. Rev. William Arthur Heywood and Eliza Reynolds. Jesus, Cambridge 1800, BA1804, dn05 (Win.), p10 (Ex.). R. Ideford, Devon 1811 to death 29/5/1836 [C76928] Married by 1823 Marie Emma Thelwell, w. issue.

**HIBBERT (Henry Booth)** From Bromley, Kent, s. Booth Hibbert. Queen's, Oxford 1801 (aged 18), BA1805, MA1807, dn08 (Win.), p09 (Win.). V. South Cockerington (Cockerington St Leonard), Lincs. 1832 to death (Louth, Lincs.) 1842 (3rd q.) [C1900. Kaye] Married North Cray, Kent 28/6/1813 Caroline Augusta Holship, w. issue.

**HIBGAME (Edward)** Bapt. Stratton St Michael (o/w Long Stratton), Norfolk 2/9/1776, s. Rev. Edward Hibgame and Mary Smith. Jesus, Cambridge 1793, BA1798, Fellow and tutor 1800-31, BA1801 [adm. Gray's Inn 1803] dn14 (Bristol), p15 (Bristol). V. Whittlesford, Cambs. 1822-30, V. Fordham, Cambs. 1830-61, PC. Norwich St George Colegate 1831-52. Died 10/11/1861, leaving £16,000 [C1056]

**HICKIN (William)** Born Handmore, Staffs., s. John Hickin (farmer) and Mary Cotton. Magdalene, Cambridge 1771 (aged 18), BA1775, dn75 (C&L), p90 (C&L). V. Audley, Staffs. 1790-1833, PC. Ellenhall, Staffs. 1817 to death 18/1/1833 aged 83 (CCEd thus) [C11673] Clerical son of same name.

**HICKS, HICKES (George)** Bapt. Yarm, Yorks. 12/3/1754, s. George Hicks and Elizabeth Burton. Lincoln, Oxford 1771, BA 1775, dn76 (C&L for ?), MA1778. R. Aunsby, Lincs. 1786-1800, V. Heydour w. Kelby and Culverthorpe, Lincs. 1786-1800, R. Burnsall (1st Portion), Yorks. 1797-1839 (res.). Died 1839 (3rd q.)? [C11726] Married Durham 28/6/1780 Elizabeth Harrison, with issue.

**HICKS (William)** Probably born Holborn, London 25/12/1775, s. William and Elizabeth Hicks. Peterhouse, Cambridge 1793, BA1798, dn98 (London), p01 (Nor.), MA1806. R. Little Braxted (Braxted Parva), Essex 1802-10, V. Great Marlow (Marlow Magna), Bucks. 1802-11, R. Whittington, Glos. 1811 and R. Coberley (Cubberley), Glos. 1816 to death. Dom. Chap. to Mary, 4th Countess of Orkney 1816. Died 12/3/1866 aged 91, leaving £7,000 [C64391] Married (1) Marylebone, London 3/7/1824 Amelia Maria Alt (d.1830) (2) Charlton Kings, Glos. 4/5/1833 Mary Grisdale (w).

**HICKS (William)** Bapt. St Columb Major, Cornwall 22/12/1788, s. Richard Hicks (of Tranoweth, Cornwall) and Martha Peter. Lieut. R.N. [wounded at Trafalgar]. Magdalene, Cambridge 1819, BA1823, dn23 (Bristol for Ely), MA1826, p29 (London). R. Sturmer, Essex 1829 to death 11/1/1874, leaving under £200. Chap. to Risbridge Poor Law Union 1836 [C52955. Boase] Married Cambridge 28/8/1823 Catherine Willimott (dau. of a Cambridge alderman), w. clerical son Herbert Sawyer Hicks.

**HIDES (John)** Bapt. Trowell, Notts. 17/11/1787, s. of William (S/M Watnall School, Greasley, Notts.) and Luna [*sic*] Hides. Literate: dn12 (York), p14 (York). V. Greasley 1819 (w. Brinsley Chapel 1838), to death 21/8/1865, leaving £2,000 [C131491. YCO] Wife Mary, and clerical son.

**HIERN (Charles)** Born Barnstaple, Devon 25/6/1762, s. James Hiern. St Catharine's, Cambridge 1780, dn85 (Ex.), p86 (Ex.), LLB 1787. R. Huntshaw, Devon 1787 and R. (and patron) of Stoke Rivers, Devon 1792 to death 16/4/1834 [C145037] Married Stoke Rivers, Nov. 1788 Hannah Caton, with clerical son.

**HIGGINS (Joseph)** Bapt. Eastnor, Heref. 28/11/1770, s. Thomas Higgins and Sarah Wood. Worcester, Oxford 1788, BA1792, dn93 (Wor.), p95 (Wor.), MA1808. R. Eastnor 1795 and R. Pixley, Heref. 1808 to death 7/9/1847 [C121389] Married Eastnor 27/6/1796 Mary Hussey, with son below.

**HIGGINS (Thomas)** Bapt. Eastnor, Heref. 16/3/1797, s. Rev. Joseph Higgins (above) and Mary Hussey. BNC, Oxford 1814, BA1818, dn19, MA 1822, p22 (Heref.). PC. Stoulton, Worcs. 1830-43. Died at his London home 9/10/1879, leaving £35,000 [C105741] Married Stratford on Avon, Warwicks. 19/11/1829 Maria Stanley Mills (w). *J.P.* Herefordshire.

**HIGTON (William)** Born Manchester. St John's, Cambridge 1814, dn14 (Chester), p15 (Chester), BA1815, MA1818. PC. Croxden (o/w Croxton), Staffs. 1818-59, PC. Tean, Staffs. 1843-59. Died Southport, Lancs. 14/4/1863, leaving £8,000 [C11731] Married Stafford 28/9/1843 Ellen Spendelow Townsend (w).

**HILDYARD (William, sen.)** Born Grimsby 6/7/1762, s. of William Hildyard (attorney and alderman) and Frances Whichcot. Sidney, Cambridge 1780, dn85 (Lin.), LLB1786, then Queens' 1789, p92 (Lin.). V. Killingholme cum Habrough, Lincs. 1792, R. East Halton, Lincs. 1792, R. Winestead, Yorks. 1795-1842, R. Ludborough, Lincs. 1815-25. Died 25/2/1842 [C64405. Kaye] Married Monks Eleigh, Suffolk 12/12/1793 Catherine Grant, of Ruckland, Lincs. (9 of their 10 sons were graduates of Cambridge, many clerical (one below), and six were Fellows of their Colleges).

**HILDYARD (William, jun.)** Bapt. Barton upon Humber, Lincs. 12/12/1794, s. Rev. William Hildyard, sen. (above) and Catherine Grant. Trinity, Cambridge 1808, BA1817, dn19 (Nor. for Bristol), MA18207, p20 (Bristol), then Trinity Hall, Fellow and Tutor 1824-30. R. Market Deeping, Lincs. 1828 to death 11/2/1875, leaving £3,000 [C52958] Married Bromley, Kent 1/5/1838 Sophia Hildyard (w) (a clergy dau.), *s.p.*

**HILL (Benjamin)** From Little Billing, Northants., s. Rev. Benjamin Hill, sen. BNC, Oxford 1807 (aged 21), BA1811, MA1815, dn19 (Ox. for Peterb.), p20 (Peterb.). R. (and patron) of Collingtree and Plumpton, Northants. 1820 to death 22/10/1855 [C110310]

**HILL (Charles)** Bapt. Old Swinford, Staffs. 3/1/1787, s. Thomas and Ann Hill. Jesus, Cambridge 1805, BA1809, dn11 (C&L), MA 1812, p12 (C&L). R. Bromsberrow, Glos. 1823 and R. Madresfield, Worcs. 1832 to death. Dom. Chap. to 3rd Earl Beauchamp 1832. Died 14/1/1856 aged 69 [C11683] Had issue. Brother Henry William, below.

**HILL (Dennis)** Bapt. Wells-next-the-Sea 3/10/1782, s. John Hill and Elizabeth March. Christ's, Cambridge 1801-4, BA 1805, dn06 (Nor.), p07 (Nor.). R. Gressenhall, Norfolk 1807 to death 18/2/1873, leaving £12,000 [C113517] Wife (1) Gressenhall 3/4/1804 Lydia Page. (2) Stanfield, Norfolk 28/7/1831 Mrs Elizabeth Senkler.

**HILL (Edmund)** Bapt. Snailwell, Cambs. 22/8/1798, s. Rev. Nicholas Isaac and Frances Hill. Christ's, Cambridge 1817, dn23 (Nor.), BA1824, p26 (Nor.), MA1827. V. Kirtling, Cambs. 1831 to death 6/2/1854 aged 56 [C113518]

**HILL (Edward)** Born Kingswinford, Staffs., s. John Hill. Queen's, Oxford 1793 (aged 19), BA

1797, dn97 (C&L), p98 (C&L). PC. Hindley, Wigan, Lancs. 1830 to death 1853 (2nd q.) aged 79 [C11734] Wife Ellen.

**HILL (Henry William)** Bapt. Old Swinford, Staffs. 27/2/1782, s. Thomas and Ann Hill. Worcester, Oxford 1801, then Jesus, Cambridge 1804, BA1806, dn06 (C&L for Wor.), p06 (C&L. for Wor.). R. Rock w. Heighington, Worcs. [net income £1,001] 1812 to death 3/5/1840 [C11684] Brother Charles, above.

**HILL (John)** Born London, s. John Hill [*pleb*]. St Edmund Hall, Oxford 1806, BA1809, dn09 (Ox.), p10 (Ox.), MA1812, tutor, etc., Vice-Principal, BD1844. PC. Hampton Gay, Oxon. 1809-51, V. Wyke Regis, Dorset 1851 to death 22/2/1855 aged 63 [C31222. ODNB. Boase. DEB] Married 1811 Sophia Warriner, 8 ch.

**HILL (John)** Born Ravenstonedale, Westmorland 1800. [Possibly St Bees adm. 1819?] dn23 (Car.), p24 (Car.). R. Scaleby, Cumberland 1826 to death 5/5/1859 aged 59, leaving £800 [C6002. Platt] Wife Mary.

**HILL (John)** Born Hawkestone, Weston under Redcastle, Shropshire 11/3/1802, s. Col. John Hill and Elizabeth Rhodes Cornish. Oriel, Oxford 1820, BA1824, dn25 (C&L), MA 1835, p27 (C&L). R. Great Bolas (Bolas Magna), Shropshire 1831-77. Died Hawkestone 15/6/1891, leaving £27,585-18s-4d. [C11851] Married Pradoe, Shropshire 17/12/1833 Charlotte Kenyon.

**HILL (John Oakley)** Born Knighton, Radnor, s. Benjamin Hill and Sally Oakley. Christ Church, Cambridge 1820 (aged 16), BA1824, dn26 (Heref.), p27 (Ox.), MA1828, Chap. 1827-29. S/M Monmouth G/S 1829; PC. Dorton, Bucks. 1829, PC. Ashendon, Bucks. 1829, V. Bledington (Bladington), Glos. 1843-71, R. Little Rollright, Oxon. 1871 to death. Chap. to Stow on the Wold Poor Law Union 1852. Died (Chipping Norton, Oxon.) 9/9/1888 aged 85, leaving £225-17s-5d. [C31223] Married Oxford 27/1/1848 Anne Maria Bagnall (w), w. clerical son Percival Oakley Hill.

**HILL (Justly)** Born Bonchurch, IoW 16/12/1781, s. Col. William Hill and Elizabeth Popham. New, Oxford 1800, Fellow 1802-20, BA1805, dn05 (Win.), p06 (Win.), MA1808. R. Tingewick, Bucks. 1819-53, Archdeacon of Buckingham 1825-53, R. Bonchurch w. Shanklin 1829 to death 18/3/1853 [C64465. Boase] Married Melcombe Regis, Dorset 1/5/1820 Jane Helena Shute, with issue.

**HILL (Matthew)** From Hereford, s. Thomas Hill. New, Oxford 1790 (aged 18), then Magdalen, BA1795, dn95 (Ox.), p97 (Heref.). Vicar Choral Hereford Cathedral 1795, PC. Putley, Heref. 1798, R. Sutton St Nicholas, Heref. 1805-47, V. Norton Canon, Heref. 1811, V. Marden w. Amberley, Heref. 1820 to death 27/1/1847 [C31225]

**HILL (Nicholas Isaac)** Born London 31/10/1760, s. Haydock (*or* Hayder) Hill and Elizabeth Bosquet. Christ Church, Oxford 1779, BA1783, dn83 (Ox.), MA1786. R. Snailwell, Cambs. 1796 to death 29/10/1854 [C31226] Married Marylebone, London 16/3/1790 Frances Gibson, with issue.

**HILL, *later* NOEL-HILL (Richard Noel, 4th Baron Berwick)** Born London 7/11/1774, s. 1st Baron Berwick (Attingham Hall, Atcham, Shropshire) and Anne Vernon. St John's, Cambridge 1792, BA1793, MA1795, dn97 (Glos.), p98 (Glos.). R. Sutton, Shropshire 1799-1845, R. Berrington, Shropshire 1799-1845, R. Thornton le Moors, Cheshire 1799-1846. Died Attingham Hall 28/9/1848 aged 73 [C11863] Married Shrewsbury, Shropshire 16/1/1800 Frances Maria Mostyn-Owen, with clerical son. Assumed title as Noel-Hill 1824. Mayor of Shrewsbury 1824-5. en.wikipedia.org/wiki/Richard_Noel-Hill,_4th_Baron_Berwick

**HILL (Samuel)** Born Worcester. Literate: dn98 (Wor.), p00 (Wor.), [BA1820, MA1822, LLD 1822 but NiVoF or Al.Dub.] R. Snargate, Kent 1824-[40]. Died 8/4/1852 [C156516] Married Kent April 1816 Jane Stephana Bond (w).

**HILL (Thomas)** Bapt. Bromsberrow, Glos. 18/3/1772, s. Joseph Hill. Trinity, Oxford 1789, BA1793, dn95 (Wor.), p96 (Wor.). R. Staunton, Worcs. 1799 to death on or about 18/1/1861, leaving £5,000 [C121395] Widow Susannah.

**HILL (Thomas)** Trinity, Cambridge 1805, BA 1810, dn11 (Lin.), p12 (Lin.), MA1813, BD 1823. V. Elmton w. Creswell, Derbys. 1813-22, R. Badgeworth, Glos. 1821 [C154117], V. Chesterfield, Derbys. 1822-46, Archdeacon of Derby 1847-73 (res.), Canon Residentiary (w. Prebendal Stalls of Offley and Flixton annexed) in Lichfield Cathedral 1851-63, PC. Hasland, Derbys. 1851-63. Died Harrogate, Yorks. 14/9/1875 aged 87, leaving £14,000 [C11871. Boase. DEB]

**HILL (Valentine)** Born Wells-next-the-Sea, Norfolk, s. John Hill (of Gressenhall, Norfolk). Caius, Cambridge 1797, BA1806, dn06 (Nor.), p96 (Nor.), MA1810. R. Wells next the Sea 1806 to death 9/12/1851 aged 72 [C113522]

**HILL (William Charles)** Bapt. Bedminster, Somerset 26/1/1790, s. William Hill. Exeter, Oxford 1808, BA1812, dn16 (B&W), p19 (Ex.). R. Trentishoe, Devon 1822, V. (and patron) of Fremington, Devon 1829 to death 1855 (1st q.) [C41375]

**HILLIARD (Frederic Joseph)** Born Cowley, Middx. 9/5/1797, s. Edward Herbert Hilliard and Elizabeth Stafford Crosier. Worcester, Oxford 1815, then Peterhouse, Cambridge, dn20 (London), BA1821, p21 (London). R. (and patron) of Little Wittenham, Berks. 1821 to death 8/2/1861, leaving £7,000 [C94903] Married Ropley, Hants. 4/8/1824 Mary Duthy, with issue. Brother below?

**HILLIARD (John)** From Westminster, London, s. Edward Hilliard. Worcester, Oxford 1797 (aged 17), BCL1804 [adm. Lincoln's Inn 1797] dn04 (Ox.), p04 (Ox.). R. (and patron) of Cowley, Middx. 1807-51, R. Long Wittenham, Berks. 1813-18 (res.). Died 25/6/1851 [C31252] Brother above?

**HILLYERD, HILLYARD, HILLIARD (Samuel John)** Bapt. Rotherhithe, Surrey 14/3/1784, s. Nicholas John and Mary Hillyerd (or Hillyard). S/M Farnley Tyas, Yorks. to 1819. Literate: dn19 (Ex. for York), p23 (York), Chap. of the Donative of Tattersall, Lincs. 1824-46, V. Semperingham, Lincs. 1846 to death (Pointon, Lincs.) 29/6/1861, leaving £1,500 [C131493. Boase. YCO] Married Westminster, London 10/5/1807 Mary Chawner, with issue.

**HILTON (Richard)** Bapt. Knockin, Shropshire 11/6/1777, s. Richard Hilton. Pembroke, Oxford 1795, BA1799, dn00 (C&L), p01 (C&L). PC. Dudleston, Ellesmere, Shropshire 1823 to death 1838 (1st q.) aged 60 [C11886]

**HINCKLEY (John)** Bapt. Lichfield, Staffs. 27/7/1796, s. Thomas and Catherine Hinckley. Christ Church, Oxford 1815, then St Mary Hall, BA1819, dn19 (C&L), p20 (Chester for C&L), MA1828. PC. King's Bromley (Bromley Regis), Staffs. 1829-67, V. Alrewas, Staffs. 1830-2 (res.), V. Sheriff Hales w. Woodcote, Staffs. 1832 to death (unm.) 9/10/1867, leaving £16,000 [C11896. ODNB]

**HIND, HINDE (John)** Born Whitehaven, Cumberland 14/8/1796. St John's, Cambridge 1818, BA1817, then Sidney 1819, MA1821, dn22 (Lin.), p23 (Lin.), Fellow 1823-4 (res. on marriage). PC. Ludford, Heref. 1825-[38]. Granted Civil List pension of £100 in 1858. Died Cambridge 17/12/1867, leaving £1,000 [C64474. ODNB. Boase] Married 1824 Mary Hexham, with issue. F.R.S. Mathematician.

**HIND (Richard)** Born Kirkby Ravensworth, Yorks., s. Richard Hind (of Gaylords, Yorks.). Trinity, Cambridge 1798 (aged 19), then Clare 1801, BA1803, dn04 (Peterb.), MA1806, p09 (Lin. for Peterb.). R. Luddington (-in-the-Brook) w. Caldecote, Northants. 1831 to death (Polebrook, Northants.) 17/9/1848 [C64475] Married Oundle, Northants. 17/3/1808 Susanna Bland.

**HINDE, HIND (Thomas)** Born Dublin, s. Benjamin Hinde. Christ Church, Oxford 1805 (aged 18), BA1809, dn11 (Lin.), MA1812, Chap. 1812-25, p13 (Ox.). V. (and patron) of Featherstone, Pontefract, Yorks. 1824 to death 3/2/1874 aged 88, leaving £600 [C31259] Wife Ann, and issue.

**HINDLE (Joseph)** Bapt. Harwood, Lancs. 1/11/1795, s. Christopher and Elizabeth Hindle. St John's, Cambridge 1813, BA1818, Fellow 1818-30, BA1821, dn21 (Ely), p23 (Ely), BD1828. V. (Knowle) Higham, Kent 1829 to death 29/12/1874 aged 79, leaving £40,000 [C7151] Wife Susanna, with issue. 'An earnest, simple Christian minister'.

**HINDS (John Thomas)** Born Dundalk, Co. Louth 1801, s. of a London physician [others say born Pulham, Dorset, but of Dundalk extraction]. Trinity, Cambridge 1818, dn22 (Salis.), BA1823, p24 (C&L), MA1832. PC. Stone, Dorset 1826-30, Min. Trinity Chapel, Conduit St., London 1831, R. Pulham 1832 to death (Torquay), a widower 24/12/1873 aged 71, leaving £3,000. Lived latterly at Weymouth, Dorset [C11689] Married Stone, Staffs. 9/8/1832 1832 Margaret Dorothea Clowes, with issue.

**HINTON (Anthony)** From Holborn, London, s. Rev. Anthony Hinton, sen. Merton, Oxford 1764 (aged 21), SCL, dn65 (London), p67 (Lin.). V. Great Missenden, Bucks. 1768-87, V. Granborough, Bucks. 1775 and V. Norwood, Middx. 1775 to death 1/7/1838 aged 95 (CCEd has his father's date of death) [C64479]

**HINXMAN (Henry)** Bapt. Wishford, Wilts. 21/6/1785, s. Henry Hinxman and Mary Robinson. Oriel, Oxford 1802, BA1806, dn08 (Ex. for Salis.), p09 (B&W). PC. St Sampson (o/w Golant), Cornwall 1829-54, Min. Bentinck Proprietary Chapel, London 1833-[4]. Died Bristol 23/4/1854. Lived in Bath [C41377] Married Salisbury Cathedral 7/4/1808 Charlotte Colton, w. clerical s. Joshua Simon Hird.

**HIRD (Joshua)** Bapt. City of London 29/8/1769, s. William Hird and Sophia Lewis. King's, Cambridge 1788, BA1792, Fellow 1791-1804, dn92 (Salis.), MA1795, p95 (Salis.), DD 1811. R. Monxton, Hants. 1803 and V. Ellingham St Mary, Hants. 1811 to death 20/5/1846 [C94905] Married Old Alresford, Hants. 4/12/1808 Sophia Lockton (a clergy dau.), with issue.

**HIRD, *born* WICKHAM (Lamplugh)** Born Cottingley Hall, Bingley, Yorks., s. Lt.-Col. Henry Wickham and Elizabeth Lamplugh (a clergy dau.). Christ Church, Oxford 1787, BA 1791, dn92 (Car. for York), p92 (York), MA 1793. V. Paull, Yorks. 1793-1842, PC. Kayingham, Yorks. 1793-1821 (res.), Prebend of Botevant in York Minster 1802 to death (Boston Spa, Yorks.) 3/12/1842 aged 75. Probate granted (as Hird) 22/5/1858 at under £20 [C6453 under Wickham. YCO] Married (1) Guisley, Yorks. 2/2/1795 Sarah Elizabeth Hird (and changed surname, she d.1812), with issue (2) Thirsk, Yorks. 13/7/1813 Hannah Frances Sturdy Lascelles (a clergy dau.), further issue. Surviving ch. reverted to name Wickham in 1842. *J.P., D.L.* West Riding Yorks.

**HITCHINGS (James)** Bapt. Oxford 13/1/1790, s. Sir Edward Hitchings (Mayor of Oxford - but F. says *pleb!*) and Elizabeth Benwell. Christ Church, Oxford 1806, BA1810, dn13 (Ox.), MA1814, p18 (Salis.). [Ensign with the Oxford local militia 1812] V. Wargrave, Berks. 1826 to death 7/5/1850 [C21699] Married Sunninghill, Berks. Harriet Cooke, with clerical son Edmund John Hitchings.

**HOARE (Charles James)** Born London 14/7/1781, s. Henry Hoare (banker, and one of the founders of the C.M.S.) and Lydia Henrietta Malortie (from Hanover). St John's, Cambridge 1799, BA1803, dn04 (Win.), MA 1806, p06 (Win.), Fellow 1806-11. V. Blandford Forum, Dorset 1807-21, R. (and patron) of Godstone (o/w Walkinstead), Surrey 1821-65 (and RD South East Ewell 1829), Archdeacon of Winchester 1829-47, Canon of 8th Prebend in Winchester Cathedral 1831-65 [total income £1,190], Archdeacon of Surrey 1847-59 (res.). Died 15/1/1865, leaving £30,000 [C52959. ODNB. Boase. DEB] Married Mitcham, Surrey 4/7/1811 Jane Isabella Holden (Moorgate, Yorks.), with clerical son.

**HOARE (Edward Hatch)** Born Co. Limerick 13/7/1790, s. Rev. Edward Henry Hoare and Elizabeth Davenport. TCD1810, BA1813, p15 (Lin.), then Trinity, Cambridge 1826, MA1826. R. ('Comportioner', and patron) of Upper Isham (o/w Isham Superior), Northants. 1826, V. Barkby, Leics. 1826-73, PC. Thurmaston, Leics. 1828. Died (Malvern, Worcs.) 13/2/1873, leaving £6,000 [C64486. Al.Dub.] Married Charlotte Rebecca Stewart, with issue. Brother below.

**HOARE (Henry)** Born Co. Limerick, s. Rev. Edward Henry Hoare and Elizabeth Davenport. TCD1810 (aged 17), BA1813, dn26, p27. V. (and patron) of Framfield, Sussex 1830 to death 16/4/1866, leaving £10,000 [C63888. Al.Dub.] Married Chobham St Lawrence, Surrey 5/10/1820 Margaret Bainbridge, with issue. Brother above.

**HOARE (Richard Peter)** Born Kelsey Park, Bromley, Kent 25/12/1807, s. Peter Richard Hoare (banker) and Arabella Penelope Eliza Greene. Trinity, Cambridge 1826, BA1830, dn31 (Salis.), p32 (Salis.), MA1833. R. Stourton w. Gasper, Wilts. 1832 to death, living at Southfeld House, Frome. Died 3/4/1846, *s.p.* [C94907]

**HOBART, *later* HOBART-HAMPDEN (Augustus Edward, 6th Earl of Buckinghamshire)** Born Ripon, Yorks. 1/11/1793, s. Hon. George Vere Hobart and Jane Cataneo. BNC, Oxford 1812, BA1815, dn17 (Lin.), p17 (Lin.), MA1818. R. Benington, Lincs. 1817-20 (res.), Prebend of Kinvaston in Wolverhampton Collegiate Church 1818, R. Welbourn, Lincs. 1818-20 (res.), R. Walton le Wolds, Leics. 1820.

Died Hampden House, Bucks. 29/10/1885 aged 91, leaving £32,747 [C11913. Boase] Married (1) Leamington, Warwicks. 12/9/1816 Mary Vaughan-Williams (d.1825), with issue (2) 15/8/1826 Maria Isabella Egremont (a clergy dau.), with clerical son. Assumed the title 1849, and the additional surname of Hampden 1878.

**HOBART (Henry Charles)** Born Richmond, Surrey 30/11/1773, s. Hon. Henry Hobart (and grandson of the 1st Earl of Buckinghamshire) and Anne Margaret Bristow. Christ's, Cambridge 1792, MA before 1797, dn97 (Nor.), p97 (Nor.). R. Bere Ferrers, Devon 1797, Bishop's (o/w Episcopi) Prebend and Canon Residentiary in Hereford Cathedral 1819-44, V. Kempley, Glos. 1821-39. Died 17/1/1844 aged 70 [C105752] Married 5/5/1800 Langley, Norfolk Mary, dau. Sir Thomas Beauchamp-Proctor, 2nd Bart., 2s.

**HOBART (Henry Lewis, Hon.)** Born Nocton, Lincs 1774, s. 3rd Earl of Buckinghamshire and Albinia Bertie. Christ's, Cambridge 1793, MA 1797, dn97 (Win.), p98 (Win.), DD1816. R. Chipping Warden, Northants 1798-1815, R. Edgcote, Northants 1801-15, 2nd Prebend of Canterbury Cathedral 1804-16, V. Nocton 1815-46, R. St Dionis Backchurch, City of London 1815-28, R. Great Haseley, Oxon. 1816-46, Dean of Windsor (with Dean of Wolverhampton Collegiate Church *in commendam*) 1816 (and Registrar of the Order of the Garter) to death, V. Fulmer, Bucks 1823-42, V. Wantage, Berks. 1828. Died (Nocton) 8/5/1846 [C31264. Kaye] Married Richmond upon Thames, Surrey 5/10/1824 Charlotte Selina Moore, with issue.

**HOBBS (Thomas)** Born Cossington, Som., s. Rev. Charles Hobbs. Oriel, Oxford 1794 (aged 16), BA1798, MA1801, p01 (Ex. for B&W). V. Shapwick, Som. 1801-6, R. Cossington 1801 and R. Templeton, Devon 1821 both to death. Dom. Chap. to Marquess of Headfort 1801. Died 24/10/1833 (CCEd says 2/1/1834) [C41378]

**HOBLYN (Edward)** Born Gwennap, Cornwall 22/4/1782, s. Rev. Robert Hoblyn. University, Oxford 1801, BA1805, dn08 (Win. for Roch.), p09 (Roch.). V. Mylor w. Mabe, Cornwall 1823 to death 8/2/1868 aged 85, leaving £2,000 [C7153] Married Bath 1808 Mary Parker, w. issue.

**HOBLYN (Robert)** Born Perranzabuloe, Cornwall 27/12/1751, s. Samuel Hoblyn and Joan/Jane Hawke. Christ Church, Oxford 1768, BA1771, MA1774, dn75 (Ox.), p76 (Ox.). PC. West Molesey, Surrey 1830 to death (Bath) 20/1/1839 [C31265] Married 26/3/1778 Mary Mallet, with clerical son.

**HOBSON (Leonard Jasper)** Born Leeds 24/12/1777, s. John Hobson and Mary Crampton. Literate: dn00 (York), p02 (York). S/M Doncaster G/S, Yorks. 1811; PC. Mexborough, Yorks. 1817-60 [blank in ERC], PC. High Melton (on the Hill), Yorks. 1826 to death Mexborough) 2/7/1860, leaving £600 [C85980. YCO] Married Mexborough 10/10/1803 Dorothy Varah, with issue.

**HOBSON (Thomas)** Bapt. Holwell, Somerset 26/8/1763, s. Rev. Thomas, sen. and Elizabeth Hobson. Queen's, Oxford 1781, BA1785, dn86 (Ox.), MA1788, p89 (Ox.). V. Hermitage, Dorset 1796-1832 and R. Pentridge, Dorset 1801-32, R. Nether Compton w. Over Compton, Dorset 1814-24, R. Lydlinch, Dorset 1818 to death. Dom. Chap. to 16th Baron Le Despencer 1818. Died 6/12/1832 (CCEd says 11/2/1833) [C31571] Married Poole, Dorset 24/2/1801 Elizabeth Whitehead Oke.

**HOBSON (William)** Literate: dn16, p17, then St Catharine's, Cambridge 1818 (a Ten Year Man, BD1830). R. (and patron) of Sisland (o/w Sizeland), Norfolk 1819-67, PC. Welshampton, Shropshire 1827, PC. Thurton, Norfolk 1829 to death 31/12/1867, leaving £5,000 [C11970] Clerical son.

**HOCKER (William)** Born St Enoder, Newlyn, Cornwall 24/2/1772, s. Rev. William Hocker, sen. Trinity, Cambridge 1790, then Pembroke 1791, BA1794, dn94 (Salis. for Ex.), p96 (Ex.), MA1806. R. St Mewan, Cornwall 1802 and V. Lanteglose by Fowey, Cornwall 1806 to death. Dom. Chap. to 3rd Viscount Falmouth 1806. Died 5/4/1842 aged 70 [C145051] Married Nymet Tracey (o/w Bow), Devon 18/8/1806 Maria Wreford, with issue. Confusion between father and son.

**HOCKIN (William)** Born St Phillack, Cornwall. 19/12/1776, s. Rev. William Hockin, sen. Jesus, Cambridge 1795, dn00 (Ex.), p01 (Ex.), LLB1802. R. (and patron) of St Phillack w. Gwithian 1809 to death 22/4/1853 [C145055] Married 3/1/1804 Peggy Williams (a clergy dau.), with clerical son.

**HODGE (John)** Bapt. Clyst Honiton, Devon 30/6/1752 (CCEd thus). Emmanuel, Cambridge 1769, migrated to Exeter, Oxford 1770, no degree, dn75 (Ex.), p76 (Ex.). PC. Newton Poppleford, Devon 1806, V. Cullompton, Devon (and Preacher throughout the Diocese of Exeter) 1830 to death 10/10/1833 [C145058] 'He was of a most benevolent disposition with a highly cultivated mind', etc.

**HODGE (Matthew)** Born North Petherton, Som. 30/11/1776, s. Rev. Matthew Hodge, sen. and Elizabeth Davey. Balliol, Oxford 1795, Fellow 1798-1818, BA1799, dn99 (B&W), p01 (Ox.), MA1804. V. Hurstbourne Priors, Hants. 1807-17, R. Fillingham, Lincs. 1817 and V. Ingham, Lincs. 1823 to death 15/1/1852 [C31572. Kaye. Bennett1] Married St Pancras, London 7/12/1848 Mrs Sarah (Keith) Shephard.

**HODGES (Charles Bishope)** Born Holmes Chapel, Cheshire 17/7/1795, s. Rev. Thomas Hodges and Mary Hilditch. Queen's, Oxford 1813, BA1817, dn18 (Chester), p19 (Chester), MA1820. PC. Congleton, Cheshire 1831-8, PC. Byley cum Lees, Middlewich, Cheshire 1838 (and Chaplain of Somerford Park Chapel, Astbury, Cheshire 1831) to death (Holmes Chapel) 16/2/1864, leaving £3,000 [C169191] Married Astbury 27/1/1829 Jane Reade, w. issue.

**HODGES (Henry)** Born Wirksworth, Derbys. 25/7/1779, s. Thomas Hallett Hodges. Trinity, Cambridge 1796, BA1801, dn02 (Win.), p03 (Win. for Cant.), MA1804. V. Benenden, Kent 1803-37, R. Beckley, Sussex 1805 and R. Frittenden, Kent 1805 to death. Dom. Chap. to Henrietta Laura, Countess of Bath 1804. Died 1/7/1837 [C63890]

**HODGES (James)** From Leicester, s. George Hodges (banker). Emmanuel, Cambridge 1793, BA1798, dn99 (Lin.), Fellow 1800, MA1801, p01 (Lin.), BD1808. V. Owlesbuy w. Twyford, Hants. 1814 and R. Chilcomb, Hants. 1826 to death 24/4/1849 aged 72 [C64494]

**HODGES (Thomas [Frederick Amelius Parry]** *or* **F.T.A.H.?)** Bapt. Easton Gray, Glos. 19/11/1796, s. Walter Parry and Mary Hodges. New, Oxford 1821, Fellow 1821-31, BCL1829, dn29, p30, DCL 1838. Fellow of Winchester College 1851-80. V. North Clifton, Notts. 1832-80, V. Lyme Regis, Dorset 1832-80, Prebend of Lyme and Halstock in Salisbury Cathedral, and Prebend of Clifton in Lincoln Cathedral to death 27/10/1880, leaving £14,000 [C94908] Some say 'Frederick Thomas' only. Surrogate.

**HODGES (Thomas Stephen)** Born Canterbury 12/5/1794, s. John Hodges and Hannah Long. University, Oxford 1814, BA1817, dn18 (Salis.), p20 (London), MA1821. R. Little Waltham, Herts. 1828 to death 18/5/1842 [C119494] Married Canterbury 18/1/1820 Julia Boteler, w. issue.

**HODGKIN (John)** Born Drigg, Cumberland. Trinity, Cambridge 1811, BA before 1817, dn17 (Ex.), p19 (Salis. for Ex.). V. North Molton, Devon 1820 to death. Dom. Chap. to 1st Earl of Morley 1817. Died 5/1/1840 aged 57 [C94911]

**HODGKINSON (Edmund)** Bapt. Matlock, Derbys. 17/2/1788, s. Joseph and Abigail Hodgkinson. Literate: dn17 (Chester for York), p17 (York). PC. Stainburn, Yorks. 1819, PC. Baildon, Otley, Yorks. 1825, PC. Burley, Yorks. 1834 to death 1848 (2nd q.) [C131500. YCO] With issue.

**HODGKINSON (Henry)** From Anderton, Cheshire, s. James Hodgkinson. BNC, Oxford 1776 (aged 21), BA1779. dn79 (Ox.), p81 (Ox.), MA1782. R. Arborfield, Berks. 1797 and R. Shadingfield, Suffolk 1805 to death 20/8/1839 [C31582]

**HODGKINSON (Joseph)** Born Prescot, Lancs. 15/8/1773, s. Joseph Hodgkinson. BNC, Oxford 1792, BA1796, Vice-Principal 1814, Fellow to 1819, dn98 (Wor.), MA1798, p98 (Chester), BD 1811. V. Didcot, Berks. 1817 to death 6/6/1851 [C94912] Married Thornton-le-Moors, Cheshire 3/4/1820 Ann Dutton.

**HODGSON (Charles)** Born Oxford 29/11/1786, s. Rev. Bernard and Harriet Hodgson. Christ Church, Oxford 1804, BA 1808, dn10 (York), MA1810, p10 (Ox.), Student [Fellow] to 1818. PC. Great Torrington, Devon, 1812-17, PC. Hawkhurst, Kent 1817, R. St Tudy, Cornwall (and Preacher throughout the Diocese of Exeter) 1817 to death 17/5/1846 aged 59 [C31585. YCO]

**HODGSON (Charles)** Born Everton, Liverpool 23/7/1801, s. Ellis Ashton Hodgson (merchant, of Snydale Hall, Ferrybridge, Yorks.) and Annabella Dixon. [Sandhurst Military

College] Magdalene, Cambridge 1820, BA1824, dn25 (Bristol for York), p25 (York), MA1830. R. Barton le Street, Selby, Yorks. 1833 (living at Snydale Hall) to death (Hastings) 21/12/1869 aged 68. Will not traced [C52963. YCO. *Memorial volume of the late Rev. Charles Hodgson, MA. With a biographical preface,* by G.T. Fox (1872 and photo.)] Married Rippingale, Lincs. May 1831 Jane Cracroft (a clergy dau.), many ch. C.M.S. District Secretary for Yorks.

**HODGSON (Charles)** [BA but NiVoF] V. Gatton, Surrey 1827-[33]. Died? [C76960]

**HODGSON (Charles [Henry])** Born Leeds 20/12/1781, s. William Hodgson and Mary Mortimer. Queen's, Oxford 1799, BA1803, dn04 (Salis.), p05 (Ox.), migrated to Pembroke, Cambridge, MA1812. S/M Salisbury Close Free G/S 1805; R. Berwick in Tisbury (or Berwick St Leonard), Dorset 1822-3 (res.), V. Kington St Michael (o/w Keinton), Wilts. 1824 [blank in ERC] and Vicar Choral in Salisbury Cathedral 1825 to death 26/4/1856 aged 76 [C94913] Married Calne, Wilts. 17/12/1805 Elizabeth Margaret Greenwood (a clergy dau.), with clerical son George Mortimer Hodgson. Surrogate.

**HODGSON (Christopher)** Born Whitchurch, Leeds 23/2/1760, s. Christopher Hodgson (a Cambridge tax collector). Pembroke, Cambridge 1787, dn90 (Peterb.), p91 (Peterb.), LLB 1794. R. Marholm, Northants. 1791 to death. Dom. Chap. to Earl Fitzwilliam. Died 11/3/1849 [C110317]

**HODGSON (Edward)** Born Buxton, Derbys. 19/5/1776, s. Brian and Ellen Hodgson. Peterhouse, Cambridge 1793, then Corpus Christi 1795, BA1797, Fellow 1798, dn98 (London), p99 (London), MA1800. R. Laindon (w. Basildon), Essex (and Preacher throughout the Diocese of London) 1803 and V. Rickmansworth, Herts. 1805 to death. Chap. to 'the last Embassy to Paris'; to Bishop of London 1803. Died 4/9/1853 [C119497] Married (1) London 10/2/1807 Jane Fullerton (d.1809) (2) Hatfield, Herts. 18/6/1812 Georgiana Franks (d.1813) (3) St George's Hanover Square, London 21/9/1815 Charlotte Pemberton (of Bombay), with distinguished issue.

**HODGSON (Francis)** Born Croydon, Surrey 16/11/1781, s. Rev. James Hodgson (R. Humber, Heref.) and Jane Coke. King's, Cambridge 1800, Fellow 1803-15, BA1804, MA1807, dn14 (Lin.), p14 (Nor. for Bristol), BD1840. Private tutor to sons of Lady Ann Lambton 1803-5; S/M Eton College 1807, Provost of Eton College 1840-52; V. Bakewell, Derbys. 1816-36, Archdeacon of Derby 1836-40, V. Edensor ['in Chatsworth Park'] w. Bakewell 1838-40, R. Cottisford, Oxon. 1842 to death (Eton) 29/12/1852 [C21945. ODNB. Boase. J.T. Hodgson, *Memoir of the Rev. Francis Hodgson, scholar, poet and divine. With numerous letters from Lord Byron and others* (1878. 2v.)] Married (1) 15/8/1815 Susanna Matilda Taylor (of Boreham House, Herts., d.1833) (2) Marylebone, London 1838 Elizabeth, dau. of Lord Denman, w. clericasl s. James Thomas Denman. 'Close' to Byron.

**HODGSON (George Marmaduke)** Born Stapleton Park, Darrington, Yorks. 22/10/1784, s. Ellis Leconby and Annabella Hodgson. Literate: dn27 (York), p28 (York). V. Frodingham, Lincs. 1829 to death (York) 16/11/1858, leaving £600 [C64503. YCO] Married York 23/2/1841 Annabelle Hird (w).

**HODGSON (Hugh)** Born Holborn, London 20/4/1795, s. John Hodgson (of Buckden, Hunts.) and Sarah St Barbe. St Catharine's, Cambridge 1813, BA1818, dn18 (Lin.), p19 (Lin.), MA1821, then Trinity 1825. Usher at Westminster School 1820-46; V. Idmiston w. Porton, Wilts. 1820-62 [C94914 as Hodson], PC. Otham, Kent 1850 to death 27/1/1862, leaving under £600 [C64509] Married Sonning, Berks. 7/8/1826 Harriet Knyvett (w). Brothers John, and Thomas Douglas, below.

**HODGSON (Jacob)** Literate: dn87 (Car.), p87 (Chester). PC. (Great) Crosby, Sefton, Lancs. 1817 to death 27/3/1840 aged 77 [C6012]

**HODGSON (John)** Bapt. Shap, Westmorland 13/11/1779, s. Isaac Hodgson (a stonemason) and Elizabeth Rawes. Schoolmaster. Literate: dn04 (Car. for Durham) [but note a second man of same name ordained deacon at Durham in same year], p05 (C&L for Durham). PC. Jarrow, Durham 1808-33 (res.), V. Kirkwhelpington, Northumberland 1823-33 (res.), V. Hartburn, Northumberland 1833 to death 12/6/1845 aged 66 [C130507. J. Raine, *A memoir of the Rev. John Hodgson, Vicar of Hartburn* (1857. 2v.)] Married 11/1/1810 Jane Bridget Kell, Heworth, 9 ch. Raised public concern for mine safety after the Felling Mine Disaster 1812 in his parish (92 died; created the Sunderland Society for Mine Safety, and was instrumental in the development of the Davy Lamp). The most important historian of Northumberland.

**HODGSON (John)** Born Holborn London 5/5/1790, s. John Hodgson and Sarah St Barbe. Trinity, Cambridge 1814, dn16 (Bristol), p17 (London), BA1818, MA1822. PC. Oare, Kent 1820-6, V. Kennington, Kent 1821-35, V. Sittingbourne, Kent 1826-35, V. St Peter in Thanet, Kent 1835-57 (and RD of Westbere 1852-56). Dom. Chap. to 1st Baron Harris of Seringapatam and Mysore 1826; Sec. to the Clergy Mutual Assurance Society (London) 1857-70. Died 28/11/1870, leaving £9,000. [C136949] Married (as a minor) Throwley, Kent 2/10/1809 Sarah Harris, with clerical s. John George Hodgson. Brothers Hugh (above), and Thomas Douglas (below): freepages.genealogy.rootsweb.ancestry.com/~kingsman/kingsman/.../indiI11260.html

**HODGSON (John)** [NiVoF] Literate. Curate of Lye, Old Swinford, Worcs. 1816 [ERC thus], R. Sheinton, Shropshire 1823-[44]. Died? [C11978]

**HODGSON (Joseph)** [NiVoF] S/M Reigate Free G/S 1814; R. Leigh, Surrey 1823-[43]. Died? [C76965] A man of this name in YCO.

**HODGSON (Robert)** Bapt. Congleton, Cheshire 22/9/1773, s. Robert Hodgson and Mildred Porteous (a clergy dau.). Peterhouse, Cambridge 1791, BA1795, dn96 (London), Fellow 1796, p97 (London), MA1798, DD1816. R. Laindon, Essex 1797-1803, R. St George's Hanover Square, London [net income £1,550] 1803-44, V. Hillingdon w. Uxbridge, Middx. 1810-40, Archdeacon of St Albans 1814-16, Dean of Chester 1816-20, Dean of Carlisle 1820 to death. Chap. to Bishop of London (his great-uncle); Chap. General to the Forces 1824; Chap. in Ordinary. Died 10/10/1844 [C3408] Married London 23/2/1804 Mary Tucker (a military dau.), with issue.

**HODGSON (Robert)** Bapt. Bootle, Cumberland 10/5/1782, s. Robert Hodgson and Bridget Parker. Literate: dn05 (York), p06 (York). PC. Kirkstall, Leeds, Yorks. 1829 to death 18/12/1838 aged 56 (from lockjaw as the result of a carriage accident, 'the jury returning a verdict of manslaughter against the hackney coachman who occasioned the accident')

[C136370. Venn to distinguish him from a Cambridge contemporary. YCO] Married 1812 Mary Hobson.

**HODGSON (Thomas Douglas)** Born Buckden, Hunts. 31/8/1796, s. John Hodgson and Sarah St Barbe. Trinity, Cambridge 1814, BA1819, dn20 (Ely for Salis.), p20 (Salis.), MA 1822. R. East Woodhay, Hants. 1825 [gross income £1,480 in CR65] to death. Dom. Chap. to Bp of Winchester 1806. Died 8/2/1884, leaving £4,348-1s-3d. [C64518] Married (1) Norton, Kent 18/3/1828 Sarah Rice (a clergy dau. of Great Holland, Essex, she d.1842), w. issue (2) Buckland, Surrey 15/7/1845 Maria Sophia Carbonell (Haling Park, Surrey). J.P. Hants. Brothers Hugh, and John, above.

**HODSON (George)** Born Carlisle 1788, s. George Hodson (merchant) and Ann Hewitt. Trinity, Cambridge 1805, BA1810, then Magdalene 1810, Fellow 1810, dn11 (Ex. for Ely), p12 (Peterb.), MA1814. PC. St Katharine Cree, City of London 1814-29 (res.), PC. Birmingham Christ Church [blank in ERC] 1824-32 (res.), V. Colwich, Staffs. 1828-51, 4th Canon Residentiary of Lichfield Cathedral 1829-33 (res.) (Chancellor and 2nd Canon 1833-55), Archdeacon of Stafford 1829-55, V. Lichfield St Mary 1850 to death. Chap. to Stanstead Park and tutor there. Died (cholera) at Riva, Lake Garda, Italy 13/8/1855 [C11983. Boase. D. Robinson (ed.), *Visitations of the Archdeaconry of Stafford, 1829-1841* (HMSO, 1980 and photo.) is exhaustive] Married Chesterton, Cambs. 8/7/1815 Mary Somerrell Stephen, and had issue.

**HODSON (John Johnston)** From Wigan, Lancs., s. James Hodson. St Mary Hall, Oxford 1817 (aged 25), BA1820, dn21 (Lin.), p22 (Lin.), MA1823. V. Yelvertoft, Northants. 1828 to death 22/1/1869, leaving £45,000 [C11986]

**HODSON (Septimus)** Born Huntingdon 17/2/1763, s. Rev. Robert Hodson and Mary Barnes. Caius, Cambridge 1779 [CCEd adds BA] MB1784, dn87 (Chester for Lin.), p87 (Lin.). PC. Little Raveley, Hunts. 1787-1833, R. Thrapston, Northants. 1789-1828. Chap. in Ordinary; Chap. to the Asylum for Female Orphans. Died 12/12/1833 (CCEd says 14/11/1834) [C64574. ODNB] Married (1) St Pancras, London 9/6/1783 Ann Bell (d.1784) (2) Stamford, Lincs. 15/3/1786 Charlotte Affleck (a clergy dau., d.1809) (3) Doncaster 114/3/1809 Francis

Fenwick /(d.1824) (4) South Kirkby, Yorks. 16/10/1826 Margaret Holford. Port. online.

**HOE (Thomas)** Bapt. Dalby-on-the-Wolds, Leics. 25/12/1759, s. Thomas Hoe (*or* Hooe) and Elizabeth Hawley. Literate: dn83 (York), p84 (Nor. for York). V. Kinoulton, Notts. 1800 (a Peculiar) and V. Long Clawson, Leics. 1803 to death 1848 (1st q.) aged 88 [C102409. YCO]

**HOGARTH (John Henry)** Bapt. Rickmansworth, Herts. 29/6/1787, s. Henry Spence Hogarth and Lucy Baker. Emmanuel, Cambridge 1813, dn14 (Ely for London), p15 (London), LLB1819, then Wadham, Oxford 1824, DCL1824. V. Harlington, Beds. 1818-22, R. (and patron) of Stifford, Essex 1821-34 (res.). Died St Servan, St Malo, France 13/7/1863, leaving under £450 [C64626] Married St James, Westminster, London 18/5/1808 Harriot Hole, with issue. *J.P.* Essex.

**HOGG (Edward)** From King's Lynn, Norfolk. Peterhouse, Cambridge 1801 (aged 17), s. George Hogge and Dorothy Tayler, BA1806, dn07 (Nor.), p18 (Nor.). R. Fornham St Martin, Suffolk 1814 to death 21/6/1869, leaving £8,000 [C113538] Married Elizabeth Ferrier by 1841, with child. Brother Martin, below.

**HOGG (James)** Literate: dn97 (Peterb.), p99 (Peterb.). S/M Kettering Free G/S 1801; R. Glendon, Northants. 1808-14, V. Geddington, Northants. 1814 (and Chap. of the Donative of Newton, Northants. 1814, and of the Donative of Great Oakley, Northants. 1814) to death 1844 (4th q.) [C110319]

**HOGGE (Martin)** Bapt. King's Lynn, Norfolk 10/7/1777, s. George Hogge and Dorothy Tayler. Oriel, Oxford 1795, BA1800, dn00 (Ex. for Nor.), p01 (Nor.), MA1802. R. Beachamwell, Norfolk 1801-24, R. Little Shelford, Cambs. 1802-6, R. South Acre, Norwich 1802 and R. West Winch, Norfolk 1823 to death. Dom. Chap. to 1st Marquess of Cholmondeley 1802. Died Swaffham, Norfolk 24/5/1846 [C100062] Married Castle Herdingham, Essex 3/2/1803 Elizabeth Swaine, w. clerical son George Hogge. Brother Edward, above.

**HOLBECH (Charles)** Bapt. Farnborough, Warwicks. 14/5/1782, s. William Holbech and Anne Woodhouse. Christ Church, Oxford 1801, BA1804, dn05 (Peterb.), p06 (Peterb.), MA1808.

V. Farnborough 1812 and PC. Radstone, Northants. 1812 to death 28/11/1837 [C11988]

**HOLBREY (William)** Bapt. Leeds 28/2/1794, s. James and Ann Holbrey. Literate: dn17 (York), p18 (York). Curate Sykehouse, Fisklake, Yorks. 1818, V. Barnby upon Don, Yorks. 1835 to death 10/5/1839 [C131505. YCO]

**HOLCOMBE (George)** Born St David's, Pembroke, s. Rev. George Holcombe, sen. (R. Pwllcrochan, Pembroke) and Catherine Stackhouse. St John's, Cambridge 1775 (aged 19), BA1779, Fellow, dn79 (Peterb.), p80 (St David's), MA1791, DD1806. R. Matlock, Derbys. 1780-1836, R. Osgathorpe, Leics. 1796-1836, R. East Leake w. West Leake, Yorks. 1804-36, 12th Prebend of Canterbury Cathedral 1815-22, Prebend of Westminster Abbey 1822 to death. Chaplain in Ordinary 1804. Died West Leake 7/2/1836 [C11992] Married Matlock 23/2/1781 Catherine Hurt (Derbys.), s. below.

**HOLCOMBE (George Francis)** Bapt. Wirksworth, Derbys. 15/10/1788, s. Rev. George Holcombe (above) and Catherine Hurt. St John's, Cambridge 1806, BA1811, Fellow 1811-19, dn11 (York), p12 (York), MA1814. V. Arnold, Notts. 1812 and R. Brinkley, Cambs. 1817 to death (Sherwood Lodge, Notts.) 24/8/1872 aged 84, leaving £18,000 [C109731. YCO] Married 1819 Isabella Hoason (Hodson?), with issue.

**HOLCOMBE (James Robertson)** Bapt. Cosheston, Pembroke 15/4/1799, s. Rev. John Holcombe and Sarah Mary Robertson. Jesus, Cambridge 1817, BA1820, Fellow 1821-40, dn22 (Ox.), MA1823, p23 (Ox.), BD1832. V. Steventon, Bucks. 1825, R. Nash w. Upton, Pembroke 1827-31, Prebend of Clydey in St David's Cathedral 1830, V. Pwllcrochan, Pembroke -- to death 24/3/1840, leaving under £20 (left unadministered) [C31589] Married Cosheston 4/4/1839 Mary Sophia Woods (w).

**HOLDEN (Charles Edward)** Born Great Yarmouth, Norfolk 20/1/1765, s. Rev. Edward Holden (R. Barsham, Suffolk) and Susanna Nissenden. Caius, Cambridge 1784, BA1788, dn88 (Nor.), p89 (Nor.). R. Laughton, Leics. 1797 (only), V. Great Cornard, Suffolk 1803-44. Died London 20/11/1849 [C64632] Married Sarah Sparrow (Gosfield Place, Essex).

**HOLDEN (George)** Bapt. Horton in Ribblesdale, Yorks. 12/6/1783, s. Rev. George Holden, sen. (schoolmaster) and Ann Procter. University of Glasgow, MA1805, dn07 (Car. for York), p08 (York). R. Maghull, Liverpool 1811-65, PC. Horton in Ribblesdale 1821-5. Died Maghull (unmarried) 19/3/1865 aged 81, leaving his library and half his wealth (£6,000) to Ripon Diocese [C130572. ODNB. Boase. YCO] For many years compiled the *Liverpool Tide Tables*, following his father and grandfather.

**HOLDEN (Hyla Willets)** Born Birmingham 8/6/1792, s. Hyla Holden and Mary Willets. Pembroke, Oxford 1810, BA1814, MA1819, p23 (Chester for C&L). PC. Erdington St Barnabas, Warwicks. 1824 to death (Kings Norton, Warwicks.) 4/8/1849 [C11996] Married Aston (juxta Birmingham) 28/2/1820 Ann Richards, with issue.

**HOLDEN (James Richard)** Born Aston on Trent, Derbys. 2/1/1807, s. Rev. Charles Edward Shuttleworth Holden (formerly Shuttleworth) and Rosamond Amelia Deane. Christ's, Cambridge 1823, BA 1830, dn30 (Lin.), p31 (C&L), MA1864. R. Pleasley, Derbys. 1831-56, R. Aston on Trent 1865-7, R. (and patron) of Lackford, Suffolk 1867 (living at Lackford Manor) to death 13/11/1876, leaving £25,000 [C11744] Married 16/7/1840 Mary Moore, of Ruddington, Notts. *s.p.* J.P. Suffolk and Notts.

**HOLDEN (John Rose)** Born Birmingham 9/9/1772, s. Rev. John Rose Holden, sen. (R. Upminster, Essex) and Mary Emily Tovey. Trinity, Cambridge 1790, BA1795, dn95 (London), p97 (London), then Clare, MA1819. (succ. his father as) R. Upminster 1799 to death 28/1/1862 aged 89, leaving £16,000 [C128047] Married 1795 Margaret Wheeler.

**HOLDICH (Thomas)** Born Thrapston, Northants. 14/10/1771, s. Edward Holdich (of Farndon, Northants.) and Anne Peach. Clare, Cambridge 1790, BA1794, dn94 (Ely for Peterb.), p96 (Peterb.), MA1797. R. Burton Overy, Leics. 1801-11 (res.), R. Maidwell, Northants. 1808 and R. Draughton, Northants. 1841 to death. Dom. Chap. to 1st Earl of Lonsdale 1808. Died Brixworth, Northants. 15/4/1866 aged 94, leaving £1,500 [C64640] Married (1) Whittlesey, Cambs. 28/3/1802 Anne Haynes (d.1806), w. clerical s. Thomas Preach Holdich (2) Little Ponton, Lincs. 3/6/1808 Elizabeth Laura Maydwell (of Whittlesey), with further (and clerical) issue.

**HOLDSWORTH, *born* KELLY (George Kelly)** Born Featherstone, Yorks. 10/6/1793, s. Rev. George Desmeth Kelly and Catherine Dewelda (?). Christ Church, Oxford 1813, no degree, dn16 (York under Kelly), p18 (Chester for C&L), MA1827 (Lambeth). V. Withernwick, Yorks. 1818 [blank in ERC] and V. Aldborough (2nd Mediety), Yorks. 1822 to death (Sharp's Hotel, London) 22/8/1863, leaving £9,000 [C14231 under Kelly. YCO] Married York 29/6/1829 Albinia Dalton, with issue.

**HOLDSWORTH (Robert)** Born Dartmouth, Devon 8/1/1783, s. Arthur and Elizabeth Holdsworth. Merton, Oxford 1800, BA1805, dn06 (B&W), p07 (Ex.), MA1807. V. Stockenham, Devon 1807, V. Brixham, Devon 1809 and V. Townstall, Devon 1811 (w. Prebend of Exeter Cathedral 1824) to death. Dom. Chap. to 1st Earl Morley 1809-11. Died (Brixham) 30/12/1860, leaving £6,000 [C43383] Married Marylebone, London 16/3/1820 Eleanor Cutler, with issue.

**HOLE (Francis)** Bapt. Georgeham, Devon 29/12/1797, s. Rev. Thomas Hole and Elizabeth Irwin. Queen's, Oxford 1817, BA1821, dn21 (Ex.), p22 (Ex.), MA1824. R. (and patron) of Georgeham 1831 to death 14/10/1866 aged 58, leaving £3,000 [C145066] Married Barnstaple, Devon. 23/1/1823 Frances Spurway (a clerical dau.), with clerical son.

**HOLE (George)** Born Teignmouth, Devon 28/11/1798, s. Rev. Humphrey Aram Hole and Sarah Horne. Trinity, Cambridge 1814, LLB 1821, dn22 (Ex.), p22 (Ex.). R. Doddiscombsleigh, Devon 1823-28, R. (and patron) of Chumleigh, Devon 1823-59 (with five Prebends of Brokeland, Dennes, Lowerline, Penell and Higherline in Exeter Cathedral 1823 attached, then amalgamated 1842), Preacher throughout the Diocese of Exeter 1829, R. (and patron) of North Tawton, Devon 1829-36. Died Exmouth 14/5/1859 aged 60, leaving £40,000 [C136956] Married St James's, Westminster, London 28/8/1821 Jane Crew, with clerical son.

**HOLE (John Radford)** Bapt. Dunsford, Devon 3/4/1763, s. Rev. Joshua Hole and Anne Radford. Exeter, Oxford 1780, BA1783, dn85 (Ex.), p87 (Ex.). R. (and patron) of Woolfardisworthy, Devon 1793 and R. (and patron) of

Broadwoodkelly, Devon 1794 to death 3/6/1841 [C145067] Married (1) Madron, Cornwall 1793 Lydia Harris Arundell (d.1797), with issue (2) Westminster, London 5/9/1806 Sophia Brassey, with further issue.

**HOLIWELL (George Marshall)** Bapt. Wraby, Lincs. 14/5/1794, s. Rev. George Holiwell and Anna Maria Marshall. Literate: dn17 (Lin.), p18 (Lin.). R. Swallow, Lincs. 1822 to death 7/4/1854 [C64663] Married 13/8/1823 Diana Ann Holgate, with clerical son Walter Currer Holiwell.

**HOLLAND (Erskine William)** Born St Giles, London 15/4/1804, s. Rev. Samuel Holland (below) and Frances Erskine. Worcester, Oxford 1827, BA1830, dn31 (Roch.), p31 (Chich.), MA 1834. R. Warehorne, Kent 1832, V. Arlington, Sussex 1833-7, R. Dunsfold, Surrey 1838 to death. Dom. Chap. to 2nd Baron Erskine 1834. Died Brighton 20/5/1888, leaving £2,317-9s-3d. [C63903] Married Tunbridge Wells, Kent 29/9/1836 Caroline Bennett, with issue. Brother Thomas Agar Holland, below.

**HOLLAND (Henry Eveleigh)** Bapt. East Retford, Notts. 1/8/1780, s. William and Mary Holland. Emmanuel, Cambridge 1798, BA 1803, dn03 (York), Fellow 1804, MA1805, p05 (Lin.), BD1812. R. Thurcaston, Leics. 1832 to death 21/9/1837 [C64669. YCO]

**HOLLAND (John)** From Tenbury, Worcs., s. Thomas Holland. Balliol, Oxford 1776 (aged 17), BA1780, dn81 (Heref.), p83 (Ox.), MA1783. R. Emmington, Oxon. 1785-90, R. Greete, Shrop-shire 1790, V. Aston Rowant, Oxon. 1795 to death 13/11/1844 [C31593]

**HOLLAND (Richard)** Bapt. Fremington, Devon 13/9/1791, s. Robert Holland and June Jeffery. Christ's, Cambridge 1795, BA1800, dn01 (Ex.), p02 (Roch. for Ex.), MA1803. V. (and patron) of Spreyton, Devon 1802-56 and R. Inwardleigh, Devon 1803-45, R. Hittisleigh, Devon 1845 to death. Dom. Chap. to 2nd Baron Arden 1803. Died 30/12/1856 [C7156] Married Kenn, Devon 9/12/1801 Frances Diana Slack, with issue.

**HOLLAND (Samuel)** Born Greenwich, Kent 25/7/1771, s. Rev. Nicholas Holland. Worcester, Oxford 1788, BA1792, MA1795, MB1796, MD1799. A physician to 1806. dn06 (Win.), p06 (Win.). (Sinecure R. Llangwm, Denbigh 1806), R. Beaudesert, Warwicks. 1806-57, R. Poynings, Sussex 1807-46, R. Warehorne, Kent 1807-32 (res.), Thorney Prebend in Chichester Cathedral 1817-22, then Woodhorne Prebend 1822 (and Precentor 1825) to death. Dom. Chap. to 1st Baron Erskine 1807. Died Brighton 16/4/1857 aged 85 [C63904. Boase] Married Dublin 20/6/1802 Hon. Frances Erskine, with clerical son (below) and Erskine William Holland (above). *F.R.C.P.* (1800)

**HOLLAND (Thomas Agar)** Born St Giles, London 16/1/1803, s. Rev. Samuel Holland (above) and Frances Erskine. Worcester, Oxford 1821, BA1825, dn26 (Lin.), p27 (Chich.), MA1828. V. Oving, Sussex 1827-38, R. Greatham, Hants. 1838-46, (succ. his father as) R. Poynings, Sussex 1846-64. Died (Poyntings) 18/10/1888, leaving £1,106-8s-6d. [C63905. ODNB as a poet. Boase] Married Brighton, Sussex 23/8/1831 Magdaline Stewart, with legal issue. Brother Erskine William, above.

**HOLLAND (Thomas Edwardes Mytton)** Born Tenbury, Worcs. 1793, s. Samuel and Harriott Holland. Balliol, Oxford 1811, BA1814, dn16 (Heref.), MA1817, p17 (Heref.). V. Stoke Bliss, Heref. 1823 to death 13/12/1864, leaving £5,000 [C171760]

**HOLLAND (William)** Born South Molton, Devon 13/2/1797, s. Rev. William Holland, sen. Christ Church, Oxford 1815, Student [Fellow] 1817-25, BA1819, dn20 (Ox.), MA1821, p21 (Ox.). R. Cold Norton, Essex (and RD) 1824 to death. Dom. Chap. to 9th Duke of Somerset 1820. Died 1/2/1867, leaving £35,000 [C31594] Married 25/2/1831 Mary Brown.

**HOLLAND (William Woollams)** Bapt. Birmingham 25/5/1785, s. Thomas Holland [*pleb*]. New, Oxford 1800, then Hertford, BA 1806, MA 1807, dn08 (Roch.), p09 (Ox.). Vicar-Choral in Chichester Cathedral 1809, R. Chichester St Andrew w. St Martin 1817 [sequestrator], V. Burpham, Sussex 1809 and V. Bapchild, Kent 1825 to death 17/1/1855 [C7157. LBSO] Married Bridgnorth, Shropshire 1809 Jane Murray (sister of the publisher), w. clerical s. John Murray Holland.

**HOLLEST (George Edward)** Bapt. Farnham, Surrey 7/6/1799, s. John Hollest and Mary Leigh Willis. Emmanuel, Cambridge 1820, SCL, dn24 (London), p25 (London). PC. Seale, Surrey 1831, PC. Frimley, Surrey 1832 to death

29/9/1850 aged 54 'from a *shot-wound* received from a burglar who had entered his bedroom' [C76971] Widow Caroline, and issue. Cricketer.

**HOLLEY (Edward)** Born Blicking, Norfolk 6/11/1807, s. James Hunt Holley and Anne Adela Pinckard. Caius, Cambridge 1825, BA 1829, dn30 (Nor.), p31 (Nor.). R. Burgh St Peter, Norfolk, 1831-73, R. Hackford w. Whitwell, Norfolk 1836-55 (family living). Died 16/6/1873, leaving £20,000 [C113545] Married (1) Norwich 19/5/1830 Eliza Helwys Thomasine Laton (of Drayton, Norfolk, d.1850), with issue (2) Kensington, London 1/6/1853 Mrs Emma Sophia (Mark) Morrice (dau. of the British Consul at Malaga, Spain).

**HOLLEY (George Hunt)** Born Aylsham, Norfolk 10/2/1787, s. John Holley and Elizabeth Hunt. St John's, Cambridge 1804, BA1810, dn10 (Nor.), p11 (Nor). R. (and patron) of Hackford w. Whitwell, Norfolk 1812 to death (London) 3/5/1836 [C113546]

**HOLLINGWORTH (John Banks)** Born London 14/12/1779, s. John and Elizabeth Hollingworth. Peterhouse, Cambridge 1799, BA 1804, dn04 (London), p04 (London), Fellow 1807-16, MA1807, BD1814, DD1819, Norris Professor of Divinity, Cambridge 1824-38. V. Cambridge Little St Mary (St Mary the Less) 1807-14, R. St Margaret Lothbury w. St Christopher le Stocks, City of London 1814-56, PC. St Botolph without Aldgate, City of London 1815, Archdeacon of Huntingdon 1828 to death 9/2/1856 [C64691. Boase] Married (1) Stafford 24/7/1814 Lydia Amphlett (Hadzor Hall, Worcs., a clerical family, d.1831) (2) City of London 12/4/1836 Mary Ann Tabor (Finsbury, London), with issue.

**HOLLINGWORTH (Nathaniel John)** Bapt. Battersea, Surrey 20/5/1771, s. John Hollingworth and Honoria Newnham. St John's, Oxford 1789, Fellow 1792, BA1793, MA1796, dn94 (Ox.), p98 (Durham). PC. Hartlepool, Co. Durham 1807-12, V. Haltwhistle, Northumberland 1809-29, R. Boldon, Durham 1829 to death 3/10/1839 aged 69 [C31598] Married before 1797 Lucy Compton (a clergy dau.), with issue.

**HOLLIS (George Parry)** Born Winchester 2/11/1796, s. George Hollis and Jane Parry. Trinity, Oxford 1815, dn21 (Salis. for Win.), then St Alban Hall, BA1824, p24 (Win.). R. Dodington, Som. 1831 to death 1867 (1st q.). No will traced [C41385] Married Southampton, Hants. 16/7/1825 Martha Welles, with issue.

**HOLLIST (John)** Bapt. Duncton, Sussex 2/1/1785, s. William and Mary Hollist. Literate: dn14 (York), p15 (York). PC. Manchester St James 1818-59. Died Eccles, Lancs. 17/2/1861 aged 76, leaving £1,500 [C131507. YCO] Married Manchester 14/7/1824 Elizabeth Heaton, with issue.

**HOLLOWAY (Charles)** Born Reading, Berks. 28/11/1798, s. John Shotter Holloway and Elizabeth Richards. Queens', Cambridge 1822, BA1826, dn26 (Lin. for Nor.), p26 (Nor.). R. Norwich St Simon and St Jude 1830-61, R. Sandford Dingley, Berks. 1830 to death (Folkestone, Kent) 23/9/1863, leaving £2,000 [C64735] (1) Great Witchingham, Norfolk 7/1/1834 Catherine Juliana Kett Tompson (d.1841), w. clerical s. Edward John Holloway (2) Reading 3/6/1845 Charlotte Richards (w), w. further issue.

**HOLLOWAY (Henry)** Bapt. City of London 28/11/1799, s. John Peter and Mary Holloway. St John's, Cambridge 1824, no degree, dn24 (Chester), p24 (Nor.). R. Longstowe, Cambs. 1832-6 [C109734]. Alive (unm) 1861 [C113548] In Fleet Prison, London to 1838.

**HOLLOWAY (James Thomas)** Born Newington, Surrey 30/7/1780, s. Jeremiah Holloway and Mary Ann Cranston. Exeter, Oxford 1797, BA1802, dn05 (Win.), p06 (Win.), Fellow 1806-13, MA1807, BD and DD1818. Min. Fitzroy Episcopal [Proprietary] Chapel, London --, V. Stanton upon Hine Heath, Shropshire 1819 to death (London) 7/8/1855 [C12005] Married Newington 9/9/1813 Elizabeth Bentham, with issue.

**HOLLWAY (Thomas)** Bapt. Boston, Lincs. 7/7/1801, s. John Palmer Hollway (attorney) and Esther Hardwick. St John's, Cambridge 1819, BA1823, dn24 (Salis. for Win.), p25 (Bristol for Lin.), MA1829. R. Partney, Lincs. 1825-54, PC. Spilsby, Lincs. 1825-54, Canon and Prebend of Stow Longa in Lincoln Cathedral 1843-79. Lived latterly and died Leamington, Warwicks. 24/1/1879. No will traced [C52966. Bennett2. Kaye] J.P. Lindsey.

**HOLME (Frederick William)** Bapt. Upholland, Lancs. 1/2/1772, s. Rev. Thomas Holme and Mary Meyrick. Corpus Christi,

Oxford 1789, BA1792, MA1796, dn97 (Chester), p97 (Ox.), BD1804, Fellow to 1812. R. Meysey Hampton, Glos. 1810 to death 16/1/1853 [C31632] Married Moreton Saye, Shropshire 1/5/1811 Mary Elizabeth Pigott, with issue.

**HOLME (James)** Literate: p09 (Salis. for London). PC. Sandiacre, Derbys. 1815-[49]. Died? [C94918. IE as Holmes]

**HOLME (James)** Bapt. Orton, Westmorland 12/3/1801, s. Thomas Holme (a mercer) and Ellen Redman. Trinity, Cambridge 1819, then Caius 1822, BA1825, dn25 (Durham for Ox.), p26 (Durham). PC. Low Harrogate St Mary, Pannal, Yorks. 1830-38, V. Kirk Leatham, Yorks. 1838-54. Died Grange over Sands, Lancs. 27/3/1882 aged 81, leaving £2,955-15s-6d. [C31629. Boase] Married Leeds 25/7/1850 Elizabeth Mary Rhodes (w), with clerical son.

**HOLME (John)** Born Westmorland. Literate: dn00 (Car.), p01 (Car.). (first) PC. Hollinwood, Prestwich, Lancs. 1809 to death (Blackburn, Lancs.) 1861 (3rd q.). Will not traced [C6024] Was married. *J.P.* Lancs. 1819.

**HOLME, HOLMES (Robert)** Literate: dn23 (Chester), p24 (Chester). PC. of Weaverham, Cheshire 1823 [C169257 as Holmes], Chap. of the Donative of Alvanley (Chapel), Frodsham, Cheshire 1825 to death 1840 [C169252]

**HOLME (William)** Born Mardale, Westmorland. Emmanuel, Cambridge 1789. BA1793, p93 (London), Fellow 1796, MA1796, BD1803. R. Loughborough, Leics. [net income £1,848] 1826 to death 12/2/1848 aged 83 [C64745]

**HOLMES (Archibald)** Probably born Malew, IoM 1/1/1774, s. Archibald Holmes and Elizabeth Gell. Literate: dn24 (S&M), p26 (S&M). Chaplain Ramsey St Paul, IoM 1825-42, V. Patrick, IoM 1842 to death 1/11/1865. Will not noted [C8066 is blank. Gelling] Married Malew 10/4/1845 Charlotte Alice Tellet.

**HOLMES (Edmund)** Literate: dn89 (Bristol for York), p89 (Bristol for York). V. Millington w. Great Givendale, Yorks. 1789 to death March 1836 aged 79 [C52967. YCO] 'His ardent love of rural pleasures', etc.

**HOLMES (Gervase)** Born Fressingfield, Suffolk, s. Rev. Gervase Holmes, sen. Emmanuel, Cambridge 1793, BA1797, dn99 (Nor.), MA 1801, p01 (Nor.). V. Tugby, Leics. 1808-10, R. Copford, Essex 1810 to death. Chap. to HRH Duke of Kent. Died 3/9/1845 aged 68 (CCEd has date of his father). [C64751] Married Dedham, Essex Nov. 1807 Charlotte Isabella Williams (dau. of an *H.E.I.C*. official), with issue.

**HOLMES (James)** Born Donaghmore, Co. Donegal, s. Thomas Holmes (farmer). MA (Glasgow), dn85 (Nor.), p88 (Nor.). R. Colesbourne, Glos. 1789, PC. Compton Abdale, Glos. 1824. Died? [C113552]

**HOLMES (Robert Bartholomew)** Born Leeds 26/8/1794, s. Robert Holmes. Literate: dn21 (Salis. for York), p21 (York). R. Gloucester Christ Church 1830 to death 6/5/1867 aged 75, leaving £450 (Will as Bartholomew only) [C94919. YCO. CR65 as Richard] Married Leeds 17/1/1827 Margaret Lapage.

**HOLMES (Thomas)** Born Acomb, York 14/4/1793, s. of John Holmes (carpenter) and Sarah Darby. Literate: dn17 (York), p18 (York). PC. Wilberfoss, Yorks. 1822 [income £67] to death 6/2/1869 aged 75, leaving £1,000 [C135893. YCO] Married York 6/7/1819 Mary Newstead, with issue.

**HOLMES (Thomas Pattison/Patteson)** Bapt. Alconbury Weston, Hunts. 26/5/1793, s. John and Elizabeth Holmes. St John's, Cambridge 1811, BA1815, dn17 (Ely), p18 (Ely). PC. Guyhirn, Cambs, 1818, PC. Wisbech New Chapel 1831 to death 16/2/1877, leaving under £300 [C109736] Widow Elizabeth Usill, and issue.

**HOLMES (William)** From Oxford, s. Robert Holmes [*pleb*]. Chorister at Magdalen 1779-87; matr. New, Oxford 1786 (aged 17), BA1790, MA1794. 3rd Minor Canon of St Paul's Cathedral 1796, V. St Giles Cripplegate, City of London 1802 and R. Aveley, Essex 1810 to death. Priest in Ordinary 1833 and Sub-Dean of Chapel Royal 1833. Died 15/6/1833 (CCEd says 20/6/1833) [C119520]

**HOLROYD (James John)** Born Camden, London 25/10/1800, s. Sir George Sowley Holroyd (Judge of the King's Bench, *q.v.* ODNB) and Sarah Chaplin. Christ's, Cambridge 1818, BA1830, dn30 (London), p30 (London), MA1835. R. Abberton, Essex 1830 to death

(Colchester) 1/8/1875, leaving £6,000 [C66869. Venn corrected] Married Norwich 12/9/1833 Sophia Tyssen (Narborough Hall, Norfolk), with issue.

**HOLROYD (John)** Bapt. Leeds 11/12/1797, s. Joseph Holroyd (a dyer) and Hannah Parkinson. Trinity, Cambridge 1814, BA1819, then St Catharine's, Fellow 1821, MA1822, dn22 (Ely), p29 (Lin. for Ely). (first) PC. Leeds Christ Church 1829-49, V. Bardsey, Yorks. 1849 (and RD) to death 12/1/1873 aged 75, leaving £16,000 [C64957] Married (1) Leeds 27/1/1825 Ann Lambert Knowles, with issue (2) Anne Atkins, 1 dau.

**HOLT (John)** Born Newark upon Trent, Notts. 14/7/1771, s. William Holt (of Wraby, Lincs.). Clare, Cambridge 1791, BA1795, Fellow 1795, dn96 (Peterb.), p97 (Peterb.), MA 1798. V. Wrawby w. Brigg, Lincs. 1799-1835, V. Gringley on the Hill, Notts. 1802-35, V. Wootton, Lincs. 1803-14, V. Kelstern, Lincs. 1806 and R. Elston, Notts. 1819 to death. Dom. Chap. to Cassandra, Dowager Baroness Hawke 1806; to Hester Elizabeth, Dowager Baroness Selsey 1819. Died Wrawby 25/12/1835 [C64973. Kaye] Married Barrow upon Humber, Lincs. 25/3/1806 Sarah Uppleby, with clerical son.

**HOLT (William)** Probably bapt. Rochdale, Lancs. 7/4/1776, s. James (of Bury, Lancs., *pleb.*) and Betty Holt. BNC, Oxford 1795, BA1799, MA 1802, dn02 (Salis.), p02 (Salis.). PC. Holcombe, Bury 1810 and PC. Edenfield, Bury 1810 to death 12/10/1849 [C94921]

**HOLT (William Henry)** From Bury, Lancs., s. George Holt. St John's, Cambridge 1822, BA 1827, dn27 (C&L), p31 (C&L). V. (Church) Biddulph, Staffs. 1831 to death 18/2/1878, leaving £800 [C11750] Had issue.

**HOLWORTHY (Charles)** Bapt. Elsworth, Cambs. 24/10/1764, s. Samuel Smith Holworthy and Elizabeth Haddock. University, Oxford 1783, BA1786, dn87 (Nor.), p91 (Ely). V. Bourn, Cambs. 1795 to death. Dom. Chap. to 2nd Baron Riversdale 1809. Died 25/6/1853 [C100068] Married 21/8/1791 Henrietta Want, with issue.

**HOLWORTHY (Matthew)** Bapt. Elsworth, Cambs. 7/7/1783, s. Rev. Matthew Holworthy, sen. and Ann Desborough. [Capt. 63rd Foot 1799-1805] Caius, Cambridge 1805, dn09 (Nor.), BA1810, p16 (Ely). R. Elsworth 1827 to death 13/11/1836 aged 53 [C109737] Brother William Henry, below.

**HOLWORTHY (Samuel)** Born Bury St Edmunds, Suffolk 14/3/1785, s. Capt. Samuel Holworthy and Deborah Stephenson. University, Oxford 1803, BA1808, dn08 (Win. for Salis.), p09 (Salis.), MA1810. V. Croxall, Derbys. 1809 to death (Bath) 5/3/1838 [C12139] Married Cheshunt, Herts. 6/4/1811 Diana Sarah Bayley, with issue.

**HOLWORTHY (William Henry)** Bapt. Elsworth, Cambs. 31/3/1792, s. Rev. Matthew Holworthy and Ann Desborough. Clare, Cambridge 1816, no degree, dn16 (Nor.), p17 (Nor.). V. Earlham w. Bowthorpe, Norfolk 1817 [blank in ERC], R. Blicking and Erpingham, Norfolk 1836 to death 28/12/1838 [C113563] Married Blicking 2/4/1818 Sarah Churchill, with issue. Brother Matthew, above.

**HOMER (William)** Born Birdingbury, Warwicks. 11/6/1768, s. Rev. Henry Homer (*q.v.* ODNB) and Sarah Pitt. Christ's, Cambridge 1784, BA1789, dn92 (C&L), p93 (C&L), MA 1793. V. Wolfhampcote, Worcs. 1794 (and S/M Great Appleby Free G/S, Leics. 1799) to death 6/6/1838 aged 69 [C11939] Married Atherstone, Leics. 3/11/1814 Sarah Homer [*thus*].

**HOMFRAY (Edward)** Born Stourbridge, Worcs. 12/1/1796, s. Thomas Homfray and Elizabeth Stephans. Emmanuel, Cambridge 1814, BA1818, dn19 (Ely for C&L). R. Easthope, Shropshire 1820-5 (res.), PC. Longdon, Shropshire 1827 and PC. Ratlinghope, Shropshire 1833 to death 24/6/1856 [C11751] Married Shrewsbury, Shropshire 31/10/1820 Ann Sarah Everett (a military dau.), with issue.

**HOMFRAY (John)** Born Derby 27/8/1768, s. John Homfray [*pleb*] and Sarah Parr. Merton, Oxford 1790, dn94 (C&L), BA1803, p14 (Nor.). Min. Great Yarmouth St George, Norfolk 1821 (res.); R. Sutton, Norfolk 1839 to death 25/12/1842 [C12149] Married Great Yarmouth 13/6/1797? Hetty Symonds, with issue.

**HONE (Joseph Frederick)** Bapt. Marylebone, London 14/1/1802, s. Joseph Terry Hone and Augusta Maria Sinclair. University, Oxford 1821, dn25 (Glos.), BA1826, p26 (Glos.), MA 1829 (as F.J.H.). V. Tirley (o/w Trinley), Glos. 1827 to death 28/1/1888, leaving £8,580-11s-1d.

[C154478] Married Cranford, Beds. 28/6/1840 Ann Grimshaw (Gorton, Manchester).

**HONIATT (Thomas)** Bapt. Hereford 11/8/1760, s. Thomas Honiatt and Elizabeth Owen. University, Oxford 1782, BA1783, dn83 (Heref.), p84 (Heref.). V. Breinton, Heref. 1797 to death 1834 [C171770] Married Breinton 24/4/1794 Mary Ann Jones, with issue. Known as 'the poor man's friend.'

**HONY (William Edward)** Born Liskeard, Cornwall 7/2/1788, s. Rev. Willliam Hony and Selina Byam. Exeter, Oxford 1805, Fellow 1808-27, BA1811, dn11 (Ox.), MA1812, p12 (Ex.), BD1823. V. South Newington, Oxon. 1818-27, R. Baverstock, Wilts. 1827-75, V. Compton Chamberlayne, Wilts. 1832 [blank in ERC], Prebend of Grimston in Salisbury Cathedral 1841-75, Archdeacon of Salisbury 1846 and Canon Residentiary 1857 to death 7/1/1875, leaving £10,000 [C31680. Boase] Married Oxford 3/7/1827 Margaret Earle (w), with issue.

**HOOK (Walter Farquhar)** Bapt. St George's Hanover Square, London 13/3/1798, s. Rev. James Hook (later Dean of Worcester) and Ann Farquhar. Christ Church, Oxford 1817, Student [Fellow] 1817-27 [student of Lincoln's Inn 1819] BA1821, dn22 (Ox.), p22 (Ox.), MA1824, BD &DD 1837. V. Coventry Holy Trinity 1828-37, Prebend of Caistor in Lincoln Cathedral 1832-59, reforming V. Leeds 1837-59, Dean of Chichester 1859 to death. Chap. in Ordinary 1827 to death. Anglo-Catholic leader. Died 20/10/1875, leaving £5,000 [C12151. ODNB. Boase. W.R.W. Stephens, *The life and letters of Walter Farquhar Hook, DD, FRS* (1878. 2v.). C.J. Stranks, *Dean Hook* (1954)] Married Edgbaston, Warwicks. 4/6/1829 Anna Delicia Johnstone (dau. of a Birmingham physician), with issue. F.R.S. (1862). Photos. online.

**HOOKER (Thomas Redman)** Bapt. City of London 2/4/1762, s. Thomas Hooker and Ann Redman. Oriel, Oxford 1780, BA1784, dn84 (Roch.), p86 (Lin. for Roch.), MA1786, BD & DD1810. V. Rottingdean, Sussex 1795 (he got the parish by a throw of the Duke's dice!) to death. Dom. Chap. to 3rd Duke of Dorset 1785 (and accompanied his sons on the Grand Tour). Died 13/4/1838 [C2915] Married (1) Boxted, Essex 28/7/1789 Mary Cooke ('a cousin of Jane Austen', she d.1797), w. issue (2) Marylebone, London 9/4/1801 Emma Jane Greenland, w. further issue. An interesting man: S/M – huntsman – cellist – smuggler.

**HOOLE (Samuel)** Bapt. London 31/1/1758 (in an Independent Chapel), s. John Hoole (chief auditor of *H.E.I.C., q.v.* ODNB) and Susannah Smith. Magdalen Hall, Oxford 1780, no degree, dn81 (Lin.), p82 (Lin.), MA by 1813. R. Poplar All Saints, Stepney, London 1823 to death (Tenterden, Kent) 26/2/1839 [C64986] Married (1) Hackney, Middx. 15/9/1791 Elizabeth Young (dau. of the agricultural writer) (2) Dorking, Surrey 10/12/1803 Catherine Warneford, with issue. Minor literary figure.

**HOOPER (Thomas)** Born Bathford, Som. 6/2/1776, s. James Hooper. Jesus, Cambridge 1798, BA1799, LLB, dn00 (Glos.), MA1802. R. Castle Combe, Wilts. 1811-45 [blank in ERC], R. Syde, Glos. 1813-45, R. Yatton Keynell, Wilts. 1822-45, R. Elkstone, Glos. 1840 to death. Dom. Chap. to 2nd Baron Nugent 1822. Died 19/9/1845 [C94930] Married Yatton Keynell 2/1/1804 Elizabeth Godfrey, with issue.

**HOOPER (Thomas Poole)** Born Marylebone, London 14/5/1774, s. John Hooper and Mary Fawler. Pembroke, Oxford 1791, BA1797, MA 1800. R. New Shoreham, Sussex 1802-15 (res.), R. Kingston by Sea, Sussex 1809, V. Sompting, Sussex 1815 to death. Dom. Chap. to 2nd Viscount Lake 1815. Died 29/1/1837 aged 63. [C7477]

**HOOPER (William Nixon)** Bapt. Reading, Berks. 12/2/1802, s. John Hopper and Sarah Nixon. Corpus Christi, Cambridge 1820, BA 1824, dn25 (Lin.), MA1827, p28 (Salis.). PC. Littleton, Hants. 1832-71, Minor Canon (and Precentor) of Winchester Cathedral 1839. Chap. to Bishop Morley's College, Winchester 1839. Died Winchester 24/7/1877, leaving £3,000 [C64990] Married Ashbourne, Derbys. 16/7/1840 Lucy Blakiston, with issue.

**HOPE (Charles Stead)** Born Derby 29/10/1762, s. Rev. Charles Hope and Susanna Stead. St John's, Cambridge 1779, BA1784, dn85 (C&L), p86 (C&L). V. Youlgreave w. Middleton, Derbys. 1797-1802, Chap. Derby All Saints 1798 and V. Derby St Alkmund 1802 to death (Duffield, Derbys.) 13/1/1841 [C11942] Married Alsop le Dale, Derbys. 6/4/1793 Ellen Mellor with clerical son. Five times Mayor of Derby.

**HOPE (John)** Born Langholm, Dumfries 20/1/1797, s. James Hope (a chandler) and Elizabeth Jepson. Literate: dn21 (York), p22 (York). PC. Halifax St Ann in the Grove (o/w Brier's Chapel) 1822 to death 9/2/1853 aged 56 [C131512. YCO] Married (1) Halifax 27/7/1824 Catherine Hobson (d.1841), w. clerical sons James, and John (2) Halifax 27/12/1842 Elizabeth Patchett.

**HOPER (Henry)** Bapt. Lewes, Sussex 10/4/1788, s. John Hoper and Sarah Cossum. Magdalen, Oxford 1805, BA 1810, dn11 (Win.), p12 (Ox.), MA1813. V. Portslade, Sussex 1815 and R. Hangleton, Sussex 1815 to death. Dom. Chap. to 1st Earl Whitworth 1813. Died 3/12/1858, leaving £12,000 [C31687] Married Cowfold, Sussex 17/6/1829 Sarah Constable (w).

**HOPKINS (Adolphus)** Born Falmouth, Cornwall 31/8/1797, s. Capt. John William Hopkins and Mary Bruish (?). Emmanuel, Cambridge 1818, BA1823, MA1826. V. Clent, Staffs. 1825 to death 19/1/1855 [C121403] Married Harborne, Staffs. 14/4/1830 Sara Bacchus.

**HOPKINS (Daniel John)** Bapt. Huntingdon 8/4/1779, s. Daniel, F.R.S., and Ann Hopkins. Trinity Hall, Cambridge 1798, BA1802, dn02 (Lin.), p04 (Lin.), MA1805. R. Woolley, Hunts. 1817-57, V. Hartford, Hunts. 1828 to death 16/6/1857 [C64992] Married (2) St Pancras, London 12/4/1825 Esther Barnard Hammond (d.1827) (3) Hartford 2/10/1838 Ann Okes; with issue.

**HOPKINS (David)** From London, s. William Hopkins. Trinity, Cambridge 1808, BA1813, dn13 (Lin.), p15 (Lin.), MA1820. V. Bucknell and Buckton, Shropshire 1816-36. Died Cheltenham, Glos. 26/1/1842 aged 56 [C64993] Married Westbury, Wilts. 1824 Ann Cockell (1 ch. who died).

**HOPKINS (Henry John)** Bapt. Hursley, Hants. 16/4/1795, s. John and Martha Hopkins. Magdalen Hall, Oxford 1815, BA1819, dn19 (Heref.), p19 (C&L for Win.). R. Winchester St Maurice 1819. Chap. to Winchester Workhouse. Died 4/9/1854 [C12162] Married Andover, Hants. 13/5/1847 Jane Tarrant, with issue.

**HOPKINS (James)** Probably born Dublin, s. Francis Hopkins (physician). TCD1797 (aged 15), BA1802, MA1805. R. Stambourne, Essex 1809 to death 3/12/1858 aged 76, leaving £3,000 [C119528. Al.Dub.?] Widow Mary Esther, and issue.

**HOPKINS (Thomas)** Born Sully, Glamorgan, s. Rev. Nehemiah Hopkins [*pleb*]. Jesus, Oxford 1768 (aged 17), dn73 (Ox.), p74 (Ox.), BA1771, MA 1774 and Fellow, BD1781. R. Donyatt, Som. 1788-1821, R. Tredington (2nd Portion), Worcs. 1789 to death, R. Earnshill. Som. [no church] 1799-1821, R. Buckland St Mary, Som. 1813-[32]. Died (Honington, Warwicks.) 25/8/1838 (CCEd death of 1821 is wrong) [C31691]

**HOPKINS (William)** Born Shrewsbury, s. Rev. William Hopkins, sen. Oriel, Oxford 1793 (aged 17), BA1797, dn98 (C&L), p00 (C&L), MA1804. PC. Ford, Shropshire 1819, R. Fitz, Shropshire 1821. Probate granted 4/5/1848 [C12166]

**HOPKINS (William)** From Stone, Bucks, s. Rev. Thomas Hopkins. Oriel, Oxford 1810 (aged 17), BA1814, MA1817. V. Honington, Warwicks. 1817-41. Died Leamington, Warwicks. 14/9/1859, leaving £16,000 [C121405]

**HOPKINS (William Toovey)** Bapt. Cholsley, Berks. 14/10/1793, s. Joseph Hopkins and Alice Toovey. Pembroke, Oxford 1811, BA1816, dn17 (Ox.), MA1822. R. Nuffield, Oxon. 1826-67 (and RD). Died 24/2/1869, leaving £12,000 [C31692] Wife Jane, and clerical s. Thomas Henry Toovey Hopkins. Good online photo.

**HOPKINSON (John)** Born Burton-le-Coggles, Lincs., son of 'J. Hopkinson'. Clare, Cambridge 1769, BA1773, Fellow 1773-7, dn74 (Ely), p75 (Lin.), MA1776. R. Westborough w. Dry Doddington, Lincs. 1775-7 (res.), R. Glatton, Hunts. 1778-1834 and R. Market Overton, Rutland 1782 to death. Dom. Chap to 8th Lord Napier 1778. Died 17/4/1834 aged 82 (CCEd says 22/5/1834). [C65002]

**HOPKINSON (John)** Born Christchurch, Surrey, s. Rev. Samuel Edmund Hopkinson (below) and Elizabeth Portington. Clare, Cambridge 1814, BA1818, dn18 (Lin.), p19 (Peterb.), MA1821. R. Etton, Northants. 1828-53, R. Alwalton, Hunts. 1833 (and Precentor of Peterborough Cathedral) to death. Dom. Chap. to Earl Fitzwilliam. Died 4/2/1853 [C65003]

Married Elizabeth Longdell, and had issue. *J.P.* Peterborough.

**HOPKINSON (Samuel Edmund)** Born Sutton, Northants. 20/8/1754, s. Rev. William Hopkinson and Elizabeth Wise. Clare, Cambridge 1773, Fellow 1776-82, BA1777, MA1780, dn81 (Ely), p81 (Peterb.), BD1793. R. Etton, Northants. 1786-1828, V. Morton by Bourne w. Hacconby, Lincs. 1795-1841, V. Thorpe St Peter, Lincs. 1834-8. Died 17/7/1841 [C65004. Bennett2] Married Northampton 13/5/1782 Elizabeth Portington, with clerical son, above. *J.P.* Kestervan and the Liberty of Peterborough 'for about 30 years.' 'An assiduous priest and devoted to his flock; every Sunday two poor men, in rotation through the parish, dined at Morton vicarage'.

**HOPPER (John Robert)** Bapt. Witton-le-Wear, Co. Durham 20/7/1799, s. John Thomas Hendry Hopper (Witton Castle) and Ann Sparling. Christ's, Cambridge 1817, BA1823, dn23 (Nor.), p24 (Nor.), MA1830. R. Bedingfield, Suffolk 1830-3, R. (and patron) of Wells next the Sea, Norfolk 1852 to death. British Chap. Baden-Baden, Germany 1849-52. Died Wandsworth, London 18/10/1863, leaving £4,000 [C113567] Married Norwich 18/10/1824 Lucinda Caroline Bedingfield, with issue. Sold Witton Castle after it had been gutted by fire.

**HOPPER (Ralph)** Bapt. Durham 12/9/1756, s. John Hopper and Elizabeth Hilton. Peterhouse, Cambridge 1775 [took part in a College riot in Jan. 1776] BA1779, dn79 (Durham), p80 (Durham). S/M Durham Charity School 1778; PC. Hamsterley, Durham 1809-25, PC. Witton le Wear, Durham 1809 to death 3/5/1834 [C130514] Married Isleham, Cambs. 31/10/1793 Elizabeth Arthy, 1s.

**HOPTON, *born* PARSONS (John)** Born Chaceley, Worcs. 5/10/1782, s. Rev. William Parsons (*later* Hopton) and Mary Graves. BNC, Oxford 1800, BA1805, MA1807 (as Parsons). V. (and patron) of Canon Frome 1810 (w. Munsley 1859), Heref. (living at Canon Frome Court) to 1870, V. Stretton Grandison, Heref. 1812, Prebend of Bartonsham in Hereford Cathedral 1832 to death 28/11/1870 aged 88, leaving £16,000 [C171789] Married Lugwardine, Heref. 5/5/1807 Grace Ann Williams, with issue. Stepbrother below.

**HOPTON, *born* PARSONS (William Parsons)** Bapt. Stretton Grandsome, Heref. 27/9/1802, s. Rev. William Parsons (*later* Hopton, of Canon Frome Court) and Ann Poole. Trinity, Oxford 1820, BA1824, dn26 (Heref.), p26 (Heref.), MA1828. V. Bishop's Frome >< Heref. 1827-79, Prebend in Hereford Cathedral 1858-78. Died 14/4/1879 aged 76, leaving £5,000 [C171791] Married Downton, Wilts. 8/9/1830 Diana Christian Shuckburgh, with clerical son Michael Hopton. Step-brother above.

**HOPWOOD (John)** Literate: dn12 (York for Chester), p14 (Chester). S/M Cockermouth G/S, Cumberland 1817; PC. Accrington, Lancs. 1817 to death 1853 (4th q.) [C131514. YCO] Wife Alice, and issue. *J.P.* Lancs. 1826; 'His grizzled, round and partially bald head …'

**HORDERN (James)** Bapt. Prestwich, Lancs. 2/2/1800, s. Rev. Joseph Edward Hordern and Ellen Allen. BNC, Oxford 1818, then St Mary Hall --, BA1823, dn23 (Chester), p23 (Chester). PC. Shaw, Prestwich 1823-41, R. Dodington, Kent 1841-2, V. Chislett, Kent 1841. Died Marylebone, London 6/5/1872 aged 72, leaving £1,000 [C169273] Married Doddington, Kent 30/6/1828 Mary Owen Ratcliffe (w), with issue. *J.P.* Oldham. Kept a school at Royton Hall, then at Failsworth Lodge. Brother below.

**HORDERN (Joseph)** Born Prestwich, Lancs. 1/4/1794, s. Rev. Joseph Edward Hordern and Ellen Allen. BNC, Oxford 1813, BA1816, dn17 (Chester), p19 (Chester), MA1820. V. Rostherne, Cheshire 1821-55 (and RD of East Frodsham), R. Burton Agnes, Hull, 1855 (and RD of Bridlington 1820) to death (Knutsford, Cheshire) 12/8/1876 aged 82, leaving £1,500 [C169274 mixes in his father. Boase] Married Knutsford 12/10/1831 Maria Frances Cotton (w), with clerical s. Brother above. *J.P.*

**HORLOCK (Holled Darrell Cave Smith)** Bapt. Box, Wilts. 8/9/1807, s. Rev. Isaac William Webb Horlock and Anne Holled Smith. Magdalen Hall, Oxford 1826, BA1830, dn30 (Salis.), p31 (Salis.), MA1834, BD1842, DD1843. V. (and patron) of Box 1831-74, V. Newton Poppleford, Devon 1878 to death 28/12/1901 (the longest-living clergyman here), leaving £79-5s-7d. [C94932] Married (1) Box 3/10/1832 Elizabeth Sudell (d.1858), w. clerical son Darrell Holled Webb Horlock (2) Westminster, London

3/9/1863 Charlotte Butler Horton Clarke, with further issue.

**HORNBUCKLE (Thomas Waldron)** Born Goldington, Beds. 12/11/1774, s. Rev. Thomas Hornbuckle and Alice Edwards. St John's, Cambridge 1793, BA1797, Fellow 1799-1827, dn99 (Lin.), p99 (Lin.), MA1800, BD1807, Tutor 1809-27. V. Kilkhampton, Cornwall 1800-4 (res.), V. Madingley, Cambs. 1807-37, R. Staplehurst, Kent 1826 to death 11/4/1848 aged 73 [C65482] Married (1) King's Lynn, Norfolk 3/4/1827 Elizabeth Whincop (d.1829) (2) Congham, Norfolk 13/6/1831 Elizabeth Forster Nelson (a clergy dau.); w. issue.

**HORNBY (Geoffrey)** Born Preston, Lancs. 4/4/1780, s. Rev. Geoffrey Hornby, sen. (Scale Hall, Lancaster) and Lady Lucy Smith Stanley (sister of the 12th Earl of Derby). Peterhouse, Cambridge 1798, LLB1809, dn09 (Chester), p09 (Chester). V. Huyton, Lancs. 1809-13, V. Ormskirk, Lancs. 1812-13, R. Bury St Mary, Lancs. [net income £1,937] 1818 (and RD of Bury) to death (Leamington, Warwicks.) 4/3/1850 [C169277] Married Middleton, Lancs. 12/4/1810 Hon. Georgiana Byng, dau. of 5th Viscount Torrington, with issue. Brother James John, below. *D.L.*

**HORNBY (Hugh)** Born Ribby Hall, Kirkham, Lancs. 22/8/1765, s. Hugh Hornby (dry salter) and Margaret Hankinson. Christ's, Cambridge 1783, BA1787, dn88 (Chester), p89 (Chester), MA1790. V. St Michael on Wyre, Lancs. 1789-1847, PC. Whitworth, Rochdale, Lancs. 1804-29 (res.). Died Garstang, Lancs. 4/1/1847 aged 81 [C169278] Married (1) Bury, Lancs. 9/9/1792 Anne Starkey (dau. of a physician), w. issue (2) Blackburn, Lancs. 5/2/1794 Alice Backhouse, w. clerical s. Robert.

**HORNBY (James John)** Born Preston, Lancs. 27/8/1777, s. Rev. Geoffrey Hornby (Scale Hall, Lancaster) and Lady Lucy Smith Stanley (sister of 12th Earl of Derby). Trinity, Cambridge 1795, BA1799, dn00 (Chester), MA1802, p02 (Chester). R. Northrepps, Norfolk 1806-13, PC. Penwortham, Lancs. 1809-14 (res.), RD, R. Winwick, Lancs. 1813-55, PC. Longton, Lancs. 1820. Died Winwick Hall 14/9/1855 aged 78 [C113569] Married (1) Preston 14/10/1800 Hester Atherton (of Atherton, Lancs.), with issue (2) Winwick, Warrington, Lancs. 23/6/1830 Catherine Boyle, with further issue. *J.P.* Lancs. 1816. Brother Geoffrey, above.

**HORNDON (David)** Born St Dominic, Cornwall, s. Rev. Thomas Horndon. Exeter, Oxford 1777 (aged 17), Fellow 1779-94, BA 1782, dn82 (Ox.), MA1784, p84 (Bristol). R. Merton, Devon 1794 and R. Bicton, Devon 1811 to death. Dom. Chap. to 1st Baron Rolle 1811. Died 6/4/1845 [C31697] Married (1) Bristol 22/11/1794 Jane Smathes (d.1797), 1 ch. (2) Bath 23/6/1802 Mary Ann Glubb, with issue.

**HORNE (Thomas)** Born Chiswick, London, s. Rev. Thomas Horne and Frances Ann Price. Christ Church, Oxford 1790 (aged 17), BA1794, MA1797, BA1805. S/M Manor House School, Chiswick 1824-35; R. St Katharine Coleman, City of London [net income £1,019] 1812 to death 19/2/1847 [C119534] Married Chiswick, London 27/6/1799 Cecilia Clementina Elizabeth Zoffany (dau. of the painter), with issue.

**HORNE (William)** Born London 27/7/1801, s. Sir William Horne (barrister and *M.P.*, of Epping House, Heref.) and Ann Hesse. Christ Church, Oxford 1819, BA1822, dn24 (Lin.), p25, MA1825. R. Humber, Hereford 1830-45 [CC171802], R. Hotham, Yorks. 1831-44, R. Limber Magna, Lincs. 1844-9, R. Barming, Kent 1849 to death 4/11/1865, leaving £9,000 [C65484 merges 2 men] Married 4/7/1831 (*or* 1/8/1831) Elizabeth Busk, with military issue.

**HORNER (John)** Bapt. Helmsley, Yorks. 23/5/1786, s. John (a dealer in hardware) and Eleanor Horner. Clare, Cambridge 1805, BA 1810, dn10 (Nor.), p10 (Nor.), Fellow 1812, MA 1813. Lived at Kilburn, Easingwold, Yorks. 1821-6; R. South Reston, Lincs. 1826 and V. Tathwell, Lincs. 1837 to death (Louth, Lincs.) 16/2/1839 [C65485. Kaye]

**HORNSBY (George)** Born Oxford, s. Rev. Professor Thomas Hornsby (astronomer, *q.v.* ODNB) and Anne Cherrill. Christ Church, Oxford 1799 (aged 18), BA1803, dn04 (Ox.), MA1805, p05 (Ox.). V. Turkdean, Glos. 1807 to death 29/8/1837 [C12171] Married Stockport, Cheshire 1808 Cordelia Emma Astley, with issue.

**HORSEMAN (James)** Bapt. Souldern, Oxon. 24/9/1778, s. Rev. John and Ursula Horseman.

Magdalen, Oxford 1794, BA1798, MA1801, dn01 (C&L), p02 (C&L), Fellow 1803-7. R. Whipsnade, Beds. 1804 [Joseph in C65487. ERC links], R. Little Gaddesden, Herts. 1813-29, R. Myddle (Middle), Shropshire 1829 to death. Dom. Chap. to 7th Earl of Bridgewater 1813; to Jane, Countess Macartney 1818. Died 10/8/1844 [C12172] Brother below.

**HORSEMAN (John)** Bapt. Souldern, Oxon. 21/6/1775, s. Rev. John and Ursula Horseman. Corpus Christi, Oxford 1792, BA1795, MA 1799, dn99 (Chester for Ox.), p00 (Ox.), BD 1807, Fellow to 1812. V. West Hendred, Berks. 1810 (only), R. Heydon w. Little Chishill, Essex 1810 (then Little Chishill only 1838) to death (Royston, Herts.) 14/8/1844 [C31800] Married Whipsnade, Beds. 12/10/1810 Emma Jones, with issue. Brother above.

**HORTON (Joshua Thomas)** Born Howroyd Hall, Halifax 12/11/1790, s. Thomas Horton and Lady Mary Gordon (dau. of 3rd Earl of Aberdeen). Trinity, Cambridge 1807, BA1808, MA1811, dn14 (C&L for Chester), p16 (Chester). V. Ormskirk, Lancs. 1818-45 (with leave of absence as Chaplain *R.N.* to HMS *Gloucester* 1826) to death 21/5/1845 aged 54, living at Rufford Hall [C11946] Married Howroyd, Ripponden, Yorks. 6/11/1832 Harriet (d.1836), dau. of Sir Thomas Dalrymple Hesketh, 3rd Bart., Rufford Hall, with issue. *J.P.* 1819, *D.L.*

**HOSKING (Thomas)** Bapt. Madron, Cornwall 11/10/1772. Peterhouse, Cambridge 1790, BA 1795, dn95 (Ex.), MA1798, then Sidney 1801, Fellow 1801, p05 (Lin.), BA1808, BD? R. Rempstone, Notts. 1811 and V. Basford (St Leodegarius), Notts. 1818 to death (Rempstone, Notts.) 8/7/1839 aged 66 ('after a long and painful illness') [C145142] Married Kimbolton, Hunts. 4/11/1824 Ann Blount, w. issue.

**HOSKINS (Henry)** Born North Perrott, Som. 21/4/1780, s. William Hoskins and Elizabeth Addinton. Oriel, Oxford 1808, BA1812, dn13 (B&W), p14 (Glos.), MA1817. R. (and patron) of North Perrott 1814-76, Prebend of Ewithington in Hereford Cathedral 1817-58 (res.), R. Frome St Quintin, Dorset 1827-65, Prebendary of Shalford in Wells Cathedral 1828 to death 26/5/1876 aged 86, leaving £12,000 [C41395] Married Cucklington, Som. 4/9/1818 Mary Phelips/Philips (a clergy dau.), with distinguished issue.

**HOSKINS (James Williams)** Born Witney, Oxon., s. Rev. Charles Hoskins. Jesus, Oxford 1774 (aged 16), then Magdalen 1776-92, BA 1778, MA1781, p84 (Ox.), Fellow 1792-1803, BD1794, DD1797. R. Appleton, Berks. 1802 (and Prebend of Combe XI in Wells Cathedral 1813) to death (Abingdon, Oxon.) 10/7/1844 [C31804] Married St George's Hanover Square, London 28/5/1803 Frances Jane Taylor, with issue.

**HOSKYNS (Bennet)** Born Herefordshire 1/5/1782, s. Sir Hungerford Bennet Hoskyns, 6th Bart. and Catherine Stanhope. Balliol, Oxford 1801, BA1806, dn08 (Win.), MA1808. R. Bacton, Heref. 1818, V. Montacute, Som. 1838 to death 18/4/1843 [C77709] Married Llangattock, Brecon 5/9/1815 Amelia Chamberlain, *s.p.* Port. miniature online.

**HOSTE (James)** Bapt. Tittleshall cum Godwick, Norfolk 31/5/1791, s. Rev. Dixon Hoste and Margaret Stanforth. Christ's, Cambridge 1810, BA1814, dn14 (Nor.), p15 (Nor.), MA1818. V. Empingham, Rutland 1822-31, PC. Longham, Norfolk 1824-42, PC. Wendling, Norfolk 1824, V. Stanhoe (o/w Barwick [in the Brakes]), Norfolk 1825 and R. Ingoldisthorpe, Norfolk 1831 to death 1842 (4th q.) aged 52 [C65495] Married Great Yarmouth, Norfolk 23/10/1817 Theophilia Elisabeth Turner, with issue.

**HOTCHKIN (Robert Charles Herbert)** Born Frome, Somerset 8/4/1801, s. Ralph Hotchkin and Mary Griffith. Emmanuel, Cambridge 1819, BA1824, dn24 (Peterb.), p25 (Peterb.). R. Thimbleby, Lincs. 1831 to death 19/5/1874, leaving £14,000 [C65496] Married Spilsby, Lincs. 4/8/1840 Julia Pearson Banks (w), with issue.

**HOTHAM (Frederick, Hon.)** Born London 16/1/1774, s. Beaumont, 2nd Baron Hotham and Susannah Hankey. Christ Church, Oxford 1791, then All Souls, BA1794, dn97 (Ox.), MA 1798, p98 (Ox.). V. Derby St Werburgh 1799, R. Burnham Sutton, Norfolk 1802-54 (3 Medieties), Canon of 3rd Prebend in Rochester Cathedral 1807 and R. Dennington, Suffolk 1808 to death 11/10/1854 [C1907] Married Bloomsbury, London 23/11/1802 Anne Elizabeth Hodges, with issue.

**HOUGH (George)** Born London 1/7/1797, s. Samuel and Margaret Hough. Literate: dn24 (York), p25 (York). PC. Earls Heaton, Dewsbury, Yorks. 1830, PC. South Crosland, Almondbury, Yorks. 1830 to death 6/6/1879 aged 81, leaving £12,000 [C131522. Boase. YCO] Married Almondbury 6/1/1831, w. issue. Founder and Secretary of the Almondbury Clerical Society 1828-78. Brother below.

**HOUGH (James)** Born Cumberland 14/2/1789 (bapt. London), s. Samuel and Margaret Hough. Literate: dn14 (Car.), p15 (Car.), then Queens', Cambridge 1828, BA1832, MA1835. Chap. *C.M.S.* missionary in India 1812-22, 1824-6. Minister of the Episcopal Floating Church on the River Thames 1829, PC. Ham St Andrew, Surrey 1832 to death (Hastings, Kent) 2/11/1847 aged 58 [C6032] Married (1) Kirklinton, Cumberland 5/3/1816 Elizabeth Pattinson (d.1824), with clerical s. Thomas George Pattinson Hough (who succ. his father at Ham) (2) Edmonton, Middx. 5/6/1828 Harriet Lewis, with further issue. Brother above.

**HOUGHTON** see under **HAUGHTON**

**HOULDITCH (Edward)** Bapt. Ottery St Mary, Devon 23/7/1801, s. Rev. Richard Houlditch and Alice Maria Ann Carter. St John, Cambridge 1819, BA1823, dn24 (Chester), p25 (Ex.). R. Exeter St Leonard 1831-40, R. Staplegrove, Som. 1840-5, R. Ashley, Wilts. 1845-52, R. Matson, Glos. 1853 to death (Bath) 9/8/1870 aged 69, leaving £3,000 [C145144] Married 1832 Frances Elizabeth Cowper (w), w. issue.

**HOUSMAN (Robert)** Bapt. Lancaster 27/2/1759, s. Robert Housman (a maltster) and Agnes Gunson. Apprenticed to a surgeon 1773. St John's, Cambridge 1780 (but others say literate, so a Ten Year Man?), dn81 (York), p83 (Peterb. for London), BA1784. (founder and first) PC. Lancaster St Anne 1796-1836 (and Preacher throughout the Diocese of Lincoln [*sic*] 1820). Dom. Chap., to 4th Duke of Portland 1820. Died 22/4/1838 near Liverpool aged 79 [C110346. ODNB. YCO. DEB. R.F. Housman, *The life and remains of Rev. Robert Housman … incumbent of St Anne's, Lancaster* (Lancaster, 1841)] Married (1) Cambridge 30/12/1784 Mary Audley (d.1785), 1 ch. (2) Leicester 24/9/1788 Jane Adams, with issue, some clerical. *J.P.*; intimate of Charles Simeon and the other Cambridge evangelicals.

**HOUSON (Henry)** Bapt. Southwell, Notts. 8/12/1788, s. Rev. Henry Houson and Ann Clay. University, Oxford 1807, then St John's, Cambridge 1809, BA1811, dn11 (York), p12 (York), MA1814. R. Brant Broughton, Lincs. 1820 and R. Great Coates, Lincs. 1820 [total income in CR65 £1,545] to death 30/5/1873 aged 84, leaving £25,000 [C65505. YCO. Austin2] Married Averham, Notts. 25/2/1819 Frances Ann Chaplin (w), with issue.

**HOUSTON, *later* DOUGLAS (Alexander)** From Aikenhead, Lanarkshire, s. Robert Houston. Exeter, Oxford 1808 (aged 19), then Queens', Cambridge 1809, BA1813, dn13 (Salis.), p14 (Salis.), MA1816. R. Hartley Mauditt, Hants. 1816-33. Died? [C77711] Returned to Scotland to inherit 'the name and arms' of Douglas of Baads, Midlothian.

**HOW, HOWE (Christopher)** Literate: dn89 (Car.), p90 (Car.). PC. Newlands, Crosthwaite, Cumberland 1792-4 (res.), V. Glossop, Derbys. 1793-1849, PC. Woodhead, Mottram, Cheshire 1807. Died 1849 (3rd q.) [C6035. Platt] Married with issue.

**HOWARD (Henry)** Born Quendon, Essex, s. Rev. Robert Howard (R. Chickney, Essex). Clare, Cambridge 1805, BA1809, dn10 (Salis. for Bristol), p10 (Bristol), MA1812. PC. Stoke Ferry, Norfolk 1810-43, R. Chickney 1843-56. Probate granted 19/12/1856 [C52979] Married St Pancras, London 19/4/1816 Juliana Bettina Beevor (dau. of a baronet), with issue.

**HOWARD (Henry Edward John, Hon.)** Born Castle Howard, Yorks. 14/12/1795, s. Frederick, 5th Earl of Carlisle and Lady Margaret Caroline Leveson-Gower (dau. of 1st Marquess of Stafford). Christ Church, Oxford 1814, BA 1818, dn20 (York), p20 (York), MA1822, BD 1834, DD1838. V. Stainton, Yorks. 1820-24, Succentor and Prebend of Holme Episcopi in York Minster 1822-68, R. Slingsby, Yorks. 1823-34, V. Sutton on the Forest (o/w Sutton Galtries), Yorks. 1824-34, R. Donington, Shropshire 1834-68, Dean of Lichfield (with Prebend of Brewood and R. Tattenhall annexed) 1833 [total income in CR65 £2,485] to death. Dom. Chap. to his father 1824. Died Donington 8/10/1868 aged 72, leaving £60,000. [C21946. ODNB. Boase. YCO] Married Mapperley, Notts. 13/7/1824 Henrietta Elizabeth (dau. of Ichabod Wright), w. clerical son.

**HOWARD (John)** From London. Corpus Christi, Cambridge 1788, BA1794, dn94 (Nor.), p95 (Nor.), MA1797. R. Morley St Botolph w. St Peter, Norfolk 1800-32, R. Burnham Deepdale, Norfolk 1816-24 (res.), R. Tacolneston, Norfolk 1824 to death 19/10/1832 (CCEd thus) [C113599]

**HOWARD (John Flory)** Born Yattendon, Berks. 16/10/1800, s. Rev. Thomas Aubrey Howard and Charlotte Stow. Trinity, Oxford 1818, BA1822, MA1824, dn24 (Chester for Salis.), p14 (Salis.), BCL 1829. R. Frilsham, Berks. 1828, R. (and patron) of Yattendon 1829 to death 3/9/1873, leaving £5,000 [C94938] Married Norwich 15/9/1836 Jane Hansell, with issue.

**HOWARD (John Garton)** Born Sculcoates, Hull 30/3/1785, s. John Howard and Jane Broadley. Queens', Cambridge 1804, BA1809, dn09 (Nor.), p10 (Nor.), MA1812. V. Derby St Michael 1816-56, V. Stanton by Dale (o/w. Dale Abbey), Derbys. 1816 to death. Dom. Chap. to 5th Viscount Downe 1816; to Earl of Sandwich 1856. Died (Scarborough) 21/9/1862 aged 76, leaving £9,000 [C12267] Married Charlotte Christana Gorham, with issue.

**HOWARD (Robert)** From London, s. John Howard. Worcester, Oxford 1796 (aged 18), BA1800, dn01 (Ox.), p02 (Win.), MA1803. R. Burythorpe, Yorks. 1807 and PC. Scarborough Christ Church, Yorks. 1828 to death (Throxenby Hall, Scarborough) 19/5/1848 aged 70 [C77712] Married before 1814, with clerical son.

**HOWARD (Thomas)** Born IoM 2/9/1785. S/M Peel Academy [Ensign in Royal Manx Fencibles 1803-6, 'much loved by his men']. Literate: dn07 (S&M), p09 (S&M). Chap. Ballure, IoM 1807-09, V. Braddan, IoM 1810-36 (w. Braddan St George, Douglas 1832), V. Ballaugh, IoM 1836 to death 7/11/1876 aged 91, leaving £1,500 [C7292. Gelling] Married Braddan June 1810 Nessy Stowell (aged 16), 14 ch. (8 predeceased him).

**HOWARD (William)** Bapt. Hoggeston, Bucks. 1/1/1804, s. Thomas Howard and Mary Selby Lowndes. University, Oxford 1822, then New 1823-37, dn27 (Heref.), p28 (Win.), BCL 1830. R. Tattenhoe, Bucks. 1828, R. Great and Little Witchingham, Norfolk 1836 to death 20/1/1886, leaving £20,342-10s-1d. [C65511] Married Marylebone, London 2/6/1837 Isabella Hankey, with issue.

**HOWARD (William George, 8th Earl of Carlisle)** Born London 23/2/1808, s. George, 6th Earl of Carlisle and Lady Georgiana Dorothy Cavendish (dau. of 5th Duke of Devonshire). Christ Church, Oxford 1826, dn31 (York), p32 (York). Londesborough, Yorks. 1832-66 , R. Whiston, Yorks. 1841. Dom. Chap. to Lord Effingham 1841. Died (unm.) Ticehurst, Kent 29/3/1889 aged 81 ('of unsound mind' - unspecified), leaving £140,000 [C131635. YCO] Succeeded to the title 1864.

**HOWE** see under **HOW**

**HOWELL (Benjamin)** [NiVoF] R. Hughley, Shropshire 1826, PC. Acton Round, Shropshire 1833. Probate granted 9/7/1851 [C171825] Married 14/11/1840 Anne Lloyd (Acton Round Hall, Bridgnorth, Shropshire).

**HOWELL (James)** Bapt. Lanreath, Cornwall April 1748, s. Rev. Joshua and ?Dunnet Howell. Christ Church, Oxford 1766, Student [Fellow] 1766, BA1773, dn73 (Ox.), p74 (Ox.). V. Honiley, Warwicks. 1778-83 (res.), V. Ardington, Berks. 1778 [blank in ERC] to death 8/11/1838 [C12270]

**HOWELLS (Edward)** From Whitchurch, Shropshire, s. William Burghill Howells [pleb] and Mary Vere Fisher. Christ Church, Oxford 1806 (aged 19, as Howell), BA1809, dn10 (Salis. for Heref.), p11 (Heref.), MA1825. Custos [Head] of the College of Vicars Choral in Hereford Cathedral, etc. 1810-64-, V. Yarkhill, Heref. 1813-22 (res.), PC. Morton Jeffries, Heref. 1817, V. Blakemere w. Preston on Wye >< Heref. 1821 to death (Abergavenny, Monmouth) 29/10/1873, leaving £14,000 [C94966] Married Hereford 23/8/1821 Elizabeth Mary Morgan.

**HOWES (Francis)** Born Morningthorpe, Norfolk 29/2/1776, s. Rev. Thomas Howes and Susan Linge. Trinity, Cambridge 1793, BA 1798, dn00 (London), p01 (London), MA1804. V. Shillington, Beds. 1801-16, V. Wickham Skeith, Suffolk 1809-44, R. Buckenham, Norfolk 1811-14 (res.), PC. Norwich St George's Collegiate 1814-31, V. Bawburgh, Norfolk 1814-29 (res.), Minor Canon of Norwich Cathedral 1814, R. Alderfold w. Attlebridge, Norwich 1825, R. Framingham Pigot, Norfolk 1829 to death

26/3/1844 aged 68 [C1059. ODNB] Married King's Lynn, Norfolk 23/3/1802 Sarah Smithson, w. issue. Brothers below.

**HOWES (George)** Born Morningthorpe, Norfolk, s. Rev. Thomas Howes and Susan Linge. Trinity, Cambridge 1788, BA1793, MA 1797, dn97 (Nor.), p97 (Nor.), then St Catharine's, Fellow 1803, then Trinity Hall, Fellow and Tutor 1804-9. R. Gazeley, Norfolk w. R. Kentford, Suffolk 1808, R. Spixworth, Norfolk 1808-55, R. Kentford, Cambs. 1807 to death 27/9/1855 [C113603] Had issue. Brothers above and below.

**HOWES (Thomas)** Born Morningthorpe, Norfolk 30/11/1770, s. Rev. Thomas Howes and Susan Linge. Caius, Cambridge 1788, then Clare 1789, BA1792, dn03 (Nor.), Fellow 1793-99, p94 (Nor.), MA1795. V. Tharston, Norfolk 1796-1844, R. Fritton St Catherine, Norfolk 1797-1848, R. (and patron) of Spixworth, Norfolk 1806-8, R. (and patron) of Thorndon All Saints, Norfolk 1825 [C113606], R. Great Moulton, Norfolk 1845 to death 12/12/1848 [C100071] Married Attleborough, Norfolk 18/12/1798 Anne Franklin, *s.p.* Brothers above.

**HOWLETT (John Henry)** Bapt. Maidstone, Kent 6/7/1781, s. Rev. John Howlett (V. Dunmow, Essex) and Sarah Baron. Pembroke, Cambridge 1800, BA1804, dn04 (London), p05 (London), Fellow 1806-7, MA1807. V. Hollington, Sussex 1812-34, R. Foston, Leics. 1834 [pop. 27] to death. 'Morning Reading Chaplain' at the Chapel Royal, Whitehall 1809-67. Founder and Secretary of Kensington G/S 1831. Died (Hawkhurst, Kent) 10/10/1867, leaving £16,000 [C63867. Boase] Married Hawkhurst 16/7/1818 Sarah Ayherst, with clerical son of father's name.

**HOWLETT (Robert)** Bapt. Frostenden, Suffolk 23/12/1797, s. Samuel Howlett and Maria Smith. Pembroke, Oxford 1817, dn20 (London), BA1822, p22 (Nor.). PC. Dunwich St James, Suffolk 1832, PC. Blythburgh w. Walberswick >< Suffolk 1835, PC. Longham w. Wendling, Norfolk 1841-61, V. Hopton St Mary, Suffolk 1861 to death 1867. No will traced [C113609] Married Norwich 20/11/1827 Harriet Marsant, with issue [incl. Robert Howlett, pioneering photographer, whose work included the iconic photo. of Brunel besides the chains of the Great Eastern]. 'Around 1845, the parsonage in Longham had an electrical telegraph link to the local manor house only eight years after Samuel Morse filed his telegraphy patent in America' (Wikipedia).

**HOWLEY (William, Bishop of London,** *then* **Archbishop of Canterbury)** Born Ropley, Hants. 12/2/1766, s. Rev. William Howley and Mary Gauntlett. New, Oxford 1783, BA1787, dn89 (Cheshire), p90 (Ox.), MA1791, Fellow and tutor. Regius Prof. of Divinity, Oxford 1809. Fellow of Winchester College 1794. Dom. Chap. to Marquess of Abercorn (his patron). (succ. his father as) V. Bishops Sutton 1796, V. Andover, Hants. 1802, Canon of Chichester 1804, V. Bradford Peverell 1811, Bishop of London 1813-28, Archbishop of Canterbury 1828 to death 11/2/1848 aged 82 less one day, leaving £120,000 [C81317. ODNB refers to an unpublished PhD thesis] Married St George's Hanover Square, London 29/8/1805 Mary Frances Belli, 2s, 3 dau.

**HOWMAN (Arthur Edward)** Bapt. Gissing, Norfolk 1/4/1765, s. Rev. Edward Howman and Anne Preston. Queens', Cambridge 1781, BA 1786, dn87 (Nor.), MA1789, p89 (Car.). R. Burstow, Surrey 1790-1848, V. Shiplake, Oxon. 1799-1848, Durnford Prebend in Salisbury Cathedral 1810-48, Master of St Nicholas' Hospital [almshouses], Salisbury 1818-24, Minor Canon of Windsor Chapel 1823-7. Died 28/9/1848 aged 84 [C6037] Married Gissing 29/9/1790 Louisa Jane Cheveley, with issue. Brother Roger Freston, below. 'Passé' (Wilberforce).

**HOWMAN (Edward John)** Born Hockering, Norfolk 6/1/1797, s. Rev. Roger Freston Howman (of Beccles, Suffolk, below) and Rhoda Lens. Corpus Christi, Cambridge 1814, BA1819, dn20 (Nor.), p21 (Nor.), MA1826. R. Hockering w. Mattishall Burgh 1821, R. Gunthorpe, Norfolk 1830-1 (res.), R. Bexwell, Norfolk 1831-74, PC. West Dereham, Norfolk 1842-70. Died Bexwell 15/10/1874, leaving £1,000 [C113611] Married Alnwick, Northumberland 1822 Margaret Davison, with clerical son.

**HOWMAN,** *later* **LITTLE (George Ernest)** Born Bristow, Surrey 31/7/1797, s. Rev. Arthur Howman and Louisa Jane Cheveley. Balliol, Oxford 1815, BA1818, MA 1821, dn21 (Salis.), p22 (Chester for Salis.). R. Sonning, Berks. 1822-41, Master of St Nicholas' Hospital [almshouses], Salisbury 1824-78, R. Barnsley,

Glos. 1841-74. Hon. Canon of Bristol Cathedral 1845-74. Died Newbold Pacey Hall, Warwicks. 3/8/1878, leaving £36,000 [C94968. F. under Little] Married (1) Marylebone, London 15/11/1821 Jane Sarah Wightwick Knightley (of Warwick, she d.1845), w. clerical s. Edward James Howman (2) Rendcomb, Glos. 29/4/1854 Mary Ann Fullerton.

**HOWMAN (Roger Freston)** Born Gissing, Norfolk, s. Rev. Edward Howman and Anne Freston. Pembroke, Cambridge 1780, BA1785, dn85 (Nor.), p87 (Nor.). R. Hockering, Norfolk 1787-1821, R. Shipmeadow, Suffolk 1803 to death [vacant in ERC] 4/9/1832 (CCEd says 7/2/1833) aged 69 [C113612] Married Norwich 19/7/1786 Rhoda Lens, w. son Edward John, above. J.P. Suffolk. Brother Arthur Edward, above.

**HOWORTH** see under **HAWORTH**

**HOYLE (Charles)** Bapt. Halifax, Yorks. 1/9/1772, s. Robert Hoyle. Trinity, Cambridge 1789, BA1794, dn94 (Lin.), p96 (Lin.), MA 1797, etc. PC. Portsea St George, Hants. 1800, V. Overton w. Fyfield, Wilts. 1812 to death. Dom. Chap. to 7th Duke of Marlborough 1817. Died 13/11/1848 [C65520]

**HOYLE (James)** Bapt. Grantham, Lincs. 18/1/1802, s. Rowland Hoyle and Elizabeth Rawlinson. St John's, Cambridge 1823, BA 1827, dn27 (Lin.), p28 (Lin.). V. Strubby w. Woodthorpe, Lincs. 1832-60, V. Burton Dassett, Warwicks. 1860 to death 26/1/1883. No will traced [C65521] Married (1) Swaby, Lincs. 25/11/1829 Ann Edwards (d.1845), with issue (2) Bloomsbury, London 25/4/1848 Margaret Harber Diggle.

**HUBBARD (Henry)** Born Bury St Edmunds, Suffolk, s. George Hubbard (surgeon) and Susan Pretyman. St Catharine's, Cambridge 1814, BA1818, dn18 (Lin.), p19 (Lin.), MA 1822. R. Hinton Ampner, Hants. 1822-78, R. Cheriton, Hants. [net income £1,192] (and Preacher throughout the Diocese of Winchester) 1825 [total income in CR65 £2,191] to death. Chap. St Cross Hospital [almshouses], Winchester. Died 13/2/1878 aged 82, leaving £450 [C65526] Married Stamford, Lincs. 11/3/1843 Mary Gouger, with issue. Brother below.

**HUBBARD (Thomas)** Born Bury St Edmunds, Suffolk 29/4/1798, s. George Hubbard (surgeon) and Susan Pretyman. Corpus Christi, Cambridge 1817, BA1821, dn21 (Nor.), p22 (Nor.). R. West Stow w. Wordwell, Suffolk 1828 to death 12/12/1845 [C113614] Brother above.

**HUCK (Richard)** From Soho, London, s. Samuel Huck. Christ Church, Oxford 1795 (aged 19), BA1779, dn01 (York), p01 (Ox.), MA1802. V. Corton, Suffolk 1801, R. Gunton, Suffolk 1801, R. Fishley, Norfolk 1801 [one house only in this parish]. Buried Shoreditch, London 28/1/1837 [C31945. YCO]

**HUDLESTON (Andrew)** Bapt. Whitehaven, Cumberland 3/1/1779, s. Rev. Wilfrid Hudleston and Elizabeth Airy. Trinity, Cambridge 1795, BA1801, dn02 (Chester), p02 (Chester), MA1808, DD1832. (succ. his father as) PC. Whitehaven St Nicholas 1811-51, R. Moresby, Cumberland 1821-29, R. Bowness, Cumberland 1828 (non-res.) to death (unmarried) Whitehaven 22/11/1851 aged 72 [C6038. Platt]

**HUDSON (John)** Born Beetham, Westmorland, s. John Hudson (farmer) and Isabella Muckalt. Trinity, Cambridge 1793 (aged 20), BA1797 (Senior Wrangler), Fellow 1798, MA 1800, dn05 (Llandaff), p07 (Ely). V. (Kirkby) Kendal Holy Trinity, Westmorland 1815 to death (Haversham, Bucks.) 31/10/1843 aged 71 [C100072] Married Beetham 22/2/1816 Frances, dau. of Capt. William Culliford, with issue.

**HUDSON (Joseph)** Born Caldbeck, Cumberland 14/12/1761, s. Christopher and Sarah Hudson. Literate: dn83 (Car.), p88 (Car.). PC. Ivegill (o/w High Head) Cumberland 1784-1800-, C.-in-C. Warkworth, Northumberland 1790-1839 and V. Stanwix, Cumberland 1808 to death 14/11/1839 aged 77 [C6042. Platt] Married Castle Sowerby, Cumberland 1/7/1790 Rachel Monkhouse, with clerical son Samuel (below). Brother Samuel, below.

**HUDSON (Richard)** Bapt. Bingley, Yorks. 9/7/1746, s. Rev. Thomas Hudson. Queens', Cambridge 1764, BA1768, dn68 (London), Fellow 1769, p70 (York), MA1771. S/M Halifax Free G/S 1772, then Hipperholme Free G/S, Halifax 1782-1835; PC. Bolsterstone, Yorks. 1818 and V. Cockerham, Lancs. 1828 to death (Hipperholme) 28/3/1835 (CCEd says 14/4/1835) aged 89 [C119547. YCO] Married

Halton, Lancs. 25/5/1779 Elizabeth Harrison, with clerical son.

**HUDSON (Samuel)** Probably bapt. Caldbeck, Cumberland 8/5/1764, s. Christopher and Sarah Hudson. Literate: dn90 (Car.), p92 (Car.), Hon. LLB1811 (Lambeth). Minor Canon of Carlisle Cathedral 1794-1807, V. Castle Sowerby, Cumberland 1801-41, R. Hutton in the Forest, Cumberland 1811 to death, V. Cumwhitton 1826-32. Dom. Chap. to Bishop of Carlisle 1811-[19]. Buried 18/8/1842 aged 78 [C3414. Platt] Married Carlisle 24/11/1812 Letitia Scott. Confusion with the man below. Brother Joseph, above.

**HUDSON (Samuel)** Bapt. Warkworth, Northumberland 20/8/1802, s. Rev. Joseph Hudson (above) and Rachel Monkhouse. Peterhouse, Cambridge 1820, BA1825, dn25 (Car.), MA 1829. Minor Canon Carlisle Cathedral 1825-34, PC. Cumwhitton 1826-32, R. Castle Carrock, Cumberland 1831 to death 15/5/1834 aged 32 (CCEd says 23/6/1834) [C3413. Venn is confused with the man above. Platt] Married Stanwix, Cumberland 30/4/1833 Margaret Baty, with issue.

**HUDSON (Thomas Dawson)** Born Dulwich, Surrey 5/9/1804, s. William Hudson and Margaret Dawson. Exeter, Oxford 1822, BA 1827, dn28 (Ely for Chich.), MA1830, p30 (Chich.). R. Buscot, Berks. 1830. Lived at Frogmore House, Aston, Herts. Died Upper Norwood, Surrey 16/11/1889 aged 85, leaving £85,832-5s-10d. [C63951] Married Water Stratford, Bucks. 15/5/1839 Isabella Mary Bennett, with issue.

**HUDSON (William)** Probably bapt. Caldbeck, Cumberland 11/5/1800, s. William Hudson and Jane Scott. St Bees adm. 1822, dn23 (Car.), p24 (Car.). PC. Hesket in the Forest, Cumberland 1829 and PC. Armathwaite, Cumberland 1838 to death 21/1/1865 aged 65, leaving £800 [C3415. Platt] Married Edenhall, Cumberland 2/11/1827 Anne Wilson (w), (Dolphenby Hall), with issue.

**HUE (Corbet)** Born St Helier, Jersey, Channel Islands 3/7/1769, s. John Hue and Anne Dolbert. Exeter, Oxford 1786, then Jesus, Fellow 1790-1820, BA1790, MA1792, dn94 (Ox.), p94 (Ox.), BD1800, DD1818. R. Braunston, Northants. 1819 and R. Jersey St Helier 1823 (w. All Saints Chapel 1825) and Dean of Jersey 1823 to death. Buried 15/12/1837. 'Supposed' to have died (unm.?) worth £80,000 [C31949] Port. online.

**HUGHES, *later* HUGHES-HALLETT (Charles)** Born Betteshanger, Kent 5/4/1778, s. William Hughes. Oriel, Oxford 1796, BA1799, dn01 (London or Nor. for Cant.), p02 (Win. for Cant.), MA1803. PC. Little Dunmow, Essex 1802-24, (Sinecure R. Gestingthorpe, Middx. 1802), R. Wixoe, Suffolk 1808-31, V. Patrixbourne w. Bridge, Kent 1813. Dom. Chap. to 3rd Baron Sondes 1813. Died 10/5/1846 [C78224] Married Mersham, Kent 15/5/1806 Frances Anne Knatchbull, with issue.

**HUGHES (Charles William)** From Bucks. Corpus Christi, Cambridge 1822, BA1826, dn26 (Lin.), p26 (Lin.), MA1829. (first) PC. Lacey Green, Bucks. 1826, PC. Princes Risborough, Bucks. 1826-44, PC. Burcombe, Wilts. 1845 to death 15/8/1853 aged 57 [C65539]

**HUGHES (David)** [MA1808 but NiVoF] V. (and patron) of Englishcombe, Som. 1808-38. Probate granted Bath 7/3/1854 [C99177] Wife Sarah.

**HUGHES (Edward)** From Amlwch, Anglesey, s. William Hughes. Jesus, Oxford 1804 (aged 17). BA1808, dn09, MA1810, p10 (Ox.), p11 (Ox.), BD1818, Fellow to 1833, Vice-President Jesus College 1823. V. Nutfield, Surrey 1832 to death 23/12/1864, leaving £1,500 [C31955]

**HUGHES (John)** From Pill, Som., s. John Hughes. St Alban Hall, Oxford 1790 (aged 23), then Exeter, BA1794, dn94 (Glos.), p95 (Glos.), then St John's, Cambridge 1808, MA1808. V. Evesbatch, Heref. 1812 and R. Cranford, Middx. 1814 to death. Chap. in Ordinary 1814; Dom. Chap. to Mary, Countess of Berkeley 1813. Died 5/6/1837 [C119553]

**HUGHES (John)** From Hereford, s. Rev. Samuel Hughes. BNC, Oxford 1823 (aged 18), BA1827, dn27 (Heref.), dn28 (Heref.), MA1836. R. Coddington, Heref. 1831, R. Wombourne w. Trysall, Staffs. 1836 to death 18/11/1848 [C171841]

**HUGHES (John William)** Bapt. Chichester 1/4/1796, s. John Conway and Ann Hughes. Trinity, Oxford 1813, BA1817, dn19 (Ox.), MA 1820, p20 (Ox.), All Souls, Chaplain 1826-50. R. Oxford St Clement 1831 to death there

16/3/1850 [C31966] Married Holborn, London 27/1/1818 Lucy Maria Vickery, with clerical son John William Conway Hughes.

**HUGHES (Joseph)** Born Llanfihangel-y-Creuddyn, Cardigan, s. John and Anne Hughes. Literate: dn23 (Chester for York), p24 (York). Chaplain of the Donative of Lockwood, Almondbury, Yorks. 1830, PC. Meltham, Almondbury 1838 to death 8/11/1863, leaving £6,000 [C135902. YCO] Married Appleton, Yorks. 29/8/1837 Catherine Laycock (w), with issue.

**HUGHES (Richard)** From Towyn, Merioneth, s. William Hughes. Jesus, Oxford 1783 (aged 29), no degree, dn84 (C&L), p92 (C&L). R. Shelsley Walsh, Worcs. 1816 to death 24/7/1835 (CCEd says 24/9/1835) [C12506]

**HUGHES (Richard, Sir, 4th Bart.)** Born 2/6/1768, s. Rev. Sir Robert Hughes, 3rd Bart. and Gratiana Mangles. Trinity, Cambridge 1784, BA1789, dn91 (Ex.), p92 (C&L for Ex.), MA1796. V. Walkhampton, Devon 1792 to death (East Bergholt, Suffolk) 3/1/1833 aged 64 [C12508?] Married Tavistock, Devon 8/12/1798 Sarah Perring Sleeman (a clergy dau.), and had issue. Assumed title 1814.

**HUGHES (Robert Edward)** Bapt. Shenington, Glos. 20/12/1775, s. Rev. Edward Hughes and Rebecca Chamberlain. Magdalen, Oxford 1792, BA1796, dn98 (Ox.), MA1799 (as Robert), p99 (Ox.). R. Shenington 1801-46, R. Broughton, Oxon. 1814-19 (res.), R. Alkerton, Oxon. 1835 to death. Dom. Chap. to 5th Earl of Jersey 1815-35 [C33234] Married Ambrosden, Oxon. by 1807 Martha Pyner, with clerical son of father's name, also in Shenington.

**HUGHES (Roger Barnston)** Born Kettering, Northants., s. Rev. William Hughes. Lincoln, Oxford 1790, dn94 (C&L for Peterb.), p97 (Peterb.), BA1808, then Emmanuel, Cambridge, MA1808. V. Rothersthorpe, Northants. 1797-1849, R. (and patron) of Kislingbury, Northants. 1801 to death. Dom. Chap. to 1st Baron Dundas 1808. Died 11/7/1849 [C12513] Married Heyford, Northants. 22/10/1801 Elizabeth Jephcott (a clergy dau.), with issue.

**HUGHES (Thomas)** Born Ruthin, Denbigh 1756, s. Rev. Thomas Hughes, sen. and Elizabeth Salusbury. St John's, Cambridge 1773, BA1777, dn77 (C&L), MA1780, p81 (Peterb. for C&L), DD1807 Lambeth. Tutor in Royal Family to Dukes of Cumberland, Cambridge and Clarence; 5th Prebend of Worcester Cathedral 1788-1793 (res.), PC. Putney, London 1788-1803, Prebend of Westminster Abbey 1793-1807, R. Shenley, Herts. 1799-1801 (res.), R. Peasemore, Berks. 1801-7 (res.), R. Turweston, Bucks. 1802-4 (res.), Canon Residentiary and Prebend of Consumpta per Mare in St Paul's Cathedral, London 1807-33, V. Chiswick, London 1808-9, V. Cilcain (or Kilkern), Flint. 1809-33, R. Uffington, Berks. 1816 to death. Chap. in Ordinary 1802 and Clerk of the Closet. Died 6/1/1833 aged 76 (CCEd says 1/2/1833) [C12307] Married Walcot, Bath 26/1/1789 Mary Anne Watts ('Mrs Hughes of Uffington', a clergy dau.), with issue. 'Intimate friend of Walter Scott, Southey and other eminent literary men'.

**HUGHES (Thomas Smart)** Born Nuneaton, Warwicks. 25/8/1786, s. Rev. Hugh Hughes. St John's, Cambridge 1803, BA1808, Fellow 1810-15, MA1811, then Trinity Hall, Fellow and Tutor 1815, dn15 (Ely), then Fellow of Emmanuel 1817, p19 (Bristol), BD1818, DD by 1827, Christian Advocate to the University 1822-9. S/M Harrow School 1809-11; travelling tutor to Robert Townley Parker (Cuerdon Hall. Preston, Lancs.) 1812-14; Canon and 6th Prebend of Peterborough Cathedral 1827-47, R. Fiskerton, Lincs. 1829-47, R. Hardwycke, Northants. 1832-6, PC. Edgware, London 1846 to death 11/8/1847 [C52992. ODNB] Married Peterborough 13/4/1823 Ann Maria Forster (a clergy dau., Great Yarmouth), with issue.

**HUGHES (William Jones)** From Chester, s. William Hughes. BNC, Oxford 1809 (aged 18), BA1812, dn14 (C&L), p15 (C&L), MA1817. V. Cardington, Shropshire 1819 to death 19/9/1865, leaving £600 [C12524] Had issue.

**HUGHILL** see under **HEWGILL**

**HUISH** see under **HUYSHE**

**HULL (John)** Bapt. Stevenage, Herts. 5/10/1767, s. Rev. William Hull and Janet Fishwick. St John's, Cambridge 1787, BA1791, dn91 (London), MA1794. p95 (Lin.). R. Little Wymondley, Herts. 1798-1816, R. Upper (o/w Over) Stondon, Beds. 1809 and V. Shillington, Beds. 1816 to death 8/11/1844 aged 77 [C65553] Married (1) Hackney, London 6/11/1794 Caroline Dove (d.1800), w. issue (2)

Stevenage, Herts. Mary Smith (d.1826), w. further issue (3) Upper Stondon, Beds. 16/2/1832 Margaret Dixon. *J.P.* Beds.

**HULSE (Thomas)** Born Marylebone, London 16/8/1780, s. Sir Edward Hulse, 3rd Bart. and Mary Lethieullier. Merton, Oxford 1798, dn05 (Ox.), p06 (Ox.), All Souls, Fellow to 1837, BCL1807, LLB. R. Sutton on Trent, Notts. 1808-32 (res.), V. Upchurch, Kent 1809-18, R. North Ockenden, Essex 1817-27, R. Wickford, Essex 1827-32, R. Buckland, Surrey 1836 to death 7/10/1853 [C33241]

**HULTON (Thomas)** Born East Dereham, Norfolk 24/9/1802, s. Rev. Edward Hulton (R. Gaywood, Norfolk) and Plesance Bagge (of Gaywood Hall). Caius, Cambridge 1819, BA 1826, dn26 (Nor.), p27 (Nor.), MA1829. R. Gaywood 1827-53, PC. Ashmanleigh, Norfolk 1832, R. Beeston St Lawrence, Norfolk 1837 to death 16/9/1853 [C113625] Married (1) Bishop's Tawton, Devon 1/7/1830 Anne Chichester (d.1834), w. issue (2) Barnstaple, Devon 4/12/1838 Jane Penelope Bencroft, w. further issue. Surrogate for Norwich Diocese 850.

**HUME (Charles John)** Born Dunchurch, Warwicks. 6/7/1798, s. Abraham Hume and Sally Wheler. Wadham, Oxford 1816, BA1821, dn22 (Ox.), p24 (Ox.), Fellow 1824-30, MA 1826. R. Meonstoke, Hants. 1832 [gross income £1,037 in CR65] to death 25/7/1893 aged 95, leaving £1,583-19s-7d. [C33243] Married Caroline Oxenham, w. clerical son. Brother William Wheler Hume, below.

**HUME (George [Shuldham])** Born Broad Hinton, Wilts. 4/3/1800, s. Rev. Thomas Henry Hume and Anne Wingfield. King's, Cambridge 1819, Fellow 1822-5, BA1823, dn23 (Salis.), p24 (Salis.), MA1828. V. Warminster, Wilts. 1824-5, V. Melksham, Wilts. [gross income £1,265 in CR65] (and Preacher throughout the Diocese of Salisbury) 1825 to death (Clifton, Bristol) 25/11/1872, leaving £8,000 [C85944] Married Melksham 21/8/1833 Helena King (w). Surrogate. Brother below.

**HUME (John Henry)** Bapt. Broad Hinton, Wilts. 4/10/1796, s. Rev. Thomas Henry Hume (below) and Anne Wingfield. Balliol, Oxford 1814, BA1818, dn19 (Salis.), p20 (Salis.), MA 1821. V. Calne, Wilts. 1821-35 (res.), V. Figheldean, Wilts. 1821-81, V. Hilmarton, Wilts.

1835 to death. Dom. Chap. to 2nd Earl of Rosslyn 1821. Died (Cripplegate, London) 22/1/1848 [C95010] Brother above.

**HUME (Thomas Henry)** Bapt. City of London 10/7/1765, s. Rt. Rev. John Hume (Bishop of Salisbury) and Lady Mary Hay (dau. of the 7th Earl of Kinnoull). Christ Church, Oxford 1783, BA1788, dn89 (Salis.), p89 (Salis.), MA 1790. R. Broad Hinton, Wilts. 1789-1804, Prebend of Yatesbury in Salisbury Cathedral 1795-9, then Prebend of Bitton 1799-1806, Treasurer with Prebend of Calne 1806-34 (and Canon Residentiary 1803-34), V. Kewstoke, Som. 1799-1834, R. (and patron) of Brixton Deverill, Wilts. 1804 and PC. Stratford sub Castro, Wilts. 1804 until death. Dom. Chap. to 2nd Marquess of Bath 1799. Died Lyme Regis, Dorset 6/1/1834 aged 66 (CCEd says 16/1/1834) [C41400] Married Covent Garden, London 1793 Anne Wingfield, 3 dau., clerical sons John Henry, and George [Shuldham], above.

**HUME (William Wheler)** Born Bilton Grange, Dunchurch, Warwicks. 23/3/1802, s. Abraham Hume and Sally Wheler. Clare, Cambridge 1821, then St John's 1824, dn26, BA 1828, p29 (Win.), MA. PC. Aldershot, Hants. 1830, R. Scaldwell, Northants. 1836-52, R. St Leonard's-on-Sea St Mary Magdalene, Sussex 1852 to death 23/3/1890 aged 88, leaving £7,282-14s-2d. [C78230] Married (1) Newbold on Avon, Warwicks. 8/5/1827 Lucy Towers (d.1845), with issue (2) Chelsea, London 15/12/1847 Augusta Middleton. Brother Charles John, above.

**HUMFREY (John)** Bapt. Thorpe next Norwich, Norfolk 22/7/1764, s. Richard Humfrey and Elizabeth Maltby. Corpus Christi, Cambridge 1781, BA1786, dn87 (Nor.), p87 (Nor.), MA1789. R. Great Dunham, Norfolk [blank in ERC] 1788-1847, Prebend of Bedford Major in Lincoln Cathedral 1793 (living at Wroxham Hall, Norfolk) to death 25/6/1847 [C5661]

**HUMFREY (Lebbeus Charles)** Bapt. Kibworth Beauchamp, Leics. 5/8/1772, s. Lebbeus Humfrey (High Sheriff of Leics.). Peterhouse, Cambridge 1788, LLB1796, dn96 (Peterb. for Lin.), p97 (Lin.). R. Laughton, Leics. 1797 (and Prebend of Milton Ecclesia in Lincoln Cathedral 1802) to death 10/7/1833 (CCEd thus) [C65559] Married (1) Stretton-en-le-Field,

Derbys. 9/1/1797 Anna Maria Cave-Brown [Cave], w. child (2) Brant Broughton, Lincs. 30/10/1817 Mary Swann (a clergy dau., of Carlton, Lincs.); with issue.

**HUMFREY (Nathaniel)** Born Thorpe Mandeville, Northants. 6/5/1781, s. Rev. Ptolemy Humfrey and Mary Parrott. Lincoln, Oxford 1798, BA1801, dn03 (Peterb.), p05 (Peterb.), MA1806. (succ. his father and grandfather in the family living of) R. Thorpe Mandeville 1806 to death 10/12/1840 [C110354] Married Elizabeth Hill, with issue.

**HUNT (George)** Born Baswich, Shropshire 15/8/1785, s. Rowland Hunt and Susannah Ann Cornish. University, Oxford 1804 [Student of Lincoln's Inn 1806] BA1807, dn10 (Salis. for Win.), p10 (Win.), MA1820. V. Cardington, Shropshire 1816-19, R. Barningham w. Coney Weston, Suffolk 1818-50, R. Boughton, Norfolk 1820 to death (Wadenhoe, Northants.) 7/3/1853 [C78237]

**HUNT (George)** Born Plymouth, s. Nehemiah Augustus Hunt. Trinity, Oxford 1806 (aged 17), BA1810, dn12 (Ex.), p13 (Ex.), MA1813. V. Egg Buckland (o/w East Buckland), Devon 1818 to death on or about 20/2/1861, leaving £4,000 [C145156. Boase] *F.R.S.* Freemason.

**HUNT (John Higgs)** Born Gainsborough, Lincs. 27/1/1780, s. Joseph and Martha Hunt. Trinity, Cambridge 1796, BA1801, Fellow 1803, MA1804, dn15 (Chester), p16 (Chester). V. Weedon Beck, Northants. 1823 to death. Edited *The Critical Review*. Died 17/11/1859 aged 79, leaving £3,000 [C110356. ODNB. Boase] Married Adlington, Lancs. 20/6/1807 Maria Ann Manesty (dau. of the British Resident at Basra).

**HUNT (Philip)** Bapt. Newcastle upon Tyne 31/1/1772, s. Thomas Hunt and Cicely Hodgson. Trinity, Cambridge 1788, BA1793, dn94 (Lin.), p96 (Lin.), MA1799. V. Bedford St Peter de Merton (o/w Bedford St Peter w. St Martin) 1799-1835, V. Ravensden, Beds. 1810-17, V. Willington, Beds. 1810-34, V. Goldinton, Beds. 1817-28, V. Bedford St John the Baptist 1828-35 (with Mastership of St John's Hospital [almshouses] annexed), 10th Prebend in Canterbury Cathedral 1833, V. Aylsham, Norfolk 1835 to death 17/9/1838. [C65575] Reforming *J.P.* Beds. 'for nearly 30 years'; *F.S.A.*

'A powerful preacher, an elegant scholar, an efficient and active magistrate.'

**HUNT (Richard)** Born Aldgate, City of London 19/6/1765, s. George Hunt [*pleb*]. St Alban Hall, Oxford 1785, BA1788, dn88 (Heref.), p90 (Lin.), MA1791. V. Medmenham, Bucks. 1801 and V. Felkirk, Yorks. 1801 to death (Medmenham) 7/2/1837 aged 71 [C65576] Married Great Marlow, Bucks. 24/6/1799 Ann Banks Lovegrove, with issue.

**HUNT (Thomas)** Born Baschurch, Shropshire 12/12/1786, s. Rowland (F. says Thomas). Hill and Susannah Ann Cornish. Christ Church, Oxford 1805, BA1809, dn10 (Durham), p11 (Ox.), BA1812, Student [Fellow] to 1817. R. Wentnor, Shropshire 1816 and R. West Felton, Shropshire 1817 to death 15/9/1860, leaving £10,000 [C12565] Married Alveston, Warwicks. 23/10/1822 Jane Harding (w), w. clerical son Thomas Henry Hunt.

**HUNT (William)** From Tiverton, Devon, s. John Hunt. Balliol, Oxford 1783 (aged 17), then Corpus Christi, BA1791, MA 1794. Priest-Vicar Wells Cathedral 1793-7, V. Castle Cary, Som. 1801 to death 11/1/1845 aged 75 [C43720]

**HUNTER (George Rivers)** Bapt. Burton Bradstock, Dorset 4/11/1796, s. Rev. William Hunter and Marion Anderson. Wadham, Oxford 1815, BA1819, dn20 (Llandaff for Bristol), p20 (Lin. for Bristol). R. Okeford Fitzpaine, Dorset 1820 to death (Mayfair, London) 26/5/1872, leaving £1,000 [C4031] Married (1) Walcot, Bath 24/11/1835 Mary Sarah Avarne (d.1839) (2) Walcot Bath 22/9/1846 Lydia Mosse.

**HUNTER (Ralph Bates)** Bapt. Lisburn, Co. Antrim 19/6/1788, s. John Hunter and Hannah Bates. University, Oxford 1807, BA1812, dn13 (York), MA1815, p16 (London for York). V. Pannal, Harrogate, Yorks. 1816-35, R. Whalton, Northumberland 1824 to death 15/11/1842 [C119616. YCO]

**HUNTER (Richard)** From Ravenstonedale, Westmorland, s. Robert Hunter. Queen's, Oxford 1790 (aged 16), BA1795, dn98 (Ox. for Win.), MA1798, p99 (St Asaph for Win.), Fellow to 1817. R. Newnham, Hants. 1816 (w. Mapledurwell 1828) to death 18/8/1844 [C1911]

**HUNTINGFORD (George Isaac, Bishop of Gloucester, *then of* Hereford)** Born Winchester 9/9/1748, s. James Huntingford (a dancing master) and Sarah Oliver. New, Oxford 1768, Fellow 1770, MA1776, DD1793. V. Milborne Port, Som. 1789-1825. Fellow of Winchester College 1785, Warden 1785 to death (residing there) while also Bishop of Gloucester 1802-15, Bishop of Hereford 1815 to death 29/4/1832 [C32254. ODNB. H.M. Stowell, *George Isaac Huntingford, Warden of Winchester College* (Southampton, 1970). A. Bell, 'Warden Huntingford and the old conservatism', in *Winchester College: sixth-centenary studies,* ed. R. Custance (Oxford, 1982)] Huntingford never married, although banns were read at Headborne Worthy, Hants, Jan. 19, 26 & Feb 2 1777, but no marriage followed. On the death of his brother Thomas he took over the upbringing of his brother's family.

**HUNTINGFORD (Henry)** Bapt. Warminster, Wilts. 2/11/1787, s. Rev. Thomas Huntingford (schoolmaster) and Mary Seagram. New, Oxford 1807, Fellow 1807-14, dn11 (Glos.), p11 (Glos.), BCL1814; Fellow of Winchester College 1814 to death. Prebend of (Barton) Colwall in Hereford Cathedral 1817, R. Hampton Bishop, Heref. (with RD) 1822-67, Canon Residentiary 1838 (w. Master of Ledbury Hospital [almshouses], Heref. 1857) [total income £1,005] to death. Dom. Chap. to Bishop of Gloucester, and of Hereford 1814. Died Great Malvern, Worcs. 2/11/1867, leaving £8,000 [C146537. ODNB as classical scholar is slight. Boase] Married Ledbury 1840 (3rd q.) Eugenia Jane Money (w). Brother, below.

**HUNTINGFORD (Thomas)** Born Warminster, Wilts. 20/4/1783, s. Rev. Thomas Huntingford (schoolmaster) and Mary Seagram. New, Oxford 1801, BA1805, dn07 (Glos.), p07 (Glos.), MA1809, Fellow to 1812. V. Kempsford, Glos. 1810, Prebend of East Withington in Hereford Cathedral 1815-17 (res.), Precentor 1817, V. Dormington w. Bartestree, Heref. 1826-32 (res.), R. Weston under Penyard, Heref. 1831 to death. Dom. Chap. to 6th Duke of Leeds 1810-31. Died 13/2/1855 [C139688] Married Gloucester 4/12/1811 Mary Apperley, w. clerical s. George William. Brother, above.

**HUNTINGTON (William)** Born Sculcoats, Hull 23/8/1797, s. William Huntington and Mary Capstick. Trinity, Cambridge 1814, dn22 (Salis.), p26, MA1826. R. Manchester St John, Byrom Street 1831 to death. Dom. Chap. to Earl of Zetland; and to Lord Dundas. Died (Barton on Irwell) 13/5/1874 aged 77, leaving £1,500 [C169326] Married Hull 24/5/1828 Eleanor Ann Lambert, many ch.

**HUNTLEY (James Webster)** Born 9/9/1794, s. Rev. Richard Huntley (Boxwell Court, Tetley, Glos.) and Anne Webster (dau. of an Archdeacon of Gloucester). Queen's, Oxford 1813, migrated to St John's, Cambridge 1819, BA 1822, dn22 (Ely for Salis.), p23 (Ely for Salis.), MA1825. V. Clanfield, Oxon. 1823-36, R. Alderley, Glos. 1829-31, V. Thursby, Cumberland 1830 and V. Kirkland, Cumberland 1836 to death (Thursby) 30/7/1878, leaving £1,000 [C3416. Platt] Married Broughton Poggs, Oxon. 3/2/1829 Ann, dau. Rev. Canon Samuel James Gooodenough, 2 dau. Brothers Richard Webster, and Wadham, below.

**HUNTLEY (John Thomas)** Bapt. Newcastle upon Tyne 10/4/1792, s. Richard Huntley. Trinity, Cambridge 1808, BA1814, dn15 (Lin.), p16 (Lin.), MA1817. R. Swineshead, Hunts. 1819-45, V. Kimbolton, Hunts. 1819-45 [blank in ERC], R. Binbrooke St Mary w. Binbrooke St Gabriel, Lincs. 1845. Dom. Chap. to 7th Earl of Sandwich 1819. Retired to and died Falmouth, Cornwall 27/7/1881, leaving £3,210-15s-0d. [C65567] Married Derby 18/9/1809 Mary Blount, with issue. *J.P.* Lincs.

**HUNTLEY (Richard Webster)** Born Boxwell Court, Wotton under Edge, Glos. 2/4/1793, s. Rev. Richard Huntley and Anne Webster (dau. of an Archdeacon of Gloucester). Oriel, Oxford 1811, BA1815, then All Souls, Fellow 1815-31, dn17 (Ox.), p18 (Ox.), MA1819. V. Alberbury, Shropshire 1829-57, R. Boxwell w. Leighterton 1831-57, RD of Hawkesbury and Bitton 1840-51. Died Boxwell Court 4/5/1857 [C33256. Boase] Married (1) 8/7/1830 Mary Lyster (d.1857), with issue (2) Mary Huntley. Brothers James Webster (above), and Wadham, below.

**HUNTLEY (Wadham)** Born 18/12/1771, s. Rev. Richard Huntley (Boxwell Court, Wotton under Edge, Glos.) and Anne Webster (dau. of an Archdeacon of Gloucester). Merton, Oxford 1787, BA1791, MA1794, dn94 (Glos.), p96 (Glos.). V. Aston Blank, Glos. 1802-44, R. Eastington, Glos. 1817-31 (res.). Died (unm.) 27/11/1844 [C134507] Brothers James Webster, and Richard Webster, above.

**HURD (John)** Born 8/12/1782. Emmanuel, Cambridge 1800 (re-adm. 1804), BA1804, dn05 (Heref. for Wor.), p06 (Heref. for Wor.), MA 1807. R. Naunton, Glos. 1807-60. Died 1866 (4th q.) aged 83. No will traced [C121532] Married Longdon, Worcs. 19/10/1830 Emma Mainwaring (Chambers Court, Worcs.).

**HURD (William)** Usher at Wirksworth Free G/S, Derbys. 1769. Literate: dn70 (C&L), p82 (C&L). R. Hognaston, Derbys. 1782-1834, V. Heath, Derbys. 1796-1821 (res.), PC. Kniveton, Derbys. 1797. Died 2/5/1834 (CCEd thus) [C12310. Austin]

**HURLOCK (James Thomas)** Born Lamarsh, Essex 10/4/1766, s. Rev. Brooke Baines Hurlock and Charlotte Laprimaudaye. St John's, Cambridge 1784, BA1789, dn89 (Nor.), MA1792, p92 (St Asaph), DD1809. Prebend of Hurstbourne and Burbage in Salisbury Cathedral 1821 and R. Langham, Essex 1829 to death 2/2/1847 aged 81 [C95019] Married 28/12/1805 Mrs Barbara (Barrett-Lennard) Hitchens. Cowper the poet describes him as 'gentle and amiable, and well-suited to his post'. Brothers, below.

**HURLOCK (Robert Allen)** Born Stratford St Mary, Suffolk, s. Rev. Brooke Baines Hurlock and Charlotte Laprimaudaye. Caius, Cam-bridge 1790, then St John's 1792, dn93 (London for Nor.), p93 (Nor.), St John's re-adm. 1796, LLB1797. V. Whaddon, Cambs. 1797-52, V. Shepreth, Cambs. 1804. Died Camberwell, London (a widower) 12/1/1852, leaving £450 (the will left unadministered until 1871) [C100074] Married Holme-next-the-Sea, Norfolk 30/8/1799 Anne Elizabeth Vitty (of Cambridge), 1 dau. Brothers above and below.

**HURLOCK (William Milton)** Born Dedham, Essex, s. Rev. Brooke Baines Hurlock and Charlotte Laprimaudaye. Pembroke, Cambridge 1800, BA1805, MA1808, dn10 (Salis. for Win.), p12 (Win.). R. Hellington, Norfolk 1823 to death 17/6/1840 (residing at Dedham), leaving £600 (unadministered until 1871) aged 57 [C78242] Married before 1814 Elizabeth Swanton (w), with clerical son of father's name. Brothers above.

**HURST (John Day)** Bapt. Wakefield, Yorks. 3/5/1801, s. Rowland (a printer) and Ann Hurst. Trinity, Cambridge 1819, then Caius 1821, dn24 (York), p25 (York), dn25, MA1829. H/M Falmouth G/S, Cornwall 1840-1; R. Croyden cum Clopton >< Cambs. 1828-40, sequestrator of Arrington, Cambs. 1834, R. Dublin St Catherine's 1841 to death 26/11/1849 [C109743. YCO] Married Newtown Blossomville, Bucks. 14/10/1825 Louisa Laughton, with issue.

**HURST (Thomas Toller)** Bapt. Stamford, Lincs. 18/7/1762, s. Rev. Thomas Hurst and Margaret Toller. Worcester, Oxford 1781, migrated to St John's, Cambridge 1781, then Emmanuel 1781, BA1785 (Oxford), dn85 (Lin.), MA1788 (Ox.), p90 (Peterb.). R. Carlby, Linc. 1791 and R. Braceborough, Lincs. 1792 to death. Dom. Chap. to 10th Duke of Somerset 1792. Died 18/6/1844 [C67014] Married Braceborough 28/10/1806 Elizabeth Isabella Smith (dau. of a Stamford draper). Brother, below.

**HURST (Thomas William)** Born Stamford, Lincs., s. Rev. Thomas Hurst and Margaret Toller. Clare, Cambridge 1786, BA1791, dn91 (Bristol), Fellow 1794, p92 (Peterb.), MA1794. R. Wittering, Northants. 1794-1808 (res.), R. Brington w. Bythorn and Old Weston, Hunts. (and Preacher throughout the Diocese of Lincoln) 1814 to death 1839 [C67019] Brother above.

**HURT (Thomas)** Bapt. Teversal, Notts. 19/7/1773, s. Rev. Thomas, sen. and Amelia Hurt. Jesus, Cambridge 1791, BA1796, dn96 (Glos. for York), p97 (York). R. Linby (Lynby), Notts. 1797 and PC. Papplewick, Notts. 1797-1853, V. Sutton cum Lound w. Scrooby, Notts. 1804 to death (Papplewick, a widower) 14/8/1853 aged 79 [C117439 has death as 1820 and some benefices belonging to the father. YCO] Married Papplewick 12/11/1799 Henrietta/Harriet Unwin, with clerical son.

**HUSBAND (John)** Bapt. Masham, Yorks. 10/8/1785, s. William Husband and Mary Dalla. St John's, Cambridge 1806, BA1810, dn10 (York), p11 (York). PC. Whixley, Yorks. 1817 [C123940] and PC. Allerton Mauleverer, Yorks. 1829 to death (Whixley) 17/10/1846 aged 62 [C169296 as Hubbard. YCO] Another man of this name.

**HUSSEY (Thomas John)** Born Lamberhurst, Kent 4/4/1797, s. John Hussey and Catharine Jennings ('who was much put upon by an Irish barrister' who embezelled £50,000 from her).

TCD1814, BA1819, p23 (London), MA by 1831, BD and DD1835, incorporated at Oxford and Durham. R. Hayes, Kent 1831-54 (res.). disappeared (presumed dead) in Algiers 'on or since' 1866, leaving £1,233-9s-10d. His mysterious disappearance was never solved. Probate granted 19/3/1902 on his presumed death [C119660. Al.Dub.] Married 18/8/1831 Anna Maria Reed (noted mycologist and botanical illustrator, *q.v.* ODNB'), 6 ch. (2 survived). Strong Darwin connections. An astronomer on whose death his equipment was sold to Durham University. https://en.wikipedia.org/wiki/Thomas_John_Hussey

**HUSTLER (James Devereux)** Born Bury St Edmunds 24/12/1784, s. Thomas Hustler and Ann Nesfield. Christ's, Cambridge 1801, then Trinity 1802, BA1806, Fellow 1807, dn08 (Nor.), MA 1809, p09 (Nor.), Tutor 1814, BD1816. R. Fakenham. Suffolk 1828-9, R. Euston w. Barnham, Suffolk 1829. Dom. Chap. to 4th Viscount Gage 1813. Died 1846 (2nd q.) [C112720. Venn corrected] Married Norwich 14/2/1823 Elizabeth Mansel (dau. of a Bishop of Bristol and Master of Trinity College), with issue. *F.R.S.*

**HUTCHESON (William)** Born Portbury, Bristol, s. Robert Hutcheson. BNC, Oxford 1811 (aged 18), then St Mary Hall, BA1818, dn20 (Glos.), MA1820, p21 (Glos. for Bristol). R. Ubley, Som. 1827 to death (Clifton, Bristol) 10/10/1873, leaving £2,000 [C41401] Married Bath 10/3/1831 Marianne Whitaker (w).

**HUTCHINS (James)** From Douglas, IoM, s. Rev. James Hutchins. St John's, Oxford 1814 (aged 18), BA1818, dn18 (Ox.), p19 (Ox.), then Christ Church, Chaplain 1818-25, MA1822. V. (and patron) of Piddinghoe, Sussex 1825 and R. (and patron) of Telscombe, Sussex 1825 to death 21/9/1866, leaving £600 [C50482]

**HUTCHINS (John)** From Westminster, London, s. John Hutchins. St John's, Oxford 1783 (aged 22), dn84 (Lin.), then Magdalen Hall, BA1793, p95 (Lin.), then St John's, Fellow to 1812, MA1796. R. of the United Parishes of St Anne and St Agnes w. St John Zachary, City of London 1796 to death 28/12/1839 [C165388]

**HUTCHINS (Joseph)** From Westminster, London, s. Thomas Hutchins. Pembroke, Cambridge 1769 (aged 18), BA1773, dn73 (C&L), p74 (London for C&L). V. Offchurch, Warwicks. 1777-9, V. Lillington, Warwicks, 1778-95 (res.), V. Ansley, Warwicks. 1779 to death 30/6/1835 (CCEd thus) aged 85 [C12313] Clerical sons Edward, and William.

**HUTCHINS (Richard William)** Born Monkston, Hants. 2/9/1782, s. John D'Oyly Hutchins and Mary Borman. Queen's, Oxford 1800, then Magdalen 1802-11, BA1805, dn05 (Win.), p06 (Ex. for Win.), MA1807, Fellow 1811-28, BD1814, Vice-Principal 1819. V. New Shoreham, Sussex 1819-28, R. East Bridgford, Notts. 1827 to death 11/9/1859, leaving £3,000 [C63971] Married New Shoreham 30/10/1827 Eliza Marriott (w), with issue.

**HUTCHINSON (Benjamin)** Born Kimbolton, Hereford 8/8/1768, s. Rev. Benjamin Hutchinson, sen. (R. Holywell, Hunts.) and Jane Peet. Sidney, Cambridge 1793, SCL, dn96 (Peterb.), p00 (Peterb.). R. Oving, Bucks. 1803-21, R. Cranford St Andrew, Northants. 1805-22, R. Rushden, Northants. 1808, V. Kirkburton, Yorks. 1822 to death (Kettering, Northants.) 2/3/1843 [C67028] Married Peterborough 18/4/1796 Harriet Vinter, w. clerical son, also Benjamin.

**HUTCHINSON (Charles Edward)** From Beeding, Sussex, s. Rev. Thomas and Elizabeth Hutchinson. Trinity, Oxford 1810 (aged 16), BA1813, dn16 (Salis. for Chich.), MA1816, p17 (Ex. for Chich.). V. Seaford, Sussex 1817-24, V. West Firle w. Bedingham, Sussex 1824, Ipthorne Prebend 1824 (and Canon Residentiary 1828) in Chichester Cathedral to 1870, R. Eastergate, Sussex 1832, R. Amport, Hants. 1864 to death. Dom. Chap. to 3rd Earl of Chichester 1832. Died 27/10/1870, leaving £10,000 [C63975] Married London 2/2/1829 Lucy Cayley, with issue (and a possible earlier marriage?).

**HUTCHINSON (Cyril George)** Bapt. Manchester Collegiate Church 26/2/1800, s. Rev. George and Elizabeth Hutchinson. Christ Church, Oxford 1818, Student [Fellow] 1818-43, BA1822, MA1824, dn26 (Ox.), p28 (Ox.). PC. Hawkhurst, Kent 1832, R. Batsford, Glos. 1842, RD of Campden 1839, Hon. Canon of Gloucester Cathedral 1852. Died Bath 2/11/1887 aged 87, leaving £6,069-12s-10d. [C33652] Married Plumstead, Kent 19/8/1874 Ellen Frances Stevens (w).

**HUTCHINSON (Henry Matthew)** Bapt. Drighlinton, Yorks. 1/1/1787, s. Rev. George Hutchinson and Ann Finlison. University, Oxford 1807, BA1811, dn11 (Chester), p12 (York). PC. Middlesmoor, Kirkby Malzeard, Yorks. 1827 to (burial) Sandal Magna, Yorks. 21/6/1864. Will not traced [C131642. YCO] Married St George's Hanover Square, London 21/1/1819 Sarah Munday, with issue. Brother, below.

**HUTCHINSON (John)** Bapt. Tong, Yorks. 18/7/1776, s. Rev. George Hutchinson (PC. Drighlington, Yorks.) and Ann Finlison. University, Oxford 1796, BA1800, dn01 (York), p02 (Chester), MA1815. S/M Bradford Free G/S 1801; R. Ashton under Lyne St Michael, Lancs. 1810-16 (res.), (first) PC. Ashton under Lyne St Peter, Lancs. 1826 to death 26/5/1847 [C134797. Boase. YCO] Brother, above.

**HUTCHINSON (John)** [NiVoF] PC. Little Marsden, Whalley, Lancs. 1814-51, PC. Beckermet St Bridget, Calder Bridge w. Beckermet St John, Cumberland 1851 to death 26/4/1859 aged 68, leaving £6,000 [Possibly C169346?] Wife Charlotte, and issue.

**HUTCHINSON (John)** Born Edgbaston, Birmingham 21/9/1793, s. Elisha Hutchinson. Trinity, Cambridge 1811, BA1816, dn17 (C&L), MA1819. PC. Hanford, Staffs. 1828-50, PC. Blurton, Staffs. 1843-65, Prebend of Hansacre 1850-1 in Lichfield, Canon Residentiary and Precentor (w. Prebend of Bishop's Itchington annexed) 1850 to death (Blurton) 27/4/1865, leaving £4,000 (will revoked?) [C12315. Boase. *In memoriam: John Hutchinson, MA, Trinity College Cambridge*, by E.J.E. [(Newcastle, 1865)]. Had issue.

**HUTCHINSON (Thomas)** Bapt. Blooms-bury, London 3.11/1766, s. Capt. Norton Hutchinson and Judith Catherine Schrom (married in Madras). New, Oxford 1785, BCL1794 [barrister, Gray's Inn 1796] dn09 (Win. for Cant.), p11 (Cant.). V. Sawbridge-worth, Hants. 1817 to death 13/9/1856 aged 91 [C78246]

**HUTCHINSON (Walter, 9th Lord Aston of Forfar)** see under **ASTON**

**HUTTON (Charles James)** Born Combe Raleigh, Devon 31/7/1798, s. Rev. James Harriman Hutton and Elizabeth Paddon. Magdalen Hall, Oxford 1821, BA1824, dn25 (Win.), p26 (Lin. for Win.). PC. Chalford, Bisley, Glos. 1827, R. Ilketshall, Suffolk by 1851 to death 25/6/1855 aged 57 [C67037] Married High Wycombe, Bucks. 22/5/1832 Elizabeth Baly, with clerical son.

**HUTTON (Henry)** From Nymet St George, Devon, s. Rev. Charles Hutton. Balliol, Oxford 1768 (aged 18), BA1772, dn72 (Ox.), p74 (Ox.), Fellow, MA1775. V. St Lawrence Jewry w. St Mary Magdalene Milk Street, City of London 1780-93, R. Beaumont w. Moze, Essex 1793 to death (Clapham, Surrey) 24/6/1833 (CCEd says 16/8/1833) [C33660]. Married Westminster, London 29/6/1791 Elizabeth Royall Pepperell, with clerical son, also Henry.

**HUTTON (James Harriman)** Bapt. Exeter 10/10/1765, s. John Hutton and Mary Seward. Exeter, Oxford 1783, BA1790, dn90 (Ex.), p90 (Ex.). V. Leckford, Hants. 1823 to death 8/9/1847 [C78247] Married Exeter 31/12/1793 Elizabeth Paddon, with clerical s. Charles James Hutton, above (and 2 other clerical sons). Port. online.

**HUTTON (James Long)** Bapt. Sherfield-on-Lodden, Hants. 3/2/1765, s. Rev. William Hutton (formerly Long?) and Mary Turner. Christ Church, Oxford 1782, then University, BCL1789. R. Maids Moreton, Beds. 1790. Died Oxon. 25/9/1846 [C67041]

**HUTTON (John)** Probably born Burgh, Cumberland, s. John Hutton. Queen's, Oxford 1796 (aged 19), BA1800, p03 (Chester). R. Wyfordby, Lincs. 1816-[46], R. Granby w. Sutton, Yorks. 1826-[36], R. Knipton, Leics. 1835-[42]. Died before 1851 [C135906]

**HUTTON (William)** Born Beetham, West-morland 8/5/1805, s. William Hutton and Catherine Pedder. Queen's, Oxford 1825, BA 1829, dn30 (Chester), p30 (Chester), MA1833. PC. Helsington, Kendal, Westmorland 1832-7, V. Warton, Lancs. 1837-44, V. Beetham 1844 to death (Beetham House) 20/11/1881 aged 76, leaving £7,520-17s-10d. [C169351] Married Bramhall, Cheshire 12/7/1838 Margaret Denton, with issue [But note at Helsington Rev. William Moore 1802-31, and Rev. William Slater 1831-2, neither in ERC. This is probably the best example of several appointments within the actual period of the compilation of the ERC Report].

**HUYSHE,** *or* **HUISH (John)** Born Pembridge, Heref. 15/9/1800, s. Rev. John Huyshe, sen. (of Exeter) and Milborough Anne Harris. BNC, Oxford 1819, BA1823, MA1825, dn28 (B&W?), p29 (Ex.). R. Clyst Hydon, Devon (a family living) 1831 to death 18/10/1880 aged 80, leaving £4,000 [C145163. Boase] Married Mayfield, Staffs. 4/5/1831 Lydia Anne Greaves (w). Brother below. Freemason.

**HUYSHE (Rowland)** Born Clyst Hydon, Devon 26/8/1801, s. Rev. John Huyshe and Milborough Anne Harris. Sidney, Cambridge 1823, dn25 (Ex. for B&W), p25 (B&W), BA 1827 (as Roland). V. East Coker, Som. 1825 and R. Chedington, Dorset 1848 to death 31/8/1863, leaving £5,000 [C41406] Married East Coker 25/8/1827 Hannah Bullock, *s.p.* Brother above.

**HYDE (John)** From Oxford, s. William Hyde. Balliol, Oxford 1791 (aged 16), BA1795, dn97 (Chester), p99 (Chester), MA1803. PC. Pott Shrigley, Cheshire 1799-1804, V. Hellidon, Northants 1806-38, R. Oxford St Martin 1800, PC. Hailey, Oxon. 1810 to death 11/12/1838. Dom. Chap. to 1st Baron Churchill of Wychwood 1816 [C33665]

**I'ANS (Francis)** Bapt. Ilfracombe, Devon 7/4/1760, s. Thomas and Margaret I'Ans. Exeter, Oxford 1778, BA1782, dn83 (Ex.), p84 (Ex.). R. Cruwys Morchard, Devon 1804 to death 1835 [C146164. ERC as J'ans. F. as Jans]

**IBBETSON (Joseph)** Born and bapt. Knaresborough, Yorks. 17/3/1801, s. Christopher and Elizabeth Ibbetson. St John's, Cambridge 1818, BA1823, dn24 (Bristol for Durham), p25 (Lin. for York), MA1843. PC. Nunthorpe (in Cleveland), Yorks. 1825, PC. Newton in Cleveland, Yorks. 1825, V. Great Ayton (in Cleveland), Yorks. 1827-78 (res.). Died Darlington, Yorks. 18/10/1887 aged 89, leaving £6,262-11s-5d. [C52996. YCO] Married Ayton 6/1/1834 Elizabeth Simpson (Nunthorpe Hall, Great Ayton - 'a faithful shepherdess and exemplary handmaid of the Lord').

**IBBOTSON (Anthony)** Bapt. Giggleswick, Yorks. 16/6/1799, s. Robert and Isabella Ibbotson. St Bees 1822, dn23 (York), p23 (York). PC. (and patron) of Rawdon, Guiseley, Yorks. 1823 to death (Knaresborough, Yorks.) 3/4/1858, leaving £300 [C131645. YCO] Married Leeds, Yorks. 19/10/1844 Jane Rawling (w), with clerical son, also Anthony.

**IBBOTSON (Thomas)** Bapt. Kilham, Yorks. 10/2/1783, s. Rev. Adam Ibbotson and Elizabeth Rudd. Literate: dn06 (York), p07 (Car. for York). PC. Skerne, Yorks. 1808-52, PC. Lowthorpe, Yorks. 1808-52, V. Garton on the Wolds, Yorks. 1817-52, PC. Skerne, Lowthorpe and Little Ruston, Yorks. 1828 to death (Nafferton Hall, Driffield, Yorks.) 28/6/1852 aged 79 [C111306. YCO] Married Kilham 11/6/1807 Ann Cranswick, with issue.

**IMAGE (Thomas)** Born Etton, Northants. 1772, s. Rev. John Image and Mary Cox. Corpus Christi, Cambridge 1790, BA1795, dn95 (Lin. for Peter.), p97 (Peterb.), MA1798. R. (and patron) of Whepstead, Suffolk 1798 and R. Stanningfield, Norfolk 1809 to death 8/3/1856 [C67056. ODNB. Boase] Married Castor, Norfolk 15/1/1799 Frances Freeman, with issue. Assembled 'the greatest collection of fossils in England', which was bought by Cambridge University in 1856. *F.G.S.*

**INCE (Edward)** Born Herts. 21/8/1779, s. James Piggot Ince and Anna Maria Cumming. Corpus Christi, Cambridge 1798, BA1802, dn03 (Lin.), p05 (Lin.). V. Wigtoft w. Quadring, Lincs. 1817 to death 6/8/1840 [C278] Married Fareham, Hants. 21/8/1822 Mary Sophia Bouchier, with clerical s. Edward Cumming Ince.

**INCHBALD (Joseph William)** Bapt. Malton, Yorks. 21/2/1797, s. Elias Inchbald and Mary Rider. St Catharine's, Cambridge 1816, dn23 (York), p24 (York), a Ten Year Man? PC. Hundersfield, Rochdale, Lancs. 1827-57. Died Scarborough, Yorks. (a widower) 12/4/1861, leaving £600 [C131646. YCO] Married (1) Handsworth, Staffs. 1/2/1825 Anne Smeller (d.1833), with child (2) Rochdale 11/11/1833 Lucy Ann Royds, w. child.

**INGE (Charles)** Born Sutton Coldfield, Warwicks. 6/9/1760, s. Rev. William and Elizabeth Inge. Christ Church, Oxford 1778, BA1781, dn83 (C&L), MA1784, p74 (C&L). V. Rugeley, Staffs. 1784 and R. Newton Regis, Staffs. 1784 to death 4/10/1833 (CCEd says 2/1/1834) [C12927]

**INGE (Charles)** Born Benn Hill, Leics. 15/12/1796, s. Richard Inge and Mary Fowler. St John's, Cambridge 1815, BA1820, dn21 (Lin.), p22 (Lin.), MA1823. V. Weston upon Trent, Staffs. 1826 to death (Shrewsbury, Shropshire) 5/9/1858, leaving £20,000. Lived at Ravenstone, Leics. (w. Chap. of Ravenstone Hospital) [C12828. Hodson] Married Tarvin, Cheshire 11/9/1824 Mary Anne Oldershaw (a clergy dau.), w. clerical son William Inge.

**INGE (George)** Born Thorpe Constantine, Staffs., s. William Philips Inge and Lady Elizabeth Euphemia Stewart (dau. of the 8th Earl of Galloway). Christ Church, Oxford 1818 (aged 18), BA1821, then All Souls, Fellow 1822-80, dn23 (Ox.), p24 (C&L), MA1826. R. Thorpe Constantine 1824 to death 1/8/1881 aged 81, leaving £74,067-13s.-3d. [C12929] Widow Mary Anne.

**INGILBY (Henry John, Sir, 1st Bart.)** Born North Deighton, Yorks. 28/1/1790, s. Rev. Henry Ingilby and Isabella Jane Bates. University, Oxford 1808, BA1812, p14 (Salis.), MA1816. R. West Keal, Lincs. 1822-55, R. Cold Hanworth, Lincs. 1823-7 (non-res.), PC. Arkendale, Yorks. 1824-7. Died 4/7/1870, leaving £16,000 [C67059. Bennett2] Married 19/8/1824 Elizabeth Macdowall (Walkinshall, Renfrew), with issue. Baronetcy re-created for him 1866 on inheriting the Ripley Castle (Yorks.) estates of a titled relation 1866.

**INGLE (Charles)** Bapt. Cambridge 3/3/1795, s. John Ingle and Elizabeth Haggeston. Trinity, Cambridge 1809, BA1814, dn17 (Lin.), MA1817, Peterhouse, Fellow 1817-25-, p18 (Lin.). V. Orston w. Thoroton, Notts. 1821-7, V. Strensall and Osbaldwick, Yorks. 1827 to death ('*shot himself* through the heart with a pistol which he had grasped in his left hand') 18/11/1843, having married his housekeeper in Liverpool a few days beforehand (she bore his posthumous son) [C67060. Romilly2].

**INGRAM, *born* WINNINGTON (Edward Winnington-)** see under **WINNINGTON**

**INGRAM (James)** Born Codford, Wilts. 21/12/1774, s. John and Elizabeth Ingram. Trinity, Oxford 1793, BA1796, dn97 (Ex. for Salis.), MA1800, p04 (Ox.), BD1808, DD1824, Fellow until 1817. Rawlinson Prof. of Anglo-Saxon, Oxford 1803-8, Keeper of the University Archives 1815-18, President of Trinity College, Oxford 1824-50. R. Rotherfield Greys, Oxon. 1816-24, R. Garsington, Oxon. 1824 to death 4/9/1850 [C33671. ODNB and port.] Wife Elizabeth, *s.p.* Portrait online. Archaeologist and antiquary. A former Cornish wrestler fond of using strong arm techniques with his undergraduates. Author of *Memorials of Oxford* (1832-7. 3v.). F.S.A. (1824).

**INGRAM (John Richard)** Bapt. Claines, Worcs. 30/6/1783, s. Richard Ingram and Mary Thomas. Pembroke, Oxford 1802, BA1805, dn06 (Glos. for Wor.), p08 (Win.), MA1808. R. Droitwich St Peter, Worcs. 1810 to death (Feckenham, Worcs.) 31/10/1854 [C78257] Married Ilfracombe, Devon 9/10/1814 Mary Fortescue, w. issue. *J.P.* Worcs.

**INMAN (George)** Born Neachill Hall, Wednesfield, Staffs. 26/8/1777, s. John [*pleb – sic*] Inman and Anthea Ferremen. Pembroke, Oxford 1796, BA1800, dn00 (London for York), p01 (York), MA1805. PC. Easington, Yorks. 1813, V. Kilnsea, Yorks. 1813, V. Skeffling, Yorks. 1813 to death. Buried Kirk Hammerton, Yorks. 26/10/1856 [C111308. YCO] Married Louth, Lincs. 1/5/1816 Elizabeth Clayton Raines, w. issue.

**INMAN (Richard)** Born Dent, Sedbergh, Yorks. 25/1/1778, s. John Inman. Literate: dn00 (Exeter for York), p02 (York). S/M Bedale G/S, Yorks. V. York Holy Trinity, King's Court 1816 and R. Todwick, Rotherham, Yorks. 1816 to death 16/4/1866 aged 88, leaving £600 [C111309/135908. YCO] Married Bedale 21/12/1808 Deborah Inman (no relation, she d.1826), 14 ch.

**INNES (George)** From Devizes, Wilts., s. Rev. Edward Innes. Merton, Oxford 1778 (aged 18), then Magdalen 1781-8, BA1782, dn82 (Ox.), p85 (C&L), MA1785, Fellow 1788-93. S/M Rugby School 1783-92; S/M King's School, Warwick 1792; S/M Warwick G/S 1810; PC. Milverton, Warwicks. 1792-1831 (res.), R. Hilperton, Wilts. 1798 to death (Warwick) 17/7/1842 [C12933]

**ION (John)** Bapt. Bubwith, Yorks. 19/7/1789, s. Rev. George and Ann Ion. Pembroke, Cambridge 1816, BA1820, dn20 (York), p21 (York), MA1825, Fellow. R. Halsham, Yorks. 1825 and V. Hemingbrough, Yorks. 1825 to death. Dom. Chap. to Elizabeth, Viscountess Sydney. Died 9/10/1860, leaving £29,000 [Not yet in CCEd. YCO] Married Hull 27/5/1835 Ann Marshall, with issue. *J.P.* East Riding 1840.

**IRBY (Adolphus Frederick, Hon.)** Born Boston, Lincs. 24/2/1797, s. Frederick Irby, 2nd Baron Boston and Christiana Methuen. St Mary Hall, Oxford 1816, BA1819, MA1822. PC. Hythe St John, Fawley, Kent 1823 to death (a bachelor) 29/4/1863, leaving under £300 [C78259] Brother below.

**IRBY (Paul Anthony, Hon.)** Born 16/12/1784, s. Frederick Irby, 2nd Baron Boston and Christiana Methuen. St John's, Cambridge 1803 [admitted Lincoln's Inn 1804] MA1807, dn07 (Win.), p09 (Peterb.). R. Whiston w. Denton, Northants. 1809-51, R. Cottesbrooke, Northants. 1814-56, Hon. Canon of Peter-borough Cathedral 1845. Died 10/2/1865, leaving £9,000 [C67067] Married (1) Fawley, Hants. 2/12/1814 Patience Anne (d.1831), dau. Sir William Champion de Crespigny, 2nd Bart., w. issue (2) Loughton, Essex 8/9/1835 Wilhelmina Powell (d.1842), with further issue (3) Westminster, London 9/8/1849 Augusta Cowell. Brother above.

**IRELAND (John)** Born Ashburton, Devon 8/9/1761, s. Thomas (a butcher - *pleb*) and Elizabeth Ireland. Oriel, Oxford 1779, BA1783, MA1810, BD and DD1810. V. Croydon 1793-1816, Canon in the Succession of Hohn

Sudbury 1802-16, then Dean of Westminster 1816-42, R. Islip, Oxon. 1816-35. Dom. Chap. to 1st Earl of Liverpool. Died 2/9/1842 [C33694. ODNB and port.] Married Exeter 29/1/1774 Susanna Short, *s.p.* Endowed the Chair of the Exegesis of Holy Scripture at Oxford. Carried the Crown at the Coronations of George 4th and William 4th (see engraving in Wiki).

**IRELAND (John)** Bapt. Arkholme, Melling, Lancs. 3/5/1777, s. John and Alice Ireland. Literate: dn00 (York), p02 (York). PC. Skelmersdale, Lancs. 1804 (with S/M Skelmersdale Endowed School 1804-24). Buried 13/7/1853? [C134808. YCO] Married (2?) Melling 24/6/1844 Ann Downham; and issue.

**IRELAND (John)** From Frome, Somerset, s. Rev. William Ireland. Queen's, Oxford 1812 (aged 18), BA1816, dn17 (B&W), MA1820. V. Queen Charlton, Som. 1829 to death 4/5/1856, living at Nunney, Frome, Som. [C41409]

**IRELAND (Joseph)** Bapt. Tynemouth, Northumberland 26/6/1774, s. Rev. John and Catharine Ireland. Literate: dn00 (York), p01 (York). [Another J.I. ordained in York at same time]. R. Croglin, Cumberland 1804 to death 1837/8 [C117655. YCO. Platt] Married Wallsend, Durham 15/7/1801 Ann Cunningham, with issue. Another notes that a second marriage in May 1832 to a Mrs Mary Parker 'did not take place'.

**IRELAND (Thomas)** Probably bapt. Newton Reigny, Cumberland 1/7/1763, s. Joseph Ireland. Literate: dn03 (Car.), p04 (Car.). PC. Walton, Cumberland 1832 to death 28/4/1836 aged 73 [C6058. Platt] Married Wetheral, Cumberland 26/11/1812 Jane Young (w), with issue.

**IRVIN (Joseph)** Born Scarborough, Yorks. 4/3/1802, s. Rev. Thomas Irvin and Sarah Ann Ramsden. Literate: dn25 (York), p26 (York). V. Brompton w. Snainton, Yorks. 1829-56, PC. Hackness w. Harwood Dale, Yorks. 1842-56, V. Brotherton, Yorks. 1856 to death 20/12/1873, leaving £7,000 [C131649. YCO] Married Holborn, London 26/1/1841 Christiana Louisa Massingberg (w), and issue. Brother, below.

**IRVIN (Thomas)** Born Scarborough, Yorks. 17/5/1795/6, s. Rev. Thomas Irvin, sen. and Sarah Anne Ramsden. Literate: dn18 (York), p19 (York). H/M Thornton le Dale G/S, Yorks. 1829-40; PC. Hackness w. Harwood Dale, Yorks. 1818, V. Ormesby, Middlesborough, Yorks. 1837-64. Died there 23/6/1883 aged 88, leaving £1,306-15s-7d. [C131650. YCO] Brother, above.

**IRVINE (Andrew)** Literate; then Emmanuel, Cambridge 1811 (and again 1822), a Ten Year Man, BD1823. V. North Molton, Devon, 1814, V. Leicester St Margaret 1830 to death. Will proved 24/2/1847 [C67072] Wife Elizabeth Rawlinson.

**IRVING (Jonathan)** Probably bapt. Scots Presbyterian Church, Maryport, Cumberland 23/9/1784, s. Thomas Irving. S/M Sebergham G/S, Cumberland 1817. St Bees adm. 1818, dn18 (Car.), p19 (Car.). V. Gilcrux, Cumberland 1824-6, V. Wigton, Cumberland 1826 to death 16/10/1857 aged 69, leaving under £100 [C6059. Platt] Married Sebergham 8/10/1818 Mary Gill, with issue.

**IRVING (Matthew)** Born Langholm, Dumfries 8/8/1779, s. Matthew Irving. Edinburgh MA, then Pembroke, Oxford 1806, migrated to Trinity, Cambridge 1806 (a Ten Year Man), dn06 (Nor.), p07 (Nor.), BD1817, DD1831. R. Redmile, Leics. 1809-19, V. West Tarring and R. Patching, Sussex 1819-22, V. Sturminster Marshall, Dorset 1822-57, Canon of 4th Prebend in Rochester Cathedral 1824-57, PC. Chatham, Kent 1827 (w. Governor of Sir John Hawkins Hospital [almshouses] 1831) to death. Chap. in Ordinary 1825-57. Died Dover, Kent 6/10/1857 [C1432] Married Dinton, Bucks. 6/2/1817 Harriet Goodall, with issue.

**IRVING (William)** Bapt. Harrington, Cumberland 7/9/1794, s. Thomas and Peggy Irving. Literate: dn19 (York), p20 (York). Chap. of the Donative of Midhope, Ecclesfield, Yorks. 1824, PC. Bolsterstone, Yorks. 1835 to burial 24/8/1847 aged 53 [C41411 corrected. YCO. Note the entry in Venn and an Oxford namesake] Married Ecclesfield 13/9/1825 Matilda Grayson, with issue.

**ISDELL (Charles Drake)** Born South Stoneham, Hants., s. Nicholas Isdell [*pleb*] (of Hurley, Hants.). New, Oxford 1790 (aged 16), BA1796, dn96 (Ox.), p97 (Ox.). R. Winchester St Thomas 1800 (and Vicar Choral of Winchester [and Hereford?] Cathedral 1802) to 1841. Died (South Stoneham, Hants.)

28/7/1841 [C33686] Married Winchester 18/8/1831 Kitty Pitter.

**ISHAM (Charles Euseby)** Born London 24/2/1774, s. Rev. Euseby Isham and Diana Baber. Christ Church, Oxford 1791, BA1795, dn98 (Ox.), MA1798. R. Polebrooke, Northants. 1800-52, R. Oundle w. Ashton, Northants. 1807 to death 18/3/1862, leaving £25,000 [C33698] Married Stockton on Tees, Durham 9 *or* 12/9/1801 Caroline Bradford, with issue.

**ISHAM (Henry Charles)** Born London 13/2/1777, s. Sir Justinian Isham, 7th Bart. and Susannah Barret. BNC, Oxford 1795, BA1799, MA1801, dn02 (Peterb.), p03 (Lin.). R. Shangton, Leics. 1803 to death (Lamport, Northants.) 1/4/1833 aged 56 (CCEd says 8/5/1833) [C67073] Married Marylebone, London 26/9/1804 Marie Anna Buller, with clerical son Henry Isham. Brother below.

**ISHAM (Vere)** Born Marylebone, London 13/9/1774, s. Sir Justinian Isham, 7th Bart. and Susannah Barret. BNC, Oxford 1792, BA1796, MA1799, dn02 (Peterb.), p03 (Peterb.). R. Cottesbrooke, Northants. 1806-14, R. Lamport w. Faxton, Northants. [net income £1,085] (and Preacher throughout the Diocese of Peterborough) 1814 to death 27/2/1845 [C110373] Married Old Windsor, Berks. 4/8/1799 Margaret Chambers, with issue. Brother above.

**ISON (John)** Born Thornton, Leics. 18/8/1764, s. Joseph Ison [*pleb*]. St Edmund Hall, Oxford 1796, dn99 (London for York), BA1800, p01 (York). PC . Boughton Chapel, Notts. 1831 [not in CCEd], V. Kneesall, Notts. 1831 to death 14/4/1843 aged 79 [C117657. YCO. Noted in S. Slinn, 'Archbishop Harcourt's recruitment of literate clergymen: Part 2', *Yorkshire Archaeological J.*, 81 (2009) pp289-290 which shows him ordained courtesy of the Elland Society. Austin2, p134 notes his extreme poverty, 'with little or no food and fuel, and four sickly and dependent female relatives and one child living with him'] Was married, with issue.

**IVES (Cornelius)** Born Bradden, Northants. 1793, s. Cornelius Ives and Anne Van Mildert (probably dau. of the Bishop of Durham). Exeter, Oxford 1811, BA1815, dn16 (Peterb.), p17 (Peterb.), MA1818. R. (and patron) of Bradden, Northants. 1818 to death (Bradden House) 15/11/1883, leaving £11,180-15s-10d. [C110375. Foster corrected] Brother below.

**IVES (William)** Bapt. Bradden, Northants. 1799, s. Cornelius Ives and Anne Van Mildert (probably dau. of the Bishop of Durham). Balliol, Oxford 1818, BA1822, dn24 (Ely), p25 (Llandaff for Ely), MA1829. V. Caddington, Beds. 1825-29, V. Haltwhistle, Northumberland 1829-69 [income £1,095] Died Whitton le Wear, Durham 16/3/1875 aged 75, leaving £80,000 [C4039] Married (1) Humshaugh, Northumberland 26/9/1832 Mary Anne Richmond (d.1840) (2) South Shields 23/6/1842 Sarah Green (d.1857) (3) Hexham 1859 (1st q.) Ann Mewburn. Brother above.

**JACK (Thomas)** Bapt. Sowerby, Cumberland 31/7/1769, s. William and Elizabeth Jack. St John's, Cambridge 1788, BA1792, dn93 (London for Ely), p93 (Ely), MA1795, BD1804, Fellow 1804-6. Curate Hapton, Norfolk [in ERC only], R. Forncett St Mary, Norfolk 1805 to death 14/2/1844 [C100081]

**JACKSON (Benjamin)** Born Ambleside, Westmorland, s. of Thomas Jackson (a carrier). S/M Crosthwaite, Cumberland 1787-89. Literate: dn89 (Car.), p90 (Bristol for Car.). V. Alston w. Garrigill, Cumberland 1790 and R. Kirkhaugh, Northumberland 1820 to death 6/9/1834 aged 72 [C6063] Married Hexham, Northumberland 13/6/1793 Zilpah Bird, with issue. *J.P.* Cumberland.

**JACKSON (Edward)** Probably bapt. Irthlington, Cumberland 14/3/1771, s. Rev. William Jackson. Literate: dn97 (Car.), p99 (Car.). PC. Bolton in Morland, Westmorland 1799-1834 [blank in ERC] (w. Chap. Appleby County Gaol 1816-34), R. Dufton, Westmorland 1834 to death 19/6/1849 aged 76 [C6065. Platt] Married Kirkland, Cumberland 17/5/1806 Elizabeth Sewall (then a minor, 'her father consenting'), with issue.

**JACKSON (George)** Born Calcutta 9/9/1800, s. George Jackson and Mary Howard. Queens', Cambridge 1819, BA1823, dn24 (Lin.), p25 (Lin.), MA1826, then St Catharine's 1830. V. (and patron) of North Reston, Lincs. 1827 (and South Reston from 1845) to death 25/7/1868 aged 68, leaving £2,000 [C67078] Married 27/1/1834 Lydia Boughton Lister, with issue.

**JACKSON (James)** Born Cumberland 1796. Formerly a soldier, and a missionary in Nova Scotia. First student admitted St Bees College 6/1/1817, dn19 (Chester), p20 (Chester). PC. Rivington, Bolton, Lancs. 1823-56. Lived at Broom Hall, Broughton, Cumberland. *Killed* falling down Pillar Rock, Ennerdale, Cumberland 1/5/1878 aged 82, leaving £10,000. [C95027. Boase] Left a widow Agnes, and issue. Full article and photo. of this muscular Christian at: www128.pair.com/r3d4k7/HistoricalClimbingImages8.2.html

**JACKSON (Jeremiah)** Born Duddington, Northants. 29/7/1775, s. Hugh Jackson and Jane Weldon. St John's, Cambridge 1792, BA 1797, dn98 (Lin.), Fellow 1799-1801, p99 (Lin.), MA1800. H/M Wisbech G/S, Cambs. 1803-26; V. Swaffham Bulbeck, Cambs. 1814-27 (res.), V. Elm, Cambs. 1824-57, Prebend of Moughtry in Brecon Collegiate Church 1830 to death. Dom. Chap. to 3rd Lord Macdonald 1824. Died Wisbech 24/9/1857 [C67079] Married Stamford, Lincs. 8/6/1801 Mary Ann Willan (a clergy dau.), with issue.

**JACKSON (John)** Born Prestbury, Cheshire 1/9/1789, s. John Jackson [*pleb*] and Anne Hankinson. BNC, Oxford 1811, BA1814, p15 (Ox.), MA1817. PC. Pott Shrigley, Cheshire 1817-21, V. Over, Winsford, Cheshire 1821 to death 28/1/1863, leaving £6,000 [C169383] Married Prestbury 31/7/1817 Anne Molineux, w. issue.

**JACKSON (Stephen)** Born Ipswich, Suffolk 21/12/1785, s. Thomas Jackson (a printer). Caius, Cambridge 1803, BA1807, dn09 (Nor.), MA 1810, p10 (Nor.). R. (and patron of) Nettlestead w. Blakenham, Suffolk 1815 to death 4/1/1838 aged 52 [C113662] Married York 5/8/1816 Ellen Sarah Benson, w. issue.

**JACKSON (Thomas)** Probably born East Cowton, Northallerton, Yorks., s. Rev. Thomas Jackson, sen. [NiVoF]. V. East Cowton 1822 (with S/M Kirkby Ravensworth G/S 'for 28 years') to death 23/4/1842 aged 83 [C169391]

**JACKSON (Thomas)** Born Sheffield, Yorks. 31/3/1789, s. Edward and Hannah Jackson. Literate: dn17 (York), p18 (York) (some say BD, so a Ten Year Man?). PC. Slaithwaite, Huddersfield, Yorks. 1823 to death 1839 aged 50 [C131657. YCO] Married Dewsbury, Yorks. 3/10/1822 Sophia Hallilay, with issue.

**JACKSON (Thomas Norfolk)** Bapt. Beverley, Yorks. 8/12/1807, s. of John Jackson (surgeon) and Nancy Stephenson. Trinity, Cambridge 1826, then Caius 1826, then Christ's 1827, BA1831, dn32 (Lin. for York), p33 (Roch. for York), MA 1834. PC. Filey, Yorks. 1833-73 [parish sequestrated in ERC]. Died Weston-super-Mare, Som. 6/1/1891 aged 83, leaving £9,600-1s-5d. [C7165. YCO] Married Whitkirk, Yorks. 30/10/1835 Sarah Kilvington Barstow, with issue.

**JACKSON (Timothy Terry)** Bapt. Payhembury, Devon 8/12/1777, s. Rev. Timothy Terry Jackson, sen. and Catherine Rowe. Balliol, Oxford 1795, BA1799, dn00 (Ex.), p01 (Ex.). V.

(and patron) of Payhembury 1810 to death 25/1/1846 [C41414] Married Clyst Honiton, Devon 6/5/1807 Elizabeth Hodge, and had issue.

**JACKSON (William)** Bapt. Grasmere, Westmorland 17/12/1792, s. Rev. Thomas Jackson. Queen's, Oxford 1808, BA1812, MA 1815, dn15 (Chester), Fellow 1815-29, p16 (Chester), Chaplain 1820, tutor 1827, BD1828, DD1832, etc. PC. Langdale, Westmorland 1819-28, PC. Whitehaven St James, Cumberland 1821-33, R. Lowther, Westmorland 1828-78, V. Penrith St Andrew, Cumberland 1833-41, R. Cliburn, Westmorland 1840-58 and RD, Chancellor of Diocese of Carlisle 1846-55, Archdeacon of Carlisle 1856-62 (and 4th Canon in Carlisle Cathedral), Provost of Queen's College, Oxford 1861 to death. Dom. Chap. to Earl of Lonsdale. Died (Askham Hall, Westmorland) 13/9/1878 aged 85, leaving £35,000 [C6078. Boase. Platt] Married Liverpool 9/5/1829 Julia Eliza Crump, with issue.

**JACKSON (William Nelson)** Born Ireland, 1798/9. [BA but NiVoF] V. Kingsey, Bucks. 1833 to death 9/8/1876 aged 78, leaving £600 [C281] Married Wells, Som. after 5/3/1828 Isabella Smith (aged 17) (with 'the consent of Col. James Smith the lawful father').

**JACOB (John)** Born Ipswich, Suffolk, s. John Jacob. Jesus, Cambridge 1820 (aged 24, a Ten Year Man), dn20 (Glos. for Roch.), p21 (Ex.), LLD. H/M of the Classical and Mathematical School, Plymouth (o/w Devonport G/S) 1821; Min. Devonport St Aubyn, Devon [a Proprietary Chapel] 1821 [in ERC twice, again as Stoke Damerel St Aubyn], Preacher throughout the Diocese of Exeter 1824. Author of *West Devon and Cornwall Flora* (1835-7). Buried St Pancras, London 28/8/1849 aged 53 [C1920] Married Stoke Damerel 28/6/1825 Maria Johns (dau. of Henry Incledon Johns, poet and banker, and sister of Charles Alexander Johns, naturalist and friend of Coleridge), who after his death supported her family through literary works, especially on the *Illustrated London News*.

**JACOB (Philip)** From Roath Court, Glamorgan, s. John Jacob. Corpus Christi, Oxford 1821 (aged 17), BA1825, dn27 (Llandaff [for Win.?]), p28 (Llandaff for Win.), MA1828. R. Crawley, Wilts. (and Preacher throughout the Diocese of Winchester) 1831-84, Residentiary Canon (of 1st Prebend) in Winchester Cathedral 1834-84, Archdeacon of Winchester 1860 to death [total income £1,700 in CR65] 28/12/1884, leaving £6,017-12s-9d. [C4044. Boase. DEB] Married Richmond, Surrey 10/10/1832 Anna Sophia Noel, with clerical son Edgar Jacob.

**JACOB (Stephen Long)** Born Faversham, Kent 7/7/1764, s. Edward Jacob and Mary Long. Worcester, Oxford 1781, BA1784, dn87 (Chester for Cant.), MA1787, p88 (Cant.). V. Waldershare w. Whitfield, Kent 1799-1851, V. Woolavington w. Puriton, Som. 1801 to death 4/2/1851 [C43954] Married Ashford, Kent 28/12/1797 Eliza Susanna Bond, with clerical son George Andrew Jacob.

**JADIS (John)** Born and bapt. Seaton Delaval, Northumberland 26/7/1806 (but 'of London'), s. Henry Devereux Jadis and Maria Elizabeth Adderley. Corpus Christi, Cambridge 1826, BA 1830, dn31 (York), p32 (Lin. for York). V. Humbleton w. Elsternwick, Yorks. 1832 to death 22/6/1863, leaving under £100 [C67088. YCO] Married City of London 26/1/1844 Jane Ann Hopkin (w), with issue. J.P. Yorks. 1833.

**JAGO (John)** Born Tavistock, Devon 17/8/1751, s. Rev. John Jago, sen. Exeter, Oxford 1770, dn73 (Ex.), p75 (Ex.), BA1776, MA1777, BCL1781, BD and DD1793. R. Whimple, Devon 1781-6, V. Rattery, Devon 1781 and V. Milton Abbot, Devon 1796-[1835]. Died 1835? [C145303] Married Anne Darell Trelawny, with issue. Major confusion with clerical son of same name.

**JAMES (Charles)** Born Longborough, Glos. 5/1/1805, s. William and Ann James. Christ's Cambridge 1822, BA1828, dn28 (Glos.), p29 (Glos.). R. Evenlode, Worcs. 1830 to death (Torquay, Devon) 24/4/1857 aged 52 [C121609] Married Painswick, Glos. 19/11/1833 Esther Carruthers Dimock.

**JAMES (Edward)** Born Rugby, Warwicks., s. Rev. Thomas James and Arabella Caldicott. Christ Church, Oxford 1808 (aged 18), BA1813, p15 (Glos.), MA1815. PC. Mortlake, Surrey 1820-32, Canon and Prebend of St Cross in Llandaff Cathedral 1827-35, Canon of 11th Prebend in Winchester Cathedral 1828-54, V. Llangattock juxta Caerleon, Monmouth 1829-31, V. Alton, Hants. 1832 to death 6/4/1854 [C4046] Brother William James, below.

**JAMES (John)** Born Shrewsbury, Shropshire, s. of John James (a merchant tailor). Magdalene, Cambridge 1770 (aged 17), BA 1774, Fellow, dn75 (Ely), p76 (Lin.), MA1779. PC. Belford, Northumberland 1804-43 (non-res.) [C134564], V. Ford, Northumberland 1811-19. Died Belford 23/1/1843 aged 93 [C132234] Married Belford 17/8/1797 Alice Hall, with issue.

**JAMES (John)** Bapt. St Bees, Cumberland 25/3/1760, s. Rev. John James, sen. Queen's, Oxford 1778, dn81 (Car.), BA1782, p82 (Car.). PC. Nichol Forest, Cumberland 1808 to death 15/3/1846 aged 88 [C6084 and possibly 6080 and 6084? Platt says literate] Married Mary Gell, with issue. Confusion here.

**JAMES (John)** Bapt. Cambridge 9/7/1783, s. John James. St John's, Oxford 1799, BA1803, dn06 (Ox.), p07 (Nor.), MA1807, BD and DD 1834. S/M Oundle G/S, Northants.; V. Southwick, Northants. 1822-32, Canon Residentiary (of 1st Prebend) in Peterborough Cathedral 1829-68, V. Maxey, Northants. 1831, V. Peterborough St John the Baptist 1833, PC. Peakirk w. Glinton, Northants. 1850-65, V. Glinton 1865 to death [total income £1,135 in CR65]. Dom. Chap. to Bishop of Llandaff, then of Peterborough 1833. Died 15/12/1868, leaving £20,000 [C33743]

**JAMES (John)** Bapt. Redbrook Newland, Glos. 5/12/1806, s. John and Elizabeth James. Queen's, Oxford 1824, BA1828, dn30 (C&L), p31 (London for York), MA1831. R. Rawmarsh, Yorks. 1831-43, V. Pinhoe, Exeter 1844, PC. Tormohun and Cockington, Devon 1844-8, V. Headington Quarry, Oxon. 1851-3, R. Avington, Hungerford, Berks. 1853-79. Retired to Lydney (on Severn), Glos.: died there 18/12/1886, leaving £17,998-15s-7d. [C12972. Boase. YCO] Married Liverpool 4/8/1828 Elizabeth, dau. William Wilberforce, *M.P.* (she d.1832), with issue. Surrogate 1855.

**JAMES (Josiah)** Born Presteign, Radnorshire, s. David Jenkyns James (Sheriff) and Mary Kinsey. BNC, Oxford 1823 (aged 18), migrated to St John's, Cambridge, dn28 (Heref.), BA1829, p29 (Heref.), MA1832. PC. Eyton, Heref. 1830, R. Dore Abbey >< Heref. 1839 to death 25/3/1868 aged 63, leaving £5,000 [C171997]

**JAMES (Maurice)** From Bath, Somerset, s. Thomas James. Corpus Christi, Oxford 1798 (aged 15), BA1802, MA1805, dn05 (Ox.), p06 (Ox.), BD 1813, Fellow to 1830. R. Pembridge, Heref. 1829 to death (Cheltenham) 17/9/1848 [C33746] Married Marylebone, London 17/6/1830 Charlotte Chapman.

**JAMES (William)** Born Oxford 17/1/1781, s. Richard James [*pleb*]. Pembroke, Oxford 1800, then Sidney, Cambridge 1803, BA1804, dn04 (B&W), p05 (B&W), MA1815. Priest-Vicar of Wells Cathedral 1812-59, V. Long Sutton, Som. 1817-59, PC. East Lambrook, Som. 1825 to death 8/1/1859 aged 78, leaving £5,000 [C41420. YCO] Widow Mary Ann.

**JAMES (William)** Probably bapt. Exeter 30/5/1787, s. William and Hannah James. Corpus Christi, Oxford 1804, BA1810, then Exeter, Fellow 1810-15, MA1812, dn13 (Ox.), Vice-Principal of Magdalen Hall, Oxford 1812, p14 (Salis.), Chap. 1839-45. R. South Moreton, Berks. 1814 to death 21/12/1855 [C33750. Boase]

**JAMES (William)** Bapt. Rugby, Warwicks. 9/8/1787, s. Rev. Thomas James and Arabella Caldecott. Oriel, Oxford 1803, BA1807, MA 1810, dn12 (Ox.), p14 (Ox.), Fellow to 1837. V. Oxford St Mary the Virgin 1819-23, V. Cobham, Surrey 1823, R. Bilton, Warwicks. 1853 to death 11/11/1861, leaving £20,000 [C33751] Married Leamington, Warwicks. 4/1/1854 Anna Skipwith. Brother Edward, above.

**JAMESON (Joseph)** Bapt. Harbridge, Hants. 17/11/1793, s. Thomas Jameson and Mary Sympson. Literate: dn16 (York), p17 (York), then Trinity, Cambridge 1820, a Ten Year Man (BD Lambeth). Vicar Choral 1821-4, then Precentor and Minor Canon of Ripon Collegiate Church (later Cathedral) 1824-75 (Hon. Canon 1875), PC. Cleasby, Yorks. 1826 to death (Ripon) 9/9/1875 aged 81, leaving £4,000 [C131658. YCO] Married Ripon 24/10/1825 Anne Matilda Wood Schaak (w) (a clergy dau.).

**JAMESON (Joseph Bland)** Son John Jameson and Jane Bland. Literate: p17 (Chester), BD - so a Ten Year Man? PC. Heywood St James, Bury, Lancs. 1823 [sequestrated 1830] to death 17/5/1835 aged 45 [CCEd 169398 corrected] Married (1) Colne, Lancs. 1815 Anne Hargreaves (d.1825), w. issue (2) Bury 17/12/1827 Margaret Milnes, w. further issue. 'He was long suspended by the bishop, and died in an obscure beer-house where he had taken shelter from the weather. He was very poor, and left a widow and family'.

**JANE (James)** From Chepstow, Monmouth, s. Warren Jane. Jesus, Oxford 1780 (aged 14), BA 1783, MA1786, dn87 (Ox.), p89 (Ox.), BD 1793. R. Remenham, Berks. 1798 to death 15/2/1841 [C33902] Brother below.

**JANE (William Hurdman)** From Chepstow, Monmouth, s.Warren Jane. Jesus, Oxford 1771 (aged 16), BA1774, Fellow, MA1777, dn77 (Ox.), p79 (Ox.), BD1784, DD1789. V. Tredington, Worcs. (1st Portion) 1802 and R. Caldecot, Monmouth 1807 to death 10/12/1834 (CCEd says 6/1/1835) [C4069] Brother above.

**JANS (Francis)** see under I'ANS

**JARMAN (James)** From Llanfihangel Brynpabuan, Brecon. Trinity, Cambridge 1792 (a Ten Year Man). PC. Mark, Somerset 1816-44, R. Ladock, Cornwall 1844 to death (a widower) 26/9/1846 aged 87 [C41421] Married Bristol 17/5/1805 Amelia Gardiner.

**JARRATT (John)** Born Somerset 16/12/1798, s. Rev. Robert Jarratt (below) and Margaret Hey. St John's, Cambridge 1818, BA1822, dn22 (Glos.) p22 (Glos.), MA1825. PC. Stoke Hamdon (w. Montacute), Som. 1826-32, V. North Cave (w. Cliffe), Brough, Yorks. 1830-90, Prebend of Bole in York Minster 1858 to death (North Cave) 30/11/1890 aged 82, leaving £78,948-2s-1d. [C41422] Married Camden, London 2/10/1832 Elizabeth Holder, with issue.

**JARRATT (Robert)** Bapt. Hull 16/7/1765, s. John Jarratt. Trinity, Cambridge 1782, BA1787, dn88 (Lin. for York), p89 (York), MA 1790. V. Wellington w. West Buckland, Som. 1791 [income £15] to death (Leeds) 24/1/1843 [C44182. YCO. DEB] Married Leeds 18/10/1797 Margaret Hey, with son above.

**JARRETT (Thomas)** Born 1805. St Catharine's, Cambridge 1823, BA1827, Fellow and Classics Lecturer 1828-32, dn29 (Lin.), MA1830, p31 (Lin.), incorporated at Oxford 1847. Sir Thomas Acland Professor of Arabic, Cambridge 1831-54. Regius Professor of Hebrew, Cambridge 1854-82. R. Trunch, Norfolk 1832-82, Canon of Ely Cathedral 1854 to death 7/3/1882 aged 87, leaving £12,705-1s-6d [C67130. ODNB. Boase] Married (1) St Stephen's, Saltash, Devon 1/10/1832 Margaret Sarah Daw (d.1878) (2) Sarah Hume (not in FreeBMD) (w). Knew at least 20 languages, and would teach any language for whom he could find a student; 'but his really remarkable powers were dissipated by his versatility and lack of concentration.'

**JARVIS (George)** Bapt. Wymondham, Norfolk 13/8/1784, s. George Jarvis and Diana Vincent. Literate: dn11 (Nor.), p12 (Nor.). V. Tuttington, Norfolk 1826 to death 1852 (4th q.). [C113671] Married East Dereham, Norfolk 9/1/1812 Rhoda Crafer, and had issue.

**JAUMARD (Thomas James)** Bapt. Camden, London 21/11/1779, s. Samuel Jaumard and Marie Bernard. Trinity, Cambridge 1797, dn02 (Ely), BA 1803, p03 (Ely), MA1805. V. Pickhill, Yorks. 1807-25, V. Codicote, Herts. 1808-48. His death was recorded twice in the *Gentleman's Magazine* incorrectly as 1848, and correctly as Islington, London 27/1/1854 aged 74 [C67132] Married (1) Paddington, London 9/6/1808 Elizabeth Pressler (d.1809), 1 child (2) Hackney, London 5/1/1826 Sarah Sibley.

**JEAFFRESON (Christopher)** Bapt. Melton, Suffolk 15/9/1769, s. Rev. Christopher Jeaffreson, sen. (R. Tunstall, Suffolk) and Mary Syer. Pembroke, Cambridge 1788, BA 1792, dn92 (Nor.), p93 (Nor.), MA1799. R. (and patron) of Iken, Suffolk 1793, R. Tunstall w. Dunningworth, Suffolk 1793-1814, V. Longborough w. Sezincote, Glos. 1813 to death. Dom. Chap. to 2nd Marquess of Hertford 1813. Died 24/2/1846 [C113674] Married 2/3/1792 Elizabeth Syer (d.1837), w. clerical son (also Christopher). Port. miniature online.

**JEANS (Thomas)** Bapt. Christchurch, Hants. 4/10/1749, s. Thomas Jeans and Martha Gibbs. Merton, Oxford 1767, then New, Fellow, BA 1773, dn73 (Ox.), p74 (Ox.), MA1776, BD & DD1810. R. Great Witchingham, Norfolk 1786 and V. Norwich St John Maddermarket 1786 to death 20/4/1835 (CCEd thus) [C33907] Married Westminster, London 1786 Mary Springer, w. issue.

**JEE,** *or* **GEE (Thomas)** Bapt. Caldecote, Warwicks. 10/3/1776, s. Richard and Mary Jee. Pembroke, Cambridge 1794, BA1798, dn98 (London), p00 (London), MA1820. V. Thaxted, Essex 1806 to death 27/5/1853 [Probate as Jee] [C106751]

**JEE** see also under **GEE**

**JEFF (William)** Born Bolton Percy, Yorks. Literate: dn17 (Chester), p18 (Chester). PC. Farnworth, Prescot, Lancs. 1832-72. Died there 29/3/1874 aged 85, leaving £3,000 [C169402] Widow Ellen, *s.p.*

**JEFFERSON (Francis)** Born Wigton, Cumberland 25/10/1795, s. Robert Jefferson. Clare, Cambridge 1815, BA1819, dn20 (York for Lin.), p21 (Lin.), then Peterhouse, MA1822, Fellow? V. Ellington, Hunts. 1822 to death 31/7/1838 [C67136. YCO]

**JEFFERSON (Jacob)** Literate: dn75 (Chester), p76 (Car.). V. Barnby upon Don, Doncaster, Yorks. 1784 and V. Ridge, Herts. 1801 to death 28/12/1832 (CCEd thus) [C3421] Surrogate.

**JEFFERSON (Lancelot)** Born and bapt. West Ward, Cumberland 3/4/1784, s. of Lancelot Jefferson (a husbandman) and Maria Atkinson. Queen's, Oxford 1802, BA1806, dn08 (Win.), p09 (Win.), MA1810, Fellow 1815-29. V. Brough under Stainmore, Westmorland 1828-70 (with RD of Kirkby Stephen 1857 and Hon. Canon of Carlisle Cathedral 1862) to death 11/2/1870 aged 86, leaving £12,000 [C6090. Platt] Married Appleby, Westmorland Jan. 1833 Hannah Thompson, *s.p.* J.P. for Westmorland. Surrogate.

**JEFFERSON (Robert)** Born Cumberland 6/10/1782, s. Robert Jefferson. Sidney, Cambridge 1803, BA1808, dn08 (Lin.), Fellow, p09 (Lin.), MA1811, BD1818, DD1825. R. South Kilvington, Yorks. 1825 to death. Chap. to HRH Dukes of Kent (1819), and Cambridge; and to Duke of Marlborough. Died 31/1/1834 (CCEd says 25/3/1834) [C67138]

**JEFFERY (John)** Born Huntspill, Somerset, s. Joseph Jeffery and Mary Guy. Lincoln, Oxford 1787 (aged 18), BA1791, dn92 (B&W), p94 (Nor. for B&W), then St John, Cambridge 1806, MA1806, DD1822. R. Otterhampton, Som. 1794-1861, PC. St Michaelchurch, Som. 1804-22, R. Exton, Som. 1821-33. Died 19/11/1861, leaving £10,000 [C41425] Married 1838 Susannah Lewis Hole (a clergy dau.).

**JEFFREYS (John)** Bapt. Berkhampstead, Herts. 25/1/1771, s. Rev. John, sen. and Elizabeth Jeffreys. Christ Church, Oxford 1788, BA1792, dn93 (Lin.), MA1795, p95 (Lin.). R. Barnes, Surrey. 1795-1840, R. Friern Barnet, Middx. 1798-[1815]. Dom. Chap. to Amabel, Countess de Grey 1798. Died 6/6/1840 [C67145]

**JEKYLL (George)** Born Kingsthorpe, Northants. 23/9/1776, s. Rev. John Jekyll and Elizabeth Webb. Lincoln, Oxford 1793, SCL by 1799, dn99 (St Asaph), p02 (Roch. for B&W), MA by 1813, BCL1834. R. (and patron) of West Coker, Som. 1802-43, R. Hawkridge w. Withypool, Som. 1834. Died 1/3/1843 [C1925] Married Oxford 26/9/1798 Ann Brown, w. clerical son Joseph Jekyll.

**JENKINS (Clarke)** From Braunston, Northants., s. Rev. Jenkin Jenkins. Lincoln, Oxford 1796 (aged 18), BA1800, dn00 (Peterb.), p02 (Peterb.), MA1803, BD1813, Fellow to 1824. R. Winterbourne Abbas w. Winterbourne Steepleton, Dorset 1823, R. Great Leighs, Essex 1823 to death 13/11/1865, leaving £40,000 [C53012]

**JENKINS (David)** From St Clement, Cornwall, s. Rev. Francis Jenkins. Exeter, Oxford 1814 (aged 18), BA1818, dn19 (Ex.), p20 (Ex.). V. St Goran (o/w Gorans), Cornwall 1824 to death 17/3/1869 aged 72, leaving £5,000 [C145308] Wife Mary L. Richards, with issue.

**JENKINS (David)** Born Cardigan 2/2/1787, s. of Evan Jenkins (a husbandman) and Elizabeth Davis. Literate: dn10 (York), p11 (York). PC. Pudsey, Calverley, Yorks. 1814 to death 21/8/1854 aged 67 [C135917. YCO] Wife Rebecca (from Pudsey).

**JENKINS (Francis)** Born St Michael Penkevill, Cornwall 19/7/1756, s. David Jenkins (Truro). Exeter, Oxford 1775, BA1779, dn79 (Ex.), p80 (Ex.). V. St Clement, Cornwall 1789 to death 18/8/1839 [C145310] Married St Agnes, Cornwall 1786 Mary Thomas, with issue.

**JENKINS (Henry)** Bapt. Midhurst, Sussex 5/9/1786, s. Rev. Henry Jenkins and Elizabeth Marchant. Magdalen Hall, Oxford 1803, then Magdalen College 1803-27, BA1806, dn08 (Ox.), MA1809, p11 (Ox.), BD1827, Fellow 1827-31, etc. S/M 1810-28; R. Stanway, Essex 1830 to death 13/8/1874, leaving £14,000 [C33917. Boase]

**JENKINS (John)** Born Lampeter, Cardigan 30/7/1801, s. of David (a mercer) and Anne

Jenkins. St Bees 1823. Literate: dn24 (Chester). PC. Whitehaven St James 1833-52, R. Bowness-on-Solway, Cumberland 1852-5. His death (on 24/3/1852?) was reported prematurely [C169406. Platt differs substantially] Married Llangunnor, Carmarthen 12/12/1825 Catherine Lewis, with issue. *J.P.*

**JENKINS (John)** [MA but NiVoF] V. Knill, Heref. 1823, and R. Norton, Heref. 1827 to death, R. Llangua, Monmouth 1830-[43]. Died Presteign, Radnor 27/1/1860, leaving £2,000 [C172041] Widow Anne.

**JENKINS (William)** Bapt. Sidbury, Devon 7/11/1783, s. Rev. William Jenkins, sen. and Mary Pearse. Oriel, Oxford 1801, BA1805, dn06 (Ex.), p07 (Ex.), MA1808. V. (and patron) of Sidmouth, Devon 1821 to death 17/4/1856 [C145312] Married Puddletown, Dorset 1828 Mary Banger, with issue.

**JENKINS (William)** From Midhurst, Sussex, s. Rev. David Jenkins. St John's, Cambridge 1806, BA1811, dn12 (Chich.), MA1814. PC. Lodsworth, Sussex 1832 to death (Silham, Sussex) 27/7/1844 aged 56 [C64039]

**JENKINS** see also under **JENKYNS**

**JENKINSON (Fearon)** Bapt. Ennerdale, Cumberland 1/2/1774, s. William Jenkinson and Jane Fearon [BA but NiVoF] dn01 (Chester), p02 (Chester). PC. Chapel Chorlton, Staffs, 1806, PC. Gnosall, Staffs. 1817 to death 30/6/1845 aged 72 [C13080] Married Egremont, Cumberland 15/11/1802 Frances Shepard, 11 ch.:
www.gnosallhistory.co.uk/fearon_jenkinson.htm

**JENKINSON (George)** Born and bapt. Ings, Westmorland 10/7/1799, s. Thomas and Mary Jenkinson. St Bees admitted 1821, dn22 (Lin. for Durham), p23 (Durham for Ox.). PC. Whitworth, Durham 1828, PC. Lowick, Berwick upon Tweed, Northumberland 1829 to death (Belford, Northumberland) 11/10/1873, aged 74, leaving £2,000 [C33922] Was married. Suspended in June 1850 for two years for drunkenness.

**JENKINSON (John Simon)** Born Kensington, London, s. Lt.-Gen. John Jenkinson and Frances Fanshawe. Magdalen Hall, Oxford 1822 (aged 24), BA1827, p29 (B&W), MA1829. R. Sudbourne w. Orford, Suffolk 1832-5 (res.), Min. Hastings St Mary-in-the-Castle [Proprietary Chapel], Kent 1835-47, V. Battersea, Surrey 1847 [income £995] to death 17/10/1871, leaving £9,000 [C41429. Boase] Married Bathwick, Som. 17/3/1830 Harriet Caroline Augusta Grey, with issue.

**JENKS (David)** Bapt. Whipsnade, Beds. 21/12/1785, s. Rev. David sen. and Elizabeth Jenks. St John's, Cambridge 1808, dn08 (Lin.), p09 (Lin.), MA1811. R. Cheddington, Bucks. 1816-19, V. Studham, Suffolk 1811-18, R. Aldbury, Hants. 1818-62, R. Little Gaddesden, Herts. 1829 (and RD of Berkhampstead) to death. Dom. Chap. to 7th Earl of Bridgewater 1815, to Charlotte, Countess of Bridgewater 1829. Died 1/11/1869, leaving £3,000 [C67158] Married Reading, Berks. 3/11/1815 Anne Eyre (a clergy dau.).

**JENKS (John)** From Bromyard, Heref., s. Timothy Colly [*pleb*] and Frances Jenks. Pembroke, Oxford 1794, then New, BA1798, dn00 (Heref.), p01 (Glos. for Heref.). V. Thriplow, Cambs. 1832 to death 18/4/1849 [C155666]

**JENKYNS, JENKINS (Richard)** Bapt. Evercreech, Som. 21/12/1783, s. Rev. John Jenkyns (Prebendary of Wells Cathedral) and Jane Banister. Balliol, Oxford 1800, Fellow 1803-19, BA1804, dn05 (Ox.), MA1806, p06 (Ox.), BD & DD1819. Master of Balliol College, Oxford 1819-54. Vice-Chancellor 1824-8. V. Evercreech 1822-54, R. Dinder, Som. (w. Prebend of Dinder in Wells Cathedral annexed) 1824-45, Dean of Wells 1845 to death 6/3/1854 [C33925. ODNB. Boase] Married Clifton, Bristol 23/4/1835 Troth [*sic*] Grove, *s.p.* 'Known as one of the wealthiest men in the University'.

**JENNINGS (John)** Born Cardigan 14/9/1789, s. John Jennings and Margaret Lloyd. Emmanuel, Cambridge 1825 (a Ten Year Man), MA1835 (Lambeth). R. Westminster St John the Evangelist 1832-83, Canon of Westminster 1837-85 [total income in CR65 £1,555], RD, Archdeacon of Westminster 1868 to death. Dom. Chap. to Marquess of Downshire. Died 26/3/1883, leaving £4,092-16s-0d. [C120054 / 303994. Boase] Married Chertsey, Surrey 27/8/1840 Lavinia Evans Shaw (w). 'Hon. Sec. of the Star Club, London 1831-9' (?)

**JENNINGS (William)** Bapt. Cannington, Som. 21/6/1772, s. Joseph [*pleb*] and Edith Jennings. St Edmund Hall, Oxford 1801, no degree, dn05 (Win. for York), p09 (York). V. Baydon, Wilts. 1821 to death 10/1/1834 aged 62 (CCEd thus) aged 62 [C80112. YCO]

**JENYNS (George Leonard)** Born Bottisham, Cambs. 19/6/1763, s. John Harvey Jenkyns (of Eye, Suffolk) and Elizabeth Chappelow. Caius, Cambridge 1781, BA 1785, dn85 (Ely), p87 (Ely), MA1788. V. Swaffham Prior, Cambs. 1787 (and Canon of 8th Prebend in Ely Cathedral 1802) to death 25/2/1848, living at Bottisham Hall (which he built) and Anglesey Abbey, Cambs. [C16943. YCO] Married Pimlico, London 17/6/1788 Mary Heberden (engraved port. online), with clerical son below. J.P. Agriculturalist.

**JENYNS, *later* BLOMEFIELD (Leonard)** Bapt. London 25/5/1800, s. Rev. George Leonard Jenyns (above) and Mary Heberden. St John's, Cambridge 1817, BA1822, dn23 (Lin. for Ely), p24 (Bristol for Ely), MA1825. PC. West Dereham, Suffolk 1824, V. Swaffham Bulbeck, Cambs. 1827-49. Died Bath 1/8/1893, leaving £9,233-18s-5d. [C53016 under Jenyns. ODNB and Boase under Blomefield. *Chapters of my life* (2nd edn., 1889)]. Married (1) Ampney Crucis, Glos. 23/4/1844 Jane Daubeney (a clergy dau., she d.1860) (2) Stapleford, Cambs. 24/6/1862 Sarah Hawthorn (a clergy dau.). Intimate of Darwin (who replaced him as naturalist on *The Beagle*), and a member of many scientific societies.

**JEPSON (George)** Bapt. Lincoln 14/2/1752, s. William Jepson and Rebecca Yorks. Emmanuel, Cambridge 1772, dn76 (Lin.), BA 1777, p77 (Lin.), MA1780. V. Saxilby w. Ingleby, Lincs. 1778-88, Senior Vicar Choral in Lincoln Cathedral 1780-1831, Prebend of St Botolph in Lincoln Cathedral (and PC. Lincoln St Botolph) 1781-1837, V. Lincoln St Mary Magdalen at Bails 1786-95, V. Glen-tham, Lincs. 1788-1837, V. Normanby, Lincs. 1788, V. Hainton, Lincs. 1795-1831 (res.), PC. Lincoln St Peter at Gowts 1803, V. Ashby Puerorum, Lincs. 1806 to death 21/4/1837 aged 84 [C67165. Bennett1. Kaye] Married Lincoln 22/1/1782 Eleanor Gibbeson, with issue. 'Said to be 'a man of remarkable sweetness of temper, of considerable musical ability, and gifted with a good tenor voice; very modest and retiring'.

**JERMYN (Edward)** Born Halesworth, Suffolk, s. Robert Jermyn (merchant) and Mary Rye (a clergy dau.). St John's, Cambridge 1791, dn94 (Nor.), BA1795, p96 (Nor.), MA 1798, R. Carlton Colville, Suffolk 1806 to death 22/2/1848, 'having inherited a valuable property in Mells, Som.' [C113684] Married Pakefield, Suffolk 10/11/1813 Sarah Hill (a clergy dau.), with issue.

**JERRAM (Charles)** Born Blidworth, Notts. 17/1/1770, s. Charles Jerram (farmer) and Ann Knutton. S/M at a Unitarian school in Highgate, London 1790. Magdalene, Cambridge 1793, BA1797, dn97 (Lin.), p97 (Lin.), MA1800. V. Chobham, Surrey 1810-34, V. St John's Chapel, Bedford Row, London 1824-6, R. Witney, Oxon. 1834 to death 20/6/1853, living at Old Idsworth House, Horndean, Hants. [C34275. ODNB. Boase. DEB. James Jerram (ed.), *The memoirs and a selection from the letters of the late Rev. Charles Jerram, late Rector of Witney, Oxfordshire* (1855)] Married Tydd St Mary, Lincs. 24/4/1798 Ann Stanger (of Long Sutton, Lincs.), with issue. 'May be regarded as one of the very best representatives of the second generation of the Evangelical school.'

**JERVOISE, *born* CLARKE (Samuel Clarke, Sir, 1st Bart.)** Born London 25/11/1770, s. of Jervoise Clarke Jervoise (formerly Clarke), *M.P.*, and Kitty Warner. Corpus Christi, Oxford 1788, BA1792, dn94 (C&L for Win.), MA1795, p95 (Peterb. for Win.). R. Blendworth, Hants. 1795-1835, R. Charlton w. Clanfield, Hants. 1795-1834, V. Catherington, Hants. 1795. Dom. Chap. to 2nd Earl of Carnarvon 1795. Died Richmond, Surrey 1/10/1852, living at Idsworth Park, Hants. [C71742] Married Eton, Bucks., 3/2/1799, Elizabeth Griffenhoofe, with issue. Name changed 1808; created baronet 1813 (but why?).

**JESSE (William)** Born Hutton Cranswick, Yorks. 20/2/1778, s. Rev. William Jesse and Mary Sage. Trinity, Oxford 1795, BA1798, dn99 (C&L), p01 (Nor.). Chap. Pelsall, Staffs. (exempt jurisdiction) 1811 and V. Margaretting, Essex 1827 to death there 5/6/1858, leaving £1,500 [C13085] Married Melton Mowbray, Leics. 13/6/1805 Sarah Kendal (w), with issue.

**JESTON (Henry Playsted)** Born Henley on Thames, Oxon. 25/1/1795, s. Rev. Humphrey Jeston (below) and Ann Allen Playsted. Worcester, Oxford 1817, BA1821, dn21

(Chester), p22 (Chester), MA1824. R. Cholesbury, Bucks. 1830-89, PC. Wigginton, Herts. 1841-7. Died Cholesbury 24/6/1889, leaving £1,531-4s-9d. Chap. at Bad Kissingen, Bavaria 1854-61 [C13088] Married Salisbury Cathedral 14/6/1824 Elizabeth Purvis Eyre, with issue (including dau. Arima Susannah Eyre Jeston, born Arima, Trinidad and Tobago). Brother Robert Green, below. *J.P.* Bucks. and Herts.

**JESTON (Humphrey)** Born Holyhead, Anglesey 28/8/1762, s. Thomas Jeston and Jane Green. Magdalen Hall, Oxford 1781, dn84 (Wor. for Win.), BA1785, p87 (Ox. for Win.), MA1788. (succ. his father as) R. Avon Dassett 1803 to death 12/7/1839 [C13089] Married (1) St James, Westminster, London 15/6/1786 Ann Allen Playsted (d.1804), w. clerical sons, above and below (2) St James, Westminster, London 14/12/1809 Ann Allen Playsted, with further issue.

**JESTON (Robert Green)** Born Henley on Thames, Oxon. 9/4/1792, s. Rev. Humphrey Jeston (above) and Ann Allen Playsted. Trinity, Oxford 1809, BA1813, dn15 (C&L), p16 (C&L), MA1817. R. Marston Sicca, Glos. 1831, (succ. his father as) R. Avon Dassett, Warwicks. 1839 to death 8/7/1867, leaving under £200 [C13090] Married (1) 13/2/1831 Lettice Jane Torre (d.1836), with issue (2) Atcham, Shropshire 1849 (1st q.) Louisa Guise, w. further issue. Brother Henry Playsted Jeston, above.

**JEX-BLAKE (William)** see under **BLAKE**

**JODRELL (Philip Nevill)** Bapt. Broxbourne, Herts. 30/5/1777, s. Rev. Daniel Jodrell and Mary Briese. Jesus, Cambridge 1795, BA1800, dn00 (Nor.), p04 (Win.). R. Yelling, Hunts. 1805 to death 1850 (2nd q.) [C67178] Married Yelling 4/5/1808 Mary Pye, with clerical son Charles Philip Paul Jodrell.

**JODRELL (Sheldon)** Born London 6/9/1788, s. Sir Richard Paul Jodrell, 2nd Bart. and Vertue Hase. Trinity, Cambridge 1807, BA1812, dn12 (Nor.), MA1815. R. Saxlingham w. Sharrington, Norfolk 1812 to death (unmarried) 6/1/1855 [C113652]

**JOHNES, *later* KNIGHT (Samuel)** From Henly Hall, Ludlow, Shropshire, s. Thomas Johnes. Christ Church, Oxford 1774 (aged 28), BA1778, then All Souls, Fellow, dn80 (Heref.), p80 (Heref.), MA1782. V. Barking All Hallows, City of London (and Preacher throughout the Diocese of London) 1783 and R. Welwyn, Herts. 1797 to death 8/7/1852 [C67180 as Johnes. Foster as Knight. ERC as Knight, S.J.] Married Marylebone, London Anna Maria Culyer 6/6/1808. Name changed 1813.

**JOHNES (Thomas)** From Batheaston, Som. Wadham, Oxford 1804 (aged 17), BA1808, dn10 (Ex.), p11 (Ex.). R. Bradstone, Devon 1812 (with Preacher throughout the Diocese of Exeter 1815) to death, R. Ashleworth, Glos. 1815-19 (res.). Died (unm.) 19/11/1862, leaving £1,000 [C53021] Major confusion in Foster with another man of same name.

**JOHNSON (Arthur)** From Lisburn, Co. Antrim, s. William Johnson. Glasgow University 1772, MA, dn88 (London), p89 (London). V. Little Baddow, Essex 1789. Died 14/3/1842 aged 92 [C120058]

**JOHNSON (Benjamin)** [NiVoF] V. Great Gidding, Hunts. 1822 to death 1843 (1st q.) [C67181] Wife Catherine, and son Frederick, below.

**JOHNSON (Bertie Entwistle)** Bapt. Wilmslow, Cheshire 24/2/1794, s. Rev. Croxton Johnson and Frances Haughton. Peterhouse, Cambridge 1812, BA1816, dn18 (London for Chester), p19 (Chester), MA1819. PC. Over Peover, Cheshire 1823-5, R. Lymm (1st Mediety o/w High Leigh), Cheshire 1825-32, PC. Childs Ercall, Market Drayton, Shropshire 1844 and R. Hinstock, Shropshire 1850 to death (Childs Ercall) 11/2/1873 aged 79, leaving £3,000 [C120059] Married (1) Camden, London 8/2/1827 Isabel Legh (d.1855) (2) 3/7/1856 Mrs Elizabeth (Greenall) Molyneux (a clergy dau.).

**JOHNSON (Charles)** From Saxmundham, Suffolk, s. Charles Johnson. University, Oxford 1783 (aged 18), BA1786, dn88 (Nor.), p94 (Nor.). R. (and patron) of Bildeston, Staffs. 1797 to death. Chap. to Prince Regent. Died 24/2/1849 aged 72 [C113690]

**JOHNSON (Charles)** Bapt. Marylebone, London 8/2/1768, s. John and Elizabeth Johnson. Exeter, Oxford 1787, BA1790, dn90 (B&W), p92 (B&W), MA1793. V. Berrow, Som. 1792, V. South Stoke, Som. 1792-1841 (living at South Stoke Hall), V. Brent Knoll (o/w South Brent), Som. 1799 V. White Lackington, Som. to

1825 (w. Prebend of White Lackington in Wells Cathedral 1816) to death. Chap. in Ordinary 1799. Died 16/8/1841 [C44225. F. corrected] Married at Christian Malford, Wilts. 25/3/1790 Mary Willis, with clerical son Francis Charles, below.

**JOHNSON (Charles Thomas)** Born Kenilworth, Warwicks. 21/9/1786, s. Rev. Robert Augustus Johnson and Ann Rebecca Craven. BNC, Oxford 1804, BA1807, dn09 (Win.), p10 (Glos. for Win. as Charles), MA1810. R. Allington, Wilts. 1811-16, R. Hampstead Marshall, Berks. 1811-48, R. West Felton, Shropshire 1816, R. Enborne, Berks. 1816 to death. Dom. Chap. to 6th Earl of Dysart 1811. Died 29/6/1848 [C13094]

**JOHNSON (Francis Charles)** Born South Stoke, Som. 26/2/1797, s. Rev. Charles Johnson (above) and Mary Willis. Queen's, Oxford (as C.F.) 1817, BA1821, dn21 (Salis. for B&W), p22 (Glos.), MA1867. (succ. his father as) V. White Lackington, Som. 1825 to death 22/12/1874, leaving £20,000 [C95044. F. as Charles Francis] Married South Stoke, Som. 28/3/1822 Emma Frances Brooke, and had issue.

**JOHNSON (Frederick)** Born Great Gidding, Hunts., s. Rev. Benjamin (above) and Catherine Johnson. St Catharine's, Cambridge 1826, dn30 (Lin.), BA1830, p30 (Lin.), MA 1833. R. Hemington, Northants. 1832-71 [blank in ERC], (succ. his father as) V. Great Gidding 1843-59, R. Luddington, Northants. 1850 to death (Hemington) 20/1/1871, leaving £1,500 [C67182] Widow Mary Nicholls.

**JOHNSON (George)** From Ashreigney, Devon, s. Rev. John Tossel Johnson. Oriel, Oxford 1807 (aged 18), BA1811, dn12 (Ex.), p14 (Ex.), MA1816. R. Ashreigney (o/w King's Ash) 1829-53. Probate granted 1865 [C145317] Brother Peter, below.

**JOHNSON (James)** Bapt. Hereford 6/1/1787, s. Samuel and Anne Johnson. Worcester, Oxford 1810, BA1813, dn14 (Heref.), p15 (Heref.), MA1816. V. Byford, Heref. 1820-66 (resided here), V. Bridge Sollers, Heref. 1820-66 (non-res.), Prebend of Hampton in Hereford Cathedral 1825-66, V. Upper and Lower Bullinghope w. Grafton, Heref. 1828-51- (non-res.), V. Mansel Gamage, Heref. 1824 (non-res.) to death 21/2/1866, leaving £45,000 [C172066 corrects Foster] J.P. Herefordshire.

**JOHNSON (John)** Bapt. Greystoke, Cumberland 28/3/1756. Literate: dn82 (Durham), p83 (Durham). V. Alnham, Northumberland 1812, R. Ilderton, Northumberland 1812 to death 1833 [C134624] Married Alnwick, Northumberland 27/12/1788 Janet Whyte, with issue.

**JOHNSON (John)** From Westminster, London, s. John Johnson. Oriel, Oxford 1776 (aged 16), BA1779, MA1782, dn82 (Ox.), p83 (Ox.). R. Great Parndon, Essex 1784 and V. North Mimms, Herts. 1790 to death. Dom. Chap. to 15th Earl of Suffolk 1786. Died 11/9/1833 (CCEd says 27/9/1833) [C34323]

**JOHNSON (John)** Bapt. Ludham, Norfolk 15/11/1769, s. John (a tanner) and Catherine Johnson. Caius, Cambridge 1787, dn93 (Nor.), p93 (Nor.), LLB1794, LLD1803. V. Hempnall, Norfolk 1793-1807, R. (and patron) of Yaxham w. Welborne, Norfolk 1800 to death 28/9/1833 (CCEd says 5/3/1834). Dom. Chap. to Earl of Peterborough [C113692. ODNB] Married 1808 Maria Livius (dau. of the 'Head of the Commissariat in India'), with issue. A cousin of the poet William Cowper, he took care of him in the last years of his life.

**JOHNSON (John)** Born Bengal 1779, s. John Johnson. Trinity, Cambridge 1799, BA1803, MA1806, dn06 (Peterb.), p07 (Peterb.). V. Little Houghton w. Brafield (on the Green), Lincs. 1817-38 (non-res.), R. Caenby (Cainby), Lincs. 1825, R. Outwell, Norfolk 1838 to death (Leamington, Warwicks.) 8/10/1848 aged 66 [C67188. Bennett1]

**JOHNSON (Maurice)** Born Ayscough Fee Hall, Spalding, Lincs. 28/2/1757, s. Lt.-Col. Maurice Johnson (1st Regt. Foot Guards) and Mary Baker. St John's, Cambridge 1773, BA 1777, dn78 (Lin.), p80 (Nor.), MA1783, DD 1795. V. (and patron) of Moulton, Lincs. 1780-1834 (non-res.), PC. Spalding, Lincs. 1782-1825, R. Moulton All Saints, Spalding 1784 [blank in ERC], Prebend of Sexaginta Solidorum in Lincoln Cathedral 1785 to death. Dom. Chap. to 5th Duke of Ancaster and Kesteven 1784. Died 25/5/1834 (CCEd says 16/6/1834) [C67192. Venn corrected] Married Spalding 22/7/1779 Ann Elizabeth Bickworth, with issue. Brother Walter Maurice, below.

**JOHNSON (Nathaniel Palmer)** Born Burleigh Fields House, Leics., s. Nathaniel Palmer Johnson and Mary Gold. Emmanuel,

Cambridge 1783, BA1787, dn88 (C&L), MA 1790, p91 (C&L). R. Sutton Bonington St Ann, Notts. 1795-97, R. Aston upon Trent, Derbys. [net income £1,030] 1796 to death 25/10/1850 aged 85, *s.p.* [C13097]

**JOHNSON (Paul)** Bapt. London 8/1/1759, s. of Paul Johnson (Runton, Norfolk). Caius, Cambridge 1776, BA1780, dn81 (Peterb. for Nor.), p84 (Nor.). R. Sustead (Sistead), Norfolk 1784-1835, R. Ingworth, Norfolk 1788 and PC. Beeston Regis, Norfolk 1799 to death (Runton) 30/7/1835 aged 76 (CCEd says 12/8/1835) [C110403] Married Kingston-on-Thames, Surrey 14/2/1788 Ann Rachel Munnings, with clerical son, also Paul, in Sustead.

**JOHNSON (Peter)** From Ashreigney, Devon, s. Rev. John Tossel Johnson. Oriel, Oxford 1805 (aged 18), Fellow of Exeter 1808-24, dn10 (Ox.), BA1812, MA1812, p12 (Ox.), BD1823. V. Long Wittenham w. Brushfeld, Berks. 1823-5 (res.), R. (and patron) of Wembworthy, Devon 1830 (and Prebend of Exeter Cathedral 1843-58) to death 16/7/1869 aged 82, leaving £60,000 [C34328] Married Timsbury, Som. 10/4/1824 Gratiana Samborne Palmer. Brother George, above.

**JOHNSON (Richard)** [NiVoF] V. Sockburn, Durham 1816 to death, and 'who resides in the neighbouring chapelry of Eryholme in Yorkshire.'. Died before 2/5/1833 [C132242. Venn merges two men here]

**JOHNSON (Richard)** Born Stalham, Norfolk 4/3/1787, s. James Johnson. Caius, Cambridge 1803, BA1809, Fellow 1809-25, dn10 (Nor.), p11 (Nor.), MA1812. R. Ingham, Norfolk [blank in ERC] 1817-32 (res.), R. Lavenham, Suffolk 1825 to death 21/9/1855 [C113695] Married Catfield, Norfolk 25/9/1828 Mary Cubitt (Catfield Hall, Norfolk), with issue. *J.P., D.L.* Suffolk.

**JOHNSON (Richard Popplewell)** Born Wakefield, Yorks. 19/6/1749, s. Alan Johnson (an attorney) and Elizabeth Popplewell. St John's, Cambridge 1768, BA1772, dn72 (Nor. for Win.), p73 (Chester). R. Ashton upon Mersey, Cheshire 1774 to death 17/4/1835 (CCEd says 1/7/1835) [C113696] Married Linton, Kent 20/8/1778 Penelope Margaret Stafford (Macclesfield, Cheshire).

**JOHNSON (Robert Henry)** From Kenilworth, Warwicks., s. Rev. Robert Augustus Johnson. BNC, Oxford 1799 (aged 18), BA1804, dn05 (Heref.), p06 (Win. for London), MA1806. V. Claybrook, Leics. (and Preacher throughout the Diocese of Lincoln) 1816 and R. Lutterworth, Leics. 1816 to death. Dom. Chap. to 1st Earl of Craven 1816. Died 1/10/1870, leaving £5,000 [C67202] Married London 22/3/1808 Caroline Rouse Boughton, with issue.

**JOHNSON (Samuel)** Born Horwich, Lancs. 24/5/1796, s. Rev. Samuel, sen. and Jane Johnson. Lincoln, Oxford 1816, BA1820, dn20 (York), p21 (York), MA1823. R. (and patron) of Hinton Blewitt, Som. 1832, PC. Atherton, Lancs. 1836-64-. Died Upper Helios, Devon 13/8/1873, leaving £6,000 [C41435. YCO] Married Leamington, Warwicks. 16/5/1842 Elizabeth Jane Jenkins (w), w. clerical son Samuel Jenkins Johnson.

**JOHNSON (Thomas)** Probably bapt. Liverpool 6/1/1796, s. John Johnson and Ann Chisenhale. BNC, Oxford 1814, BA1817, dn20 (Chester), MA1820, p21 (Chester). (joint) PC. Liverpool St Michael 1831 to death (Inverness) 30/9/1834 (CCEd says 17/10/1835) [C169422] Married Liverpool 1830 Lydia Hankinson Roughsedge (a clergy dau.).

**JOHNSON (Walter Maurice)** Born Stanway Hall, Essex 19/12/1757, s. Lt.-Col. Maurice Johnson (1st Regt. Foot Guards) and Mary Baker. [Cornet 1775, then Lt. 1778 in 3rd (Prince of Wales) Dragoon Guards]. St John's, Cambridge 1785 (a Ten Year Man), dn85 (Win.), p86 (Lin. for Win.). V. Weston St Mary, Lincs. 1805 [vacant in ERC] to death (Spalding, Lincs.) 20/7/1832 (CCEd says 14/6/1835) [C67208] Married Melford, Suffolk 27/10/1788 Frances Weller-Poley (Boxted Hall, Suffolk), with issue. Brother Maurice, above.

**JOHNSON (William)** Born Cumberland 1784. St John's, Cambridge 1817, a Ten Year Man (BD1827). R. St Clement Eastcheap w. St Martin Orgar, City of London 1820-64; but essentially a schoolmaster in charge of the National Society's schools in Holborn, London 1812-40. Died 20/9/1864, leaving £6,000 [C120068. ODNB. Boase] Married 1822 Mary Tabrum (w), with clerical son Andrew. Known as 'The Patriarch of National Education' as organised on the Bell system. 'He became a trainer of masters, a travelling organiser, an inspector of schools, and later (1840), cashier and comptroller of accounts of the National

Society. Presented by the Czar of Russia with a diamond ring 1821, for his exertions in favour of four students sent to England to study the system of education adopted at the National Central School' (Venn).

**JOHNSON (William)** [A contemporary source says BNC, Oxford, MA, but NiF] Literate: dn10 (Llandaff for Chester), p11 (Chester). PC. Manchester St George in the Fields 1818, V. Mottram in Longendale, Cheshire 1826 (and S/M there 1827) to death 2/12/1840 aged 72 [C4091]

**JOHNSON (William Moore)** From Lisburn, Co. Antrim. St Edmund Hall, Oxford 1803 (aged 31), dn09 (Nor. for Bristol), p10 (Salis. for Bristol). R. Perranuthnoe, Cornwall 1815 to death 19/7/1849 aged 78 [C53029] Had issue.

**JOHNSON (William Wilbraham)** Born Shrewsbury, Shropshire 4/5/1807, s. Rev. William Johnson and Mary Middleton. BNC, Oxford 1825, BA1829, dn30 (Chester), p31 (Chester), MA1831. PC. Marple, Stockport, Cheshire 1832-5 (res.), Chap. 1835 then Minor Canon Manchester Cathedral 1854 to death (unmarried, Broomfields, Shropshire) 9/2/1864 aged 56, leaving £3,000 [C169426]

**JOHNSTON (Thomas)** Bapt. Darenth, Kent, s. of Leathes Johnson and Maria Bench. University, Oxford 1789, BA1793, dn93 (Nor. for Win.), p94 (C&L for Win.). R. (and patron) of Broughton, Hunts. 1797 to death 25/5/1851 [C13104]

**JOHNSTONE (Charles Vanden Bempde)** Born Hackness Hall, Hackness, Yorks. 23/8/1800, s. Sir Richard Vanden Bempde Johnstone, 1st Bart., *M.P.*, and Margaret Scott. Trinity, Cambridge 1818, BA1825, dn25 (York), p26 (York), MA1830. V. Felixkirk (Feliskirk) w. Boltby, Yorks. 1827-72, Prebendary of Wetwang in York Minster 1844-82 w. Canon Residentiary 1845-73 [value £1,200 in CR65]. Died Sutton Hall, Thirsk 14/5/1882 aged 81, leaving £45,397-4s-7d. [C131666. Boase. YCO] Married Scarborough, Yorks. 14/9/1827 Amelia Hawksworth (a clergy dau.), with clerical son Charles. Surely related to William, below.

**JOHNSTONE (Thomas Bryan)** Born Southampton 23/12/1786, s. Thomas Johnstone and Elizabeth Anna Maria Storer. Trinity, Cambridge 1808, dn11 (Salis. for Win.), BA1812, p13 (Win.), MA1815. R. Fisherton Anger, Wilts. 1790-1, R. Clutton, Som. 1815 (and Chap. of Clutton Poor Law Union 1838) to death. Dom. Chap. to Philadelphia Hannah, Dowager Viscountess of Cremone 1813. Died 23/7/12/1878, aged 91. Will not traced [C44231] Married Bishops Waltham, Hants. 28/12/1812 Mary Anne Wilson, with issue. Port. online.

**JOHNSTONE (William Vanden Bempde.** From Haverfordwest, Pembroke, s. Charles Johnstone. Trinity Hall, Cambridge 1797, then Trinity 1798, BA1803, dn03 (Heref.), p04 (Heref.). PC. Sibdon, Heref. 1804-12 (res.), R. (and patron) of Culmington, Shropshire 1804 to death 1854, *s.p.* [C172068] Surely related to Charles, above.

**JOLLANDS (Charles)** From Middlesex, s. Charles Jollands and Mary Dixon. St John's, Cambridge 1820, BA1826, dn27 (Chich.), p28 (Chich.). R. Little Munden, Herts. 1831 to death 11/5/1866 aged 64, leaving £14,000 [C64050] Married Brixton, Surrey 10/9/1835 Mary Brettle, with issue.

**JOLLIFFE (Peter William)** Born Poole, Dorset 3/1/1767, s. Peter (merchant and alderman) and Harriet Jolliffe. St John's, Cambridge 1785, BA1789, dn89 (Win.), p91 (Nor. for Salis.), MA1792. R. Poole St James 1791 to death 21/2/1861 aged 95 (the oldest beneficed clergyman in England), leaving £1,000 [C113703] Wife Harriett, and issue. Venn notes: He 'devoted two days a week ... to receiving the papers and claims of sailors and soldiers discharged from the Napoleonic War, who had previously been defrauded by dishonest agents'.

**JOLLIFFE (Thomas Robert)** Born Charlton, Somerset 12/11/1780, s. of Thomas Samuel Jolliffe, *M.P.*, and Ann Twyford (a clergy dau.). Trinity, Cambridge 1799, BA1804, MA 1807, dn09 (Killala). R. Babington, Som. 1810 to death. Chap. in Ordinary. Died 15/6/1872 aged 91, living at Ammerdown House, Somerset. Will not traced [C44237] *J.P.* Somerset.

**JONES (Anselm)** Born Brackley, Northants., s. Edward Jones. Trinity, Cambridge 1813, BA 1818, dn19 (Peterb.), p20 (Peterb.), MA1821. V. Stockton on the Forest, Yorks. 1824 to death (Brackley) 8/7/1838 aged 43 [C110404. Boase]

**JONES (Christopher)** From Hereford, s. Edward Jones. Christ Church, Oxford 1802 (aged 18), BA1805, dn05 (Heref.), p07 (Heref.), MA1808. 'Vicar in Choir' in Hereford Cathedral 1806-53, PC. Brockhampton, Heref. 1809-10, V. Yarkhill, Heref. 1810-14 (res.), V. Canon Pyon, Heref. 1813-19 [blank in ERC], PC. Wormsley, Heref. 1819 [blank in ERC] and Cormeilles Canon in Hereford Cathedral 1819 to death 8/3/1853 [C172057]

**JONES (Edward)** Bapt. Loddington, Northants. 16/3/1771, s. Rev. Edward and Sarah Jones. King's, Cambridge 1790, Fellow 1793-1801, BA1794, dn94 (Lin.), p96 (Peterb.), MA1797. R. Greetham, Rutland 1801-21 (res.), R. North Kilworth, Leics. 1804-12 (res.), PC. Little (o/w Bow) Brickhill, Bucks. 1814-56, R. Milton Keynes, Bucks. 1821 to death 19/7/1857 aged 86 [C67575] Married Tugby, Leics. 29/7/1812 Elizabeth Inwood, w. issue. Brother Francis (below). A noted cricketer.

**JONES (Edward)** King's College Cambridge, BA1797, MA1799. V. & R. Brockworth, Glos. 1801-47, and R. Mitcheldean, Glos. 1802 to death (Chosen House, Gloucester) 10/5/1847 aged 74 [C155824 has another man mixed in here. Not in Venn. *Gentleman's Magazine* links] Widow Anne.

**JONES (Edward)** [NiVoF] R. Dunnington, Yorks. 1821 to death 9/1/1835 (CCEd says 25/2/1835) [CCEd 131670 thus]

**JONES (Francis)** Born Loddington, Northants., s. Rev. Edward and Sarah Jones. Clare, Cambridge 1791, BA1796, dn96 (Peterb.), p97 (Peterb.), MA1805. R. Rockingham, Northants, 1797, R. Lutton and Washingley, Northants, 1809 to death. Dom. Chap. to 2nd Baron Lilford 1800. Died Kettering, Northants. 19/6/1854 [C67576] Brother above.

**JONES (Henry Prowse)** Bapt. Newnham on Severn, Glos. 1781, s. Roynon [*sic*] Jones and Mary Richards. Corpus Christi, Cambridge 1797, BA1801, p03 (Win. for Glos.), p04 (Glos.), MA1837. R. Edgeworth, Glos. 1820-60, V. Berkeley, Glos. 1837-9, R. Hazleton w. Yarworth, Glos. 1840 to death. Dom. Chap. to Lord Seagrove 1821. Lived at Hill House, Newnham, Glos. Died 4/5/1860, leaving under £600 [C80573] Married Doncaster, Yorks. 18/5/1805 Sarah Hussey Shafto (dau. of Sir Cuthbert Shafto, Bavington Hall, Northumberland). A fox-hunting fanatic.

**JONES (Henry Thomas)** Bapt. Rochester Cathedral 26/8/1771, s. Rev. Henry Jones and Elizabeth Austin. St John's, Oxford 1790), BA 1794, dn94 (Ox.), MA1798, BD 1803, Fellow to 1828. Chap. *R.N.*; Minor Canon Rochester Cathedral 1799-1803 (res.), V. Darenth, Kent 1799-1801, V. West Peckham, Kent 1801-30, V. Charlbury w. Shorthampton, Oxon. 1827-8, R. Tackley, Oxon. 1828 to death 12/6/1839 (Brighton, Sussex), leaving £3,000 (will left unadministered) [C1472] Married Hadlow, Kent 19/8/1828 Elizabeth Winchester (w), with clerical son Edward Jones.

**JONES (Hugh)** From Burton on Trent, Staffs., s. Rev. Hugh Jones, sen. Christ Church, Oxford 1792 (aged 18), then Jesus, BA1796, dn96 (C&L), p97 (C&L). S/M Burton on Trent Free G/S 1796; PC. Burton upon Trent 1821 to death. Dom. Chap. to 4th Duke of Newcastle 1814. Died 1839 (2nd q.) [C13125. Hodson]

**JONES (Hugh Chambres)** Born Liverpool 7/5/1783 (but of Llansantffraid, Conway, Denbigh), s. John Chambres Jones and Jane Jones. Christ Church, Oxford 1801 (aged 18), BA1805, dn06 (Ox.), MA1807, p07 (Ox.). V. West Ham, Essex 1809-45, Treasurer of St Paul's Cathedral 1816-69, R. Aldham, Essex 1823-40, Archdeacon of Essex 1823-61 (res.). Dom. Chap. to Duke of Portland 1809; to William Howley, Bishop of London, later Archbishop of Canterbury 1813-23. Died Llansantffraid 29/9/1869, leaving £45,000 [C34398, Boase] Married Winchester 6/6/1814 Helen Carstairs, *s.p.*

**JONES (John)** Born Liverpool 5/10/1791, s. Capt. Rice Jones. St John's, Cambridge 1811, BA1815, dn15 (Lin.), p15 (Chester), MA1819. PC. Seaforth, Lancs. 1815, (first) V. Liverpool St Andrew 1815-50, V. Christ Church, Waterloo, Liverpool 1850-89, Archdeacon of Liverpool 1855-86 (res.). Died 5/12/1889 aged 98, leaving £13,471-6s-9d. [C67673. ODNB. Boase. DEB] Married Ratby, Leics. 10/8/1816 Hannah Pares (dau. of a banker, Hopwell Hall, Derbys.), 5 clerical sons.

**JONES (John)** Born Bala, Merioneth 10/2/1792, s. Henry and Catherine Jones. Jesus, Oxford 1814, BA1817, dn19 (Ox.), then Christ Church, Fellow and Chaplain 1819-43, p19

(Ox.), MA1821. PC. Oxford St Thomas the Martyr 1823-41, V. Nevern, Pembroke (and Prebend of St David's Cathedral) 1841 to death 2/5/1852 [C51040. Boase. *Dictionary of Welsh Biography*] Wrote Welsh poetry under the name of 'Tegid'.

**JONES (John)** From Foy, Heref., s. Rev. John Jones, sen. Trinity, Oxford 1811 (aged 16), BA 1814, migrated to? St John's, Cambridge 1815, MA1815. V. (and patron) of Foy, Heref. 1817 to death 17/3/1862, leaving £6,000 [C172160] Widow Sarah Jane.

**JONES (John)** [NiVoF] PC. Cradley, Halesowen, Worcs. 1822-[50]. Died? [C121624] Disambiguation well-nigh impossible.

**JONES (John Applethwaite)** Born Barbados, s. Robert Burnet Jones and Elizabeth Susannah Estwick. Queens', Cambridge 1808, BA1812, dn12 (Ex. for Win.), p13 (Chester for Win.), MA1815. R. Burley-on-the-Hill, Rutland 1819-68; lived subsequently at Horsham, Surrey. Died Cuckfield, Sussex 9/10/1876, leaving £6,000 [C80576. CR65 as Joseph. LBSO] Married St George's Hanover Square, London 18/4/1816 Louisa Prevost, with issue.

**JONES (John Collier)** Born Plympton Earle, Devon 7/10/1770, s. Richard and Maria Jones. Exeter, Oxford 1788, BA1792, Fellow 1792-9, dn93 (Ex.), MA1796, p02 (Ox.), BD1807, DD 1819. Naval chaplain (HMS *Namur* at St Vincent 1819?). Rector of Exeter College, Oxford 1819-38. Vice Chancellor of Oxford University 1828-32. V. Kidlington, Oxon. 1819 to death (Oban, Argyll) 7/8/1838 [C34474] Married Plympton 1825 Mrs Charlotte (Yonge) Crawley, *s.p.*

**JONES (John Fowell)** Bapt. Longney, Glos. 4/10/1791, s. Rev. Benjamin Jones and Catharine Fowell. Balliol, Oxford 1810, BA 1813, dn14 (B&W), p15 (Glos.), MA1817. PC. Saul, Glos. 1825-77, PC. Moreton Valance, Glos. 1830-77, R. Gwernesney, Monmouth 1830-71. Died 13/3/1877, leaving £14,000 [C4168] Married Yeovil, Som. 1/12/1831 Elizabeth Greenham, with clerical son Frederick Havard Jones.

**JONES (John Pike)** Born Chudleigh, Devon 25/2/1791, s. John Jones (tradesman) and Mary Pike. Pembroke, Cambridge 1809, BA1813, dn14 ([Ex.]), p15 (Ex.). Was initially refused institution to benefices on doctrinal grounds 1819; V. Alton (or Alveton), Staffs. 1829 (non-res.) and R. Butterleigh, Devon 1832 to death (unm.) 4/2/1857 ('while entering the newsroom at Cheadle', Staffs.), leaving under £100 [C13133. ODNB. Boase. Hodson] Antiquarian; botanist; political activist.

**JONES (John Price)** [MA but NiVoF] PC. Leonard Stanley, Glos. 1818. Possibly died Nov. 1857, one of 2 men of this name in Venn [C155979]

**JONES (John Theodosius)** Bapt. Llanarth, Monmouth 12/10/1785, s. Rev. John Jones and Mary Hand. Jesus, Oxford 1806, p11 (Llandaff), BA1811. S/M King's New School, Stratford, Warwicks; R. Llansantfraed, Monmouth 1812, R. Saintbury, Glos. 1826 to death 8/4/1851 [C4170] Married (1) Elizabeth Thorp (d.1836), with issue (2) Ann Charles.

**JONES (John William)** Bapt. Towcester, Northants. 6/2/1791, s. Rev. Pryce Jones, sen. and Sarah Jemson. St Edmund Hall, Oxford 1809, then All Souls, BA1813, dn14 (London), p16 (York). Chap. of the Donative of Scropton, Derbys. 1819 and V. Church Broughton, Derbys. 1820 to death (Kelsall, Cheshire) 17/3/1864, leaving £1,000 [C13134. YCO] Married Daventry, Northants. 10/9/1814 Jane Cullingworth Worley.

**JONES (Joseph)** Born Longham, Glos. 1781, s. Rev. David Jones. Jesus, Oxford 1800, BA 1803, dn05 (Ox.), MA1807. R. Newchurch in Winwick, Lancs. 1816, PC. Repton, Derbys. 1843 to death 1856 (4th q.) [C34476. Boase] Married Derby 15/1/1817 Elizabeth Joanna Cooper, with issue.

**JONES (Lewis)** Bapt. Towcester, Northants. 13/12/1763, s. Richard Jones (Cardigan). Magdalene, Cambridge 1784, BA1788, dn89 (C&L), p93 (Wor.). V. Burton Pedwardine, Lincs. 1800 to death 19/5/1833 (CCEd says 19/6/1833) [C13135] Married Swaton, Lincs. 9/3/1799 Mary Pickworth, with clerical son Neville Jones.

**JONES (Lewis)** Born Penpronpen, Cardigan 14/2/1793, s. William Jones. Literate: St John's College, Ystrad Meurig, South Wales, dn20 (York), p21 (York). Trinity, Cambridge 1821, a Ten Year Man. S/M Clitheroe G/S, Lancs.; R. Llandevaud, Monmouth 1822-52, V. Almondbury, Yorks. 1823-66, PC. Meltham, Almondbury 1829-38. Died Almondbury 26/8/1866 aged 72, leaving £6,000 [C131673. Boase. YCO] At least one son. A 'reformed pluralist', he deliberately recruited Welshmen into Yorkshire. Photo. online.

**JONES (Morgan Walter)** Born Much Wenlock, Shropshire, s. Rev. Morgan Jones. St John's, Cambridge 1797 (aged 18), BA1801, MA1804, dn05 (Lin.), p10 (London for Ely), BD1812, Fellow 1812-15. R. Hughley, Shropshire 1813-20, (succ. his father as) V. Ospringe, Kent 1815 and PC. Oare, Kent 1826 to death 13/8/1858. Will not traced [C67715] Married Much Wenlock 18/7/1815 Eliza Collins (dau. of a Town Clerk), with an only son drowned when attempting to cross ice on Lake Sturgeon, Upper Canada.

**JONES (Richard)** From Llanfechell, Anglesey, s. John Jones [*pleb*]. Jesus, Oxford 1779 (aged 20), BA1783. PC. Little Leigh, Great Budworth, Cheshire 1826 to death 7/7/1840 aged 82 [169457]

**JONES (Richard)** Bapt. Lledrod, Cardigan 28/3/1795, s. John Jones. Literate: dn21 (York), p22 (York). V. Gisburn, Yorks. 1822-67, RD 1848, RD for West Craven 1857 to death before 22/4/1867 aged 71. Will not traced [C131674. YCO] Wife Agnes A. in 1861 Census (only).

**JONES (Richard)** From Gloucester, s. Rev. Edward Jones. Worcester, Oxford 1814 (aged 18), BA1818, dn18 (Glos.), p20 (Glos.). Minor Canon of Gloucester Cathedral, PC. Norton, Glos. 1821 [C155986], R. Brookthorpe, Glos. 1828 to death 24/12/1836 [C157464. ERC identifies]

**JONES (Richard Prankerd)** From Charfield, Glos., s. Rev. Richard Jones. Wadham, Oxford 1810 (aged 18), then Worcester, BA1815, dn15 (Glos.), p16 (Glos.), MA1817. R. (and patron) of Charfield 1816 and V. Compton, Berks. 1829 to death. Dom. Chap. to 6th Duke of Beaufort 1829. Died 4/10/1853 [C136971. ERC identifies] Married Brittleton, Wilts. 1/4/1837 Elizabeth Charlotte White.

**JONES (Robert)** Bapt. Llangynhafal, Denbigh 24/10/1769, s. of an attorney. St John's, Cambridge 1787, Fellow 1791-1808, BA1791, dn92 (St Asaph), MA1794, p96 (Ely), BD802. R. Souldern, Oxon. 1806 to death (non-res. and sequestrated for debt) 3/4/1835 (CCEd says 20/8/1835) [C34486] This was the friend of William Wordsworth, with whom he visited the Continent in 1790: www.souldern.org/history/rev-robert-jones-1787-1835/ has his date of birth as 1787.

**JONES (Robert)** From Chester, s. Richard Jones. St Edmund Hall, Oxford 1804 (aged 24), BA1808, then St John's, Cambridge 1809, p11 (London), MA1815, DD1815 (Lambeth). Chap. at Cape Town in 1811; V. Bedfont, Middx. 1823 to death (Jersey) 23/4/1844 aged 63 [C120087] Married Lewisham, Kent 7/7/1815 Agnes, dau. Rear-Admiral George Dundas, w. issue.

**JONES (Samuel)** Bapt. Dawley, Shropshire 8/1/1786, s. Thomas and Sarah Jones. Literate: dn20 (York), p21 (York). PC. New Mill, Kirkburton, Yorks. 1832-4 (sti pend £55). Died? [C131675. YCO]

**JONES (Theophilus)** Born Cardigan 1752, s. Theophilus Jones [*pleb*]. Pembroke, Oxford 1773 (aged 21), dn76 (Ox. for Salis.), BA1777, p77 (Ox. for Salis.). R. Romney Marsh St Mary, Kent 1802 to death 5/8/1835 (CCEd says 13/10/1835) [C34488] Married Brookland, Bristol 6/4/1786 Mary King, w. issue.

**JONES (Thomas)** From Mixbury, Oxon., s. Rev. Anselm Jones. Pembroke, Oxford 1767 (aged 16), no degree. V. Ilmer, Bucks. 1791 and V. Radnage, Bucks. 1805 to death 26/2/1833 aged 82 (CCEd says 9/4/1833) [C67728]

**JONES (Thomas)** Born Hafod, Cardigan 2/4/1752, s. of a small farmer. Literate: dn74. Curate for 43 years then (aged 76) R. Great Creaton, Northants. 1829-33 (res.). Died 7/1/1845 [C110421. ODNB. DEB. *Dictionary of Welsh Biography*. John Owen, *Memoir of the Rev. Thomas Jones, late of Creaton, Northamptonshire* (1851)] Promoted Welsh printing of the Bible, and a founder of the British and Foreign Bible Society.

**JONES (Thomas)** From Gloucester, s. Samuel Jones. Wadham, Oxford 1818 (aged 18), BA 1822, dn23 (Glos.), p25 (Glos.), MA1827. R. Hempsted, Glos. 1826 to death 16/4/1867, leaving £6,000 [C155996] Widow Mary, and issue.

**JONES (Thomas Le Quesne)** Born Wickwar, Glos. 16/8/1794, s. Rev. Thomas Jones and Susanna Mary Wade. Queen's, Oxford 1813,

BA1817, dn17 (Glos.), p18 (Glos.), MA1820. (succ. his father as) PC. North Nibley, Glos. 1828 to death 7/9/1856 [C155991] Married Clifton, Bristol 13/5/1834 Sarah Pinnell.

**JONES (Thomas Lewis)** Probably bapt. Rochester 23/6/1760, s. Lewis and Sarah Jones. Emmanuel, Cambridge 1777, then Corpus Christi 1778, BA1782, dn82 (Ely), p87 (Ely). R. Brettenham, Norfolk 1790 and R. Bury, Hunts. 1803 to death 10/2/1848 aged 88 [C67731]

**JONES (William)** From Wolverhampton, Staffs., s. William Jones. Christ Church, Oxford 1781 (aged 16), BA1784, MA1787. V. East Witton, Yorks. 1811 to death 23/11/1837 [C169461]

**JONES (William)** From Maentwrog / Llandefaelog Fach, Merioneth, s. Nathaniel Jones. Jesus, Oxford 1793 (aged 19), BA1797, MA1814, Fellow to 1817. R. Llandyufaelog Fach, Brecon 1823 [C131998], R. Scartho, Lincs. 1817 and R. Llanvillo, Brecon 1827 to death 14/9/1844 at Llandyfaelog House [C67736. ERC links them. Kaye].

**JONES (William)** [NiVoF] PC. Minsterley, Shropshire 1811-[38]. Died? [Not yet in CCEd] Below?

**JONES (William)** [NiVoF] PC. Lingen, Heref. 1831-[40]. Died-? [C172389] Above?

**JONES (William Pitman)** From Cheltenham, Glos., s. John Jones. Pembroke, Oxford 1804 (aged 17), BA1807, dn11 (Win.), MA1811, p11 (Win.). PC. Bentley, Hants. 1814-22 (res.), PC. Seale, Surrey 1815 (res.), R. Eastbridge, Kent 1827. Died Preston, Lancs. 29/1/1864. No will traced [C80734] Married Farnham, Surrey 7/1/1812 Fanny Cook.

**JOPE (John)** Bapt. Callington, Cornwall 24/7/1752, s. Robert Jope and Mary Pike. Exeter, Oxford 1771, dn74 (Ex.), BA1775, p76 (Ex.), migrated to St John, Cambridge, MA 1785. R. St Cleer, Cornwall 1776-1844, V. Gerrans, Cornwall 1785-1806, R. St Ives, Cornwall 1806 to death. Dom. Chap. to 1st Baron Eliot 1784. Died St Cleer 18/1/1844 aged 92 [C145330] Married Liskeard, Cornwall 28/2/1786 Joanna Saltren (of Tredulick), with clerical son. 'The spirit of his dead clerical son haunted the church and vicarage until his father … consented to his [son] remaining in the shape of a spider and gave him as a "hiding place" a crevice in the mantlepiece'.

**JORDAN, JERDAN (George Colebrook)** Bapt. Alverstoke, Hants. 28/10/1798 (nonconformist baptism), s. John and Hephzibah Jordan. Pembroke, Oxford 1818, BA1823, MA1827, dn28 (Salis.), p29 (Salis.). PC. Blakeney, Awre, Glos. 1832 to death 10/9/1842 [C95167] Married Holborn, London 1831 Elizabeth Muston.

**JORDAN (Gibbes Walker)** Bapt. St Pancras, London 11/9/1800, s. Gibbes Walker Jordan (barrister and colonial agent for Barbados) and Amy North. Pembroke, Cambridge 1818, BA1823, dn23 (Salis.), p26 (C&L). R. Waterstock, Oxon. 1827 to death (Keynsham, Som.) 13/6/1856 aged 56 [C13206. LBSO] Married Bloomsbury, London 23/6/1825 Charlotte Penelope Sclater (a clergy dau.), with issue.

**JORDAN (Richard)** From Kent. Queens', Cambridge 1775, BA1779, Fellow 1781, dn81 (Peterb.), MA1782, p83 (Llandaff). V. Mountfield, Sussex 1791, Senior Minor Canon in Rochester Cathedral 1801-35, V. Poling, Sussex 1801-2, V. Hoo St Werburgh, Kent 1801 to death. Dom. Chap. to Marquess of Camden. Died 28/8/1835 aged 71 (CCEd says 27/11/1835) [C1435] Had issue.

**JOWETT (James Forbes)** Bapt. Fleet St., London 25/4/1794, s. James Robert Jowett and Janet Forbes. St John's, Oxford 1813, Fellow 1813-29, BA1817, dn18 (Ox.), p19 (Ox.), MA 1820, BD1826, etc. R. Kingston Bagpuize, Berks. 1828 to death (Hornchurch, Essex) 3/6/1877, leaving £2,000 [C34498] Married Ardingley, Surrey 17/4/1833 Harriot Frances Crawfurd, with issue.

**JOWETT (John)** Born St John Horsleydown, Bermondsey, London 5/7/1775, s. John Jowett and Betty Bankes. Literate: dn14 (Salis. for York), p14 (York). R. (and patron) of Ancaster, Lincs. 1814, R. Hartfield, Sussex 1815 to death 29/5/1859 aged 84, leaving £14,000 [C67740. YCO] Married Cambridge 29/4/1819 Mary Clark (w).

**JOWETT (Joseph)** Born Surrey 1784. Queens', Cambridge 1802, BA1806, dn07 (Lin.), p07 (Lin.), MA1823. R. Silk Willoughby >< Lincs. 1813 to death. Dom. Chap. to 2nd Baron Barham 1819; to Earl of Gainsborough. Died

13/5/1856 [C67741. Boase. Kaye] Composer of church music.

**JOYNES (Richard Symonds)** Bapt. Gravesend, Kent 26/4/1780, s. James Leigh Joynes and Sarah Harvey. Adm. Middle Temple 1798. St Catharine's, Cambridge 1800, BA1804. Fellow 1804, dn06 (Ex.), MA1807, p10 (Ex. for Cant.), DD1825. V. Ridgewell, Essex 1816-37, R. Frindsbury, Kent 1846. Died Brighton, Sussex (2nd q.) [C297] Married Frindsbury 1/10/1816 Mary Baker, with issue.

**JUDKIN (Thomas James)** Born London 25/7/1788, s. Thomas and Elizabeth Judkin. Caius, Cambridge 1810, BA1815, dn15 (London), p17 (London), MA1818, incorporated at Oxford 1842. PC. Somers Town St Mary, London 1828-68. Died Reigate, Surrey 11/9/1871, leaving £30,000 [C120093. Boase] Married Bloomsbury, London 7/9/1845 Anne Barrow (w), with issue. 'A very good amateur painter and personal friend of Turner and Constable'.

**JUSTICE (John)** Born Market Drayton, Shropshire 8/3/1803, s. Capt. Philip Justice, R.N., and Judith Rotton. Christ Church, Oxford 1821, BA1825, dn26 (C&L), p27 (C&L), MA 1828. R. (and patron) of Ightfield, Shropshire 1827 to death (at The London and Paris Hotel, Newhaven, Sussex) 13/7/1864, leaving £1,500 [C14133] Married Tunbridge Wells, Kent 4/7/1848 Clarisse Toone (w), with issue (inc. a dau. who married a German Count).

**KARSLAKE (William)** Born Bishop's Nympton, Devon 31/7/1776, s. Rev. John Burgess Karslake and Bridget Flexman. Worcester, Oxford 1795, BA1798, dn99 (Ex.), MA1802. R. Loxbeare, Devon 1802-61, R. Dolton, Devon 1803-61, V. Littleham cum Exmouth, Devon 1809, 'Perpetual Vicar' Culmstock, Devon 1811 to death. Probably Dom. Chap. to 1st Earl Fortescue 1809 . Died 15/10/1861, leaving £16,000 [C145332] Married Exeter Cathedral 18/11/1807 Elizabeth Althea Heberden, 2 clerical s., one below. J.P. Devon.

**KARSLAKE (William Heberden)** Bapt. Dolton, Devon 18/9/1808, s. Rev. William Karslake (above) and Elizabeth Althea Heberden. Oriel, Oxford 1826, BA1830, dn31 (Ex.), p32 (Ex.). R. Creacombe and Meshaw, Devon 1832 (and RD South Measham) to death. Prebend of Exeter 1875. Died 29/10/1878 aged 70, leaving £6,000 [C145334. Boase] Married Exeter 23/4/1833 Mary Burgess, with issue. J.P. and Chairman of Quarter Session.

**KAY (William)** Bapt. Nunnington, Yorks. 25/1/1799, s. Rev. John Kay. Magdalen, Oxford 1816, BA1820, dn22 (Nor.), Chap. 1822-23, p23 (Ox.), MA1823, then Lincoln, Fellow 1823-40, BD1832 (and an unsuccessful candidate for the Rectorship in 1851), etc. PC. Kirkdale w. Nawton, Helmsley, Yorks. 1830-62. Died York 8/2/1866, leaving £5,000 [C135923 / C113742] Married York 24/6/1839 Ann Kendale (w), with issue.

**KAYE, later LISTER-KAYE (Arthur Lister Lister-)** Bapt. 14/1/1804, s. Sir John Kaye, 1st Bart. (Denby Grange, Wakefield, Yorks.) and Amelia Grey (dau. of 5th Earl of Stamford and Warrington). BNC, Oxford 1824, BA1828, dn30 (York), p30 (York), MA1831. R. Thornton in Craven, Yorks. 1832 to death (Leamington, Warwicks.) 20/2/1834 (CCEd says 4/8/1834) aged 28 [C131678. YCO]

**KAYE (John, Bishop of Bristol, *then of* Lincoln)** Born Hammersmith, London 27/12/1783, s. Abraham Kaye (linen draper) and Susan Bracken. Christ's, Cambridge 1800, BA1804, MA1807, dn09 (Win.), p09 (Win.), BD1814, DD1815. Master of Christ's College 1814-30 (aged 30), Vice-Chancellor of Cambridge 1815-16. Regius Professor of Divinity 1816 (where he revived patristic studies) w. Bishop of Bristol 1820-7. A reforming Bishop of Lincoln (1,273 benefices) 1827 to death, he reformed the educational requirements for the Anglican clergy and attacked the Tractarians for betraying the English Reformation. Died 18/2/1853 [C80737. ODNB. Boase. R.W. Ambler (ed.), *Lincolnshire parish correspondence of John Kaye, Bishop of Lincoln, 1827-53* (Lincoln, 2006)] Married Great Abington, Cambs. 18/7/1815 Eliza Mortlock (a banker's dau.), 1s., 3 dau. *F.R.S.* (1811).

**KEARY (William)** Born Tuam, Co. Galway 7/8/1789. [A former soldier]. Literate: dn16 (Nor.), p16 (Chester). R. Nunnington, Yorks. 1817 to death (London) 1856 (3rd q.). Dom. Chap. to 2nd Viscount Melville 1816 [C113743] Married Stockton-on-the-Forest, Yorks. 16/3/1814 Lucy Plumer (Bolton Hall, Yorks.), with clerical son.

**KEATE (John)** Born Wells, Som. 30/3/1773, s. Rev. William Keate and Anne Burland. King's, Cambridge 1792, Fellow 1795-1803, BA 1796, dn05 (Nor. for Win.), p06 (Cant. for Salis.), DD1810. S/M Eton College 1797-1809. H/M of Eton College 1809-34; Canon of Windsor 1820-52, V. Nether Stowey, Som. 1820-4, R. Hartley Wespall, Hants. 1824 to death 5/3/1852 [C44309. ODNB. Boase] Married Eton 3/8/1803 Frances Brown (dau. of a baronet), and had issue. 'When he was appointed ... the discipline was extremely bad ... Keate himself was subjected to such indignities as the screwing-up and smashing of his desk, the singing of songs in chorus during schooltime, and an occasional fusillade of rotten eggs ... The struggle was long and severe, but, although rough and hasty in his methods, he gained a complete victory. Renowned for his ferocity; he flogged more than 80 boys on the same day June 30 1832. His courage and real kindness of heart made him popular; the boys cheered him after the great flogging and subscribed a large sum of money to present him with a testimonial when he left'. 'A small man with bright red hair'.

**KEBBEL (Henry)** Born Lullingstone, Kent. 13/12/1772, s. William Kebbel. Worked as a customs official in London for 12 years. Sidney, Cambridge 1803, Fellow, dn06 (Peterb. for Nor.), p08 (Peterb. for Nor.), LLB1810. PC. Kilby, Leics. 1813 and PC. Wistow, Leics. 1813 to death (a widower) 13/7/1867, leaving under £20 [C67754] Married Rachel Dirs, w. clerical son Carston Dirs Kebbel.

**KEBLE (John)** Bapt. Fairford, Glos. 12/6/1845, s. Rev. John Keble, sen. and Elizabeth Wotton. Corpus Christi, Oxford 1763, BA1766, Fellow, MA1770, dn70 (Nor. for Ox.), p71 (unspecified bishop for Ox.). R. Little Staughton, Beds. 1776-82, R. Blewbury, Beds. 1781-1824, V. Coln St Aldwyn, Glos. 1782 ('but resided at Fairford in a house of his own'), V. Poulton, Glos. 1782-1819. Dom. Chap. to 21st Baron de Clifford 1782. Died 24/1/1835 aged 90 (CCEd says 31/8/1835) [C34573] Married Uley, Glos. 8/12/1785 Sarah Maule (a clergy dau.), w. sons John Keble, jun. (the 'Father of the Oxford Movement', and poet), and Thomas (below).

**KEBLE (Thomas)** Born Fairford, Glos. 25/10/1793, s. Rev. John Keble (above) and Sarah Maule. Corpus Christi, Oxford 1808, BA1811, MA1815, dn16 (Ox.), p17 (Ox.), Fellow 1820-5, BD1824. V. Bisley, Glos. 1827-73. Died 5/9/1875, leaving £60,000 [C37475. ODNB. Boase. G. Sanders, *The younger brother: a short biography of the Rev. Thomas Keble, Vicar of Bisley, 1827-1874* (1975)] Married 14/6/1825 Elizabeth Jane Clarke, with son of same name in same parish. Brother of John Keble, Tractarian leader and poet. Port. of Thomas and wife online.

**KEELING (William)** Bapt. St Botolph by Billingsgate, City of London 18/4/1766, s. William Keeling and Anne Philby. Literate: dn12 (York), p12 (York). PC. Pendleton, Salford, Lancs. 1825 to death (Ramsey, IoM) 3/7/1844 (CCEd says 4/11/1834) aged 68 [C131679. YCO] Married Manchester 3/11/1788 Mary Finndley, w. clerical son William Robert Keeling. .

**KEENE, *later* RUCK (Charles Edmund)** Bapt. St George's Hanover Square, London 3/4/1792, s. Rev. Benjamin Keene and Mary Ruck. Christ Church, Oxford 1811, then All Souls, Fellow 1814-21, BA1815, dn18 (Ox.), MA1819, p19 (Ox.). R. Buckland, Surrey 1821, Sub-Dean of Wells Cathedral 1822 (res. by 1849) w. Prebend of Wiveliscombe 1827-33 (res.). Died 18/12/1880, living at Swyncombe House, Henley on Thames, Oxon. [C34577] Married St George's Hanover Square, London 3/4/1821 Rebecca Frances Shiffner, with issue. Name changed 1841.

**KEITH (Patrick)** Bapt. Inchinnan, Renfrew 1/1/1771, s. Duncan Keith. 'A literate person': dn06 (London for York), p07 (Salis. for York). PC. Marr, Yorks. 1808 (non-res.), R. Bethersden, Kent 1815-23, R. Ruckinge, Kent 1822 and V. Stalisfield, Kent 1827 to death 25/1/1840 aged 70 [C88823. YCO] Married Colchester, Essex 3/1/1807 Sarah Cater, with issue. *F.L.S.*; A botanical writer; 'of a somewhat caustic turn … his theological views are said to have been peculiar, [his] beautiful but unfortunate daughter [Emily] is understood to have been the heroine of a book'.

**KEKEWICH (Charles)** Bapt. Islington, London 26/6/1769, s. William Kekewich and Susanna Johnson. Balliol, Oxford 1796, dn99 (Ex.), p00 (Ex.), BA1800. PC. Lynton, Devon 1816, PC. Countisbury, Devon 1816, R. Greinton, Som. 1832 to death 27/3/1849 [C41478]

**KELL (William)** Bapt. 10/2/1785, Falstone, Northumberland, s. John and Mary Kell. Literate: dn08 (Durham for York), p09 (York), then St John's, Cambridge 1811, a Ten Year Man (BD1821). Incumbent of Kelso, Roxburgh 1815-16, then Minister of Kelso Qualified Chapel 1816-26 (i.e. taking the Chapel out of the Scottish Episcopal Church in 1815 into the CoE and returning it in 1826), R. Corsenside, Northumberland 1826 to death 9/11/1863 aged 79, leaving £200 [C132347. Bertie. YCO] Married Leyton, Essex 8/11/1801 Elizabeth Blinkworth, with clerical son of father's name (and at the same place, and with whom he is confused).

**KELLAND (Philip)** Bapt. Coldridge, Devon 6/4/1774, s. Robert Kelland and Charity Stoneman. Exeter, Oxford 1793, BA1797, dn97 (Ex.), p02 (B&W). R. Landcross (o/w Lancras), Devon 1818 to death 14/5/1847 [C44321] Married Luccombe, Som. 24/11/1804 Rachel Fish, and had issue.

**KELLY (Anthony Plimley)** Bapt. Finsbury, London 12/1/1797, s. Patrick Kelly (schoolmaster) and Anne Plimley. Caius, Cambridge 1816, BA1820, dn20 (Chich.), p22 (Chester), MA1823. V. Barnham, Sussex 1824 [in ERC only], V. Littlehampton, Sussex 1824-41, PC. Hoxton St Mary, London 1841 to death there 24/11/1864, leaving £10,000 [C64123] Married Clewer, Berks. 21/8/1824 Elizabeth Jenkin, with clerical son of father's name. 'Very active in schools and other parochial work', etc.

**KELSON (Henry)** Born Sevenoaks, Kent 31/5/1794, s. Thomas Mortimer Kelson (surgeon) and Anne Whitmore. Sidney, Cambridge 1812, BA1816, MA1820, dn17 (Ex. for Cant.), p18 (Cant.). R. Folkington, Sussex 1820 and V. Lullington, Sussex [pop.16] 1840 to death 8/1/1878, leaving £3,000 [C64126] Married by 1835 Elizabeth Grace, w. issue.

**KEMP (Edward Curtis)** Bapt. Melton, Sussex 9/4/1795, s. William Kemp and Anna Curtis. St John's, Cambridge 1812, BA1817, dn20 (Bristol), MA1820, p21 (Salis.). R. Whissonsett w. Horningtoft, Norfolk 1829-65, PC. Yarmouth St George, Norfolk 1865 to death. Chap. in Berlin; Chap. to HRH Duke of Cambridge 1865-81. Died Yarmouth 10/6/1881 aged 86, leaving £1,720-7s-2d. [C53117. Boase] Married Great Yarmouth, Norfolk 28/6/1826 Elizabeth Anne Reynolds, with issue.

**KEMP (Thomas Cooke)** Born Blickling, Norfolk 28/3/1787, s. Benjamin Kemp (farmer, of Swafield, Norfolk) and Sarah Cooke. Caius, Cambridge 1806, BA1811, dn19 (Nor.), p21 (Nor.). V. East Meon, Norfolk (w. Steep and Froxfield Chapels) [income in CR65 £1,140] 1826 to death 17/10/1867 aged 81, leaving £6,000 [C80744] Married Redenhalll, Norfolk 20/12/1808 Jane Sarah Pretyman, w. clerical s. Nunn Robert Pretyman Kemp.

**KEMP (William Robert, Sir, 10th Bart.)** Born Gissing Hall, Gissing, Norfolk 14/11/1791, s. Sir William Robert Kemp, 9th Bart. and Sarah Adcock. Corpus Christi, Cambridge 1811, MA1813, dn15 (Nor.), p15 (Nor.). R. (and patron) of Gissing 1816-74 [blank in ERC], R. Flordon, Norfolk 1816-56 [blank in ERC] 1816 to death 29/5/1874, leaving £40,000 [C113751. Boase] Married Camberwell, London 10/5/1859 Mary Saunders, with issue. Succ. to title 1804.

**KEMPE (Charles Trevanion)** Bapt. Penzance, Cornwall 1/12/1777, s. Admiral Arthur Kempe (one of Captain Cook's crew) and Anne Coryton. Exeter, Oxford 1795, BA1799, dn00 (Ex.), p01 (Ex.), MA1805. R. and V. St Michael Carhays, Cornwall 1806-51, V. Grade, Cornwall 1813-17. Dom. Chap. to HRH Duke of Cambridge 1811. Died 23/12/1851 aged 74 [C145340] Married St Issey, Cornwall 1/12/1803 Elizabeth Marshall, w. clerical son Edward Marshall Kempe.

**KEMPE (John)** Bapt. St Tudy, Cornwall 1/7/1773, s. Rev. Charles Kempe and Catherine Hocken. Exeter, Oxford 1790, BA1794, dn96 (Win. for Ex.), p97 (Ex.). V. Fowey, Cornwall 1818-63 (and Prebend of Trehaverock in St Endellion Collegiate Church 1818) to death 7/1/1863, leaving £1,500 [C145343] Married Egloshayle, Cornwall 29/6/1798 Frances Cory, with clerical son.

**KEMPSON (Henry)** Born Birmingham 24/6/1778, s. Simon Kempson and Lucy Heyward. Christ Church, Oxford 1799, BA 1803, dn03 (London for Salis.), p04 (Ox.), Chap. Christ Church 1804-11, MA1806. H/M Brewood G/S, Staffs. 1811; V. Long Preston, Yorks. 1809 to death 17/10/1857 [C14234] Married Giggleswick, Yorks. 15/10/1832 Mary Ingram.

**KEMPTHORNE (John, sen.)** Born Plymouth Dockyard 24/6/1775, s. Admiral James Kempthorpe and Eleanor Sandys (a Cornish clergy dau.). St John's, Cambridge 1792, BA1796 [Senior Wrangler], Fellow 1796-1802, MA 1799, dn02 (London), p02 (London), BD1807. V. Northleach, Glos. 1816-38, V. Preston, Glos. 1817-20 (res.), Prebend of Ufton Decani in Lichfield Cathedral 1825-38, R. Gloucester St Michael w. St Mary de Grace 1826 to death. Dom. Chap. to Bishop of Gloucester 1815. Died 9/11/1838 [C13212] Married (1) Northwold, Norfolk 8/6/1802 Elizabeth Sandys Whish (a clergy dau., d.1823), w. clerical son, below (2) Droxford, Hants. 11/6/1831 Cordelia Shephard White.

**KEMPTHORNE (John, jun.)** Born Langford, Essex c.1803, s. Rev. John Kempthorne, sen. (above) and Elizabeth Sandys Whish. St John's, Cambridge 1820, BA1825, dn27 (C&L), p27 (B&W), MA1845. V. Wedmore, Som. 1827 to death 3/5/1876, leaving £3,000 [C41479] Married Lewisham, Kent 25/9/1833 Jane Handfield Burn (dau. of a general), with clerical son, also John.

**KEMSEY (Matthew)** Bapt. Lapley, Staffs. 10/6/1773, s. Matthew Kemsey and Jane Samsom. St Edmund Hall, Oxford 1793, BA 1797, dn97 (C&L), p02 (C&L). S/M Wolverhampton Free G/S 1800-6; PC. Codsall, Staffs. 1805 to death. Probate granted 11/9/1846 [C14235]

**KENDAL (Charles Edward)** Bapt. Chelwood, Somerset 5/8/1796, s. Rev. Jonathan Kendal (R. Barrowby, Lincs., below) and Charlotte Williams. Trinity, Cambridge 1814 (aged 18), BA1819, dn21 (Lin.), p22 (Lin.), MA1822. R. Brindle, Preston, Lancs. 1822 to death 25/2/1864, leaving £7,000 [C68571] Married Barrowby 26/7/1825 Catherine Downing. J.P. Lancashire.

**KENDAL (Jonathan)** 'The son of Anne Heaton' [NiVoF] Admitted Student Lincoln's Inn 1784. R. Martinsthorpe, Cambs. 1801, R. Barrowby, Lincs. [net income £1,084] (and Preacher throughout the Diocese of Norfolk) 1802 to death. Dom. Chap. to his patron 6th Duke of Devonshire 1811. Died (Grantham, Lincs.) 8/5/1849 [C80747] Married St James, Piccadilly, London 28/2/1793 Charlotte Williams (illegitimate dau. of the 5th Duke of Devonshire, *q.v.* the *All things Georgian* website), with clerical son, above.

**KENDALL (Frederick)** Born Nunnington, Yorks. 1/9/1790, s. Rear-Admiral John and Ann Kendall (of Scarborough, Yorks.). Trinity, Cambridge 1809, then Sidney 1810, BA1813 ['In that year 'Sidney College was again on fire in two places, and suspicion fell on Kendall, who was committed for trial at the Assizes. Sir William Garrow, who was specially retained, defended the prisoner, who was acquitted but finally expelled from the College'], dn16 (York), p17 (York). R. Riccall, Yorks. 1818 to death 16/2/1836 aged 44 [C131684. Venn has no mention of him as an incendiary. YCO. H.S. Torrens, 'Scarborough's first geologist? The life and works of the Rev. Frederick Kendall (1790-1836)', *Proc. Yorks. Geological Society*, 55 (2004-5) is exhaustive, but does not mention the fire] Married York 28/4/1826 Frances Hobson, w. issue. J.P. East Riding.

**KENDALL (Henry)** Bapt. Morland, Westmorland 7/10/1790, s. John Kendall and Ann Smith. Literate: dn13 (York), p14 (York). V. Startforth, Yorks. 1826 to death 31/3/1867 aged 77, leaving £1,500 [C131685. YCO] Brother William below.

**KENDALL (John)** Bapt. Whitehaven, Cumberland 5/10/1763, s. Wilfrid Kendall. St Alban Hall, Oxford 1785, dn86 (C&L), BA1790, MA 1791, p91 (Wor.). Master of the Earl of Leicester's Hospital [almshouses], Warwick 1794, V. Budbrooke, Warwicks. 1802 to death 23/4/1844 [C14238]

**KENDALL (Nicholas)** Born Pelyn, Cornwall 30/9/1781, s. Rev. Nicholas Kendall and Elizabeth Cotes. Exeter, Oxford 1800, BA1804, dn04 (Chester), p06 (Ex.), migrated to Pembroke, Cambridge 1815, MA1815. V. (and patron) of Talland, Cornwall 1806-44 and V. Lanlivery, Cornwall 1815-44, V. Lanhydrock, Cornwall 1831 (and Prebend of Heredum Marney in St Endellion Collegiate Church 1838) to death. Dom. Chap. to 2nd Earl of Mount Edgcumbe 1815. Died 29/4/1844 aged 62 (by falling from his gig) [C145351] Married Guernsey 25/9/1807 Susan Goodwin, with clerical son, also Nicholas. 'He was much beloved by his parishioners', etc.

**KENDALL (William)** Bapt. Morland, Westmorland 16/6/1783, s. John Kendall and Ann Smith. Literate: dn06 (York), p07 (Car. for York). PC. Grindale, Yorks. 1816-35, PC. Flamborough, Yorks. 1817-35, R. Marske w. Downholme, Yorks. 1834 to death 2/9/1855 aged 72 [C135924. YCO] Married Penrith, Cumberland 29/6/1812 Mary Fisher (a clergy dau.), with issue. Brother Henry above.

**KENDALL (William Charles)** Bapt. Mansfield, Notts. 4/1/1794, s. Rev. William and Ann Kendall. Magdalene, Cambridge 1811, BA 1817, dn17 (Chester for York), p18 (Chester for York), MA1820. V. (and patron) of Swinderby, Lincs. 1821, PC. Ravenstonedale, Westmorland 1842-9. Without cure of souls 1861. Died Newark on Trent, Notts. 1/4/1879 aged 85, leaving £30,000 [C68575. YCO. Platt] Married 12/11/1829 Albina Fisher, 1 dau.

**KENNARD (George)** Born Cripplegate, City of London 3/1/1806, s. John Kennard and Harriet Elizabeth Pierse. St Alban Hall, Oxford 1824, BA1829, dn30 (Salis.), p31 (Salis.), MA 1833. PC. Speeton, Bridlington, Yorks. 1832. Died Gayton, Towcester, Northants. 11/12/1847 aged 41 [C95174] Married Hawkshead, Lancs. 26/9/1839 Mary Jeanette Jackson, with issue.

**KENNAWAY (Charles Edward)** Born Exeter, 3/1/1800, s. Sir John Kennaway, 1st Bart. (*q.v.* ODNB) and Charlotte Amyatt. St John's, Cambridge 1817 [adm. Lincoln's Inn 1820] BA 1822, Fellow 1824-30, MA1825, dn28 (B&W), p29 (B&W). V. Chipping Camden,

Glos. 1832-73, (first) PC. Cheltenham Christ Church, Glos. 1840-3, PC. Brighton Holy Trinity 1843-47, Hon. Canon of Gloucester Cathedral 1861 to death (Great Malvern, Worcs.) 3/11/1875 aged 75, leaving £18,000 [C41481. Boase] Married (1) Richmond, Surrey 17/6/1830 Emma Noel (dau. Rev. the Hon. Gerard Thomas Noel, she d.1843) (2) St Margaret, Westminster, London 30/12/1845 Olivia Way (a clergy dau., of Stanstead Park, Sussex), with clerical son Charles Lewis Kennaway. Surrogate 1861-75.

**KENNEDY (Rann)** Bapt. Birmingham 28/8/1772, s. Benjamin Kennedy (a surgeon working in Maryland) and Damaris Maddox. St John's, Cambridge 1791, BA1795, dn95 (C&L), MA1798, p15 (C&L). S/M King Edward's School, Birmingham 1807-36; V. Birmingham St Paul 1817-47. Died 2/1/1851 [C13217. ODNB. Boase] Married Swansea, Glamorgan 3/8/1802 Julia Hall, w. clerical son. 'One of the most able and popular preachers in Birmingham'. Classicist and friend of Wordsworth and Coleridge at Cambridge. Port. online.

**KENNEY (Arthur Henry)** Born Cork 1/9/1776, s. Rev. John K. Kenney and Frances Herbert (dau. of an *M.P.*). TCD1790, BA1795, Fellow 1800-9, MA1800, BD1806, DD1812. R. Kilmacrenan (Raphoe Diocese) 1810, Dean of Achonry 1812-21, R. Southwark St Olave, South London 1821 (sequestrated 1844) to death (Boulogne - 'because of pecuniary difficulties') 27/1/1855 aged 78 [C80749. ODNB. Boase. Not in Al.Dub.] Married (1) Ireland Feb.1802 Mary Lucinda Herbert (his cousin, she d.1806), w. clerical s. Arthur Robert (2) Ireland by 1816 Elizabeth Morton, w. issue. Controversialist and anti-Papal writer. Port. online.

**KENNEY (Richard)** Bapt. Ashby Magna, Leics. 25/10/1778, s. John and Mary Kenney. Literate: dn10 (Chester for York), p11 (Chester). C.M.S. missionary in India 1820-6; PC. Preston St Peter, Lancs. 1827 to death (Ashby Magna) 3/1/1835 aged 56 [Obliquely found in CCEd 169625 as Kenny. YCO]

**KENNICOTT (Benjamin)** Bapt. Dartmouth, Devon 15/12/1755, s. Gilbert Kennicott [*pleb*] and Elizabeth Peaty/Peate. Christ Church, Oxford 1773, BA1777, dn77 (Ox.), p79 (Ex.). R. Dodbrooke, Devon - [not noted in CCEd], R. Woodhorn, Northumberland 1798-1842, PC. Monkwearmouth, Durham 1816. Died (Woodhorn) 21/3/1842 aged 87 [C34585] Married (1) Stoke Damerel, Devon 7/5/1780 Ann Dutton (d.1803), w. clerical s. Benjamin (2) Tynemouth, Durham 13/11/1806 Mrs Ann Henderson.

**KENNION (Thomas)** Born London. Trinity, Cambridge 1822 (aged 34), then Christ's 1822, dn25 (Chester), BA1826, MA1829. PC. Harrogate St John (o/w Bilton w. Harrogate), Knaresborough, Yorks. 1825 to death (Cheltenham, Glos.) 8/1/1846, with issue [C169624] Married Holborn, London 28/11/1810 Martha Winter ('the compassionate Mrs Kennion'), w. issue.

**KENRICK (Jarvis)** Born Chilham, Kent 26/2/1774, s. Rev. Jarvis Kenrick, sen. and Dorothy Seward. [adm. Middle Temple 1796]. Jesus, Cambridge 1799, dn03 (Win.), p03 (Win.), LLB 1805. R. Bletchingley, Surrey 1803, Prebend of Teinton Regis in Salisbury Cathedral 1806 to death 21/11/1838 [C80752] Married Soho, London 12/4/1804 Mary Perkins, many ch. (inc. an eminent lawyer of the father's name).

**KENT (George Davies)** Born Lincoln 13/4/1773, s. George Kent and Justina Davies. BNC, Oxford 1791, BA1795, dn95 (Lin.), then Lincoln, p97 (Lin.), MA1797. V. Lincoln St Martin (and Prebend of St Martin in Lincoln Cathedral) 1803-49, V. Scothern, Lincs. 1809, R. Sausthorpe, Lincs. 1813-19, R. Conisholm, Lincs. 1819. Died 31/10/1849 to death. Dom. Chap. to 4th Earl of Buckinghamshire 1809. Died 31/10/1849 [C68579. Kaye] Married Lincoln 7/10/1800 Ann Chaplin, with clerical son George Davies Kent.

**KENT (George Edward)** Born Little Dunham, Norfolk 11/10/1796, s. Edmund Kent and Charlotte Shene. Corpus Christi, Cambridge 1815, BA1819, dn20 (Nor.), p20 (Nor.), MA 1822. V. East Winch, Norfolk 1820-42, living St John's Wood, North London 1848-52. Died (a widower) North Walsham, Norfolk 18/8/1870, leaving £5,000 [C113755] Married Norwich 23/4/1821 Mary Decker, w. issue.

**KENT (Samuel)** Bapt. Middlewich, Cheshire 14/10/1758, s. Samuel [*pleb*] and Elisabeth Kent. BNC, Oxford 1774, BA1778, dn80 (Lin. for Win.), MA1781, p91 (Ox. for Win.). R. Carleton St Peter, Norfolk 1823 to death 21/11/1837 aged 88 [C34589] Brother below.

**KENT (William)** Bapt. Middlewich, Cheshire 11/5/1759, s. Samuel [*pleb*] and Elisabeth Kent. BNC, Oxford 1775, BA1778, MA1781. S/M Whitchurch Free G/S, Shropshire 1789; PC. Calverhall, Shropshire 1813. Will proved 1841 [C14243] Married Whitchurch 18/12/1805 Mariana Dod. Brother above.

**KEPPEL (Edward Southwell, Hon.)** Born Eldon/Elvedon, Norfolk 16/8/1800, s. William Charles Keppel, 4th Earl of Albermarle and Elizabeth Southwell. Caius, Cambridge 1818 [as a nobleman], MA1820, dn23 (Nor.), p24 (Nor.). R. Quidenham w. Snetterton, Norfolk 1824-83, R. Tittleshall w. Godwick and Wellingham 1826-35, RD of Rockland 1842, Hon. Canon of Norwich Cathedral 1844. Deputy Clerk of the Closet 1841-75. Died 1/12/1883, leaving £43,645-3s-7d. [C113756] Married Marylebone, London 24/7/1828 Lady Maria Clements (dau. of 2nd Earl of Leitrim), *s.p.*

**KEPPEL (William Arnold Walpole)** Born London 7/10/1804, s. Frederick Keppel (of Lexham Hall, Norfolk) and Louisa Clive (dau. of an *M.P.*). Trinity, Cambridge 1821, BA1826, dn28 (Nor.), p29 (Nor.). R. St Devereux, Heref. 1830, R. Brampton, Norfolk 1830-6, R. Haynford, Norfolk 1836-77. Died (Lexham Hall) 26/11/1888 aged 84, leaving £17,028-4s-10d [C113757] Married Stratton Strawless, Norfolk 7/9/1830 Frances Georgiana Sophia Marsham, with issue. Online photo. LNCP.

**KER, *later* COKBURNE (Hugh)** Bapt. Hull 6/4/1794 (Independent Chapel), s. Hugh and Sarah Ker. Trinity, Cambridge 1812, BA1816, dn17 (Ely for C&L), p18 (Glos. for C&L), MA 1819. V. (and patron) of Etwall, Derbys. 1830, R. (and patron) of Norton in Hales, Shropshire 1830-45 (res.). Lived latterly at Bellaport Old Hall, Norton in Hales (and Llanddwywe, Merioneth). Died Norton (as Hugh Ker Cokburne) 22/5/1866, leaving £100,000 [C13221] Name change 1833.

**KERBY (Cranley Lancelot)** Bapt. Salisbury 13/9/1763, s. Rev. Lancelot Kerby and Louisa Gauntlett. New, Oxford 1784, dn87 (Ox.), p88 (Chester for Ox.), BCL1791. V. Whaddon, Bucks. 1793-1810, R. Wheatfield, Oxon. 1807-20, R. Chinnor, Oxon. 1810-16, R. Stoke Talmage, Oxon. 1820 and 'Perpetual V.' Bampton Low (1st Portion), Oxon. 1824 to death 19/9/1857 [C21811] Married Chinnor 1793 Mary Clerke. A cousin of William Howley, Archbishop of Canterbury (*q.v.*).

**KERR (Henry, Hon., *actually* Lord Henry Francis Charles)** Born Newbattle Abbey, Midlothian 17/8/1800, s. William John Kerr, 6th Marquess of Lothian and Harriet Hobart-Hampden (dau. of 2nd Earl of Buckinghamshire). St John, Cambridge 1819, MA1821, dn24 (Ex.), p25 (Ex.). R. Dittisham, Devon (and Preacher throughout the Diocese of Exeter) 1827-52. Died (Huntlyburn House, Melrose, Roxburgh) 7/3/1882 aged 81, leaving £23,098-3s-10d. [C113758] Married Aberlady, East Lothian 12/9/1832 Louisa Dorothea (w), dau. Gen. Hon. Sir Alexander Hope, 6 ch. (2 clerical).

**KERRICH (Walter John)** Born Chigwell, Essex 24/1/1768, s. Rev. Walter Kerrich and Christian Wenyeve [*sic*]. St John's, Cambridge 1786-7, then New, Oxford 1787, Fellow 1787-1819, BA1791, MA1795. Prebend of Alton Australis in Salisbury Cathedral 1792 and R. Paulerspury, Northants. [blank in ERC] 1818 to death 31/8/1842 [C34592] Married Salisbury 23/5/1823 Emma Elizabeth Wapshare.

**KERSHAW (George William)** Bapt. Rochdale, Lancs. 25/12/1800, s. James Kershaw. Queen's, Oxford 1819, then Worcester, BA 1830, dn30 (Nor.), p31 (Nor.), MA1833. PC. Charsfield, Suffolk 1832, R. Thwaite St George, Suffolk 1841 to death 12/11/1867, leaving £4,000 [C113762] Married Woodbridge, Suffolk 13/2/1832 Charlotte Page (w).

**KEWLEY (Thomas)** Bapt. Arbory, IoM 6/12/1795, s. John Kewley and Eleanor Quick. Literate: dn19 (S&M), p22 (S&M). V. Santan (St Ann), IoM 1827 to death 24/6/1835 aged 39 (CCEd thus) [C7295. Gelling] Married Braddan, IoM 11/9/1820 Anne Moore.

**KEYSALL (John)** Bapt. Holborn, London 21/1/1761, s. John Keysall.l and Mary Browne. BNC, Oxford 1778, BA1783, dn85 (Cant. for London), p85 (Nor.), MA1785. R. Groton, Norfolk 1785-1806, R. Bredon, Worcs. 1805 [net income £1,498] to death. Dom. Chap. to 1st Earl of Uxbridge 1785. Died 27/12/1836 [C113764] Married Heston, Middx. 26/8/1782 Anne Eleanora Woodcock, w. issue.

**KIDD (Thomas [George])** Born Giggleswick, Yorkshire, s. Thomas Kidd and Alice Howson. Trinity, Cambridge 1789 (aged 19), BA1794,

MA1797, dn98 (London), p99 (London). S/M Merchant Taylors' School, London; S/M King's Lynn School, Norfolk 1818; S/M Wymondham School, Norwich; S/M Norwich G/S; R. St James Garlickhithe, City of London 1802, R. Croxton St James, Cambs. 1814-1835, V. Eltisley, Cambs. 1814-21 (and then both parishes again 1835-50), R. Norwich St Swithin 1825 [C19854 as Stipendiary Curate] Died 27/8/1850 [C109770. ODNB] Married Shoreditch, London 22/9/1801 Elisabeth Smith, with clerical son, below.

**KIDD (Thomas George)** Born City of London 24/9/1803, s. Rev. Thomas Kidd (above) and Elisabeth Smith. Caius, Cambridge 1823, dn31 (Peterb. for Nor.), p31 (Nor.), BA1832. V. Bedingham, Norfolk 1831-5, R. Catwick, Yorks. 1835 to death there 1/1/1862, leaving under £200 [C119431]

**KILBY (Thomas)** Born York 19/11/1794, s. John Kilby (Lord Mayor of York) and Ann Shaw. Queen's, Oxford 1816, no degree, dn18 (Chester for York), p21 (York). PC. Wakefield St John, Yorks. 1825 to death 5/9/1868 aged 73. Will not traced [C131688. YCO] Married Scarborough, Yorks. 11/8/1818 Mary Ann Hall, w. issue. Port. online. Topographical artist. Freemason.

**KILDERBEE (Samuel)** Bapt. Ipswich, Norfolk 11/3/1759, s. Samuel Kilderbee (Town Clerk of Ipswich and close friend of Thomas Gainsborough) and Mary Wayth. University, Oxford 1777, BA1780, dn81 (Ox.), p83 (Glos. for Nor.), MA1783, BD and DD1811. R. Campsey Ash, Suffolk 1784-1817, R. Trimley St Martin, Suffolk 1787 [*not* St Mary] and R. Easton, Suffolk 1817 to death 5/9/1847, living at Glemham Hall, Suffolk [C34807] Married Bury St Mary, Suffolk 10/4/1787 Mrs Caroline (Horsey) Waddington, w. issue (incl. Spencer Kilderbee Horsey de Horsey, *M.P.* ,'renowned for his wit and amusing conversation'. *J.P.*

**KILLETT (William)** Bapt.Spitalfields, London 25/6/1770, s. William and Mary Killett (merchant). Pembroke, Cambridge 1787, BA 1792, dn92 (Nor.), p94 (Nor.). V. Middleton, Norfolk 1797-1810 (res.), V. Kenninghall, Norfolk 1820 to death 14/4/1846 aged 78 [C100091]

**KILNER (William)** Born Dufton, Yorks. 6/10/1765, s. Rev. William Kilner, sen. and Elizabeth Bellasis. Queen's, Oxford 1783, BA 1789, dn91 (Car.), MA1792, p93 (Car.), BD and DD1813, Fellow to 1814. R. Weyhill, Hants. 1812 to death 27/9/1853 [C6106] Married Appleby, Westmorland 12/10/1812 Emily Camilla Robinson, with issue.

**KILVINGTON (Edward)** Born Wakefield, Yorks. 10/3/1766, s. Edward Kilvington (of Stoke Newington, Middx.) and Hephzibah Pickering. Jesus, Cambridge 1783, BA1787, dn88 (Cant.), p90 (Ely), MA 1790, then Sidney, Fellow 1791. PC. Ossett cum Gawthorpe, Yorks. 1799-1826, (first) R. Ripon Holy Trinity 1827 to death. Dom. Chap. to 1st Baron Carrington 1818. Died 28/1/1835 (CCEd says 21/5/1835) [C100092] Married Mepal, Cambs. 23/4/1794 Catharine Adams.

**KILVINGTON (Orfeur William)** Born Dulwich, London 16/11/1780, s. John William and Anne Kilvington. Christ Church, Oxford 1800, BA1805, dn07 (Car. for York), p08 (York), MA1808. Military Chaplain in 1813. V. Brignall, Yorks. 1816-54, V. Snaith, Yorks. 1824-8. Died Hatfield, Doncaster. Yorks. 17/10/1854 [C105953. YCO] Married Enfield, Middx.. 29/8/1816 Hon. Maria Margaret Napier (dau. 8th Baron Napier of Merchistoun), with issue.

**KILWICK (William)** From Sussex. Corpus Christi, Cambridge 1778, dn82 (Lin. for Chich.), BA1782, p84 (Chester for Chich.). Minister Funtington, Sussex to 1805, V. Alciston, Sussex 1805-34, V. Bosham, Sussex 1805 to burial (Pagham) 22/11/1837 aged 76 [C64136]

**KING (Isaac)** Bapt. Lee, Missenden, Bucks. 23/6/1804, s. Rev. Isaac King, sen. Christ Church, Oxford 1822, BA1826, dn27 (Lin.), p28 (Lin.), MA1829. R. Bradenham, Bucks. 1832-65. PC. Lee 1832. Died Turin 9/7/1865, leaving £4,000 [C68600] Married Reading, Berks. 25/11/1833 Maria Golding Rickford (w), with issue.

**KING (James)** Born Marylebone, London 13/6/1801, s. of Rt. Rev. Walker King (Bishop of Rochester) and Sarah Dawson. Oriel, Oxford 1818, BA1822, MA1825. R. Henley on Thames, Oxon. 1825 and R. Longfield, Kent 1825 (living at Longfield Court) to death 21/6/1864, leaving £20,000 [C7170] Married Walcot, Bath 23/7/1825 (Hon.?) Maria Carleton, with clerical son. Brother Walker King, below.

**KING (John)** Bapt. Little Bentley, Essex 28/11/1761?, s. of Robert (a farmer) and Elizabeth King. St John's, Cambridge 1780, re-admitted 1782, dn83 (Ely for London), BA1789, MA1792, p01 (York). (builder and first) PC. Leeds St James [blank in ERC] 1801-31, (builder and first) PC. Hull Christ Church, Yorks. 1822 to death 12/9/1858, leaving £12,000 [C88840, YCO. DEB] Wife Ann, and clerical son Samuel King.

**KING (John)** From Middleton, Yorks., s. Rev. John King, sen. Magdalene, Cambridge 1782 (aged 17), BA1787, dn88 (London), MA1798, Fellow. R. Bisley, Surrey 1810 to death 1845 aged 80 [Not yet in CCEd]

**KING (John Myers)** Bapt. Askham, Westmorland 21/3/1804, s. Edward King and Dorothea Myers. Balliol, Oxford 1820, BA1824, MA 1827, dn27 (Nor.), p28 (B&W). PC. Edington, Som. 1829, V. Cutcome, Som. 1832 to death 25/5/1887, leaving £18,487-5s-8d. [C41487. Boase] Married Norton, Kent 6/9/1827 his first cousin Sarah Frances King (dau. of a Bishop of Rochester), with clerical son. Photo. online.

**KING (John William)** Bapt. Lincoln 26/9/1793, s. Neville King. Corpus Christi, Oxford 1810, BA1814, MA1818, dn19 (Ox.), p20 (Ox.), Fellow 1820-33, BD1827. V. (and patron) of Ashby de la Launde, Lincs. 1822 and R. (and patron) of Bassingham, Lincs. 1832-74 (res.). Died 9/5/1875, leaving £25,000. A sporting parson ('Mr Launde'), living at Ashby Hall, Lincs., his horse won the 1000 Guineas and the St Leger. [C34811] Married (2?) Ashby (aged 73) 12/2/1866 Hannah Maria Blake (aged 21, who later remarried).

**KING (Joshua)** Bapt. Birkenhead, Cheshire, 17/12/1778, s. Rev. Bryan King and Ellen Peacock. BNC, Oxford 1796, BA1800, MA1802, Fellow to 1812, dn03 (Ox.), p04 (Ox.). PC. Liverpool St Stephen 1807, R. Bethnal Green St Matthew,London 1809-51 (non-res., his curate being his nephew Bryan King, the ritualist), R. (and patron) of Woodchurch, Cheshire 1821 to death 15/2/1861 aged 82, leaving £14,000 [C34812] Married Leamington, Warwicks 3/4/1838 Hamilton Georgiana Aveling, *s.p.*

**KING (Richard Fitzgerald)** Bapt. Dublin 10/5/1779, s. of Robert King (*later* 2nd Earl of Kingston) and his (later to be separated) wife Caroline Fitzgerald. Exeter, Oxford 1796, then St Mary Hall 1799, BA1799, dn13 (Nor.), p13 (Nor.), MA1828. [Capt. 6th Dragoon Guards]. V. Great Chesterford w. Little Chesterford, Essex 1824 to death. Dom. Chap. to HRH Duke of York 1814. Died Winkfield, Berks. 22/9/1856 aged 77. [C110432] Married Faversham, Kent 6/1/1800 Williamina Ross, w. clerical son Robert Henry King.

**KING (Robert Jarrold)** Bapt. Clare, Suffolk 6/10/1788, s. Robert Frederick Eagle (farmer) and Elizabeth King. St John's, Cambridge 1810, BA1814, dn14 (Nor.), p19 (Ely) V. West Bradenham, Norfolk 1831-5, V. Wymondham, Norfolk 1852 to death (Boston, Lincs.) 3/4/1854 aged 66 [C109773] Widow Elizbeth and at least 13 ch.

**KING (Samuel)** From Middx. Queens', Cambridge 1809, dn13 (Clonmacnois for Peterb.), p14 (Lin.), BA1814, MA1817. Chap. Latimer, Chesham, Bucks. 1820-56, V. Flaunden, Bucks. 1834 and Min. St Aubyn's Chapel, Jersey 1852 to death there 13/12/1856 [C68605]

**KING (Walker)** Born Marylebone, London 1798, s. Rt. Rev. Walker King, sen. (Bishop of Rochester) and Sarah Dawson. Oriel, Oxford 1816, BA1821, dn22 (Roch.), MA1822, p22 (London for Roch.). R. Frindsbury, Kent 1822-5 (res.), R. Stone, Kent 1822-59, R. Bromley, Kent 1824-7 (res.), V. Dartford, Kent 1825, Archdeacon of Rochester (w. Canonry of 6th Prebend in Rochester Cathedral annexed) 1827 to death 13/3/1859, leaving £45,000 [C1944. Boase] Married Westminster, London 15/5/1823 Anne Heberden, with clerical son Edward King, the saintly Bishop of Lincoln (*q.v.* ODNB, *et al*). Brother James King, above.

**KING (William] Moss)** Born London 1795, s. of John King (Under-Secretary of State to the Home Office) and Harriot Margaret Moss. Christ Church, Oxford 1813, Student [Fellow] 1813-21, BA1817, dn19 (Ox.), MA1820, p20 (Ox.). R. Moor Crichel w. Long Crichel, Dorset 1820 to death 14/7/1864, leaving £25,000 [C34813] Married St George's Hanover Square, London 9/3/1825 Elizabeth Margaret Coddington (w) (an Irish clergy dau.), with issue: www.natgould.org/robert_moss_king_1832-1903

**KING (William Poore)** Bapt. Knipton, Leics. 3/6/1789, s. William Anthony King and Sarah Foster. Trinity Hall, Cambridge 1809, no degree, dn21 (Chester), p22 (Chester). PC. Martindale, Westmorland 1828-43. Died Carlisle 12/2/1848 aged 57 [C6109. Platt. Venn says d.1867 - a son?] Married Kendal, Westmorland 5/2/1815 Ann Bigland, with issue.

**KINGDON (John)** Bapt. Bridgerule, Devon 3/11/1768, s. Rev. John Kingdon, sen. and Jane Hockin. Exeter, Oxford 1785, BA1789, dn91 (Ex.), p93 (Ex.), MA1818. R. Hollacombe, Devon 1793-1843, R. (and patron) of Whitstone, Cornwall 1793, R. (and patron) of Marhamchurch, Cornwall 1818-43, V. North Petherwin, Cornwall 1833. Dom. Chap. to Sir Thomas Plumer 1818. Died 17/1/1843 [C145356] Married Bideford, Devon 21/2/1792 Mary Marsh, w. clerical s. William. Brothers, below.

**KINGDON (Roger)** Bapt. Holsworthy, Devon 12/10/1769, s. Rev. John Kingdon and Jane Hockin. Exeter, Oxford 1788, BA1792, dn96 (Bristol for Cant.), p97 (Ex.). R. (and patron) of Holsworthy, Devon 1819 to death 20/11/1837 [C53230] Married Nether Petherwin, Devon 5/5/1800 Thomasin Ware, w. issue. Brothers, above and below.

**KINGDON (Thomas Hockin)** Born Bridgerule, Devon 1/2/1775, s. Rev. John Kingdon and Jane Hockin. Exeter, Oxford 1791, BA1797, dn97 (Ex.), MA 1800, BD1808. V. (and patron) of Bridgerule 1808 and R. (and patron) of Pyworthy, Devon 1808 to death 31/1/1853 [C145358] Married Finsbury, London 24/7/1804 Caroline Nicholson, w. issue. Brothers, above.

**KINGSLEY (Charles)** Bapt. Tamford, Herts. 22/11/1782, s. Charles Kingsley and Elizabeth Westneys. BNC, Oxford 1800, migrated to Trinity Hall, Cambridge 1807, then Sidney 1814, SCL, dn14 (Nor.), LLB1816, p16 (Nor.). V. North Clifton, Notts 1821, R. Barnack, Northants. 1824-30, R. Clovelly, Devon 1830-6, R. Chelsea St Luke, London 1836 to death. Dom. Chap. to Earl Cadogan. Died 29/2/1860 aged 78 [C68654. ODNB. DEB] Married Hampton Wick, Surrey 24/8/1813 Mary Lucas (dau. of a judge in Barbados); father of the more famous Rev. Charles Kingsley, jun. (novelist, Christian Socialist, muscular Christian and sexual athlete), who said of his father that he was 'a magnificent man in body and mind, and possessed of every talent except that of using his talents'.

**KINGSTON (George)** From London, s. George Kingston. Queen's, Oxford 1790 (aged 17), BA1794, dn97 (Car.), p98 (Car.). R. Barningham Norwood >< Norfolk 1800, R. Sidestrand (o/w Syderstone), Norfolk 1800 to death 21/1/1844 [C6110]

**KINLESIDE (William)** Bapt. City of London 8/2/1750, s. William and Elizabeth Kinleside. St John's, Oxford 1767, BA1771, MA1775, dn75 (Ox.). V. Angmering, Sussex 1775-1836 [61 years], R. Clapham, Sussex 1775-86, R. Earnley and Almodington, Sussex 1795-1802, V. Poling, Sussex 1802-36, Hampstead Prebend in Chichester Cathedral 1781-1822. Dom. Chap. to 7th Viscount Montagu 1775; to 2nd Earl of Chichester 1802. Died (Angmering) 17/3/1836 [C34819] Married (1) Angmering 18/10/1791 Frances Gratwicke (aged 19, she d.1798), with issue (2) Valentine House, Ilford, Essex 19/6/1804 Martha Mathew Raikes, w. clerical s. Charles Raikes Kinleside.

**KINSMAN (Andrew Guyse)** Bapt. Plymouth, Devon 30/3/1788 (into an Independent Congregation), s. Andrew Kinsman (Paymaster and Major, *Royal Marines*) and Catherine Poole. Clare, Cambridge 1810, BA1814, dn14 (B&W), p14 (B&W), MA1817. PC. Gildersome, Batley, Yorks. 1821 to death 29/5/1867 aged 79, leaving £600 [C41490. Boase] Married Shrewsbury 19/8/1818 Anne Brown, with issue.

**KIPLING (Charles)** Bapt. Dorton, Bucks. 24/2/1769, s. Rev. Charles, sen. and Penelope Kipling. Wadham, Oxford 1786, dn91 (Lin.), p94 (Ox.), BCL1809. V. Stony Stratford, Bucks. 1809, R. Newport Pagnell, Bucks. 1810-22 (res.), R. Coston, Leics. 1822 to death 28/5/1841 [C34822] Brother below.

**KIPLING (John)** Bapt. Dorton, Bucks. 16/1/1767, s. Rev. Charles and Penelope Kipling. Lincoln, Oxford 1783, BA1787, dn89 (Lin.), MA1790, p91 (Lin.). PC. Chearsley. Bucks. 1791-39, PC. Nether (or Lower) Winchendon, Bucks. 1802-33 (res.), PC. Chilton, Bucks. 1810-29 (res.), V. Oakley, Bucks. 1810 to death 26/11/1839 [C68657] Brother above.

**KIRBY (John)** Literate: dn80 (Car.), p81 (Car.). PC. Newlands, Crosthwaite, Cumberland 1780-92, PC. Matterdale, Greystoke, Cumberland 1828 to death 22/9/1833 (CCEd thus) [C6113. Platt]

**KIRBY (John)** Born Kirby, Mayfield, Sussex 26/3/1786, s. Rev. John Kirby and Anne Ruth Baker. St John's, Cambridge 1805, BA1810, dn10 (Salis. for Chich.), p10 (Cant.), MA1813. V. (and patron) of Mayfield 1810-31. Died 27/10/1844 aged 58 [C64145] Married London 2/1/1816 Louisa Murdoch, with issue.

**KIRBY (John Lawrence)** Born Dedham, Essex, s. Rev. John Robert Kirby and Ann Fogg. Pembroke, Cambridge 1816 (aged 17), dn19 (London), BA1820, p20 (London). V. Little Clacton, Essex 1832 to death 1850 (1st q. as Laurence) [C120152] Married 2/9/1851 Margaret Manthorp (of Thorpe Abbey, Thorpe, Essex), with issue.

**KIRBY (William)** Bapt. Witnesham, Suffolk 19/9/1759, s. William Kirby (attorney) and Lucy Meadows. Caius, Cambridge 1776, BA 1781, dn82 (Nor.), p83 (Nor.), MA1816. V. Barham, Suffolk 1797 (and RD of Claydon) to death 4/7/1850 [C113783. ODNB] Married (1) Debenham, Suffolk 1784 Sarah Ripper (d.1814) (2) Baylham, Suffolk 27/6/1816 Charlotte Rodwell; *s.p.* An eminent parson-entomologist (he identified 130 different specimens of bees in his own parish), and one of the first Fellows of the Linnean Society (Hon. President 1837); *F.R.S.* (1818).

**KIRKBANK (Joseph Thompson)** Bapt. Whicham, Cumberland 11/9/1784, s. of William Kirkbank, *J.P.*, and Elizabeth Thompson. Queen's, Oxford 1812, BA1816, dn18 (Chester), p18 (Chester), MA1819. S/M Bury, Lancs.; PC. Royton, Lancs. 1820, V. Dalton in Furness, Lancs. 1823 to death 29/12/1848, leaving £2,000 [C169690] Married Bury 29/6/1837 Mary Anne Clegg [her will of 1880 left £20,000]

**KIRKBY (John)** From Notts. Queens', Cambridge 1774, BA1779, MA1783, dn88 (Ely), p88 (York). R. Gotham, Notts. 1788-1841 (license of non-res. 1828-35 'on account of actual bodily infirmity'). Died there 1847 (2nd q.) [C100095. YCO] Married Frances Allanson (a clergy dau.).

**KITCHEN, KITCHIN (Joseph)** Born Gosforth, Cumberland *c.*1797, s. John Kitchen and Elizabeth Porter. St Bees adm. 1818, dn19 (Chester), p19 (Chester). PC. Wasdalehead 1819-72 [pop. 49]. Died 4/9/1878 aged 84. Will not traced in England [C169699] Married Gosforth 19/10/1824 Frances Turner, with issue.

**KITCHINGMAN (Henry)** Bapt. Sessay, Yorks. 11/10/1753, s. Rev. Richard Henry Kitchingman. Clare, Cambridge 1773, BA1777, dn77 (Chester), p78 (Chester), MA1780. V. Kirby on the Moor (o/w Kirby Hill), Yorks. 1778-1839, Canon and Prebend of Bole in York Minster 1786-1839, R. North Witham, Lincs. 1788-1829 (non-res.). Dom. Chap. to 1st Duke of Montagu 1779. Died Clifton, Yorks. 17/1/1839 aged 85 [C68677. Bennett2] Married Chipping Warden, Northants. 5/2/1786 Sarah Knowler (a clergy dau.), with clerical s. Richard Henry Kitchingman.

**KITSON (Walter)** Born Torquay, Devon 8/12/1777, s. Rev. Walter Kitson, sen. Oriel, Oxford 1795, BA1799, dn00 (Ex.), p01 (Ex.), MA1804. V. St Eval, Cornwall 1803-43, R. Marksbury, Som. 1815-16 then again 1835 to death and PC. Brislington St Luke, Bristol 1815-43, R. Chilton Foliat, Berks 1816-35. Died 25/1/1843 [C41491] Married (1) Exeter 5/6/1806 Mary Ann Andrew (d.1820), w. issue (2) Exeter 1815 Mary Jones, w. further issue.

**KITSON (William)** Born Shiphay House, Torquay, Devon 14/4/1769, s. Rev. William Kitson, sen. and Martha Addicott. Oriel, Oxford 1787, BA1791, dn91 (Ex.), p93 (Ex.), MA1795. R. Northlew, Devon 1807 and V. Abbotskerswell, Devon 1807 to death. Dom. Chap. to Bishop of Exeter, then of Salisbury 1807. Died 1/2/1847 [C145369] Married Woodland, Devon 26/9/1797 Susan Abraham, with issue.

**KNAGG (Richard)** Bapt. Selside, Kendal, Westmorland 22/2/1784, s. Robert Knagg and Alice Sutton. Literate: dn07, p08 (Chester). PC. Silverdale, Lancs. 1808, PC. Lunds, Aysgarth, Yorks. 1829 (and S/M) to death 1842 (2nd q.) [C169703] Married Warton, Lancs. 1/2/1813 Eleanor Ellen Burrow.

**KNAPP (Henry Hartopp)** Bapt. Stamford, Lincs. 24/8/1782, s. Rev. Henry Ryder Knapp (R. Woodford, Northants.) and Elizabeth Hartopp. King's, Cambridge 1801, Fellow 1804-21, BA1806, MA1809, dn09 (Ely), p20 (Ely). S/M Eton College 1808-34 (where Gladstone was amongst his pupils); R. Ampthill, Beds. 1820 to death (Rome, unmarried, of malaria) 18/12/1846 aged 64. Lived for 'some time' on the Island of Elba [C68681] 'Passionately fond of the theatre'. Brother Samuel Hartopp Knapp, below.

**KNAPP (Henry John)** Bapt. Jersey, Channel Islands 29/1/1779, s. Gabriel Knapp and Anne Taylor. Pembroke, Oxford 1795, BA1800, MA1804, p04 (Win.), BD and DD1840. V. Willesden, Middx. 1803, Minor Canon of St Paul's Cathedral, London 1804 (4th Minor Prebend 1817, 9th Minor Prebend 1821, etc.), V. Mucking, Essex 1821-4, V. Barling, Essex 1824, V. Kingsbury 1834 to death 18/7/1850 [C80770]

**KNAPP (Primatt)** Born Shenley, Bucks. 11/10/1764, s. Rev. Primatt Knapp, sen. and Keturah French (an American?). Worcester, Oxford 1783, dn22 (Lin.), p24 (Lin.), BA1787. R. (and patron) of Shelly Mansell, Berks. 1793 to death 21/1/1838 [C68679] Married Little Dalby, Leics. 11/5/1796 Rebecca Ann Goodwin, w. clerical son of same name (d.1834).

**KNAPP (Samuel Hartopp)** Born Stoke Albany, Northants., s. Rev. Henry Ryder Knapp (R. Woodford, Northants.) and Elizabeth Hartopp. Merton, Oxford 1813 (aged 18), BA1820, dn20 (Lin.), p21 (Lin.), MA 1827. Chap. H.E.I.C. 1827; R. Letchworth, Herts. 1831 to death 23/6/1858, leaving £10,000 [C68680] Married Richmond on Thames, Surrey 15/4/1824 (Mrs) Marianne Jane James, with issue. Brother Henry Hartopp Knapp, above.

**KNATCHBULL (Wadham)** Born Cholderton Lodge, Marlborough, Wilts. 9/8/1794, s. Wyndham Knatchbull and Catherine Maria Knatchbull (thus). Christ Church, Oxford 1813, BA1816, dn18 (Salis.), p19 (Salis.), MA 1823. Prebend of Combe the Second in Wells Cathedral 1822 (value £3-15s-6d.), R. Sutton Mandeville, Wilts. 1831-9. Died Cholderton 9/1/1876, leaving £70,000 [C34830] Married Teffont Magna, Wilts. 5/7/1825 Louisa Elizabeth Wyndham, with issue.

**KNATCHBULL (Wyndham)** Born Norton, Kent 23/8/1786, s. Sir Edward Knatchbull, 8th Bart. and Frances Graham. Christ Church, Oxford 1804, MA1808, then All Souls, Fellow 1809-24, dn10 (Ox.), p11 (Cant.), MA1812, BD 1820, DD1823. Laudian Professor of Arabic, Oxford 1823-40. R. Westbeare, Kent 1811-68, R. Bircholt, Kent 1821-36, R. Aldington w. Smeath, Kent 1823 [net income in CR65 £1,014] to death (Smeath) 5/4/1868, leaving £8,000 [C34831. Boase] Married Folkestone, Kent 16/12/1826 Anna Maria Elizabeth Dawkins, with issue.

**KNIGHT (James)** Bapt. Winteringham, Lincs. 25/4/1793, s. Rev. Samuel and Frances Knight. Lincoln, Oxford 1811, BA1814, dn16 (B&W), p17 (B&W), MA1817. PC. Halifax St John in the Wilderness, Yorks. 1821-2, PC. Sheffield St Paul 1824-60, R. Foulness, Essex 1832. Died Barton on Humber, Lincs. 30/8/1863, leaving £5,000 [C41493. Boase. DEB. S. Slinn, 'Archbishop Harcourt's recruitment of literate clergymen: Part 2', *Yorkshire Archaeological Journal*, 81 (2009), 294, note 60] Wife Frances (w), with clerical son. Brother William, below. Surrogate 1829.

**KNIGHT (John)** Bapt. Lynton, Devon 20/7/1789, s. Rev. Richard and Elizabeth Knight. Magdalen, Oxford 1808, BA1812, dn12 (B&W), p14 (Ex.), MA1815. R. Huish, Devon 1825-44 and R. Petrockstowe, Devon 1825 to death 2/11/1844 [C45325] Married Shebbear, Devon 18/4/1827 Mary Ann Dovell.

**KNIGHT (Robert Hervey)** Bapt. Weston Favell, Northants. 26/3/1764, s. Rev. Robert Knight and Mary Hervey. Lincoln, Oxford 1781, BA1785, MA 1788. R. Earls Barton, Northants 1789 and R. (and patron) of Weston Favell 1797 to death 19/7/1842 [C110439 is the son of the same name who succ. him at Weston Favell] Married by 1793 Ann Walker, w. issue.

**KNIGHT (Samuel Johnes)** see under **JOHNES (Samuel)**

**KNIGHT (Thomas)** Born Norham, Northumberland 4/9/1795, s. of William Henry Knight (the village schoolmaster) and Jane Young. Peterhouse, Cambridge 1812, BA1818, dn18 (York for Durham), p19 (Durham). R. Ford, Northumberland 1819 [income £1,380 in CR65] to death 29/3/1872 aged 76, leaving under £6,000 [C132352. YCO] Married Berwick-on-Tweed 23/6/1820 Sarah Crowther Norris, with issue. Typescript biography online.

**KNIGHT (William)** Born Winteringham, Lincs. 8/12/1790, s. Rev. Samuel and Frances Knight. St Catherine's, Cambridge 1819, BA 1823, dn22 (York), p23 (York), MA1826. V. Hull St James 1831 to death 3/1/1862, leaving £3,000 [C132426. YCO] Brother James, above.

**KNIGHT (William)** From Painswick, Glos., s. William Knight. Balliol, Oxford 1809 (aged 19), BA1813, dn13 (Ex.), p14 (Heref. for Glos.), MA 1816. R. Bristol St Michael and All Angels 1816-55, Hon. Canon of Bristol Cathedral 1864 to death. Chap. to Earl of Winchelsea and Nottingham 1827. Died 5/8/1878, leaving £2,000 [C53235. Boase] Clerical son.

**KNIGHT (William)** Born 1798 Godmersham Park, Kent, s. Edward Knight (born Austen, brother of Jane Austen) and Elizabeth Bridges. Exeter, Oxford 1818, BA1822, dn22 (Win.), p23 (Win.), MA1824. R. Steventon, Hants. 1823 to death 5/12/1873, leaving £7,000 [C80773] Married London 24/6/1856 Jane Hester Hope (a Scot), with clerical son Edward Bridges Knight.

**KNIPE (Francis)** Bapt. Hawkshead, Lancs. 9/6/1757, s. William Knipe. Queen's, Cambridge 1886, BA1780, dn80 (C&L for Peterb.), Fellow 1781, MA1783, p82 (Peterb.), tutor. V. Oakington, Cambs. 1791-1800, R. Sandon, Essex 1800 to death 9/5/1834 aged 76. Chap. at British Embassy at Hamburg to death 10/4/1834 aged 76 [C13587 says 18/7/1834]. Married Finchley, London 19/10/1802 Jane Sawrey, w. issue.

**KNIPE (John)** Bapt. Middleton in Lonsdale, Westmorland 3/2/1760, s. William Knipe and Margaret Garnet. Literate: dn84 (Chester), p85 (Chester). PC. Middleton, Kirkby Lonsdale, Westmorland 1785 to death 20/4/1838 aged 78, leaving £3,000 [C169706] Married (1) Middleton 19/8/1799 Dorothy Cooke (d.1800), with issue (2) St James's, Piccadilly, London 8/1/1807 Mary Holmes.

**KNIPE (John)** Bapt. Grasmere, Westmorland 29/12/1765, s. Rev. Isaac Knipe. Queen's, Oxford 1781, BA1785, dn88 (Ox.), MA1789, p89 (Chester for Ox.). R. Charlton on Otmoor, Oxon. [blank in ERC] 1805 to death.Chap. at British Embassy at Hamburg. Died 1/9/1845 aged 82. [C34836]

**KNIPE (Randolph Richard)** Bapt. London 26/1/1773, s. Robert Knipe (Berkhamsted, Herts.) and Jane Davis. Queen's, Oxford 1791, BA1795, dn95 (Salis.), MA1799, p02 (Win.). R. (and patron) of Water Newton >< Hants. 1807-60, R. Denton, Hants. 1816, (Sinecure R. Grand Tey, Essex 1827-8 (res.)). Died Bath 20/4/1859, leaving £3,000 [C69128] Married Westminster, London 23/2/1810 Harriet Willard, with issue.

**KNOLLIS (James)** From Burford, Oxon., s. Rev. Francis Knollis and Mary Hallifax. Trinity, Oxford 1794 (aged 18), then Lincoln, Fellow 1798-1815, BA1798, dn99 (Lin.), p00 (Ox.), MA1801, BD1809. V. Penn, Bucks. 1823 and Curate Maidenhead, Bucks. 1819 to death. Chap. to HRH Duke of Clarence 1812. Died 8/5/1860, leaving £1,000 [C34839] Married Harpsden, Oxon. 1814 Frances Hall, and issue.

**KNOTT (James Monkhouse)** From Everdon, Northants., s. Rev. Isaac Knott and Jane Boyce. Lincoln, Oxford 1813 (aged 17), BA 1818, dn18 (Peterb.), p24 (C&L). V. Worm-leighton, Warwicks. 1824, V. Priors Hardwick >< Warwicks. 1837 to death 28/9/1861, leaving £3,000 [C14759] Married Fenny Compton, Warwicks. 17/6/1822 Anne Maria Reading, with issue.

**KNOTTESFORD, born FORTESCUE (Francis Fortescue-)** Bapt. Edmonton, Middx. 22/4/1772 , s. Francis Fortescue and Maria [Knottesford?]. Queen's, Oxford 1790, BA 1793, dn95 (London), p96 (London), MA1798. R. Billesley, Warwicks. 1823 to death (Alveston Manor, Stratford on Avon) 31/5/1859, leaving £25,000 [C120160] Married Maria Downing (a clergy dau.), w. clerical son Edward Bowles Knottesford-Fortescue (later RC)

**KNOWLES (Thomas)** Probably bapt. Ledsham, Yorks. 4/5/1769, s. William Knowles (Ferrybridge, Yorks.). Magdalene, Cambridge 1791, BA1795, dn95 (Lin.), p96 (Lin.). R. South Somercotes, Lincs. 1817 (and RD) to death 4/1/1848 aged 77 [C69135. Kaye]

**KNOX (Thomas)** Born Tonbridge, Kent, s. Rev. Vicesimus Knox (Headmaster Tonbridge School, *q.v.* ODNB) and Mary Miller. BNC, Oxford 1802 (aged 19), BA1806, dn06 (Ex. for Roch.), p07 (Roch.), MA1809, BD and DD1824. H/M Tonbridge G/S 1819; R. Runwell, Essex 1821 and R. (and patron) of Ramsden Crays, Essex 1821 to death 23/7/1843 ('He died in a fit while in the vestry where he gone to put on a surplice for Communion'). Succ. by his son of same name in same two places [C303] Married Tonbridge 19/8/1815 Frances Woodgate, with issue.

**KNYVETT (Charles William)** Bapt. Marylebone, London 21/9/1796, s. Charles William Knyvett and Jane Laney. Christ Church, Oxford 1815, Student [Fellow] 1815-30, BA 1819, dn19 (Salis.), p20 (Salis.), MA1821. Usher Westminster School 1823 Bradley w. Yarnfield, Wilts. 1829-42, Canon of Windsor Chapel 1834-47, R.

West and East Helserton, Yorks. 1847 to death (Wallington, Surrey) 20/12/1881, leaving £4,004-17s-4d. [C80775] Married Beddington, Surrey 2/7/1829 Julia Ferrers, with issue.

**KYNASTON (Edward, Sir, 2nd Bart.)** Born Shrewsbury 7/1/1758, s. Roger Kynaston and Mary Powell. St John's, Cambridge 1775, dn80 (Heref.), p82 (Heref.). V. Madeley, 1785-6 (res.), R. Risby, Suffolk 1786-1839, V. Kinnerley, Shropshire 1795-1834 (res.), R. Knockin 1800-15, R. (and patron) of Hordley, Shropshire 1803-39, R. Fornham St Genevieve, Suffolk 1804 to death. Chap. in Ordinary 1790. Died 26/8/1839 [C14762] Married Shrewsbury 9/4/1783 Letitia Owen (of Dublin). Succ. to the title 1822.

**KYNASTON (John)** Bapt. Wem, Shropshire 1/1/1801, s. John [*pleb*] and Mary Kynaston. Christ Church, Oxford 1822, BA1822, MA1826, dn26 (C&L), p27 (C&L), MA1829. S/M Free Market Drayton G/S 1829; PC. Child's Ercall, Shropshire 1829-37, V. Billingborough Lincs. 1855-85, V. Tideswell, Derbys. 1837-55. Died 4/8/1885, leaving £4,238-2s-7d. [C14763. Bennett1] Married Wem 23/7/1829 Elizabeth Rowe Muckley, with issue.

**LA TOUR, *or* LATOUR (Peniston)** Born Marylebone, London 18/6//1769, s. Peniston La Tour. Peterhouse, Cambridge 1786, migrated to St Mary Hall, Oxford 1794, BA1795, dn95 (Ox.), p95 (Ox.), MA1798. V. Greasley, Notts. 1797-1819, R. Boothby Graffoe, Lincs. 1801 and R. Scorborough [*not* Scarborough], Yorks. 1819 to death. Dom. Chap. to 2nd Earl of Dorchester 1801. Died 10/11/1851 aged 82 [C34944. Foster under Tour] Married Lincoln 10/9/1811 Elizabeth Mason.

**LACY (Charles)** Born Salisbury Jan. 1795, s. James Lacy and Margaret Bernister. All Souls, Oxford 1814, BA1818, dn18 (Ox.), Chap. Christ Church 1818-20, p19 (Ox.), MA1824, incorporated at Cambridge, MA1833. PC. Tring, Herts. 1819-39 and PC. Wigginton, Herts. 1819-39, R. Althorpe, Lincs. 1837-9, R. All Hallows London Wall, City of London 1839 [income £1,250 in CR65] to death (Finsbury, London) 17/5/1890, leaving £23,134-9s-0d. [C34845. Boase] Wife Mart, w. issue (incl. son Charles Sethward de Lacy Lacy). *J.P., D.L.* Herts.

**LACY (Richard)** Born Northumberland, s. Richard Lacy and Dorothy Appleby. Queens', Cambridge 1789, BA1794, dn94 (Lin.), p95 (Lin.). R. Newbold Verdon, Lincs. 1795-1803, R. Shelfanger, Norfolk 1800-12, R. Dore Abbey >< Heref. 1802-9, R. Whiston, Rotherham, Yorks. 1807 to death 16/9/1836 aged 62 [C69173] *J.P.*

**LADE (William)** Bapt. Boughton under Blean, Kent 2/11/1761, s. John Lade and Hester Hobday. Jesus, Cambridge 1778, BA1783, then Clare, dn84 (Ely), p85 (Lin. for Cant.), Fellow 1786, MA1786. R. Knowlton, Kent 1792-1834, V. Ringwould, Kent 1802-8, V. Graveney w. Goodnestone >< Kent 1806-34, R. Wickhambreaux, Kent 1807 to death. Dom. Chap. to 4th Earl of Guilford 1806. Died April 1842 aged 80 [C69176]

**LAFONT (John)** Bapt. Whitechapel, London 20/11/1792, s. of John Lafont (a merchant from King's Langley, Herts.) and Jane Steavenson. Emmanuel, Cambridge 1815, dn18 (Lin.), p19 (London), BA1820, MA1823, incorporated at Oxford 1835. R. (and patron) of Hinxworth, Herts. 1822-44 and R. Sutton Bonnington (1st Mediety, o/w St Ann), Notts. 1827 to death (Hinxworth) 13/10/1844 aged 51 [C69179] Married Baldock, Herts. 19/7/1825 Eliza Pryor (Clay Hall, Herts.), with clerical son Ogle Russell Lafont.

**LAING (Francis)** Born Edinburgh 1/5/1773, s. Alexander Laing (architect) and Charlotte Polson. Edinburgh University; Glasgow University 1795; Worcester, Oxford 1795, then Snell Exhibitioner to Balliol, BA1799, dn99 (Salis.), p99 (Salis.), MA1801. Private Secretary to Governor of Malta 1803, then to the Government to 1814; R. Llanmaes, Glamorgan 1815-24, PC. Humshaugh, Northumberland 1820-32. Died Tewksbury, Glos. 24/11/1861 aged 88, leaving £30,000 [C4216. Snell] Married Dudmaston Hall, Quatt, Shropshire 8/3/ 1817 Mary Dorothea Whitmore, with clerical son Francis Henry Wolryche Whitmore.

**LAKE (Atwell)** Born London 1/7/1774, s. Sir James Winter Lake, 3rd Bart. (Deputy-Governor of the Hudson's Bay Company) and Joyce Crowther. Trinity Hall, Cambridge 1794, no degree, dn97 (Nor.), p03 (Nor.). Chap. to Prince of Wales Island (i.e. Penang) with *H.E.I.C.* 1805; R. West Lynn, Norfolk 1803-12, R. West Walton (2nd Mediety, o/w Lewis), Norfolk 1811 to death (Weymouth, Dorset) 8/11/1847 [C113793] Married London 31/10/1832 Sophia Turner.

**LALLY (William Michael)** Bapt. Whitegate, Cheshire 4/9/1775, s. Rev. Edmund Lally and Catherine Holme. Adm. Lincoln's Inn 1794. Peterhouse, Cambridge 1797, dn99 (York), p99 (York), LLD1803, then Oxford, St John's 1829, DCL1829. R. Drayton Bassett, Staffs. 1799-1857, V. Little Middenden, Bucks. 1809-10. Died 15/6/1857 [C14766. YCO] Married Bloomsbury, London 4/3/1800 Susannah Cooper.

**LAMB (George Augustus)** Bapt. Rye, Kent 6/2/1782, s. Thomas Phillips Lamb and Maria Davis. Oriel, Oxford 1799, then Magdalen 1800-6, BA1803, dn04 (Ox.), p96 (Ox.), MA 1806, BD1817, DD1827. R. (and patron) of Iden, Sussex 1807 and R. (and patron) of East Guldeford w. Playden, Sussex 1807 to death 31/10/1864 [total income £1,398], leaving under £800 [C34849] Married Marylebone, London 25/6/1806 Julia Louisa Bancroft, with clerical s. Thomas Davis Lamb. Magnificent natural online photo. of him reading a newspaper. Apparently a political 'fixer' in Rye before the Reform Bill.

**LAMB (John, sen.)** Born Ely, Cambs. 7/3/1758, s. Joseph Lamb. Christ's, Cambridge 1776, BA 1780, dn80 (Nor.), p83 (Glos. for Nor.). R. of Hasketon, Suffolk 1783, PC. Ixworth, Norfolk 1789-1805, R. Woodbridge, Suffolk 1792, R. Charwelton, Northants. 1805, R. Stretton, Rutland 1810 and V. Haxey, Lincs. 1810 to death 14/5/1842 [C69180] Married City of London 22/5/1792 Maria Hovell (a clergy dau., Badwell Ash, Suffolk), with son, below.

**LAMB (John, jun.)** Born Ixworth, Norfolk 28/2/1789, s. Rev. John Lamb, sen. (above) and Mary Hovell. Corpus Christi, Cambridge 1807, BA1811, Fellow 1812, dn12 (Bristol), p13 (Bristol), MA1814, BD1822, DD1827. Master of Corpus Christi College, Cambridge 1822 to death, Vice Chancellor 1823-4. PC. Cambridge St Benedict 1821, Dean of Bristol 1837 and V. Olveston, Glos. 1845 to death 19/4/1850 [C53240. ODNB] Married Cranford, Northants. 19/3/1822 Anne Hutchinson (a clergy dau.), with issue. Historical and antiquarian writer.

**LAMBARDE (Thomas)** Born Sevenoaks Park, Kent 4/1/1798, s. Milton Lambarde and Aurea Otway. Christ Church, Oxford 1816, Student [Fellow] 1816-23, dn21 (Ox.), BA1820, p22 (Ox.), MA1822. R. Ridley, Kent 1822 and R. Ash, Kent 1822-40, Died (unm.) Notting Hill, London 20/5/1870, leaving £14,000 [C1956]

**LAMBERT (Johnson)** Bapt. Bowes, Barnard Castle, Yorks. 28/9/1794, s. Rev. Joseph Lambert (Gilmonby Hall, Bowes) and Ann Johnson. Literate: dn20 (Chester), p21 (Chester). PC. Bowes 1823 to death 27/1/1867. Will not traced [C169737] Married Bowes 3/2/1831 Jane Adamthwaite, with issue.

**LAMBERT (Joseph)** Bapt. Morland, Westmorland 1/7/1763, s. Joseph Lambert. Literate: dn97 (York), p98 (York). PC. Marrick, Yorks. 1815 and V. Seaham, Durham 1846 to death 31/12/1849 aged 87 [C120007. YCO *as* John] Married Bowes, Yorks. 11/11/1791 Nancy Johnson, with issue.

**LAMBERT (Richard William)** Bapt. Redlands, Bristol 2/3/1801, s. Richard Lambert and Hester Jones. Pembroke, Oxford 1819, BA 1823, p24 (Bristol), MA1826. Master of Choristers in Bristol Cathedral 1824-40, PC. Puxton, Som. 1832 and PC. Churchill, Som. 1832-40, V. Fivehead w. Swell, Som. 1840. Died Clifton, Bristol 3/7/1888, leaving £1,355-12d-9d. [C41515] Had issue.

**LAMBERT (Robert)** Bapt. Kendal, Westmorland 14/6/1764, s. John Lambert. Trinity, Cambridge 1782, BA1787, dn90 (Bristol for Car.), p90 (Car.). PC. Troutbeck, Westmorland 1792-79 (non-res.), PC. Stalling Busk, Aysgarth, Yorks. 1799-1836, R. Thornton cum Bagworth, Leics. 1803. Died 29/4/1836 aged 71, leaving under £200 [C6117] Married Aysgarth 30/5/1830 Alice Tennant, with issue.

**LAMPEN (John [Skinner])** Born Stoke Damerel, Devonport, Devon, s. Richard Lampen and Anne Skinner. Exeter, Oxford 1822 (aged 18), BA1826, dn27 (Ex.), p28 (Ex.), MA1830. Min. Stoke Damerel St John the Baptist 1831-65, R. Anthony, Cornwall 1863. Died Plymouth 20/1/1874, leaving £14,000 [C145393] Married Stoke Damerel 22/9/1825 Lavinia Gilbard, w. issue. Surrogate.

**LAMPEN (Robert)** From Plymouth, Devon, s. Robert Lampen and Elizabeth Snow. Exeter, Oxford 1808 (aged 18), BA1812, dn13 (Ex), MA1816. Chap. Plymouth St Andrew 1823, V. St Enoder, Cornwall 1823-[28], V. Probus, Cornwall 1828, Canon Residentiary of Exeter Cathedral 1844 to sudden death 18/8/1849 aged 59 [C145394] Married Elizabeth Gandy by 1817, w. issue.

**LANCASTER (Joseph)** Literate: dn92 (Car.), p92 (Car.). PC. Thornthwaite, Crosthwaite, Cumberland 1792 to death April 1841 aged 74 [C6119. Platt]

**LANCASTER (Richard Hume)** Born London 19/9/1772, s. Richard Lancaster and Mary Tofts. Merton, Oxford 1790, BA1793, dn96 (Ox.), MA1796, p97 (Ox.). R. Warneford, Hants. 1802 to death 25/6/1853 [C34923] Married (1) by 1804 Elizabeth Burne (d.1822), with clerical son Thomas Burne Lancaster (2) Jane Martha (d.1828), with further issue. A talented landscape artist, and father of the marine painter Hume Lancaster (*q.v.* ODNB).

**LANCASTER (Thomas William)** Born Fulham, London 24/8/1787, s. Rev. Thomas Lancaster (PC. Wimbledon, Surrey) and Anne Burney. Oriel, Oxford 1804, BA1807, then Queen's 1808, Fellow 1809-16, MA1810, dn10 (Ox.), p12 (Ox.). Usher Magdalen College School 1840-9; V. Banbury, Oxon. 1815-49 [blank in ERC] (exchanged for) R. Over Worton, Oxon. 1849 to death. Dom. Chap. to Dowager Countess of Guilford. Died 12/12/1859 ('found dead in his bed'), leaving under £300 [C34926. ODNB. Boase] Married Banbury 23/4/1816 Anne Walford, *s.p.*

**LANCE (John Edwin)** Bapt. Southampton, Hampshire 16/3/1794, s. Rev. William Lance and Mary Fitzhugh. Corpus Christi, Cambridge 1813, BA1817, dn17 (Salis.), p19 (Salis.), MA 1853. R. Buckland St Mary, Som. 1830 (with RD and Prebend of Combe 12th in Wells Cathedral 1844) to death 7/5/1885, leaving £7,060-1s-6d. [C41516] Married (1) St George's Hanover Square, London 6/5/1822 Madelina Louisa Dupré Porcher (a minor, d.1839), with clerical son (2) Paddington, London 1841 (4th q.) Clara Pearse, with further issue.

**LANCE (William)** Bapt. Gosport, Hants. 15/8/1761, s. William and Mary Lance. Corpus Christi (Benet Hall), Cambridge 1778, BA 1782, dn84 (Ox. for Win.), Fellow 1785, MA1785, p86 (Ely for Win.). V. Horsford, Norfolk 1787-91 (res.), R. Helmington, Suffolk 1790-2, R. Faccombe, Hants. 1792 to death 1848 (1st q.) [C34927] Married Greenwich, Kent 13/12/1787 Catherine Elizabeth Elliot, with issue.

**LANDON (Charles Richard)** Born London 21/2/1766, s. James Landon and Anna Palmer. Trinity, Cambridge 1781, BA1786, MA1789, dn89 (London), then Sidney, Fellow 1794, BD 1796. R. Vange, Essex 1809 to death (Billericay, Essex) 11/2/1834 (CCEd says 25/4/1834) [C120168] Married Strand, London 17/6/1802 Caroline Harrop, with issue.

**LANDON (George)** Born Oxford 22/4/1805, s. of Very Rev. Whittington Landon, Dean of Exeter (below) and Maria Augustina Ready. Worcester, Oxford 1823, BA1827, dn28 (Ex.), p29 (Ex.), MA1830, BCL1834. V. Branscombe, Devon 1828-37, R. Richards Castle, Shropshire 1837 to death (near Ludlow) 6/10/1873 aged 67, leaving under £200 [C145398] Married Bishopsteignton, Devon. 1/6/1830 Joanna Maria Commyns, w. issue. Brothers James, and J.W.R., below.

**LANDON (James)** Bapt. Tedstone Delamere, Hereford 2/11/1764, s. Rev. John Landon and Elizabeth Higgins. Worcester, Oxford 1783, BA 1787, then Oriel, Fellow, MA1789, BD1789, dn90 (Ox.), p91 (Ox.). V. St Mary the Virgin, Oxford 1797-1800, V. Aymestrey, Heref. 1797 and V. Aberford, Yorks. 1805 to death (Tedstone Delamere) 2/3/1850 [C34928 is wrong] Married (1) Margaret Mary Dent, 1s. (2) Aberford 7/6/1808 Ann Bainbridge, with further issue. Brother Whittington, below.

**LANDON (James)** Bapt. Oxford 24/10/1803, s. of Very Rev. Whittington Landon, Dean of Exeter (below) and Maria Augustina Ready. Worcester, Oxford 1822, dn27 (Nor.), p27 (Nor.). V. Tawton Bishop >< Devon 1827, PC. Saxton, Yorks. 1829-32 (res.). Died Malden, Surrey 13/12/1878 aged 76. Will not traced [C113797] Married Astley, Worcs. Frances Harbour (ahed 19) 12/9/1853, w. issue. Brothers George (above), and J.W.R. Landon (below).

**LANDON (John Whittington Ready)** Born Oxford 28/6/1801, s. of Very Rev. Whittington Landon, Dean of Exeter (below) and Maria Augustina Ready. Worcester, Oxford 1818, BA 1822, MA1824, Fellow of Exeter 1826, Chap. 1826-7. V. Braunton, Devon 1826-80, V. Bishopstone, North Wilts. 1825-60, R. Lillingstone Lovell, Oxon. 1825-6, PC. Slebech, Pembroke 1851-77. Died Braunton 14/2/1880 aged 78, leaving under £100 (left unadmin--istered) [C34929. CR65 as Henry Whittington Landon] Married (1) Bishops Tawton, Devon 22/5/1828 Jane Chichester (d.1848), with issue (2) Paddington, London 9/8/1855 Sarah Anne Parker, with further issue (w). Brothers, above.

**LANDON (Thomas Jones)** Born Tedstone Delamere, Heref., s. Thomas Sylvanus Landon and Ann Jones (*or* Lane). Worcester, Oxford 1805 (aged 19), BA1809, dn09 (Ox.), Chap. of Worcester, p10 (Win.), MA1814. V. St Bruard, Cornwall 1815 [blank in ERC] to death 1/11/1850 ('in consequence from injuries after falling from his horse') aged 62 [C34931] Had a child, therefore presumably married? Admonished for 'public drunkenness and profane swearing in Bodmin in b1847). Surely related to the other Landons here?

**LANDON (Whittington)** Bapt. Tedstone Delamere, Heref. 12/9/1758, s. Rev. John Landon and Elizabeth Higgins. Worcester, Oxford 1775, BA1779, Fellow 1782, MA1782, p82 (Ox.), BD1790, DD1795. Provost of Worcester College, Oxford 1796 to death. Keeper of the University Archives 1796-1815. Vice-Chancellor of Oxford 1802-6. R. Denchworth, Berks. 1790-6 (res.), R. Uttoxeter, Staffs. 1791-1816, PC. Elton, Heref. 1796, R. Croft w. Yarpole, Heref. 1797 to death, Canon of 1st Prebend in Norwich Cathedral 1811-13 (res.), Dean of Exeter 1813-38 (w. Canon Residentiary and Prebend of Exeter Cathedral 1813-38), R. Bishopstone, Wilts. 1817-25, Prebend of Bishopstone in Salisbury Cathedral 1821 to death (Barthomley, Cheshire) 29/12/1838 [C1063] Married Barthomley 19/6/1800 Maria Augustina Ready, with sons George, James, and John Whittington Ready Landon (above). Brother James (b.1764), above; and other Landons here?.

**LANDOR (Charles Savage)** Born Warwick 7/5/1777 ['about 1130 in the morning, Dr Holyoak, Mrs Cockbill, Mary Perry and Anne Crutchley were present'], s. of Walter Landor (physician) and Elizabeth Savage. Worcester, Oxford 1795, BA 1798, dn00 (C&L), MA1801, p01 (C&L). V. Leighton Bromswold, Hunts. 1802 [C1802], R. Colton, Staffs. 1829-49, PC. Penkridge, Staffs. 1833. Died 7/7/1849 [C14847] Married 9/12/1812 Catherine Willson, with issue. Brother of Walter Savage Landor, writer and poet, and of the man below.

**LANDOR (Robert Eyres)** Born Warwick 10/5/1781, s. Walter Landor (physician) and Elizabeth Savage. Worcester, Oxford 1797, BA1801, MA1804, dn04 (Ox,), p06 (Ox.). R. Hughenden, Bucks. 1817-25 (res.), V. (and patron) of Birlingham, Worcs. 1829 to death. Chap. to Prince Regent. Died (unm.) 26/1/1869 aged 87, leaving £20,000 [C34930. ODNB. Boase] Brother of Walter Savage Landor, writer and poet, and of the man above.

**LANE (Charles)** Born London 2/2/21793, s. Thomas Lane and Barbara Fowler. Queen's, Oxford 1813, BA1815, dn16 (Ely), p17 (London), MA1817. PC. Torquay St John's, Devon 1831, V. Wasperton, Warwicks. 1834, PC. Bognor, Sussex 1834-8, R. Deal, Kent 1838-45, R. Wrotham, Kent 1845-79, Hon. Canon Canterbury Cathedral 1869 to death 23/3/1879, leaving £8,000 [C109774] Married Edinburgh 1/7/1816 Frances Catherine Sandford (dau. of the Episcopal Bishop of Edinburgh), with issue.

**LANE (Charlton)** Bapt. Croydon Surrey 7/5/1797, s. William Lane and Susanna Pollock. Trinity, Cambridge 1815, then Jesus 1817, BA 1820, dn20 (London), p21 (London), MA 1823, incorporated at Oxford 1842. Chap. Kennington St Mark, London 1832-64, RD of Southwark 1854-64, V. Hampstead, London 1864-72. Chap. in Brussels 1863-72 and Professor of Rhetoric, Gresham College, London 1863-72. Died St John's Wood, London 28/5/1875, leaving £10,000 [C80786. Boase] Married Wellingborough, Northants. 22/2/1832 Jane Hill, with issue.

**LANE (Joseph)** Bapt. Hingham, Norfolk 20/6/1759, s. Rev. Matthew Lane (R. Scoulton, Norfolk). Clare, Cambridge 1776, BA1780, dn81 (Nor.), MA1789, p89 (Nor.). V. Carbrooke, Norfolk 1788-97, V. Belstead, Norfolk 1789, R. Scoulton 1797 to death. Buried Norwich 19/11/1846 aged 88 [C113798] Married (2 - 'a widower') Old Buckenham, Norfolk 10/10/1839 Mary Leedon.

**LANE (Newton Charles)** Born London 16/2/1763, s. John Lane (of King's Bromley, Staffs.) and Sarah Fowler. Christ's, Cambridge 1780, BA1784, dn85 (Ely), Fellow 1785-1811, p87 (Peterb.), MA1787. V. Alveston, Warwicks. 1789-1846, R. Ingoldsby, Lincs. 1810 to death 6/3/1846, *s.p.* [C69255] Married St Marylebone, London 16/8/1814 Mary Clarke. 'His acquaintance was chiefly with men of dissipated habits and sporting propensities'.

**LANE (Richard)** Born Coflette House, Brixton, Devon 18/2/1771, s. Thomas Lane and Penelope Tothill. Trinity, Cambridge 1791, BA 1795, dn96 (Chich. for Ex.), p96 (Ex.), MA 1800. PC. Brixton 1802 to death 17/3/1858 [C145400] Married Tiverton, Devon 18/2/1800 Lucy Dennys.

**LANE (Samuel)** Born Totnes, Devon 1/12/1802, s. Rev. Samuel Lane, sen. and Bridget Birdwood. Exeter, Oxford 1821, dn25, BA1825, p26, MA1828. R. Holme, Devon 1827-8, V. Frome Vauchurch w. Batcombe, Dorset 1828 (RD 1836) to death (a widower) 10/12/1868, *s.p.*, leaving £10,000 [C53242]

**LANE (Theophilus)** Born Walcot, Bath 2/6/1797, s. Theophilus Lane and Sophia Gardiner. Queens', Cambridge 1815, then Magdalene 1818, BA1820, dn21 (London), p21 (London), MA1823. V. Horndon on the Hill, Essex 1827 to death 9/7/1844 aged 47 (in Brompton/Kensington 'Licensed Madhouse') [C120170]

**LANE (Thomas Leveson)** Born King's Bromley, Staffs. 28/9/1802, s. John Lane and Mrs Sarah (Lloyd) Amler. St John's, Cambridge 1818, BA1823, dn27 (Heref.), MA1828, p28 (C&L), incorporated at Oxford 1853. V. King's Bromley 1827-8 (res.), R. Withington, Glos. 1828-34 (res.), V. Wasperton, Warwicks. 1835-83, V. Berkswich (o/w Baswick) w. Walton, Staffs. 1836 (and RD) to death (unmarried) 8/10/1883, leaving £1,403-9s.-9d. [C13590. Hodson]

**LANGDALE (Edward)** From East Hoathly, Sussex, s. Rev. Edward Rudston Langdale (below) and Elizabeth Delves. Jesus, Cambridge 1820 (aged 17), BA1824, dn25 (Chich.), p26 (Chich.). R. East Hoathly 1828 to death 29/1/1882 aged 79, leaving £7,727-8s-0d. [C64189] Married Wortling, Sussex 2/6/1835 Emily Mary Fuller, with issue.

**LANGDALE (Edward Rudstone)** Born London 21/6/1754, s. William Langdale (merchant) and Lucy Rudstone. Pembroke, Cambridge 1772, BA1777, dn77 (Chester for Cant.), p81 (Glos. for Cant.), MA1780. R. Chignal Smealy, Essex 1790 to death 16/2/1838 [C64188] Married Frant, Sussex 22/6/1790 Elizabeth Delves, with clerical son above.

**LANGDON (Charles)** Bapt. Sherborne, Dorset 30/5/1792. Queens', Cambridge 1824, dn27 (C&L), BA1829, p29 (C&L). V. Queen Camel, Som. 1832 to death 13/12/1882 aged 93, leaving £1,886-18s-6d. [C14857] Married (2) Ryme Intrinsica, Dorset 20/7/1830 Margaretta Fitzherbert.

**LANGDON (Gilbert Henry)** Born Puddletown, Dorset 23/1/1780, s. Rev. Gilbert Langdon and Elizabeth Plowman. Exeter, Oxford 1797, dn02 (Bristol), LLB1802, p08 (B&W). PC. Weston Patrick Chapel and PC. Rotherwick Chapel, Odiham, Hants. 1813, R. Athelhampton w. Burleston >< Dorset 1818 to death 28/10/1840 [C46335] Married Chideock, Dorset 22/9/1803 Anna Fitzherbert, w. clerical s., also Gilbert Henry, and George Leopold.

**LANGLEY (John)** Bapt. Warminster, Wilts., 10/10/1800, s. William Langley and Ann Cockrell. Magdalen Hall, Oxford 1818, BA 1823, dn23 (Salis.), MA1826, p27 (Salis.). R. Wallingford St Mary le More w. All Hallows, Berks. [separate in ERC] 1829, R. Wallingford St Leonard, Berks. 1829-72, PC. Southampton St Peter 1846 ('income from pew rents'). Died 30/7/1875, leaving £7,000 [C95311] Wife Mary Emma, and issue. Another cleric of this name, with potential confusion. Surrogate.

**LANGLEY (Samuel)** Bapt. Checkley, Staffs. 20/6/1755, s. Rev. Samuel Langley, sen. and Dorothy Clasy. Worcester, Oxford 1773, BA 1777, MA1780. R. Checkley 1791 to death 10/2/1839 [C15006] Married (1) Alton, Staffs. 7/7/1785 Sarah Mellor (d.1789), with issue (2) Checkley 7/8/1798 Mary French, with distinctively named children: Kezia - Tychicus - Eusebius - Epaphras - Boniface - Parmenas. Someone noted 'the impracticable temper of the rector'.

**LANGLEY (William Hawkes)** From Newport, Shropshire, s. Rev. John Langley. Christ Church, Oxford 1814 (aged 18), BA1819, dn19 (Salis.), p20 (Ox.), MA1821. PC. Wheatley, Oxon 1823. In 1861 'assistant chap.' Isleworth Poor Law Union'. Died Marylebone, London (unm.) 16/2/1870 (but not noted as a cleric), leaving £450 [C24279] Tried in 1843 for 'quarrelling, chiding, and *brawling by words* in the parish church'; and was in constant 'pecuniary difficulties'.

**LANGSTON (Stephen Hurt)** Born Little Horwood, Bucks. 20/10/1792, s. Rev. Stephen Langston (R. Hulcot, Bucks.) and Rebecca Gines. Wadham, Oxford 1810, 1812-19, BA 1814, dn15 (Glos.), p16 (Nor.), Fellow 1819-25, MA1820. R. Little Horwood 1817, PC. Sheffield St George 1825-42, R. Aston Sandford, Bucks. 1828 ('exhausted and voiceless'), V. Jersey St James 1842-47, PC. Southborough, Kent 1847-72. Died Tunbridge Wells, Kent 15/3/1878 aged 85, leaving £14,000 [C69306. Bertie says Hurst. DEB] Married (1) Camberwell, Surrey 11/8/1825 Maria Cattley (d.1835), 3 dau. (2) St Pancras, London 28/7/1836 Maria Rotch, with further issue.

**LANGTON (Charles)** Born Lincoln 14/11/1800, s. George Langton and Elizabeth Mainwaring. [One year in the Royal Navy?] Trinity, Oxford 1820, MA1827 [Student of Lincoln's Inn 1823] BA1824, dn24 (Lin.), p25 (Lin.). R. Onibury, Heref. 1832-41, then without cure. Lived at Maer Hall, Shropshire 1841-7, then Hatfield Grove, Tunbridge Wells, Kent 1847-63, then Bournemouth. Died at the Hotel Russie, Frankfurt 26/8/1886 aged 86, leaving £103,941-6s-1d. [C69308] Married (1) Maer

22/3/1832 Charlotte Wedgwood (d.1862), with issue (2) Regent's Park, London 12/10/1863 Emily Catherine Darwin (sister of Charles Darwin, she d.1866) (3) Wellington, Som. 21/2/1884 Augusta Ann H. Dawkins: www.lostlangtons.co.uk/humogen/family/humo_/F90/I126/

**LANGTON (George Thomas)** From Buckingham, s. Rev. William Langton and Elizabeth Mary Ford. St Edmund Hall, Oxford 1797 (aged 21), no degree, p07 (Win.). V. Kempston, Norfolk 1809 and R. Barton St Andrew, Norfolk 1837 to death 18/11/1841 [C80788] Married York 8/12/1801 Martha White.

**LANGTON (Wenman Henry)** Born Dublin, s. Rev. William Langton and Elizabeth Mary Ford. Wadham, Oxford 1783 (aged 19), dn86 (C&L), p87 (York), BA1787, MA1793, BD 1800, DD1810. V. Arnold, Notts. 1797-9, R. Warham St Mary w. Waterden, Norfolk 1789 (and Sinecure R. Longford, Derbys. 1807) to death. Chap. in Ordinary to Prince of Wales 1800. Died 4/11/1836 [C15012. YCO. Austin] Married Leicester 27/10/1791 Elizabeth Henshaw Arnold, with clerical sons Wenman Cavendish, Arthur John, and Augustus Wenman Langton.

**LAPRIMAUDAYE (Charles John)** Born Calcutta 9/11/1806, s. Stephen Laprimaudaye and Elizabeth Catharine Letch. Left India 1817. St John's, Oxford 1825, BA1829, dn29 (London), p30 (London), incorporated at Cambridge, MA1833. V. Leyton, Essex 18-- (ERC is wrong here) to 1848. Resigned Orders and became (w. his wife) Roman Catholic. Died of smallpox 20/1/1858 aged 58 (at the Collegio Pio, Rome, leaving £12,000 [C120174] Married Leyton 17/4/1834 Ann Frances Hubbard (d. Rome 1854), with issue. He was (Cardinal) Edward Manning's curate at Lavington, Sussex.

**LARDEN (George Edge)** Born Chester, s. Rev. George Harrison Larden and Catherine Edge. BNC, Oxford 1816 (aged 17), BA1820, dn21 (Chester), MA1822, p22 (Chester). R. Doverdale, Worcs. 1831, V. Brotherton, Yorks. 1843 and V. High Ercal, Shropshire -- to death 18/10/1859, leaving £800 [C121651] Married (1) Christchurch, Hants. 12/8/1824 Eliza Ellen Marsden (of Liverpool, d.1837), with issue (2) Pitchford, Shropshire 10/11/1840 Mrs Emily Elizabeth (Corfield) Jervis (a military widow, d.1844), with further issue (3) Rugby, Shropshire 15/10/1847 Mary Lydia Fanny Bucknill (w), with yet more issue.

**LARKING (Lambert Blackwell)** Bapt. East Malling, Kent 5/2/1797, s. John Larking (High Sheriff of Kent, Clare House, East Malling) and Dorothy Style (dau. of a baronet). BNC, Oxford 1816, BA1820, dn20 (London), p21 (London), MA 1823. V. Ryarsh, Kent 1830 and V. Burham, Kent 1837 to death. Dom. Chap. to Viscountess Falmouth. Died 2/8/1868 aged 71, leaving £6,000 [C6723. ODNB. Boase] Married West Malling, Kent 27/7/1831 Frances Twysden (dau. of a knight). Local historian and founder of the Kent Archaeological Society. Freemason.

**LASCELLES (Robert)** Bapt. Brafferton, Yorks, Yorks. 25/2/1779, s. Rev. Lascelles Sturdy Lascelles and Jane Butterwick. Merton, Oxford 1796, then Christ's, Cambridge 1802, dn16 (Nor.), p16 (Nor.), BA1822, MA1825, re-adm. Cambridge 1830. PC. Sand Hutton, Yorks. 1830-32, PC. Thirsk w. Carlton Miniott, Yorks. 1830, V. Chrishall, Essex 1832 to death (Cambridge) 1/8/1839 aged 60 [C109296] Married Cambridge 19/1/1812 Hannah Isabel Barker, *s.p.*

**LATEWARD (Frederick James)** Born London 10/1791, s. John Lateward. St John's, Cambridge 1805, BA1809, dn11 (Chich.), MA 1812, p12 (London). R. Perivale (o/w Little Greenford), Middx. 1812-61, Min. Brompton Proprietary Chapel, London 1833. British Chap. at Berne 1853-60 . Died (Hastings) 1/6/1861 aged 71, leaving £600 [C120178] Married Tunbridge Wells, Kent 14/7/1813 Mary Kirby, with clerical son Marsack Henry Richard Lateward.

**LATEY (John)** Bapt. South Molton, Devon 13/6/1780, s. Richard Latey and Elizabeth Simkins. St Edmund Hall, Oxford 1802, BA 1806, dn06 (Ex. for Bristol), p07 (Bristol), MA 1809. Minor Canon of Bristol Cathedral, R. Rumney, Monmouth 1815, R. West Deeping, Lincs. 1818-21 (res.), R. Rede, Suffolk 1821 and R. Doynton, Glos. 1822 to death 21/10/1846 [C4221] Married Bristol 16/12/1815 Susannah Davis.

**LATHAM (Thomas)** Bapt. Waltham on the Wolds, Leics. 13/1/1771, s. Charles and Sarah Latham. BNC, Oxford 1788, BA1793, dn93 (Lin.), MA1794, p95 (Lin.). V. Billingborough,

Lincs. 1803 and V. Sempringham w. Pointon and Birdthorpe, Lincs. 1826 to death 11/5/1846 aged 76 [C69316. Bennett1] Married Catherine Smithers before 1813, w. issue.

**LATIMER (Edward William Forty)** Born Oxford 25/11/1803, s. Edward Latimer and Elizabeth Jones. Lincoln, Oxford 1822, BA 1827, dn27 (Ox.), p28 (Ox.), MA1828. R. Waddesdon, Bucks. (1st Portion 1829 and 2nd Portion 1830), and Chap. of Donative of Sandford on Thames, Oxon. 1831 to death. Dom. Chap. to 5rd Duke of Marlborough 1830. Died (Shepherds Bush, London) 14/3/1881 (widower) aged 78, leaving £1,500 [C34943]

**LATOUR** see under **LA TOUR**

**LAUGHARNE (Hugh)** From Ashton, Lancs., s. David Laugharne [*pleb*]. Christ Church, Oxford 1775 (aged 16), no degree, dn80 (Wor.). V. Radford Semele, Warwicks. 1789 and V. Rowington, Warwicks. 1812 to death, Chap. of the Donative of Baddesley Clinton, Warwicks. 1830 [C121652] Chap. Warwick Gaol. Died 2/7/1843 [C121652. Not linked in ERC] Note the man below.

**LAURENCE, LAWRENCE (Robert -** *not* **Thomas - French)** Born Eltham, Kent 2/4/1807, s. John Laurence and Hannah Ardlie. Christ Church, Oxford 1824, Student [Fellow] 1824-33, BA1828, dn28 (Ox.), p29 (Ox.), MA 1831. PC. Great and Little Hampton, Worcs. 1832 (only), V. Chalgrave, Oxon. 1832-85, V. Reading St Lawrence, Berks. 1834. Died 23/4/1885, leaving £47-7s-0d. [C34954 corrected. Boase] Married (1) Chalgrave 15/1/1835 Elizabeth Coates (d.1868), with issue (2) Aylesbury, Bucks. 1872 (1st q.) Annie Jolly (w).

**LAURENCE** see also **LAWRENCE**

**LAW (Edmund)** Bapt. Haweswater, Westmorland 20/8/1748, s. Joseph Law and Mary Kinson. Peterhouse, Cambridge 1771, BA1775, p75 (Ely). V. Comberton, Cambs. 1775-78, R. Great Musgrave, Westmorland 1777-1804, V. Whittingham, Northumberland 1804 to death 2/6/1835 (CCEd says 23/6/1835) aged 87 [C3426] Married 5/8/1780 Elizabeth Harrison, 15 ch. (12 survived, inc. clerical son). *J.P.* Cumberland.

**LAW (Francis)** Born Tenby, Pembrokeshire 4/6/1800, s. Rev. Francis Law, sen. (of Dublin) and Belinda Isabella Comerford. Queens', Cambridge 1823, BA1827, dn27 (Killaloe), p28 (Cloyne). PC. Samlesbury, Blackburn, Lancs. 1832 to death 20/9/1881 (a widower) aged 81, leaving £590-4s-2d. [But note also Henry Walter McGrath, PC. Samlesbury 1830-32, not noted in ERC nor this work] [C169756] Married (1) Dublin 6/5/1828 Marianne Cuppage, 1s. (2) Nice, France 15/11/1865 Mrs Sophie Elizabeth (Perkins *or* Parker) Wahl, w. step-children. Brother Patrick Comerford, below.

**LAW (George Henry, Bishop of Carlisle,** *then of* **Bath and Wells)** Born 12/9/1781, s. Edmund Law (Bishop of Carlisle) and Mary Christian. Queen's Cambridge 1776, BA1781, Fellow 1781-1804, MA1784, dn85 (Car.), p85 (Car.), DD 1804, admitted Oxford 1834. 1st Canon Carlisle Cathedral 1785-1824, V. Torpenhow, Cumberland 1787-91, Prebend of Bilton in York Minister 1787-1812, R. Kelshall, Herts. 1791-1804, V. Great Carleton, Lincs. 1797-1812, R. Willingham, Cambs. 1804-24, Bishop of Chester 1812-24 (when he established the College of St Bees for the training of non-graduate clergy), Bishop of Bath and Wells 1824 to death (Wells) 22/9/1834 (after 'a gradual decay of mind and body', which 'for many years' prevented him from performing the duties of his office') [C3427. ODNB] Married 1784 Jane Adeane (dau. of an M.P. and general), w. clerical sons Henry, James Thomas, and Robert Vanbrugh, all here. *F.R.S.* (1814), *F.S.A.*

**LAW (Henry)** Born Westmill, Herts. 1781, s. Rev. John Law. St John's, Cambridge 1799, dn04 (Roch.), p05 (Roch.), LLB1806. V. Standon, Herts. 1805-56, R. Stretham, Cambs. 1812-18, R. Downham, Cambs. [net income £1,108] 1818 to death (Bath) 28/12/1862, leaving £12,000 [C1962] Married Alderley, Cheshire 3/10/1808 Elizabeth Hibbert, with issue. *J.P.* for Herts. and Isle of Ely.

**LAW (Henry)** Born Kelshall, Herts, 28/9/1797, s. of Rt. Rev. George Henry Law (above) and Jane Adeane. St John's, Cambridge 1816, BA1820, dn21 (Chester), p21 (Chester), Fellow 1821-6, MA1823. V. St Anne, Manchester 1822-23, V. Childwall, Liverpool 1821-4, Archdeacon of Richmond (Yorks.) 1824-6 (res.), R. West Camel, Som. 1824-35, Archdeacon of Wells 1826 (w. Prebendal Stall of Huish and Brent annexed) to 1862, Vicar General 1827,

Canon Residentiary 1828-62, R. Yeovilton, Som. 1830-4, R. Weston super Mare, Som. 1834-8 and 1840-62, R. Bath 1838-9, V. East Brent, Som. 1839, Dean of Gloucester 1862 [income in CR65 £1,224] to death (unmarried) 25/11/1884, leaving £15,583-14s-2d. Dom. Chap. to his father 1830 [C41524. ODNB. Boase. DEB] Two brothers below.

**LAW (James Thomas)** Born Carlisle 8/12/1790, s. Rt. Rev. George Henry Law (above) and Jane Adeane. Christ's, Cambridge 1807, BA1812, dn14 (Chester), Fellow 1814-17, p14 (Chester), MA1815. R. Tattenhall, Cheshire 1816, V. Childwall, Liverpool 1818-21, V. Bowden, Cheshire 1815-21, Canon of Chester Cathedral 1818-28 (res.), Prebend of Bobenhull in Lichfield Cathedral 1818-37 (res.), Chancellor 1821-73, V. Harborne, Staffs. 1825-45, Master of St John's Hospital [almshouses], Lichfield 1821. Dom. Chap. to Bishop of Chester, then of Bath and Wells 1814. Died Lichfield (a widower) 22/2/1876, leaving under £450 [C13759. ODNB. Boase] Married Bowden, Cheshire 16/12/1820 Lady Henrietta Charlotte Grey (dau. of the 6th Earl of Stamford and Warrington), w. clerical s. Frederick Henry Law. Brothers Henry (above), and Robert Vanburgh (below). Hon. Warden of Queen's College, Birmingham 1846.

**LAW (John)** Bapt. Bishops Tawton, Devon 16/6/1799, s. John and Sarah Law. Exeter, Oxford 1817, BA1821, dn22 (Ex.), p23 (Ex.), MA1824. V. Bradworthy, Devon 1823 to death 12/1/1845 [C145506]

**LAW (Patrick Comerford)** Born Tenby, Pembroke 21/8/1797, s. Rev. Francis Law and Belinda Isabella Comerford. TCD, BA1818, dn28 (Killaloe), p28 (Killaloe). R. Samlesbury, Lancs. 1829-30, PC. Hawkshead, Lancs. 1830, R. Northrepps, Norfolk 1830-64- and RD of Repps 1842. Dom. Chap. to Marquess of Cholmondeley. Died Northrepps 15/4/1869. No will traced in England [C113811. Not in Al.Dub.] Married Balbriggan, Co. Dublin 17/10/1828 Frances Arbuthnot (an Irish clerical dau.), w. issue. Brother Francis, above.

**LAW (Robert Vanburgh)** Bapt. Nov. 1799, s. Rt. Rev. George Henry Law (above) and Jane Adeane. Peterhouse, Cambridge 1817, BA1822, dn23 (Chester), p24 (Chester), MA1825. V. Weaverham, Cheshire 1823-35, R. Wallasey, Cheshire 1825-34, Prebend of Easton in Gordano in Wells Cathedral 1825-34, Treasurer 1829-84, (nominated but resigned before installation as Prebend of Dulcote 1834), Canon of Chester Cathedral 1828-34 (res.), R. Yeovilton, Som. 1834-5, R. West Camel, Som. 1835, R. Christian Malford, Wilts. 1835-77 (and RD). Dom. Chap. to 1st Earl of Ellenborough 1835. Died Bath 4/2/1884 aged 84, leaving £2,798-16s-0d. [C41525] Married Chester 3/11/1829 Sidney Dorothea Davison (a military dau.), with clerical son. Brothers Henry, and James Thomas (above). 'A first-rate rider to hounds'.

**LAWRENCE (Alfred Charnley)** Born Camberwell, Surrey 9/2/1791, s. Richard Lawrence and Henrietta Henshaw. Christ's, Cambridge 1808, BA1813, dn14 (Salis. for Chich.), p15 (London), MA1818. R. Sandhurst, Kent 1831-54. Died Clifton, Bristol 17/3/1874, leaving £16,000 [C64228] Married Marylebone, London 7/2/1826 Emily Mary Finch-Hatton, with issue.

**LAWRENCE (Benjamin)** From Builth Wells, Brecon, s. John Lawrence. Jesus, Oxford 1777 (aged 16), BA1782, p85 (Lin.). R. Carsington, Derbys. 1798-1808, R. Darley, Derbys. 1808 to death 18/2/1838 [C15279]

**LAWRENCE (Charles Washington)** Born Liverpool 5/9/1804, s. Charles Lawrence and Rosetta Dagueler. Literate: dn19 (Chester), then BNC, Oxford 1823, BA1827, MA1830. (first and joint) PC. Liverpool St Luke 1831 to death 20/11/1861, leaving £35,000 [C169758] Married Cookham, Berks. 22/7/1839 Lucia Young, with issue.

**LAWRENCE (John Alexander)** Bapt. Manchester 3/11/1790, s. John Lawrence and Mary Irwin. Clare, Cambridge 1810, BA1814, dn14 (Lin.), p15 (Lin.). V. Keddington, Lincs. 1816-46 and V. Marnham, Notts. 1824 to death 9/6/1844 [C69333. Kaye] Married (1) Grantham, Lincs. 19/8/1816 Theodosia Manners (d.1835, 'leaving 12 small children') (2) East Retford, Notts. 1838 (4th q.) Hannah Dudley, with further issue.

**LAWRENCE** see also **LAURENCE**

**LAWSON (George)** Bapt. Renwick, Cumberland 8/4/1764, s. William Lawson and Tamar Sander. Trinity, Cambridge 1785, BA1789, dn89 (Bristol for Lin.), p89 (Bristol for Lin.), Fellow 1791, MA1792. V. Heversham, Westmorland

(and 'Preacher within Chester Diocese') 1797 (the living being sequestrated in 1812 for debt, and still an insolvent debtor in 1817) to death 17/6/1842 aged 77 [C53249] Married Edinburgh 19/10/1798 Henrietta Ronaldson (Blair Hall, Perthshire), with clerical son (below).

**LAWSON (Gerrard George)** Born Heversham, Westmorland 12/1/1803, s. Rev. George Lawson (above) and Henrietta Ronaldson. Literate: dn27 (Chester). V. Kirkoswald, Cumberland 1828 to death 4/12/1854 aged 51 [C6131. Platt] Married Kirkoswald 11/5/1837 Frances Carruthers (dau. of a surgeon), w. issue.

**LAWSON (John)** Bapt. Aldborough, Suffolk 14/1/1808, s. Rev. Marmaduke Lawson (Boroughbridge Hall, Yorks.) and Barbara Isabella Wilkinson. St Alban Hall, Oxford 1825, BA1829, dn31 (Durham for York), p32 (York), MA1833. PC. (and patron) of Seaton Carew, Durham 1831 to death 10/8/1890 aged 83, leaving £461-6s-11d. [C132357. YCO] Married Copgrove, Yorks. 23/10/1834 Mary Crowe, with issue.

**LAWSON (William)** Bapt. Leeds 14/3/1751, s. Richard Lawson. Trinity, Cambridge 1769, BA1774, dn74 (Peterb.), p76 (Peterb.), Fellow 1776, MA1777. V. Kirkby Malzeard (w. Commissary of the Peculiar of Masham), Yorks. 1791 to death (Southwell, Notts.) 15/3/1833 [C108197]

**LAWSON (William Morell)** Bapt. Brafferton, Yorks. 20/3/1803, s. George Lawson. St John's, Cambridge 1821, BA1826, dn27 (C&L), p28 (C&L), MA1833. PC. Moseley, Worcs. 1831-57. Died Brafferton 24/12/1862, leaving £6,000 [C13760]

**LAWTON (Joseph Thomas)** Bapt. Walthamstow, Essex 6/7/1774, s. Thomas Lawton and Cecilia Cannadine. Trinity, Cambridge 1793 (aged 18), BA1798, dn98 (Nor.), p01 (Nor.), MA1805. R. Elmswell, Suffolk 1809-63, PC. Walsham le Willows, Suffolk 1813-52. Died 19/3/1863 aged 88, leaving £7,000 [C113819] Married Walthamstow 22/12/1798 Catherine Warner, with issue.

**LAX (William)** Born Ravensworth, Yorks. c.1761, s. William and Hannah Lax. Trinity, Cambridge 1780, BA1785 (Senior Wrangler), Fellow 1786, p87 (Peterb.), MA1788, Lowndean Professor of Astronomy and Geometry, Cambridge 1795-1836. V. Orwell, Cambs. 1827 to death [not in ERC; but also Sinecure R. here], V. Marsworth, Bucks. 1801 and V. St Ippolyts w. Great Wymondley >< Herts. 1801 (where he built a small observatory) to death. Dom. Chap. to 2nd Earl of Courtown 1801. Died 29/10/1836 [C15282. ODNB] Married Gilling West, Yorks. 1801 Margaret Hannah Craddock, with issue. F.R.S. (1796). Port. online.
https://en.wikipedia.org/wiki/William_Lax

**LAYARD (Brownlow Villiers)** Born 19/1/1779, s. Very Rev. Charles Peter Layard (Dean of Bristol) and Elizabeth Ann Carver Ward. [Lieut. Royal Fusiliers 1795 and ADC to HRH Duke of Kent] Literate: dn03 (St Asaph), p03 (St Asaph), then St John's, Cambridge 1803, a Ten Year Man (MA1810 Lambeth). R. Uffington, Lincs. 1803 and V. Tallington, Lincs. 1820 to death (Wembley, London) 26/3/1861 aged 82, leaving £18,000. Latterly in Boulogne (debt?) [C69343. Boase. CR65 says Benjamin] Married (1) Derby 6/10/1803 Louisa Port (of Ilam, Staffs. d.1817), with issue (2) Kensington, London 1/2/1821 Sarah Jane Margary (of Clapham, Surrey), with further issue (w); clerical sons John Thomas, and Charles Clement Layard.

**LAYNG (William Wright)** Born Marholm, Northants. 1/12/1779, s. Rev. Thomas Layng and Frances Wright. Queens', Cambridge 1796, BA1801, dn02 (Lin.), p03 (Lin.), MA1804. V. York St Lawrence 1804-8, V. Great Harrowden w. Little Harrowden, Northants. 1808 to death (Wellingborough, Northants.) 31/5/1843 [C69349] Married (1) York 31/7/1806 Frances Helena Bulmer (d.1808), with issue (2) Stibbington, Hunts. 26/2/1816 Elizabeth Beecroft Cook, with further issue; some clerical.

**LAYTON (James)** Born London 1/1/1780, s. Nicholas Layton and Hannah Roach. Corpus Christi, Cambridge 1798, BA1802, dn02 (Nor.), p06 (Nor.). R. Sandwich St Peter, Kent 1831-6 (and S/M Sandwich Free G/S 1835). Died Swinbrook, Oxon. 26/8/1859 aged 79 [C113820] Married Norwich 1/7/1817 Lydia Roach.

**LAYTON (Thomas)** From London, s. Henry Layton (a baker). Trinity, Cambridge 1783, BA 1788, dn88 (London), p89 (London), MA 1791. R. East Hatley, Cambs. 1798-9 (res.), V. Chigwell, Essex 1803 and R. Theydon Bois,

Essex 1803 to death 14/6/1833 (CCEd thus) [C100106] Had issue.

**LE BAS (Charles Webb)** Born Westminster, London 26/4/1779, s. Charles Le Bas (a linen draper of Huguenot extraction) and Anna Maria Webb. Trinity, Cambridge 1795, BA1800, Fellow 1802 [adm. Lincoln's Inn 1802: called to the Bar 1806, 'but deafness compelled him the abandon the law'] MA1803, dn09 (Bristol, CCEd thus), p09 (Bristol, CCEd thus). Professsor of Mathematics and Dean of the East India College, Haileybury, then Principal 1837-43 (res.)]. R. Shadwell, Middx. 1812-43, R. Darfield, Yorks. 1812-25, Prebend of Marston St Lawrence in Lincoln Cathedral 1812-61. Died Brighton 25/1/1861 [C53250. ODNB. Boase] Married Bromley, London 28/6/1814 Maria Hodgson (dau. of the owner of the Bow Brewery, the inventor of India Pale Ale). The Le Bas Prize, to perpetuate his memory at Cambridge, was founded in 1848, chiefly by his old Haileybury pupils.

**LE CORNU (John)** see under **CORNU**

**LE GEYT (Philip)** Bapt. Canterbury Cathedral 1/4/1776, s. Robert Le Geyt and Anne Marie Chandler. Magdalen, Oxford 1793, BA1797, dn99 (Chester), Fellow, MA1800, p00 (Cant.). V. St Nicholas at Wade, Isle of Thanet, Kent 1803-8, R. Ringwould. Kent 1808-11 (res.), PC. Wingham, Kent 1811-17, V. Marden, Kent 1817-47, R. Ightham, Kent 1818-27 (res.). Chap. to HRH Duke of Kent 1803-18; to HRH Duke of York and Albany 1821. Died 6/1/1847 [C34957. Foster under Geyt] Married Canterbury Cathedral 8/4/1801 Jane Cairnes, with issue.

**LE GRICE (Frederick)** Born Bury St Edmunds, Suffolk 22/3/1798, s. John Le Grice and Mary Holdsworthy. Clare, Cambridge 1815, BA1820, dn21 (Ex.), Fellow 1823, MA1823, p24 (London). V. Great Gransden, Hunts. 1832 to death 25/1/1884 aged 85, leaving £21,698-6s-9d. [C69354] Married Wisbech, Cambs. 7/3/1837 Eliza Gregory Peers Swaine, with issue. Silhouette online.

**LEA (Thomas)** Bapt. Henley in Arden, Warwicks. 31/12/1792, s. Thomas Lea. Trinity, Oxford 31/12/1792, BA1815, MA1820. V. Bishops Itchington, Warwicks. 1820 and R. Tadmarton, Oxon. 1824 (non-res.) to death. Dom. Chap. to 5th Earl Cornwallis 1824. Died 26/10/1866, leaving £3,000 [C15288] Married (1) Wootten Wawen, Warwicks. 23/5/1826 Mary Ward, 1 dau. (2) Harbury, Warwics. 12/12/1848 Henrietta Catherine Newsham (a clergy dau.). 'Middling in every way' (Wilberforce).

**LEACH (John)** Bapt. Cumwhitton, Cumberland 29/9/1793, s. William Leach and Deborah Dixon. St Bees adm. 1817, dn18 (Car.), p23 (Durham). PC. Tweedmouth, Durham 1827 to death (a widower) 5/10/1864 aged 71, leaving £800 [C35021 and 6134] Wife Dorothy (?Bell), and a step-daughter. Surrogate.

**LEACH (Richard Ebenezer)** Born Hurst, Bucks. 10/10/1798, s. James and Mary Leach. Literate: dn22 (Chester for York), p23 (York). PC. Holmfirth, Yorks. 1832 to death 3/1/1873 aged 73, leaving £4,000 [C132356 as Ibenezer. YCO] Married Sunderland, Co. Durham 3/7/1828 Mrs Sarah (Walton) Dowdall.

**LEACH (Walter Burton)** Born Sutton Montis, Som. 10/5/1801, s. Robert Leach and Sarah Goodsell Francis. Wadham, Oxford 1819, BA1823, p25 (Ely), MA1827. PC. Lovington, Som. 1825, R. Sutton Montis 1825, V. Chilthorne Dormer, Som. 1846 to death there 24/2/1860, leaving £5,000 [C41531] Married Chilthorne Dormer 5/6/1827 Jane Bowden (w), with issue.

**LEACH (William Crawley)** Bapt. Mold, Flintshire 25/7/1798, s. Rev. Robert Leach. Trinity, Cambridge 1817, BA1821, dn21 (Ely), p23 (Nor.), MA1825. Minor Canon (and Precentor) of Ely Cathedral 1827 (w. PC. Ely St Mary 1827-32 res.), V. Dilham w. Honing, Norfolk 1831-3, V. St Albans St Peter, Herts. 1833-42, R. Stonham Parva, Suffolk 1843 to death 31/7/1856, leaving £4,000 [C109289] Married London 4/10/1832 Matilda Harriet Alexander.

**LEAK(E) (John Custance)** Born Holt, Norfolk 2/1/1806, s. Rev. John Custance Leak, sen. and Catherine Knight Lombe (*or* Graver). Trinity Hall, Cambridge 1825, SCL1828, dn29 (Nor.), p30 (Nor.), LLB1833. R. Little Barningham, Norfolk 1831 to death (unm., Plumstead, Norfolk) 5/4/1876, leaving £1,500 [C113827]

**LEAPINGWELL (George)** From Chelmsford, Essex, s. William Leapingwell. Christ's, Cambridge 1788, dn93 (Salis.), LLB 1794, p94 (Salis.). V. High Easter and Good Easter, Essex

1816 to death 24/5/1849 aged 79 [C95320] Married Mary Anne Toke/Tuke (a clergy dau.) by 1803, w. issue. A 'very companionable but remarkably idle' man.

**LEAR (Francis)** Bapt. Downton, Wilts. 21/3/1789, s. Rev. Thomas Lear and Ethelinda Hewett. Oriel, Oxford 1806, then Magdalen 1809-19, BA1810, MA1813, Fellow 1819-22, dn20 (Salis.), p20 (Salis.), BD1821. R. Chilmark, Wilts. 1824-42, Prebend of Stratford in Salisbury Cathedral 1830-4 (then Prebend of Netheravon 1834), R. Bishopstone, Wilts. 1842-50, Archdeacon of Salisbury 1836-46, Dean of Salisbury 1846 to death 23/3/1850 [C83518] Married Marylebone, London 6/6/1822 Isabella Mary Majendie (dau. of a Bishop of Bangor), with clerical son Francis.

**LEATHES (Edward)** Bapt. Reedham, Norfolk 13/4/1777, s. Rev. Edward Leathes, sen. and Elizabeth Reading (a clergy dau.). Trinity, Cambridge 1794, BA1799, then Queens' 1800, dn01 (Nor.). R. Reedham w. Freethorpe, Norfolk 1801 to death (Milan) Buried Reedham 16/1/1844 aged 66 [C113832] Brother George Reading, below.

**LEATHES (Frederic)** Born Kirby, Norfolk, s. George Augustus Leathes (Bury St Edmunds, Suffolk) and Mary Moore. Emmanuel, Cambridge 1812, BA1816, dn17 (Nor.), p18 (Nor.). R. Great Livermere and Little Livermere, Norfolk 1820, R. Ringsfield w. Little Redisham, Norfolk 1829, R. Wickhampton, Norfolk 1836-70, R. Reedham, Norfolk 1844 to death 1/6/1870, leaving £12,000 [C113833] Married 1821 his cousin Elizabeth Tompson (a clergy dau.), w. issue. Doubtless related to the men above and below.

**LEATHES (George Reading)** Born Reedham, Norfolk 19/2/1779, s. Rev. Edward Leathes and Elizabeth Reading (a clergy dau.). Jesus, Cambridge 1797, BA1801, dn03 (Nor.), p03 (Nor.), MA1813. R. Wickhampton, Norfolk 1803-36, R. Limpenhoe w. Southwood >< Suffolk 1803-36, R. Flordon, Norfolk 1811-16 (res.), R. Gissing, Norfolk 1811-16 (res.). Died Shropham, Norfolk 1/1/1836, 'having been stricken on Christmas Day by a fit of apoplexy while at his reading desk' [C113830] Married 1/1/1821 Sarah Barker (later Hethersett, dau. of a general, Shropham Hall, Norfolk), *s.p.* Brother Edward, above.

**LEATHES (Isaac)** Bapt. Brigham, Cumberland 19/6/1764, s. Thomas Leathes and Ruth Fearon. Jesus, Cambridge 1783, BA1787, dn88 (Nor.), MA1790, Fellow 1792-6, p92 (B&W). R. Mepal w. Sutton, Cambs. [net income £1,267] 1802 to death (London) 27/1/1838 [C35027] Married Cambridge 14/1/1796 Mary Winifred Pulleine Haggerston, with issue.

**LECHMERE (Anthony Berwick)** Born Hanley Castle [*a parish*], Worcs. 28/5/1802, s. Sir Anthony Lechmere, 1st Bart. and Mary Berwick. Christ Church, Oxford 1820, BA1824, dn26, MA1826, p26. V. Eldersfield, Worcs. 1828, R. Welland, Worcs. 1826-76, V. (and patron of) Hanley Castle 1839-76, Hon. Canon of Worcester Cathedral 1849 to death. Dom. Chap. to 3rd Earl of Beauchamp 1828. Died 8/10/1878 aged 76, leaving £12,000 [C136975] Married Upton on Severn, Worcs. 11/10/1842 Emily Mary Darell (dau. of a baronet), *s.p.*

**LEDIARD (James)** Bapt. Bristol 10/6/1759, s. Thomas Lediard. Balliol, Oxford 1777, BA 1781, dn82 (B&W), p83 (B&W). V. Devizes St John the Baptist w. Lediard St Mary, Wilts. 1788 to burial 25/4/1833 (CCEd says death date 18/4/1833) [C46355] Accused of 'unnatural practices' 1796 (the accuser was hanged for blackmail).

**LEE (Charles)** Born Leeds 12/6/1789, s. Richard Lee (merchant) and Jane Fenton. Clare, Cambridge 1813, dn15 (Ex. for York), p15 (Bristol for York), BA1818, MA1821. PC. Lee St John's >< Hexham, Northumberland 1815-62 (w. PC. of the Peculiar of St Oswald in Lee 1824-5), PC. Bingfield St Mary, Northumberland 1825, V. Yaxley, Hunts. 1836 (and Hon. Canon of Durham) to death. Dom. Chap. to 1st Viscount Keith 1815. Died Lee St John's 12/4/1862 aged 72, leaving £8,000 [C53255. YCO] Married Swillington, Yorks. 7/9/1825 Mary Louisa Ikin (w), Leventhorpe House, Yorks., with issue.

**LEE (Frederick)** Born Thame, Oxon. 4/12/1798, s. Rev. Thomas Tripp Lee (below) and Elizabeth Smith. Chorister Magdalen, Oxford 1806-16; matr. Pembroke, Oxford 1816, then Merton 1817-21, BA1821, dn21 (Ox.), p22 (Ox.), Chap. Magdalen 1822-6, MA1823. R. Easington, Oxon. 1832-41, Minor Canon of Windsor Chapel 1833, R. Stantonbury, Bucks. 1838 and R. Stowe, Shropshire [1838?] to death 4/11/1841 aged 42 [C35028] Married

Aylesbury, Bucks. 10/2/1831 Mary Ellys, with clerical son of father's name. Ports. of both online.

**LEE (Harry, sen.)** Born Winchester, s. Rev. Harry Lee and Caroline Michel. New, Oxford 1782 (aged 16), Fellow 1782-9, BA1785, dn88 (Ox.), MA1789, p89 (Chester for Ox.). Fellow of Winchester College 1789. V. Sydling St Nicholas, Dorset 1797-1800 (res.), R. Bradford Peverell, Dorset 1800-10 (res.), V. Hound, Hants. 1812, R. Ash, Surrey 1813 [not in CCEd], PC. Hamble (le Rice), Hants. 1815, Prebendary of Putson Major in Hereford Cathedral 1821 and R. Vowchurch, Heref. 1831 to death. Chap. to Bishop of Gloucester 1805. Died Winchester 5/2/1838 [C35029] Married Winchester 8/5/1790 Philippa Blackstone, with son below. Brother Lancelot Charles, below. *J.P.*

**LEE (Harry, jun.)** Bapt. Winchester 10/9/1793, s. Rev. Harry Lee, sen. (above) and Philippa Blackstone. New, Oxford 1811, Fellow 1812-27, BA1815, MA1819, etc., BD 1827; Fellow of Winchester College 1828. V. North Bradley, Wilts. 1832 to death (a widower) 16/9/1880, leaving £25,000 [C159386] Married Orcheston, Wilts. 28/6/1831 Julia Lowther.

**LEE (Lancelot Charles)** Bapt. Winchester 15/5/1768, s. Rev. Harry Lee and Caroline Michel. New, Oxford 1785, Fellow 1785-1826, BA1788, MA1793 [but a prisoner of war at Verdun, France 1803-15]. R. Wootton, Oxon. 1825-36. Died unmarried 28/11/1841 [C35031]. Brother Harry Lee, sen. (above). John Parry-Wingfield, *Napoleon's Prisoner: a country parson's ten-year detention in France* (online?)

**LEE (Richard [Henry Beaumont])** Bapt. Leeds 6/5/1802, s. Thomas Lee. Lincoln, Oxford 1820, dn28 (Lin.), p29 (Lin.), BA1830, MA 1840. V. Aslackby, Lincs. 1829-38, R. Darley, Derbys. 1838-47, R. Stepney, London 1847 to death. Dom. Chap. to Earl of Mexborough. Died 6/8/1869. Will not traced [C69467. Bennett1] Married Southwark, Surrey 23/1/1832 Charlotte Longton, with issue.

**LEE (Samuel)** Born Longnor, Shropshire 14/5/1783, s. William Lee and Hannah Rupel. A carpenter and self-taught orientalist (18 languages by 1833). Queens', Cambridge 1814, BA1818, dn18 (Ely for London), p18 (Glos.), MA1819, DD1823, BD1827, then Trinity 1831. Professor of Arabic, Cambridge 1819-31. Regius Professsor of Hebrew, Cambridge 1831-48. R. Bilton cum Harrogate, Yorks. 1825-31, V. Banwell, Som. 1831-8, Canon of 4th Prebend in Bristol Cathedral 1831 and R. Barley, Herts. 1838 to death 16/12/1852 [C41532. ODNB. Boase. DEB. [Anna Mary Lee], *A scholar of a past generation: a brief memoir of Samuel Lee, DD …* (1886)] Married (1) Worcester 30/1/1810 Sabina Farrell (d.1822), with issue (2) Berkeley, Glos. 9/9/1840 Anne Jenkins (a clergy dau.), with further issue. One of the great linguists of the 19th century. Photo online.

**LEE (Timothy Tripp)** Born Thame, Oxon. 22/12/1769, s. Timothy Newmarch Lee and Elizabeth Simeon. Pembroke, Oxford 1817, Fellow 1787, BA1791, dn92 (Lin.), p94 (Lin.). V. Thame w. Towersey (and H/M Thame G/S 1814 to death 29/12/1840. Married Islington, London 2/2/1792 Elizabeth Smith, with son Frederick (above) [C69469] Splendid portrait sketch online!

**LEECH (John)** see under **LEACH**

**LEEKE (Ralph Harvey)** Born Longford Hall, Longford, Shropshire 5/10/1793, s. Col. Ralph Leeke, *H.E.I.C.*, and Honoria Frances Harvey Thursby. Christ Church, Oxford 1811, BA1816, dn18 (Glos. for C&L), MA1820, p20 (Peterb. for Cant.). R. Longford 1825 to death 4/4/1849 [C15293]

**LEEKE (Robert)** Literate: dn81 (Lin.), p85 (Lin.). V. Fulstow, Lincs. 1792 and PC. Marsh Chapel, Lincs. 1784 to death 27/1/1835 (CCEd thus) [C69474]

**LEGG, LEGGE (Joseph)** Born Market Lavington, Wilts. 1754, s. Richard Legg and Elizabeth Palmer. Queen's, Oxford 1775 (aged 21), no degree, dn77 (Salis.), p81 (Glos. for Salis.). R. Holton, Som. 1786 and PC. Maddington, Wilts, 1813 to death 8/2/1833 (CCEd thus) [C41535] Had issue.

**LEGGE (Henry)** Bapt. Wonston, Hants. 22/7/1803, s. Rev. Hon. Augustus George Legge and Honora Bagot. Christ Church, Oxford 1821, BA1824, dn16 (Win.). R. East Lavant, Sussex 1828 to death 8/11/1879, leaving £16,000 [C64283] Married Funtington, Sussex 4/5/1830 Elizabeth Louisa Douglas (an admiral's dau.), with issue. Brother William, below.

**LEGGE (Henry, Hon.)** Born 25/9/1803, s. of George, 3rd Earl of Dartmouth and Lady Frances Finch. Christ Church, Oxford 1822, BA 1825, then All Souls, Fellow 1825-42, dn26 (Cashel: - but in Oxford), p27 (Ox.), BCL1835, Hon. DCL 1840. V. Lewisham, Kent 1831 [income £1,113 in CR65] to death (Blackheath, Kent) 13/2/1887, leaving £22,470-12s-11d [C7181] Married Lewisham 12/5/1842 Marion Rogers (dau. of a baronet).

**LEGGE (William)** Bapt. Wonston, Hants. 29/7/1802, s. Rev. Hon. Augustus George Legge and Honora Bagot. Christ Church, Oxford 1821, Student [Fellow] 1821-5, BA1825, dn25 (Ox.), p26 (Heref.). R. Ashtead, Surrey 1826 (living at Ashtead Park) to death 6/11/1872, leaving £45,000 [C35038] Brother Henry, above.

**LEGGETT (John)** Literate: dn82 (Lin.), p83 (Lin.). R. East Tisted, Hants. 1822 to death. Probate granted 13/3/1841 [C69510] His widow remarried after his death.

**LEGH, LEIGH (Edmund Dawson)** Born London 2/3/1801, s. John Legh and Isabella Dawson [Foster says of Booth Hall, Cheshire]. Balliol, Oxford 1818, BA1821 [adm. Middle Temple 1826] MA1830, dn30 (London), p31 (London). PC. St Giles in the Fields, London 1831, PC. St Botolph Aldersgate, City of London 1838 to death 14/3/1845 aged 44 [C120195] Married Marylebone, London 8/8/1826 Catherine Robinson, with issue.

**LEGH, LEES (Peter)** Probably born Lyme Hall, Cheshire Venn says London), s. Thomas Peter Legh, *M.P.* (perhaps one of his 7 natural children). Trinity, Cambridge 1816 (aged 21), BA1821, dn22 (Chester), p22 (Chester), MA 1824. PC. Newton-in-Makerfield (o/w. Newton-le-Willows, Lancs. 1823-64 (living at nearby Golborn Park). Died Shap, Westmorland 21/6/1867 (a widower) aged 69, leaving £2,000 [C169818] *J.P.* Lancs. and Cheshire 1825.

**LEGREW (James)** Born Spitalfields, London 16/12/1769, s. Obadiah Legrew (a weaver of Huguenot descent) and Martha Hesse. St John's, Cambridge 1788, BA1792, dn92 (Nor.), p93 (Nor.), MA1795. R. Chaldon, Surrey 1830 and R. Caterham, Surrey 1832 to death 5/8/1856 age 86 [C82117] Married Haughley, Suffolk Mar. 1797 Elizabeth Harrison, w. clerical son Arthur (and James, a sculptor, *q.v.* ODNB). 'The Rector … was a quaint old gentleman of the old school, who wore black breeches and gaiters like our Bishops wear at the present day. He was very kind-hearted and much beloved by his parishioners. I was present in church the last time he officiated, when he fainted at the Reading Desk. I well remember his funeral; he was carried to the church by eight of his parishioners all robed in white smock-frocks as was customary in those days.'

**LEICESTER (Charles)** Born Tabley House, Knutsford, Cheshire, 29/9/1795, s. Henry Augustus Leicester (Grenadier Guards) and Letitia Sophia Smyth-Owen. Trinity, Cambridge 1813, then Trinity Hall 1814, dn19 (B&W), p19 (Nor. for B&W), LLB1825. R. Westbury, Shropshire (Sinister Parte) 1820-52. Died 16/3/1858. No will traced [C41536] Married (1) Westbury, Shropshire 5/7/1821 Sally Topp (d.1843), w. issue (2) Paris 24/10/1846 Mrs Susannah (Crowther) Müller (a military widow).

**LEICESTER (Robert)** Bapt. Liverpool 25/10/1799, s. Peter Leicester and Ellin Hume. Clare, Cambridge 1818, BA1822, dn22 (Lin.), p23 (Lin.), MA1825. V. Harlington, Beds. 1823-6, (first) V. (Much) Woolton St Peter, Childwall, Liverpool 1828 to death 14/8/1875 aged 75, leaving £8,000 [C69654] Wife Ann, with issue.

**LEIGH (Clement)** Bapt. Cheadle, Staffs. 30/8/1774, s. Thomas and Mary Leigh. Christ's, Cambridge 1793, BA1797, dn99 (Lin.), MA 1800, p01 (Lin.). PC. Stoke on Trent Chapel, Newcastle under Lyme, Staffs. 1803-15 (res.), R. Newcastle under Lyme St Giles 1815 to death (a widower) 16/2/1853 aged 77 [C15299. Hodson]

**LEIGH (Edward Trafford)** Born Stockport, Cheshire 8/8/1801, s. Rev. George Edward Leigh and Elizabeth Phillips. BNC, Oxford 1820, BA1824, MA1826. R. Cheadle, Cheshire 1829 to death (Clifton, Bristol) 7/1/1847 [C169820] Married York 20/11/1828 Frances Barlow. Brother, below.

**LEIGH, *later* LEIGH MALLORY (George)** Born Stockport, Cheshire 16/7/1806, s. Rev. George Edward Leigh and Elizabeth Phillips. BNC, Oxford 1824, BA1828, dn29 (Chester), p30 (Chester), MA1830. R. Mobberley, Cheshire 1832 to death 26/7/1885 at the Old Hall there, leaving £28,296-0s-1d. [as Mallory] [C169821] Married (1) 28/2/1832 Julia Houldsworth Mallory (a clergy dau., d.1835), w. clerical s.

George Mallory (2) Lymm, Cheshire 7/6/1836 his cousin Henrietta Trafford (w) (Oughrington Hall, Cheshire), with another clerical s. Herbert Leigh Mallory. Brother, above.

**LEIGH (John)** Born Liverpool 8/2/1798, s. Joseph Leigh (merchant) and Margaret Sherlock. BNC, Oxford 1815, BA1820, dn21 (Chester), MA 1822, p22 (Chester). R. Eggington, Derbys. 1824 to death (Belmont Hall, Great Budworth, Cheshire) 5/8/1856 or 24/10/1856 [C18066]

**LEIGH (Thomas)** Bapt. Cheadle, Staffs. 27/7/1771, s. Edward Leigh and Elizabeth Hodgson. Christ's, Cambridge 1789, BA1793, dn93 (Car. for Nor.), p95 (London), MA1796. R. Little Tey, Essex 1796-1805, V. Aveley, Essex 1800-3, R. Wickham Bishops >< Essex 1803-48, R. Pattiswick, Essex 1805-8, R. St Magnus the Martyr w. St Margaret New Fish Street, City of London 1808 to death. Dom. Chap. to Viscount Cremorne 1808. Died 10/6/1848 aged 77 [C6137] Married Soho, London 2/6/1808 Emma Mason Morris, with issue.

**LEIGH (Thomas Gerard)** Born Liverpool 17/1/1804, s. John Leigh and Elizabeth Gerard. BNC, Oxford 1821, BA1825, dn25, p28 (Chester), MA1827. Lecturer (or 2nd Minister) Liverpool St George 1829, R. Walton on the Hill, Liverpool [income £2,100 in CR65] 1847 to death 3/11/1867 aged 63, leaving £14,000 [C169822] Married Cheltenham, Glos. 7/6/1831 Henriana Matilda Murray.

**LEIGH (William)** From Atherston, Warwicks., s. Richard Leigh. Hertford, Oxford 1795 (aged 17), BA1800, dn01 (C&L), p03 (C&L), then Worcester, MA1820. PC. Bilston St Leonard, Staffs. 1813, R. Pulham, Norfolk 1835 to death 12/4/1858, leaving £5,000 [C18074] Wife Mary Proud.

**LEIGH** see also under **LEGH**

**LEIGHTON (Francis)** Born India 5/12/1801 (bapt. 4/9/1803), s. Maj.-Gen. Thomas Leighton and Mary Louisa Everett. Trinity, Cambridge, dn26 (Heref.), BA1827, p27 (Heref.), MA1830, R. Cardeston, Shropshire 1828 to death 15/12/1870, leaving £450 [C172538] Married Thenford, Northants. 12/2/1829 Catherine Severne, with issue.

**LEIR (Paul)** Born Charlton Musgrove, Som. 9/6/1770, s. Rev. Thomas Leir and Mary Shore. Queen's, Oxford 1788, BA1793, dn93 (B&W), p95 (B&W), MA1808. R. (and patron) of Charlton Musgrove 1812 and PC. Shepton Montague, Som. 1823 to death 14/2/1845 [C41540] Married 11/4/1825 Mrs Frances (Freke) Pleydell. J.P. Somerset. Brother below.

**LEIR (William)** Born Charlton Musgrove, Somerset 10/9/1768, s. Rev. Thomas Leir and Mary Shore. Queen's, Oxford 1787, BA1791, dn91 (B&W), p93 (B&W), MA1808. R. (and patron) of Ditcheat, Som. (and Preacher throughout the Diocese of B&W) 1812 to death. Dom. Chap. to 2nd Baron Boston 1812. Died 23/12/1863, leaving £30,000 [C46391] Married Clifton, Bristol 4/4/1804 Harriet Mariott, with clerical son. Brother above. Port. online.

**LEMAN, *born* ORGILL (George Orgill)** Bapt. Beccles, Suffolk 14/6/1789, s. of Rev. Naunton Thomas Orgill (below) and Henrietta Jane Anderson. University, Oxford 1807, BA 1811, dn12 (Nor.), p13 (Nor.), MA1814. PC. Stoven, Suffolk 1823. Died Brampton Hall, Suffolk 14/12/1867, leaving £9,000 [C113846] Surname added 1808. Brother Thomas Orgill, below.

**LEMAN, *born* ORGILL (Naunton Thomas)** Born Brampton, Suffolk 11/12/1759, s. William Orgill and Sarah Leman. Caius, Cam-bridge 1777, BA1782, dn82 (Lin.), p85 (Lin.), MA1787. R. Lea, Lincs. 1789-92, V. Croft, Lincs. 1792-3, R. Worlingham, Suffolk 1793-1837, R. Brampton, Suffolk at death. Dom. Chap. to Earl of Mansfield. Died 3/1/1837 [C71654] Married York 2/12/1783 Henrietta Jane (dau. Rev. Sir William Anderson, 6th Bart., of Lea), with clerical sons above and below. Changed to his mother's surname 1808.

**LEMAN, *born* ORGILL (Thomas Orgill)** Born Brampton, Suffolk 31/3/1804, s. Rev. Naunton Thomas Leman (above) and Henrietta Jane Anderson. Worcester, Oxford 1822, BA1826, dn27 (Llandaff), p28 (Lin.), MA1849. R. (and patron) of Brampton 1837 to death 7/6/1873, leaving £5,000 [C4229] Married Taunton, Som. 23/2/1838 Emily Antonia Guerin (w). Brother George above.

**LEMPRIERE (Everard)** Bapt. Abingdon, Berks. 1/7/1800, s. Rev. John Lempriere and Lucy Willince. Literate: dn23 (Chester), p24 (Ex.). R. Meeth, Devon 1824 to death 17/8/1886 aged 86, leaving £1,005-2s-6d.

[C145414] Married Buckland Filleigh, Devon 30/5/ 1826 Lucy Foulkes. Brother below.

**LEMPRIERE (Francis Drocus *or* Drouet)** Born Abingdon, Berks. 11/11/1794, s. Rev. John Lempriere and Lucy Willince. Trinity, Cambridge 1812, BA1818, dn18 (Chester for Ex.), p19 (London), MA1823. H/M St Olave's G/S Southwark, Surrey 1824; R. (and patron) of Newton St Petrock, Devon 1824-68, R. Kirkley, Lowestoft, Suffolk 1872 to death 27/10/1875 aged 80. Will not traced [C82118. CR65 says Drouet] Married (1) Westminster, London 12/10/1817 Elizabeth Sarah Butcher (d.1865), with issue (2, at age of 71) Bideford, Devon 1867 (1st q.) Fanny Davey (aged 23). Brother above.

**LENDON (Abel)** Bapt. Westminster, London 29/10/1770, s. William Lendon and Ann Evans. Christ Church, Oxford 1791, BA1795, dn95 (Ox.), p96 (Ox.), MA1798. PC. Totteridge, Herts. 1815, R. Friern Barnet, Herts. 1815 to death 4/8/1846 [C35093] Married (1) Clerkenwell, London 15/7/1799 Lucy Fletcher (d.1801), with issue (2) Bristol 13/1/1806 Sibylla Seyer (a clergy dau.), with further issue. Brother below.

**LENDON (Richard)** Born Westminster, London 5/3/1767, s. William Lendon and Ann Evans. Trinity, Cambridge 1787, dn90 (London), BA1791, p91 (London), MA1794. R. Clerkenwell St John's, London 1794-1812, R. St Edmund the King w. St Nicholas Acons, City of London 1811 (and Oxgate Prebend in St Paul's Cathedral 1812) to death 15/11/1833 aged 66 [C120203] Married 27/10/1796 Hannah Bellamy, with clerical son. Brother above.

**LENNARD (Dacre Barrett)** Born Ramsden Bellhouse, Essex 3/1/1801, s. Sir Thomas Barrett Lennard, 1st Bart. and Dorothy St Aubyn. Jesus, Cambridge 1819, BA1824, dn24 (Lin.), p25 (Lin.). R. Norwich St Michael at Plea 1825 to death (Catton, Norfolk) 21/1/1839 [C51345] Married Norwich 5/10/1825 Rachel Anna Ives, with issue.

**LEONARD (Richard Weston)** Born Abingdon, Berks. 4/10/1774, s. William Leonard [*pleb*] and Sarah Weston. Queen's, Oxford 1790, BA 1796, dn96 (Bristol for Peterb.), p98 (Peterb.), MA 823. S/M Aynhoe School, Northants. 1810; R. Newbottle w. Charlton, Northants. 1809 and V. King's Sutton >< Lincs. 1823 [not listed in CCEd] to death (Charlton) 4/10/1861, leaving £3,000 [C53281] Married Brackley, Northants. 5/4/1801 Frances Burford, with clerical son Francis Burford Leonard.

**LEONARD (William)** From Abingdon, Berks., s. William Leonard. All Souls, Oxford 1775 (aged 16), then Magdalen, then Exeter, BA1779, dn82 (Lin.), p94 (Ox.). R. Hardwick, Oxon. 1799 to death 2/12/1840 [C35095]

**LESITER (Charles)** Born and bapt. North Collingham, Notts. 8/6/1777, s. Charles Lesiter and Ann Jebb. Clare, Cambridge 1796, BA 1800, dn00 (York), p01 (Lin.). V. North Collingham 1802 to death 24/1/1858 aged 81, leaving £20,000 [C51479. YCO] Married North Collingham 7/3/1814 Hannah Rachel Pym (*or* Fox) (w).

**LESLIE (Henry, Sir, 3rd Bart.)** Born London 22/9/1783, s. Sir Lucas Pepys Leslie, 1st Bart. (physician) and Jane Elizabeth Leslie, Countess of Rothes. St John's, Cambridge 1800, MA1802, dn03 (Win.), p06 (Win.). R. Shephall, Herts. 1806-49, Prebendary of Exeter Cathedral 1809 and R. Wetherdon, Suffolk 1809 to death. Chap. in Ordinary 1809. Died 9/12/1849 [C82119] Married Tostock, Suffolk 15/2/1816 Elizabeth Jane Oakes (a clergy dau.), *s.p.* Succ. to title 1833.

**LETHBRIDGE (Charles)** Bapt. Launceston, Cornwall 9/5/1763, s. Rev. John Lethbridge and Sibylla Luxmoor. Oriel, Oxford 1780, BA1785, dn85 (Ex.), p87 (Ex.), migrated to St John's, Cambridge 1791, MA1792, R. Landulph, Cornwall 1787-1805, R. Launceston St Thomas 1791-1840, R. Sutcombe, Devon 1797 and PC. Stoke Climsland, Cornwall 1805 to death. Probably Dom. Chap. to Marquess Townshend 1797, 1805. Died St Stephens by Launceston 14/12/1840 aged 88. [C145416] Married Plymouth 1789 Mary Brent, with clerical son, below.

**LETHBRIDGE (Charles Henry)** Bapt. St Stephens by Launceston, Cornwall 17/1/1793, s. Rev. Charles Lethbridge (above) and Mary Brent. Wadham, Oxford 1810, BA1815, dn16 (B&W), p17 (Glos.). PC. St Stephens by Launceston 1819 (and perhaps Chap. HMS *Isis* in 1823?). Died 18/1/1845 aged 53 [C41543] Married Newhaven, Sussex 22/2/1832 Sarah Anne Stone.

**LETTICE (John)** Born Rushden, Northants. 27/12/1737, s. Rev. John Lettice (V. Bozeat, Northants.) and Mary Newcome (a clergy dau.). Sidney, Cambridge 1756, BA1761, dn61 (Lin.), Fellow 1763, MA1764, p64 (Lin.), BD 1771, DD 1797. Chap. and Sec. to the British Embassy at Copenhagen (where he witnessed the Palace Revolution of 1772); tutor to William Beckford and his lifelong friend. V. Peasmarsh, Sussex 1795 and Prebend of Seaford in Chichester Cathedral 1804 to death. Chap. to 10th Duke of Hamilton 1804-32. Died 21/10/1832 aged 94 [C51483. ODNB. Long obit. in *Gentleman's Magazine*. M.J. Barber, *The Vicar's tin box: the life of John Lettice, Vicar of Peasmarsh 1785-1832* (Peasmarsh, 2002), but which fails to mention the forenames of either of his wives!] Married (1) Cambridge 3/10/1786 Ann Newling (d.1788), 1 dau. (2) 25/5/1788? the widow of Dr Hickley, a physician, 1 more dau. A poet, translator and academic: https://en.wikipedia.org/wiki/John_Lettice

**LEVESON-GOWER (Granville)** see under **GOWER**

**LEVETT (Thomas)** Bapt. Whittington, Staffs. 25/2/1770, s. Thomas Levett and Catherine Floyer. Christ Church, Oxford 1788, BA1792. PC. Wychnor, Staffs. 1794-1832 (res.), PC. Whittington 1796. Died 9/10/1843, living at Packington Hall, Warwicks. [C18088] Married Leamington, Warwicks. 21/9/1802 Wilmot Maria Gresley.

**LEVETT (Walter)** Born Stafford 9/5/1784, s. Rev. Richard and Lucy Levett. Christ Church, Oxford 1802, BA1806, dn07 (Ox.), p08 (Ox.), MA1808, Student [Fellow] until 1818. V. Carlton in Craven, Yorks. 1816-49, V. Bray, Berks. 1822-[53], Sub-Dean 1827-52 (res.). Died Reading, Berks. 27/10/1860, leaving £25,000 [C35096] Married Knaresborough, Yorks. 21/10/1823 Susan Sheepshanks (w), of Leeds. Founded the Lich Gate Charity in Bray.

**LEWES (Thomas)** Born Llysnewydd, Carmarthen, s. John Lewes and Joan Lloyd. BNC, Oxford 1811 (aged 17), BA1815, dn16 (B&W), MA1817, p17 (St David's). V. Llanfihangel-ar-Arth, Carmarthen 1818-60, V. Taynton, Oxon. 1819 and V. Great Barrington, Glos. 1820 to death 8/4/1873, leaving £6,000 [C35154]

**LEWIN (Richard)** Born Eltham, Kent 19/12/1790, s. Richard Lewin and Hendrina Alette nan der Poel (of Cape Town). Literate: dn20 (Nor.), p20 (Nor.). PC. Yateley, Hants. 1821 to death 13/11/1874, leaving £3,000 [C82123] Married (1) Cheshunt, Herts. 21/9/1830 Sarah Sandon (a clergy dau., d.1863) (2, at age 80) Lydiard Tregoze, Wilts. 12/1/1871 Ellen Katharine Daubeney (w).

**LEWIN (Spencer James)** Born Bushy, Herts., s. James Lewis and Martha Amy Spencer. Worcester, Oxford 1784 (aged 17), BA1788, p90 (Bristol), MA1791. V. Ifield, Sussex 1790, R. (and patron) of Rushden, Northants. 1804, and R. Crawley, Sussex 1815 to death 25/4/1842 [C53292] Married St Pancras, London 19/7/1791 Elizabeth Capper, with issue.

**LEWIS (Daniel Carter)** From Gloucester, s. Joseph Lewis. Pembroke, Oxford 1781 (aged 16), BA1784, dn86 (Glos.), MA1787, p88 (Glos.). PC. Colnbrook, Bucks. 1788. Minor Canon of St George's Chapel, Windsor 1794, V. Ruislip, Middx. 1797, and V. Newington next Sittingbourne, Kent 1807 to death. Dom. Chap. to 17th Earl of Erroll 1807. Died 21/3/1834 aged 70 [C69665] Wives Martha (d.1819); Julia.

**LEWIS (Edmund Burke)** Bapt. West Molesey, Surrey 9/3/1789, s. James and Sarah Lewis. Christ Church, Oxford 1809, BA1813, dn15 (C&L for Roch.), MA1816, p16 (Ely for Roch.). R. Toddington, Beds. 1816 to death 1/11/1846 [C1967] Married Cheriton, Kent 24/5/1821 Anne Brockman (a clergy dau. who remarried another clergyman in 1847).

**LEWIS (Francis)** Born Chepstow, Monmouth 4/7/1782, s. Charles Lewis and Susannah Davies. University, Oxford 1798, BA1802, MA 1805, dn05 (Llandaff), p06 (Glos.), BD1826. R. Machen, Monmouth 1807-31 (res.), R. Cadoxton-juxta-Neath, Glamorgan 1812-15 (res.), R. Holme Lacy, Heref. 1826 and R. Llanfair Kilgeddin, Monmouth 1831 [total income £1,063 in CR65] to death (Bath) 20/2/1872, leaving £30,000 [C4257] Married (1) 25/3/1828 Mary Lewis (d.1846), with issue (2) Mathan, Monmouth 7/6/1853 Mrs Jane (Gordon) Burr (w). who remarried.

**LEWIS (Gilbert Frankland, Sir, 3rd Bart.)** Born Tiberton Court, Gloucester 21/7/1808, s. Sir Thomas Frankland Lewis, 1st Bart., *M.P.*, and Harriet Cornewall. Magdalene, Cambridge, BA 1830, dn31 (Heref.), MA1833, p33 (Heref.). R. Gladestry, Radnor 1832, R. Monnington on

Wye, Heref. 1832-64, Prebend of Church Withington in Hereford Cathedral 1845-56, RD and Canon of Worcester Cathedral 1856-81 (res.). Died (Harpton Court, Radnor) 18/12/1883, leaving £32,185-11s-4d. [C130026. Boase. ERC links them] Married St George's Hanover Square, London 3/8/1843 Jane Antrobus (dau. of a baronet), with issue.

**LEWIS (Henry John)** Bapt. St George's, Hanover Square, London 6/3/1799, s. John Lewis and Elizabeth Phillips. Worcester, Oxford 1818, BA1821, MA1827. V. Worcester St Peter the Great, 1831-5, Warden St Oswald's Hospital [almshouses] 1831 and Minor Canon of Worcester Cathedral to death 15/2/1835 (CCEd says 29/5/1835) [C121824] Married Bredwardine, Heref. 11/10/1831 Elizabeth Clifton, with issue.

**LEWIS (Israel)** From Cayo, Carmarthen, s. Rev. Leyson Lewis. Jesus, Oxford 1781 (aged 20), dn82 (Ox. for Glos.), p83 (Bristol), then St Alban Hall, BA1792, MA1793. V. Long Ashton, Som. 1794-1841, PC. Whitchurch (o/w Filton), Som. 1794, V. Foxcote, Som. 1806. Died Bedminster, Bristol 20/1/1841 aged 81, leaving £28,500 to 3 ch. [C46415. LBSO] Married Long Ashton, Som. 21/7/1800 Anne Orton, w. issue. Inherited the slave estates of Lady Elizabeth Smyth.

**LEWIS (John)** From Llangattock, Monmouth, s. Rev. John Lewis. Christ Church, Oxford 1767 (aged 19), BA1771, dn71 (Ox.), p72 (Ox.), MA 1775, Chaplain 1775-9. V. Charlton, Wilts. 1779-1838, but parish sequestered 1789; he disappeared 1798 following a tithe dispute. Died? [C35162]

**LEWIS (John)** Probably s. Rev. John Lewis, sen., Essex. Queens', Cambridge 1783, BA1788, MA1791, p92 (London). R. Ingatestone w. Buttsbury, Essex 1796 and R. Rivenhall, Essex 1824 to death. Dom. Chap. to HRH Duke of Sussex 1824. Died 25/2/1853 [C120209] Was married with issue.

**LEWIS (John)** Born Bungay, Suffolk. Emmanuel, Cambridge 1789, BA1793, dn93 (Nor.), p94 (Nor.), MA1796. R. Kirstead w. Langhale, Norfolk 1794 and R. Gillingham All Saints w. St Mary, Norfolk 1797 to death 13/5/1855 aged 80 [C113865] Wife Mary and dau. Deaf.

**LEWIS (John)** [NiVoF] R. East Blatchington, Sussex 1804, V. Bishopstone, Sussex 1821-[46]. Died? [C64295. ERC links them]

**LEWIS (John)** [MA but NiVoF] V. Timsbury, Hants. 1823-[43] Died? [C82126 - and perhaps 82125?] Probably one of the others above?

**LEWIS (Morgan)** Born Nethley, Radnor. St John's, Cambridge 1779, BA1783, dn84 (Chester for London), p85 (Lin. for London), MA1786. V. Great Sampford w. Hempstead, Essex 1801 to death (Lambourne, Essex) 22/5/1834 (CCEd says 17/7/1834) [C69670]

**LEWIS (Thomas Taylor)** Bapt. Ludlow, Shropshire 26/1/1801, s. Edward and Ann Lewis. St John's, Cambridge 1819, BA1825, dn25 (Heref.), p26 (Heref.), MA1828. PC. Leinthall Earles, Aymestrey, Heref. 1832-3 (res.), V. Bridstow, Heref. 1842 to death there 28/10/1858, leaving £6,000 [C172600. ODNB. Boase] Married (1) Cheam, Surrey 24/4/1827 Eliza Penfold (d.1828), 1 dau. (2) 21/6/1838 Elizabeth Jane Woodhouse Ferguson (w) (Yatton Court, Heref.), w. further issue. Antiquary and fossil collector.

**LEWIS (William)** Bapt. Hythe, Kent 11/11/1795, s. William and Margaret Lewis. BNC, Oxford 1815, then St Mary Hall, BA1819, MA1821. V. Abbots Langley, Herts. 1821 to death 19/7/1858, leaving £25,000 [C120215] Widow Lucy.

**LEWORTHY (William)** Bapt. Bratton Fleming, Devon 16/12/1766, s. Humphrey (a farmer) and Rebecca Leworthy. Caius, Cambridge 1784, BA1789, dn89 (Ex.), Fellow 1791, p91 (Ely), MA1792. V. Harston, Cambs. 1796 to death 1837 [C100110] Married Melbourn, Cambs. 16/5/1793 Charlotte Hitch. *J.P.* Cambs.

**LEWTHWAITE (George)** Born Millom, Cumberland 18/7/1772, s. William Lewthwaite and Mary Nicholson. Queen's, Oxford 1791, BA1795, dn96 (Peterb.), MA1797, p97 (Peterb.), BD1805. V. Stanway, Glos. 1807-9, R. Adel, Yorks. 1809 to death 28/6/1854 [C110467] Married St Bees 21/5/1816 Martha Burley, with clerical son. *J.P.* West Riding.

**LEY (Carrington)** Bapt. Tiverton, Devon 27/11/1788, s. Rev. John Ley and Sarah Carrington. Balliol, Oxford 1806, Fellow 1806-18, BA1810, dn12 (Ox.), p13 (Ox.), MA1814.

S/M Tiverton Free G/S 1825; R. Bere Regis, Dorset 1818 to death 24/9/1864, leaving £2,000 [C35208] Married East Putford, Devon 29/8/9/1837 Lucretia Dayman (w), w. issue.

**LEY (Henry)** Born St Paul, Devon 14/8/1781, s. Henry Ley and Mary Smith. Christ Church, Oxford 1799, BA 1803, dn04 (Ox.), p05 (Ex.), MA1806. R. Kenn, Devon 1805 to death (unm.) 8/1/1856 [C35209]

**LEY (Jacob)** Born Cockington, Devon 5/8/1768, s. Jacob Ley. Balliol, Oxford 1787, BA1791, dn91 (Bristol), p93 (Bristol), MA 1796. R. Ashprington, Devon 1795 to death 2/2/1859, leaving £20,000 [C145440] His wife predeceased him, leaving a clerical son.

**LEY (Thomas Hunt)** Bapt. Exeter 29/4/1786, s. John Ley and Mary Browne. Exeter, Oxford 1802, dn09 (Ex.), BA1812, p12 (Ex.), MA1813. V. Landrake w. St Erney, Cornwall 1820 and R. Rame, Cornwall 1824 to death. Dom. Chap. to 2nd Earl of Mount Edgecumbe 1824, the patron of both livings. Died 4/3/1866 aged 79, leaving £600 [C145442] Married Maker, Cornwall 25/3/1812 Sarah Hillyer, with clerical son William Henry Ley.

**LEYCESTER (Oswald)** Bapt. Chester 21/3/1752, s. Ralph Leycester (Toft, Cheshire) and Charlotte Lushington. King's, Cambridge 1769, Fellow 1772-86, BA1774, dn76 (Chester), MA1777, p77 (Chester). V. Knutsford, Cheshire 1785-1809, R. Stoke upon Tern, Shropshire 1806-46, V. Ashton under Lyne St Michael, Lancs. 1797-99 (res.), R. Lymm, Cheshire (1st Moiety), 1799-1806, V. Harlington, Beds. 1822, R. Hodnet w. Weston under Redcastle, Shropshire 1831. Dom. Chap. to 1st Earl of Kilmorney 1831. Died 25/6/1846 aged 94 [C18113] Married (1) Bowdon, Cheshire 21/1/1790 Mary Johnson (d.1812), with issue (2) Ashton-on-Mersey, Cheshire 20/6/1814 Eliza White. Port. online.

**LICKORISH (Richard)** Born Brandon, Warwicks. 3/12/1791, s. Rev. Richard Lickorish, sen. (R. Wolston, Warwicks.) and Sarah Scotten. Sidney, Cambridge 1814, BA 1818, dn18 (Lin.), p21 (Wor. for C&L). PC. Ryton on Dunsmore, Warwicks. 1821 to death (Wolston) 28/8/1871, leaving £6,000 [C18130] Married Southam, Warwicks. 29/4/1824 Alice Griffin.

**LIDDELL (Henry George)** Bapt. 22/7/1787, s. Sir Henry George Liddell, 5th Bart. (Ravensworth Castle, Gateshead, Co. Durham) and Elizabeth Steele. BNC, Oxford 1805, BA1809, dn10 (Durham), p11 (Durham), MA1812. R. Redmarshall, Durham 1811-24, R. Boldon, Durham 1814-29, R. Romaldkirk, Yorks. 1824-28, R. Whickham, Durham 1829-32, R. Easington, Durham 1832-62 [net income £1,311]. Died Charlton Kings, Glos. 9/3/1872 aged 84, leaving £80,000 [C132360] Married 11/11/1809 Charlotte, dau. of Hon. Thomas Lyon; their son was Dean of Christ Church, Oxford, and the father of Lewis Carroll's 'Alice'.

**LIEVRE (John Sturges)** Born Deptford, Kent 16/5/1790, s. Rev. Peter Lievre and Mary Sturges. St John's, Cambridge 1809, dn14 (Lin.), p17 (Ely for Win.), BA1815, MA 1819, incorporated at Oxford 1860. R. Ashby Parva (Little Ashby), Leics. 1832 to death (South Hackney, London) 26/4/1864, leaving £3,000 [C69658] Married Westminster St James, London 25/8/1818 Sarah Ord West (w) (a clergy dau., Guildford, Surrey).

**LIGHTFOOT (John)** Born Uxbridge, Kent, s. Rev. John Lightfoot, sen. (a noted botanist, q.v. ODNB) and Matilda Raynes. Merton, Oxford 1802 (aged 18), BA1806, dn08 (Ox.), p09 (Ox.), MA1809, BD1819, tutor 1822, Fellow to 1824. PC. St Peter in the East, Oxford 1815-24, V. Ponteland, Northumberland 1823-63. Chap. Harefield, Uxbridge, Middx. 1823 [C35235] to death 23/11/1863 aged 79, leaving £7,000 [C132361 death is of the father] Married Cheltenham 25/8/1825 Cordelia Kettilby (a clergy dau., Sutton, Beds.), with issue.

**LIGHTFOOT (Joseph)** From Abbey Holm, Cumberland, s. John Lightfoot. Literate: dn83 (Glos.), p84 (Glos.). Queen's, Oxford 1784 (aged 19), BA1790, MA1793, Fellow and Tutor to 1814. V. Stanway, Glos. 1795-1814, V. Knight's Enham, Hants. 1814 and PC. Upton Gray, Hants. 1814 to death 24/3/1835 [C82131 has the wrong death date]

**LIGHTFOOT (Nicholas)** Bapt. Moretonhampstead, Devon 27/9/1772, s. Nicolas Lightfoot and Jane Hannaford. Balliol, Oxford 1790, BA1794, dn95 (B&W for Ex.), p97 (Ex.). R. Kennerley, Devon 1807, PC. Oldridge, Devon 1819 and R. Stockleigh Pomeroy, Devon 1831 to death 7/4/1847 [C46425] Married

Rockbeare, Devon 13/7/1801, w. issue. Schoolfriend of Robert Southey.

**LILLINGSTON (George)** Born Southend, Essex 6/4/1807 (bapt. Walcot, Bath 25/5/1810), s. Abraham Spooner (later Lillingston) and Elizabeth Mary Agnes Lillingston. Worcester, Oxford 1828, BA1832, p33 (C&L), MA1836. V. Bisham, Berks. 1833 [Inc. of Southend, Essex?] Died Ipswich, Suffolk 29/3/1848 [C18134. F. differs] Married Cheltenham, Glos. 26/6/1832 Barbara Ann Spooner.

**LILLINGSTONE (John)** Bapt. Beccles, Suffolk 6/8/1797. s. Samuel and Elizabeth Lillingstone. Corpus Christi, Cambridge 1815, BA1819, dn20 (Nor.), p21 (Nor.). R. Barsham, Suffolk 1828 to death (Gravesend, Kent) 23/6/1839 aged 41 [C113869] Married Whepstead, Suffolk 10/11/1829 Adelaide Image (a clergy dau.), with issue.

**LINCOLN (Bishop of)** see under **KAYE (John)**

**LINDLEY (Thomas)** Bapt. Halifax, Yorks. 25/7/1753, s. James Lindley. Literate: dn76 (York), p77 (York). PC. Halton Gill, Arncliffe, Yorks. 1777-1847 (res.) (and S/M Halton Gill 1777-1847), PC. Hubberholme, Arncliffe 1802-32. Died Halton Gill 8/1/1847 aged 94 [C117359. YCO]

**LINDSAY (Henry)** Probably born Blackheath, Kent. Trinity, Cambridge 1808, BA1812, dn13 (Bristol), p14 (Chester for Cant.), MA1817. Chap. to British Factory at Constantinople 1817; PC. Wimbledon, Surrey 1819-46, V. Croydon, Surrey 1830-46, R. Sundridge, Kent 1846 to death 4/6/1859 aged 70, leaving £2,000 [C53311] Married 7/7/1819 Maria Marryat (dau. of an *M.P.*), with clerical sons Henry, and James Lindsay.

**LINDSAY (John)** Born Donaghmore, Co. Tyrone, s. Waterhouse Crymble Lindsay and Elizabeth Lee. TCD1803 (aged 16), BA1807, dn09 (Lin.), p10 (Lin.), then Trinity, Cambridge 1811, BA1811, MA1811. V. Swinford, Leics. 1818 and V. Stanford upon Avon, Northants. 1818 to death (a bachelor) 31/5/1875, leaving £16,000 [C69677]

**LINGARD (Joshua)** Bapt. Shaw, Lancs. 21/10/1798, s. Thomas Lingard and Elizabeth Shaw. St Mary Hall, Oxford 1823, BA1827, MA1831. PC. Manchester St George [in the Fields], Hulme 1828 to death 30/11/1842 [C169832] Wife Elizabeth in 1841.

**LINTON (Henry)** Born Freiston, Lincs. 5/12/1752, s. Rev. John Linton and Elizabeth Boulton. Lincoln, Oxford 1770, then Magdalen 1771-4, BA1774, dn75 (Ox.), p76 (Ox.), MA 1776, BD1786, DD1797, etc. R. Leverton (North Moeity), Lincs. 1776-99, V. Freiston 1782-99, V. Fritwell, Oxon. 1799-1833, V. North Aston, Oxon. 1799-1833, V. Dinton w. Teffont Magna, Wilts. 1800-41, V. Fringford, Oxon. 1833. Died 14/2/1841. Dom. Chap. to 5th Duke of Ancaster and Kesteven 1782 [C35240]

**LINTON (Hewett)** Bapt. Fotheringhay, Northants 5/1/1797. s. Rev. Robert Linton and Mary Thomlinson. St John's, Cambridge 1813, BA1818, dn20 (Peterb.), MA1821, p21 (Peterb.). V. Nassington, Northants. 1829 to death (Sydenham, Surrey) 8/3/1879 (residing at Torquay and Sydenham for health reasons), leaving £600 [C69679] Married (1) Ashby-de-la-Launde, Lincs. 5/4/1826 Sarah Marshall (d.1837), w. issue (2) Wainfleet All Saints, Lincs. 10/6/1841 Catherine Atkinson (w), w. further issue. Brother, below.

**LINTON (Thomas)** Bapt. Fotheringhay, Northants. 15/5/1798, s. Rev. Robert Linton and Mary Thomlinson. St John's, Cambridge 1816, BA 1821, dn21 (Peterb.), p22 (Peterb.), MA1824. (succ. his father as) V. Fotheringhay 1832-58, PC. Woodneston, Northants. 1832, (succ. his father as) V. Warmington, Northants. 1833-51, PC. Woodnewton, Northants. to 1832, V. Apethorpe, Northants. to 1833. Died 23/11/1858, leaving £4,000 [C69681] Brother Hewett, above.

**LINZEE (Edward)** Born Newport, IoW, s Admiral Robert Linzee and Anne Redstone, Christ's, Cambridge 1791 (aged 16), BA1796, dn97 (Nor.), MA1799. R. Charlton next Woolwich, Kent 1799-1806 (res.), V. Shrewsbury St Alkmund, Shropshire 1806-18, R. West Tilbury, Essex 1818 to death (Binfield, Berks.) 4/8/1842 aged 68, living at Kelvedon Hall, Essex, then Penn, Bucks. [C1972] Married Hornsey, Middx. 25/10/1803 Caroline Warner, with issue. Port. online.

**LIPSCOMB (Francis)** Born Welbury, Yorks. Feb. 1798, s. Rev. William Lipscomb and Margaret Cooke. Corpus Christi, Oxford 1817, then University 1818-24, BA1821, dn21 (London), p22 (Bangor for Cant.), MA1824. PC. Sevenoaks Weald, Kent 1823-33, R. Welbury, Northallerton, Yorks. 1832 (with part RD of Cleveland) to death (Exmouth, Devon) 4/8/1885 aged 87, leaving £3,135-3s-3d [C120221] Married (1) Sevenoaks 30/9/1824 Sarah Woodgate (d.1866), with issue (2) Welbury 17/4/1866 Adelaide Augusta Mercer (w).

**LIPTROTT (John)** Bapt. Egham, Surrey 22/12/1773, s. Rev. James and Amelia Ann Liptrott. Wadham, Oxford 1792, then Trinity, BA1796, MA1806. R. Steventon, Berks. 1805-12, R. Broughton Astley, Leics. 1812 to death 16/12/1848 [C69778] Married Egham 18/11/1806 Frances Burnett, with issue.

**LISTER (James Stovin)** Bapt. Whitgift, Yorks. 5/12/1806, s. James Stovin Lister and Alice Spofforth. Worcester, Oxford 1825, BA 1829, dn30 (York), p30 (Lin.), MA1833. V. Luddington w. Garthorpe, Lincs. 1830 to death (Crowle, Lincs.) 1/3/1844 [C69780. YCO]

**LISTER (John Joseph)** Bapt. Manchester 1/4/1770, s. Matthew Dymoke Lister and Lydia Bancroft. BNC, Oxford 1789, BA1793, dn96 (Lin.), p07 (Lin.). V. Farlesthorpe, Lincs. 1814-37, R. Muckton, Lincs. 1815-17, R. Cranoe, Leics. 1817 and R. Caunton, Notts. 1817 to death (Alford, Lincs.) 23/7/1837 [C69781] Married Alford 25/3/1805 Olivia West, with issue.

**LISTER (Robert)** Bapt. Batley, Yorks. 1/4/1770, s. of James (an innkeeper) and Hannah Lister. Pembroke, Cambridge 1791, BA1795, dn99 (Chester), p00 (Chester). PC. Lytham, Lancs. 1800-34 (res.). Died there 29/1/1836 aged 66 [C169833]

**LISTER-KAYE (Arthur Lister)** see under **KAYE**

**LITCHFIELD (Francis)** Bapt. Northampton 31/7/1792, s. Francis Litchfield and Anna Miller. Merton, Oxford 1819, BA1815, dn17 (Peterb.), MA1818, p19 (Ox. for Peterb.). R. Farthinghoe, Northants. 1817-76, R. Elham, Kent 1830-76, R. Ryhall and Essendine, Rutland 1834, R. Great Linford, Northants. 1836 to death 9/9/1876, leaving £16,000 [C110469] Married Combrook, Warwicks. 1/12/1852 Frances Ann Richmond.

**LITTLE (George Ernest)** see **HOWMAN**

**LITLER, LITTLER (Robert)** Born Northwich, Cheshire 28/10/1800, s. Rev. Robert, sen. and Elizabeth Litler. BNC, Oxford 1817, BA 1821, dn23 (Chester), MA1824, p24 (Chester). PC. Goostrey, Cheshire 1823, PC. Chadkirk, Romiley, Cheshire 1826, PC. Marple, Cheshire 1826, PC. Poynton, Macclesfield, Cheshire 1832 to death. Dom. Chap. to Earl of Winterton. Died 23/6/1864, leaving £4,000 [C169834] Married Stockport, Cheshire 20/6/1833 Mary Bellot, with clerical son.

**LITTLEDALE (Osborn)** Bapt. Arlecdon, Westmorland 8/6/1771, s. John Littledale. Literate: dn96 (Chester), p97 (Chester). PC. Admarsh (o/w Bleasdale), Lancs. 1828 to death 11/1/1833 aged 63 [C169837] Married Cockermouth, Cumberland 20/6/1808 Barbara Scott, with issue.

**LITTLEHALES (Joseph Gascoyne)** Born 5/2/1775, s. Rev. Joseph Lawrence Littlehales (PC. Clerkenwell, London) and Margaret Gascoigne/Gascoyne). BNC, Oxford 1793, BA 1797, dn97 (Lin.), p99 (Ex. for Glos.), MA 1800. R. Condicote, Glos. 1799, PC. Biddlesden, Bucks. 1809-54, V. Langham Episcopi, Norfolk 1814-22 (res.), V. Westbury, Bucks. 1817 (res.), R. Shalstone, Bucks. 1822, R. Lillingstone Dayrell, Bucks. 1840 to death 2/6/1854 [C35247] Married Bicester, Oxon. 13/8/1798 Elizabeth Davis, with issue.

**LITTLEWOOD (Samuel)** Bapt. Manchester 14/7/1795, s. John Littlewood (Walworth, London) and Susannah Davis. St John's, Cambridge 1816, dn19 (Salis.), p20 (Salis.), BA1823 (a Ten Year Man: BD 1834). PC. Edington, Wilts. 1826-79. Died Croydon, North 4/1/1884, leaving £15,002-3s-11d. [C95339] Married (1) Beechingstoke, Wilts. 24/6/1820 Mary Ann Hayward (d.1831), w. clerical son Alfred Samuel (2) Liverpool 14/9/1833 Mrs Ellen (Lawrence) Nunns, with clerical sons James Lawrence, and John Littlewood.

**LIVESEY (John)** Born Manchester 17/5/1803, s. of John Livesey (a warehouseman). St John's, Cambridge 1822, BA1827, dn27 (London for Ely), p28 (Ely), MA1830. PC. Sheffield St Philip, Yorks. 1832 to death.

Military Chap. at Sheffield 1836. Died 11/8/1870 aged 66, leaving £6,000 [C109775. Boase] Married (1) Manchester 17/6/1824 Mary Wright (d.1853) (2) Cambridge 8/10/1857 Mrs Sarah (Pennington) Owen (d.1863, widow of 'the first missionary to the Zulus') (3) York 12/5/1864 Mrs Emily (Cockayne) Jervis (w). Convicted in 1862 for falsifying a burial record: much online about this at: www.chrishobbs.com/sheffield/agraveaffair1862.htm

**LIVINGSTON (Terence)** An Irishman. TCD, BA, p21 (Ex.). R. Bigbury, Devon 1821 to death (unm., Surbiton, Surrey) 22/5/1861 aged 60, leaving £4,000 [C145445. Not in Al.Dub.]

**LLOYD (Arthur Forbes)** Born Co. Tipperary, s. Rev. Richard Walter Lloyd and Priscilla Lord. Corpus Christi, Cambridge 1812, BA 1816, dn16 (Ex.), p17 (Ex.), MA1819. R. Instow, Devon (and RD) 1822 to death (Marylebone, London) 3/7/1866 aged 73, leaving £4,000 [C145446] Married Walthamstow, London 26/3/1825 Harriet Forster (who died two days before he did), with issue.

**LLOYD (George Wood)** Bapt. Mavesyn Ridware, Staffs. 16/11/1768, s. Owen Lloyd and Margaret Wood. Trinity, Cambridge 1785, BA 1790, dn91 (Ely for C&L), MA1793, p93 (C&L), DD1821. PC. Church Gresley, Derbys. 1793 to death (Stapenhill, Derbys.) 8/3/1860, leaving £600 [C18161] Married Clifton Campville, Staffs. 22/12/1812 Elizabeth Flavell, w. clerical son George Lloyd.

**LLOYD (Griffith/Gryffydd)** From Llanfyllyn, Montgomery, s. Bell Lloyd (brother of 1st Lord Mostyn) and Ann Pryce. Christ Church, Oxford 1793 (aged 18), BA1797, Fellow All Souls 1801-9, dn97 (Ox.), p98 (Ox.), MA1801. V. Trefeglwys, Montgomery 1799, V. Audlem, Cheshire 1799-1802 (res.), R. Newton Purcell, Oxon. 1805, V. Upchurch, Kent 1806-9, R. Christleton, Cheshire 1809 to death 25/1/1843 [C35257] See also William Henry Cynric Lloyd, below.

**LLOYD (John)** [NiVoF] V. Hindolveston ('vulgarly called Hilveston'), Guist, Norfolk 1798. Probate granted 11/8/1848 [C1085] Widow Elizabeth.

**LLOYD (Maurice)** Born Abermule, Montgomeryshire 1801, s. John and Anne Lloyd. Emmanuel, Cambridge 1820, BA1824, dn25 (Heref.), p26 (Heref.), MA1827. (succ. his uncle as) R. Montgomery (Diocese of Hereford) 1831 and RD to death 9/6/1873. leaving £4,000 [C172640] Married Clun, Shropshire 16/7/1861 Hariett Louisa More (w) (a clergy dau., Linley, Shropshire).

**LLOYD (Maurice Head)** Born Lenham, Kent 8/5/1794, s. Rev. Maurice Lloyd. Pembroke, Cambridge 1812, BA1816, dn17 (Roch.), p18 (London for Cant.). PC. Goodnestone, Kent 1825-54, PC. Nonington w. Wymynswold, Kent 1835-45. Died 30/5/1854 [C332]

**LLOYD (Owen)** Born Brathay, Westmorland 31/3/1803, s. Charles Lloyd. Trinity, Cambridge 1822, BA1827, MA1830. PC. Langdale, Grasmere, Westmorland 1829 to death (Manchester) 18/4/1841 [C120227] Married 1826 Mary Dudley, with issue.

**LLOYD (Richard)** From Wrexham, Denbigh, s. Rev. John (R. Thorpe, Derbys.) and Mary Lloyd. Magdalene, Cambridge 1783, BA1787, dn88 (London), Fellow 1790, MA1790, p90 (London). V. Midhurst, Sussex 1796-1805, R. Lynch, Sussex 1805, V. St Dunstan in the West, City of London 1805 to death 27/6/1834 (CCEd thus) [C64325. ODNB]

**LLOYD (Robert Watkin)** Born Caerwys, Flintshire 10 or 19/11/1783, s. Rev. John Lloyd and Martha Williams. St John's, Cambridge 1800, BA1804, dn06 (C&L), MA1807, p07 (C&L). H/M Ashby de la Zouche G/S, Staffs. 1811-14 ('replaced'); PC. Wigginton, Staffs. 1818 and PC. Wilnecote w. Castle Liberty, Tamworth, Warwicks. 1818 to death 12/12/1860, leaving £2,000 [C18192] Married 10/2/1812 Anne Blick (a Tamworth clergy dau.), with clerical son Francis Llewellyn Lloyd.

**LLOYD (Samuel)** Born Uley, Glos. 27/10/1793 (bapt. in an Independent Chapel), s. Nathaniel and Elizabeth Lloyd. Magdalen, Oxford 1815. [Student of Lincoln's Inn 1817] BA1819, MA 1822, dn23 (Glos.), p23 (Glos.). V. Horsley, Glos. 1825 to death (Stanley Hall, King's Stanley, Glos.) 16/3/1863, leaving £6,000 [C157603] Married Horsley 26/1/1832 Eliza Young (w), with issue.

**LLOYD (Thomas)** Bapt. Frogmore, Herts. 26/8/1772, s. Rev. William Lloyd and Elizabeth Bourchier. Peterhouse, Cambridge 1792, BA 1796, dn96 (Lin.), MA1799, p00 (Lin.). R.

Fordwich, Kent 1802 (non-res.) and R. Sacombe, Herts. 1807 to death. Dom. Chap. to Earl Cowper 1838. Died 5/12/1851 [C69722] Married Tewin, Herts. 7/12/1799 Frances Mackay, with issue.

**LLOYD (William)** Bapt. Chetwynd, Shropshire 27/10/1787, s. Thomas and Mary Lloyd. Merton, Oxford 1806, LLB1813, p13 (Ox.). R. Hanwell, Oxon. 1813, R. Drayton, Oxon. 1813 to death 20/10/1861, leaving £450 [C35268] Had issue. 'Not a man one likes to speak about' (Wilberforce).

**LLOYD (William)** From London, s. John Lloyd. BNC, Oxford 1818 (aged 18), BA1822, dn23 (Lin.), p24 (Lin.), MA1825. R. Lillingstone Lovell, Oxon. 1827 to death. Dom. Chap. to Viscount Dungannon 1837. Died 24/5/1889, leaving £3,604-15s-0d. [C35269] A 'very good man' (Wilberforce).

**LLOYD (William Henry Cynric)** Born Woodstock, Oxon. 13/1/1802, s. Bell Lloyd (brother of 1st Baron Mostyn) and Ann Pryce. Jesus, Oxford 1819, BA1822, MA1825, dn26 (Ox.), p26 (Ox.). R. Norbury, Staffs. 1826-49, V. Ranton, Staffs.1826-49. In South Africa from 1849, Archdeacon of Durban, Natal 1869 to death there. Dom. Chap. to his cousin 1st Earl of Lichfield. Died 3/1/1881 aged 78. No will traced in England [C18205. Boase. Hodson] Married (1) 3/7/1832 Lucy Anne Jeffreys (a clergy dau., d.1843), with issue (2) Newport, Shropshire 23/5/1844 Ellen Norman (a clergy dau.), with further issue. Photo. online. See also Griffith Lloyd, above.
https://en.wikipedia.org/wiki/William_Lloyd_(archdeacon_of_Durban)

**LOCK (George)** Born Marylebone, London 30/5/1771, s. William Lock (Mickleham Park, Surrey) and Frederica Augusta Schaub. Christ Church, Oxford 1789, BA1794. p95 (B&W), MA1796. R. Norton sub Hamdon, Som. 1795-1804, R. Lee, Kent 1802 to death 17/11/1864, leaving £6,000 [C1974] Married (1) Marylebone 5/4/1805 Harriet Poulett Thompson (d.1838) (2) Mickleham 1839 Elizabeth Oak, with issue.

**LOCKETT (William)** Born Sandbach, Cheshire 24/10/1800, s. William Lockett. Literate: dn24 (Chester), p25 (Chester), then Queens', Cambridge 1825 (a Ten Year Man, BD1835). PC. Wetenhall, Cheshire 1829 to death (Over, Cheshire, income £75) 13/1/1867 aged 66, leaving £2,000 [C169846] Married Davenham, Cheshire 27/12/1826 Mary Dudley, w. clerical son Francis Hall Lockett.

**LOCKEY (Francis)** Bapt. Reading, Berks. 27/7/1797, s. Francis and Anna Lockey. Adm. Middle Temple 1814. St Catherine's, Cambridge 1820, then Magdalene 1821, SCL1822, dn22 (Lin.), p23 (Lin.), LLB1826. PC. Blackford in Wedmore, Som. 1825-35, Chap. to Bath Female Home, Penitentiary and Lock [venereal disease] Hospital 1834. Retired to Swainswick near Bath and died there 14/5/1869, leaving £5,000 [C41552] Widow Susannah Emm [sic], with issue. Important early photographer, q.v. D. McLaughlin and M. Gray. *Shadows and light: Bath in camera, 1849-1861* … (1989).

**LOCKEY (Ralph)** Bapt. Cam, Glos. 1/6/1770, s. Richard Lockey and Ann Beard. Peterhouse, Cambridge 1788, BA1792, dn93 (Nor. for Glos.), p94 (Glos.), MA1796, incorporated at Oxford 1810. V. Much Dewchurch, Heref. 1812, PC. Much Birch, Heref. 1812 and R. Llanwarne, Heref. 1818 to death. Dom. Chap. to 1st Baron Rous 1818. Died 1833 [C113887] Married Lugwardine, Heref. 22/5/1817 Mary Phillipps, w. issue. .

**LOCKTON (Thomas)** From Weyhill, Hants., s. Rev. Thomas Lockton. Pembroke, Oxford 1784 (aged 14), then Corpus Christi, BA1788, MA1792, dn92 (Salis.), p94 (Salis.), BD1800. R. Church Brampton, Northants. 1807 to death 9/2/1853 [C82143] Married Whissenden, Rutland 11/1/1810 Jane Langton, w. clerical s. Philip Langton Lockton.

**LOCKWOOD (Frederick Vernon)** Born Maldon, Essex 1803, s. Thomas Lockwood (Glamorgan) and Charlotte, dau. Lord George Manners-Sutton. Trinity, Cambridge 1819, BA 1824, dn26 (B&W for Cant.), p26 (London for Cant.), MA1828. R. Musham, Isle of Thanet, Kent 1827-40, Prebend of Asgarby in Lincoln Cathedral 1828-45 (res.), 6th Canon of Canterbury Cathedral 1838-51, V. Minster in Thanet, Kent 1839 to death (from smallpox caught visiting a parishioner) 1/7/1851. Chap. to House of Commons 1828-[45?] [C41553. Boase] Married 21/7/1840 his cousin Mary Isabella Percy (dau. of a Bishop of Carlisle).

**LOCKWOOD (John William)** Born Yoxford, Suffolk 1800, s. Rev. John Cutts Lockwood and Amelia Boddington. Christ Church, Oxford

1816, Student [Fellow] 1816-38, BA1821, MA 1823, dn25 (Ox.), p26 (Cashel for Ox. - in Oxford). V. Chalgrove, Oxon. 1832, R. Chelsea St Luke, London 1832-6 [income in CR65 £1,003], R. Kingham, Oxon. 1836 to death 29/11/1879, leaving £3,000 [C35275] Married Marylebone, London 2/10/1832 Alicia Davis (w), with issue.

**LOCKWOOD (John William Knollis *or* Knowles)** Bapt. Beverley, Yorks. 7/8/1808, s. (alderman) John Lockwood and Sarah Dickens. Trinity, Cambridge 1826, BA1831, dn32 (Lin. for York), p32 (York). PC. Ulrome Chapel, Barmston, Yorks. 1833-48, V. Everingham, Yorks. 1842 to death (Pocklington, Yorks., a widower) 4/3/1871 aged 63, leaving under £50 [C69804. YCO] Married Clifford, Yorks. 8/10/1856 Jane Isabella Gordon Fleming.

**LOCKWOOD (William)** Born Easingwold, Yorks. 28/8/1804, s. William Lockwood (an attorney) and Jane Key. University, Oxford 1821, BA1825, dn27 (Durham for York), p28 (York), MA1829. PC. Brighouse, Halifax 1832-43, V. Kirkby Fleetham, Yorks. 1843 to death 29/5/1854 aged 49 [C132539. YCO] Married (1) Easingwold 17/12/1827 Jane Smith (d.1829) (2) 28/6/1831 Kirkby Fleetham Elizabeth Glaister (a clergy dau.), with issue.

**LODGE (Oliver)** Born Co. Tipperary 9/4/1765, s. Oliver William Lodge and Joanna Barton. BA (probably TCD where there are two men of this name). PC. Great Ilford Chapel, Barking, Essex 1819, R. Elsworth, Cambs. 1837 to death 15/6/1845 [C120234. Al.Dub.?] Married (1) Dublin Dec. 1784 Dorcas Cromie (d.1791) (2) Dublin 1801 *or* 1805 Anne Supple, c.19 ch. (2 clerical). Port. online. Grandfather of Sir Richard Lodge, historian.

**LOFT (John)** Bapt. Marsh Chapel, Lincs. 27/3/1792, s. John Loft (Market Stainton, Lincs.) and Mary Codd. Caius, Cambridge 1810, BA1814, dn15 (Lin.), p16 (Lin.), MA 1817. Chap. of the Donative of Market Stainton 1818 [and living at Market Stainton House in 1834] (CCEd says PC), V. Nun Ormesby (o/w North Ormesby), Lincs. 1818-72, R. Wyham w. Cadeby. Lincs. 1818 (with RD of Louthesk) to death (Worthing, Sussex) 4/5/1884, leaving £24,433-12s-6d. [C69813. Kaye] Married (1) Ancaster, Lincs. 27/10/1824 Frances Wyndham Pennell (d.1837), with issue (2) Wyham cum Cadeby, Lincs. 15/4/1843 Frances Jane Robson (d.1844, probably in childbirth) (3) Hull, Yorks. 28/10/1846 Mary Ann Phillips.

**LOFTUS (Arthur)** Bapt. Marylebone, London 28/7/1795, s. Gen. William Loftus and Lady Elizabeth Townshend (dau. of 1st Marquess Townshend). Clare, Cambridge 1814, BA1819, dn19 (Nor.), p20 (Nor.), MA1822. V. and R. Helhoughton w. Rainham St Peter, Norfolk 1822 to death, R. and V. Fincham St Michael w. St Martin, Norfolk 1826-45 (deprived: a delinquent clergyman accused of cruelty and abuse towards his wife, who had left him. He brought a case against her for restitution of conjugal rights). Dom. Chap. to 1st Earl of Kilmorney 1819. Died 8/2/1878 aged 83. Will not traced [C113888. Tom Hughes, *Blame it on the Norfolk vicar* ... (Wellington, 2009)] Married 10/8/1836 Mary Anne Ray Clayton (a clergy dau.), with issue.

**LOMAS (Thomas)** From Prestbury, Cheshire, s. Edward Lomas. BNC, Oxford 1780 (aged 20), BA1784, MA1786, dn02 (London), p03 (London). PC. Leeds w. Broomfield, Kent 1814 to death 8 *or* 15/11/1843 aged 84 [C120235. Foster corrected]

**LONDON (Bishop of)** see under **BLOMFIELD (Charles James)**

**LONG (John)** Literate: dn17 (Car.), p18 (Car.). PC. Winster, Kendal, Westmorland 1821 to death 20/8/1841 aged 48 [C6140] Married Crosthwaite, Westmorland 12/8/1820 Mary Norman, with issue.

**LONG (Phipps)** From Shabbington, Bucks., s. Rev. Samuel Long and Catherine Weston. Magdalen, Oxford chorister 1784-90, matr. 1789 (aged 18), then All Souls, BA1793, dn94 (Nor. for Salis.), p96 (Salis.), MA1797. R. East Shefford, Berks. 1797-1800, V. Shabbington 1799 to death (Thame, Oxon.) 8/8/1846 [C69821] Married Aylesbury, Bucks. 24/5/1803 Elizabeth Bull, with issue.

**LONG, *born* KELLETT (Robert Churchman)** Bapt. City of London 20/11/1761, s. Robert Cowan Kellett and Anne Churchman. Pembroke, Cambridge 1779, BA1783, MA1786, dn87 (Nor.), p87 (Nor.). R. (and patron) of Illington, Norfolk 1787-1841, R. (and patron) of Newton Flotham, Norfolk 1790-1835 (consolidated w. Swainsthorpe 1825), PC. (and patron) of Dunstan, Norfolk 1796-1841 (living at Dunstan Hall), R. Pulham, Norfolk 1808-35. Died 1841 aged 79 [C113747] Married Bergh Apton, Norfolk 12/11/1794 Jane Walter (a clergy dau.), w. issue. Name changed 1797.

**LONG (Walter)** Born Melksham, Wilts. 15/4/1795, s. John Long and Mrs Lucy Ann (Warneford) Kinnear (a clergy dau.). St John's, Cambridge 1816, LLB1816, dn19 (Salis.), p19 (Salis.). R. Tytherton Kellaways (o/w Calloes), Wilts. 1819 to death 9/9/1857 aged 62 [C95348] Married Bath 21/4/1829 Sarah Anne Gunning (a clergy dau.).

**LONG (William)** Born Carshalton, Middx. 24/8/1763, s. Beeston Long and Sarah Cropp. Emmanuel, Cambridge 1781, LLB1788, dn88 (Nor.), p88 (Nor.). R. Dennington, Suffolk (w. Preacher throughout the Diocese of Norwich) 1788-1808, R. Sternfield, Suffolk 1788-1835, Canon of 10th Stall in St George's Chapel, Windsor 1804 and R. Pulham, Norfolk 1808 to death 16/7/1835 (CCEd says 18/9/1835) [C113891] Brother of 1st Baron Farnborough.

**LONG (William)** Born Applethwaite, Cumberland 12/5/1788, s. William and Agnes Long. Literate: dn11 (York), p12 (York). V. Lythe, Whitby, Yorks. 1826 to death 23/12/1857 aged 69 [C135602. YCO] Married Stanhope, Co. Durham 11/5/1822 Alice Sowerby.

**LONGE (John)** Born Spixworth, Norfolk 24/4/1765, s. John Longe and Dorothy Elwin. Corpus Christi, Cambridge 1782, then Trinity 1784, BA1787, dn87 (Nor.), p89 (Nor.), MA 1790. V. (and patron) of Coddenham, Suffolk [net income £1,009] 1797 to death 3/3/1834 aged 68 (CCEd says 22/5/1834) [C113894] Married (1) Norwich 2/11/1790 Charlotte Browne (of Ipswich, d.1812) (2) Salthouse, Norfolk 14/4/1817 Frances Ward (a military dau.), with issue.

**LONGFORD (William Hawes)** Born Stretton on the Fosse, Warwicks. 10/4/1771, s. Rev. William Longford, sen. and Elizabeth Hawes. Pembroke, Oxford 1787, BA1792, dn93 (Wor.), MA1794, p96 (Wor.). R. Stretton on the Fosse 1809 to death 28/10/1835 aged 67 [C121832. Foster as William only] Married Northfield, Birmingham 28/8/1813 Sarah Harrison Greaves, with clerical son of same name.

**LONGLANDS (Thomas) From** Westminster, London, s. Thomas Longlands. Trinity, Cambridge 1797, BA1801, dn01 (London for Cant.), p02 (Roch. for Cant.), MA1804. V. Great Canfield, Essex 1810-22, V. Damerham, Wilts. 1822-50, V. Porchester, Hants. 1829 to death 30/11/1856 aged 79 [C1978]

**LONGMORE (James)** Possibly born Boyndie, Aberdeenshire 15 *or* 17/4/1772, s. William Longmore and Jean Bremner. Literate: dn94 (London), p94 (London), then Clare, Cambridge 1806 (a Ten Year Man, BD 1816). R. Yealmpton, Devon 1810 to death 13/9/1855 aged 83 [C120239] Married Yealmpton 2/12/1830 Elizabeth Wyatt, w. clerical son.

**LONSDALE (Henry Gylby/Gilby)** Born Sandal Magna, Wakefield, Yorks. 5/8/1791, s. Rev. John Lonsdale (V. Darfield, Barnsley, Yorks.) and Elizabeth Steer. Jesus, Cambridge 1810, BA 1814, dn16 (York), MA1817, p18 (York). R. Bolton by Bowland, Yorks. 1826-30, V. Lichfield St Mary, Staffs. 1830 to death 31/1/1851 [C135604. YCO] Married 5/8/1824 Anna Maria Heywood (Stanley Hall, Wakefield), with clerical son James Gylby Lonsdale. Brother, below.

**LONSDALE (John, *later* Bishop of Lichfield)** Born Newmillerdam, Wakefield, Yorks. 17/1/1788, s. Rev. John Lonsdale (V. Darfield, Barnsley, Yorks.) and Elizabeth Steer. King's, Cambridge 1806, Fellow 1809-15 [adm. Lincoln's Inn 1811] BA1811, BA1814, dn15 (B&W), p15 (Salis.), BD1824, Fellow of Eton College 1827-8, Hon. DD1844. R. Mersham, Kent 1822-7, Prebend of Haydour cum Walton in Lincoln Cathedral 1825-7, Canon Residentiary and Precentor of Lichfield Cathedral 1828-31, R. Bloomsbury St George, London [net income £1,153] 1828-34 (res.), Prebend of Newington in St Paul's Cathedral 1831-43, third Principal of King's College, London 1839-44, Archdeacon of Middlesex 1842, Bishop of Lichfield 1843 [income £4,000] to sudden death 19/10/1867 'of haemorrhage of the brain occasioned by excessive letter writing after a trying diocesan meeting'. Chap. to Archbishop of Canterbury 1815. Left £90,000 (as John Lichfield) [C18306. ODNB. Boase. E.B. Denison, *Life of John Lonsdale, Bishop of Lichfield. With some of his writings* (1868. photo.)] Married Clapham, London 25/11/1815 Sophia Bolland (dau. of an *M.P.*), with clerical sons James Gylby, and John Gylby Lonsdale. Brother above.'There was but one opinion of Lonsdale's episcopate during his time that he was the best bishop the diocese had ever had. A perfect model of justice, kindness, humility and shrewd sense.'

**LORD (Henry)** Born Northiam, Sussex 18/8/1760, s. Rev. William Lord and Mary Frewen. St John's, Oxford 1778, Fellow 1781, BA1782, p86 (Ox.), MA1792. S/M Merchant Taylors' School, London 1783-96; R. Barfreystone, Kent 1800-36, V. Lydden, Kent 1807-14, R. Northiam 1815 to death 20/5/1836 aged 75 [C35286] Married Newbery, Berks. 26/1/1802 Sarah Minter, many children.

**LORD (James)** Bapt. Drayton Parslow, Bucks. 14/10/1758, s. Rev. James Lord, sen. and Mary Alston. St Mary Hall, Oxford 1778 [CCEd says Magdalen Hall], BA1781, dn81 (Ox.), p85 (Ox.), BD1792, DD 1801. (succ. his father as) R. (and patron) of Drayton Parslow 1817 to death 13/11/1835 aged 77 [C35287]

**L'OSTE (Charles Nettleton)** Bapt. Horncastle, Lincs. 2/6/1784, s. Rev. Charles L'Oste and Susannah Benee. Corpus Christi, Cambridge 1805, BA1809, dn08 (Lin.), p10 (Lin.), MA 1815. Curate (and patron) of the 'exempt donative' of Revesby, Lincs. 1815, R. Claxby Pluckacre, Lincs. 1822 and R. Moorby, Lincs. 1826 to death (Horncastle) 1833 aged 53 [C69139. Kaye]

**L'OSTE (Joseph)** Bapt. Louth, Lincs. 31/12/1763, s. Frederick L'Oste ('seven times Warden of Louth') and Elizabeth Hill. Trinity Hall, Cambridge 1781, dn86 (Lin.), LLB1788, p89 (Nor.). R. Hungerford, Norfolk 1792-1817, R. Framingham Pigot, Norfolk 1814-29, R. Postwick, Norfolk 1817-41, R. (and patron) of Caistor w. Marketshall, Norfolk 1829 to death 22/10/1841 aged 79 [C69141. Venn corrected]

**LOVE (Edward Missenden)** Born Great Yarmouth, Norfolk 26/1/1783, s. Rev. John Love and Suannna Jane Holden. Caius, Cambridge 1800, BA1806, dn07 (Nor.), MA1809, p09 (Nor.). R. Ashby, Suffolk 1810-17, R. Blundeston w. Flixton, Suffolk 1817 and R. Somerleyton 1817 [total income in CR65 £1,063] to death 25/11/1865, leaving £10,000 [C113899] Married Great Yarmouth 28/3/1811 Charlotte Maria Fisher, many issue.

**LOVEDAY (Thomas)** Born Williamscote, Oxon. 11/2/1789, s. Rev. John Loveday and Anne Taylor Loder. Magdalen, Oxford 1806, BA1810, MA1813, dn13 (Ox.), p14 (Ox.), Fellow 1817, BD1820, etc. R. East Ilsey, Berks. 1831-66. Died Williamscote 22/8/1873, leaving £18,000 [C35294] Married Tamworth, Staffs. 28/7/1831 Mary Churton, with issue.

**LOVELL (Trefusis)** Bapt. Plymouth, Devon 14/11/1766, s. Abraham Lovell and Elizabeth Pitman. Exeter, Oxford 1796, BA1780, dn90 (Ex.), p90 (Ex.). R. Aghadoe and Duboe, Co. Derry 1796-8 and Archdeacon of Derry, R. St Luke Old Street, City of London 1813-44, V. Northampton Holy Sepulchre 1822. Died London 10/8/1844 aged 78 [C64340] Married (1) Plymouth 1781 Honor Suger (d.1783) (2) Lurgan, Co. Armagh 2/4/1802 Margaret Macan, with issue.

**LOWE (Edward Walter)** Born Southwell, Notts. 4/10/1797, s. Edward Richard Lowe and Elizabeth Mather. St John's, Cambridge 1818, BA1823, dn23 (Chester for C&L), p26 (C&L), MA1831. R. North Wingfield, Derbys. 1826 to death (London) 23/4/1861, leaving £25,000 [C18313]

**LOWE (Henry)** Bapt. Derby 31/7/1779, s. Thomas Lowe and Margaretta Snelson. Literate: dn21 (Nor.), p22 (Nor.). R. Hawnby, Yorks. 1830 to death (York) 6/11/1851 aged 72 [C135930] Married Hawerby [some say Whippingham, IoW] 21/7/1828 Susanna Lomas, with issue.

**LOWE (John, sen.)** From Ferrybridge, Yorks., s. John Lowe and Elizabeth ?Argyll. Lincoln, Oxford 1779 (aged 21), BA1782, dn82 (Salis. for Ox.), p82 (Ox.), MA 1785. V. Brotherton, Ainsty of York 1784-91-, V. Huddersfield 1784-90, PC. Wentworth, Yorks. 1798-1837, R. Tankersley, Yorks. 1803 (and Prebend of Ricall in York Minster 1831) to death. Dom. Chap. to Earl Fitzwilliam. Died 2/5/1837 aged 80 [C35292] Married York 15/6/1785 Elizabeth Jackson, w. son (below). *J.P.* Port. online.

**LOWE (John, jun.)** Bapt. Brotherton, Yorks. 3/12/1790, s. Rev. John Lowe, sen. (above) and Elizabeth Jackson. Lincoln, Oxford 1809, BA 1813, dn13 (York), p14 (York), MA1839. PC. Swinton, Wath, Yorks. 1814-44, R. Ardley, Bicester, Oxon. 1815-74, PC. Wentworth, Yorks. 1837. Died 18/3/1874. Will not traced

[C135605. YCO] Married Ardley 1/4/1815 1815 Susanna Hind (a clergy dau.), with issue.

**LOWE (Richard)** Born Derby. St John's, Cambridge 1805-6, then as a Ten Year Man 1818, p24 (Nor.), BD1830. PC. Crewkerne, Som. 1826 and V. Misterton, Som. 1826 to death (Whaplode, Lincs.) 7/8/1852 aged 75 [C18320] Married Marylebone, London 5/7/1821 Martha Conran, w. clerical s. Julius Conran Lowe.

**LOWE (Robert)** Bapt. Southwell, Notts. 27/10/1779, s. of Robert Lowe (High Sheriff of Notts.) and Ann Becher. St John's, Cambridge 1797, BA1802, dn03 (York), p06 (York), MA 1814. R. Bingham, Notts. 1810 (and Prebend of Halloughton in Southwell Collegiate Church 1834) to death 23/1/1845 aged 65 [C120134. YCO] Married Hadzor, Worcs. 1/7/1795 Ellen Pyndar (a clergy dau., Windsor, Berks.), with issue (including the (albino) politician Robert Lowe, 1st Viscount Sherbrooke, *q.v.* ODNB, etc.).

**LOWE (Samuel)** Born Cornhill, London 28/5/1776, s. Edward and Anne Lowe. Trinity, Cambridge 1793, BA1798, dn00 (York), p01 (York), then Magdalene, MA1802, Fellow 1802-14, Tutor. R. Darlaston, Staffs. 1814 to death 24/11/1834 (CCEd says 27/2/1835) [C18322. YCO] Married Nottingham? Marianne Maddock.

**LOWE (Thomas)** Born Atherton, Lancs., s. Rev. Thomas Lowe, sen. Literate: dn23 (Chester), p24 (Chester). Prebend of Chester Cathedral 1828, (first) PC. Warrington St Paul, Lancs. 1831 to death 1857 (4th q.) [C169859] Was married. Surrogate.

**LOWE (Thomas Hill Peregrine Fury)** Born Bromsgrove, Worcs. 21/12/1781, s. of Thomas Humphrey Lowe and Lucy Hill. Trinity, Oxford 1799 [Student of Lincoln's Inn 1804] BA1805, MA1818, LLD. V. Grimley w. All Hallows, Worcs. 1820-32 (res.), R. Holgate (2nd Portion or Deaconry), Shropshire 1821, R. Silvington, Shropshire 1827, Canon Residentiary of Exeter Cathedral 1832-61 (and Precentor 1832-9) , R. Exeter Holy Trinity 1837-40, Dean of Exeter 1839-61, V. Littleham w. Exmouth, Devon 1840-3. Dom. Chap. to 4th Viscount Gage 1812. Died 7/1/1861, leaving £25,000 [C121833. Boase] Married Ludlow, Shropshire 24/2/1808 Ellen Lucy Pardoe, with clerical sons George, and Noel Lowe.

**LOWNDES (Matthew)** Born Buckfastleigh, Devon 29/10/1787, s. Rev. Matthew Lowndes, sen. and Margaret Bovey. Exeter, Oxford 1804, BA1810, dn10 (Ex.), p12 (Ex.). V. Buckfastleigh 1825 (and succ. by son of same name there) to death 2/6/1856 (apoplexy) [C145454] Married Buckfastleigh 29/6/1829 Sophia Elizabeth Templer White, with clerical son Matthew Lowndes.

**LOWNDES (Robert)** From Winslow, Bucks., s. William Lowndes and Mary Goostrey (of Missenden Abbey). Magdalen Hall, Oxford 1787 (aged 18), BCL1794, dn95 (Ox.), p97 (Ox.). V. Astwood, Bucks. 1798 [blank in ERC] and R. North Crawley, Beds. 1798 [blank in ERC] to death (probably unm.) 23/9/1837 [C35301. Foster corrected] Brother below.

**LOWNDES (Thomas)** From Winslow, Bucks., s. William Lowndes and Mary Goostrey (of Missenden Abbey). Merton, Oxford 1794 (aged 18), then Magdalen 1795-1804, BA1797, dn98 (Ox.), p99 (Ox.), MA1800, Fellow 1804-24, BD1807, etc. V. East Worldham, Hants. 1823 and PC. West Tisted, Hants. 1823 to death 19/4/1860, leaving £12,000 [C35302] Brother above.

**LOWRY (James)** From Bucks. Queens', Cambridge 1814, dn18 (Ely), BA1819, p21 (Lin. for Ely). R. Waddesdon (3rd Portion), Bucks. 1823 to death (Huntingdon, a widower) 20/6/1859, leaving under £450 [C69848]

**LOWRY (Thomas)** Born Carlisle, s. Richard and Jane Lowry. St John's, Cambridge 1782, BA1786, dn89 (Car.), p89 (Car.), MA1789, DD 1815. V. and R. Crosby on Eden, Cumberland 1791 and V. and R. Ousby, Cumberland 1807 (non-res.) to death 3/1/1833 (CCEd says 26/1/1833) [C6146. Platt] Married Workington, Cumberland 14/1/1799 Barbara Stamper, with clerical son. Mayor of Carlisle 1804-5.

**LOWRY (Thomas [Barnes])** Bapt. Stanwix, Cumberland 4/7/1802, s. William Lowry and Jane Barnes. Literate: dn25 (York for Car.), p26 (Car.). PC. Watermillock, Penrith, Cumberland 1826 (with S/M Watermillock 1825-40, and living at Watermillock House) to death 14/5/1876 aged 74, leaving £3,000 [C6147. YCO. Platt] [Married (1) Stanwix, Cumberland

20/11/1821 Ann Noble Scurrah (d.1866), with clerical son (2) Longtown, Cumberland 1870 (1st q.) Elizabeth Jefferson (w).

**LOWTHER (Gorges Paulin)** Born Lyons, France 2/2/1792 (a British subject), s. Gorges [*sic*] Lowther (Clifton, Bristol) and Julia Tanhourdin Huntingford. St Mary Hall, Oxford 1812, BA1815, MA1823. R. Barton Blount, Derbys. 1821. R. Orcheston St George, Wilts. 1830-81, RD1832, Prebend of Salisbury Cathedral 1841 to death. Dom. Chap. to Earl of Lonsdale. Proctor in Convocation for the Diocese of Salisbury from 1835. Died 25/4/1881, leaving £1,500 [C18326] Married East Teignmouth, Devon 22/8/1815 Elizabeth Windsor, with clerical son.

**LOWTHER (Henry)** Born Kensington, London 1787, s. Col. James Lowther, *M.P.*, and Mary Forsyth Codrington. Trinity, Cambridge 1806, BA1810, dn11 (Car.), p12 (Car.), MA 1813. R. Lowther, Cumberland 1812-28, R. Moresby, Cumberland 1821-13, R. Distington, Cumberland 1813-14, R. Bolton, Cumberland 1822-72. Dom. Chap. to Mary, Countess of Lowther 1813. Died Cannes (where he wintered) 6/2/1874 aged 86, leaving £2,000 [C6151. Platt] Married Whitehaven, Cumberland 14/9/1813 Eleanor How Younger, with issue. *J.P.* 'A very red and somewhat passionate old gentleman.'

**LOWTHER (Joseph)** Bapt. Cumberland 28/4/1798. Literate: dn21 (Chester), p22 (Chester). PC. Embleton, Cumberland 1822-43, PC. Brigham, Cumberland 1834. Died 2/3/1843 aged 44 ('after a few weeks illness') [C169863] Married Cockermouth, Cumberland 1824 Juliana Jefferson, with issue.

**LOWTHER (Richard)** Bapt. Dalton, Lancs. 18/3/1792, s. Richard and Elizabeth Lowther. Literate: dn17 (York), p18 (York). PC. Muker, Yorks. 1827 (and S/M 1846) to death 30/8/1863, leaving £1,500 [C135606. YCO] Married Grinton, Yorks. 8/7/1845 Susan Garth, with issue.

**LOWTHER (Robert)** Bapt. Kirk Bampton, Cumberland 9/10/1773, s. Robert and Mary Lowther. Literate: dn97 (Car. for Durham), p98 (Durham). PC. Birtley, Northumberland 1805 (and Minor Canon of Durham Cathedral) to death 4/8/1853 aged 79 [C6152]

**LOWTHIAN (John)** Born Sebergham, Cumberland, s. of Isaac Lowthian (a tailor). Trinity, Cambridge 1792 (aged 20), BA1797, Fellow 1799, MA1800, dn06 (Peterb.), Ass. Tutor 1806-13, p07 (Ely). V. Kellington, Yorks. 1818 to death 24/2/1840 [C100115] Married Sebergham 15/10/1818 Jane Wallas, with clerical son.

**LOWTHIAN (Joseph)** Bapt. Kirkoswald, Cumberland 11/3/1759, s. John Lowthian [*pleb*] and Mary Folder. Queen's, Oxford 1778, BA 1782, dn82 (Ox.), p83 (Ox.), MA1793. V. New Windsor, Berks. 1800 and R. Thatcham, Berks. 1804 to death there 23/2/1842 [C35306] Married Ipswich, Suffolk 1796 Elizabeth Layton (a clergy dau.), with issue.

**LOXHAM (Richard)** Born Stickney, Lincs., s. Rev. Richard Loxham, sen. and Elizabeth Nundy. Jesus, Cambridge 1779, BA1783, dn84 (Lin.), p86 (Chester). PC. Liverpool St John's the Baptist 1815-43 and R. Halsall, Lancs. [net income £3,051] 1816 to (burial) 17/5/1843 aged 82 [C69852] Married Liverpool 2/4/1793 Ann Preston.

**LUBBOCK (John)** Bapt. Norwich 26/1/1800, s. Richard Lubbock (physician) and Bridget Postle. Caius, Cambridge 1819, dn23 (Nor.), BA1824, p25 (Nor.), MA1827. V. Potter Heigham, Norfolk 1830-4, V. Scottow and Lelaugh, Norfolk 1834 to death (Alysham, Norfolk) 18/5/1857 [C113903] Married by 1829 Marianne L'Oste, and had issue.

**LUCAS (George)** Born Bury St Edmunds 11/8/1768, s. Rev. Gibson Lucas (R. Filby, Norfolk) and Mary Anne Ward. Caius, Cambridge 1785, BA1790, dn90 (Nor.), p01 (Nor.). R. and V. Catfield, Norfolk (2 Medieties) 1801-33 and R. Billockby, Norfolk 1820 to death 8/8/1833 (CCEd says 22/8/1833) [C113906] Married Ormesby, Norfolk 9/2/1809 Mrs Mary Anne (Doughty) Montague (and living at her house there). Brothers Gibson, and Richard, and step-brother William, all below.

**LUCAS (Gibson)** Born Bury St Edmunds 16/2/1767, s. Rev. Gibson Lucas, sen. (R. Filby, Norfolk) and Mary Anne Ward. Pembroke, Cambridge 1785, BA1790, dn90 (Nor.), p92 (Nor.). V. Billockby, Norfolk 1792-1820, R. (and patron) of Stokesby w. Herringby, Norfolk 1795 and R. Filby 1820-48 to death 8/1/1848 [C113907] Married Ormesby, Norfolk 15/1/1796 Mary Anne Wymberley Salmon (a clergy dau., Caistor, Norfolk), with clerical sons William (below) and Charles Lucas. Brothers George and Richard, and step-brother Willam, below.

**LUCAS (Richard)** Born Bury St Edmunds, Suffolk, s. Rev. Gibson Lucas and Mary Anne Ward. Caius, Cambridge 1786 (aged 17), BA 1791, Fellow 1791, MA1794, etc., dn04 (Nor.), p04 (Nor.). V. Oxborough w. Foulden, Norfolk 1811 to death (unmarried) 11/12/1847 [C113908] Brothers George, and Gibson (above), and step-brother William (below).

**LUCAS (Richard)** Born Cardigan, s. Rev. William Lucas. Worcester, Oxford 1788 (aged 17), BA1792, dn93 (Heref.), p95 (Ox.), MA 1795. R. Little Birch, Heref. 1810 to death 9/3/1846 [C35310]

**LUCAS (Richard)** Bapt. Casterton, Rutland 19/9/1787, s. Rev. Richard, sen. and Elizabeth Lucas. St John's, Cambridge 1804, then Clare 1805, BA1809, dn11 (Lin. for Peterb.), p11 (Ely for Peterb.), MA1812. R. (and patron) of Edith Weston, Rutland 1827 to death 13/2/1846 [C69859] Married Wensley, Yorks. 28/10/1819 Mary Dorothy Costobadie.

**LUCAS (St John Wells)** Born Alford, Lincs., s. Richard Lucas and Sarah Wells. [In army 1804-27; wounded and taken prisoner at Battle of Roleia (now Rolica), Portugal 1808]. Downing, Cambridge 1823 (aged 40), dn27 (Lin.), BA1828, p29 (Lin.), MA1831, Chap. Downing in 1840. V. Arrington, Cambs. (sequestrator) 1832-4, R. and V. Astwick w. Arlesley, Beds. 1833, R. East Hatley and V. Tadlow, Cambs. 1840 to death 4/7/1853 [C69860]

**LUCAS (Thomas Burton)** Born Hasland, Derbys. 26/6/1790, s. Bernard Lucas and Esther Lax. St John's, Cambridge 1807, BA1812, dn13 (Chester for C&L), p14 (C&L), MA1816. R. Sawtry All Saints, Hunts. 1823-34. Died 24/4/1866, living at Barton under Needwood, Staffs. 1852-36, then near Chesterfield [C18330] Married Newcastle upon Tyne 7/6/1834 Anne Cram.

**LUCAS (William)** Born Bury St Edmunds 12/5/1784, s. Rev. Gibson Lucas and Charlotte Pearce Nelson. Caius, Cambridge 1800, BA 1805, Fellow 1805, MA1808, dn08 (B&W), p09 (B&W). Prebend of Wedmore 11 in Wells Cathedral 1815-59, R. (and patron) of Burgh St Margaret and St Mary, Norfolk 1816-59, R. Billocksby, Norfolk 1833 to death (Padding-ton, London) 28/2/1859, leaving £25,000 [C46491] Clerical sons William Nelson, and Charles John; step-brothers George, Gibson, and Richard, above.

**LUCY (John)** Bapt. Charlecote, Warwicks. 20/8/1790, s. Rev. John Lucy, sen. (born Hammond) and Maria Lane. Trinity, Cambridge 1810, BA1814, dn14, MA1819, p15. R. Hampton Lucy (o/w Bishop's Lucy), Warwicks. 1815 [income £1,147] and V. Charlecote 1823 to death 14/10/1874, leaving £70,000 [C121834 has the father's date of death] J.P. Warwicks. Port. online.

**LUDBEY (Thomas)** Born Chalfont St Peter, Bucks. 25/1/1785, s. Thomas Ludbey and Jane Evans. St John's, Cambridge 1802, BA1806, dn08 (Ely), MA1809, p09 (Ely). R. Cranham (o/w Bishop Ockendon), Essex 1818 to death 18/5/1859, leaving £20,000 [C95362] Married Battersea, Surrey 3/9/1806 Anna Maria Leech, and clerical son Thomas Ludbey.

**LUDERS (Alexander)** Bapt. Bloomsbury, London 13/2/1789, s. Alexander Luders (legal writer, *q.v.* ODNB) and Sarah Seawell. BNC, Oxford 1806 (aged 17), BA1810, MA1815. R. Birlingham w. Nafford, Worcs. 1814-29, R. Woolston, Glos. 1829 to death 24/3/1851 [C121835] Married Hadzor, Worcs. 25/2/1812 Penelope Bradstock, with issue.

**LUGGER (John Lloyd)** Bapt. Stoke Damerel, Devon 30/11/1785, s. Joseph Lugger and Elizabeth Tom. Christ's, Cambridge 1821, SCL, dn24 (Nor.), p24 (Nor.), LLB1828. PC. Bilton w. High Harrogate, Yorks. 1825 (only), R. Tregony w. St Cuby, Cornwall 1831 to death 7/8/1847 aged 61 [C41556] Married East Stonehouse, Devon 5/4/1825 Mary Williams.

**LUKE (Francis Vyvyan)** Bapt. Helston, Cornwall 17/11/1794, s. Stephen Luke (Exeter physician) and Harriet Walter Vyvyan. Jesus, Cam-bridge 1812, dn17 (London), BA1818, p18 (London), MA1826. R. Frinton (on Sea), Essex 1818 [pop. 30] to death (Jersey) 29/8/1875, leaving £361-14s.-0d. [C53340] Married Marnhull, Dorset 31/12/1829 Agnes Ramsden (a clergy dau.), 'with a son now residing in Madras'.

**LUKIN (John)** Bapt. Saltash, Cornwall 10/6/1782, s. Rev. George William Lukin (later

Dean of Wells) and Catherine Susanne Doughty. Oriel, Oxford 1801, BA1804, dn05 (B&W for Win.), p06 (Nor. for Win.), MA 1807. Prebend of Combe 5th in Wells Cathedral 1808-46, V. Combe St Nicholas, Som. 1809-10, V. Nursling, Hants. 1809, again 1822, R. Chilton, Suffolk 1822. Died Nursling 15/12/1846 [C46505] Married (1) Etchingham, Sussex 18/12/1810 Emma Easton Gimmer (d.1813), 1 dau. (2) Catherine Ann Wynell-Mayow (d.1823), 3 ch. (3) Nursling 10/6/1825 Elizabeth Timson (d.1833), 5 further ch. (4) Kingston on Thames, Surrey 28/7/1836 Lucy Elizabeth Byng (dau. 5th Viscount Torrington).

**LUMLEY (Benjamin)** Born Stockton on Tees 27/5/1774, s. Benjamin Lumley and Esther Ferrand. Jesus, Cambridge 1792, BA1796, dn97 (York), p98 (York), MA1799, Fellow 1801-7. R. Dalby, Yorks. 1806-48 and V. Sheriff Hutton, Yorks. 1824 to death (Leamington, Warwicks.) 21/8/1848 aged 74 [C100116. YCO] Married Pontefract, Yorks. 2/8/1810 Eleanor Bennett, with issue.

**LUNDY (Francis)** Born Lockington, Beverley, Yorks. 10/8/1780, s. Rev. Francis Lundy, sen. and Elizabeth Barber. University, Oxford 1798, BA1802, dn03 (York), p04 (York), MA1805. V. (and patron) of Lockington 1817-53 and PC. Kilnwick (on the Wolds), Yorks. 1817 to death 21/11/1853 [C102272. YCO] Married Full Sutton, Yorks. 27/5/1813 Agnes Elizabeth Rudd, with issue.

**LUNN (Francis)** Born Brasted, Kent 14/10/1795, s. Griggs and Maria Lunn. St John's, Cambridge 1814, BA1817, dn20 (Glos. for London), p20 (Chester for London), MA 1821. V. Butleigh, Som. 1828 to death 4/8/1839 [C41559] Married Wells 5/12/1837 Elizabeth Periam Hood. *F.R.S.* (1819) for his work in experimental chemistry.

**LUNN (Matthew [Florence])** Bapt. Norton, Worcs. 19/4/1780, s. Robert Lunn [*pleb*] and Mary Rock. Magdalen Hall, Oxford 1799, BA 1807, dn97 (C&L), MA1810. Minor Canon of Worcester Cathedral 1814, R. Worcester St Peter the Great 1815-16 (res.), V. Kempsey, Worcs. 1816 to death (unm.) 9/3/1852 [C18337]

**LUPTON (James)** Born York 1800, s. James Lupton [*pleb*] and Sarah Watts. Christ Church, Oxford 1819, BA1823, dn23 (Ox.), Chaplain 1823-7, p24 (Ox.), New College, Chaplain 1823-29, MA1825. V. Black Bourton, Oxon. 1827-73, Minor (8th) Canon of St Paul's Cathedral, London 1829-73 and of Westminster Abbey 1829-73, V. St Michael Queenhithe w. Holy Trinity the Less, City of London 1832 to death 21/12/1873, leaving £5,000 [C35313] Married Oxford 1827 Ann Dry, w. issue. 'Attends to his parish very well' (Wilberforce).

**LUPTON (John)** Born Leeds 24/6/1764, s. Rev. William Lupton and Frances Lowry. Trinity, Cambridge 1781, BA1786, dn87 (York for Cant.), p88 (Lin. for Cant.), MA1789. R. Lewes St Thomas at Cliffe, Sussex 1807-41, V. Ulting Essex 1823-40, R. Ovingdean, Sussex 1841 to death 12/2/1844 [C64350. YCO] Married Covent Garden, London 7/10/1790 Philadelphia Davies, with issue.

**LUSCOMBE (Richard James)** Born Totnes, Devon 4/1/1781, s. Richard Luscombe and Mary Cuming. St Mary Hall, Oxford 1799, migrated to Emmanuel, Cambridge 1802, SCL, dn03 (B&W), LLB1815. V. (and patron) of Moorlinch w. Stawell and Sutton Mallet, Som. 1818-47, PC. Chilton-super-Polden, Som. w. PC. Edington, Som. 1835. Died Bath 1/6/1865, leaving £5,000 [C41561] Married Plymouth 30/10/1806 Phillis King, with clerical son of the father's name at Moorlinch.

**LUTTRELL (Alexander Fownes)** Born Dunster Castle, Dunster, Somerset, s. of John Fownes Luttrell, *M.P.*, and Mary Drewe. Exeter, Oxford 1812 (aged 18), dn16 (B&W), SCL1817, p17 (B&W). R. (and patron) of East Quantoxhead, Som. 1818 to death 12/10/1888 aged 95, leaving £67,325-18s-2d. [C41565. Boase] Married Westminster, London 1824 Jane Leader, with clerical son. Note in Venn another family member of this name the R. East Quantoxhead until 1816. Brother Thomas, below.

**LUTTRELL (Alexander Henry Fownes)** Son Rev. Alexander Fownes Luttrell (above) and Jane Leader. Pembroke, Cambridge 1827, BA 1831, dn31 (B&W), p32 (B&W). V. Minehead, Som. 1832 to death 20/2/1899 aged 90, leaving £15,075-1s-1d. [C41564] Married Moorlinch, Devon 3/1/1837 Margaret Charlotte Ann Jeremy (a clergy dau.), and had issue.

**LUTTRELL (Thomas Fownes)** Born Dunster Castle, Dunster, Som., s. John Fownes Luttrell, *M.P.*, and Mary Drewe. Exeter, Oxford

1814 (aged 19), BA1817, dn17 (B&W), p19 (Ely for B&W). PC. Dunster 1821, V. Minehead, Som. 1821-32, V. Carhampton, Som. 1832. Died Dunster 17/12/1871 aged 77, leaving £50,000 [C41566] Brother Alexander Fownes, above.

**LUXMOORE (Charles Scott)** Bapt. Eton, Bucks. 5/11/1791, s. Rt. Rev. John Luxmoore (Bishop of Hereford, then of St Asaph) and Elizabeth Barnard. St John's, Cambridge 1811, BA1815, dn15 (Heref.), p15 (Heref.), MA1818. (Sinecure R. Bromyard (2nd Portion, Heref. 1814-54), Prebend of Inkberrow in Hereford Cathedral 1815-54, R. Cradley, Heref. 1815-54, (Sinecure R. Darowen, Montgomery. 1819-54), Cursal Canon of Adam Rekensall in St Asaph's Cathedral 1816, then of Melfod 1819 (and Chancellor 1826), then Dean of St Asaph's 1826 to Dom. Chap. to his father the Bishop 1815. Died Cradley)27/4/1854 [C112631. ODNB. Boase] Married 10/9/1829 Catherine Nicoll (dau. of the Dean of Arches, Glamorgan), with issue. 'The death of the Dean of St Asaph removes another gigantic pluralist. The late Dean held, beside his deanery, which was worth £1200 per annum, the rectory of Cradley, worth £1000 per annum, a sinecure rectory at Bromyard, £200 per annum, another of the same value at Darowen, the Chancellorship of the Cathedral and a Canonry of Hereford' (*The Clerical J*. 1854).

**LUXMOORE (Coryndon)** Bapt. Okehampton, Devon 23/4/1760, s. Henry (surgeon) and Grace Luxmoore. St John's, Cambridge 1778, BA1782, Fellow 1784-8, MA1785, dn86 (Ex.), p86 (Ex.). R. Bridestowe, Devon 1786 and R. Lanteglos by Camelford, Cornwall 1794 to death. Dom. Chap. to 2nd Earl Spencer 1824. Died 10/8/1845 [C145461] Married Plymouth 31/7/1792 Caroline Putt, with clerical son, below.

**LUXMOORE (Henry)** Bapt. 11/3/1794, s. Rev. Coryndon Luxmoore (above) and Caroline Putt. St John's, Cambridge 1812, BA1816, dn17 (St Asaph), p18 (St Asaph), MA1820. V. Barnstaple, Devon 1820-60, V. Everdon, Northants. 1860 to death. Dom. Chap. to 6th Marquess of Lothian 1820. Died 15/6/1876 aged 82 [C112633] Married Barnstaple, Devon 7/6/1838 Mary Jane, dau. of Admiral Noble, with issue.

**LUXTON (John)** Bapt. Witheridge, Devon 28/12/1768, s. George and Elizabeth Luxton. St Mary Hall, Oxford 1788, BA1791, dn92 (C&L for Ex.), p93 (Ex.). PC. (and patron) of Brushford, Devon 1793 to death 1836 [C18339]

**LYALL (William Rowe)** Born London 11/2/1788, s. John Lyall (merchant and shipowner) and Jane Comyn. Trinity, Cambridge 1804, BA1810, dn12 (Win.), p14 (Glos. for Win.), MA1816. R. Weeley, Essex 1823-33, Archdeacon of Colchester 1824-41, R. Fairstead, Essex 1827-33, R. Hadleigh, Suffolk 1833-42, Archdeacon of Maidstone (w. Canon of 9th Prebend in Canterbury Cathedral) 1841-45, R. Great Chart, Kent 1842-52, Dean of Canterbury 1841 to death. Dom. Chap. to Bishop of London, then Archbishop of Canterbury 1822; Chap. St Thomas' Hospital London 1817. Died 17/2/1857 [C82194. ODNB. Boase. C. Dewey, *The passing of Barchester* (1991) is almost entirely concerned with the inter-relation of the Dean's extended family of eight clergy] Married Toxteth Park, Liverpool 2/10/1817 Catharine Brandreth (dau. of a Liverpool doctor). Edited the *British Critic* 1816-7, and re-edited the *Encyclopedia Metropolitana* 1820.

**LYE (Edward Barton)** From Warminster, Wilts., s. George Lye. Exeter, Oxford 1813 (aged 18), BA1816, dn17 (Salis.), p19 (Salis.), MA1822. V. Raunds, Northants. 1820 to death 6/11/1854 [C95365] Married Bratton, Wilts. Sophia Whitaker.

**LYNE (Charles Philip)** Born West Marden, Sussex, s. Philip Lyne and Sarah Poole. Queen's, Oxford 1803 (aged 17), BA1808. MA 1826. V. East Marden 1817, R. West Thorney, Sussex 1833 to death. Buried 1/6/ 1869. No will traced [C64355] Married Westbourne, Sussex 21/4/1817 Maria Amy Harriet Bean, with issue.

**LYNE (Richard)** Bapt. St Ives, Cornwall 22/12/1779, s. Rev. John Lyne (V. Liskeard, Cornwall) and Elizabeth Cowling. Exeter, Oxford 1779, BA1783, dn83 (Ex), p85 (Ex.). S/M Liskeard G/S 1785; R. St Petroc Minor (o/w Little Petherick), Cornwall 1812 to death 1834 [C145167]

**LYNES (John)** Born Kirkby Moorside, Leics. 24/2/1782, s. John Lynes (of Corley, Warwicks. and Kirkby Mallory) and Sarah Webb. Trinity Hall, Cambridge 1806, dn09 (Win.), p10 (Win.), LLB1812. R. (and patron) of Elmley Lovett, Worcs. 1822-35, PC. Hatton, Warwicks. at death 22/7/1843, living at Tooley Park, Leics.

[C82202] Married Hatton, Warwicks. 17/9/1822 Caroline Sobieski Wynne (of Corwen, Denbigh), with issue. *J.P.* Worcs.

**LYNN (James)** Born Rochester, Kent (bapt. Aylesbury, Bucks. 29/9/1776), s. John [*pleb*] and Lydia Lynn. Wadham, Oxford 1794, BA 1799, MA1803, incorporated at Cambridge MA1827. Minor Canon of Rochester Cathedral 1803-14, R. Strood, Kent 1805-20, R. Sebergham, Cumberland 1811-20, R. Caldbeck, Cumberland 1814-55, V. Crosthwaite, Cumberland 1820 to death. Dom. Chap. to 1st Marquess of Westminster 1809; and to Bishop of Carlisle 1820. Died (Hampstead, London) 1/2/1855 aged 78 [C1438. Platt] Married London 24/1/1805 Charlotte Alicia Goodenough (dau. of Bishop of Carlisle), 12 ch. (including clerical, and also Mrs Lynn Linton, novelist and feminist); lived at Gads Hill, Rochester 'for about thirty years', his dau. selling the property to Charles Dickens.

**LYON (James)** Born Appleton Hall, Warrington, Lancs. 26/10/1757, s. Matthew Lyon and Ellen Fairclough. BNC, Oxford 1776, BA1780, dn81 (Ox. for Chester), p81 (Chester), MA1783. R. Prestwich, Lancs. [net income £1,230] (and Public Preacher in the Diocese of Chester) 1783 to death. Dom. Chap. to 2nd Earl Grosvenor 1809. Died 13/8/1836 [C169869] Married Prestwich 7/10/1782 Mary Radcliffe, w. clerical son (below).

**LYON (James Radcliffe)** Born Preston, Lancs. 11/7/1785, s. Rev. James Lyon (above) and Mary Radcliffe. BNC, Oxford 1804, BA 1808, dn08 (Chester), p10 (Chester), MA1811. PC. Ringley, Prestwich, Lancs. 1817 and R. Pulford, Cheshire 1818 to death 6/12/1869 aged 84, leaving £20,000 [C169870] Married Lostock, Lancs. 18/5/1814 Frances Clayton, w. clerical son.

**LYS (John Thomas)** Bapt. Guildford, Surrey 26/4/1792, s. James Lys and Martha Thomas. Exeter, Oxford 1809, BA1813, Fellow 1813-71, dn15 (Ox.), p15 (Ox.), MA1816, BD1826. V. Merton, Oxon. 1826-33, V. Waterperry, Oxon 1833. Died 4/10/1871, leaving £16,000 [C35319]

**LYSONS (Daniel)** Born Rodmarton, Glos. 28/4/1762, s. Rev. Samuel Lysons and Mary Peach. St Mary Hall, Oxford 1779, BA1782, dn84 (Glos.), MA1785, p86 (Glos.). R. (and patron) of Rodmarton 1804 to death. Dom. Chap. to Horace Walpole at Strawberry Hill. Died 3/1/1834, living at Hempsted Court, Glos. [C157711. ODNB] Married (1) Bath 12/5/1801 Sarah Carteret Hardy (a military dau., she d.1808), with issue (2) Bath 2/7/1813 Josepha Catherine Susannah Gilbert-Cooper, with further issue. The famous topographical writer. *F.R.S.* (1797).

**LYTE (Henry Francis)** Born Ednam, Kelso, Scotland 1/6/1793, s. of Capt. Thomas Mohum Lyte ('an itinerant soldier') and Anna Maria Oliver. TCD1809, BA1814, dn14, MA1820, incorporated at Oxford 1834. PC. Lower Brixham, Devon 1826 to death (Nice, France) 20/11/1847 [C145472. ODNB. Al.Dub. B.G. Skinner, *Henry Francis Lyte: Brixham's poet and priest* (Exeter, 1974)] Married Bath 21/1/1818 Anne Maria Maxwell (an Irish clergy dau.), and had issue. Hymn writer, including 'Abide with me'.

**MABERLY (Charles [Housley])** Born London, s. John Maberly. TCD1820 (aged 21), dn24 (Win.), BA1825, p25 (Win.), MA1830. PC. Owslebury Chapel, Twyford, Hants. 1832-53. Died 1852 (2nd q.) [C82207. Al.Dub.] Wife Charlotte, 8 ch.

**MACAULAY (John)** Bapt. Clapham, Surrey 20/12/1805, s. Zachary Macaulay (the anti-slaver and reformer, *q.v.* ODNB) and Selina Mills. Queens', Cambridge 1825, then Peterhouse 1827, BA1829, dn30 (Chester), p30 (Chester), MA1856. R. Pwllcrochan, Pembroke 1832, V. Loppington, Shropshire [blank in ERC] 1832-41, V. Bovey Tracey, Devon 1842-9, R. Aldingham and PC. Dendron, Lancs. 1849 [income in CR65 £1,100] (and Hon. Canon of Carlisle Cathedral 1867) to death 5/4/1874, leaving £5,000 [C18357] Married Malpas, Cheshire 30/12/1812 Jane Emma Large (w), and issue. Brother of Thomas Babington Macaulay, *M.P.* Surrogate.

**MacBEAN (William)** Born St Ann, Jamaica 4/10/1797, s. William MacBean and Mary Brady Barnett. Christ Church, Oxford 1817, BA1823, MA1823, p23 (Ex.). R. Peter Tavy, Devon 1825 [blank in ERC] to death 13/7/1855 [C145680] Married Kildale, Yorks. 2/9/1823 his first cousin Frances Bell, with issue.

**McCARTHY (Charles)** From Westminster, London, s. Charles McCarthy. Exeter, Oxford 1788 (aged 19), BA1792, dn92 (London), p92 (London). V. Lyminster, Sussex 1815-23 (res.), V. Madehurst, Sussex 1815, V. Harlton, Cambs. 1824-[39]. Buried 1Holborn, London 5/5/1839 aged 72 [C64528]

**McCREIGHT (William Walkinshaw)** Born Armagh, Ireland. [NiVoF] PC. Huddersfield All Saints, Paddock, Yorks. 1830, V. Little Horwood, Bucks. 1834, V. Winslow, Bucks. in 1846 and at death (Worthing, Sussex) 16/10/1871 aged 70, leaving £18,000 [C120516 as Mc Creight] Wife Catherine Puckle, and issue.

**MacDONALD (Alexander)** Born Glasgow, s. Lachlan Macdonald (merchant). St John's Cambridge 1823 (a Ten Year Man), dn24 (Lin.), p25 (Lin.), re-adm. 1830, then Queens' 1833, BD1834. V. Cotterstock w. Glapthorne, Northants. 1831 to death 23/6/1853 [C69877] Wife (2?) Louisa.

**MacDONALD (William)** Born Carriden, Linlithgow 10/8/1783, s. John Macdonald and Cecilia Maria Douglas Kinnear. Balliol, Oxford 1801, BA1805. dn06 (Salis.), MA1807, p07 (Salis.). Prebend of Bitton in Salisbury Cathedral 1807-62 (Canon Residentiary 1823-62), V. Minety, Wilts. 1807-10, V. Broad Hinton, Wilts. 1807-15, V. Cricklade St Sampson, Wilts. 1809-17, V. Chitterne, Wilts. 1812, RD of Avebury w. Winterbourne Monkton, Wilts. 1812, V. Bitton, Glos. 1817-23, PC. Kingswood, Bitton, Glos. 1822, Archdeacon of Wiltshire 1828-62, V. Bishops Cannings, Wilts. 1815 to death 24/6/1862, leaving £12,000. Dom. Chap. to 17th Lord Sinclair 1809-17 [C78657. Boase] Married (1) Chresberry, Wilts. 16/6/1810 Frances Goodman (d.1838), with issue (2) St James, Westminster, London 20/7/1847 Frances Laura Dawson, with further issue.

**MacDONOGH, MacDONOUGH (Terence Michael)** Born Falmouth, Cornwall 24/5/1785, s. Capt. Michael Terence MacDonough and Patty Bell. Queens', Cambridge 1826 (a Ten Year Man), dn27 (Llandaff), p27 (Llandaff). PC. Bransgore, Hants. 1830-67, R. Dengie, Essex 1867 to death (Christchurch, Hants.) 28/7/1876, leaving £450 [C4305]

**McDOUALL (William)** Born 29/4/1775, s. John McDouall (Glasgow merchant and brother of 5th Earl of Dumfries) and Mary Isabel MacCulloch. Glasgow University 1787-1791, then Snell Exhibitioner Balliol, Oxford 1791, BA1795, MA1798, dn98 (C&L), p99 (C&L). R. Ashby de la Zouche, Leics. 1799-1827, PC. Smisby, Derbys. 1812-28, V. Luton, Beds. 1827, 2nd Canon of Peterborough Cathedral 1831 to death. Chap. in Ordinary 1809. Died Copt Hall, Luton, Beds. 15/12/1849 [C18359 has wrong death date. Snell] Married Uphemia Gaudin (d.1824), w. clerical sons Patrick George, and William Sutherland.

**McEVOY (John Nesbitt)** Literate: dn79 (London), p85 (Wor.), MA (so a Ten Year Man?). V. Kington, Worcs. 1787, V. Kineton Worcs. 1787-1834, V. Butler's Marston, Worcs. 1789 to death 15/2/1834 (CCEd thus) [C121839 as Mac Evoy and says Magdalen Hall, Oxford but NiF - who has yet another man, probably a son] Married (1) Juliana -- (d.1786) (2) St Pancras, London 30/11/1814 Ann Hewlett (d.1821).

**MacFARLAN (George)** Bapt. Richmond, Yorks. 1/2/1780, s. of Philip MacFarlan (attorney). Trinity, Cambridge 1798, BA1802, Fellow 1804-23, MA1805, dn08 (York), p09 (York). V. Arrington, Cambs. 1813, V. Shudy Camps, Cambs. 1823, V. Gainford, Co. Durham 1824 to death 18/7/1862 aged 82, leaving £8,000 [C109835. YCO] Married Bishopwearmouth, Co. Durham 21/2/1832 Emma Mary Bussell, with issue.

**McGRATH (Henry [Walter])** Born Dublin 1803, s. Nicholas M'Grath. TCD, BA1825, dn29, p29, MA1830. PC. Salmlesbury, Lancs. 1830-2, PC. Walton le Dale, Preston, Lancs. 1832-7, R. Manchester St Ann 1837-52, (first) R. Kersal Moor, Manchester 1852-65, Hon. Canon of Manchester Cathedral 1858 (but lived at Torquay 1878) to death (Harrogate, Yorks.) 17/7/1884 aged 81, leaving £29,841-4s-5d. [C169985. Boase. Not in Al.Dub.] Married Walton 6/6/1836 Frances Jane Swainson, with issue.

**McGUIRE (Thomas William)** Peterhouse, Cambridge 1807, BA1811, dn11 (Glos.), p12 (Glos.). R. Deptford St Paul, Kent 1819 to death 5/12/1833 aged 44 (CCEd says 6/3/1834), 'after a protracted illness of several years' [C361. Venn as McGwire]

**MACHELL (James)** Born Colton, Lancs. 6/2/1803, s. James Penny Machell and Ann Penny. BNC, Oxford 1821, BA1827, dn27 (Chester), p29 (Chester), MA1829. (first) PC. Haverthwaite, Lancs. 1830, PC. Egton cum Newland, Lancs. 1833. Died unmarried Penny Bridge Hall, Ulverston, Lancs. 14/5/1864, leaving £18,000 [C169872]

**MACK (William Bumpstead)** From Norfolk, s. Rev. William Mack. Corpus Christi, Cambridge 1818, BA1823, dn23 (Bristol), p24 (Bristol). R. Horham, Suffolk 1829 to death 1850 (4th q.), living at Metfield, Suffolk [C53352] Married Gorleston, Suffolk 25 or 29/3/1825 Sarah Warner.

**MACKENZIE (Charles)** Born 28/2/1807, s. John Mackenzie (of Torridon, Isle of Skye and Welwyn, Herts.) and Anne Isabella Van Dam. Pembroke, Oxford 1825, BA1828, dn30 (Salis.), MA1831, p31 (Salis.). H/M St Olave's G/S, Southwark, Surrey 1832-55; Curate Colnbrook Chapel, Horton, Bucks. 1834, V. St Helen Bishopsgate, City of London 1836-46, R. St Benet Gracechurch, City of London 1846-66, Principal of Westbourne College 1855-64, Prebend of Hoxton in St Paul's Cathedral 1852, R. All Hallows Lombard Street, City of London 1867 to death 11/4/1888 aged 81, leaving £5,738-15s-4d. [C69881] Married 9/7/1832 Henrietta Simonds, with issue.

**MACKENZIE (William)** King's College Aberdeen, MA, dn82 (Chester for Durham), p82 (Nor. for Durham). R. South Collingham, Notts. 1791-4, R. Smarden, Kent 1793-1821 (res.), (Sinecure R. 1821) and V. Burwash, Sussex 1824, R. Hascombe, Surrey 1824-35. Dom. Chap to Mary, Baroness Seaforth 1817. Died 4/6/1840 aged 82 [C108200] Wife Christian, and 2 dau. (died as infants).

**MACKERETH (Charles)** Bapt. Thornton le Dale, Yorks. 12/8/1794, s. Rev. Michael Mackereth and Elizabeth Scott. Literate: dn17 (York), p18 (York). V. Middleton, Helmsley, Yorks. 1829-68, Chap. of the Donative of Old Byland, Yorks. 1829-66, Inc. Newton upon Radcliffe, Yorks. at time of death (Pickering, Yorks.) 18/4/1871 aged 76, leaving under £200 [C135614. YCO. CR65 as Mackerith] Married York 9/6/1823 Ellen Ward (w), w. issue. Brother below.

**MACKERETH (George)** Bapt. Thornton le Dale, Yorks. 24/6/1792, s. Rev. Michael Mackereth and Elizabeth Scott. Literate: dn15 (York), p16 (York). V. Bilton in Ainsty, York 1831 (non-res.) to death. Examining Chap. to Bishop of Quebec 1836-58, and the same Bishop's Official and Ecclesiastical Commissary 1843-58. Died (Whitby, Yorks.) 20/2/1866 aged 74, leaving £1,000 [C135615. YCO] Married Sculcoates, Hull 2/2/1825 Maria Hemsworth, with issue. Brother above. An arresting oil painting and a good late photograph online.

**MACKERETH (John)** Bapt. Grasmere, Westmorland 1/6/1762, s. Thomas Mackereth and Mary Squire. Literate: dn87 (Car.), p88 (Car.). PC. Ottringham, Yorks. 1811 to death (living at Ottringham Hall). Probate granted 14/4/1848 [C6160] Married 28/12/1786 Ann Wilson, with clerical son Miles Wilson Mackereth in the same parish.

**MACKERETH (Thomas)** Born Kendal, Westmorland. Literate: dn12 (York for Chester), p13, then Peterhouse, Cambridge 1817 (aged 24), a Ten Year Man (BD1828), DD1859

(Lambeth). PC. Natland, Kendal 1819-25, PC. Poulton le Sands, Lancs. 1824, R. Halton, Lancs. 1825-70, Vice Commissary of the Archdeaconry of Richmond and RD of Lancaster 1847, Hon. Canon Manchester Cathedral 1854. Died Halton 4/1/1871 aged 81, leaving £9,000 [C135617. YCO] Married (1) Lancaster 27/6/1822 Mary Thomas (a clergy dau., d.1828), with issue (2) Natland 10/11/1835 Elizabeth Inman, with further issue. *J.P. Lancs. 1826.*

**MACKEY (Bryan)** Born Kingston, Jamaica, s. William Mackey and Mary Welsh. BNC, Oxford 1788 (aged 18), BA1792, dn93 (Ex. for Salis.), p94 (Salis.). R. Coates, Glos. 1799 to death 25/11/1847 [C87225] Married Marylebone, London 24/1/1824 Anna Bell, with issue.

**MACKIE (Charles)** Edinburgh University, MA, dn21 (London for Win.), p21 (Lin. for Win.). R. Quartley, Hants. 1821 to death 5/11/1872, leaving under £600 [C69886]

**MACKINNON (John)** Born Bloxholme w. Digby, Lincs. 25/12/1791, s. Rev. Daniel and Sarah Mackinnon. St John's, Cambridge 1809, then Pembroke 1809, BA1814, dn14 (Lin.), p15 (Lin.), MA1817. R. Bloxholme w. Digby 1825 to death 8/2/1873, leaving £5,000 [C69973. Kaye] Married Grantchester, Cambs. 19/2/1850 Jane Anne Harding (w).

**MacLEOD (Roderick)** Born Drynock, Ross-shire 1755, s. Donald MacLeod. King's College Aberdeen, MA1773, dn79 (London for Lin.), p79 (C&L for Lin.), DD1793. St Paul's Qualified Chapel, Aberdeen 1782-93; V. Great Bentley, Essex 1791-1806, R. Weeley, Essex 1791-1806, R. Soho St Ann's, Westminster, London 1806 to death 1845 aged 91 [C18345. Bertie] Married Edinburgh 17/8/1784 Helen Middleton, w. clerical son Charles MacLeod.

**MacLEOD (William)** Bapt. Gateshead, Co. Durham 20/4/1782 (nonconformist chapel), s. John and Agnes MacLeod. University, Oxford 1802, BA1808 [Barrister Inner Temple 1812] dn23 (Nor.), p26 (London), MA1835. PC. Canvey Island, Essex 1828-35, V. Goxhill, Lincs. 1834, R. Biscathorpe, Lincs. 1835 to death. Dom. Chap. to 2nd Viscount Clifden 1826. Probate granted 3/7/1851 [C113931]

**McNEILE (Hugh [Boyd])** Born Ballycastle, Co. Antrim 15/7/1795, s. Alexander McNeile (High Sheriff of Antrim) and Mary McNeale [*thus*]. TCD1810, BA1815, dn20 (Raphoe), MA 1821, p21 (Raphoe), BD and DD1847, incorporated at Trinity, Cambridge 1860. [adm. King's Inn, Dublin and Lincoln's Inn]. R. Albury, Surrey 1822-34, Min. Liverpool St Jude 1835-48, PC. St Liverpool St Paul, Prince's Park 1848-67 (built for him by the congregation, salary £900), Hon. Canon of Chester Cathedral 1845-60, then Canon Residentiary 1860-8, Dean of Ripon ('over the protest of Queen Victoria') 1868-75 (res.). Retired to Bournemouth and died there on or about 28/1/1879, leaving £25,000 [C82249, ODNB. Boase. Al.Dub. DEB] Married 1822 Anne Magee (dau. of the then Archbishop of Dublin), 12s, 3 dau. A virulent Catholic hater and demagogue, there is an excellent and full article about this deeply unpleasant 6 foot 3 inch tall man at:
https://en.wikipedia.org/wiki/Hugh_M'Neile

**MADAN (Spencer, sen.)** Born 25/8/1758, s. Rt. Rev. Spencer Madan (Bishop of Peterborough) and Lady Charlotte Cornwallis (dau. of 1st Earl Cornwallis). Adm. Middle Temple 1776. Trinity, Cambridge 1776, MA1778, dn82 (Peterb.), p82 (Peterb.), DD1809. V. (Bishop's) Tachbrook, Warwicks. 1785-7 (w. Prebend of Tachbrook in Lichfield Cathedral 1785-6), then Treasurer (and Prebend of Sawley) 1787-1809, R. Ibstock, Leics. 1786-1836, R. Birmingham St Philip 1787-1811, Chancellor of Diocese of Peterborough 1794 (and 5th Prebend of Peterborough Cathedral 1800-33), Canon Residentiary 1809 (then 5th in 1812-17), R. Thorpe Constantine, Staffs. 1809-24. Dom. Chap. to Mary, Dowager Duchess of Walsingham; Chap. in Ordinary 1788. Died (Ibstock) 9/10/1836 aged 78, after a stroke in 1833 [C18347. ODNB] Married Lichfield 5/1/1791 Henrietta Inge (of Thorpe Constantine), 11 ch. (inc. clerical son, below)

**MADAN (Spencer, jun.)** Born Lichfield 6/10/1791, s. Spencer Madan, sen. (above) and Henrietta Inge. Christ Church, Oxford 1810, Student [Fellow] 1812-25, BA1814, p15 (Ox.), MA1816. Tutor to Duke of Richmond's sons in Brussels for 18 months. 5th Residentiary Canon and Prebend of Flixton and Offley in Lichfield Cathedral 1817 to death, V. Batheaston, Som. 1824 and V. Twerton (on Avon), Som. 1825 to death. Chap. in Ordinary 1830-51. Died Lichfield 27/8/1851 [C18346] Married Seal, Leics. 26/7/1825 Louisa Elizabeth Gresley, with issue.

**MADDEN (Wyndham Carlyon)** Born Tripasore, Madras 31/8/1793, s. Major William Molesworth Hatch Madden and Elizabeth Barber Ridewood (a clergy dau.). [Capt. in the 43rd Regiment of Foot]. Queens', Cambridge 1820, dn23 (Nor. as William), p23 (Nor.), BA 1824, MA1835. PC Bradford Christ Church, Yorks. 1825-45, V. Fareham, Hants. 1846-51, R. Bergh Apton w. Holverstone, Norfolk 1852 to death 13/5/1864 aged 71, leaving £3,000 [C113932. DEB] Married (1) Woodhouse, Yorks. 9/6/1826 Mary Whiteacre (d.1844), with issue (2) Ticehurst, Hants. 1846 (1st q.) Charlotte Leeke (w) (of Longford Hall, Newport, Shropshire), with clerical son.

**MADDISON (John George)** Bapt. Coromandal, East Indies 2/5/1793, s. Capt. Charles Maddison (Bengal Cavalry, and Blandford, Dorset) and Mary Harington (a clergy dau.). [Officer in 7th Hussars]. Magdalene, Cambridge 1822 (aged 30), dn24 (Nor.), p25 (Ely), BA1828. R. West Monkton, Som. 1825-47. Resided latterly in Bath. Died Doe Castle, Co. Donegal 11/5/1856 aged 64 'two days after falling on a rock when fishing' [C41606] Married Marylebone, London 22/6/1815 Thomasine Ann Macrae ('of Edinburgh and Jamaica'), with issue.

**MADDOCK (Benjamin)** Bapt. Nottingham 7/6/1782, s. Benjamin Maddock (surgeon) and Mary (North?). Magdalene, Cambridge 1806, then Corpus Christi 1806, BA1810, dn10 (Lin.), p11 (Lin.), MA1814. PC. Holy Trinity, Huddersfield 1826-30, V. Tadcaster, Yorks. 1830 to death. Dom. Chap. to Duke of Rutland 1826. Died Leamington, Warwicks. 16/12/1871 aged 90, leaving £16,000 [C69985] Married (1) 21/8/1810 Jane Wilson (a Leicester clergy dau., d.1848), 5 ch. (2) Marylebone, London 1858 (2nd q.) Mary Ann Williams. Brother Samuel below. Excellent online article: www.biblicalstudies.org.uk/pdf/churchman/099-04_336.pdf

**MADDOCK (Henry William)** Born Chester 2/12/1804, s. Rev. Thomas Maddock and Emma Anne Scott. St John's, Oxford 1823, then BNC, dn27 (Ox.), Fellow 1827-36, p28 (Ox.). PC. Bethnal Green St John, London 1829-31 (res.), V. Kington, Heref. 1835-50, PC. St John's Wood, London 1859 to death 18/2/1870, leaving £5,000 [C35330] Married 18/8/1836 Elizabeth Grey (w), with issue.

**MADDOCK (Samuel)** Bapt. Nottingham 8/5/1783, s. Benjamin Maddock (surgeon) and Mary (North?). Literate: dn11 (York), p11 (York), MA1834 (Lambeth). V. Bishops Sutton w. Ropley, Hants. 1818 to death 13/5/1871 aged 86, leaving £5,000 [C82211. Foster and CR65 have another man of BNC mixed in here. YCO] Clerical son Edward Knight Maddock. Brother Benjamin, above, and the online link.

**MADDOCKS (Evan)** Literate: dn98 (Llandaff), p02 (Llandaff). Chap. of Donative of Kinsham, Heref. 1815. Died? [C4306/C1723694]

**MADDOCKS (Robert)** Born Shelwick, Heref., s. Maddox Maddocks (of Royton, Shropshire). Pembroke, Oxford 1792 (aged 17), BA1797, p99 (C&L). V. Leighton, Shropshire 1816, R. Sidbury, Shrop-shire 1819 to death 2/8/1851, aged 76 [C18372] Wife Mary.

**MADDRELL (Henry)** Bapt. Arbory, IoM 11/3/1766, s. Robert Maddrell and Elinor Waterson. Literate: dn89 (S&M). Chaplain Ballure, IoM 1790-1803, V. Lezayre, IoM 1803 to death 23/7/1842 aged 76 [C7298. Gelling]

**MADDY (John)** From Dorstone, Heref., s. Joseph Maddy [*pleb*]. Jesus, Oxford 1784 (aged 18), BA1788, dn89 (Chester for Ox.), p90 (Ox.), MA 1791, BD and DD1835, incorporated at Cambridge. R. Somerton, Suffolk 1799-1853, Min. Berwick Street Chapel, London 1806, R. Hartest w. Boxted, Suffolk 1819, R. Stansfield, Suffolk 1820, 4th Canon in Ely Cathedral 1835 to death. Chap. in Ordinary 1803-53. Died Bury St Edmunds 17/6/1853 [C17629. Boase] Married (1) Westminster, London Sarah Jessup (d.1830), with issue (2) City of London 24/10/1830 Finetta Hale. *F.R.S.* (1817), *F.S.A.*

**MADEL(E)Y (Clement)** From Uttoxeter, Staffs, s. John Bailey Madely. BNC, Oxford 1792 (aged 18), BA1795, dn96 (C&L), p97 (C&L), MA1798, BD and DD1828. V. Horncastle, Lincs. 1802 and V. Stickford, Lincs. (non-res.) 1829 to death 21/3/1845 [C18375. Kaye. Bennett].

**MAGENIS (John Balfour)** Born Chanter Hill, Co. Fermanagh 1798, s. Richard Magenis and Lady Elizabeth Anne Cole (dau. of 1st Earl of Enniskillen). St John's, Cambridge 1816, BA 1821, dn22 (Lin.), p23 (Lin.), MA1825. V. Harrold, Beds. 1822-31, V. Sharnbrook, Beds. 1825-44, R. Great Horkesley, Essex 1753 to death. Dom. Chap. to 2nd Earl of Enniskillen 1825. Died 1/6/1862 aged 65, leaving £1,000 (unadministered until 1868) [C70028] Married 15/1/1827 Mrs Frances Margaretta (Moore) Ede (w) (dau. of an Irish judge), with issue.

**MAINE (John Thomas)** Born Scotland, s. Thomas Maine (of St George's Hanover Square, London). Christ's, Cambridge 1821, then Pembroke 1821, then Trinity 1823, BA1825, dn25 (Lin.), p28 (Lin.), MA1836. R. Husbands Bosworth, Leics. 1828-50, R. Harrington, Lincs. 1839-50 (living at Harrington Hall), R. Brinkhill, Leics. 1840-50, no benefice, living at Alresford, Hants. 1860 to death (Southsea, Hants.) 25/3/1881 aged 80, leaving £120,000 [C70031] Married St George's Hanover Square, London 3/3/1829 Eliza(beth) Penelope Ann Cracroft (a minor and clergy dau.) (w), w. issue. J.P. Hants.

**MAINWARING (James)** Born Avignon, France ('naturalised by Act of Parliament'), s. Rev. James Eyton Mainwaring (Boden Hall, Cheshire) and Anne Vaudrey. Emmanuel, Cambridge 1810, BA1815, dn15 (C&L), p17 (London [for C&L?]), MA1818. V. Cainham, Shropshire 1818-50, PC. Welshampton, Shropshire 1823-7, PC. Bromborough, Cheshire 1827 (living at Bromborough Hall) to death 17/9/1850 [C18349] Married Whitchurch, Shropshire 21/7/1838 his cousin Emily Jane Smith (from Northampton), with issue.

**MAINWARING (John)** Born 9/7/1806, s. George Boulton Mainwaring and Letitia Wodehouse. 'Studied in France for 2 years'. Caius, Cambridge 1823, BA1829, dn29 (Nor.), p31 (Nor.), MA1832. R. Geldeston, Norfolk 1831 to death (London) 2/11/1857 [C113935] Married Westminster, London 31/8/1842 Jane Susannah Carver, with issue.

**MAITLAND (Charles Barclay-)** Born Tillicoultry, Clackmannanshire 4/11/1789, s. Charles Barclay Maitland and Elizabeth Mary Hale. University, Oxford 1804, migrated to Jesus, Cambridge 1808, dn09 (Salis.), p20 (Salis.). R. Little Langford, Wilts. 1827 [blank in ERC] to death 12/1844 [C87229] Married Stockland, Dorset 6/9/1820 Anne Knott, with issue (inc. Charles, 12th Earl of Lauderdale). Confusion here.

**MAJENDIE (George John)** Born Windsor, Berks. 21/9/1795, s. Rt. Rev. Henry William Majendie (of Huguenot extraction, Bishop of Chester, then of Bangor) and Anne Routledge. Christ Church, Oxford 1814, dn13 (Bangor), Student [Fellow] 1815-20, p20 (Bangor), BA 1818, then Magdalen, Fellow 1820-9, MA1821, DD1828. V. Stanton St Bernard, Wilts. 1830-42, R. Headington, Oxon. 1839-1842, Prebend of Torleton in Salisbury Cathedral 1841 to death 2/11/1842 [C87230] Married Camberwell, London 2/5/1839 Susanna Maria Ward, with issue. Brothers below.

**MAJENDIE (Henry William)** Born Windsor, Berks. 23/1/1791, s. Rt. Rev. Henry William Majendie (of Huguenot extraction, Bishop of Chester, then of Bangor) and Anne Routledge. Trinity, Cambridge 1807, BA1812, dn14 (Bangor), MA 1816, p16 (Bangor). (first) V. Speen, Berks. 1819-69, Prebend of Penmynydd in Bangor Cathedral 1818-69 (and also several small Welsh parishes), and of Beaminster Prima in Salisbury Cathedral 1824-69, RD1827. Died (unm.) 17/12/1869, leaving £80,000 [C85929] Brothers above and below.

**MAJENDIE (Stuart)** Born Windsor, Berks. 20/10/1799, s. Rt. Rev. Henry William Majendie (Bishop of Chester, then of Bangor, of Huguenot extraction) and Anne Routledge. Christ Church, Oxford 1819 (aged 19), BA1822, dn22 (Bangor), p22 (Bangor). V. Longdon, Staffs. 1823-60, R. Barnwell, Notts 1860 to death. Also held several small Welsh parishes. Died Berchtesgaden, Bavaria 28/9/1871, leaving £35,000 [C18377] Married Prescot, Lancs. 13/11/1835 Mary Angelina Hughes, many ch. Brothers above.

**MALCOLM (Gilbert)** Born Burnfoot, Dumfries 14/12/1774, s. George Gilbert and Margaret Pasley. Trinity, Cambridge 1792, BA 1796, Fellow 1798, MA1799, dn00 (Peterb.), p01 (Peterb.), incorporated at Oxford 1816. V. Aysgarth, Yorks. 1806-12 (res.), R. Todenham, Glos. (and Hon. Canon of Gloucester Cathedral) 1812 to death 16/4/1855 [C110517] Married Langholm, Dumfriesshire 1806 Helen Little, w. clerical s. Archibald Malcolm. Port. online.

**MALLET (John)** Born Grouville, Jersey, s Jean Mallet and Rachel Godfray. [NiVoF] R. Jersey St Peter 1789-1800 (res.), R. Jersey St John 1800-19, R. Jersey Grouville 1808. Died 6/2/1851 aged 85 [C82213] Married Jersey St Peter 27/1/1793 Elizabeth Anne Marett. 'Respected for his stern integrity, private and public worth.'

**MALLISON (Richard)** Bapt. Horton in Ribblesdale, Lancs. 12/6/1791, s. John Mallison and Ann Jackson. Literate: dn17 (Chester), p18 (Chester). PC. Arkholme, Lancs. 1828 [income £80] to death 20/8/1866 aged 75, leaving £300 [C169880] Probably married Blackburn, Lancs. 9/2/1834 Mary Stones, with issue. Had 4 pupils in 1851.

**MALPAS (Joseph Henry)** From Knightsbridge, London, s. Henry Malpas. Exeter, Oxford 1809 (aged 21), BA1813, dn13 (C&L), p13 (Chester for C&L), MA1816. PC. Measham, Leics. 1813-27 (res.), V. Awre, Glos. 1826 to death. Dom. Chap. to 5th Viscount Boye 1819. Died Bath 28/9/1877, leaving £12,000 [C18422] Married (1) Tamworth, Staffs. 11/1816 Lucy Buswell (d.1830), with clerical son Henry (2) Forest of Dean, Glos. 7/9/1831 Mary Wait(e) (w), with further issue.

**MALTBY (Edward, Bishop of Chichester, *then* of Durham)** Born Norwich 6/4/1770, s. George Maltby (a Presbyterian master weaver) and Mary Fearman. Christ's College, Cambridge 1787/9, BA1792, dn93 (Lin.), MA1794, p94 (Lin.), BD1801, DD1806. Dom. Chap. to Bishop of Lincoln w. Prebend of Leighton in Lincoln Cathedral 1794 to death (with V. Buckden, Lincs. 1794-1823, and V. Holbeach, Lincs. 1794-1831). Bishop of Chichester 1831-36, Bishop of Durham 1835-56 (retired - the first bishop to do so since the Reformation). Died London 3/7/1859 leaving £120,000. Controversial for his liberal politics (he voted *for* the Reform Bill), for his slightly naïve ecumenism (esp. towards Unitarians), and for the great personal wealth he accumulated. [C70037. ODNB. Boase] Married (1) 10/7/1794 Mary Harvey (d.1825), w. issue (2) 31/8/1826 Mary Green. F.R.S. (1824). F.S.A. (1834). Fine port in D. Cross, *Joseph Bouet's Durham ...* (Durham, 2005).

**MALTBY (John Ince)** Bapt. Shelton, Notts. 27/12/1780, s. Brough Maltby and Mary Ince. Chorister at Southwell Collegiate Church 1796-97; St John's, Cambridge 1799, BA1803, dn03 (Lin.), p06 (C&L), MA1806. R. Shelton 1814-63, V. Whatton, Notts. 1824-63, PC. Sibthorpe and Cotham, Notts. 1837 to death (Shelton) 25/9/1863, leaving £20,000. Dom. Chap. to 4th Earl Fitzwilliam 1824 [C18353] Married Hinckley, Leics. 20/7/1807 Elizabeth Weston, with clerical son.

**MALTHUS (Henry)** Born Bath 16/12/1804, s. of the political philosopher Rev. Thomas Malthus (below) and Harriet Eckersall. Jesus, Cambridge 1822, then Trinity 1823, BA1828, dn29 (Win.), p30 (Win.), MA1831. R. Poughill, Devon 1832-5, V. Effingham, Surrey 1835-37 and V. Donnington, Sussex 1837 to death 5/8/1882 aged 76, leaving £12,680-12s-11d. [C82215] Married Strand, London 16/6/1836 Sophia Marian Frances Otter (dau. of a Bishop of Chichester), *s.p.*

**MALTHUS ([Thomas] Robert)** Born Guildford, Surrey 13/2/1766, s. Daniel Malthus and Henrietta Catherine Graham. Educ. at the nonconformist Warrington Academy. Jesus, Cambridge 1784, BA1788, MA1791, p91 (Nor. for Win.), Fellow 1793-1804. Travelled in Russia, Germany and Scandinavia 1799. R. Walesby, Lincs. 1803-34, Professor of History and Political Economy at East India College, Haileybury 1805-34 (where he was known as 'Old Pop[ulation]'), PC. Okewood, Surrey 1824. Died suddenly at Bath 29/12/1834 [C70040. ODNB. P. James, *Population Malthus, his life and times* (1979). R. J. Mayhew, *Malthus: the life and legacies of an untimely prophet* (Harvard, 2014)] Married Bath 1804 his cousin Harriet Eckersall (Claverton House, Bath, now the American Museum), with clerical son Henry (above). F.R.S. (1819). This is the great political philosopher and demographer ('Malthusian checks'). Had a cleft palate and a harelip.

**MANBY (Aaron)** Bapt. Knaresborough, Yorks. 21/4/1795, s. William Manby and Peggy Benson. Pembroke, Cambridge 1812, BA1817, dn18 (York), p19 (York), MA1821. PC. Bramhope, Yorks. 1821-35, V. Nidd, Yorks. 1833 (w. PC. Brearton Chapel 1837-51) to death (Knaresborough) 2/2/1854 aged 58 [C135618. YCO] Married Wakefield, Yorks. 21/9/1821 Harriet Took, with clerical son.

**MANBY (John)** Born Agmondesham, Bucks. 10/11/1763, s. Edward Manby. Merton, Oxford 1782, dn85 (Ox.), BA1787, p87 (Ox.), MA1789. V. Meldreth, Cambs. 1792-4, V. East Stoke w. Syerston, Notts. 1798-1804, PC. Churchill 1804 and PC. Puxton, Som. 1804-19, V. Lancaster St Mary [net income £1,709] 1806 to death. Chap. to HRH Duke of Sussex. Died 13/2/1844 aged 80 [C35335] Married Overton, Lancs. 8/9/1812 Elizabeth Margaret Hamon (d. 1821), with issue.

**MANDALE (Blain)** Born Threlkeld, Cumberland. Literate: dn18 (Chester), p19 (Chester). PC. Rusland, Lancs. 1819-22 (res.), R. Ripple, Kent 1827 to death 20/6/1870 aged 61, leaving £7,000 [C82216] Married Finsbury, North London 28/7/1822 Elizabeth Kirkbank, with clerical son of same name.

**MANESTY (Charles)** From Crondall, Hants., s. Rev. James Manesty. St John's, Oxford 1790 (aged 16), BA1794, dn98 (Ox.), MA1798, p98 (Ox.). R. Purley, Berks. 1800 to death 11/11/1844 [C35336] Married Souldern, Oxon. 13/4/1803 Elizabeth Watson, with issue. Confusion with the man below.

**MANISTY (James)** Bapt. Newcastle upon Tyne 25/11/1764, s. Henry Manisty. Literate: dn87 (Durham), p92 (Durham), Trinity, Cambridge 1792, a Ten Year Man (BD1802). S/M Durham School 1788-1804; Minor Canon of Durham Cathedral 1792, V. Edlingham, Northumberland 1803 to death 7/3/1839 aged 74 [C134179] Married (1) 1803 Northumberland, Eleanor Forster (d.1816), with issue (including Sir Henry Manisty, Judge of the Queen's Bench, and Rev. James Manisty). Confusion with the man above.

**MANLEY (John)** Bapt. Bloomsbury, London 5/5/1792, s. John Manley. University, Oxford 1809, BA1813, dn17 (London), p17 (London), MA1818. V. Godmersham, Kent 1824, V. Westwell, Kent 1824, V. Merstham, Surrey 1839 to death. Dom. Chap to 1st Marquess of Anglesey 1820. Died 28/12/1875, leaving £14,000 [C120289] Married 17/1/1823 Caroline Mary Moore (w), 1 dau.

**MANLEY (Orlando)** Bapt. Stoke Fleming, Devon 26/10/1790, s. Rev. William Manley and Maria Lewis. Exeter, Oxford 1809, dn13 (Chester), BA1814, p14 (Ex.). PC. Dartmouth St Petrox 1818-[22], R. Plymstock, Devon 1832 [blank in ERC], R. St Stephens by Launceston, Cornwall --. Died 27/4/1853 [C145688] Married Dartmouth 22/5/1821 Jane Matthew Glubb, w. 2 clerical sons.

**MANN (Charles)** Born Norwich 2/12/1761, s. George (a mercer) and Mary Mann. Caius, Cambridge 1781, BA1785, dn85 (Nor.), p86 (Nor.). PC. West Dereham, Norfolk 1818-24, PC. Ryston w. Roxham, Norfolk 1807-48, PC. Fordham, Norfolk 1830-7, R. Southery, Norfolk 1837 to death 20/1/1848 [C114005] Married Old Caton, Norfolk 29/10/1807 Susannah, dau. of Admiral John McDougall, with issue.

**MANN (Horatio)** Born Linton Place, Kent 7/4/1790, s. James Cornwallis Mann and Lucy Sherman. Trinity, Cambridge 1808, BA1813, dn13 (Salis. for Cant.), p14 (Cant.), MA1816. R. St Mawgan w. St Martin by Looe, Cornwall (and Preacher throughout the Diocese of Exeter) 1816 to death 23/10/1846 (after falling from his carriage) [C87232] Married Hernbury, Glos. 23/9/1813 Louisa Trevelyan, with issue. Brother William Henry Galfridus, below.

**MANN (William)** [MA but NiVoF] Joint Chap. Southwark St Saviour, Surrey 1804 to death (widower) 26/4/1843 aged 84 [C82219] Married Southwark, Surrey 31/12/1804 Ann Coventry (a minor), w. issue. A Calvinist associated with Lady Huntingdon's Connection.

**MANN (William Henry Galfridus or Godfrey)** Bapt.. Linton, Kent 9/5/1794, s. James Cornwallis Mann and Lucy Sherman. Trinity, Cambridge 1812, BA1817, dn20 (Chester [For Glos.?]), p20 (Salis.), MA1823. V. Bowden, Cheshire 1821-56, Registrar of Diocese of Lichfield in 1864. Died Glanllyn, Flintshire 13/1/1885 aged 91, leaving £16,361-8s-7d. [C87233] Married (1) Elmdon, Warwicks. 12/5/1826 Barbara Spooner (d.1831), with issue (2) Bowden 3/7/1838 Frances Powys, with clerical son of the same name. Brother Horatio, above.

**MANNERS (Edward)** Born London, s. Capt. Edward Manners (illeg. s. 3rd Duke of Rutland, of Goasdby Marood, Leics.) and *his* long-tern mistress Ann Stafford. Christ's, Cambridge 1822 (kept nine terms, MA?), dn24 (Chester), p25 (Lin.). R. Goadby Marwood 1825 to death (The Manor House, Kirby Bellars, Leics.) 21/12/1857 [C70232] Married City of London 18/9/1807 Elizabeth Hill, 3 dau.

**MANNERS (Moses)** Bapt. Newcastle upon Tyne 11/11/1759, s. of Edward Manners (a stonemason and *pleb.*) Lincoln, Oxford 1778, BA1782, dn82 (Ox. for Durham), p84 (Durham), MA1785. Usher, Newcastle Royal G/S 1783; PC. Newcastle upon Tyne St Anne 1786-1842, R. Carleton St Peter, Norfolk 1812 and R. Thelverton, Norfolk 1813 to death (Newcastle) 3/2/1842 aged 82 [C35338] Married Tynemouth 21/3/1785 Bridget Heslope, with issue.

**MANNERS-SUTTON (Thomas)** see under **SUTTON**

**MANNING (William)** Born Brome, Norfolk 30/9/1771, s. Rev. William Manning, sen. (R. Diss, Norfolk) and Elizabeth Adams (a clergy dau.). Caius, Cambridge 1788, BA1793, Fellow 1793, dn94 (Nor.), p95 (Nor.), MA1796. R. Weeting All Saints w. St Mary, Norfolk 1804, (succ. his father as) R. (and patron) of Diss (and Preacher throughout the Diocese of Norwich) 1811 to death 3/1/1857 [C114010] Married 28/12/1812 Elizabeth Donne (a clergy dau.), with issue.

**MANSEL (Henry Longueville)** Born Cosgrove, Northants. 5/8/1783, s. John Mansel and Mary Ann Biggin. Trinity, Cambridge 1802, BA1806, dn08 (Win.), MA1809, p09 (Win.). R. (and patron) of Cosgrove 1810 to death 4/3/1835 (CCEd says 28/7/1835) [C82220. ODNB under son of same name] Married Chelsea, London 8/9/1815 Maria Margaret, dau. Vice-Admiral Sir Robert Moorsom, and had issue.

**MANSEL (Lort)** From Pembroke, s. Thomas and Margaret Mansel. Trinity, Oxford 1811 (aged 19), BA1815, dn15 (Roch. for C&L), p17 (Glos.). V. Minsterworth, Glos. 1819 to burial (Pembroke) 9/5/1854 [C1986] Married Cambridge 5/12/1821 Isabella Haggerston, with clerical son below.

**MANSEL (William Frederick)** Born Chesterton, Cambs. 23/9/1795, s. Rev. Lort Mansel (above) and Isabella Haggerston (and godson of HRH Duke of Gloucester). Trinity, Cambridge 1814, BA1819, dn19 (Lin. for Bristol), p19 (Bristol), MA1822. V. Sandhurst, Glos. 1819 and V. Ashelworth, Glos. 1819 to death 7/8/1839 [C53372] Married Sandhurst 21/5/1821 Mary Vernon, with issue.

**MANSERGH (John)** [NiVoF] V. Climping, Sussex 1795 to death 6/3/1833 (CCEd thus), aged 82 [C64412]

**MANSFIELD (John)** Born Thrapston, Northants. Clare, Cambridge 1778, BA1782, dn83 (Ely), Fellow 1782, MA1785, p85 (C&L), BD1797. V. Litlington, Cambs. 1798-1803 (res.), R. Patrington, Yorks. 1803-37 and R. Rowner, Hants. 1805 to death 2/4/1837 aged 77 [C18378] Married IoW 3/3/1815 Winifred Blachford, with issue.

**MANSFIELD (William)** From London, s. Sir James Mansfield (Chief Justice of the Common Pleas and *M.P.*) and Susan Lane. Queens', Cambridge 1799, then Trinity 1801 (aged 20), BA1804, dn07 (Roch.), MA1807, p07 (Roch.). R. Milton Bryant, Beds. 1811, and R. Collyweston, Northants. 1813 to death. Dom. Chap. to 1st Marquess of Camden 1813. Died 23/2/1854 [C1987] Married Isabella Frances Markham.

**MANTELL (Edward Reginald)** Born London 8/9/1798 [Venn says: bapt. 30/6/1806, the 'son of Mrs Skelton, 50 Hattton Gardens, London']. Emmanuel, Cambridge 1816, BA1821, dn22 (Bristol for Salis.), p23 (Chester for Salis.), MA1824. V. Louth Lincs. 1831-59, V. Tetney, Lincs. 1831-59, R. Gretford w. Wilsthorpe, Lincs. 1831-84, Prebend of Louth in Lincoln Cathedral 1845-84, Dean of the Peculiar of Stamford, Lincs. 1863-84, RD of Ness 1864-76. Died St Albans 29/5/1884 aged 85, leaving £19,329-11s-7d. [C341. Boase] Married Dartford, Kent 14/7/1828 Susannah Minet (dau. of the High Sheriff of Kent). Surrogate 1832.

**MAPLETON (James Henry)** Born Henley on Thames, Oxon. 22/8/1778, s. Rev. David Mapleton and Mary Anne Golding. New, Oxford 1797, dn01 (Ox.), p02 (Ox.), BCL1808, Fellow to 1812. R. Southwark Christ Church, Surrey 1809, R. Whaddon, Bucks. 1810, V. Mitcham, Surrey 1829. Died (Adderbury, Oxon.) 11/1/1859, leaving £5,000 [C35344] Married Allesley, Warwicks. 10/12/1812 Elizabeth Bree (w), with issue.

**MARCON (William Mason)** Bapt. Swaffham, Norfolk 5/12/1793, s. John Marcon and Elizabeth Bailey. Sidney, Cambridge 1813, then Corpus Christi (Benet Hall) 1813, BA 1817, dn17 (Nor.), p18 (Nor.), MA by 1829. R. Edgefield, Norfolk 1829 to death 1846 (4th q. as William, 'of an infectious disease') [C114015] Married (2?) Corpusty, Norfolk 14/11/1842 Mary Farrow.

**MARDEN (Owen)** From Southwark, Surrey, s. Owen Marden and Ann Weston, Trinity Hall, Cambridge 1816, SCL, dn19 (Salis. for Win.), p20 (Glos. for Win.), LLB1823. R. Trusthorpe, Lincs. 1824-31, R. Greetham, Lincs. 1831-3, V. Climping, Sussex 1833-69 (non-res.), PC. Hove St Andrew 1838-57. Died Brighton 15/2/1869, leaving £12,000 [C64416] Wife Ann, and issue.

**MARGESSON (William)** Bapt. Broadwater, Sussex 7/2/1792, s. William Margesson and Mary Hughes. Christ Church, Oxford 1811, no degree, dn19 (Nor.), p20 (Chester for Nor.). R. (and patron) of Whatlington, Sussex 1821 and V. Mountfield, Sussex 1836 to death (Chelsea, London) 20/5/1871 aged 79, leaving £12,000 [C64417] Married 8/6/1818 Mary Frances Cooke, with clerical son Reginald Whitehall Margesson.

**MARGETTS (Henry)** Bapt. Huntingdon 28/6/1801, s. William Margetts (solicitor) and Elizabeth Brown. St John's, Cambridge 1818, BA1822, dn26 (Lin.), MA1826, p27 (Lin.). V. Huntingdon St Mary w. St Benedict 1828-46. Chap. Folkingham House of Correction 1826 Died Huntingdon 14/12/1874 aged 73, leaving £16,000 [C70262] Married St Pancras, London 6/2/1834 Elizabeth Grace Berkeley (w) (Biggin, Northants.). Surrogate 1839. Photo. online.

**MARK (Matthew)** Bapt. Burgh-by-Sands, Cumberland 24/5/1780, s. of John (a husbandman) and Jane Mark. Literate: dn03 (York), p04 (York). PC. Barnsley St George w. St Mary, Yorks. 1832 to death 7/4/1836 aged 55 [C117690. YCO]

**MARK (William)** Literate: dn82 (Car.), p83 (Car.). V. Burgh by Sands, Cumberland 1820 (w. Chap. Carlisle Gaol 1815-24) to death 6/6/1838 aged 80 [C6165. Platt] Married 1/5/1784 Jane Wilson.

**MARKBY (William Henry)** Born Duxford, Cambs. 22/10/1786, s. Thomas Markby and Sarah Pleasance. Corpus Christi, Cambridge 1804, BA1808, dn09 (Lin.), Fellow 1810-23, MA1811, p12 (Peterb.), BD1819. V. Cambridge St Benet 1814-16, R. Duxford St Peter, Cambs. 1819 to death (Wimbledon, Surrey) 4/2/1866, leaving £12,000 [C70264] Married Cambridge Jan. 1823 Sophia Randall (Wincanton, Som.), with issue.

**MARKER (Henry William)** Born Sowton, Devon 27/12/1792, s. Rev. Henry Marker and Margaretta Putt. Exeter, Oxford 1810, BA 1814, p17 (B&W), MA1825. V. (and patron) of Aylesbeare, Devon 1816 and R. Southleigh, Devon 1825 to death. Dom. Chap. to 5th Lord Nairne. Died 28/3/1865 ('now of Boulogne' - suggesting debt?) [C41613] Married Kenton, Devon 12/3/1816 Mary Swete. Brother, below.

**MARKER (Thomas John)** From Exmouth, Devon, s. Rev. Henry Marker and Margaretta Putt. Exeter, Oxford 1816 (aged 18), BA1819, dn21 (Ex.), MA1822, p22 (Ex.). R. Gittisham, Devon 1823-54, R. Farway, Devon 1833 to death. Dom. Chap. to 22nd Baron de Ros of Helmsley 1833. Died 29/1/1854 [C136976] Married 15/7/1833 Frances Amelia Drew, with issue. Brother, above.

**MARKHAM (David Frederick)** Born Becca Hall, Aberford, Yorks. 13/3/1800, s. William Markham and Elizabeth Bowles. Christ Church, Oxford 1818, BA1822, dn23 (Chester for York), p24 (Lin. for York), MA1825. V. Addingham, Cumberland 1825-9, V. Stillingfleet, Yorks. 1826-38, Canon of Windsor 1827-53, R. Great Horkesley, Essex 1838 (and RD) to death 31/3/1853 [C3451. YCO] Married Bolton Percy, Yorks. 30/8/1827 Catherine Frances Nanette, dau. of Sir William Mordaunt Milner, 4th Bart., and had issue.

**MARKHAM (Henry Spencer)** Born Bolton Percy, Yorks. 8/1/1805, s. Ven. Robert Markham (below) and Frances Egerton Clifton. Christ Church, Oxford 1823, BA1828, dn28 (York), p29 (Chich. for York), MA1830. V. Morland, Westmorland 1828, V. Addingham, Cumberland 1828-30, V. Conisbrough, Yorks. 1829-44, R. Clifton w. Glapton, Notts. (w. Prebend of Givendale in York Minster 1830-33, then Canon Residentiary and Prebend of Wetwang 1833) to death. Dom. Chap. to 1st Earl of Lonsdale 1830. Died 2/9/1844 [C3452. YCO. Platt] Married Grange, Yorks. 18/10/1831 Sophia Charlotte, dau. of Sir John Lister-Kaye, 1st Bart., with issue.

**MARKHAM (Robert)** Born 28/3/1768, s. of Most Rev. William Markham (Archbishop of York) and Sarah Goddard. Christ Church, Oxford 1786, BA1790, dn91 (York), p92 (London for York), MA1794. Prebend of Wetwang in York Minster 1792-1833 (res.), R. Barton in Fabis, Notts. 1792-6, Archdeacon of [West Riding of] York and Chancellor of Richmond 1794-1837, R. Bolton Percy, Yorks. [net income £1,540] 1796 and Prebend of Southwell Collegiate Church (with Preacher throughout the Diocese of York) 1796-1837, V. Bishopthorpe, Ainsty of York 1797-1814, 3rd Prebend of Carlisle Cathedral 1801 to death. Dom. Chap. to his father as Bishop of Chester/Archbishop of York 1797. Died 17/6/1837 [C3453. YCO] Married Marylebone, London

2/8/1797 Frances Clifton, with clerical son (above).

**MARKHAM (William Rice)** Born St Martin's in the Fields, London 3/2/1803, s. Admiral John Markham, *M.P.*, and Hon. Maria Rice. Christ Church, Oxford 1820, BA1825, dn26 (York), p27 (York). V. Addingham, Cumberland 1827-8, V. Morland, Penrith, Cumberland 1828 to death 27/3/1877 aged 74, leaving £25,000 [C3454. YCO. Platt] Married (1) 29/11/1838 Jane Eliza Tulip (d.1839) (2) Hexham, Northumberland 21/6/1840 Jane Clayton, with issue.

**MARKS (Richard)** Born North Crawley, Bucks. 31/12/1778. [In Royal Navy - was at Trafalgar]. Literate: dn12 (Nor.), p13 (Nor.), then Magdalene, Cambridge 1813 (a Ten Year Man). V. Great Missenden, Bucks. 1820 to death 22/5/1844 (after a long illness) [C70268. J.B. Marsden, *Two sermons on the life, ministry and death of the Rev. Richard Marks* (1847)]

**MARRIOTT, born WAKEFIELD (George Parry)** Born Bedfordshire. St John's, Cambridge 1795, BA1800, dn02 (Roch. for B&W), p02 (London for Cant.), MA1808. R. Hazeleigh, Essex 1804-52, V. Eynsford, Kent 1807-52 (and Prebend of Canterbury Cathedral 1824), Prebend of Osbaldwick in York Minster 1829-52 (then Hon. Canon). Died 6/3/1852 [C1993 under Marriott] Married Great Baddow, Essex 2/10/1809 Jane Bonham Bax, with issue.

**MARRIOTT (Harvey)** Born Dorking, Surrey 23/8/1782, s. William Marriott and Jane Capper. Worcester, Oxford 1798, BA1806, p08 (B&W). R. Claverton, Som. 1808-47, V. Loddiswell, Devon 1847-62, V. Wellington, Som. 1862 to death. Dom. Chap. to 2nd Baron Kenyon 1817. Died 18/8/1865, leaving £800 [C41614. Boase] Married Bathwick, Som. 22/6/1826 Caroline Paterson (w), w. clerical son Randolph Charles Marriott.

**MARRIOTT (Randolph)** Born York 18/2/1776, s. John Marriott and Margaret Gawtherne. University, Oxford 1796, no degree, dn98 (York), p00 (York). V. Ipplepen, Devon 1814-43. Died 1842 (4th q.) [C109361 and YCO say literate] Married Wapping, Middx. 13/12/1796 Ann Hilley, with issue.

**MARRIOTT (Robert)** Born Cotesbach, Leics., s. Rev. Robert Marriott, sen. BNC, Oxford 1792 (aged 18), BA1796, MA1799, dn02 (C&L), p03 (C&L). R. Bincombe w. Broadway, Dorset 1801-20, R. Cotesbach 1808 to death (Leamington, Warwicks.) 5/10/1841 [C18432 has wrong date of death] Married Hackney, London 2/5/1809 Anne Powell, with issue.

**MARRIOTT, later MARRIOTT-DODINGTON (Thomas)** Born Hardingstone, Northants. 14/12/1803, s. John Mariott and Martha Manning. Christ's, Cambridge 1824, dn27 (B&W), p27 (B&W), BA1828. R. Stowell, Som. 1828-70 (w. R. Compton Pauncefoot, Som. 1831-8). Died 22/3/1876 (Horsington House, Templecombe, Som. which he inherited), leaving £100,000 [C41615] Married Maperton, Som. 3/8/1837 Elizabeth Bird Phelps (a clergy dau.), with clerical s. Henry Phelps Marriott Dodington. Name changed 1853.

**MARRIOTT (William)** Literate: dn05 (Chester), p05 (Chester). PC. Disley, Cheshire 1810 to death 3/9/1839 [C169908] Had clerical son.

**MARRIOTT, later SMITH-MARRIOTT (William Marriott Smith-, Sir, 4th Bart.)** Born London 31/8/1801, s. Sir John Wyldbore Smith, 2nd Bart. and Elizabeth Anne Marriott. Trinity, Cambridge 1819, BA1825, dn25 (Lin. for Roch.), p25 (Lin.). R. (and patron and squarson) of Horsmonden, Kent 1825 to death 4/10/1864 aged 63, leaving £35,000 [C70380. A. Cronk, *A Wealden rector: the life and times of William Marriott Smith-Marriott of Horsmonden* (Chichester, 1975)] Married (1) 29/12/1825 Julia Elizabeth Hodges (Hempstead, Kent, d.1842), 3s, 3 dau. (2) 11/4/1844 Frances Radclyffe. Name changed 1811; succ. to title 1862.

**MARSDEN, born LISTER (Anthony)** Born Giggleswick, Yorks. 24/1/1778, s. Rev. Anthony Lister, sen. and Margaret Booth. Clare, Cambridge 1795, BA1800, dn00 (Chester), p02 (Chester), then Emmanuel 1803, MA1803. PC. Hornby, Lancs. 1802, V. Gargrave, Yorks. 1806-52, V. Tatham, Lancs. 1809-23. Dom. Chap. to 1st Baron Ribblesdale 1809. Died (Gargrave) 17/2/1852 [C157700 as Lister] Married 1807 Mary Yorke, with clerical son. To inherit Wennington Hall estate, Lancaster, he changed his name.

**MARSDEN (William)** Born Manchester 9/8/1770, s. William Marsden [*pleb*] and

Dorothy Buxton. BNC, Oxford 1790, BA1793, p94 (Chester for unspecified bishop), p95 (Chester), MA1796, BD1811. Curate Blackrod, Bolton (le Moors), Lancs. 1800 (1821?), PC. Liverpool St Matthew 1811, PC. Wigan St George 1821 (?), PC. Manchester St Michael, Angel Meadow 1821-37, V. Eccles, Lancs. 1837 to death (Bolton) 15/2/1861 aged 90, leaving £4,000 [C169912] Married Manchester 23/8/1802 Sarah Howard, with clerical son.

**MARSH (Edward Garrard)** Bapt. Salisbury 21/7/1783, s. John Marsh and Elizabeth Catherine Marsh. Wadham, Oxford 1800, BA 1804, then Oriel, Fellow 1804-14, MA1807, dn07 (Ox.), p08 (Ox.). PC. North Hinksey, Berks. 1820-41, Min. Hampstead, North London 1820 (only), Prebend of Woodborough in Southwell Collegiate Church 1821-62, V. Sandon, Herts. 1828-34, V. Ardeley, Herts. 1828-62, R. Waltham, Lincs. 1834-41, V. Aylesford, Kent 1841 to death 20/9/1862, leaving £35,000 [C35398. Boase. Kaye. DEB] Married 7/7/1813 Lydia Williams, with issue.

**MARSH (George Watkin)** Born Newport, Shropshire 5/9/1773, s. Watkin Marsh and Sarah Booth. Christ Church, Oxford 1790, BA 1794, dn96 (C&L), MA1797, p98 (C&L). R. Hope Bowdler, Shropshire 1806. Died London 7/3/1852 [C18437] Married (1) Wolverhampton 23/6/1797 Ann Shaw (d.1803), with issue (2) Shrewsbury 9/2/1809 Sarah Cheney Hart (d.1822) (3) Finsbury, London 5/5/1834 Elizabeth Shuter, with further issue.

**MARSH (Herbert, Bishop of Peterborough)** Born Faversham, Kent 10/12/1774, s. Rev. Richard Marsh and Elizabeth Frend. St John's, Cambridge 1774, Fellow 1779-1807, dn80 (Ely), p82 (Ex.), MA 1782, BD1792, DD1808; lived for some years in Leipzig, where he studied theology; Lady Margaret Professor Divinity 1816-19 (w. R. Bedwas, Monmouth *in commendam*), Bishop of Llandaff 1816-19, then Bishop of Peterborough 1819 (w. Castor annexed) to death 1/5/1839 [C108203. ODNB. G. Carnell, *The Bishops of Peterborough 1541 to 1991* (Much Wenlock, 1993)] Married Harwich 1/7/1807 Marianne Emilie Charlotte Lecarrière (dau. of a Leipzig merchant), with weird son (below). 'Regarded as the outstanding man of letters and divine in Cambridge, and the foremost Bishop on the Bench. By his writings he 'introduced into theological study at Cambridge a more scientific and liberal form of Biblical criticism.' Opposed the establishment of the Bible Society in Cambridge. Delivered his professorial lectures in English, and not, as hitherto, in Latin; his first course was given in Great St Mary's instead of the Divinity Schools, so as to accommodate the crowded audience, which listened to him 'with rapture.' A good chess player. 'A vigorous and pugnacious pamphleteer and controversialist' [Venn]

**MARSH (Herbert Charles)** Born Cambridge 3/7/1808, s. Rt. Rev. Herbert Marsh (Bishop of Peterborough, above) and Marianne Emilie Charlotte Lecarrière (dau. of 'a Leipzig merchant'). St John's, Cambridge 1825, BA 1830, dn31 (Peterb.), p32 (Peterb.), MA1833. R. Barnack, Northants. [net income £1,025] 1832-44 (suspended), Prebend of 3rd Canonry in Peterborough Cathedral 1833 to death 11/9/1851. 'Of unsound mind', he 'brought proceedings at Northampton Assizes in March 1844 against a young Frenchwoman for extorting money by means of menacing letters; the jury found her not guilty. Upon his own avowal he had bought the silence of several of his French mistresses' [C110530. ODNB]

**MARSH (Matthew)** Bapt. York 28/10/1769, s. Rev. Philemon Marsh and Mary Benson. Christ Church, Oxford 1788, BA1791, MA1794, dn99 (Ex.), p99 (St Asaph), BD1801. V. St Mary Magdalen, Oxford 1799-1803, R. Brinkworth, Wilts. 1802, R. Winterslow, Wilts. 1804, RD 1812, Chancellor of the Diocese of Salisbury 1819, Prebend of Beaminster Prima in Salisbury Cathedral 1823-4, then Sub-Dean 1824 w. Prebend of Chisenbury and Chute 1824, Canon Residentiary 1826 to death 30/7/1840 [C35402] Married West Harnham, Wilts. 1/9/1808 Margaret Brodie, with issue.

**MARSH (William)** Born Beckenham, Kent 20/7/1775, s. Col. Sir Charles Marsh (of Reading, Berks.) and Catherine Case. St Edmund Hall, Oxford 1797, dn00 (Salis.), BA1801, p01 (Salis.), MA1807, BD and DD1839. V. Basildon, Berks. 1802-14, R. Colchester St Peter, Essex 1814-29, R. Birmingham St Thomas 1835-9, Incumbent Leamington, Warwicks. 1839-51, Hon. Canon of Worcester 1848 and R. Beddington, Surrey 1860 to death 24/8/1864, leaving £3,000; having retired to Beckenham [C18439. ODNB. Boase. Kaye. DEB. [Catherine M. Marsh], *Life of Rev. William Marsh, DD* (1867)] Married (1) Chelsea, London 27/11/1807 Maria Chowne Tilson (d.1833), with issue (2) 21/4/1840 Lady Louisa Cadogan (dau. of 1st Earl of Cadogan, she d.1843) (3) Clifton, Bristol 3/3/1848 Hon. Louisa Horatia Powys (dau. of Baron Lilford), with further issue. Known as 'Millennial Marsh' because of the emphasis in his preaching.

**MARSH (William)** Probably born Exeter, s. James Marsh. Magdalen Hall, Oxford 1819 (aged 22), BA1823, dn23 (Ex.), p23 (Ex.), MA1830. V. Gwennap, Cornwall 1825-35, R. Ashburton, Devon 1835 to death 3/5/1861, leaving £4,000 [C145699] Married (1) Heavitree, Exeter 25/9/1825 Lucy Napleton, with clerical s. William Blencoe Marsh (2) Before 1846 Sarah Anna -- (w), with further issue.

**MARSH (William Heath)** Born Norwich 1770. Corpus Christi, Cambridge 1786, BA 1791, dn92 (Nor.), MA1794, p94 (Nor.). R. Wramplingham, Norfolk 1800-11 (res.), V. Calthorpe, Norfolk 1801-48, R. Eccles [by the Sea], Norfolk 1810-12 (res.), R. Hempstead, Norfolk, 1819-12. Died 1848 (1st q.) [C114036] Married Norwich 4/12/1794 Mary Leader, w. issue.

**MARSHALL (James)** Born 10/2/1748 (bapt. Kirkandrews on Eden, Cumberland 4/8/1751). Literate: dn76 (Durham), p76 (Durham). S/M 1780 then PC. Ireby, Cumberland 1800 to death 26/1/1842 [C3455. Platt - 'added to his slender means by leading coal' - *sic*] Married Ireby 14/5/1778 Mary Walker, 10 ch.

**MARSHALL (John)** [MA but NiVoF] R. Ovingdean, Sussex 1804 to death 16/10/1835 (CCEd thus) [C64425] Clerical son John Henry Marshall in same parish (*suicide* 1841).

**MARSHALL (John)** Son Rev. Charles Marshall, Lawhitton, Cornwall. Exeter, Oxford 1816 (aged 17), BA1820, dn21 (Salis. for Ex.), p22 (Ex.). PC. Exeter St Sidwell 1825-8, R. Evesham All Saints w. St Lawrence, Worcs. 1827 to death 9/12/1857, leaving £4,000 [C87243] Widow Fanny.

**MARSHALL (Lewis)** Bapt. Bodmin, Cornwall 10/6/1761, s. Lewis Marshall and Alice Wallis. Exeter, Oxford 1780, BA1783, dn84 (Ex.), p85 (Ex.). V. Warleggan, Devon 1796 and V. Davidstow, Cornwall 1797 to death (Bodmin) 3/4/1833 [C145702] Married Lanteglos, Cornwall 28/7/1795 Armenell Inch, with issue.

**MARSHALL (Thomas Horncastle)** Born Leeds, Yorks. 18/1/1757, s. James Marshall (a cabinet maker) and Susanna Horncastle. Clare, Cambridge 1774, dn79 (Chester for York), BA1780, p81 (York), MA1783, Fellow 1783-90. V. Pontefract, Yorks. 1809 to death (Tickhill, Yorks.) 1/9/1841 [C91819. YCO] Married Whitby 1/9/1789 Alice Skinner (dau. of a shipowner), and had issue.

**MARSHALL (William)** Bapt. Cambridge 15/5/1763, s. Charles Marshall and Ann Smith. Trinity, Cambridge 1780 (aged 17), BA1785, dn85 (Ely), p87 (Ely), MA1788. V. Newport Pagnell, Bucks. 1823-32, V. Naseby, Northants. 1829 to death 10/2/1847 aged 83 [C100126] Married Cambridge 31/8/1786 Elizabeth Freeman, with issue.

**MARSHALL (William)** Bapt. Totnes, Devon 23/8/1774, s. William Marshall and Dorothy Chadder. Corpus Christi, Oxford 1791, BA1795, dn97 (Ox.), MA1797, p98 (Glos. for Ex.), BD 1807. R. Chickerell, Weymouth, Dorset 1830 to death 1/3/1864, leaving £4,000 [C35415] Married by 1818 Isabella Caroline Clarke Perry Ogilvie, with issue

**MARSHALL (William)** Bapt. Middx. 15/10/1794. Queens', Cambridge 1819, BA 1823, dn23 (Glos.), p23 (Glos.), MA1826. PC. Islington St John, London 1830 to death 24/10/1834 (CCEd thus) [C120306]

**MARSHAM (Charles)** Born Thurnam, Kent 2/6/1787, s. Rev. the Hon. Jacob Marsham (below) and Amelia Frances Bullock. Christ Church, Oxford 1795, BA1809, dn10 (York), p11 (York), MA1811. V. Stoke Lyne, Oxon. 1812-67, V. Kingsey, Bucks. 1812-67, V. Caversfield, Bucks. 1812-67, R. Edgcott, Bucks. 1814-24, V. Ilsington, Devon 1826-64. Died Bicester House, Oxon. 24/8/1867 aged 80, leaving £12,000 [C1440. YCO] 'A kindly, inefficient man - the children shout out "Here comes Old Charlie" - resides with Admiral Styles at Bicester' (Wilberforce). Brothers George Frederick John, and Jacob Joseph, below.

**MARSHAM (Edward)** Bapt. Gunthorpe, Norfolk 30/4/1787, s. Robert Marsham. St John's, Cambridge 1803, BA1808, then Emmanuel 1810, Fellow 1810, dn10 (Nor.), MA1811, p11 (Ex.). R. (and patron) of Wramplingham, Norfolk 1811-49, R.

Sculthorpe, Norfolk 1811-59, R. Brampton, Norfolk 1826-8, R. Stratton Strawless 1828 to death 10/2/1859. Will not traced [C114038]

**MARSHAM (George Frederick John)** Born Kirkby Overblow, Yorks. 2/6/1806, s. Rev. the Hon. Jacob Marsham (below) and Amelia Frances Bullock. Christ Church, Oxford 1824, BA1828, dn30 (C&L), MA1831. R. Allington, Kent 1831, V. Halling, Kent 1832, R. Edgcott, Bucks. at death 29/1/1852 aged 45 [C348] Married 4/6/1833 Elizabeth Marcia Jones, w. issue. Brother Charles (above), and Jacob Joseph (below).

**MARSHAM (Jacob, Hon.)** Born Mote, Kent 23/2/1759, s. Charles, 2nd Baron Romney and Priscilla Pym. Christ Church Oxford 1777, then King's, Cambridge 1783, MA1783, dn83 (Glos. for Cant.), p83 (Chester for Cant.), DD 1797. Prebend of Worminster in Wells Cathedral 1787-1840, R. Allington, Kent 1789-1830, R. Caversfield, Bucks. 1795-1812, R. Thornton, Bucks. 1795-7, 1st Prebend of Rochester Cathedral 1797-1840, R. Edburton, Sussex 1797-1840, V. Stoke Lyne, Oxon. 1799-1812, V. Wilmington, Kent 1799-1840, R. Kirkby Overblow, Yorks. 1804-40 (non-res.), Canon of Windsor 1805-40, V. Wateringbury, Kent 1827 to death. Dom. Chap. to 7th Lord Fairfax of Cameron 1783. Died Rochester 28/1/1840 [C349] Married 28/6/1784 Amelia Frances Bullock, 13 ch. (4 clerical sons, incl. Charles, and George Frederick John (above), and Jacob Joseph (below)). A classic, non-resident pluralist.

**MARSHAM (Jacob Joseph)** Born Rochester 8/2/1804, s. Rev. the Hon. Jacob Marsham (above) and Amelia Frances Bullock. Christ Church, Oxford 1823, BA1826, dn27 (Durham for York), p28 (London for York), MA1830. R. Edgcott, Bucks. 1828, R. Kirkby Overblow, Yorks. 1828, V. Shorne, Kent 1837 to death. Dom. Chap. to Earl of Harewood. Died 23/10/1894, leaving £48,630-3s-8d. [C70414. YCO]

**MARTIN (Charles Herbert)** Bapt. Chester 5/1/1794, s. Lt.-Col. Charles Martin and Elizabeth Williams. Exeter, Oxford 1813, BA 1817, dn18 (Glos.), p19 (Glos.), MA1820. PC. Maisemore, Glos. 1829-57. Died Reading, Berks. 22/11/1865, leaving £4,000 [C145707] Married (1) Rockbeare, Devon 29/12/1818 Elizabeth Porter Sloane (d.1845), with issue (2) Glanford Brigg, Lincs. 1849 (2nd q.) Frances Anne Goodwin, with further issue.

**MARTIN (George)** Bapt. Bourton on the Hill, Glos. 13/10/1791, s. Rev. Joseph and Isabella Martin. New, Oxford 1810, BA1813, Fellow until 1817, MA1818. Prebend and Canon Residentiary 1815 in Exeter Cathedral 1815-60, Chancellor of the Diocese of Exeter 1820 and V. Harberton, Devon 1820 to death (by *cutting his throat*) 27/8/1860 aged 69, leaving £4,000. Principal of the Exeter Training School from 1839 (the first in England) [C171724. Boase] (1) Westminster, London 26/7/1825 Lady Charlotte Sophia Eliot (dau. of Earl of St Germans, she d.1839), with issue (2) St James, Westminster, London 21/7/1842 Renira Henrietta Aldenburgh Bentinck (an admiral's dau.), with further issue. Brothers Richard and William, below. *www.eliotsofporteliot.com/eliots/eliot-charlotte-sophia.html*

**MARTIN (John)** Born Greystoke, Cumberland. Literate: p14 (Chester). PC. Bunbury, Tarporley, Cheshire 1814 to death 3/9/1861, leaving £450 [C169917] Married Bunbury 9/11/1816 Phoebe Young (w).

**MARTIN (Joseph William)** Bapt. Hayes, Kent 9/8/1776, s. Joseph and Elizabeth Martin. Trinity Hall, Cambridge 1792, LLB 1799, dn00 (London for Cant.), p00 (London for Cant.). R. Keston, Kent 1800 to death 12/11/1858 aged 82, leaving £16,000 [C120310] Married York 28/7/1807 Ann Pickard, and had issue.

**MARTIN (Richard)** [NiVoF] PC. Satterthwaite, Hawkshead, Lancs. 1830-3 (res.). Died? [C169918]

**MARTIN (Richard)** Born Exeter 7/9/1802, s. Rev. Joseph and Isabella Martin. Oriel, Oxford 1819, BA1823, then Exeter, Fellow 1824-31, MA1826, dn27 (Ox.), p29 (Ox.). V. Menheniot, Cornwall 1831-83 [income in CR65 £1,140] and Hon. Canon Truro Cathedral 1878 to death (Upton on Severn, Worcs.) 3/2/1888, leaving £26,261-1s-5d. [C35429] Brothers George (above), and William (below).

**MARTIN (Robert)** Born Anstey Pastures, Leics. 19/11/1809, s. William Martin and Ann Wood. Queens', Cambridge 1827, BA1832, dn33 (Lin.), p33 (Lin.), MA1835. V. Ratby w. Groby, Leics. 1833-71, V. Breedon on the Hill, Leics. 1833 and V. Newtown Linford, Leics.

1834 to death. Dom. Chap. to Earl of Stamford and Warrington 1838. Died 11/7/1871, leaving £7,000 [C70405] Married (1) Rutland 14/3/1839 Selina Turner (a clergy dau., Cold Overton Hall, Oakham, Rutland, d.1852), w. issue (2) Blaby, Leics. 20/9/1860 Marian Cecil Wood, with further issue. J.P.

**MARTIN (Samuel)** Bapt. Nottingham 3/4/1770, s. Rev. Samuel and Elizabeth Martin. Glasgow University 1787-9, then St John's, Cambridge 1788, BA1792, dn94 (York), p95 (York). R. Warsop, Notts. [net income £1,020] 1806 to death 4/4/1859 aged 89, leaving £30,000 [C109403. YCO] Married Ashbourne, Derbys., 21/10/1794 Selina Beresford, with clerical son.

**MARTIN (Thomas)** Born c.1753. Literate. Curate and S/M Bromfield Cumberland 1790; R. Moorby, Lincs. 1798 to death 1837 [C70429. Platt]

**MARTIN (William)** Born Bourton on the Hill, Glos., s. Rev. Joseph and Isabella Martin. Merton, Oxford 1816 (aged 18), BA 1819, dn22 (Ex.), p22 (Ex.), MA1825. V. Gwennap, Cornwall 1822-5, V. Staverton, Devon 1825 to death 10/4/1850 [C145709] Married Dartington, Devon 12/8/1828 Jane Champernowne, with clerical son Richard Martin. Brothers George, and Richard Martin, above.

**MARTYN (John Lee)** Bapt. Bloomsbury, London 18/11/1766, s. Nicholas Martyn and Hannah Russell (*or* Weller?). Trinity, Oxford 1786, BA1792, MA1793, BD and DD 1826. R. St George the Martyr, Bloomsbury, London 1806 to death 19/8/1836 [C120313] Wife Mary, with clerical son Charles Martyn. Brother two below.

**MARTYN (Richard)** [NiVoF] PC. Poulton, Wilts. 1819-[45]. Died? [C87248]

**MARTYN (Richard Lomax)** Bapt. Blooomsbury, London 27/4/1769, s. Nicholas Martyn and Hannah Russell (or Weller?). Oriel, Oxford 1789, BA1792, dn94 (Lin.), MA1795. R. Lurgashall, Sussex 1819 to death 21/9/1851 [C64431] Brother two above.

**MARTYN (Thomas)** Born Ludgershall, Bucks. 21/4/1792, s. Rev. Claud Martyn and Mary Stalley. Queen's, Oxford 1810, no degree, dn15 (Lin.), p19 (Glos.). R. Ludgershall 1821 to death 6/10/1869, leaving £800 [C70433] Married Evenley, Northants. 24/10/1814 Catherine Horner Strangeways, w. clerical s. Claudius Robert..

**MARTYN (Thomas)** Born Pertenhall, Beds. 1802, s. Rev. John King Martin and Eulalia Maria Longmire. Queen's, Oxford 1820, BA 1823, dn24 (Lin.), p25 (Lin.), MA1828. R. Pertenhall 1825-42 (res.). Died? [C70434] Married Pertenhall 1829 Elizabeth Sturgess (d.1831).

**MARTYN (Thomas Waddon)** Born Luffincott, Devon 18/3/1766, s. Rev. Robert Martyn and Letitia Waddon. Exeter, Oxford 1783, BA 1787, dn88 (Ex.), p90 (Ex.). R. Luffincott 1794-1837, R. Lifton, Devon 1833 to death 31/1/1837 [C145711] Married Lifton, Devon 20/2/1800 his first cousin Mary Martyn, with clerical sons William Waddon Martyn, and Thomas Waddon Martyn.

**MARTYN** see also **MARTIN**

**MARVIN (William Staresmore)** Born Clifton upon Dunsmore, Warwicks. 16/9/1794, s. William Marvin and Christiana Staresmore. University, Oxford 1813, BA1816, dn17 (Chester), p18 (Chester), MA1820. V. Shawbury, Shropshire 1826 to death 31/11/1854 [C18449] Married Brinklow, Warwicks. 28/7/1824 Mary Ann Brierley.

**MASON (Christopher)** Literate: dn99 Chester), p00 (Chester). PC Brusyard, Suffolk 1818 and V. Bramfield, Suffolk 1830. Died May 1842 aged 71 [C114048]

**MASON (George)** Bapt. Osberton, Notts. 16/1/1787, s. William Mason and Jane Cleaver. Clare, Cambridge 1806, BA1810, dn12 (York), p13 (York), MA1813. R. Whitwell, Derbys. 1831 (living at Cuckney, Notts.) to death there. Dom. Chap. to Duke of Portland. Died 25/10/1851 [C18470. YCO] Married Anmer, Norfolk 28/5/1816 Harriet Coldham, with issue. His account book for 1841-51 survives.

**MASON (James Holman)** Bapt. Okehampton, Devon 5/1/1780, s. Holman Mason. Exeter, Oxford 1797, BA1801, dn02 (Ex.), p04 (C &L for Ex.), MA1804. V. Treneglos, Cornwall 1804 and V. Widdicombe in the Moor, Devon 1815 (with Chap. of Princeton - o/w Dartmoor - Prison Chapel) to death. Chap. to Prince of Wales 1815. Died 'on or about' 19/1/1861, leaving £35,000 [C18471] 'The Bishop of the Moor'.

**MASON (John, sen.)** Bapt. Dent, Sedbergh, Yorks. 13/5/1773, s. James and Ann Mason. Literate: dn96 (Bristol for York), p97 (York). PC. Bothamsall, Elksley, Notts. 1812-27. Died Tuxford, Notts. 29/10/1844 aged 72 [C53390. YCO] Married (2?) Dent 22/6/1836 Margaret Sedgwick (a clergy dau.), with clerical son (below).

**MASON (John, jun.)** Bapt. Bothamsall, Notts. 14/2/1806, s. Rev. John Mason (above) and Margaret Sedgwick. Literate: dn31 (York), p32 (York). V. Skipsea, Yorks. 1831, V. Hayton, Notts. 1833, V. Sherburn, Yorks. 1834-73, PC. Knapton, Yorks. 1842-66, RD of East Buckrose 1855. Died Scarborough, Yorks. 20/7/1873, leaving £4,000 [C136818. YCO] Married York 10/9/1834 Sarah Knowlson, with clerical sons John, and James Mason.

**MASON (William)** Bapt. Keddington, Lincs. 11/2/1799, s. James Mason and Susanna Ludlow. Queens', Cambridge 1819, BA1823, dn22 (Lin.), p23 (Lin.). V. Bilsby, Lincs. 1826 and V. Farlesthorpe, Lincs. 1840 to death 11/12/1856 ('*accidentally killed* at Louth railway station') [C70447] Married (1) Wife Maria and 6 ch. (2) Alford, Lincs. 1851 (2nd q.) Henrietta Holmes.

**MASON** see also **MAYSON**

**MASSEY (John)** Born Northenden, Cheshire 7/8/1793, s. John Massey and Mary Baxter. Literate: dn16 (Chester), p17 (Chester). PC. Ringway, Cheshire 1818 to death 2/2/1862, leaving £3,000 [C169925 says Ringley] Married Stockport, Cheshire 7/9/1819 Elizabeth Worsley, with issue.

**MASSIE (Richard)** Born Covent Garden, London 12/1/1771 (but from Coddington, Cheshire), s. Thomas Massie and Elizabeth Marriot. St John's, Cambridge 1789, BA1794, dn94 (Chester), p95 (Chester), MA1805. R. Chester St Bridget 1810-32, R. Aldford, Cheshire 1811-32, PC. Goostrey, Cheshire 1832, R. Eccleston St Mary, Cheshire 1832 to death 16/4/1854 [C169928] Married Neston, Cheshire 5/10/1796 Hester Lee Townshend (Wincham Hall, Northwich, Cheshire), with 22 children (including clerical), of whom 18 lived to maturity - the record! (and she lived to be 97).

**MASSINGBERD (Charles Bolle)** Bapt. Ingatestone, Essex 10/7/1771, s. Thomas Meux Massingberd (Millgreen, Essex) and Elizabeth Emerson. St Mary Hall, Oxford 1792 (as Bolles), SCL, dn96 (Bristol for York), p01 (Lin.). V. Upton w. Kexby, Lincs. 1801-6, R. Kettlethorpe w. Laughton and Fenton, Lincs. 1806-36, PC. Stow in Lindsey, Lincs. 1827 to death (at the Oak Inn, Grantham, Lincs.) 27/3/1836 aged 65 [C53392. YCO] Married Gainsborough, Lincs. 11/11/1805 Mary Smith, with issue. Freemason.

**MASSINGBERD (Francis Charles)** Bapt. Washingborough, Lincs. 30/12/1800, s. Rev. Francis and Elizabeth Massingberd. Magdalen, Oxford 1818, BA1822, dn24 (Ox.), MA1825, p25 (Lin.). R. South Ormsby, Lincs. 1825-72, Prebend of Thorngate in Lincoln Cathedral 1847-62, then Chancellor of the Diocese 1862 to death (London) 5/12/1872, leaving £12,000 [C35435. ODNB. Boase. Frances Knight, *The Nineteenth century Church and English Society* (Cambridge, 1995), 141-150 for his revealing diary] Married Putney, London 15/1/1839 Fanny Baring (w), with issue.

**MASSINGBERD (Hompesch, '*sometimes* Edward')** Born Lincoln 25/6/1797, s. Capt. Thomas Massingberd, *R.N.*, and Elizabeth Hawkesmore Waterhouse. Downing, Cambridge 1824, dn27 (Lin.), p27 (Lin.), BA1828. V. Upton w. Kexby, Lincs. 1829-58. Appears to be unbeneficed thereafter, living on Jersey (without cure of souls) until at least 1881, then aged 83. Died? [C70450] Married by 1838 Sarah Fretwell, with issue.

**MASTER (Edward)** Bapt. Vron, Flintshire 23/11/1770, s. Rev. Robert Master and Elizabeth Whalley. Balliol, Oxford 1790, BA 1794, dn94 (Bristol), p94 (London for Chester). R. Rufford, Lancs. 1798-1834, PC. Tarleton, Lancs. 1800 to death 17/7/1834 [C53393] Brothers John Whalley, and Streynsham, below.

**MASTER (Frederick)** From Lymington, Hants., s. Henry Master. Christ Church, Oxford 1802 (aged 19), Student [Fellow] 1802-17, BA1806, dn06 (Win.), p07 (Ox.), MA1808. V. Runcorn, Cheshire 1816 to death 2/5/1845 [C35438]

**MASTER (John Whalley)** Born Croston, Preston, Lancs. 15/8/1768, s. Rev. Robert Master and Elizabeth Whalley. BNC, Oxford 1786, BA1790, dn92 (Chester), p93 (C&L for Chester), MA1794, BD1803. PC. Clifton (Bristol) 1793-5, R. (and patron) of Chorley, Lancs. [net income £1,022] 1798 to death (Cheltenham, Glos.) 13/8/1846 aged 77 [C18473] Was married. Brothers Edward (above) and Streynsham (below).

**MASTER (Robert Mosley)** Born Croston, Preston, Lancs. 12/2/1794, s. Rev. Streynsham Master (below) and Elizabeth Mosley. Balliol, Oxford 1811, BA1815, dn17 (Chester), p18 (Chester), MA1818. PC. Burnley, Lancs. 1826-55, Hon. Canon Manchester Cathedral 1850-67 with Archdeacon of Manchester 1854-67, PC. Leyland, Lancs. 1855-64, R. (and patron of) Croston 1864 and RD of Leyland to death. Chap. to Earl of Derby 1827; to Lord Carrington 1830. Died Blackpool 1/7/1867 aged 83, leaving £9,000 [C169931. Boase] Married Marylebone, London 11/4/1822 Frances Mary (dau. George Smith, *M.P.*, Selsden Park, Surrey), with clerical son.

**MASTER (Streynsham)** Born Croston, Preston, Lancs. 10/6/1766, s. Rev. Robert Master and Elizabeth Whalley. Balliol, Oxford 1784, BA1788, dn89 (Chester), p90 (Chester), MA1791. PC. Becconsall, Lancs. 1790-1864, R. (and patron) of Croston [net income £1,538] (with Preacher throughout the Diocese of Chester) 1798-1864, PC. Hesketh, Lancs. 1824-64, R. Tarleton, Lancs. 1834 to death. Dom. Chap. to 6th Viscount Torrington 1813. Died Croston (a widower) 19/1/1864 aged 97, leaving £1,500 [C157944. Boase] Married Rolleston, Staffs. 26/8/1790 Elizabeth, dau. Sir John Parker Mosley, 1st Bart., 11 ch. (with clerical son Robert Mosley Master, above). 'Got into financial trouble so had to leave the country for some time', hence Chap. at Ghent 1820-6. Brothers Edward, and John Whalley, above

**MASTERMAN (Henry)** Bapt. Admiston, Dorset 11/4/1777, s. William Masterman. Wadham, Oxford 1795, BA1799, dn99 (Bristol), p01 ((Win. for Bristol), Chaplain 1812-19. V. Alton Pancras, Dorset 1811 and V. Milton Abbas, Dorset 1823 to death 7/12/1841 aged 64 [C53394]

**MASTERS (William)** [MA but NiVoF?]. V. Overton 1790-6 (res.), R. Sparsholt, Hants.
1794-[42], V. Shalbourne, Berks. 1796-[42]. Died? [C82231 and could be 35442?]

**MASTIN (Thomas)** [NiVoF] dn82 (Peterb.), p85 (Peterb.). PC. Fifield, Oxon. 1815, PC. Idbury, Oxon. 1815, PC. Swinbrook, Oxon. 1816. Probably died 1838 (2nd q.) [C35443]

**MATCHETT (Jonathan Chase)** Bapt. Norwich 20/11/1798, s. Jonathan Matchett and Catherine Cole. St John's, Cambridge 1816, BA1821, dn21 (Bristol for Nor.), p23 (Nor.), MA1824. R. Norwich St Augustine 1824-32, V. Norwich St Mary in the Marsh 1824-79, Minor Canon and Sacrist in Norwich Cathedral 1824-79, V. Catton, Norfolk 1827-36, PC. Norwich St Saviour 1832-6, V. Easton, Norfolk 1836-73. Died 4/4/1879 aged 80, leaving £4,000 [C1092] Married Great Yarmouth, Norfolk 24/8/1824 Eliza Janette Dade (a clergy dau.), with clerical son Henry Horace Matchett.

**MATHEW (Edward William)** Born Pentlow Hall, Essex 14/1/ 1789, s. William Mathew and Elizabeth Maria Coldham. Pembroke, Cambridge 1810, dn13 (Nor.), p13 (Nor.), then Peterhouse 1814, no degree. V. Coggeshall, Essex 1815 to death (heart attack following a swim) 9/8/1834 (CCEd says 7/1/1835) [C114060] Married Earls Colne, Essex 10/12/1815 Charlotte Olivia Johnson, with issue.

**MATHEW (George)** Bapt. Croydon, Surrey 2/2/1785, s. James Mathew (Bury St Edmunds, Suffolk). Trinity, Cambridge 1785, BA1790, dn91 (Cant.), Fellow 1792, p92 (Cant.), MA 1793. PC. Brauncewell (w. Dunsby and Anwick), Lincs. 1799-1812, V. Greenwich w. Greenwich St Mary, Kent [net income £1,013] 1812 to death. Dom. Chap. to the 1st Marquess of Bristol 1809; and to Princess Augusta Frederica, Duchess of Brunswick 1809. Died 4/7/1833 [C1997] Married Greenwich 4/9/1824 Mary Enderby, with issue.

**MATHEW (John)** From Norfolk. St John's, Cambridge 1809, BA1814, dn14 (Nor.), p15 (Nor.), MA1817. R. (of Moiety) of Reepham w. Kerdiston, Norfolk 1817 to death 1842 aged 52 [C114062]

**MATHEW** see also under **MATTHEW**

**MATHEWS (John Staverton)** Bapt. Wargrave, Berks. 7/4/1776, s. Richard Mathews and Ann

Staverton. Trinity, Oxford 1795, BA 1799, dn99 (Win. for Salis.), p00 (Salis.), MA 1801. R. Hitcham, Suffolk 1801 to death 4/6/1837 [C87425] Married Deene, Northants. 9/2/1815 Mary Webster, with clerical son Henry Staverton Mathews.

**MATHEWS (Stephen)** BA [possibly Jesus, Cambridge as Stephen Britannicus?], dn12 (Nor. for Cant.), p12 (Nor. for Cant.). PC. Knockholt, Kent 1832-37, PC. Hanging Heaton, Halifax, Yorks. 1840-51. Died? [C87428. Venn mentions]

**MATHEWS (Thomas)** [NiVoF] R. (and patron) of Bentworth, Hants. 1806 to death 12/4/1847 [C82232]

MATHEWS  see also under  **MATTHEWS**

**MATHIAS (Daniel)** Bapt. Warrington, Lancs. 28/11/1767, s. John Mathias. BNC, Oxford 1786, BA1789, MA1792, dn93 (Ex. for C&L), Fellow 1793-1810, p93 (Ox.). R. Whitechapel St Mary, London 1807 to death 24/7/1837 [C18476]

**MATHIAS (Octavius)** Bapt. Mundham, Norfolk 10/3/1805. Corpus Christi, Cambridge 1823, LLB1826/7, BA1828, dn28 (Nor.), p29 (Nor.). V. Horsford, Norfolk 1829-50, PC. Horsham St Faith, Norfolk 1829 [blank in ERC], R. Canterbury Christ Church, New Zealand 1850-5 and Archdeacon of Akaroa 1855 to death there. Chaplain *R.N.* at some date; Chap. to British Consulate in Algiers. Died 18/6/1864, leaving £2,000 and a further £20 in England [C114061. Boase] Married (1) 10/1837 Marianne Taylor (d.1851), 6 ch. (2) Christ-church, New Zealand 28/12/1854 Harriet Brown (his children's governess, 29 years his junior), 7 sons. Freemason. 'Took his beer, and allowed others to do so'.
*www.peelingbackhistory.co.nz/octavius-mathias/*

**MATTHEW (Charles)** Born Chudleigh, Devon 10/8/1768, s. Philip Matthew and Margaret Hugo. Balliol, Oxford 1786, BA1790, dn91 (Ex.), p93 (Ex.), MA1810. S/M Saltash G/S, Devon 1805; V. (and patron) of Maldon All Saints w. St Peter, Essex 1809, R. Langford, Essex 1832, R. Layer Marney, Essex 1841 to death. Chap. to HRH Duke of Cumberland, King of Hanover 1832. Died 13/6/1844 [C120340] Brother below.

**MATTHEW (John, sen.)** Born Chudleigh, Devon 30/9/1761, s. Philip Matthew and Margaret Hugo. Balliol, Oxford 1779, BA1782, MA1785, dn85 (Ox.), p86 (Ox.). R. Klive w. Stringston, Som. 1797 to death 10/3/1837 [C35452] Married Bridgwater 11/5/1798 Mary Codrington, with clerical son (below). Brother Charles, above.

**MATTHEW (John, jun.)** Born Kilve, Som. 2/4/1799, s. Rev. John Matthew, sen. (above) and Mary Codrington. Balliol, Oxford 1817 (aged 18), BA1821, dn22 (Glos.), p23 (Salis.), MA1830. R. Chelvey, Som. 1831 to death (Brighton) 28/1/1886, leaving £666-6s-1d. [C41619] Married Flax Bourton, Som. 2/4/1839 Charlotte Letitia Maudant (w), with issue.

**MATTHEWS (Andrew Hughes)** Born Oxford, s. of James Hughes. Jesus, Oxford 1794 (aged 12 [*sic*]), BA1798, MA1801, dn06 (Ox.), p06 (Ox.), BD1809, Fellow to 1812. V. Stanton Harcourt, Oxon. 1810, V. Weston on the Green, Oxon. 1822-54, R. Aspenden, Herts. 1827-30, R. Tilbrook, Beds. 1830 to death 1/9/1854 [C35445] Wife Frances.

**MATTHEWS (Arthur)** Born Clehonger, Heref. 7/2/1788, s. John Matthews and Elizabeth Ellis. BNC, Oxford 1804, BA1808, MA1811, dn12 (Heref.), p12 (B&W), BD1818 Fellow to 1850, etc. V. Linton, Heref. 1812, Prebend of Withington Parva in Hereford Cathedral 1818-40 (Canon Residentiary 1831), V. Woolhope, Heref. 1831 and V. Fownhope w. Fawley, Heref. 1831 to death (Evesham, Worcs.) 23/9/1840 [C46747]

**MATTHEWS, MATHEWS (James)** Bapt. Ambrosden, Oxon. 1/8/1803, s. Rev. Thomas Pardoe and Mary Matthews. Wadham, Oxford 1820, BA1826, dn26 (Cashel for Ox - in Oxford), p27 (Ox.), MA1828. V. Kirk Fenton, Yorks. 1830-69, V. Sherburn in Elmet, Yorks. 1831 to death 24/1/1885 aged 82, leaving £4,812-17s-4d [C16490 as Mathews] Married (1) Eliza Matthews (d.1859) (2) Knaresborough, Yorks. 1869 Mary Allen (w); clerical son. Confusion here.

**MATTHEWS (James Thomas)** From Worcs. Literate: dn13 (Llandaff), p13 (Llandaff), then St John's, Cambridge 1817 (a Ten Year Man, BD1828). S/M Shifnal G/S 1839; PC. Priors Lee, Shropshire 1825-57. Probate granted 21/12/1857 [C4313]

**MATTHEWS (John)** From Fisherton Anger, Wilts., s. Rev. Richard Matthews. St John's, Cambridge 1787, BA1790, dn90 (Win.), p92 (Salis.), MA1823. V. Berwick St James, Wilts. 1799-1809, V. Stapleford, Wilts. 1808 (w. Shrewton 1823) to death. Dom. Chap. to Bishop of Exeter / Salisbury 1823. Died 14/10/1853 aged 86 [C82233] Had issue.

**MATTHEWS, MATHEWS (Marmaduke Harvey)** Bapt. Mavesyn Ridware, Staffs. 9/11/1774, s. Rev. Marmaduke Mathews [*sic*]. BNC, Oxford 1793, then Magdalen 1796-1806, BA1797, dn97 (Wor.), p99 (Wor.), MA1801, Fellow 1806-27, BD1809, etc. R. Horsington, Lincs. 1816 to death 24/2/1855 [C70460. Foster as Mathews] Married Holborn, London 27/4/1820 Margery Strongitharm.

**MATTHEWS (Richard Buck)** Bapt. Norwich 25/11/1773, s. Richard Matthews (a worsted weaver) and Elizabeth Buck. Caius, Cambridge 1790, MB1796, Fellow 1800, dn02 (Nor.), p06 (Nor.).V. Westhall, Suffolk 1808 to death (Hingham, Norfolk) 27/10/1857, leaving £1,500 [C1093] Married Duddingston, Edinburgh 7/7/1797 Janet ('Jessie') Macpherson, with issue.

**MATTHEWS** see also under **MATHEWS**

**MATTHIE, MATHER (Hugh)** From Greenock, Scotland, s. Hugh Matthie. Pembroke, Oxford 1825 (aged 20), BA1829, MA 1839. R. Worthenbury, Flintshire (Chester Diocese) 1831 to death (Wirral, Cheshire) 9/12/1842 [C169932 as Mather]

**MAUDE (Francis)** Born Wakefield, Yorks. 2/1/1778, s. Francis and Hannah Maude. BNC, Oxford 1816, BA1820, dn22 (York), p23 (York), MA1823. PC. (Nether) Hoyland, Yorks. 1823 to death 5/7/1850 [C135624. YCO] Married Doncaster, Yorks. 6/5/1830 Frances Ann Branson, *s.p.*. Brother Ralph, below.

**MAUDE (Frederick)** Born Blackburn, Lancs. 24/2/1806, s. William Maude and Jane Greenway. BNC, Oxford 1824 [Student Inner Temple 1825] BA1828, dn29 (Peterb.), MA1830. p30 (Peterb.). PC. Longridge, Preston, Lancs. 1831. Died (unm.) Kensington, London 2/7/1843 [C36566]

**MAUDE, *later* ROXBY (Henry Roxby)** Born Newcastle upon Tyne 27/9/1799, s. Thomas Maude (Stockton-upon-Tees) and Jane Roxby. Trinity Hall, Cambridge 1823, dn26, p27, LLB 1829 [Inner Temple 1830]. PC. Arkendale, Yorks. 1827-32 (res.), V. St Olave Old Jewry w. St Martin Pomery, City of London 1833-60. Died (Clapham Rise, Surrey) 14/1/1860, leaving £800 [C82234] Married (1) Bloomsbury, London 3/11/1829 Jane Meux (d.1841), with issue (2) Camden Town, London 11/10/1843 Augusta Maria Lally, with further issue. Name changed 1837.

**MAUDE (Ralph)** Born Wakefield, Yorks. 3/7/1799, s. Francis and Hannah Maude. BNC, Oxford 1819, BA1824, dn27 (York), p27 (Durham for York), MA1827. V. Mirfield, Yorks. 1827-70 [C131706. YCO] Died (unm.) Lytham, Lancs. 15/8/1880 aged 81, leaving £25,000. Brother Francis (above). Another man of this name in YCO.

**MAULE, MAUL (John)** Born Reading, Berks., s. Richard Maul. Christ's, Cambridge 1789 (aged 19), BA1793, dn93 (C&L), p95 (C&L), MA1797, Fellow 1798-1815 ('one of the few Fellows of much character in the first decade of the 19th century'), etc. R. Brisley (w. Gateley), Norfolk 1814 (and Prebend of Stow Longa in Lincoln Cathedral 1828) to death 13/5/1838 aged 67 [C17911] Married Painswick, Glos. 27/9/1815 Esther Compton, with issue.

**MAULE (John)** Bapt. Greenwich, Kent 18/4/1772, s. Stephen John Maule and Arabella Leigh. Queen's, Oxford, 1778, then Merton, BA 1792, dn93 (Nor.), MA1800. PC. Dover St Mary the Virgin, Kent 1817-42, V. St Mary at Cliffe, Kent 1823-63. Died Greenwich 17/2/1866, leaving £5,000 [C114083] Married 13/11/1798 Louisa Mary March, with issue. Photo. online.

**MAUND (Charles)** Bapt. Haverfordwest, Pembrokeshire 9/8/1771, s. Joseph Maund. Jesus, Oxford 1792, BA1795, dn97 (Wor.), p98 (Wor.). V. Avenbury, Heref. 1831-[50]. Died? [C121845]

**MAVOR (John)** Born Woodstock, Oxon., s. Rev.William Mavor (below) and Ann Harris. Wadham, Oxford 1802, then Lincoln, Fellow 1806-26, BA1806, MA1808, dn08 (Ox.), p09 (Ox.), BD1816, etc. PC. Forest Hill, Oxon. 1823-47, R. (Castle) Hadleigh, Essex 1825 to death (unmarried, 'in his cell, on the debtor side of Oxford County Gaol', having been there nine years) 19/6/1853 [C36568, Boase] 'Probably insane' (Wilberforce), or, alternatively, a nasty piece of work: www.hadleighhistory.org.uk › People

**MAVOR (William Fordyce)** Born New Deer, Aberdeenshire 1/8/1758, s. John Mavor and Elspeth Low. S/M Burford, Oxon. 1775. Literate: dn81 (Ox), p84 (Ox.), LLD (Aberdeen) by 1789. H/M Woodstock G/S 1810. V. Hurley, Berks 1789-1837, V. Tysoe, Warwicks. 1790-5, R. Stonesfield, Oxon. 1806-10, R. Bladon w.Woodstock, Oxon. 1810 to death. Dom. Chap. 2nd Marquess of Bute 1803-15. Died 29/12/1837 [C36569. ODNB] Married (1) Shipton-under-Wychwood, Oxon. 17/10/1782 Ann Harris (d.1822), with issue (inc. clerical son above) (2) Castle Ashby, Northants. 5/12/1823 Harriet Seagrave, with further issue. J.P. and 10 times mayor of Woodstock. Author of a famous children's spelling book.

**MAWDESLEY (Henry)** Bapt. Standish, Lancs. 1/5/1763, s. Henry Mawdesley and Ellen Worsley. St Catharine's, Cambridge 1784, dn86 (Chester), BA1789, MA1792, p02 (Lin.). PC. Ramsey, Hunts. 1802 to death 5/7/1840 aged 77 [C70519] Married Morley, Derbys. 7/11/1799 Elizabeth Smith, with issue.

**MAWDESLEY (Thomas, sen.)** Bapt. Prescot, Lancs. 26/3/1758, s. Rev. Thomas Mawdesley, sen. and Francis Cross. BNC, Oxford 1776, BA 1779, MA1782, dn83 (Chester), p83 (Chester). V. Chester St Oswald 1803-19, R. Chester St Mary on the Hill 1819 to death 2/9/1833 aged 75 (CCEd says 25/10/1833) [C169972] Wife Mary Anne, with clerical son (below) [and a naval son Othuell].

**MAWDESLEY (Thomas, jun.)** Born Chester 11/8/1788, s. Rev. Thomas , sen. (above) and Mary Ann Mawdesley, BNC, Oxford 1805, BA 1809, MA1812, p14 (Chester). R. Chelford, Cheshire 1816 to death (Adderley Hall, Salop) 21/1/1839 [C169973]

**MAWSON (William)** Bapt. St Bees, Cumberland 17/10/1768, s. of a miller. Literate: dn94 (Chester), p95 (Chester). PC. Flimby, Cumberland 1798 to death 1838 aged 68 [C169975. Platt] Probably married Loweswater, Cumberland 6/3/1793 Elizabeth Bewsher.

**MAXWELL (James)** From Lewes, Sussex, s. James Maxwell. Trinity, Cambridge 1804 (aged 18), BA1809, dn10 (Ex.), p11 (Nor.) MA1813. R. Thorpe next Norwich 1812-57. Died? [C145720]

**MAY (James Six)** Bapt. Maidstone, Kent 14/11/1794, s. George May and Mary Six. Christ Church, Oxford 1812, BA1815, dn17 (London for Cant.), p18 (Cant.), MA1820. V. Herne, Kent 1831 to death (Ramsgate, Kent) 17/5/1866, leaving £5,000 [C120511] Married (1) Foots Cray, Bromley, Kent 10/3/1843 Sophia Warriner (d.1844), with son (2) 1856 Mary Sophie Goddard (?)

**MAY (Thomas)** Bapt. Fremington, Devon 19/12/1753, s. Emanuel May and Elizabeth Radman (*or* Radmore). Exeter, Oxford 1772, BA1776, dn76 (Ex.). R. (and patron) of Roborough, Devon 1781 to death 28/3/1837 [C145726] Married Fremington 27/2/1772 Ann Dowden, with issue.

**MAY (Thomas)** Bapt. Digswell, Herts. 5/5/1798, s. Rev. Nathaniel May (V. Leigh, Kent) and Isabella Oliphant. Christ's, Cambridge 1816, BA1820, dn21 (Chester), p22 (Chester), MA1823. (succ. his father as) V. (and patron) of Leigh, Kent 1830-76. Died there 19/2/1888 aged 89, leaving £25,170-14s-1d. [C359] Married Leigh 29/9/1826 Emily Catherine Saint, w. clerical s. James Thomas May. Good photo. online.

**MAY (Thomas Charles)** Born Lisbon, Portugal 8/9/1772, s. Joseph May and Mary Coppendale. Oriel, Oxford 1791, BA1796, dn96 (Salis.), p96 (Salis.). R. (and patron) of Breamore, Hants. 1797-37, Chap. of the Donative of Hale, Hants. 1802, V. Chertsey, Surrey 1805. Died 26/3/1837 [C87815] Married (1) Bloomsbury, London 4/3/1798 Mary Mawby (d.1799) (2) Stanwell, Middx. 13/7/1807 Rebecca Gibbons (dau. of a baronet), with clerical son Henry Thomas May.

**MAYD (William)** Bapt. Epsom, Surrey 29/8/1797, s. John Winslow and Harriet Mayd. Exeter, Oxford 1817, BA1822, dn22 (Nor.), MA 11823, p24 (Nor.). V. Ewell, Surrey 1824-[31], R. (and patron) of Withersfield, Suffolk 1827 (and RD) to death (a widower) 22/2/1879, leaving £7,000 [C114088] Married Wixoe, Suffolk 5/4/1827 Emily Matilda Jardine, with issue.

**MAYDWELL (Richard John Lockwood)** From Kennington, Northants., s. Rev. William

Maydwell. Wadham, Oxford 1823 (aged 17), BA1827, dn29 (Lin.), p30 (Peterb.). V. Southwick, Northants. 1832. Died Brighton, Sussex 14/9/1886, leaving £2,228-8s-0d. [C70527] Married Bengeo, Herts. 10/8/1843 Susanna Manston Teed, and issue.

**MAYNE (Charles Otway)** Born Limpsfield, Surrey 6/9/1807, s. Rev. Robert Mayne. Christ Church, Oxford 1825, Student [Fellow] 1825-34, BA1829, dn30 (Ox.), MA1831, p31 (Ox.). V. Midsomer Norton, Som. 1833-67, RD of Frome and Prebend of Haselbere in Wells Cathedral 1840 to death 28/4/1867, leaving £800 [C36574] Married Sanderstead, Surrey 5/8/1833 Emily Smith, with issue.

**MAYNE (Robert)** Born Westminster, London 26/2/1778, s. Robert Mayne, *M.P.*, and Sarah Otway. Christ Church, Oxford 1796, BA1800, dn01 (Ox.), p02 (Ox.), MA1803. R. Limpsfield (Lympsfield), Surrey 1806 to death (Tunbridge Wells, Kent) 7/3/1841 aged 63 [C36575] Married Canterbury 8/6/1803 Charlotte Cunningham Graham, with issue.

**MAYO (James)** Born Wimborne, Dorset 9/9/1784, s. Rev. James Mayo, sen. and Jane Barfoot. Queen's, Oxford 1802, then Pembroke BA1805, dn06 (B&W), p08 (Salis.), MA1810. S/M then H/M Wimborne G/S 1802-22-; Chap. Sturminster Marshall, Dorset 1807, V. Gussage All Saints, Dorset 1817-35, V. Shaftesbury St Peter (o/w Shafton) 1819-23, R. (and patron) of Blackland, Berks. 1822, R. Avebury cum Winterbourne Monkton, Wilts. 1823 to death 18/8/1851 [C88023] Married Jane Willis.

**MAYO (Joseph)** Born Westminster, London 15/6/1764, s. Joseph Mayo and Mary Hutchinson. University, Oxford 1782, BA1786, dn87 (Salis.), p88 (Salis.), MA1789. R. Ozleworth, Glos. 1821 to death 30/12/1851 aged 87, living at Nibley House, Glos. from 1806, where he kept a large school [C88026] Married Seend, Wilts. 2/3/1789 Mary Jane Gibbes, with clerical sons Joseph Mayo, and William Mayo.

**MAYOR (Joseph)** Born Shawbury, Salop 4/9/1788, s. Rev. John and Ann Mayor. St John's, Cambridge 1807, BA1812, dn12 (York), p12 (Peterb.), Fellow 1812-4, MA1819. R. South Collingham, Notts. 1813-60 and PC. Langford, Notts. 1838 (with RD) to death (South Collingham) 19/4/1860 aged 71, leaving £6,000 [C110543. YCO] Married Peterborough 5/10/1813 Charlotte Pratt (a clergy dau.), with clerical son, also Joseph.

**MAYOR (Robert)** Born Shawbury, Shropshire 6/2/1791 (nonconformist baptism), s. Rev. John Mayor and Anne Hollings. [MA by 1833 but NiVoF]. Missionary in Ceylon 1818-28; PC. Burslem St Paul, Staffs. *post* 1828, R. Coppenhall [now Crewe], Cheshire 1833, V. Acton, Cheshire 1844. Died Nantwich, Chershire 14/7/1846 [C169982] Married Everton, Liverpool 4/9/1817 Charlotte Bickersteth, with clerical sons Robert Bickersteth Mayor, and John Eyton Bickersteth Mayor (*q.v.* ODNB).

**MAYSON (John)** Born Penrith, Cumberland, s. John and Esther Mayson. Literate: dn85 (Car.), p86 (Car.). PC. Great Orton, Cumberland 1825 to death 1/4/1845 aged 83 [C6189. Platt] Married 1793 Isabella Trimble, with issue. Grandfather of Mrs Beeton (the cookery writer), who lived with him as a child, and called one of her sons after him.

**MAYSON (Martin)** Born Crosthwaite, Cumberland 2/1/1799, s. John Mayson and Mary Fisher. Trinity, Cambridge 1819, then Christ's 1819, BA 1823, dn24 (Chester), MA1828. R. Knapwell, Cambs. 1833 to death 5/8/1856 [C109325] Wife Frances, and issue.

**MEAD (Francis)** Born Wellsborne, Warwicks. 18/10/1760, s. Joseph and Harriet Mead. Trinity, Oxford 1778, BA1781, dn83 (Wor.), then Magdalen, MA1784, p85 (Ox.), BD1792, DD1809. R. Gayton le Marsh, Lincoln 1809 and R. Candlesby, Lincs. 1809 to death 19/9/1833 (CCEd thus) [C36585]

**MEAD (Thomas Wynter)** Bapt. Houghton Regis, Beds. 23/9/1783, s. Rev. William Mead and Mary Elizabeth Wynter Hemmings. St John's, Oxford [*not* Cambridge] 1802, BA1806, dn06 (Lin.), p07 (Ox.), MA1810, BD1816, Fellow to 1831. V. Studham, Beds. 1818 and V. Great Staughton, Hunts. 1831 to death 1/11/1849 [C36586] Married Studham 23/6/1831 Harriet Parkinson, with issue.

**MEADE (Richard)** Born Cripplegate, City of London 10/12/1782, s. Edward Meade and Ann Lampey. Wadham, Oxford 1801, BA1805, dn05 (Lin.), p06 (Lin.). PC. Princes Risborough, Bucks. 1811, R. Horsenden, Bucks. 1811 to death 2/8/1844 [C70537] Married Islington,

London 1811 Frances Aldwin Soames, with issue.

**MEADE (Richard John)** Born Cuddesdon, Oxon. 11/6/1793, s. Thomas Meade and Catherine Barnston. Balliol, Oxford 1812, BA 1815, dn16 (Peterb.), p19 (Bangor for B&W), MA1822. R. Marston Bigot, Som. 1821-34, PC. Frome Selwood, Som. 1834-45, Prebend of Combe XV in Wells Cathedral 1863 (Residentiary Canon 1865, Precentor 1868), V. Castle Cary, Som. 1845 to death 23/5/1880, leaving £45,000. Chap. to Earl of Cork [C41623] Married Marylebone, London 29/7/1817 Frances Arnold, with clerical sons Willam Meade, and John Michael de Courcy Meade.

**MEADOWS (Philip)** Born Botesdale, Suffolk 20/8/1777, s. Philip Meadows (solicitor, later of Witnesham Hall, Suffolk) and Catherine Rust. Corpus Christi, Cambridge 1794, BA1799, dn00 (Nor.), p01 (Nor.). R. Great Bealings, Suffolk 1804 to death 18/12/1837 [C114093] Married Claverton, Som. 24/1/1804 Elizabeth Graves (a clergy dau.), with many ch. (some clerical).

**MEAKIN (James)** From Sutton, Shropshire, s. George Meakin [*pleb*] and Elizabeth Poole. Christ Church, Oxford 1779 (aged 19), BA1782, dn89 (Chester for Ox.), p90 (Ox.), MA1795. PC. Oxford St Thomas the Martyr 1796, Curate of Lathbury, Bucks. 1801, Canon of 7th Prebend in Worcester Cathedral 180442, PC. Putney, Surrey 1805-11 (res.), V. Wolverley, Worcs. 1811-13 (res.), R. Harvington, Worcs. 1813-14 (res.), V. Bredwardine St John, Worcs. 1814-18 (res.), V. Lindridge, Worcs. 1817-42, V. Cropthorne, Worcs. 1818 (res.). Died 6/10/1842 ('of natural decay'). Dom. Chap. to 2nd Earl Romney 1811 [C36587]

**MEARS (Thomas)** From Southampton, s. Thomas Mears. Wadham, Oxford 1785 (aged 18), BA1789, dn90 (Win.), p92 (Salis. for Win.), MA1792. V. Southampton St Michael 1793-1817, V. Southampton St Laurence w. St John >< 1794, R. Southampton All Saints 1817 to death 24/4/1835 (CCEd says 15/5/1835). Dom. Chap. to Frances, Baroness Brownlow 1817 [C82267]

**MEDHURST, *later* WHELER (Charles)** Born Kippax, Yorks. 25/5/1794, s. Granville William Wheler Medhurst (Ledsham Hall, Wetherby, Yorks.) and Anne Jennings. Corpus Christi, Oxford 1812, BA1817, dn17 (Cant.), p18 (Cant.), MA1824. V. Collingham, Yorks. 1818-27, V. Ledsham w. Fairburn 1827-54. Died Ledsham Hall 20/11/1877 aged 83, leaving £120,000], living at Otterden Place, Kent [C124130 as Medhurst. Foster as Wheler] Married Aberford, Yorks. 17/5/1831 Anne Landon (a clergy dau.), w. clerical s. Charles Wheler. J.P. Hereford and West Riding.

**MEDLEY (John, *later* Bishop of Frederickton)** Born Chelsea, London 19/12/1804, s. George Medley and Henrietta Lockhart. Wadham, Oxford 1822, BA1826, dn28 (Ex.), p29 (Ex.), MA1830, Hon. DD Cambridge and Durham. PC. Kenwyn St John, Cornwall 1831-38, V. Exeter St Thomas the Apostle 1838-45, Prebend of Exeter Cathedral 1842-5, Bishop of Fredericton 1845 and Metropolitan of Canada 1879 to death 9/9/1892, leaving in England £4,470-4s-1d. [C145946. ODNB. Boase. W.J. Ketchum, *The life and work of the Most Rev. John Medley, DD, first Bishop of Fredericton and Metropolitan of Canada* (St John, New Brunswick, 1893); *Dictionary of Canadian Biography Online* has an exhaustive bibliography] Married (1) Salcombe Regis, Devon 10/7/1827 Christiana Bacon (d.1841), 3 clerical sons (2) Campobello Island, New Brunswick, 15/6/1863 Margaret Hudson. The first Tractarian to be made a bishop. Port. online.

**MEECH (Giles)** Born 1764 (bapt. Dorchester, Dorset 29/12/1769), s. Thomas and Betty Meech. Christ Church, Oxford 1782, BA1785, dn86 (Ox. for Bristol), p89 (Bristol), MA1801. R. West Compton (o/w Compton Abbas West), Dorset 1790, PC. Charminster, Dorset 1797-1813, V. Toller Porcorum, Dorset 1800-49, R. Hammoon, Dorset 1808-32. Died 1/1/1849. Dom. Chap. to 7th Earl of Cavan 1810 [C36591] Married 1800 Charlotte Templeman, with clerical son, below.

**MEECH (William John)** Born Charminster, Dorset 21/3/1802, s. Rev. Giles Meech (above) and Charlotte Templeman. New, Oxford 1823, Fellow 1823-37, BA1827, MA1832. (succ. his father as) R. Hammoon, Dorset 1832 to death 28/3/1858, leaving £12,000 [C53402] Married Sturminster Newton, Dorset 24/3/1838 Sarah Marwood Yeatman, with issue.

**MEGGISON (Septimus Stanley)** Born Hatton Gardens, London 21/8/1791, s. of Thomas Meggison (a solicitor from Whalton, Notts.) and Catherina Elizabetha Thorpe.

Trinity, Cambridge 1809, BA1814, dn15 (London), p16 (London). V. Bolam, Newcastle upon Tyne 1817 to death 15/3/1879 aged 87, leaving £400 [C106748] Married (1) Wendens Ambo, Essex 22/1/1818 Martha Robinson (of Wenden Hall, she d. 1829), with clerical son (2) Newcastle upon Tyne 2/3/1836 Elizabeth Maria Batson.

**MELHUISH (Thomas)** Bapt. Ashwater, Devon 27/7/1777, s. Rev. Thomas Melhuish, sen. and Elizabeth Warren. Exeter, Oxford 1796, BA1800, dn00 (Ex.), Fellow 1800-9, p01 (Ex.), MA1803. R. (and patron) of Ashwater 1811-61, PC. (and patron) of Clawton, Devon 1811-61, R. St Ervan, Devon 1811-[17]. Died 28/10/1861, leaving £8,000 [C145953] Married Portisham, Devon 10/8/1809 Elizabeth Walter, with issue.

**MELHUISH (Thomas Abraham)** Bapt. Exeter 10/2/1780, s. John Melhuish. Magdalen Hall, Oxford 1815 (aged 36), SCL, dn19 (Ex. - says from Wadham, aged), p19 (Ex. - says from Wadham). R. (and patron) of Exeter St Mary Steps 1825 to death (unm.) 1849 (1st q.) [C145950. Foster as Thomas only] Two men here?

**MELLARD (William)** From Cardiff, s. Thomas Mellard. Magdalen Hall, Oxford 1817 (aged 24), dn21 (Lin), p22 (Lin.), BA1824, MA 1825. V. Caddington, Beds. 1829 to death 3/6/1862, leaving £800 [C41624]

**MENCE (Benjamin)** Bapt. Barnsley, Yorks. 7/5/1765, s. Rev. John Mence and and Jane Ryall. Worcester, Oxford 1781, BA1785, dn88 (Ox.), MA1788, p89 (Ox.). PC. Barnsley St Mary 1793 to death 28/5/1847 [C36593]

**MENCE (Samuel)** Born Worcester 4/6/1781, s. Richard Mence. Trinity, Oxford 1798, dn03 (London for Wor.), BA1805, p08 (Ox.), BD 1814, Fellow to 1815. S/M Highgate G/S, London 1816; V. Driffield, Glos. 1825, R. Ulcombe, Maidstone, Kent 1838 to death 28/11/1860, leaving £14,000 [C36595] Wife Anna in 1851, w. clerical son Richard.

**MERCER (Thomas Warren)** Bapt. Clapham, Surrey 30/8/1797, s. William Mercer and Margaret Warren. Trinity, Oxford 1815, dn20 (Heref.), p21 (Heref.), BA1823, MA1825. Chap. of Donative of Southwark St Thomas, Surrey 1830, R. Weeley, Essex 1833, R. Northallerton, Yorks. 1849 to death. Dom. Chap. to Duke of Bedford. Died 24/12/1876, leaving £1,000 [C114101] Married Aldeburgh, Suffolk 2/9/1817 Sarah Campbell Butcher, with issue.

**MEREDITH (Richard)** From Worcester, s. Thomas Meredith. St Edmund Hall, Oxford 1819 (aged 23), BA1823, dn23 (Chester), p24 (Heref.), MA1826. R. Hagbourne, Berks. 1825, R. Westborough w. Dry Doddington, Lincs. 1868-85. Died Grantham, Lincs. 3/9/1886, leaving £783-3s-0d. [C85169]

**MEREST (John William Drage)** Born Soham, Cambs. 10/6/1789, s. James Merest and Elizabeth Drage (d.1791). St John's, Cambridge 1806, re-adm. 1807 [M.P. for Ilchester 1818-20] re-adm. again 1824 (as a Ten Year Man, BD 1834), dn24 (Bristol for Nor.), p24 (Glos.). V. Cockfield w. Staindrop, Durham 1829-46, PC. Darlington, Durham 1830-46, V. Stottes-don, Salop 1846-73 and R. Wem, Salop 1846 [income in CR65 £2,192] to death. Chap. to Duke of Grafton 1825; and to Duke of Cleveland 1842. Died 1/10/1873 aged 84, leaving £20,000 [C53404] Married Bury St Edmunds 20/2/1810 Susannah Jenkin, *s.p.*

**MEREWETHER (Francis)** Born Calne, Wilts. 1/2/1784, s. Henry Merewether and Mary White. Christ Church, Oxford 1802), BA1805, dn07 (Ex.), p08 (Ely for Nor.), then St John's, Cambridge 1809, MA1809. V. Haverhill, Suffolk 1808-15, R. Coleorton, Leics. 1815 and V. Whitwick, Leics. 1819 to death. Dom. Chap. to 3rd Marquess of Lansdowne 1810. Died Ashby de la Zouche, Leics. 21/7/1864, leaving £1,500 [C70545. Boase] Married Great Yeldham, Essex 24/4/1819 Frances Elizabeth Way (w) (a clergy dau.), w. clerical s. Henry Robert Merewether. Port. online. 'He wrote and printed many letters to politicians and theologians'.

**MEREWETHER (Francis)** Born Marshfield, Glos. 9/3/1800, s. John Francis Merewether (of Blackland, Wilts.) and Ann Lean. St John's, Cambridge 1825 (a Ten Year Man), then Trinity Hall 1826, dn29 (Heref.), p29 (Heref.), LLB 1832. V. Allensmore, Heref. 1833 [blank in ERC]. V. Cleongher, Heref. 1833-75, V. Woolhope, Heref. 1841-81. Died Ramsgate, Kent 25/12/1891, leaving £298-0s-2d. [C145955] Married Kington, Heref.) 17/10/1829 Margaret Wall (a clergy dau.), Brother below. Photo. online.

**MEREWETHER (John)** Born Marshfield, Glos. 1797, s. John Francis Merewether (Blackland, Wilts.) and Ann Lean. Queen's, Oxford 1814, BA1818, dn19 (Salis.), p20 (Salis.), MA1822, BD and DD1832. R. New Radnor, Radnorshire 1828, Prebend of Pion Parva in Hereford Cathedral 1830 and Dean of Hereford Cathedral (and Residentiary Canon) 1832, V. Madeley, Heref. 1836 to death. Chap. to HRH Duchess of Clarence 1824 and as Queen Adelaide 1830; Deputy Clerk of the Closet 1833. Died 4/4/1850 [C85171. ODNB] Married Fifehead Magdalen, Dorset 30/12/1821 Mary Ann Baker (Wiley, Wilts.), 6s., 3 dau. Brother above. F.S.A. 1836. Strongly opposed the election of Renn Dickson Hampden to the Bishopric of Hereford in 1847.

**MESMAN (Charles)** Born Spitalfields, London 30/10/1764, s. Daniel Mesman and Marie DeVimes (both of Huguenot extraction). Hertford, Oxford 1789, BA1793, dn93 (Lin.), p94 (Lin.). R. Duntisbourne Abbots, Glos. 1794 to death 20/9/1842 aged 77 [C70548]

**MESSENGER (George)** From Ham, Surrey, s. James Messenger. Magdalen Hall, Oxford 1805 (aged 23), no degree, dn13 (Win.), p13 (Salis. for Win.). V. Barton St David, Som. 1831 to death 13/5/1841 [C41626]

**MESSENGER (John)** Born Bewcastle, Cumberland 2/8/1794, s. Rev. Thomas Messenger and Phoebe Sewell. Literate: dn19 (Chester), p20 (Chester). PC. Whittonstall, Northumberland 1829-36, PC. Shotley, Northumberland 1829 to death 18/12/1841 [C131553] Married 1823 Sarah Redpath, Berwick upon Tweed, Northumberland, with issue.

**MESSENGER (Robert)** Bapt. Isel, Cumberland 26/12/1765, s. John Messenger. Literate: dn88 (Car.), p90 (Durham). S/M Newcastle upon Tyne 1790; PC. Horton, Northumberland 1813-37 and PC. Ninebanks, Co. Durham 1813 to death (Newcastle) 13/6/1837 aged 68 [C135938] Was married.

**MESSITER (Richard)** Born Wincanton, Som. 2/6/1800 (bapt. 9/8/1809), s. Rev. John Messiter and Effie Dyne. Wadham, Oxford 1817, then Corpus Christi, BA1821, dn23 (Salis.), p24 (B&W), MA1827. R. Marsh Caundle >< Dorset 1828, R. Purse Caundle >< Dorset 1828, PC. Stourton Caundle >< 1829-64, R. Bratton St Maur, Som. 1829 to death 15/5/1885, leaving £1,701-19s-6d. [C41627] Married Cotleigh, Devon 25/6/1`830 Laura Michell, with issue.

**METCALF (Robert)** Literate: dn12 (Chester), p13 (Chester), then Trinity Hall, Cambridge 1824, a Ten Year Man. (first) PC. Sunk Island, Yorks. 1830 to death 4/9/1858, leaving £1,500 [C135939] Had clerical son. J.P. East Riding.

**METCALFE (Francis)** Born and bapt. Brandesburton, Yorks. 19/3/1791, s. Rev. Francis Metcalfe, sen. and Harriet Clough. Trinity, Cambridge 1807, BA1812, dn14 (York), p15 (York), MA1815. (succ. his father as) R. Kirkbride, Cumberland 1823-34 ('his mother retained the advowson'), V. Reighton (Righton), Yorks. 1824 and PC. Bessingby, Yorks. 1828 to death 30/10/1834 (CCEd says 25/3/1835) [C6196. YCO. Platt] Married Bridlington, Yorks. 1825 Margaret Rickaby, *s.p.* J.P. East Riding.

**METCALFE (James)** Bapt. Hawes, Yorks. 19/11/1798, s. Warren and Nancy Hawes. St John's, Cambridge 1821, BA1825, dn25 (Peterb.), p26 (Peterb.), MA1828. PC. Hardrow, Aysgarth, Yorks. 1827-54. Died there 25/1/1876 aged 77, leaving under £100 [C110546]

**METCALFE (John)** Born Ely. Queens', Cambridge 1807, BA1812, dn13 (Ely), p14 (Ely), MA1821. Minor Canon of Canterbury Cathedral 1816-62, V. Little Halstow, Kent 1816-25, V. Stone in Oxley, Kent 1825 to death. Chap. to Canterbury Gaol 1822. Died 25/7/1862 aged 73, leaving £9,000 [C109328] Married York 29/10/1816 Elizabeth Eamonson, w. clerical son Joseph Powell Metcalfe.

**METCALFE, METCALF (William)** Bapt. Muker, Yorks. 1/2/1759, s. John and Mary Metcalfe. Literate: dn81 (York), p83 (York). V. Bishop Wilton >< Pocklington, Yorks. 1786. Died? [C118838. Noted in Venn. YCO] Married June 1810 Isabel Seymour.

**METCALFE (William)** Born Ely 25/12/1785, s. Rev. William Robert Metcalfe and Anna Maria Harwick. Sidney, Cambridge 1803, LLB 1809, p09 (Salis. for Ely), p10 (London for Ely). R. Fulmer (o/w Fowlmere), Cambs. 1814 to death 22/6/1850 [C85174] Married Ely 13/9/1814 Susanna Golborne, with clerical son Frederick Metcalfe. J.P. Cambs.

**METCALFE (William)** Bapt. Kirklington, Yorks. 1/6/1789. St Catharine's, Cambridge 1811, then Clare 1812, BA1815, dn15 (London for Win.), p17 (Chester). PC. Kirk Hammerton, Yorks. 1822, PC. Yeadon, Guisley, Yorks. 1844-67. Died there 17/10/1870 aged 81, leaving £4,000 [C82275] Probably married Ripon 28/1/1818 Ann Elizabeth Hancock, with issue.

**METHOLD (Thomas, sen.)** Born Stonham Aspal, Suffolk 14/7/1764, s. Thomas Methold and Catharine Toller. Trinity, Oxford 1781, BCL 1787, dn88 (Cant.). R. Stonham Aspal 1789, R. Wetheringsett, Suffolk (and Preacher throughout the Diocese of Norwich) 1791, Canon of 2nd Prebend in Norwich Cathedral 1804 to death 17/6/1836 [C1095] Married (1) Ipswich, Suffolk 7/2/1793 Maria Turner (d.1795), with clerical son, below (2) Bury St Edmund, Suffolk 30/6/1799 Dorothea Frances Rose, with clerical sons John William Methold, and below.

**METHOLD (Thomas, jun.)** Born Stonham Aspal, Suffolk 28/2/1794, s. Rev. Thomas Methold, sen. (above) and Maria Turner. Caius, Cambridge 1812, BA1816, dn17 (Nor.), p18 (Nor.), MA1819. R. Kilverstone, Norfolk 1826 to death (Thetford) 14/3/1853 aged 71 [C114171] Married Norwich 16/10/1824 Susannah Mary Forster, with issue. *J.P.* Norfolk.

**METHUEN (Thomas Anthony)** Born Marylebone, London 23/5/1789, s. Paul Cobb Methuen (Corsham House, Wilts.) and Matilda Gooch. Oriel, Oxford 1799 [adm. Inner Temple 1801] BA1803, dn04 (B&W), p05 (Cant.), MA1806. R. All Cannings w. Etchilhampton, Wilts. 1809 [net income £1,100] and R. Garsdon w. Lea and Cleverton, Wilts. 1814 to death. Dom. Chap. to 6th Duke of Beaufort 1809. Died 15/6/1869, leaving £16,000 [C46795. Boase. DEB. *The autobiography of T.A. Methuen. With a memoir ...*, by T.P. Methuen (1870)] Married Herne, Kent 2/7/1810 Eliza Maria Plumptre (a clergy dau.), w. clerical sons Henry Hoare, and Francis Paul Methuen.

**METTAM (George)** Bapt. Nottingham 20/7/1768, s. Thomas and Frances Mettam. Merton, Oxford 1786, BA1790, dn91 (Ox.), p92 (Ox.), MA1793. R. (and patron) of Barwell w. Stapleton and Potters Marsden, Leics. 1803-53, V. Hillesden, Bucks. 1816 (only), V. Arnesby, Leics. 1820 to death 18/6/1853 [C36608] Married Barwell 2/5/1803 Frances Ashby.

**MEYRICK (Arthur)** Born Ramsbury, Wilts. 13/7/1786, s. Rev. Edward and Anne Meyrick. Trinity, Oxford 1803, BA1806, MA1809, dn09 (Salis.), p11 (Win. for Salis.). R. Urchfont w. Stert, Wilts. 1811-38. Died 31/12/1855 [C82276] Married Hants. 3/2/1811 Mary Ann Foxton, with 5 sons matriculated.

**MEYRICK (Edward Graves)** Born Hungerford, Wilts., s. Rev. Edward Graves and Anne Graves. Queen's, Oxford 1795 (aged 14), then St Mary Hall, BA1799, MA1801, dn02 (Salis.), p04 (Win. for Salis.), BD and DD1814 (from Queen's). V. Fisherton Delamere, Wilts. 1804-20 (res.), V. Ramsbury w. Axford, Wilts. 1811 (& H/M Ramsbury School), R. Winchfield, Hants. 1820 to death. Dom. Chap. to Frances, Countess of Jersey 1811. Died 29/3/1839 [C82277] Married Ramsbury 7/1/1823 Myra Howard, with issue. Port. online.

**MEYRICK (Thomas)** Bapt. Holsworthy, Devon 13/10/1774, s. Rev. Owen Lewis Meyrick, and Elisabeth Manley. Exeter, Oxford 1792, BA1796, dn97 (Ex.), p99 (Chester) PC. Upholland, Lancs. 1802, R. Covenham St Mary, Lincs. 1810 to death 27/5/1841 aged 66; but living at Lezant, Cornwall [C70560]

**MICHELL (Bennett)** Born Bodmin, Cornwall 29/10/1792, s. Bennett Michell and Ann Cole Knight. St John's, Cambridge 1809, then Emmanuel 1813, BA1814, Fellow 1816-24, dn16 (Ex.), p17 (Ex.), MA1817, BD1824. V. Winsford, Som. 1824 to death 6/6/1857 aged 64 [C41629] Married Exton, Som. Matilda Euphemia Wilson (of Tobago, West Indies) 19/3/1829, 7 ch. *J.P.* Somerset.

**MICHELL (James)** From Kingston Russell, Dorset. Emmanuel, Cambridge 1793, dn99 (Bristol), BA1799, LLB1799, p99 (Bristol). V. Isle Brewers, Som. 1800 and V. Sturminster Newton [*not* Marshall], Dorset 1800 to death 1838 (4th q.) aged 64 [C46827] Married 1831 Margaretta Pleydell, Whatcombe House, Long Bredy, Dorset.

**MICHELL (John Henry)** Born Brighton, Sussex 23/4/1759, s. Rev. Henry Michell. King's, Cambridge 1778 [adm. Lincoln's Inn 1780] Fellow 1781-1804, BA1782, MA1785. R. Buckland, Herts. 1803-44, R. Waterbeach, Cambs. 1813-21, R. Kelshall, Herts. 1822 to death. Dom. Chap. to 11th Duke of Somerset 1822. Died Bath 10/3/1844 [C6199] Married

12/6/1804 Margaret Wagner (dau. of a hatter, Pall Mall, London).

**MICHELL (Thomas Penruddocke)** Born Doller, Hants. 12/12/1796, s. Thomas Michell and Elizabeth Juliana Pearce. Merton, Oxford 1815, BA1819, dn20 (Chester), p21 (Chester), MA1823. V. Histon, Cambs. 1821-56. Died Clifton, Bristol 24/6/1866, leaving £9,000, living at Standon Hussey, Berks. [C82361] Married (1) Caroline Patience, with clerical s. Thomas Hungerford Michell (2) St Pancras, London 1/7/1834 Arabella Elisabeth Wyld.

**MICHELL (William)** Born and bapt. Cotleigh, Devon 21/6/1802, s. Rev. Richard Michell and Mary Newton. Trinity Hall, Cambridge 1820, dn26 (Salis. for Ex.), LLB 1827, p27 (B&W). R. Cotleigh 1827-61 (a family living; sold the advowson for £400 and retired to Axminster, Devon), R. Barwick, Som. 1827-64-, PC. Wincanton, Som. 1829 (only). Died Axminster 18/9/1869, leaving £4,000 [C41631] Married Wincanton 23/7/1828 Lucy Messiter, with issue.

**MIDGLEY (Richard)** [NiVoF] Literate: dm77 (Peterb.), p77 (Peterb.). PC. Fenny Stratford, Lincs. 1803 [blank in ERC] and R. Bletchley, Bucks. 1818 to death 4/12/1832 (CCEd thus) [C70574]

**MIDLETON (William John Brodrick, 2nd Viscount)** see under **BRODRICK**

**MILDMAY (Carew Anthony St John)** Born Winchester 2/2/1800, s. Sir Henry Paulet St John Mildmay, 3rd Bart. (Dogmersfield Park, Hartford Bridge, Hants.) and Jane Mildmay (*thus*). Oriel, Oxford 1818 [adm. Inner Temple 1825] BA1822, MA1825, dn25 (Win.), p26 (London for Win.). R. Chelmsford, Essex 1826-78, V. Burnham on Crouch, Essex 1827, (Sinecure R. Shorwell and Mottistone, IoW 1824-35), Archdeacon of Essex 1861 to death. Dom. Chap. to 7th Marquess of Lothian 1827. Died Hamburg 13/7/1878, leaving £25,000 [C82364] Married Marylebone, London 16/12/1830 Hon. Elizabeth Caroline Waldegrave (dau. Admiral William Waldegrave, 1st Baron Radstock), with issue. Brother below.

**MILDMAY (Walter St John)** Born 12/10/1798, s. Sir Henry Paulet St John Mildmay, 3rd Bart. (Dogmersfield Park, Hartford Bridge, Hants.) and Jane Mildmay (*thus*). BNC, Oxford 1817, then Magdalene, Cambridge 1819, then St John's 1820, BA1823, dn23 (Ely for Salis.), p24 (Win.). V. (and Sinecure R.) Shorwell and Mottistone, IoW 1824-35, V. and R. Abbotstone and Itchenstoke, Hants. 1829-30, R. Dogmersfield 1830 to death (Chiandola, near Nice) 31/7/1835 (CCEd says 8/10/1835) [C82365] Married 17/7/1834 Kitty Anne Warde. Brother above.

**MILES (John)** From Leicester, s. Samuel Miles. Magdalene, Cambridge 1794, dn98 (Lin.), p99 (Lin.), LLB1801. V. and R. Willoughby Waterless w. Peatling Magna, Leics. 1815-46, V. Ashby Magna (Great Ashby) Leics. 1825-46, R. Reynoldstone, Pembroke 1825-34. Died? [C70598]

**MILES (Richard)** Bapt. Wootton Bassett, Wilts. 26/3/1748, s. Thomas Miles. Balliol, Oxford 1766, BA1770, dn70 (B&W), p72 (B&W), MA 1792. R. Lydiard Tregoze, Wilts. 1780 to death 4/9/1839 aged 92. Probate granted 8/10/1839 [C46831]

**MILL (Thomas Harrison Valletort)** Born Stoke Damerel, Devon 9/3/1782, s. Nicholas Mill and Elizabeth Jeredl. Exeter, Oxford 1800, BA1804, dn05 (Ex.), p06 (Ex.). V. Northam, Devon 1812 to death 1/7/1844 [C145959. Foster spells him differently] Wife Elizabetha.

**MILLARD (Charles Freeman [Salter])** Bapt. Norwich Cathedral 17/8/1774, s. Rev. Charles Millard and Elizabeth Salter (a clergy dau.). Pembroke, Cambridge 1794, BA1798, dn98 (Nor.), p98 (Nor.), MA1798. Usher, Norwich G/S 1802-07; R. Didlington w. Colveston, Norfolk 1802-7, V. Hicking, Norfolk 1811-49, V. Sedgeford, Norfolk 1831-49, V. Norwich St Martin at Place 1807 and PC. Norwich St Giles 1811 (and Minor Canon of Norwich Cathedral) to death 1849 [C1097] Married London 5/1/1806 Mary Ann Berry (dau. of a naval knight), with issue.

**MILLER (Charles)** From Harlow, Essex, s. Rev. Charles Miller, sen. Worcester, Oxford 1813 (aged 16), then Magdalen 1814-31, BA 1817, MA1819, dn19 (Ox.), p20 (Ox.). V. Harlow 1831 to death 10/5/1885, leaving £2,401-7s-6d. [C36794]

**MILLER (Charles Sanderson)** Bapt. Radway, Warwicks 13/12/1761, s. Sanderson Miller and Susannah Trotman. St John's, Oxford 1778, BA

1782, dn84 (Ox.), MA1785, p86 (Ox.). V. Harlow, Essex 1789-1831 (res.), V. Lindsell, Essex 1790-1801, V. Latton, Essex 1801-20, V. Matching, Essex 1825 to death. Dom. Chap. to Elizabeth, Baroness Saye and Sele 1790; to Charlotte, Viscountess Chetwynd 1825. Died 21/4/1837 [C36795] Married Charlotte Mead.

**MILLER (Edward)** Born Radway, Warwicks. 7/10/1784, s. Fiennes Sanderson Miller and Henrietta Mead. Queen's, Oxford 1801, BA 1805, MA1808, Fellow to 1819. PC. Chesterton, Warwicks. 1822 and V. Radway w. Ratley 1822 to death. Buried 16/1/1858 aged 73, leaving £9,000 [C18522] Married 28/4/1824 Charlotte Miller [*sic*], 4 s. (3 clerical – Edward, Henry, George).

**MILLER (George Oakes)** Born Malta, s. Rev. John Castleton Miller and Sarah Paget. Caius, Cambridge 1822 (aged 19), BA1826, MA1829, dn29 (Peterb.), p30 (Peterb.). R. (and patron) of Milton Malsor,, Northants. 1830 to death. Dom. Chap. to Lord Croftes; British Chap. at Genoa. Died Genoa 17/9/1840 aged 36 [C110549] Married Canterbury 29/7/1830 Jane Starr.

**MILLER (James)** Possibly bapt. Monzievaird, Perthshire 20/6/1781, s. Andrew Miller and Ann Drummond. St Andrews University 1801, MA1806, dn10 (Durham), p11 (Durham), DD1832. Minor Canon Durham Cathedral 1821 and V. Pittington, Durham 1822 to death 15/1/1854 [C131694. Smart] Married (as Millar) St Andrews , w. issue.

**MILLER (John)** Born Bockleton, Worcs. 20/1/1787, s. Rev. Peter Miller and Mary Kirkman. Worcester, Oxford 1804, BA1808, Fellow 1810-23, dn12 (Ox.), p13 (Ox.), MA 1813. R. Benefield, Northants. 1822-42, V. Bockleton, 1855 to death 18/1/1858, leaving £3,000 [C36797. Boase. In J.M. Chapman, *Reminiscences of three Oxford worthies* (1870)] Brother below.

**MILLER (Joseph Kirkman)** Born Bockleton, Heref. 1785, s. Rev. Peter Miller and Mary Kirkman. Trinity, Cambridge 1803, BA1807, Fellow 1808, dn11 (Win.), p12 (Win.), MA 1810. V. Walkeringham, Notts. 1819-53, PC. Bockleton 1830 and PC. Leysters, Heref. 1830 to death (Walkeringham) 11/5/1855 [C136824] Married 1812 Susan Duppa (a clergy dau., Pudleston Court, Heref.), with clerical son. Brother above.

**MILLER (Michael Hodsoll)** Born West Farleigh, Kent 16/1/1793. St John's, Cambridge 1811, BA1815, then Clare, Fellow 1816-27, dn17 (Ely), p18 (London for Cant.), MA1818. V. Scarborough, Yorks. 1828-48, PC. Hopton, Suffolk 1848-61, PC. Longham and Wendling, Norfolk 1861-4. Chap. to Duke of Buccleuch 1838-70. Died Hampstead, London 22/4/1870 aged 77, leaving £6,000 [C109329] Married York 10/12/1829 Eliza Stibbert Belcomb, Yorks., with issue.

**MILLER (Robert Marratt)** Bapt. Warwick. 18/9/1786, s. Rev. Robert Miller. Wadham, Oxford 1806, BA1810, dn10 (Ox.), p10 (Ox.), MA1813, BD and DD1826. V. Dedham, Essex 1819 to death. Resident Chaplain at Lisbon 1811. Dom. Chap. to 2nd Earl of Warwick 1811; to Baron Beresford 1814. Died 11/6/1839 aged 52 [C36798] Had issue.

**MILLER (Saunders William)** Bapt. City of London 14/11/1760, s. William Miller and Elizabeth Saunders. Pembroke, Oxford 1778, BA1782, dn83 (Ox.), MA1810. R. Hasfield, Glos. 1787-1833, V. Faringdon w. Little Coxwell, Berks. 1799-1800. Died 13/11/1833 (CCEd thus) [C36799] Married Harwell, Berks. 7/9/1784 Maria Blake, w. clerical son Frederick William.

**MILLER (Thomas Combe, Sir, 6th Bart.)** Born 1780, s. Sir Thomas Miller, 5th Bart. and Hannah Black. St John's, Cambridge 1796: re-adm. 1799, LLB1802, dn02 (Win.), p03 (Win.). V. Froyle, Hants. 1803 (living at Froyle Place) to death 29/6/1864, leaving £60,000 [C82370. Boase] Married Bungay, Suffolk 5/5/1824 Martha Holmes (a clergy dau., Brook Hill, Norfolk), with issue. Succ. to title 1816. 'Miller's grandson, Sir Hubert Miller, said of him in 1936: "My grandfather hunted hard to hounds and drank two bottles of port with his dinner'".

**MILLER (William)** Born Newington Bagpath, Glos., s. Richard Miller and Hester Parslow. Trinity, Oxford 1799 (aged 18), MA by 1804, dn04 (Ox.), p05 (Ox.). V. Friston, Sussex -1815-, V. East Dean, Sussex 1815-17, R. East Wittering, Sussex 1817, V. Bapchild, Kent 1821-5, R. Birdham, Sussex 1825. Died Ozleworth, Glos. 6/12/1846 [C36801. Foster is unhelpful] Married Jane Carpenter, with clerical son, also William.

**MILLERS (George)** From Kendal, Westmorland, s. Thomas Millers and Esther Abbot. St John's, Cambridge 1793, BA 1798, dn98 (Lin. for Ely), p00 (Ely), MA1801. PC. Chettisham, Cambs. 1800, V. Winston, Suffolk 1803-6, Minor Canon, etc. of Ely Cathedral 1803-52 (and S/M King's School, Ely), V. Stanford, Norfolk 1808-45, V. Runham, Norfolk 1811-52, R. Hardwicke, Cambs. 1825 to death. Chap. Ely House of Correction 1822. Died Ely 3/1/1852 aged 76 [C70604] Married Alysham, Norfolk 9/7/1801 Mary Forby (a clergy sister!). Inherited £5,000 a year in 1847 on the death of a niece (Romilly2)

**MILLS (Francis)** Bapt. Barford, Warwicks. 13/7/1759, s. Rev. John Mills. Christ Church, Oxford 1777, BA1781, dn83 (Glos. for Wor.), p83 (Wor.), MA1784. R. Hinton on the Green, Glos. 1783-96 (res.), R. Barford 1785-1841. Dom. Chap. to 2nd Earl of Shelburne 1785. Died 23/4/1851 [C121864] Married 25/10/1811 Catherine Maudant, with issue.

**MILLS (Malkin)** Bapt. Bishop Auckland, Co. Durham 8/12/1793, s. John Mills. Literate: dn17 (York), p18 (York). PC. Longstone, Derbys. 1823, V. Thorpe Arnold, Melton Mowbray, Leics. 1852-[66]. Died (Melton Mowbray, a widower) 26/5/1870 aged 76, leaving under £100 [C32582. YCO] Married Sarah Eaton by 1830, with issue.

**MILLS (Thomas)** Bapt. Cowbit, Lincs. 23/3/1774, s. Rev. Joseph Mills. Christ Church, Oxford 1792, BA1796, dn96 (Lin.), p98 (Lin.), MA1800. R. Dembleby, Lincs, 1805 (non-res.), Minor Canon, etc. 1806-45 in Peterborough Cathedral (Canon 1845-56), PC. Eye, Sussex 1816-32, V. Bringhurst cum Great Easton, Leics. 1824-33, R. Northborough, Northants. 1833 to death 21/7/1856, living at Coval Hall, Chelmsford, Essex [C70612. Bennett1] Had issue.

**MILLS (Thomas)** From London, s. John Mills. Trinity, Cambridge 1791, BA1796, Fellow 1798, MA1799, dn99 (Peterb.), p00 (Peterb.). V. Helions Bumpstead, Essex [vacant in ERC] 1809 and V. Eye, Northants. 1809 to death 4/1/1833 (CCEd thus) [C110551] Had issue.

**MILLS (Thomas)** Born Sudbury, Suffolk 17/11/1791, s. Thomas Mills (Grove House, Surrey) and Mary Story. Christ Church, Oxford 1810, BA1814, dn14 (Nor.), p16 (Nor.). R. (and patron) of Little Henny w. Stutton, Essex 1821-79, R. (and patron) of Great Saxham, Suffolk 1829 and Hon. Canon of Norwich Cathedral 1859 to death. Chap. in Ordinary at death. Died 29/9/1879, leaving £9,000 [C114179. Boase] Married (1) Marylebone, London 12/4/1815 Anne Barnardiston (d.1827), with clerical son Barnardiston Stopford Thomas Mills (2) 13/12/1836 Hon. Elizabeth Frances Barrington (dau. Rev. 5th Viscount Barrington) (w), *s.p.*

**MILLS (Thomas Sturges)** Born Deddington, Oxon. 3/10/1790, s. Moses Mills. Magdalen Hall, Oxford 1818, dn19 (Chester), p21 (Chester). PC. Dobcross, Saddleworth, Yorks. 1821-45 (res.), PC. Littleborough, Lancs. 1848 to death 1/10/1864, leaving £4,000 [C170010] Married St Dunstan in the West, City of London 3/9/1816 Charlotte Mary Jane Roberts [but some online confusion here], with issue. *J.P.* Lancs., Cheshire, West Riding of Yorks.; *D.L.*

**MILLS (William)** Bapt. Miserden, Glos. 26/10/1769, s. John Mills and Ann Ady. Trinity, Oxford 1785, BA1785, MA1792, dn95 (Glos.), p96 (Glos.), BD1802. R. (and patron) of Miserden 1797 and R. Shellingford, Glos. 1810 to death 15/3/1848 [C158004] Married 1808 Hester Howes, with clerical son William Yarnton Mills.

**MILMAN (Henry Hart)** Born 10/2/1791, s. Sir Francis Milman, 1st Bart. (physician to George 111) and Frances Hart. BNC, Oxford 1810, BA 1814, Fellow 1814-19, dn15 (Ox.), MA1816, p16 (London), BD and DD1849. R. Reading St Mary 1817-35, R. St Margaret's, Westminster (w. Canon of Westminster Abbey annexed) 1835-49, Dean of St Paul's Cathedral, London 1849 ('The Great Dean', income £2,000) to death 4/9/1868, leaving £20,000 [C36807 has wrong ord. dates. ODNB. Boase. A. Milman, *Henry Hart Milman, DD, Dean of St Paul's: a biographical sketch* (1900). LNCP] Married 11/3/1824 Mary Anne Cokell (a general's dau.), 3s., 2 dau. (and clerical s. William Henry). Historian; Professor of Poetry, Oxford 1821.

**MILNE (Robert)** Bapt. Dundurcas, Morayshire 19/8/1787, s. William Milne. Edinburgh University, MA1814, dn20 (York), p22 (York), St John's, Cambridge 1827, a Ten Year Man. V. Swine, Yorks. 1824-38 (sequestrated 1836 and deprived of his benefice, 'but continued to live nearby'), Min. Bayswater Proprietary Chapel

London 1827-9, PC. West Molesey, Surrey 1827-30. Died? [C82371. YCO as Literate]

**MILNER (Henry Stephen)** Born Pudsey, Yorks. 1764, s. Sir William Milner, 2nd Bart. and Elizabeth Mordaunt. Christ Church, Oxford 1781, BA1785, then All Souls, BCL 1788, dn86 (St Asaph), p88 (Llandaff), DCL 1793. Prebend of Meliden and Treasurer in St Asaph Cathedral 1788-91, R. Dunton, Bucks. 1788-1811, R. Monk's Risborough, Bucks. 1801-11, R. Thrybergh, Yorks. 1811 and R. Adwick le Street, Yorks. 1811 to death (unmarried, Uxbridge, Middx.) 6/5/1843 aged 78 [C4326] J.P. West Riding of Yorks.

**MILNER (James George)** Born Bolton on Swale, Yorks. 14/8/1796. s. John Milner & Ann Thompson. Literate: dn20 (Chester), p23 (Chester). PC. Hamsterley, Durham 1825-85, PC. Bellerby, Yorks. 1829-82. Died a widower 16/3/1885 aged 88, personal estate £177-6s-10d. [C131695] Married West Witton, Yorks. 13/5/1823 Nancy Kirkbank, with issue.

**MILNER (Joseph)** Born North Ferriby, Yorks. 3/9/1793, s. Rev. Joseph Milner, sen. (nephew of Dean Milner of Carlisle) and Elizabeth Needham. St Catherine's, Cambridge 1815, dn17 (Glos.), p17 (York), BA1820, MA 1824. V. Appleby St Laurence, Westmorland 1817 (with Chap. St Anne's Hospital [almshouses]) to death (a widower) 28/11/1864, leaving £1,000 [C135636. YCO. Platt] Married his cousin Mary Wilberforce, with clerical son. J.P., D.L. Westmorland. Mayor of Appleby at death.

**MILNER (Robert)** Born Orton, Westmorland 21/8/1767, s. Holme Milner and Esther Newton. Literate: dn96 (Car.), p97 (Car.). V. Orton 1802 to death 15/3/1849 [C5670. Platt] Married Orton 2/4/1792 Peggy Burn (a clergy dau.), with issue. J.P.

**MILNES (Christopher)** Bapt. Stixwold, Lincs. 8/2/1801, s. John and Elizabeth Milnes. Lincoln, Oxford 1819, BA1822, dn24 (Lin.), MA1825, p25 (Lin.), BD1833. R. Scampton, Lincs. 1828, R. Aisthorpe w. Thorpe in the Fallows (o/w West Thorpe), Lincs. 1833 to death 7/2/1850 [C70621. Kaye]

**MILNES (Edward)** From Henley, Oxon., s. Rev. Thomas and Elizabeth Milnes. All Souls, Oxford 1808 (aged 19), BA1811, p12 (Salis). V. Watlington, Oxon. 1814 to death 11/7/1841 [C36810] Married Highworth, Wilts. 18/10/1814 Charlotte Sanders.

**MILNES (Thomas)** Born Halton, Lincs. 14/6/1764, s. Rev. James Andrew Milnes. Christ's, Cambridge 1783, BA1788, dn87 (Lin.), p88 (Lin.), MA1791. V. Burton Agnes, Yorks. 1806 to death 9/1/1833 [C70623] Married Eaton Socon, Beds. 10/10/1796 Eleanor Gery, with clerical son.

**MILWARD (Joseph)** Possibly born Long Marton, Westmorland, s. Rev. Thomas Milward. PC. Denby, Derbys. 1799, V. Horsley, Derbys. 1801. Died Basford, Notts. 2/9/1836 aged 74 (*Gentleman's Magazine* thus) [C5677 and Foster have to be incorrect] 2 people?

**MINGAY, MINGAYE (George)** Born Thetford, Norfolk 23/4/1789, s. William Robert Mingay and Mary Harvey. Caius, Cambridge 1807, BA1812, dn12 (Nor.), p13 (Nor.), MA 1815. R. Kennett, Cambs. 1813-36, R. Wistow, Hunts. 1827-40, R. (and patron) of Wilby, Suffolk 1838-69. R. West Barkwith, Suffolk 1869-73. Resigned his Orders under the Clerical Disabilities Relief Act, 1873 (though still called Reverend in his will). Dom. Chap. to 5th Duke of Rutland 1827. Died Bury St Edmunds, Suffolk 17/5/1879, leaving £16,000 [C70676] Married Sunbury-on-Thames, Middx. 15/10/1818 Mary Webb Giraud, with issue.

**MINTON (Thomas Webb)** Born Stoke on Trent, Staffs. 24/12/1791, s. Thomas Minton and Sarah Webb. Queens', Cambridge 1823 (a Ten Year Man), dn25 (Lin.), p26 (Dur.). PC. Brimington, Derbys. 1832-46, V. Darlington Holy Trinity, Co. Durham 1846-65. Died 15/3/1870 aged 78, leaving £25,000 [C18530 as Literate. CR65 Thomas William] Married Everton, Liverpool 12/4/1819 Jane Senhouse, with clerical son Samuel Minton Senhouse.

**MIREHOUSE (Thomas Henry)** Born Castlemartin, Pembroke 21/12/1790 (a twin), s. John Mirehouse and Mary Edwards. Clare, Cambridge 1809, then Christ's 1810, BA1814 [adm. Lincoln's Inn 1817] MA1817, p17 (Salis.). V. Easton in Gordano, Som. 1818-67 (and Prebend of Grantham Australis in Salisbury Cathedral 1824) and R. (and patron) of Harlaxton, Lincs. 1826 to death. Dom. Chap. to Bishop of Salisbury 1824. Died 7/1/1867, leaving £45,000 [C41634] Married Westminster, London

26/3/1835 Millicent Miles (dau. of an *M.P.*), with issue. *J.P.* for Somerset and Pembroke. Twin brother below.

**MIREHOUSE (William Squire)** Born Castlemartin, Pembroke 21/12/1790 (a twin), s. John Mirehouse and Mary Edwards. Clare, Cambridge 1809, BA1814, dn16 (B&W), p17 (Salis. for Bristol), MA1817. V. Sandhurst, Glos. 1817-21, (first and only) PC. Fishponds Chapel, Bristol 1821 and R. Colsterworth, Lincs. 1826 (non-res.) to death. Chap. to HRH Princess Sophia. Died 26/3/1864, living at Hambrook Grove, Glos., leaving £30,000 [C41603. Bennett2] Married Montgomery 2/2/1832 Eliza Brunetta Herbert (w), with clerical son succeeding at Colsterworth. *J.P.* Glos. and Pembrokeshire. Twin brother above.

**MISTER (Samuel Wright)** Bapt. Shipston on Stour, Worcs. 20/10/1769, s. John and Ann Mister. St John, Oxford 1788, BA1792, dn92 (Ox.), p93 (Ox.), Fellow, MA1796, BD1801. R. Little Rollright, Oxon. 1797 to death 7/5/1836, living at Basford, Glos. [C36815]

**MITCHELL (James [Dyke Molesworth])** Bapt. Exeter 1/1/1780 (but of Lismoy, Co. Longford), s. Knight Mitchell and Charlotte Amelia Molesworth. Trinity Hall, Cambridge 1798, no degree, dn03 (Chester). R. Quinton, Northants. 1813 to death (Shanklin, IoW) 15/12/1838, leaving £99 (left unadministered until 1885) [C53415] Married Beddington, Surrey 20/9/1820 Mary Ann Spragge (w), 1 dau. Two forenames added 1803/6.

**MITCHELL (John)** Probably bapt. Chatham, Kent 5/12/1792, s. Thomas and Isabella Mitchell. St John's, Cambridge 1812, BA1816, dn16 (B&W), p17 (Glos.). R. St Nicholas Cole Abbey w. St Nicholas Olave, City of London 1817 [C120592 as Mitchel], V. Kingsclere (w. Sydmorton & Ecchinswell Chapels 1829), Hants. 1817 (and S/M Kingsclere G/S 1833) to death 19/2/1849 [C41635]

**MITCHELL (Thomas)** Bapt. Helmsley, Yorks. 5/8/1788, s. Thomas Mitchell and Martha Swales. Literate: dn11 (York), p12 (York). PC. Holme on the Wolds, Yorks. 1817-53-, V. Saundby, Notts. 1835-58. Died 1858? Will not yet traced [C135639. YCO] Married Pocklington, Yorks. 16/11/1826 Mary Ann Clubley, with issue.

**MITCHINSON (Thomas, sen.)** Bapt. North Ormsby, Lincs. 22/2/1765. Literate: dn85 (Car.), p86 (Car.). V. Helpringham, Lincs. 1799 to death 17/6/1836 [C5680] Married Catherine Hollingworth, w. clerical son, below.

**MITCHINSON (Thomas, jun.)** Bapt. Helpringham, Lincs. 24/12/1793, s. Rev. Thomas Mitchinson, sen. (above) and Catherine Hollingworth. St John's, Cambridge 1811, then Sidney 1813, BA1815, dn16 (Lin.), p17 (Lin.), MA1819. S/M Boston G/S 1817; PC. Carrington, Lincs. 1819-62 (and where he kept a boarding school), PC. West Fen (o/w Frithville), Lincs. 1822-62, (succ. his father as) V. Helpringham 1836-54. Died 13/4/1862 aged 70, leaving £1,000 [C70680. Bennett2] Married Boston, Lincs. 28/12/1824 Elizabeth Clarke, with issue.

**MITFORD (John)** Born Richmond, Surrey 13/8/1781, s. John Mitford (Commander in navy of *H.E.I.C.*) and Mary Allen. Oriel, Oxford 1801, BA1804, dn05 (Win. for Cant.), p08 (Nor.). V. Benhall, Suffolk 1810-59 (and Dom. Chap. to his patron Lord Redesdale 1815) [C11650], R. Weston St Peter, Norwich 1815 and R. Stratford St Andrew, Suffolk 1817 (these parishes united 1824) to death. Editor of the *Gentleman's Magazine* 1834-50; and of Gray's works. Died Benhall 27/4/1859, leaving £5,000 [C82377. ODNB. Boase. *Letters and reminiscences of the Rev. John Mitford...*, ed. M.C. Houstoun (1891)] Married 21/10/1814 Augusta Boodle ('the marriage was not attended with happiness'; and 'he excited much gossip by taking under his wing a 12-year-old village girl'), 1s.

**MITTON (Henry)** Born Knaresborough, Yorks. 18/2/1782, s. Rev. Robert Mitton and Jane Gilbertson. University, Oxford 1800, BA 1804, dn05 (Win. for York), p06 (York), MA 1807. R. Harswell, Yorks. 1816-54 [blank in ERC] and R. Wold Newton (o/w Newton le Wold), Lincs. 1832 to death (Harswell) 30/8/1854 [C70681. YCO] Married 1828 Anne Hutchinson, dau. of a Harrogate physician.

**MITTON (James)** Bapt. Bentham, Cumberland 19/7/1772, s. Joseph Mitton and Mary Wilkinson. Literate: dn95 (York), p96 (York). V. Thornthwaite, Pateley Bridge, Yorks. 1804 to death 21/8/1852 [C130230. YCO] Married Leeds 16/7/1799 Jane Garforth, w. clerical son.

**MOGG (Henry Hodges)** Born Farrington Gurney, Som. 28/4/1770, s. Jacob Mogg and

Sarah Hodges. Oriel, Oxford 1787, BA1791, p93 (Ex. for B&W), MA1794, p95 (Glos.). R. Tellisford, Som. 1797-1804, V. ('Treasurer') High Littleton, Som. 1804 and V. Chewton Mendip, Som. 1814 to death (Ston Easton, Som.) 17/1/1850 [C46997] Married Chippen-ham, Wilts. 13/8/1799 Maria Singer, with issue.

**MOGRIDGE (William Henry)** Born Pershore, Worcs. 28/7/1795, s. Rev. John and Maria Mogridge, Jesus, Oxford 1816, BA1821, MA1822. PC. Wick (juxta Pershore) 1824 and Min. Balham Proprietary Chapel, Surrey 1828 to death 15/10/1847 [C82379 is blank]

**MOISES (Edward)** Born Masham, Yorks. 23/8/1762, s. Rev. Edward Moises, sen. Trinity, Cambridge 1779, BA1783, dn85 (York), MA 1787, p11 (Durham). H/M Newcastle upon Tyne G/S 1787-1828; Master of the Virgin Mary Hospital [almshouses], Newcastle 1806 and V. Hart and Hartlepool, Durham 1811 to death (Jesmond, Newcastle) 2/4/1845 aged 83 [C130233. YCO] Married 1788 Mary Bowes, a surgeon's daughter. Port. in: S. Harbottle, *The Reverend William Turner ...* (Newcastle, 1997).

**MOLESWORTH, *later* MOLESWORTH ST AUBYN (Hender)** Born St Breock, Cornwall 12/3/1798, s. Rev. John Molesworth and Catherine St Aubyn. Exeter, Oxford 1817, BA 1820, dn22 (Ex.), p22 (Ex.). R. (St Ewny juxta) Redruth, Cornwall 1822-67. Died 13/12/1867 aged 69, leaving £18,000 (as Hender St Aubyn) [C145969 as Molesworth] Married Heavitree, Exeter 6/6/1829 Helen Matilda Isabella Napleton, with clerical son St Aubyn Hender Molesworth-St Aubyn.

**MOLESWORTH (John Edward Nassau)** Born Westminster, London 4/2/1790, s. John Molesworth and Frances Caroline Hill. Trinity, Cambridge 1808, BA1812, dn13 (Chester for Win), p14 (Glos. for Win.), MA 1817, BD and DD1838. V. Wirksworth, Derbys. 1828, V. Canterbury St Martin and St Paul 1829-39, V. Minster-in-Thanet, Kent 1839, V. Rochdale, Lancs. [income in CR65 £1,730] 1839 to death 21/4/1877 aged 87, leaving £60,000 [C18536. ODNB. Boase] Married (1) London 28/11/1815 Harriet Mackinnon (d.1850), with distinguished issue (2) Eastry, Kent 31/10/1854 Mrs Harriet Elizabeth Bridges (dau. of Rev. Sir Robert Affleck, St Nicholas Court, Thanet, Kent). *ghgraham.org/johnmolesworth1790.html*

**MOLESWORTH (William)** Bapt. Egloshayle, Cornwall 5/11/1792, s. Sir William Molesworth, 6th Bart. and Caroline Treby Ourry. St John, Cambridge 1810, BA1814, dn15 (Ex.), p16 (Ex.), MA1817. R. Beaworthy, Devon (and Preacher throughout the Diocese of Exeter) 1816-51, R. St Breock, Cornwall 1816 and R. St Ervan, Cornwall 1817 to death. Dom. Chap. to 2nd Marquess of Exeter 1816. Died 28/3/1851 [C145971] Married (1) Plympton, Devon 6/11/1817 Katherine Treby (d.1823), w. clerical sons Sir Hugh Henry, 9th Bart., and Sir Paul William, 10th Bart. (2) 10/2/1829 Frances Susanna Buller, w. further issue.

**MOLINEUX (George [Fieldhouse])** Born Wolverhampton 4/11/1773, s. George Molineux, (banker and ironmaster, J.P. and High Sheriff of Staffs.) and Jane Robinson. Christ Church, Oxford 1793, BA1796, dn96 (C&L). R. Ryton, Shropshire 1798-1840, Prebend of Wobaston in Wolverhampton Collegiate Church 1800, PC. Acton Trussell w. Bednall, Staffs. 1832. Died 30/9/1840 [C18537] Married Manchester 21/2/1801 Maria Hardman, with issue.

**MOLYNEUX (George More)** Born Farnham, Surrey 29/3/1797, s. James More Molyneux (Loseley House, Surrey) and Ann Merritt. Trinity, Oxford 1815, BA1820, MA1822, dn23 (Chester), p23 (Lin. for Chich.). R. Compton, Surrey 1823 to death 5/11/1872, leaving £4,000 [C64565] Married Marylebone, London 26/4/1825 Anne Spurstow Skrine, with clerical son.

**MONCKTON (Hugh)** From London, s. Edward Monckton. Christ Church 1810-18, Student [Fellow] 1812-17, BA1814, dn15 (Ox.), MA1816, p16 (Lin.). R. Seaton w. Thorpe, Rutland 1816 and V. Harringworth, Northants. 1816 to death. Dom. Chap. to Millicent, Countess of Gosford 1816. Died 31/10/1842 [C36826]

**MONCRIEFFE (David Stewart)** Bapt. Bristol 26/5/1773, s. Rev. William Moncrieffe (a Scot) and Forrester Suttie Bruce. Queen's, Oxford 1792, BA1796, dn97 (B&W), p98 (Bristol), MA 1798. R. Loxton, Som. 1801 and R. Weston-in-Gordano, Som. 1817 to death. Dom. Chap. to 1st Baron Lynedoch 1817. Died 9/8/1850 aged 77 [C41639] Married (1) 20/8/1803 Sarah Anne Simmons, with issue (2)

30/5/1820 Elizabeth Young Monkland. *J.P.* Port online.

**MONEY (Frederick)** Bapt. Framingham Earl, Norfolk 'spring of 1795', s. Gen. John Money (an early balloonist, Trowse Hall, Norfolk) and an unknown mother. Caius, Cambridge 1817, dn18 (Nor.), p21 (Nor.), BA1822. R. Offham, Kent 1832 to death (Southsea, Hants.) 26/4/1869, leaving £12,000 [C6986] Married Intwood, Norfolk 3/7/1817 Elisabeth Lydia Clarke (Keswick, Norfolk), with issue.

**MONEY (Kyrle Ernle)** Born Durham 23/1/1781, s. William Money (Hom House, Much Marcle, Heref.) and Mary Webster. Oriel, Oxford, BA by 1808, dn08 (Glos.), p09 (Ex.). V. Much Marcle w. Yatton 1809, Prebend of Gorwell and Overbury in Hereford Cathedral 1830 to death (Great Malvern, Worcs.) 17/1/1846 aged 64 [C158899. Confusion in Foster] Married Woolwich, Kent 16/1/1806 Mary Thomasina ffrench, with clerical s. Kyrle Ernle Aubrey Money. Much confusion here as other family members changed names to Money-Kyrle 1809. Brother William, two below.

**MONEY (William)** Born Norwich 12/7/1752, s. William Money and Elizabeth French. Christ's, Cambridge 1769, BA1773, dn74 (Nor.), p85 [*sic*] (Nor.). R. Warham, Norfolk 1789, V. Wiggenhall St Mary Magdalen, Norfolk 1800-35. Buried Fakenham, Norfolk 23/2/1835 [C114189] Married Maria Riches.

**MONEY, *later* MONEY-KYRLE (William)** Born 13/10/1776, s. William Money and Mary Webster, Hom House, Much Marcle, Hereford. Oriel, Oxford 1794, BA1798, p01 (Salis.), MA 1824. R. Yatesbury, Wilts. 1801-43. Died Ely 18/1/1848 [C88401] Married 16/7/1805 Emma Down, and had issue. Inherited his brother's estates (Hom House, etc.) in 1843 and changed name in 1844. Brother Kyrle Ernle, above.

**MONINS (John)** Bapt. Margate, Kent 6/11/1786, s. John Monins and Sarah Price. St John's, Cambridge 1803, BA1808, dn09 (Salis. for Cant.), MA 1811, p11 (Cant.). R. Ringwould, Kent 1811-53, R. Charlton by Dover, Kent 1811-29, R. Hurst (o/w Fawkenhurst), Kent 1818-43. Died 7/10/1853 aged 66 [C86627] Married 18/10/1808 Mary Lee Carter (Kennington Hall, Kent), with issue.

**MONK (Edward Gould)** Born Windsor, Nova Scotia 4/9/1798, s. Capt. George Henry Monk (of Montreal) and Elizabeth Wentworth Gould. Adm. Lincoln's Inn 1815. Trinity, Cambridge 1816, BA1821, dn24 (London for Cant.), MA 1824, p25 (Chich.). V. Newport, Essex 1828-50, V. Much Cowarne, Heref. 1851 to death (Church Stretton, Shropshire) 26/8/1861 aged 62, leaving £1,000 [C106755] Married St Pancras, London 12/7/1823 Marie Anne Amanda Moulon (w), with issue.

**MONK (George)** Bapt. Upholland, Lancs. 18/5/1752, s. Richard (a farmer and *pleb*). BNC, Oxford 1773, BA1776, dn76 (Chester), p77 (Chester). (joint) Minister Liverpool St Paul 1827 to death 13/1/1835 (CCEd thus) [C170015] Clerical son (two below?)

**MONK (James Henry, Bishop of Gloucester, *then of* Gloucester and Bristol)** Born Buntingford, Herts. 12/12/1784, s. Charles Monk (an army officer) and Sarah Waddington (a clergy dau.). Trinity, Cambridge 1799, Fellow 1805-22, Tutor to 1822, BA1804, MA1807, dn09 (Bristol), p10 (Bristol), BD1818, DD 1822, incorporated at Oxford 1831. Regius Professor of Greek 1809-23. Dean of Peterborough 1822-30 and R. Fiskerton, Lincs. 1822-32, R. Peakirk cum Glinton, Northants. 1829-50, Canon of Westminster 1830 to death, Bishop of Gloucester 1830 (the See being amalgamated with that of Bristol in 1836) to death 6/6/1856 aged 73. Buried Westminster Abbey [C53420. ODNB. Boase] Married Nuneaton, Staffs. 18/9/1822 Jane Smart Hughes, and had issue.

**MONK (John Boughey)** Born Liverpool 22/4/1791, s. Rev. George Monk (above?). Trinity, Cambridge 1807, BA1812, Fellow 1813, dn14 (Bristol), MA1815, p15 (Chester), incorporated at Oxford 1843. (joint) PC. Liverpool St George 1829 to death 20/11/1861, leaving £25,000 [C53421] Married Liverpool 19 or 26/6/1820 Jane Ward.

**MONKHOUSE (Henry)** Bapt. Raughton Head, Castle Sowerby, Cumberland 24/10/1802, s. Rev. William Monkhouse and Ann Relph. St John's, Cambridge 1820, BA1825, dn26 (Chester), p27 (York for Car.). PC. Raughton Head, Castle Sowerby 1828-43 (where he also took pupils), PC. Laxfield, Suffolk 1844-7, PC. Great Tey, Essex 1848 to death 29/12/1849 [C5688. YCO. Platt] Married Castle Sowerby 29/2/1832 Charlotte Berry Fallowfield.

**MONKHOUSE (Isaac)** Bapt. Ivegill, Cumberland 15/2/1752, s. Isaac Monkhouse [*pleb*]. Queen's, Oxford 1772, BA1776, MA1780, BD1796. R. Holwell, Dorset 1797 and R. Wootton Glanville, Dorset 1814 to death 29/12/1834 aged 81 (CCEd says 9/2/1835) [C53422] Married Langwathby, Cumberland 3/5/1773 Sarah Williamson. J.P. Dorset.

**MONSON (John Joseph Thomas)** Born Essex 7/7/1791, s. Rev. Hon. Thomas John Monson (below) and Anne Shipley Greene. Trinity, Cambridge 1808, BA1813, dn14 (Chester), p15 (Nor. for Chester), MA1821. PC. Leeming, Yorks. 1815, R. Burton by Lincoln, Lincs. 1815-43, (succ. his father as) R. Bedale, Yorks. 1843 to death. Chap. in Ordinary 1828. Died 31/7/1861 aged 70, leaving £9,000 [C70692. Kaye] Married Burton Constable, Yorks. 26/8/1813 Elizabeth Anne Wyvill (a clergy dau.), *s.p.*

**MONSON (Thomas John, Hon.)** Born Lincs. 10/5/1764, s. 2nd Baron Monson and Theodosia Maddison. Trinity, Cambridge 1782, MA1785, dn88 (Lin.), p88 (Lin.). R. Burton by Lincoln 1788-97, R. Donington on Bain, Lincs. 1789-1803, PC. South Carlton, Lincs. 1797, R. Bedale, Yorks ('the Rector's son assists him, no regular stipend') [net income £1,936] 1797-1843, PC. Leeming, Yorks. 1813-15. Died 3/4/1843 aged 78 [C70693. BBV] Married (1) Heckfield, Hants. 29/7/1790 Anne Shipley Greene (d.1818), with clerical son (above) (2) Bedale 11/8/1824 Sarah Wyvill (a clergy dau.), with further and clerical son.

**MONTAGU (George)** Born Burlingham, Norfolk, s. Gerard Montagu and Mary Anne Doughty. Peterhouse, Cambridge 1811 (aged 18), BA1815, re-adm. 1816, dn16 (Nor.), p17 (Nor.). R. South Pickenham, Norfolk 1827 to death (Swaffham, Norfolk) 6/7/1865, leaving £30,000 [C114191] Married Swaffham 23/10/1817 Emily Yonge (a clergy dau.), with clerical son Edgar William Montagu.

**MONTGOMERIE (George Stephen Molineux)** Bapt. Garboldisham, Norfolk 29/3/1790, s. George Montgomerie (Garboldisham Hall) and Elizabeth White. Christ's, Cambridge 1812, dn15 (Nor.), p15 (Ely), BA1816, MA1827. R. Garboldisham St John w. All Saints 1815 to death (unm.) 17/1/1850, leaving £50 (unadministered) [C109332]

**MONTGOMERY (George Augustus)** Born Islington, London 5/4/1794, s. Augustus Retnuh [his mother's surname spelt backwards!] Reebkomp (an anagram of Pembroke!) (later Montgomery), the natural s.10th Earl of Pembroke and Kitty Hunter. Oriel, Oxford 1813, BA1817, dn18 (Salis.), p20 (Salis.), MA 1821. R. Bishopstone, South Wilts. 1821-42, Prebend of Ruscombe Southbury in Salisbury Cathedral 1828 to death 1/12/1842 [C36828] Married Ightham, Kent 26/6/1827 Cecilia Markham, with issue.

**MONTGOMERY (Robert)** Bapt. 10/2/1801, s. Rev. Francis Montgomery, Northants. Peterhouse, Cambridge 1819, BA1823, dn24 (Peterb.), p25 (Peterb.), MA1827. R. (and patron) of Holcot, Northants. 1825 to death 12/12/1880, leaving £18,000 [C110555] Married Holborn, London 15/11/1825 Jane Walker, with issue.

**MONYPENNY (Phillips)** From Maytham Hall, Tenterden, Kent, s. James Monypenny and Silvestra Blackwell. Peterhouse, Cambridge 1778, BA1783, dn84 (Lin. for London), MA 1786, p87 (Roch.). V. Hadlow, Kent 1797-1841, V. Benenden, Kent 1799-1803. Dom. Chap. to Theodosia, Baronesss Monson 1799 (*q.v.* Thomas John Monson, *opposite*). Died (Hadlow House) 4/1/1841 aged 79 [C393] Married 13/1/1803 Charlotte (dau. Sir Edward Dering, Bart.).

**MOODY (Henry Riddell)** Born Marylebone, London 22/7/1792, s. Robert Sadleir Moody and Jane Riddell. Oriel, Oxford 1811, BA1815, dn17 (Chester for London), p17 (London), MA 1817. R. Chartham, Kent (and Preacher throughout the Diocese of Canterbury) 1822 to death, Hon. Canon Rochester Cathedral 1866. Died 16/3/1873, leaving £25,000 [C120639] Married Westminster, London 29/10/1819 Althea Jane Wollaston, with issue. Online photo.

**MOODY (Robert)** Bapt. Everton Notts. 18/8/1782, s. Robert and Jane Moody. Corpus Christi, Cambridge 1800, BA1805, dn08 (York), p09 (York). R. Beckingham w. Fenton and Stragglethorpe, Lincs. 1810 to death 1837 [C70696. YCO]

**MOOR (Edward James)** Born Bombay 19/7/1799, s. Major Edward Moor and Elizabeth Lynn. Trinity, Cambridge 1817, BA 1821, dn22 (Nor.), p23 (Nor.). PC. Kesgrave,

Suffolk 1828-43, PC. Brightwell w. Foxhall, Suffolk 1831-43, R. Great Bealings, Suffolk 1844 to death 10/6/1886, leaving £1,153-0s-0d. [C114196] Wife Harriet Jane, and issue.

**MOOR (James Hoare Christopher)** Born Rugby, Staffs. 28/1/1780, s. Rev. Christopher Moor (an Irishman) and Mary Blackbourn. Magdalen, Oxford 1796, BA1800, MA1803, dn03 (C&L), p04 (C&L), Fellow 1810-15, BD 1811. R. Swaby, Lincs. 1814-31, V. Clifton upon Dunsmoor, Warwicks. 1831 and PC. Donington Wood, Shropshire 1832 to death 20/3/1853 [C18539] Married (1) Clifton upon Dunsmore 24/7/1815 Mary Sale (d.1836), with issue (2) Louth, Lincs. 10/8/1837, with further issue.

**MOOR (Richard Watson)** Bapt. Hardraw, Yorks. 18/5/1804. Literate: dn29 (B&W), p29 (B&W). PC. Stoke St Gregory, Som. 1829. Died Bath 11/3/1884, leaving £2,216 [C41640] Married Bradford (?Mrs) Anna Maria Trapp (w), w. issue.

**MOORE (George)** Born 19/11/1770, s. Most Rev. John Moore (Archbishop of Canterbury) and Catherine Eden (dau. of a baronet). Christ Church, Oxford 1788, BA1792, dn94 (Cant.), p94 (Cant.), MA1795. 'Registrar of the Faculty Office' 1790; Principal Registrar of the Prerogative Court of Canterbury 1795. Canon of the 6th Prebend in Canterbury Cathedral 1795-1845, R. Brasted, Kent 1795, V. (and Sinecure R.) Wrotham cum Stansted, Kent 1800-24 [net income £2,655], V. East Peckham, Kent 1805 to death. Chap. to his father 1804. Died 9/12/1845 aged 75 [C158207] Married (1) Wrotham 29/6/1795 Lady Maria Elizabeth Hay (dau. of 15th Earl of Erroll, d.1804) (2) St George's Hanover Square, London 11/10/1806 Harriet Mary Brook Bridges (dau. of a baronet), with clerical s. Edward Moore. Brother Robert, below.

**MOORE (George)** Born Middlesex, s. George Moore (of Lincoln). St John's, Cambridge 1807 (aged 15), then Pembroke 1809, BA1813, dn14 (Lin.), p16 (Lin.). R. Lincoln St Peter in Eastgate w. St Margaret in the Close 1819 >< and R. Owmby by Spital, Lincs. 1823 (non-res.) to death 19/10/1841 aged 49 [C50549. Kaye] Married 1823 Mary Fardell. 'The best minister in Lincoln'.

**MOORE (Henry)** From Sherborne, Dorset, s. Thomas Moore. Trinity, Cambridge 1814 (aged 19), then Clare 1814, BA1819, dn19 (C&L), p19 (C&L), MA1822. V. Eccleshall, Staffs. 1822-56, V. Dunchurch, Warwicks. 1822-36, V. Penn, Staffs. 1836-56, Archdeacon of Stafford 1855-76, V. Lichfield St Mary 1856-65, Prebend of Hansacre 1851 (and Precentor of Lichfield Cathedral 1865) to death (Tettenhall Wood House, Wolverhampton) 18/7/1876, leaving £10,000 [C18387. Boase] Widow Rebecca Harriet.

**MOORE (Henry)** [MA but NiVoF] A curate from 1815. V. Willingdon, Sussex 1830 to death 21/6/1843 aged 56 [C64576]

**MOORE (James)** Born London 16/12/1769, s. James Moore (merchant). Magdalene, Cambridge 1787 [adm. Inner Temple1792] dn95 (Salis.), LLD1795, incorporated at Oxford St John's 1817, DCLOxford 1817. R. Sutton on Derwent, Yorks. 1809-14, V. St Pancras New Church, London 1814-45 'In 1822 the new parish church was opened, the vicar going thither from the Old Church' Died 19/6/1845 [C88450]

**MOORE (John)** From Clerkenwell, London, s. Rev. John Moore, sen. Worcester, Oxford 1806 (aged 18), BA1809, LLB1810, dn10 (London), MA1812, p12 (Ox.), Fellow, etc. 1814-18. V. Alrewas, Staffs. 1832 to death 11/6/1851 aged 63 [C18541]

**MOORE (John)** see also under **STEVENS**

**MOORE (John Vaux)** From Aspley Guise, Beds., s. John Patrick Moore. Exeter, Oxford 1816 (aged 18), BA1819, dn21 (Lin.), p22 (Lin.), MA1822. R. Wilden, Beds. 1822-35, R. Brampton, Hunts 1826, R. Aspley Guise 1844 to death. Dom. Chap. to 8th Duke of Bedford 1826. Died 12/1/1864, leaving £3,000 [C70710]

**MOORE (Joseph Christian)** Born Douglas, IoM 12/8/1802, s. James Moore and Elizabeth Jeale. Initially in business. St Edmund Hall, Oxford 1823, BA1827, dn28 (C&L [for S&M?]), p29 ([C&L for?] S&M), MA1844. PC. Measham, Derbys. 1830-44, R. (Kirk) Andreas, IoM and Archdeacon of Man 1844 to death 26/2/1886. No will traced in England [C8051. Boase. Gelling]

**MOORE (Peter Wallond)** From Middlesex. St John's, Cambridge 1802, BA1806, dn08 (Heref.), p08 (Glos.), MA1809 (as Wallond only). V.

South Hayling, Hants. 1809-10, R. Bixley, Norfolk 1810-13, R. Thakeham, Sussex 1815 to death 28/1/1849 aged 49 [C64577]

**MOORE (Richard)** Born Halsall, Lancs. 3/8/1792, twin s. Rev. Glover Moore and Ann Tarleton Antrobus. BNC, Oxford 1810, BA 1814, dn15 (Chester), p17 (Chester), MA1817. V. Lund (o/w Clifton), Kirkham, Lancs. 1820 to death 19/4/1886, leaving £3,214-0s-8d. [C170051. Boase] Married (1) Mary Ann Hodgson (d.1872), with issue (2) Portsea, Hants. 1879 (2nd q.) Ellen Green. J.P. Lancashire from 1820.

**MOORE (Robert)** [LLD by 1801 but NiVoF] V. Thurleigh, Beds. 1803-33 (res.). Died St Albans, Herts. 1834 aged 77 [C70712]

**MOORE (Robert)** Born c.1778, s. Most Rev. John Moore, Archbishop of Canterbury, and Catherine Eden (dau. of a baronet). Christ Church, Oxford 1795 (aged 17), BA1799, MA 1802. Registrar of the Prerogative Court of Canterbury; (Sinecure R. Hollingbourne, Kent 1801), R. Hunton, Kent [income in CR65 is £1,057] 1802-65. (Sinecure R. Eynsford, Kent 1803), R. Latchington, Essex (RD, and Preacher throughout the Diocese of Canterbury) 1804, Canon of 1st Prebend in Canterbury Cathedral 1804-62 (res.). Dom. Chap. to his father 1802. Died 5/9/1865, leaving £250,000 (derived from being Principal Registrar of the Prerogative Court of Canterbury from his boyhood to 1858, drawing for 60 years an average income of £10,000) [C158243. Boase] Married Lambeth, Surrey 2/1/1800 Dulcibella Bell, with clerical s., also Robert. Brother George, above.

**MOORE (Robert)** From Putney, Surrey, s. Rev. Robert Moore, sen., a 'celebrated' S/M. Trinity, Cambridge 1801 (aged 17), BA1805, dn07 (Win.), MA1808, p08 (Win.). R. Wimborne St Giles, Dorset 1823, RD, Prebend of Teignton Regis in Salisbury Cathedral 1841 to death 26/1/1865, leaving £4,000 [C53430] Widow Sophia Elizabeth.

**MOORE (Uriah)** see under **TONKIN**

**MOORE (William)** Born 20/7/1784, s. Edward Moore, Stockwell House, Surrey (a barrister) and Sarah Gray. St John's, Cambridge 1803, BA1807, dn08 (Lin.), MA1810, p10 (Nor.), DD 1826. PC. Moulton, Lincs. 1814-66, PC. Spalding, Lincs. 1825-66 [total income in CR65 £1,477], RD, Prebend of Sexaginta Solidorum in Lincoln Cathedral [value £3] 1834 to death. Chap. at Spalding Gaol 1816. Died 11/3/1866, leaving £25,000 [C36831. Kaye] Married Spalding 11/6/1807 Anne Elizabeth Johnson (a clergy dau., Ayscough Fee Hall, Lincs.), with clerical son Edward. J.P. for Lincs. and Norfolk, and Chairman of South Holland Quarter Sessions; President of the Spalding Gentlemen's Society (which survives).

**MOORE (William)** Born Bisley, Glos. 29/5/1796, s. Rev. William Moore. Pembroke, Oxford 1810, BA1814, MA1817, dn19 (Glos.), p20 (Glos.). R. Brimpsfield w. Cranham, Glos. 1829 to death. Dom. Chap. at Chavenage House, Horsley, Glos. 1819-[23]. Died 11/6/1879, leaving under £200 [C158934] Married by 1825 Sarah Elizabeth Mary Worthington, w. issue.

**MOORE (William Gurden)** Bapt. Lincoln 24/2/1794, s. George and Susanna Moore. Corpus Christi, Cambridge 1812, BA1816, dn17 (Ex. for York), p19 (Chester for York), MA 1834. R. West Barkwith, Lincs. 1832-40, Chap. of the Donative of Wykeham, Spalding, Lincs. 1832 , V. Stixwould, Lincs. 1833-9, V. Aslackby, Lincs. 1840 to death (Kensington, London) 30/3/1850 [C70720. YCO] Married Hackney, London 18/3/1834 Emily Ann Andrews, w. issue.

**MOORE** see also under **MOOR and MORE**

**MORE (Robert Henry Gayer)** Born Larden Hall, Much Wenlock, Shropshire 20/6/1798, s. Thomas More and Harriett Mytton. Trinity, Cambridge 1817 (2 terms), then Christ's 1820, BA1825, dn26 (Heref.), p29 (Heref.), MA1836. R. Acton Round, Shropshire 1833 [blank in ERC], PC. Bourton, Heref. 1833-69 [income £56], PC. of Donative of Shipton, Heref. 1833 to death 28/4/1880, s.p., leaving £2,000, living at Larden Hall, Shropshire after 1804 [C172851]. Port. online. Doubtless related to the man below.

**MORE (Thomas Frederick)** Born Linley Hall, Bishop's Castle, Shropshire 19/1/1790, s. Robert More and Eliza Taylor. Exeter, Oxford 1808, then Pembroke, Cambridge 1813, BA 1815, dn15 (Nor.), p27 (Nor.). R. Coreley, Shropshire 1830-3, R. Shelve, Shropshire 1833 and R. More, Shropshire 1833 to death 17/12/1869, leaving £8,000; living at Linley Hall

[C114201] Married his cousin Harriet Mary More (of Larden House, Shipton, Shropshire) 29/8/1831, and had issue. Doubtless related to the man above.

**MOREHEAD (Robert)** Born Herbertshire, Stirling 19/3/1777, s. William Morehead, J.P. Glasgow University 1792-4, Edinburgh University 1792-4, Snell Exhibitioner to Balliol, Oxford 1795, BA1799, dn02 (Salis.), MA1802, p03 (Salis.), DD1828 St Andrews University. Scottish curacies including St Paul's Episcopal Chapel, York Place, Edinburgh 1818-32, Dean of Edinburgh 1818-32, Dean of Fife 1822-32; R. Easington, Yorks. 1832-40 [C136828], R. Lofthouse (or Loftus), Yorks. --. to death 13/12/1842 [C88516. Bertie. Snell. Smart] Married Nov. 1804 Margaret Wilson (a clergy dau.), and had issue.

**MORETON (William)** Born Madeley, Staffs. 7/7/1759, s. William Moreton (who may not have been his biological father) and Mary Beech (who definitely seems to have been his mother). [BA but NiVoF] PC. Willenhall St Giles, Wolverhampton 1789 to death 16/7/1834 [C18547] His diary for 1815 survives.' A drunkard, a poacher, a bull and dog-baiter, and a cock-fighter.'

**MORETON (William Moreton)** Born Little Moreton Hall, Cheshire 2/4/1759, s. Rev. Richard Moreton (born Taylor) and Frances Moreton. Magdalen, Oxford, BA [but NiF?]. R. West Dean, Sussex 1785-1815, R. Lewes St John sub Castro, Sussex 1785-1795. Dom. Chap. to 1st Earl Talbot 1784; to 2nd Earl Winterton 1803. Died 4/10/1840 [C64584] Married (1) Cranford, Middx. 14/6/1787 Louisa Board (d.1811) (2) 1815 Elizabeth Hutton, with issue (inc. an Anglican nun).

**MORETON** see also under **MORTON**

**MORGAN (Edward)** Born Pyle, Glamorgan, s. David Morgan and Alice Howell. Jesus, Oxford 1802 (aged 18), BA1806, dn07 (St Asaph), p07 (St Asaph), MA1811. V. Syston, Leics. 1814-64-, PC. Ragdale, Leics. 1815-64 [not in CCEd], V. Radcliffe on the Wreake, Leics. 1818 to death. Dom. Chap. to 7th Earl Ferrers 1818. Died Syston 7/1/1869, leaving £4,000 [C112646] Wife Ann Roberts.

**MORGAN (Evan)** [NiVoF] PC. Nafferton, Yorks. 1826-35. Died? [C135942. YCO has someone of this name - possibly a son - here]

**MORGAN, *later* MORGAN-PAYLER (Frederick)** From Buddesden, Bucks., s. George Morgan. St John's, Oxford 1822 (aged 19), BA1827, dn28 (Lin.), p29 (Lin.), MA1832. PC. Biddlesden 1829, R. Willey, Warwicks. 1843 to death 3/8/1888, leaving £51,425-9s-0d. [C70768 as Morgan] Married 1832 Charlotte Clara Payler, w. clerical son, alsdo Frederick. Changed name 1854.

**MORGAN (George)** Born Lamphey, Pembrokeshire, s. Thomas Morgan [*pleb*]. Christ Church, Oxford 1807 (aged 18), BA1811, dn13 (Ox.), Chap. 1813-18, MA1814, p14 (Ox.). PC. Great Torrington w. St Giles in the Wood, Devon 1817 to death 12/6/1849 [C36835]

**MORGAN (George) From** Newent, Glos., s. Rev. William Morgan. Wadham, Oxford 1812 (aged 21), then St Mary Hall, BA1815, dn15 (Glos.), p15 (Glos.), MA1819. R. (and patron) of Stoke St Milborough w. Heath, Shropshire 1819 to death 16/12/1866, leaving £14,000 [C159045]

**MORGAN (Hector Davies)** From London, s. Hector Morgan. Trinity, Oxford 1803 (aged 18), BA1806, dn07 (Roch. for London), p09 (Salis. for London), MA1815. Chaplain of the Donative of Castle Headingham >< Essex 1809, Prebend of Trallwng in Brecon Collegiate Church 1820. Dom. Chap. to 2nd Baron Kenyon 1816. Died 23/12/1850 [C2025] Clerical son John Blackstone Morgan.

**MORGAN (Henry) From** Newent, Glos., s. Rev. Henry Morgan. Worcester, Oxford 1814, then St John's, Cambridge 1818, dn20 (Glos.) [adm. Middle Temple 1821] LLB1822, p22 (Heref.). PC. Withington, Shropshire 1825-41, Chap. of Nunhead Cemetery, London 1842-70, R. Stoke Lacy, Heref. 1871 to death (Moreton Jefferies, Heref.) 3/11/1886 aged 88, leaving £1,471-8s-0d. [C18550] Clerical son Henry George Morgan.

**MORGAN (Henry Charles) From** Mortimer, Berks., s. Rev. James Morgan. BNC, Oxford 1809 (aged 18), BA1813, dn15 (St Asaph for Heref.), p15 (B&W), MA1816. R. Winstone, Glos. 1819-30 (res.), V. Brinsop, Heref. 1820-31 (res.), V. Goodrich, Heref. 1830-64-, V. Dilwyn,

Heref. 1831 (and Curate Beachley Chapel, Tiddenham, Glos. 1833) to death. Dom. Chap. to Eleanor, Baroness de Blaquiere 1820. Died 29/7/1875, leaving £200,000 [C41643]

**MORGAN (Hugh Hanmer)** Born Ross on Wye, Heref. 20/5/1783, s. Rev. Hugh Morgan and Elizabeth Edward. Christ Church, Oxford 1800, BA1804, dn06 (Heref.), MA1807, p07 (Heref.), BD1814. R. Slapton, Bucks. 1805, Prebend of Putson Minor in Hereford Cathedral 1808 (Canon 1821, Chancellor 1830) to 1861, R. Moccas, Heref. 1808. V. Lydney, Glos. 1831. Died 30/6/1861, leaving £20,000 [C65538] Married Marylebone, London 12/1/1814 Helen Mary Beale, with clerical son Hanmer Morgan-Stratford.

**MORGAN (John)** [NiVoF] H/M Steyning G/S, Sussex G/S; V. Scalford, Leics. 1805 to death 19/9/1834 aged 88 [C70773]

**MORGAN (John)** From Oxford, s. Thomas Morgan [*pleb*]. Christ Church, Oxford 1775 (aged 16), BA1779, MA1782. V. Burton Dassett, Warwicks. 1787, V. Tenbury, Warwicks. 1845 to death 21/8/1848 aged 90 [C18551]

**MORGAN (John)** Born Caio, Carmarthen, s. Rev. Morgan Morgan. Jesus, Oxford 1809 (aged 22), then to Sidney, Cambridge 1827, LLB1832. Chap. *R.N.* 'for sixteen years'; R. Croxton, Lincs. 1831 to death 16/7/1858 aged 71, leaving £2,000 [C70777. Kaye]

**MORGAN (John)** Probably born Wexford, Ireland, s. John Morgan (physician in Paris). Educated at the Collège Bourbon there. Caius, Cambridge 1823 (aged 20), BA1828, dn29 (Lin.), p29 (Lin.), MA1831. R. Normanton, Lincs. 1829-44, R. Kirby Laythorpe w. Asgarby, Lincs. 1829, R. Pyecombe, Sussex 1844 to death 22/5/1875, leaving £1,000 [C70776. Kaye. CR65 says Joseph] Married Bathwick, Som. 4/6/1844 Mary Jane Macdonnell (w), with issue.

**MORGAN (John Woodroffe)** Bapt. Chelmsford, Essex 18/9/1793, s. Rev. John Morgan and Anna Maria Tindal. University, Oxford 1811, BA1814, dn17 (London), MA1817, p17 (London). R. Colchester St Giles, Essex 1818 to death 13/6/1857 [C120655 name corrected]

**MORGAN (Nathaniel)** Bapt. Charlcombe, Bath, Somerset 15/8/1780, s. Rev. Nathaniel Morgan, sen. and Mary Webster. King's, Cambridge 1799, Fellow 1802-12, BA1803, MA1806, dn09 (Peterb.), p12 (Lin.). R. Rearsby, Leics. 1812-56 [blank in ERC], V. Aston (juxta Birmingham), Warwicks. 1831-4 [net income £2,075] Chap. *R.N.* 1834. Died 25/11/1856 [C17902] Married Deene, Northants. 29/6/1813 Anne Webster, and had issue.

**MORGAN (Rowland)** [LLB but NiVoF] R. Wattisfield, Suffolk 1808, V. Rendham, Suffolk 1817 to death 13/2/1855 aged 76 [C114206]

**MORGAN (Thomas)** From Bewdley, Worcs., s. Rev. William Morgan. Magdalen Hall, Oxford 1788 (aged 21), BCL and DCL1808. Prebend of Combe 1 in Wells Cathedral 1804-26, V. King's Langley, Herts. 1812. Chap. to HRH Duke of Cambridge -1815-21-. Died? [C41646] Married Hampton 19/5/1800 Augusta Hinuber ('dau. of an Hanoverian courtier'), 7 ch. (two having godparents from the Royal Family).

**MORGAN (Thomas)** [MA by 1814 but NiVoF]. H/M Kidderminster G/S. R. Rushock, Worcs. 1814 to death (Stone, Worcs.) 27/3/1845 aged 78 [C121877]

**MORGAN (William)** From Barnstaple, Devon, s. William Morgan. Exeter, Oxford 1795 (aged 23), BA1799, MA1817. V. Tollesbury, Essex 1826 to death 17/8/1842 aged 71 [C120659]

**MORGAN (William)** Bapt. Crickadarn, Breconshire 20/4/1781. Literate: dn04 (St David's), p05 (St David's), then Emmanuel, Cambridge 1813, then Queens' 1816 (a Ten Year Man, BD1823). PC. Bierley, Yorks. 1812, PC. Bradford Christ Church, Yorks. 1815-51, R. Hulcott, Bucks. 1851 to death (Bath) 25/3/1858 aged 76 [C135943 - but several men of this name] Married (1) Guiseley, Yorks. 29/12/1812 Jane Branwell Fennell (a clergy dau., d.1827), w. clerical son (2) Calverley, Yorks. 28/9/1836 Mary Alice Gibson (d. 1852) (3) Aylesbury, Bucks. 1854 Mary Howell. 'A portly, loquacious Welshman.'

**MORGAN (William Augustus)** Bapt. South Pool, Devon 23/3/1773, s. Rev. John and Mary Morgan. Wadham, Oxford 1796, SCL, dn01 (Ex.), p01 (Ex.). V. Lewannick, Cornwall 1811, PC. Tresmere, Cornwall 1824 to death 19/8/1869 aged 96. No will traced [C145982] Married St Giles on the Heath, Devon 12/4/1803 Grace Fry, with issue.

**MORGELL (Crosbie)** Born Dublin, s. Thomas Morgell (lawyer). TCD1820 (aged 18), BA1824, dn25 (Bristol), p26, incorporated at Trinity, Cambridge, MA1830. R. Chilbolton, Hants. 1830-48, R. East Knoyle, Wilts. [income in CR65 £1,100] 1848 (and RD) to death. Chap. to Bishop of Winchester. Died 9/9/1865, leaving £3,000 [C53434. Al.Dub.] Married by 1829 Sarah Warren (w), with issue.

**MORICE (Henry)** Born Holborn, London 12/2/1777, s. Rev. William Morice and Hannah Voyce. St John's, Oxford 1795, BA1798, dn99 (London), p01 (London), MA1804, incorporated at Cambridge, 1835? V. Dagenham, Essex 1801-7 (res.), V. Ashwell, Herts. 1812 and Canon of Lincoln Cathedral 1846 to death (London) 20/12/1850 [C70874] Married St George's Hanover Square, London 31/12/1801 Mary St Aubyn, with issue. *J.P.* Herts. and Cambs.

**MORLAND (George)** Bapt. Ravenstonedale, Westmorland 19/3/1791, s. John (a yeoman farmer) and Ann Dent. Literate: dn14 (Chester), p15 (Chester), then Peterhouse, Cambridge 1817, a Ten Year Man. S/M Lancaster Royal G/S 1812-24 (and Ass. Chap. Lancaster Gaol 1817), PC. Lancaster St John 1824 to death 5/10/1862 (a widower) aged 71, leaving £10,000 [C170057] Wife Martha, with issue. Brother (below).

**MORLAND (John)** Bapt. Ravenstonedale, Westmorland 28/8/1792, s. John (a yeoman farmer) and Ann Dent. Literate: dn16 (Chester), p16 (Chester). PC. Aughton, Halton, Lancs. 1817-51 [C170058] Died Bolton le Sands, Lancs. 20/7/1877, leaving £7,000. Married Halton 15/8/1835 Margaret Cock, with issue. Brother (above).

**MORLEY (George)** Literate: dn25 (Lin.). V. Newport Pagnell, Bucks. 1832 to death 24/1/1865 aged 63, leaving £40,000 [C70951] Married Leverton, Lincs. 8/5/1834 Martha Rebecca Dawson (w), and issue.

**MORLEY (John)** Born Elworthy, Som., s. Rev. John Morley and Amanda Shaw. Oriel, Oxford 1780 (aged 16), no degree, dn86 (Wor.), p87 (Wor.). V. Wasperton, Warwicks. 1791, V. Kineton, Warwicks. to 1792, V. Aylesbury, Bucks. 1816-42, R. Bradfield Combust, Suffolk by 1815. Died 29/9/1842 aged 79 [C71076] Married (1) Wellington, Som. 10/1/1783 Mary Lyddon (d.1824) with issue.

**MORLEY (Thomas Wilson)** Bapt. Carlisle 28/6/1784, s. Thomas Wilson and Martha Morley. Trinity, Cambridge 1802, BA1807, dn07 (Chester), p08 (Chester), MA1810. PC. Bolton on Swale, Yorks. 1808, R. Kirklington, Yorks. 1815-27, R. Birkby, Northallerton, Yorks. 1828 to death. Dom. Chap. to 1st Earl Lonsdale 1784. Died (Birkby Hall, Huddersfield) 29/12/1866 aged 82, leaving £25,000 [C131701] Married Marylebone, London 8/6/1822 his cousin Henrietta Downes (a clergy dau.), with clerical son. *J.P.*

**MORLEY (William)** Born Hampton Lacy, Warwicks. 15/3/1793, s. John and Mary Morley. Literate: dn18 (Lin.), p19 (Lin.). PC. Midville Chapel, East Fen, Lincs. 1832-4 (res.), R. (and patron) of Mavis Enderby, Lincs. 1834 to death (Raithby, Lincs.) 5/5/1869 aged 76, leaving £6,000 [C71077] Wife Eliza, and issue.

**MORRES (Robert)** Bapt. Hinckley, Leics. 3/6/1767, s. Rev. Thomas and Ann Morres, BNC, Oxford 1774, BA1777, MA1780, p82 (Ox.). V. Britford, Wilts. 1796, R. Great Cheverell (Cheverell Magna), Wilts. 1806, Prebend of Netherbury in Terra in Salisbury Cathedral 1805-12, then of Alton Borealis 1812 to death. Dom. Chap. to Bishop of Bangor 1806. Died 18/10/1841 [C36855] Son below?

**MORRES (Thomas)** From Isleworth, Middx., s. Rev. Robert Morres (above?). BNC, Oxford 1813 (aged 17), BA1817, dn18 (Salis.), p19 (Salis.), MA1820. R. Wokingham, Berks. 1820-72 (w. Master of Lucas Hospital [almshouses]). Died 2/4/1877 aged 81, leaving £2,000 [C85934] Married Marianne Forster, with clerical son Hugh Redmond Morres. Surrogate.

**MORRICE (Andrew Ducarel)** Born Battersea, Surrey 22/1/1782, s. Rev. James Morrice (R. Barford, Warwicks.) and Marie Coltée Ducarel [dau. of Marquis Du Carel, of Huguenot extraction; formerly governess to Clive of India]. Christ Church, Oxford 1799, BA1803, MA1806, dn08 (Ox.), p09 (Ox.), Student [Fellow] to 1812. R. Betteshanger, Kent (a family living: 3 houses) 1815 to death (Heath and Reach, Beds.) 30/9/1866, leaving £4,000 [C36847] Married Flore, Northants. 12/9/1812 Emma Darby, 8s., 2 dau.

**MORRIS (John)** From Hagworthingham, Lincs., s. John Morris [pleb]. Lincoln, Oxford 1796 (aged 17), then Queen's, Fellow, BA1799,

MA1802, BD and DD1822. R. Elstree, Herts. 1822 to death 6/11/1848 [C120661]

**MORRIS (Joseph)** Bapt. Hope Bagot, Staffs. 10/5/1772, s. Joseph Morris and Elizabeth Camel. Wadham, Oxford 1772, BA1777. R. Tasley, Shropshire 1778. Died Bridgnorth, Staffs. 19/7/1837 aged 84 [C18556] Married Bridgnorth 9/7/1789 Mary Ann Noyes, with issue.

**MORRIS (Joseph)** Born Eastcheap, London 14/5/1791, s. Joseph Morris and Margaret Turney. Trinity, Cambridge 1808, then Corpus Christi 1809, BA1812, dn14 (Lin.), MA1815, p15 (Lin.). V. (and patron) of Feltham, Middx. 1818 (where he also kept a boarding school) to death 17/6/1833 aged 42 (CCEd says 8/11/1833) [C70942] Married Stone in Otney, Kent 20/5/1819 Margaret Hodges, with issue. *F.S.A.*

**MORRIS (Robert)** From Clun, Shropshire, s. Rev. Thomas Morris. Jesus, Oxford 1785 (aged 19), BA1789. PC. Knighton (on Teme Chapel), Lindridge, Radnor 1813-[44]. Died? [C18557]

**MORRIS (Thomas)** From Llangyfelach, Glamorgan, s. Sir John Morris, 1st Bart. (a coal and ironmaster) and Henrietta (dau. of Sir Philip Musgrave, 6th Bart.). Oriel, Oxford 1800 (aged 19), BA1804, dn08 (St David's), MA1807, p10 (Win. for St David's). R. Dover St James the Apostle, Kent 1818 and R. Hougham (*not* Hingham), Kent 1818 to death 5/4/1854 [C132503]

**MORRIS (Thomas Brooke)** Born Middx. c.1771. St John's, Cambridge 1788, BA1792, MA1795, dn96 (C&L), p97 (Win. for C&L). V. Tortington, Sussex 1815-17, R. Shelfanger, Norfolk 1812 to death 26/3/1863 aged 92, leaving £450 [C17894]

**MORSE (John)** Bapt. Newent, Glos. 28/2/1792, s. John and Mary Morse. Pembroke, Oxford 1810, BA1814, dn15 (Glos.), p15 (Glos.), MA 1824. V. (and patron) of Huntley, Glos. 1817, V. Oxenhall, Glos. 1824. Arrived New South Wales, Australia as an immigrant 13/9/1839. (first) Inc. Scone, NSW 1839 to death 11/4/1852 aged 69 [C159159] Married Gloucester St Mary de Lode 24/6/1817 Helen Elizabeth Mary Williams, with issue.

**MORSHEAD (Edward)** Bapt. Meheniot, Cornwall 29/6/1764, s. William Morshead and Olympia Treise. Exeter, Oxford 1782, Fellow 1785-97, dn87 (Ox.), BA and MA1789. R. Hascombe, Surrey 1791-1823, R. Calstock, Cornwall 1796, St Dominic, Cornwall 1800-3, R. St Petroc Minor, Cornwall 1801, V. Quethiock, Cornwall 1801, R. Beaworthy, Devon 1807, R. Kelly, Devon 1823. Chaplain to Prince of Wales 1800 and HRH Duke of York 1823. Died 17/9/1852 aged 89 [C36868] Married Tavistock, Devon 12/4/1798 Mary Kelly w. clerical s. Henry John Morshead.

**MORTIMER (Hans Sanders)** Born Harborne, Staffs., s. Hans Winthrop Mortimer (*M.P.* and barrister, Caldwell Hall, Derbys.) and Ann (dau. of Lord Hamilton). St John's, Cambridge 1801, BA1805, dn05 (Win.), p05 (Win.), MA1808. V. Sandwich St Clement, Kent 1824-6 (res.), R. Kington Magna (Great Kington), Dorset 1826-9 (res.), R. Winchelsea St Thomas the Apostle, Sussex 1829-31 (res.), V. Throwley, Kent 1829 to death. Dom. Chap. to 5th Earl of Shaftesbury 1809; to 1st Baron Manners 1829. Died 31/1/1846 [C53436] Married St George's Hanover Square, London 25/5/1799 Mary Tilbe, and had issue.

**MORTIMER (Thomas)** Born Middx. 5/2/1785, s. Harvey Walklate Mortimer (gunmaker to George 111 and *H.E.I.C.*) and Elizabeth Ritchie. Queens', Cambridge 1817 (a Ten Year Man), dn18 (Chester), p19 (Chester), re-adm. 1820, BD 1830. PC. Clerkenwell St Mark, Pentonville, London 1828-36, Minister Gray's Inn Lane Proprietary Chapel, London 1841 to death (Broseley, Shropshire) 25/11/1851 [C71087. DEB claims more parishes] Married (1) Shrewsbury 30/6/1818 Letitia Pritchard (d.1836, w. issue (2) Kendal, Westmorland 1841 (2nd q.) Mrs Favell Lee Bevan (Belmont, Middx., dau. of a banker, photo. online). With adopted clerical son Lethbridge Charles Edward Mortimer.

**MORTLOCK (Henry)** Born Cambridge 16/7/1789, s. John Mortlock and Elizabeth Mary Harrison. Trinity Hall, Cambridge 1805 [In Madras Civil Service 1808-24], re-adm. St John's, Cambridge 1824 (a Ten Year Man), dn24 (Nor.), p24 (Nor.). R. Farthingstone, Northants. 1828 to death. Took pupils, and was Chap. to the Workhouse. Died Brighton, 13/2/1837 aged 48 [C110623] Married Newington, Surrey

4/9/1817 Elizabeth Thomas, 7 ch. A fine linguist.

**MORTON (David)** Bapt. East Harsley, Yorks. 2/9/1799, s. Edward and Elizabeth Morton. Trinity, Cambridge 1817, BA1822, dn23 (Bristol for London), p26 (Ely for London), MA1827. Chaplain *R.N.* 1823-31; R. Harlestone, Northants. 1831-81, RD of Haddon 1847-64. Died (Ventnor, IoW) 2/8/1884 aged 84, leaving £9,799-8s-7d. [C53437] Married Portsea, Hants. 1/10/1835 Elizabeth Morgan.

**MORTON (James)** A weaver from Kelso, Roxburgh (where 'he used to study with a book on his loom'). Literate: dn11 (Durham), p12 (Durham), then St John's, Cambridge 1812 (a Ten Year Man, BD1824). V. Holbeach, Lincs. 1831 and Prebend of Leighton Buzzard in Lincoln Cathedral 1831 to death 31/7/1865 aged 82, leaving £3,000 [C71088. Boase] Married Chelsea, London 14/11/1833 Margaret Bruce, with issue. *J.P.* Lincs.

**MOSELEY (Thomas)** Born Westminster, London, s. Richard and Mary Anne Moseley. St Edmund Hall, Oxford 1821 (aged 18), BA 1824, MA1827, dn28 (London for Cant.), p30. R. Birmingham St Martin [net income £1,048] 1829-46. Died Brighton, Sussex 8/7/1882, leaving £56,307-6s-1d. [C18565. DEB] Married Edgbaston, Birmingham 8/6/1832 Margaret Augusta Tilson, with issue.

**MOSLEY (John Peploe)** Born 13/12/1766, s. Sir John Parker, 1st Bart. (a failed Manchester hatter, who inherited the estates and the re-created title of his cousin) and Elizabeth Bayley. Queens', Cambridge 1783, BA1787, dn88 (C&L), MA1789, p89 (C&L). R. Rolleston, Burton on Trent, Staffs. 1799-1834 (living at Rolleston Hall), R. Standon, Staffs. 1789-1812. Died 28/1/1834 (CCEd says 4/3/1834) [C17897] Married (1) Wells, Som. 7/10/1790 Sarah Maria Paget (d.1823), with clerical son Peploe Paget Mosley (2) Derby 9/8/1827 Mrs Frances (Bingham) Pole (a clergy widow).

**MOSS (Anthony)** Bapt. Warcop, Westmorland 7/5/1749, s. Anthony and Margaret Moss. Literate: dn72 (London for York), p73 (York). PC. Luddenden, Halifax, Yorks. 1773-9, PC. Illingworth, Yorks. 1779 to death 15/1/1836 aged 85 [C117632. YCO] Was married, with issue.

**MOSS (John)** [NiVoF] V. Aldingbourne, Sussex 1819 to death ('for whom the Rev. J. Graham officiates'). Buried 5/10/1852 [C64607]

**MOSS (Thomas)** Born Preston, Lancs. 10/11/1764, s. Robert and Elizabeth Moss. University, Oxford 1782, BA1786, MA1789, dn90 (York), p07 (Chester). V. Liverpool St Mary, Walton on the Hill 1816 to death 22/11/1842 [C130246. YCO]

**MOSSOP (Charles)** From Deeping St James, Lincs., s. Rev. John Mossop (below, 1778) and Ann Berridge. St John's, Cambridge 1812 (aged 17), BA1816, dn16 (Lin.), p17 (Lin.), MA1819. V. Helpston, Northants. 1817-53, R. Etton, Northants. 1853 to death. 'Private Chap'. to Duke of Somerset. Died 4/4/1883 [C71144] Married 27/9/1836 Mrs Lucy (Burrough) Booth (a clergy widow).

**MOSSOP, MOSCROP (George Edward)** Bapt. St Bees, Cumberland 23/3/1759, s. John Mossop (or Moscrop) and Ann Vicars. Literate: p83 (London), then St John's, Cambridge 1786 (a Ten Year Man). V. Langford, Beds. 1783 to death 6/11/1837 aged 76 [C71145] Brother John (1778) below.

**MOSSOP, MOSCROP (Isaac)** Bapt. 16/11/1776, s. Clement Mossop (Rottington Hall, St Bees, Cumberland) and Eleanor Walker. Literate: dn99 (York), p01 (York). Stipendiary Curate Cranbrook, Kent 1813-34, PC. Nonington w. Wymynswold, Kent 1821-34, R. Smarden, Kent 1834-51-. Died (unm.) St Bees 10/1/1857 aged 80 [C130247. YCO] Brother John (2 below).

**MOSSOP, MOSCROP (John)** Born Whale House, Seascale, Cumberland 14/10/1753, s. John Mossop (or Moscrop) and Ann Vicars. St John's, Cambridge 1778, a Ten Year Man, dn78 (Lin.), p79 (Lin.). V. Baston, Lincs. 1781 and V. Langtoft, Lincs. 1801 to death 14/7/1834 (CCEd says 16/8/1834) [C71146. *Gentleman's Magazine* is wrong in saying of Queen's, Oxford] Married Deeping St James 30/4/1787 Ann Berridge, with s. Charles, above. Brother George Edward (above). His Charity survives.

**MOSSOP (John)** Born Rottington Hall, St Bees, Cumberland 1774, s. Clement Mossop and Eleanor Walker. Queen's, Oxford 1792), BA 1795, MA1799. R. Hothfield, Kent 1802 to death 3/10/1849 [C82406] Brother Isaac, above.

**MOSSOP (John)** Born St Bees, Cumberland 1797. St John, Cambridge 1823, BA1828, dn28 (Lin.), p29 (Lin.). R. Covenham St Bartholomew, Lincs. 1829 to death (unm.) 28/2/1873, leaving £600 [C71149. Kaye] Much confusion here. 'A devoted ornithologist.'

**MOSSOP (Joseph)** Literate: dn10 (Chester), p11 (Chester). PC. Holland Fen, Lincs. 1813 to death 26/6/1835 (CCEd thus) [C71150]

**MOULD (William)** [NiVoF] R. Challacombe, Devon 1800. Died 17/4/1839 aged 75 [2 possibles in CCEd] Married Mary Scott (a clergy dau.)

**MOULD (William)** Bapt. Appleby, Westmorland 24/9/1777, s. Rev. Thomas and Penelope Mould. Peterhouse, Cambridge 1794, BA1800, dn01 (York), p03 (York), MA1803, Fellow 1803-5. H/M Retford G/S 1801-37; V. Misterton, Notts. 1809-37, PC. Stowe, Staffs. 1821-9 w. PC. Gayton, Staffs. 1821, V. West Burton (o/w Burton Joyce cum Bulcote), Notts. 1819-37, V. Gringley on the Hill, Notts. 1836 to death (East Retford, Notts.) 9/1/1837 aged 59 [C18602. YCO] Married York 1/11/1803 Maria Blackburn, Malton, Yorks.

**MOULE (Henry)** Born Melksham, Wilts. 27/1/1801, s. of George Moule (a solicitor and banker). St John, Cambridge 1817, BA1821, dn24 (Salis.), p25 (Lin. for Salis.), MA1828. V. Fordington, Dorchester, Dorset 1829 to death. Chap. to troops in Dorchester. Died 3/2/1880, leaving £1,500 [C53440. ODNB. Boase. DEB. T. Ward, *Henry Moule of Fordington* ... (Poole, 1983)] Married Melksham 1824 Mary Mullett Evans, with two episcopal sons (Handley Carr Glyn Moule, Bishop of Durham; George Evans Moule, Bishop of Mid-China) Important social and sanitary reformer (especially his invention of the Dry Earth System of Sanitation, 1860); private schoolmaster; friend of Thomas Hardy. Surrogate.

**MOULTRIE (George)** Born East Florida, s. John Moultrie (Governor there) and Eleanor Austin. [NiVoF] V. Cleobury Mortimer, Heref. 1800. Died St John's Wood, London 12/5/1845 [C82407] Married Marylebone, London 2/4/1799 Harriet Fendall, with clerical son, below. Port. online.

**MOULTRIE (John)** Born London 30/12/1799, ('the residence of Mrs Fendell'), s. Rev. George Moultrie (R. Cleobury Mortimer, Heref., above) and Harriet Fendall. Trinity, Cambridge 1819 [adm. Middle Temple 1822] BA1823, dn25 (Bristol for Ely), p25 (Ely), MA 1826. Tutor to sons of Lord Craven; R. Rugby, Warwicks. 1825-74 (and friend of Thomas Arnold, Headmaster of Rugby School), RD, Canon of Worcester Cathedral 1864. Died (of illness caught while parish visiting) 26/12/1874, leaving £1,500 [C18603. ODNB. Boase] Married London 28/7/1825 Harriet Margaret Fergusson, w. issue. Good photo. online. Poet.

**MOUNSEY (George)** Bapt. Barton, Westmorland 22/1/1772, s. Robert Mounsey (a husbandman) and Rachel Thompson. Literate: dn96 (Chester), p97 (Chester). PC. Macclesfield Forest Chapel, Cheshire 1799-1851-, PC. Rushton, Staffs. 1806-51-, Chap. Fairfield, Hope, Derbys. 1815-32 (w. S/M Buxton National School 1817). Died Kendal, Westmorland 8/6/1862. Will not yet traced [C32587] Married Harrington, Cumberland 16/5/1795 Nancy Hayton, with issue.

**MOUNSEY (John)** Probably bapt. Normanby-le-Wold, Lincs. 3/2/1758, s. Rev. John, sen. and Bridget Mounsey. Emmanuel, Cambridge 1775, BA1780, dn80 (Lin.), p02 (Lin.). R. Gautby, Lincs. 1783-1836, R. Withern w. Stain, Lincs. 1789 and R. Authorpe, Lincs. 1806 to death 1836 aged 77 [C71157. Kaye] J.P. Lincs.

**MOUNSEY (Thomas)** Bapt. Greystoke, Westmorland 16/8/1778, s. Richard and Sarah Mould. Literate: dn01 (York), p02 (York), then Emmanuel, Cambridge 1820, a Ten Year Man. V. Owthorne (Awthorne), Yorks. 1826 to death (Sculcoates, Yorks.) 5/1/1845 aged 66 [C130249. YCO]

**MOUNT (Charles Milman)** Bapt. Cirencester, Glos. 29/1/1784, s. Thomas and Sarah Mount. Trinity, Oxford 1800, BA1804, dn08 (Win.), MA 1808, p08 (Ox.), then Corpus Christi, Fellow to 1815. V. Hannington, Wilts. 1811, R. Helmdon w. Stutchbury, Northants. 1814, (Sinecure R. Great Tey, Essex 1814-16 (res.)), Min. of Christ Church Walcot, Bath 1821, Prebend of Combe 1V Wells Cathedral 1830, then of Dulcote 1834 to death. Dom. Chap. to 1st Marquess of Ormond 1814. Died 9/5/1855 [C36876] Married London 19/10/1815 Emilia Nisbet, with issue.

**MOUNTAIN (George Robert)** Born Buckdan, Hunts. 29/10/1791, s. Rt. Rev. Jacob Mountain (first Bishop of Quebec) and Elizabeth Mildred Wale Kentish. Trinity, Cambridge 1807 (did not reside?). Literate: p20 (Lin.). V. North Kelsey, Lincs. 1820-5, R. Havant, Hants. 1825 to death. Died Blackheath, Kent 25/6/1846 aged 55 [C71161] Married Beddington, Surrey 22/2/1821 Katherine Hinchliff (of Mitcham, Surrey). Brother below.

**MOUNTAIN (Jacob Henry Brooke)** Born 10/1/788, s. Rt. Rev. Jacob Mountain (first Bishop of Quebec) and Elizabeth Mildred Wale Kentish. Trinity, Cambridge 1805, BA 1810, dn11 (Bristol), p12 (Lin.), LLB1814, BD1837, DD1844. R. South Ferriby, Lincs. 1812-14, Prebend of North Kelsey in Lincoln Cathedral 1812-72, R. Puttenham, Surrey 1814-31, R. Chalfont St Giles, Bucks. 1814-17 (res.), V. Hemel Hempstead, Herts. 1820-46, R. Blunham, Beds. 1831 (and RD) to death. Dom. Chap. to Bishop of Bristol 1814; to 2nd Baron Suffield 1814. Died 8/9/1872, leaving £5,000 [C53442. Boase] Married (1) Little Bardfield, Essex 12/10/1812 Frances Mingay Brooke (d.1837), with clerical son George Jehosophat Mountain (2) Blunham 2/4/1850 Mrs Frances Margaretta Polhill (widow of an *M.P.*), *s.p.* J.P. Beds. and Herts. Brother above. Surrogate. Photo. online.

**MOURANT (Edward)** Literate: p92 (C&L for Win.). R. Guernsey (St Margaret of the) Forest 1797 and R. (St Philip of) Torteval, Channel Islands 1797. Died? [C18394]

**MOUSLEY (William)** Born Ashby Hall, Cold Ashby, Northants., s. Rev. William Mousley. Queens', Cambridge 1818, BA1822, dn23 (Peterb.), p23 (Peterb.), MA1825. (succ. his father as) V. (and patron) of Cold Ashby 1829 to death 12/9/1871, leaving £14,000 [C110626] Had issue.

**MOVERLEY (John)** Born Manchester 23/2/1798, s. Thomas and Elizabeth Moverley. Queens', Cambridge 1819, dn23 (Lin.), p24 (Lin.), BA1825. MA1826. PC. Halton, Runcorn, Cheshire 1827-30, V. Lyddington w. Caldecote, Rutland 1830 to death 16/10/1834 (CCEd thus) aged 36 [C71168] Married Todmorden, Lancs. 15/5/1823 Hannah Buckley.

**MOWER (James)** Bapt. Sheffield, Yorks. 8/4/1768, s. Joseph Mower (a currier). Trinity, Cambridge 1786, BA1791, dn91 (C&L), p08 (York). V. Tinsley, Yorks. 1812 and R. Dinnington, Yorks. 1818 to death 1835 aged 76 [C18395. YCO]

**MOXON (George Browne)** Born Whitechapel, London 16/4/1794 (bapt. 8/9/1797), s. Thomas Moxon (a banker) and Ann Browne. Corpus Christi, Cambridge 1818, BA1823, dn23 (Nor.), p24 (Nor.). V. Sandringham w. Babingley, Norfolk 1827 to sudden death 28/1/1866 (his funeral being attended by the Prince of Wales), leaving £18,000 [C114217] Married Twickenham, Middx. 15/2/1849 Bertha Browne (a clergy dau.).

**MOYSEY (Charles Abel)** Born London 26/11/1779, s. Abel Moysey, *M.P.*, and Charlotte Bampfield. Christ Church, Oxford 1798, BA 1802, p03 (Ox.), MA1805, BD and DD1818. V. Oxford St Mary Magdalene 1808, PC. Southwick, Hants. 1808 and R. Hinton Parva (Little Hinton), Wilts. 1808-39, R. Martyr Worthy, Hants. 1817-39, R. Walcot, Bath 1817-39, Archdeacon of Bath 1820-39 (w. Prebend of Combe X111 in Wells Cathedral 1826-1832). Had a stroke in 1839. Died (Batheaston Court, Bath) 17/12/1859, leaving £35,000 [C36878. Boase] Married (1) Clapham, Surrey 9/8/1810 Charlotte Fownes Luttrell (Dunster Castle, Som., she d.1819), with clerical s. Frederick Luttrell Moysey (2) Walcot 24/6/1820 Elizabeth Susanna Stewart. Watercolourist.

**MUCKLESTON (John)** Born Lichfield, s. Rev. John Fletcher Muckleston (below) and Louisa Preston. Christ Church, Oxford 1819 (aged 18), BA1822, dn23 (Chester for C&L), p24 (C&L). PC. Wychnor, Staffs. 1832-72. Died Lichfield 16/7/1877, leaving £25,000 [C18611] Married Teignmouth, Devon 14/3/1841 Mary Levett.

**MUCKLESTON (John Fletcher)** Born Shrewsbury Salop 14/7/1764, s. John Muckleston and Mary Fletcher. Christ Church, Oxford 1782, BA1786, dn87 (C&L), p88 (C&L), MA 1789, BD and DD1814. Prebend of Hilton in Wolverhampton Collegiate Church 1789, V. Hints w. Weeford, Staffs. 1790-1839, PC. Wybunbury, Cheshire 1802 (w. Prebend of Durnford 1790) to 1843, PC. Tong, Salop 1807-39. Died Torquay, Devon (a widower) 24/10/1843 aged 80 [C18507] Married 16/4/1793 Louisa Preston (a clergy dau.), Askham Bryan, Yorks., with clerical son, above. On the *Muckleston Family History Group Website* there is much undigested material; it says he left no will, but an estimated £2,000.

**MUDGE (John)** Bapt. City of London 3/7/1763, s. Thomas and Abigail Mudge. Pembroke, Oxford 1780, BA1784, then Christ's, Cambridge 1780, dn87 (Ex.), p88 (Ex.), MA 1792. V. Brampford Speke, Devon 1790-1847 and R. Lustleigh, Devon 1791 to death. Dom. Chap. to 1st Earl Fortescue. Died 3/5/1847 aged 83 [C145987]

**MULES (Charles)** Bapt. Marwood, Devon 14/9/1763, s. Rev. John Mules (R. Tawstock, Devon) and Mary Hawkes. Emmanuel, Cambridge 1787, then St Catharine's 1787, dn90 (Ely), p91 (Ely), BA1792, MA1798. PC. Ely St Mary 1793-1802, V. Stapleford, Cambs. 1803 and V. Pampisford, Cambs. 1806 to death. Dom. Chap. to Bishop of Ely. Promoter of and Chap. to the North Devon Infirmary. Died 10/12/1844 aged 80 [C100137] Married (1) East Down, Devon 2/10/1792 Grace Harris, w. issue (2) Ely 21/3/1797 Sarah Tooke; with issue. Brother William, below.

**MULES (John Hawkes)** Born Muchelney, Somerset, s. Rev. John Mules, sen. (R. Tawstock, Devon) and Mary Hawkes. St Mary Hall, Oxford 1798 (aged 15), BA1803, dn05 (Ex. for B&W), p07 (B&W), then St John, Cambridge 1823. R. Thorne Coffin, Som. 1812-22, PC. Kingstone, Som. 1815-58, V. Isle Abbots, Som. 1820-58, PC. Mulchelney 1822, V. Ilminster, Som. 1822 to death. Dom. Chap. to 10th Baron Dormer 1823. Died 5/1/1858, leaving £14,000 [C41653] Married (1) 1811 Mary Ann Jolly, w. clerical s. John Henry Mules (2) Marylebone, London 18/10/1836 Eleanora Augusta Mathieson, with issue (inc. Charles Oliver, third Bishop of Nelson, New Zealand). But see above and below. Confusion with three generations of same name.

**MULES (William)** Bapt. Marwood, Devon 29/12/1761, s. Rev. John Mules and Mary Hawkes. St John, Cambridge 1785, BA1789, dn89 (Ex.), p89 (Ex.). R. Bittadon, Devon 1832-9. Died 30/3/1839 aged 77 [C145989] Brother Charles, above.

**MULLINS (George)** Born Box, Wilts. 17/7/1800, s. George Mullins and Mary Cornish. Literate: dn23 (Salis.), p24 (Salis.). R. Ditteridge, Wilts. 1825-57, R. Chalfield Magna, Wilts. 1857 to death. Master of the Free School, and Master of the Almshouse, Corsham, Wilts. Died Oxford 29/4/1867, leaving £1,500 [C88992] Married Bristol 5/1/1835 Susannah Gardiner (w), and clerical sons George Henry, and Robert John. Photo. online.

**MUNCASTER (Jonathan)** Bapt. Loweswater, Cumberland 2/1/1774, s. James and Mary Muncaster. Literate: dn97 (York), p98 (York), DD (?). PC. Selby, Yorks. 1819-34, PC. Oulton, Yorks. 1834-6. Probate granted 1/12/1847 [C124139. YCO] Married Ferry Fryston, Yorks. 28/5/1801 Mary Eyre.

**MUNDEN (John Maber)** Bapt. Beer Hackett, Dorset 13/11/1782, s. Rev. George Munden (V. Chetnole, Glos.) [others say John and Jane Munden]. Queen's, Oxford 1801, BA804, dn05 (Bristol), p07 (Bristol), MA1807, Fellow to 1816, DD 1828. R. English Bicknor, Glos. 1815-22, R. (and patron) of Corscombe, Dorset 1821-42, V. Northover, Som. 1828, RD Bridport, Dorset 1832. Died 17/2/1842 [C41654] Married 1816 Caroline Matilda Chichester, with issue

**MUNDY (Frederick)** Bapt. Shipley, Derbys. 22/4/1778, s. Frederick Miller Mundy. Christ Church, Oxford 1797, BA1800, All Souls, Fellow, dn02 (Ox.), p03 (Car.), MA1805. R. Winston, Durham 1803 to death 2/1/1846 aged 68 [C5696]

**MUNNINGS (Thomas Crowe)** Born East Bilney, Norfolk 16/11/1756, s. Rev. Christopher Munnings. Caius, Cambridge 1775, then Sidney 1778, BA1779, dn79 (Nor.), Fellow 1779, MA 1782, p82 (Nor.). R. Beetley, Norfolk 1782-1733 and (succ. his father as) R. East Bilney 1782 to death 30/9/1833 (CCEd says 11/10/1833) [C114221] Married King's Lynn, Norfolk 28/11/1782 Margaret Glenton (Upwell, Cambs.). 'A somewhat eccentric character and a noted author of electioneering squibs.'

**MUNSEY (William)** Bapt. Hereford 29/11/1782, s. James and Catherine Munsey. All Souls, Oxford 1801, then Cambridge, Trinity Hall 1808, dn09 (Heref.), BA1809, p10 (Heref.). V. Arundel, Sussex 1811-28 (res.), V. Norton Canon, Heref. 1821-41, Vicar Choral in Hereford Cathedral 1822-40, V. Fownhope, Heref. 1841 to death (Brighton, a widower) 10/11/1864, leaving £1,000 [C64614] Had issue.

**MURRAY (Charles)** Son of Lt.-General John Murray (Lt.-Governor of Demerara-Essequibo,

British Guiana 1813-24, and a slave owner) and Ellen Butler. Peterhouse, Cambridge 1822, BA1827, dn27 (Lin.), p29 (Lin.), MA1830. R. Ashe, Hants. 1830 to death (Bermondsey, Surrey) 1844 (1st q.) [C71175] Married 14/10/1844 Frederica Jane Groves.

**MURRAY (David Rodney)** Born Marylebone, London 12/4/1791, s. Hon. David Murray, *M.P.*, and Elizabeth Harley. Christ Church, Oxford 1810, BA1814, dn16 (Salis. for Win.), p18 (Heref. for Win.), MA1820. PC. St Margaret w. Michaelchurch Escley >< Heref. 1825-8, R. Bampton Bryan, Heref. 1826-78, V. Beedon, Berks. 1828-74, R. Cusop, Heref. 1835. Died 4/11/1878, leaving £6,000. Dom. Chap. to Viscount Curzon 1820 [C82412] Married 4/12/1828 Frances Portal (w), with military and naval issue.

**MURRAY (Edward)** Born Hunton, Kent 5/11/1798, s. Rt. Rev. Lord George Murray (Bishop of St David's) and Ann Charlotte Grant (dau. of military *M.P.*). Trinity, Cambridge 1816, BA1820, dn21 (London), p21 (Bristol), MA 1829. V. Stinsford, Dorset 1821-30, V. Dartford, Kent 1829, R. Winterbourne Monkton, Dorset 1831-6, V. Northolt, Middx. 1837 (and Prebend of Twiford in St Paul's Cathedral 1842) to death (Northolt, Middx.) 1/7/1852. Dom. Chap. to Bishop of Sodor and Man 1831 [C6995. Boase] Married Westminster, London 14/2/1822 Ruperta Catherine, dau. Sir George Wright, 2nd Bart., with military issue. Brother below. 'He applied the archimedean screw to the purposes of navigation in 1823, and many of his lines were used in the Admiralty and in men of war. He was a member of the Chess Club and beat France when he played for England more than once' (Boase).

**MURRAY (George, *later* Bishop of Sodor and Man, *then of* Rochester)** Born Farnham, Surrey 12/1/1784, s. Rt. Rev. George Murray (Bishop of St David's, and himself s. of 3rd Duke of Atholl) and Ann Charlotte Grant. Christ Church, Oxford 1801, BA1806, MA1810, DD 1814. R. Bocking, Essex 1802, Archdeacon of Man 1808-14, V. Broadwindsor, Dorset 1813, Bishop of Sodor and Man 1813 (but See vacant for one year as he was under the canonical age of 30!) 1814-27, then Bishop of Rochester 1827 to death (w. R. Bishopsbourne, Kent 1827 [income £1,240]) w. Dean of Worcester *in commendam* 1828-45 (and V. Bromsgrove, Worcs. 1828). Died London 16/2/1860 aged 75, leaving £60,000 [C573 / 522. ODNB. Boase. Gelling is exhaustive] Married 5/5/1811 Lady Sarah Hay-Drummond (dau. of 10th Earl of Kinnoull) (w. - 'strong-willed and often domineering'), 5 s. (inc. clerical), 6 dau. Brother above.

**MURRAY (John)** Born London 1/5/1774, s. James Murray. Trinity, Cambridge 1790, BA1795, dn99 (Ely), p00 (Ely). R. Newbiggin, Northumberland 1813-18, PC. Whixhall, Shropshire 1818 to death. Dom. Chap. to 9th Earl of Kellie 1810. Died 7/1/1844 [C100140] *J.P.* Shropshire.

**MURRAY (William, Sir, 9th Bart., of Dunerne)** Born Edinburgh c.1769, s. Col. Sir Robert Murray, 6th Bart. and Susan Renton. Christ Church, Oxford 1786, BA1790, dn93 (Ox.), MA1793, p93 (Ox.). V. West (o/w Bishops) Lavington, Wilts. 1795 and R. Lofthouse, Yorks. 1802 to death 14/5/1842 [C36883] Married Camden, London 8/3/1809 Esther Jane Gayton, w. at least 9 ch. Succ. to title 1827.

**MUSGRAVE (Charles)** Born Cambridge 17/7/1792, s. Peete Musgrave (a wealthy tailor and woollen draper) and Sarah Betts. Trinity, Cambridge 1809, Fellow 1813, BA 1814, dn17 (Ely), p17 (Nor. for Bristol), MA1817, BD 1831, DD1837. V. Whitkirk, Leeds, Yorks. 1821, V. Halifax, Yorks. 1827-75 [where a dispute over small tithes in 1829 led to their commutation and an annual salary of £1,000 paid to him by the town council: ERC says £1,678], PC. Roundhay, Leeds 1826-7 (res.), RD, Prebend of Givendale in York Minster 1833 and (first) Archdeacon of Craven 1836 to death (Halifax) 17/4/1875 aged 82, leaving £18,000 [C109335. Boase. DEB] Married (1) Cambridge 14/8/1822 Selina Buxton (d.1828), with issue (2) Halifax 18/2/1830 Ellen Frances Waterhouse, with issue; clerical son. Brother Thomas (Abp of York), below. Port online.

**MUSGRAVE (Richard Adolphus)** Bapt. Marylebone. London 25/11/1799, s. Sir James Musgrave, 8th Bart. and Clarissa Blackall. Trinity, Cambridge 1818, dn23 (Ox.), p23 (Ox.), LLB 1829, DD? R. Compton Bassett, Wilts. 1825-41, Canon of Windsor 1829-41, R. Barnsley, Glos. 1829 to death (Karlsruhe, Germany) 21/1/1841 [C36887] Married St George's Hanover Square, London 3/7/1822 Katherine Lowther (dau. of an *M.P.*), and had issue. Brother William Augustus, below.

**MUSGRAVE (Thomas, *later* Bishop of Hereford, *then* Archbishop of York)** Born Cambridge 30/3/1788, s. Peete Musgrave (a wealthy tailor and woollen draper) and Sarah Betts. Trinity, Cambridge 1804, BA1810, Fellow, etc. 1812, MA1813, dn16 (Bristol), p17 (B&W), DD1837. Lord Almoner's Professor of Arabic, Cambridge 1821-37. R. Over, Cambs. 1823-5, V. Cambridge Great St Mary's 1825-33, V. Orwell, Cambs. 1835. V. Bottisham, Cambs. 1837, Dean of Bristol 1837 (only), Bishop of Hereford 1837-48. Archbishop of York 1847 to death 4/5/1860, leaving £70,000 [C41656. ODNB. Boase. DEB] Married 12/12/1839 Hon. Catherine Cavendish (dau. of 2nd Baron Waterpark). Brother Charles, above.

**MUSGRAVE (William Augustus, Sir, 10th Bart., of Hayton Castle)** Born London, s. James Musgrave, 8th Bart. and Clarissa Blackhall. Christ Church, Oxford 1809 (aged 17), BA1813, dn14 (Glos.), MA1815, p15 (Glos.). R. (and patron) of Chinnor, Oxon. 1816-75 and R. Emmington, Oxon. 1827-72. Dom. Chap. to 3th Earl of Howth 1827. Died a bachelor 20/9/1875, leaving £60,000. Succ. 1858, title thereafter extinct [C36889. Boase] Brother Richard Adolphus, above. A big farmer - very reserved - 'his voice, &c. in church are as bad as possible' (Wilberforce).

**MUTLOW (Thomas Anthony)** Bapt. Gloucester 19/8/1776, s. Thomas Mutlow and Elizabeth Hunt. Magdalen, Oxford, Chorister 1788-93; matriculated 1793, BA1797, dn99 (London), p00 (London). Minor Canon of Canterbury Cathedral 1803, R. Canterbury St Andrew.w. St Mary Bredman 1803-8, R. Canterbury St Paul w. St Martin 1808-29,V. Preston (next Wingham), Kent 1829 to death 26/3/1854 [C120680]

**MUTLOW (William Wilton)** Bapt. Gloucester 8/3/1790, s. William Mutlow (organist) and Mary Maria Wilton. Pembroke, Oxford 1808, BA1812, dn13 (Ox.), Fellow 1813-17, p14 (Ox.), MA1815. Minor Canon of Gloucester Cathedral 1815, V. Brookthorpe, Glos. 1817-20, PC. and V. Gloucester St Mary de Lode 1819-28, R. and V. Rudford, Glos. 1828 to death 27/9/1865. No will found [C36890] Married (1) Gloucester 27/5/1818 Mary Ann Wilton (d.1829), w. issue (2) Twyford, Glos. 28/10/1834 Betty Steight. Freemason.

**MUTTER (George)** Born Westminster, London, s. George Mutter. St Edmund Hall, Oxford 1795 (aged 18), BA1799, dn99 (Win. for London), p01 (London), MA1802. R. Chillenden, Kent 1807, PC. Little Stanmore, Middx. 1832. Died 1843 (3rd q.) [C120681]

**MYDDELTON (John)** Born Melton Mowbray, Leics. 6/1/1759, s. Rev. Thomas Myddelton and Sarah Edwards. Sidney, Cambridge 1777, dn81 (Nor.), BA1782, Fellow 1783-1804, MA1785, BD1792. R. Bucknall, Lincs. 1804 to death 10/5/1834 (CCEd says 24/5/1834) [C71185] Married Great Waldingfield, Suffolk 1813 Anna Maria Marshall, with issue.

**MYDDELTON (Charles Panton)** Born Prescot, Lancs. 1769, s. Thomas Myddelton. BNC, Oxford 1785, BA1789, MA1791, dn94 (C&L), p95 (C&L). PC. Manchester St Thomas, Heaton Norris 1809 (non-res.) to death. Chap. to 4th Earl of Tyrconnell 1813. Died King's Norton, Worcs.10/9/1843 [C18618]

**MYERS (Charles John)** Bapt. Stamford, Lincs. 11/8/1800, s. David Thompson Myers and Phoebe Crow. Trinity, Cambridge 1819, BA1823, Fellow 1825-9, MA1826, dn29 (Lin. for York), p29 (Lin. for York), incorporated at Oxford 1853. V. Flintham, Notts. 1829 and R. (and patron) of Ruskington, Lincs. (1st Mediety) 1832 to death. Dom. Chap. to Bishop John Kaye of Lincoln 1832 Died (Flintham) 14/11/1870 aged 70, leaving £40,000 [C71190. YCO. P. Gallon, 'Paterfamilias: the Reverend Charles John Myers, Vicar of Flintham from 1829 to 1870'. *Nottinghamshire Historian*, No.49 (1992)] Married 19/2/1835 Mary Caroline Ward, Sheffield, with clerical son. Port. online.

**MYERS (John)** [NiVoF] V. Rye, Sussex 1793 and PC. Udimore, Sussex 1799 to death 18/11/1834 (CCEd thus) [C64617]

**MYERS (Timothy)** Bapt. 16/8/1767 Whicham, Cumberland, s. Timothy Myers [*pleb*]. Literate: dn90 (York), p91 (York). Chaplain *R.N.* [present at the Battle of Copenhagen]; V. Preston w. Sutton Poyntz, Dorset 1813-15, V. Stannington, Northumberland 1815 to death 4/2/1845 [C71195. YCO] Married St George's Hanover Square, London 10/1/1808 Ann Steel, *s.p.*

**NAIRN (Fasham)** Bapt. Middx 12/12/1762, s. Fasham and Sarah Nairn. Emmanuel, Cambridge 1781, dn95 (Peterb.), BA1786, p87 (C&L), MA1790. R. Little Bealings, Suffolk 1790 and V. Walton w. Felixstow, Suffolk 1790 to death (asthma) 7/2/1845 aged 82 [C18397] Married Warwick 30/5/1793 Ann Chamberlain, with issue. Apparently 8 men of this name!

**NAIRNE (Charles)** Born Macao, China, s. James Nairne. Trinity, Cambridge 1820 (aged 18), BA1826, dn26 (Chester), p27 (Lin.), MA 1829. R. Shadoxhurst, Kent 1830-7, PC. Lincoln St Peter at Gowts 1837, PC. Lincoln St Botolph 1837-60, Prebend of St Botolph in Lincoln Cathedral 1845-67, R. Bonby, Lincs. 1860 to death 19/5/1867. No will traced [C18398] Surrogate.

**NANCE (John)** Bapt. Boxley, Kent 5/5/1777, s. Rev. William Nance and Lydia Catharine Andrew. Worcester, Oxford 1794, BA1798, dn00 (Ox.), MA1801, p01 (Ox.), BD and DD 1813. S/M Ashford Free G/S, Kent 1813; R. Old Romney, Kent 1810 and R. Hope All Saints, Kent 1827 to death 21/2/1853 [C37014] Married Ashford 17/10/08 Anne Bond.

**NANTES (Daniel)** Born Battersea, Surrey 16/10/1795, s. Willliam Henry Nantes and Marianne Voguell. Trinity, Cambridge 1813, BA1817, dn18 (Ex.), p19 (Ex.), MA1820. R. Powderham, Devon 1825 to death 11/7/1877 aged 82, leaving £800 [C146000] Married Bridport, Dorset 27/4/1826 Mary Golding, with issue.

**NAPIER (Henry Alfred, Hon.)** Bapt. Wilton, Hawick, Roxburgh 20/6/1797, s. 8th Baron Napier of Merchistoun and Maria Margaret Clavering. Christ Church, Oxford 1817, BA 1820, dn21 (Ox.), p21 (Ox.), MA1822. R. Swyncombe (w. Master of Ewelme Hospital [almshouses]), Oxon. 1826 to death (unmarried) 20/11/1871 aged 74, leaving £3,000 [C37016] 'Painstaking - ernest - zealous - prejudiced against everything new - disappointed - proud and poor.' (Wilberforce).

**NAPLETON (William Timothy)** Born Powderham, Devon 29/4/1802, s. Rev. Timothy Napleton and Decima Green. Sidney, Cambridge 1820, BA1824, dn25 (Ex.), p26 (Ex.), MA1827, Fellow, BD1834. PC. Stoke Canon, Devon 1832-48. Died Clifford, Hereford 30/11/1857 [C146003] Married Penoyre, Som. 8/8/1846 Anna Maria Rigby.

**NARES (Edward)** Born London 26/3/1762, s. Sir George Nares (a judge) and Mary Strange. Christ Church, Oxford 1779, BA1783, then Merton, Fellow 1788-90, MA1789, dn92 (Ox.), p92 (Ox.), BD and DD1814. Regius Professor of Modern History, Oxford 1813-41. R. Biddenden, Kent (and Preacher throughout the Diocese of Canterbury) 1798-1841, R. New Church, Romney (Marsh), Kent 1827-34 (res.). Died Biddenham 23/7/1841 [C37018. ODNB. G. C. White, *A versatile Professor: reminiscences of the Rev. Edward Nares* (1903)] Married (1) Henley on Thames 16/4/1797 Lady Charlotte Spencer (dau. of 4th Duke of Marlborough, she d.1802), with issue (2) Cranbrook, Kent June 1803 Cordelia Adams, with further issue.

**NASH (Robert Atkins)** Bapt. Carrigoon House, Co. Cork, 29/10/1795, s. Michael Nash and Marcella Devereux. TCD BA1821. R. Hamerton, Hunts. 1822 to death (Bath). Probate granted 27/12/1843 [C71213. Al.Dub.?]

**NASH (Thomas)** Born Huntingdon 30/10/1799, s. Thomas Nash (of London). Trinity, Cambridge 1815, dn20 (Roch.), BA1821, p22 (Lin.), MA1825. R. Lancing, Sussex 1823 to death 6/8/1834 (CCEd says 24/11/1834) [C2029] Married 24/3/1821 Dorinda Brander (Morden Hall, Surrey), with issue.

**NATT (John)** Born Netteswell, Essex 6/7/1778, s. Rev. Nathan Natt and Marie Bertrand. St John's, Oxford 1795, Fellow, etc. 1795-1838, BA1799, dn02 (Ox.), MA1803, p03 (Ox.), BD 1808. V. Oxford St Giles 1809-28 (res.), R. St Sepulchre, City of London 1830 to death (unm.) 12/2/1843 [C37025. DEB is detailed]

**NAYLER (Thomas)** Born Glos. 24/2/1799, s. Richard Nayler and Frances Blunt. St John's, Cambridge 1816, dn22 (Lin.), BA1823, p25 (Lin.), MA1828. S/M Marlborough College 1828-30; R. Lincoln St Peter at Arches 1830-51, then unbeneficed. Dom. Chap. to HRH Duke of York 1825. Died Holloway, London 15/4/1873 aged 74, leaving £18,000 [C41664] Married St George's Hanover Square, London 20/4/1826 Dorothy Blore Nayler (dau. Sir George Nayler, Garter King of Arms), with issue.

**NAYLOR (George)** Born Turnham Green, Middx. 28/9/1767, s. Rev. Christopher Naylor and Mary Bramble. St John's, Cambridge 1786, BA1790, dn90 (Roch.), p92 (Cant.). V. Bramford w. Burstall, Suffolk 1795-1854, R. Byton, Heref. 1806 to death 30/5/1854 [C2030] Married (1) Anne Bond (a clergy sister) (2) 26/5/1830 Elizabeth Caroline Smith (Chartham Place, Kent); with issue.

**NAYLOR (Martin Joseph)** Bapt. Dewsbury, Yorks. 27/12/1764, s. Abraham Naylor and Mary Taylor. Queens', Cambridge 1792, BA 1787, dn87 (London for York), p89 (Peterb.), Fellow 1789, MA1790, BD1799, DD1829. H/M Wakefield G/S 1814-37; V. Penistone, Yorks. 1809-43 (non-res.), R. Crofton, Yorks. 1837 to death. Chap. West Riding Lunatic Asylum, Wakefield 1829. Died 21/11/1843 aged 79 [C110637. YCO] Married 1800 Rebecca Ground, with issue. Suspected in 1793 of being a member of the small Jacobin party in the University; 'a man of coarse and rough manners, was known as 'the honest Yorkshireman', he also editor of the *Wakefield Journal* for 30 years. Active freemason.

**NEALE, *born* VANSITTART (Edward)** Born Bisham, Berks., s. George Vansittart, *M.P.*, and Sarah Stonhouse. New, Oxford 1788 (aged 18), dn95 (Salis.), p95 (Salis.), BCL1796. R. and V. White Waltham w. Shottesbrooke, Berks. 1795-1803 (res.), R. Stapleford, Herts. 1804-19, R. Taplow, Bucks. 1805-50, V. Bisham 1819-33. Died 21/1/1850; living at Allesley Park, Warwicks. (his mother's home) [C71246. DEB] Married (2) Bath 26/1/1809 Anne Spooner, with son Edward Vansittart Neale, Christian Socialist (*q.v.* ODNB). Changed name 1803. Port. online.

**NEALE (John)** Born Henley, Oxon. 9/2/1754, s. Rev. James Neale and Mary Ayres. Worcester, Oxford 1775, no degree, dn77 (C&L), p81 (Ex). R. Bristol St Mary le Port 1782 (non-res.) and V. Boddington w. Staverton >< Glos. 1794 to death 26/10/1841 aged 87, leaving £2,000 [C18632] Married Honiton, Devon 2/8/1783 Anne Blagdon, with clerical issue. *J.P.* Glos. 1810. Good portrait miniature online.

**NEALE (Thomas)** Born Saltash, Cornwall 26/6/1767, s. Rev. Thomas Neale, sen. (R. Tollerton, Notts.) and Susannah Falkner. Jesus, Cambridge 1785, BA1789, R. Sibson cum Upton (or Sibstone), Leics. 1791 to death 26/1/1859, leaving under £200 [C71254] Married Congerstone, Leics. 11/9/1810 Bridget Glen, and had issue.

**NEATE (Arthur)** Born Hinwick House [a Grade 1 listed Queen Anne mansion], Podington, Beds., s. Rev. Thomas Neate and Catherine Church. Trinity, Cambridge 1822, BA1827, then Oxford 1828, dn28 (Ox.), p29 (Ox.), MA1829. R. Alvescot w. Shilton, Oxon. 1829 to death 30/5/1870, leaving £4,000 [C37027] Married Witney, Oxon. 17/10/1844 Eleanor Burnaby, w. clerical s. Walter Neate.

**NEAVE (Henry Littleton)** Born London, s. Sir Thomas Neave, 2nd Bart. and Frances Caroline Digby. Christ Church, Oxford 1816 (aged 18), BA1820, dn22 (Bangor), p22 (London), MA1823. V. Epping, Essex 1822 (and Chap. to Epping Poor Law Union) to death 4/8/1873, leaving £25,000 [C120745] Married Marylebone, London 31/8/1824 Anne Agnes Sheffield (dau. of a baronet), *s.p.*

**NECK (Aaron)** Born Moretonhampstead, Devon 15/4/1783 (Presbyterian baptism 11/3/1785), s. Gregory Andrews Neck and Anne Newcombe. Wadham, Oxford 1787, BA1791, dn91 (Ex.), p93 (Ex.). PC. Kingskerswell, Devon 1832 to death 29/11/1851 *or* 4/10/1852 [C146008] Married Dartmouth, Devon 3/12/1805 Sarah Bond.

**NEESHAM (Robert)** Literate: dn12 (Lin.), p14 (Lin.). Chap. of Donative of Goltho w. Bullington, Lincs. 1816 ['*whose only income is a gratuity from the patron*'] and PC. Stainfield and Apley, Lincs. 1818 to death (Langworth, Lincs.) 1846 (1st q.) [C71263]

**NELSON (James Edmund Rose)** Born Congham St Mary, Norfolk 1/6/1784, s. Rev. Edmund Nelson and Elizabeth Forster Rose. Christ's, Cambridge 1802, BA1807, dn07 (Nor.), p08 (Nor.). (succ. his father as) R. (and patron) of Congham St Mary 1811 to death (Lincoln) aged 55. Probate granted 23/8/1839 [C112862]

**NELSON (John)** Bapt. Stokesley, Yorks. 17/2/1762, s. Thomas Nelson. Literate: dn85 (York), p87 (York), then Emmanuel, Cambridge 1787 (a Ten Year Man, BD1797). 'Provost of the College of Priest Vicars' in Lincoln Cathedral 1789-1845, PC. Lincoln St Mark 1790-1845, V. Wellingore, Lincs. 1803-45, V.

Ruskington (Second Portion), Lincs. 1804-45, V. Searby cum Owmby, Lincs. 1811 and R. Snarford, Lincs. 1828 to death 23/5/1845 aged 83 [C104301. YCO. Kaye] *J.P.* Lindsey.

**NELSON (John)** [Probably] Literate: dn01 (S&M). V. Jurby, IoM 1803-18, V. Santan (St Anne), IoM 1818-30 (res.), Vicar General of the Isle of Man from 1827, R. Bride, IoM 1830 to death 27/10/1847 aged 68 [C7308. Gelling] Married Andreas, IoM 21/11/1801 Anne Allen. In debt 1837.

**NELSON (John)** Born Dereham, Norfolk, s. John Nelson. Caius, Cambridge 1802, then Trinity Hall 1805, BA1796, dn08 (Nor.), p09 (Nor.), MA1810. R. Beeston, Norfolk 1810-65, R. Mileham 1823-5 (res.), R. (and patron) of Little Dunham, Norfolk 1830-45. Dom. Chap. to Dowager Lady Suffield. Died Beeston 9/11/1865, leaving £10,000 [C114252] Married Dereham 5/4/1808 Emily Smyth (w), with clerical son, also John.

**NELSON (John)** Bapt. Holme-next-the-Sea, Norfolk 6/5/1793, s. Matthew Nelson and Anne Thurlow. Sidney, Cambridge 1813, then Queens' 1813, dn16 (Nor.), BA1817, p17 (Nor.). R. Winterton w. East Somerton, Norfolk 1821 to death 5/5/1867, leaving £800 [C114253] Married Fring, Norfolk 8/7/1815 Elizabeth Gudgeon, and clerical son John Gudgeon Nelson.

**NELSON (John)** From Portsmouth, Hants., s. John William Nelson. St John's, Oxford 1818 (aged 18), BA1822, dn24 (London), MA1824, p24 (London). R. Fulham St John, London, 1828. Died 1843? [C120747]

**NELSON (William)** Bapt. Old Hutton, Kendal, Westmorland 21/12/1784, s. John Nelson and Mary Blamire. Literate: dn08 (Chester), p09 (Chester). S/M Over Kellet, Lancs. 1810; PC. Gressingham, Lancs. 1820 to death (Over Kellet) 7/9/1837 aged 51 [C170090] Married Warton, Lancaster 29/12/1829 Sarah Ann Hodgson (d.1831), 1 dead ch. (2) Bolton-le-Sands, Lancs. 9/11/1835 Sarah Heaton, w. issue.

**NEPEAN (Evan)** Born London 20/4/1800, s. Sir Evan Nepean, 1st Bart. (Secretary to the Admiralty, *q.v.* ODNB) and Margaret Skinner (then aged 47). Trinity, Cambridge 1818, BA 1823, dn23 (Chester for Bristol), p24 (Bristol), MA1826. PC. Bothenhampton, Dorset 1824-5, Min. Grosvenor Chapel, South Audley Street, London 1830-73, R. Heydon w. Hermingland, Norfolk 1831-61, Canon of Westminster 1860 to death. Chap. in Ordinary 1848-73. Died 13/3/1873, leaving £5,000 [C53446. Boase] Married 5/9/1832 Anne (dau. Rt. Hon. Sir Herbert Jenner Fust, a judge), with at least 14 ch.

**NESS (John Derby)** Born Hanwell, Oxon., s. Rev. Richard Ness (below?) and Elizabeth Mary Derby. Lincoln, Oxford 1821 (aged 20), BA 1825, dn26 (Ex.), p27 (Ex.). V. Morthoe, Devon 1830 to death 18/3/1884 aged 83, leaving £4,340-11s-5d. [C146009] Married Camberwell, Surrey 31/8/1837 Elizabeth Jane Thomson, with issue.

**NESS (Richard)** From Broughton, Oxon., s. Richard Ness. Merton, Oxford 1785 (aged 18), BA1788, dn89 (Ox.), p90 (Ox.), MA1801, BD and DD1823. R. Abingdon, Northants 1792 and R. West Parley, Dorset 1798 to death 7/4/1839 [C37034] Married Ringwood, Hants. 22/10/1795 Elizabeth Mary Derby, with son above?

**NETHERSOLE (William Pierce)** Bapt. Westminster, London 6/6/1781, s. William Nethersole. Hertford, Oxford 1773, BA1776, dn78 (Lin.), p79 (Lin.), LLB1799. V. Clophill, Beds. 1799 and V. Pulloxhill, Beds. 1799 to death 6/12/1842 aged 88 [C71278 has wrong death date] Married Westminster, London 7/6/1781 Anna Boote.

**NETTLESHIP (William)** Bapt. Twickenham, Middx. 1/5/1762, s. Rev. William and Ann Nettleship. Worcester, Oxford 1781, BA1784, dn85 (Ox.), p86 (Lin.), MA1787. R. Ruckland w. Farforth and Maidenwell, Lincs. 1794-1815, R. Churchill, Worcs. 1811 and R. Irby on the Humber, Lincs. 1814 to death 18/9/1841 [C37035]

**NEVE (Charles)** Born Willenhall, Staffs. 9/7/1765, s. Rev. Titus and Sarah Neve. Pembroke, Oxford 1788, BA1793, p06 (C&L). V. Kilmserdon, Som. 1806 and P.C. Brierley Hill, Staffs. 1809 to death 2/7/1833 aged 67 (CCEd says 10/8/1833) [C18638] Had issue.

**NEVE (Frederick Hervey)** Born Thame, Oxon. 31/5/1775, s. Rev. Timothy Neve and Anne Jenner. Merton, Oxford 1793, BA1797, dn99 (Salis.), p99 (Salis.), MA1802. R. Llansantfraid yr Mechan, Montgomery 1805, R. Walwyn's Castle, Pembroke 1815, V. Southill w. Old Warden, Beds. 1816 to death 15/5/1843 [C71280] Married Chiselhurst, Kent 5/8/1805 Elizabeth Marton Stone, with clerical son Frederick Robert Neve.

**NEVILE, NEVILL (Christopher)** Born Thorney Hall, Newark, Notts. 11/1/1806, s. of Capt. Christopher Nevile, *R.N.*, and Ann Elizabeth Acklom. Trinity, Cambridge 1822, BA1829, dn29 (York), p30 (York). R. Wickenby, Lincs. 1830, V. Thorney 1830-62 (having succeeded to Thorney Hall in 1830). Died Thorney Hall 8/8/1877, leaving £12,000. [C71285. YCO. Boase. Kaye] Married (1) Thorney 24 *or* 27/12/1830 Gertrude Hotham (d.1859), dau. of an army officer, with issue (2) St Pancras, London 1862 (1st q.) Margaret Wright (d.1862) (3) Cranbrook, Kent/Sussex 1865 (2nd q.) Mary Ann Tooth, of Swift's Park, Kent, with further issue. *J.P.* Notts. and Lincs. *Relinquished his Orders* 1870.

**NEVILE (Edward)** Bapt. Thorney, Notts. 23/12/1773, s. George Nevile and Catherine Nevile (thus). Jesus, Cambridge 1791, BA1795, dn96 (York), p97 (London for York), MA1798. V. Thorney w. Wigsley and Broadholme, Notts. 1798-1803, R. Wickenby, Lincs. 1798-1801, V. Prees, Shropshire 1801 to death. Dom. Chap. to 1st Viscount Hill 1816. Died 13/5/1846 [C18642. YCO] Married Prees 22/11/1807 Elizabeth Hill (dau. of a baronet).

**NEVILE (Henry William)** Born Wellingore Hall, Wellingore, Lincs. 26/3/1775, s. Christopher Nevile and Lady Sophia Noel (dau. of 4th Earl of Gainsborough). Trinity, Cambridge 1794, BA1798, dn00 (Peterb.), p00 (Peterb.), MA1801. R. Fulbeck. Lincs. 1803-7 (res.), R. Cottesmore, Rutland 1812-43, R. Blatherwycke, Northants. 1817-33, R. Walcot, Bath, Som. 1838-41. Dom. Chap. to 9th Earl of Dalhousie 1817. Died (Cottesmore) 8/11/1843 [C71286] Married Linton, Kent 28/9/1807 Amelia Mann (a minor, Hallow Park, Worcs.), with issue.

**NEVILL (Henry Walpole)** Born Flower Place, Frant, Surrey 10/11/1803, s. Hon. George Henry Nevill and Caroline Walpole. Magdalene, Cambridge 1811, MA1826. R. West Chillington, Sussex 1829-30, R. Otley, Suffolk 1831-7, R. Bergh Apton w. Holreston, Norfolk 1831 to death 3/3/1837 [C64674] Married 28/5/1833 Frances Bacon (dau. of a baronet), *s.p.*

**NEVILL, NEVILLE, *later* ROLFE (Strickland Charles Edward)** Born Eltham, Kent 31/1/1789, s. Lt.-Gen. Charles Nevill(e) and Ann Colden Williamson. Wadham, Oxford 1808, BA1812, MA1816. V. Houghton, Harpley, Norfolk 1829, V. Heacham, Norfolk 1838 to death 25/12/1852 [C114259] Married (1) Marylebone, London 22/9/1814 Agnes Fawcett (d.1831), with issue (2) Paddington, London 5/1/1833 Dorothy Thomason. Changed name 1837.

**NEVILL (William, Hon., *later* 4th Earl of Abergavenny)** Born Isleworth, Middx. 28/6/1792, s. Henry Nevill, 2nd Earl of Abergavenny (of Elridge Castle, Sussex) and Mary Robinson. Christ Church, Oxford 1812, then Magdalene, Cambridge 1816, BA, dn16 (Roch.), MA1816. R. Birling, Kent 1816-44, V. Frant, Sussex 1818-44. Chap. in Ordinary. Died Birling Manor 17/8/1868, leaving £300,000 [C392] Married 7/9/1824 Caroline Leeke (w) (Longford Hall, Shropshire), with issue. Succ. to title 1845.

**NEVILLE, *later* NEVILLE-GRENVILLE (George [Aldworth], Hon.)** Born Stanlake, Berks. 17/8/1789, s. Richard Neville (born Griffin), 2nd Baron Braybrooke, *M.P.*, and Catherine Grenville (daughter of the Prime Minister George Grenville). Trinity, Cambridge 1807, MA1810, dn13 (Bristol), p13 (Bristol), Master of Magdalen College, Cambridge 1813-53. R. Ellingham, Norfolk 1813, R. Hawarden, Flintshire [net income £2,844] (and Preacher within Chester Diocese) 1813-34, Dean of Windsor (and Chap. to Queen Victoria) 1846 to death (Butleigh Court, Som.) 10/6/1854 aged 64 [C53450. ODNB. Venn under Neville. Boase] Married 9/5/1816 Lady Charlotte Legge (dau. of 3rd Earl of Dartmouth), 6s. (some clerical), 5 dau. Name changed when he inherited the Grenville estate of Butley Court in 1825; co-discoverer of Samuel Pepys's diaries with his brother Lord Braybrooke.

**NEWBERY, NEWBURY (Thomas)** Born Manchester 17/12/1803, s. of William (a silk manufacturer) and Ann Newbery. Queens', Cambridge 1822, BA1826, dn27 (York), p28 (London for York), MA1830, incorporated at Oxford 1834. PC. Shipley cum Heaton, Yorks.

1828-45, R. Hinton St George w. Seavington St Michael, Som. 1846 to death 30/3/1861 (apoplexy) aged 57, leaving £7,000 [C135661. YCO] Married Ealing, Middx. 9/8/1848 Mary Newbery [*thus*], with issue.

**NEWBOLD (Francis [Henry] Stonhewer)** Bapt. Macclesfield, Cheshire 15/6/1799, s. Alderman Francis Newbold and Anna Ston(e)hewer. BNC, Oxford 1816, BA1820, Fellow 1821-7, MA1822, dn22 (Ox.), p24 (Chester), BD and DD1834, etc. H/M Macclesfield G/S 1830; PC. Pott Shrigley, Cheshire 1827-9 (res.), V. Stickney, Lincs. 1828-35 (non-res.). Living latterly and died Maidenhead Thicket, Berks. 16/1/1876, leaving £600 [C37042. Bennett2] Married (1) Hagnaby, Lincs. 21/8/1827 Mary Coltman (Hagnaby Priory, she d.1835) (2) Marylebone, London 9/5/1843 Martha Lawley, with issue.

**NEWBOLT (William Hill)** Bapt. Winchester 27/2/1771, s. Rev. John Monk Newbolt and Susanna Knowler. Oriel, Oxford 1790, BA1794, dn94 (Salis.), p95 (Salis.), MA1799, BD and DD1813. R. Hartley Witney, Hants. 1797, Minor Canon of Winchester Cathedral 1804-33, R. Morestead, Hants. 1804-33, V. Collingbourne Kingston, Wilts. 1814, V. Shorwell, Hants. 1814-24 (res.), R. Mottistone, Hants. 1824 (res.). Died 9/3/1833 (CCEd thus) [C47283] *J.P.* Hants.

**NEWBOLT (William Robert)** Born Bloomsbury, London 26/8/1801, s. Sir John Henry Newbolt and Elizabeth Juliana Digby. Christ Church, Oxford 1820, Student [Fellow] 1821-8, BA1824, MA1826. PC. Brentwood, Essex 1829, V. Somerton, Som. 1833 to death (Clifton, Bristol) 4/4/1857 [C37184] Married Marylebone, London 1828 Anne Frances Magens, with issue.

**NEWBY (George)** Born Stockton on Tees, Durham 11/7/1779, s. Mark Newby and Mary Bulan. Literate: dn02 Chester), p03 (Chester). PC. Witton-le-Wear, Auckland St Andrew, Durham 1806 (and proprietor of Barningham Boarding Academy there), V. Stockton on Tees 1832-44, R. Whickham, Durham 1841 to death. Dom. Chap. to Earl Poulett 1846-61. Died 8/5/1846 aged 67 [C130679] Married Barningham 29/1/1803 Margaret Crawford (of Staindrop), 2 clerical sons (one, Mark, below).

**NEWBY (John Pengree)** Bapt. Cambridge 4/6/1790, s. John Newby and Ann Harston. St John's, Cambridge 1816, BA1821, dn21 (Lin.), p22 (Lin.), BA1824. V. Enderby, Lincs. 1824 to death there 23/7/1858 aged 67, leaving £2,000 [C71296] Married (1) 16/8/1819 Mrs Ann (Milner) Murfitt (d.1841) (2) Seagrave, Leics. 26/1/1842 Mary Ann Gutch (a clergy dau.), with issue.

**NEWBY (Mark)** Born Witton-le-Wear, Co. Durham 1806, s. Rev. George Newby (above) and Margaret Crawford. Trinity, Cambridge 1824, BA1829, dn29 (Durham), p30 (Durham), MA1835. R. Crosby Garrett, Brough, Westmorland 1832 to death (Uxbridge, Middx.) 28/12/1860 aged 54. Will not traced [C5703. Platt]

**NEWCOME (Thomas)** Born Gresford, Denbigh 6/11/1777, s. Rev. Henry Newcome and Elizabeth Hughes. Queens', Cambridge 1795, BA1799, dn00 (St Asaph), p01 (Lin.), MA 1825. R. Shenley, Herts. [net income £1,244] 1801-49 and V. Tottenham All Hallows, London 1824 to death. Chap. to HRH Duke of Sussex 1824. Died 1/9/1851 [C71312] Married Shenley 9/4/1806 Charlotte Winter. 'He represented the last but one of nine generations of beneficed clergy since the Reformation'.

**NEWCOME (William)** Born Kilkenny, Ireland, s. Most Rev. William Newcome (Archbishop of Armagh, *q.v.* ODNB) and Anna Maria Smyth. Christ Church, Oxford 1796 (aged 18), BA1799, MA 1802. R. Belaugh, Norfolk 1810-24. R. (and patron) of Mundford, Norfolk 1815, R. Scottow, Norfolk 1824, R. Langford w. Ickburgh, Norfolk 1824, V. Sutton (Isle of Ely), Cambs. 1838 to death 22/5/1846 [C64681] Wife Catherine in 1841.

**NEWELL (James Edward)** From Great Missenden, Bucks., s. Rev. Jeremiah Newell. Worcester, Oxford 1815 (aged 19), BA1819, dn19 (Roch.), p19 (Chester), MA1821. PC. Bromley, Kent 1827 to death (Horswell House, South Milton, Devon) 5/1/1880, leaving £12,000 [C395] Married Halifax, Yorks. 27/8/1834 Ann Catherine Rawson.

**NEWELL (Robert Hasell)** Born Colchester, Essex, s. Robert Richardson Newell (surgeon) and Sally Mary Hassell. St John's, Cambridge 1795, BA1799, Fellow 1800-14, MA1802, dn05 (Lin.), BD1810, etc. R. Little Hormead, Herts. 1813 to death 21/1/1852 [C71315. ODNB. Boase] Married Little Hormead 27/9/1813 Mary

Alexander. A good painter, and the father of another.

**NEWELL (Thomas Blackman)** Born Cheltenham, Glos. 2/8/1793, s. Thomas Newell and Lucretia Blackman. Christ Church, Oxford 1811, BA1815, dn16 (Glos.), MA1817, p17 (Glos.). PC. Cold Salperton, Glos. 1823 to death. Dom. Chap. to 4th Duke of Argyll 1817. Died Cheltenham 14/4/1850 [C158765] Married Catherine Crane.

**NEWLAND (Henry Garret)** Bapt. Piccadilly, London 13/4/1806, s. Col. Bingham Newland and Charlotte Mitford. Educ. at Lausanne. Christ's, Cambridge 1823, BA1827, dn28 (Chich.), p29 (Ely), MA1830. (Sinecure R. 1829 and) V. Westbourne, Sussex 1833-60, V. (St) Marychurch w. Coffinswell, Devon 1855 to death. Chap. to Bishop of Exeter. Died (unm.) 25/6/1860, leaving under £20 [*sic*] [C64682. ODNB. Boase] 'A zealous Tractarian'.

**NEWLING (John)** Bapt. Shrewsbury, Shropshire 8/4/1762 s. Rev. Charles and Mary Newling. St. John's, Cambridge 1781, BA1785, dn87 (C&L), p87 (C&L), Fellow 1789-1804, MA 1789, BD1797. V. Clunbury, Shropshire 1789-1802, PC. Ford, Shropshire 1802-11, R. Ditchingham, Norfolk 1802-38, Prebend of Wellington in Lichfield Cathedral 1802-7, then Prebend of Freeford and Hanscare 1807 and Canon Residentiary 1807 to death 1/7/1838 [C18401] Married 1/12/1810 Ann Frances Lettice (a clergy dau.), with issue. J.P. Shropshire and Staffs. 'Justly considered the first amateur herald in England', with a major library.

**NEWMAN (Edward Sandys)** Born Hinkley, Leics. 24/2/1762, s. Rev. Henry Newman (R. Shepton Beachamp and Sparkford, Som.) and Ann Underwood. Magdalene, Cambridge 1780, dn85 (Lin.), LLB1791, p91 (B&W). R. Sparkford 1798 to death (Babcary - where he was also Curate) 19/4/1836 aged 74 [C41671] Married Berry Pomeroy, Devon 16/5/1797 Frances Tucker Lyde, with clerical son. Pastel port. online.

**NEWMAN (John)** Born London 22/11/1765, s. Rev. Thomas Newman and Margaret Bankes. Corpus Christi, Cambridge 1782, BA1787, dn88 (London), p90 (London). R. Childerditch, Essex 1792, V. Great Burstead, Essex 1805-22, V. Witham, Essex 1822 to death. Dom. Chap. to 4th Earl of Albemarle 1805-22; and to 8th Earl of Haddington 1805. Died 23/4/1840 [C120752] Married Holborn, London 23/12/1796 Ellen Sterry, with issue.

**NEWMAN (John Henry,** *Saint*) Born Alton, Hants. 21/2/1801, s. John Newman (a failed banker, then brewery manager) and Jemima Fourdrinier. Trinity, Oxford 1816 [Student of Lincoln's Inn 1819] BA1820, then Oriel, Fellow 1822-45, MA1823, dn24 (Ox.), p26 (Ox.), Tutor 1826-32, BD1836, Vice-Principal St Alban Hall, Oxford 1825-6, Hon. Fellow Trinity 1877. V. Oxford St Mary the Virgin 1828-43 (res.). Roman Catholic 1845; Oratorian Priest in Birmingham 1846; Cardinal 1879; canonised 13/10/2019. Died Birmingham Oratory 11/8/1890 aged 89, leaving £4,206 [C37041. ODNB. Boase. DEB. A library of primary and secondary material] The originator of the Tractarian/Oxford Movement, and one of the century's most influential religious figures; and the only *bona fide* saint amongst all these Anglican clergymen!

**NEWMAN (Thomas)** From Essex, probably s. Rev. Thomas Newman, sen. Jesus, Cambridge 1783, BA1787, dn87 (Nor.), p88 (Nor.), MA 1790. R. Little Bromley, Essex (a family living) 1792-1838, R. West Horndon w. Ingrave, Essex 1797, R. Alresford, Essex 1829 to death. Dom. Chap. to HRH Duke of Cumberland (later King Augustus 1 of Hanover) 1829. Probate granted 24/5/1838 aged 73 [C114265] Had issue.

**NEWMARCH (Henry)** Bapt. Hull 19/4/1802, s. John and Jane Newmarch. St Mary's Hall, Oxford 1823, BA1826, p26 (B&W for York), p29 (Lin.). R. Boultham, Lincs. 1829-74, V. Hessle, Yorks. 1837 to death 11/7/1883, leaving £777-2s-4d. [C71366. YCO] Married Lincoln 19/5/1829 Susannah Keyworth, with issue.

**NEWMARCH (John Ladeveze)** Born Horsforth, Yorks. 14/6/1790 s. Major Timothy Newmarch and Mary Trapaud. Trinity, Cambridge 1807, then Caius 1810, BA1813, dn15 (London), p18 (York), MA1817. PC. Frickley w. Clayton, Yorks. 1823-7, V. Hooton Pagnell, Yorks. 1823-35 and PC. Skelbrooke, Yorks. 1835 to death 16/6/1855 [C120757. YCO says Lawrence] Married Woodford, Essex 31/3/1813 Eliza Dundersdale (a clergy dau.), with issue.

**NEWNHAM (George William)** Born Bassingham, Lincs. 9/9/1806, s. Rev. William

Newnham and Susanna Townsend. Corpus Christi, Oxford 1823, BA1827, MA1830, dn31 (B&W), p32 (B&W), Fellow 1831-3, LLD by 1833. Curate <u>Coleford</u>, Som. 1831-40, PC. Shaw, Wilts. 1840-2, PC. Combe Down, Som. 1842-77, PC. Monkton Combe, Som. 1845-63. Died (Corsham, Wilts.) 21/12/1893, leaving £7,245-16s.-4d. [C41672. DEB] Married (1) St Pancras, London 11/5/1833 Helen Maria Heath (d.1834), with son (2) Chicklade, Wilts. 16/4/1839 Catherine Pennock Read (d.1865), many ch. (3) Weston-super-Mare, Som. 10/10/1866 Harriet Helen White (d.1889), with further child.

**NEWSAM (Clement)** Bapt. Dalkeith, Midlothian 26/2/1777, s. ?Rev. Clement Newsam and Henrietta Wren. Worcester, Oxford 1793, BA1797, MA1800, dn00 (Salis.), p01 (Ox.). V. <u>Portbury w. Tickenham</u>, Som. 1803 and V. <u>Harbury</u>, Warwicks. 1806 to death (Leamington, Warwicks.) 10/2/1859, leaving £6,000 [C18641] Wife Hannah, and issue.

**NEWSAM (James)** Bapt. Eckington, Derbys. 6/8/1792, s. William Newsam and Jane Alderson. Christ's, Cambridge 1810, BA1815, dn16 (Chester), p16 (Chester), MA1825. PC. Pateley Bridge, Yorks. 1819-26, PC. <u>Sharow</u>, Yorks. 1826-39. Chap. to the private chapel at Pitfour House, Old Deer, Aberdeenshire 1851-67 (res.). Died a widower (Aberdeen) 12/10/1871, leaving £450 [C135945. Bertie] Married York 16/10/1827 Sarah (Sally) Remington, York, with issue.

**NEWSAM (William)** Bapt. Richmond, Yorks. 1/7/1765, s. of James Newsam (merchant) and Elizabeth Simpson. Sidney, Cambridge 1783, BA1788, dn88 (C&L), p89 (C&L), MA1791. V. Whatton, Notts. 1790-1800, R. <u>Scruton</u>, Yorks. 1792-1834. Probate granted 19/3/1834. Chap. to 2nd Baron Alvanley 1810 [C18403] Married Eckington, Derbys. 26/4/1791 Elizabeth Alderson (a clergy dau.), with issue.

**NEWTON (John Farmer)** Born Devynnock, Breconshire 1791, s. Rev. Benjamin Newton and Mary Fendall. Jesus, Cambridge 1807, BA 1816, dn17 (B&W), p18 (Glos.). PC. <u>Whorlton</u>, Yorks. 1827-55, V. (and patron) of Kirkby in Cleveland 1841 to death 23/11/1880 aged 89, leaving £10,000 [C41674] Married Little Beswin, Wilts. 2/4/1811 Elizabeth Kent (d.1850), 1s. 'In financial straits due to their mutual extravagence'. His father left *The diary of Benjamin Newton, Rector of Wath, 1816-1818*, edited C.P. Pendall and E.A. Crutchley (Cambridge, 1933).

**NEWTON, *born* HAND (Newton Dickinson Hand)** Born City of London 7/12/1778, s. Ven. George Watson Hand (Archdeacon of Dorset) and Ann Martha Dickinson. St Mary Hall, Oxford 1802, BA1806, dn06 (Cant.), p07 (Cant.). V. (and patron) of <u>Bredwardine</u>, Heref. 1829 and R. (and patron) of <u>Brobury</u>, Heref. 1829 to death 22/11/1853 [C158766] Married Ightham, Kent 24/7/1810 Maria Julia Wyatt, with clerical son William Newton.

**NEWTON (Richard Edward)** Literate: dn83 (Chester), p83 (Chester). PC. <u>Birkenhead</u>, Cheshire 1793 (and S/M Wallasey Free G/S 1793) to death 1810/6/1834 (CCEd thus) [C70101].

**NEWTON (Thomas)** Bapt. Coxwold, Yorks. 4/5/1761, s. Rev. Thomas Newton, sen. and Ellen Whitehead. Jesus, Cambridge 1777, BA 1783. Fellow 1783-98 [candidate for Woodward Professor of Geology 1788] dn83 (Peterb. for York), p85 (Peterb. - two possible dates here), MA1786. R. <u>Tewin</u>, Herts. 1797-1843, PC. <u>Husthwaite</u>, Yorks. 1806-43, PC. <u>Coxwold</u> 1807 (and S/M Coxwold G/S 1806) to death 10/4/1843 aged 83 [C71383. YCO] Wife Lucy Maria Douglas, with clerical son. J.P. North Riding.

**NEWTON (William)** From Stowey, Somerset, s. Rev. James Newton. Pembroke, Oxford 1801 (aged 17), BA1804, dn06 (Win. for B&W), p07 (Cantab. For B&W). V. <u>Old Cleeve</u>, Som. 1807 to death. Probate granted 15/4/1848 [C41676] Wife Eliza J., and issue.

**NICHOLAS (John)** Bapt. Devizes, Wilts. 30/12/1763, s. Rev. Edward Richmond Nicholas and Jane Neate. Queen's, Oxford 1781, dn86 (Ox.), BCL1788, p89 (Wor.), DCL 1800. R. <u>Fisherton Anger</u>, Wilts. 1804, R. <u>Bremilham</u>, Wilts. 1804, V. <u>Westport St Mary</u> Wilts. 1800 (and RD of Malmesbury 1812) to death 7/10/1836 [C37200]

**NICHOLLS (Henry)** Bapt. St Gerrans, Cornwall 19/3/1773, s. Henry Nicholls and Elizabeth Dash. Exeter, Oxford 1791, BA1796, dn96 (Ex.), p97 (Ex.), migrated to Peterhouse, Cambridge 1808. S/M Barnstaple, Devon 1812; R. Goodleigh, Devon 1831 only, V. <u>Rockbeare</u>,

Devon 1831 to death 5/1/1860 aged 87, leaving £800 [C146013] Married (1) Barnstaple, Devon 25/5/1801 Ann Bremridge (d.1825) (2) St Erme, Cornwall 19/4/1827 Lucy Braithwaite Cardew (w), with issue.

**NICHOLSON (Isaac)** Probably bapt. Yelling, Hunts. 10/6/1760, s. Isaac and Dinah Nicholson. Queens', Cambridge 1788, BA1792, dn92 (Lin.), p94 (Lin.), MA1795. V. Great Paxton, Hunts. 1825 to death 27/12/1839 aged 68 [C71501] Had issue.

**NICHOLSON (John)** Bapt. Romaldkirk, Yorks. 20/4/1775. St John's, Cambridge 1793, BA1798, dn99 (Peterb.), p01 (Lin.). R. Wyddial, Herts. 1803 to death 13/4/1836 [C71503]

**NICHOLSON (John)** Bapt. Bolton, Cumberland 3/3/1786, s. Henry and Nancy Nicholson. Literate: dn09 (York), p10 (York). PC. Drax, Yorks. 1820-35 (and S/M Drax parish schools 1818). Died 1850, 'embittered and drunken' [C136499. Boase. YCO. *The life of Mrs Nancy Nicholson, of Drax* (Howden, 1855) and legible online version)] Married Oct. 1811 Nancy Jackson (a clergy dau., he separated from her Nov. 1814), the famous termagant, a 'disgusting and filthy woman', 'who died unrespected and unlamented'.

**NICOLAY (George Frederick Louisa)** Bapt. London 2/12/1764, s. George Nicolay and Albinia Lattman. Christ Church, Oxford 1781, BA1784, Student [Fellow], MA1787. R. St Michael Royal w. St Martin Vintry, City of London 1789, Minor Canon of Durham Cathedral 1801, 'Brother' and R. of St Katharine's Hospital, Tower of London (then in Regent's Park) 1802, V. Little Marlow, Bucks. 1821. Chap. to HRH Duke of York and Albany 1821. Died 13/12/1847 aged 83 [C37215] Married Durham 6/10/1796 Mary Hayes (a clergy dau.), *s.p.* Named after his sponsors the King and Queen of Denmark.

**NICOLL ([Thomas Vere] Richard)** Bapt. Bodicote, Oxon. 2/3/1770, s. Rev. Richard Nicoll and Vere Alice Wykeham. Oriel, Oxford 1788, BA1792, p93 (Ox.), MA1795. R. Cherington, Warwicks. 1794 to death 22/10/1841 [C37216] Married Wootton Wawen, Warwicks. 22/9/1801 Mary Bond Mister, with issue.

**NIHILL (Daniel)** Born Ireland *c.*1791. St John's, Cambridge 1814, dn18 (Lin.), BA1819, p19 (Lin.), MA1822. PC. Clunbury w. Clunton, Shropshire 1818-26, PC. Forden, Montgomery (and Chap. to and Governor of the General Penitentiary, Millbank, London) 1826-44, R. Bridgwater, Som. 1845-8, R. Fitz, Shropshire 1840 to death 19/7/1867, leaving £3,000 [C71510. Boase] Married Dublin 1822 Catherine Elizabeth Stephens, and issue.

**NIXON (Charles)** Born Nuthall, Notts. 19/3/1766, s. Rev. Thomas Nixon and Peggy Farnworth. Merton, Oxford 1784, BA1788, dn88 (York), p90 (York). R. Nuthall 1790-1837, R. Hucknall Torkard, Notts. 1790-1831-, V. Great Dalby, Leics. 1791 (and Prebend of Segeston (or Sacrita) in Southwell Collegiate Church) 1825 to death. Dom. Chap. to 3rd Baron Vernon 1814. Died 20/6/1837 [C71513. YCO. Kaye] Married Nuthall 3/12/1806 Phoebe Johnson.

**NOBLE (John)** Bapt. St Bees, Cumberland 21/6/1760, s. Joseph Noble and Sarah Hutchinson. Literate: p91 (Lin.). Chap. of Donative of Grimston, Leics. 1791, V. Frisby (on the Wreak), Leics. 1796-1840, PC. Kirby Bellars, Leics. 1813. Died 18/8/1840 aged 80 [C71590] Married Leicester 31/5/1796 Sarah Wragge (a clergy dau.), with clerical sons John, and Robert Turlington Noble.

**NOBLE (Richard)** Literate: dn05 (Chester), p05 (Chester). V. Whalley, Lancs. 1822-39 (w. H/M Whalley G/S 1814-29), PC. Grindleton, Yorks. 1822, PC. Church Kirk, Whalley 1824 to (burial) 3/12/1839 aged 60 [C135946] J.P.

**NOBLE (Samuel Lambert)** Born Frolesworth, Leics. 26/8/1795, s. Rev. Samuel George Noble and Margaret Lambert. Queens', Cambridge 1814, BA1818, dn18 (Lin.), p19 (Lin.). (succ. his father as) R. Frolesworth 1822 to death 21/5/1864, leaving £800 [C71595] Married Brinklow, Warwicks. 1/8/1839 Ellen Susannah Brierly, w. clerical s. Samuel Henry Brierly Noble.

**NOEL (Francis James [Edwardes], Hon.)** Born Marylebone, London 4/5/1793, s. Sir Gerard Noel Edwardes Noel, 2nd Bart. (formerly Edwardes, of Exton Park Hall, Rutland), *M.P.*, and Diana Middleton, 2nd Baroness Barham (in her own right, 1813). Trinity, Oxford 1813, BA1817, MA1820. R. Nettlestead w. West Barming, Kent 1820-54, V. Teston, Kent 1820 (and Sinecure R. 1830) and RD to death

30/7/1854 aged 60 [C398. DEB] Married Southampton 24/4/1822 Cecilia Penelope Methuen (Corsham Court, Wilts.), w. clerical son Montague Henry. Brother below.

**NOEL (Leland Noel [Edwardes], Hon.)** Born Leatherhead, Surrey 21/8/1797, s. Sir Gerard Edwardes Noel, 2nd Bart. (formerly Edwardes) and Diana Middleton, 2nd Baroness Barham (in her own right, 1813). Trinity, Cambridge 1817, MA1821, dn23 (Glos.), p24 (Glos.). V. Chipping Camden, Glos. 1824-32, V. Lavendon, Bucks. 1832, R. Horn and Exton, Rutland 1832-70, Hon. Canon of Peterborough 1850 to death (Exton Park Hall, Rutland, a widower) 10/11/1870, leaving £10,000 [C71599] Married Worksop, Notts. 30/12/1824 Mary Arabella Foljambe, w. clerical s. Horace. Brother above.

**NOEL (Thomas Noel)** Natural s. 2nd Viscount Wentworth. Christ Church, Oxford 1792 (aged 18), BA1796, MA1801. R. Kirkby Mallory, Leics. 1798-1853, (Sinecure R. Elmersthorp, Leics. ['church in ruins'] 1798), Chap. of Donative of Fleckney, Leics. 1810. Died (unm.) 22/8/1853 [C71600] He performed the marriage ceremony of his cousin Anne Isabella Noel and Lord Byron in 1815.

**NOEL-HILL (Richard)** see under **HILL**

**NOLAN, NOWLAN (Frederick)** Born Old Rathmines Castle, Co. Dublin 9/2/1784, s. Edward Nowlan and Florinda Shenton. TCD 1796 [but not in Al.Dub], then Exeter, Oxford 1803, BCL1805, p09 (London), DCL1828. V. Prittlewell, Essex 1822 to death (Geraldstown House, Co. Cavan) 16/9/1864. Will not traced [C120777. ODNB. Boase. DEB] Widow Angelina, s.p. F.R.S. (1832).

**NOLAN (John)** [NiVoF] R. Antony, Cornwall before 1806, PC. Torpoint, Cornwall 1821 to death 19/4/1835 [Not yet in CCEd] Married 1799.

**NORCROSS (John)** Bapt. Ormskirk, Lancs. 22/4/1761, s. Rev. John (schoolmaster and PC. Rivington, Lancs.) and Margaret Norcross. Pembroke, Cambridge 1778, BA1783, dn03 (Chester), Fellow 1785, MA1786, p06 (Durham). V. Saxthorpe, Norfolk 1806-13, R. Framlingham w. Saxstead, Suffolk [net income £1,201] 1813 to death (Dawlish, Devon) 10/4/1837, but an absentee due to a tithe dispute in 1815 [C114280] Wife Marian, w. issue. Archer.

**NORFORD (Charles)** 'Said to have been the 26th child' of William Norford, a Bury St Edmunds doctor (q.v. ODNB). Caius, Cambridge 1795 (aged 19), BA1800, dn00 (London), MA1803, p03 (Glos.). R. Westonbirt, Glos. 1803 to death 16/9/1867 aged 89, leaving £200 (and where he kept a night school for 60 years) [C120778] Clerical son William.

**NORGATE (Burroughes Thomas)** Bapt. Diss, Norfolk 24/5/1788, s. Thomas Norgate (physician) and Elizabeth Burroughes. Caius, Cambridge 1805, BA1810, dn11 (Norwich), Fellow 1812-23, p12 (Nor.), MA1813. PC. Badwell Ash, Suffolk 1823-47. Died (Streatham, London) 26/5/1855 aged 67 [C114281] Married Coltishall, Norfolk 10/3/1823 Sophia Marianne Johnston.

**NORGATE (Thomas Starling)** Born Hethersett, Norfolk 30/12/1807 (bapt. 13/1/1820), s. Thomas Starling Norgate ('man of letters and horticulturalist'; q.v. OBNB) and Mary Susan Randall. Caius, Cambridge 1826, BA1832, dn32 (Nor.), p32 (Nor.). PC. Briningham, Norfolk 1832-5, R. Sparham, Norfolk 1840 to death 25/11/1893, leaving £27,585-0s-0d. [C114284. Boase] Married Beeston Regis, Norfolk 1838 (3rd q.) Mary Caroline Roxalana Woodrow, with issue.

**NORMAN (Charles Manners Richard)** Born Leatherhead, Surrey 8/7/1799, s. Richard Norman, *M.P.*, and Lady Elizabeth Isabella Manners (dau. of 4th Duke of Rutland). St John's, Cambridge 1817, MA1821, dn24 (Ely), p24 (Lin. for Ely). V. St Alban St Peter, Herts. 1824-33, R. Northwold, Norfolk 1833 to death 10/1/1873, leaving £10,000 [C71601] Married 20/8/1841 Caroline Amelia Angerstein (dau. of an *M.P.*, 'whose collection was the nucleus of the National Gallery'). Photo. online.

**NORRIS (Charles)** Born Brabourne, Kent 12/4/1744, s. Rev. Charles Norris and Ann Kennett. Trinity, Cambridge 1762, BA1766, dn66 (London for Cant., 'His Grace being indisposed'), Fellow1767, MA1769, p70 (Peterb.). V. Shuddy Camps, Cambs. 1786-90, V. Orwell, Cambs. 1787 (only), V. Arrington, Cambs. 1787, R. Fakenham, Norfolk 1790-1833, R. Wolterton w. Wickmere, Norfolk 1791-1801, Canon of 9th Prebend in Canterbury Cathedral 1798 and V. Aylsham, Norfolk 1800 to death 16/12/1833 aged 90 (CCEd says 20/1/1834) [C100143]

**NORRIS (Dennis George)** Born Tatterford, Norfolk 13/3/1798, s. Rev. Robert Norris and Rose Gunton. Christ's, Cambridge 1817, no degree, dn22 (Peterb.), p23 (Salis.). R. Belaugh w. Scottow, Norfolk 1829-30, V. Kessingland, Suffolk 1830 to death 19/5/1865, leaving £16,000 [C87195] Married Portsea, Hants. 1/10/1825 Mary Pellew Wallis, w. issue.

**NORRIS (Frederick)** From Yorks. Queens', Cambridge 1826, BA1830, dn30 (C&L for Ely), p31 (Roch. for Ely), MA1833. R. Little Gransden, Cambs. 1831-56, V. Dunham, Notts. 1854 to death 28/2/1856 [C18410] Had issue.

**NORRIS (George Poole)** From Minehead, Devon, s. Rev. John Norris. Exeter, Oxford 1811 (aged 19), then St Catharine, Cambridge 1813, dn15 (Ex.), p16 (Ex.). R. East Anstey, Devon 1816 to death 24/3/1869 aged 76, leaving £80,000, living at Roscraddoc House, St Cleer, Cornwall [C146015] Married St Cleer 18/9/1823 Mary Ann Marshall, with issue. Made a fortune out of mining in Cornwall; but was absentee.

**NORRIS (Henry Handley)** Born City of London 14/1/1771, s. Henry Handley Norris (a Russia merchant) and Grace Hest (a clergy dau.). Pembroke, Cambridge 1788, then Peterhouse 1789, BA1793, MA1796, dn96 (Peterb.), p00 (Peterb.), incorporated at Oxford 1817. PC. Hackney St John, London 1809-31, then R. 1831-50, Prebend of St Dubritius in Llandaff Cathedral 1816, Holbourn Prebend in St Paul's Cathedral, London 1825 to death. Dom. Chap. to 8th Earl of Shaftesbury 1812. Died 4/12/1850 [C110649. ODNB] Married 19/6/1805 Henrietta Catherine Powell, with issue. 'Rumour secured for him the title of the Bishopmaker. From 1793-1834 he largely ruled the proceedings of the S.P.C.K.'

**NORRIS (William)** Bapt. Warblington, Hants. 28/6/1795, s. Rev. William Norris and Mary Ann Gilbert. Trinity, Oxford 1812, BA1816, dn18 (Heref.), MA1819, p19 (Salis.). (succ. has father as) R. (and patron) of Warblington 1827-64, RD South East Droxford 1846. Died 21/1/1893, leaving £29,572-1s-7d. [C82445] Wife Emily, and issue.

**NORTH (Charles Edward)** Born Hampstead, London 29/10/1780, s. Fountain North (Rougham, Norfolk) and Arabella Strutt. Trinity, Cambridge 1798, BA1802, dn03 (Win.), p04 (Win.), MA1805. R. Portland, Dorset 1811-35, R. Childe Oakford, Dorset 1815 to death. Dom. Chap. to Bridget, Viscountess Torrington. Died (unm.) 16/4/1863, leaving £60,000 [C53457]

**NORTH (Francis, 6th Earl of Guilford)** Born Chelsea, London 17/12/1772, s. Rt. Rev. Brownlow North (Bishop of Winchester) and Henrietta Maria Bannister. Christ Church, Oxford 1790, then St Mary Hall, BA and MA 1797. R. Old Alresford w. New Alresford and Medstead, Hants. (and Preacher through-out the Diocese) 1797-1850 (forced to resign), R. Southampton St Mary, Hants. 1797-1850, Master of the Hospital [almshouses] of St Cross, Winchester 1808-61, Canon of 5th Prebend in Winchester Cathedral 1802-27 (res.). Dom. Chap. to 3rd Baron Holland 1797. Died Waldershare Park, Kent 29/1/1861 aged 88, leaving £200,000 [C74032] Married (1) 20/2/1798 Esther Harrison (a clergy dau., she d.1823), *s.p.* (2) Kilmeston, Hants. 4/5/1826 Harriet G. Warde (w) (a military dau.), with issue. Assumed title 1827.

**NORTH (Henry)** Bapt. Harlow, Essex 25/7/1787, s. Rev. Edward Roper North and Catherine Styleman (a clergy dau.). Caius, Cambridge 1806, BA1810, dn10 (Nor.), p11 (Nor.), MA1813. V. Ringstead St Peter w. St Andrew (or Great Ringstead), Norfolk 1811 and V. Heacham, Norfolk 1812 [blank in ERC] to death (at the Castle Inn, Downham Market, Norfolk) 15/6/1837 aged 49 [C114292]

**NORTHCOTE (Hugh)** Bapt. Upton Pyne, Devon 26/1/1774, s. Rev. Hugh Northcote and Elizabeth Bradford. Sidney, Cambridge 1791, BA1796, dn97 (Ex.), p97 (Ex.). PC. Dowland, Devon 1797-1839 and R. Monkhampton, Devon 1797-1839 (both family livings), R. Upton Pyne 1811-20, V. Okehampton, Devon 1817. Died (Hannaford, Devon) 26/7/1839 [C146016] Married Swimbridge, Devon 12/4/1804 Ann Lewis Southcombe (a clergy dau.), *s.p.* Doubtless related to the man below.

**NORTHCOTE (Stafford Charles)** Born Upton Pyne, Devon 13/7/1806, s. Sir Stafford Henry Northcote, 7th Bart. and Jacquetta Baring. Balliol, Oxford 1816, BA1819, dn20, p21 (Salis.), MA1821. R. Upton Pyne 1821 to death 19/4/1872 aged 66, leaving £3,000 [C87203] Married Westminster, London 22/4/1830 Elizabeth Helena Robbins, with issue. Doubtless related to the man above.

**NORTON (Eardley)** Bapt. Holborn, London 31/11/1781, s. Eardley Norton and Mary Swinnerton. University, Oxford 1801, Fellow 1801-9, BA 1805, dn07 (Ox.), p08 (Ox.), MA 1808. V. Arncliffe, Yorks. 1809-35, PC. Blythborough w. Walberswick, Suffolk 1816 to death (Little Stanmore, Middx.) 26/1/1835 aged 55 [C37232] Married Southwold, Suffolk 14/12/1815 Frances Mary, dau. Sir Charles Blois, 6th Bart., with issue.

**NORTON (William Addington)** Son of John Bradbury Norton and Mary Selby. Christ's, Cambridge 1815, BA1819, dn19 (Nor.), p20 (Nor.), MA1826. V. and R. Skenfrith, Monmouth 1827-30, R. Eyke, Suffolk 1830-56, R. Alderton, Suffolk 1830 to death 24/6/1856 aged 61 [C4388] Married (1) Hambledon, Herts. 13/8/1823 Eleanor Douglas Fox (d.1824), with issue (2) Alderton, Suffolk 9/11/1839 Elizabeth Mary Weeding.

**NORWICH (Bishop of)** see under **BATHURST (Henry)**

**NORWOOD (George)** Born Mersham, Kent 16/10/1780, s. Rev. Edward Norwood and Sarah Young. Oriel, Oxford 1797, BA1801, dn03 (B&W for Cant.), p04 (Roch. for Cant.), MA 1825. R. Sevington, Kent 1831, R. Mersham 1840 to death 24/5/1876 aged 95, leaving £1,400 [C2040] Married Canterbury 17/9/1813 Anne Norwood [sic], with issue.

**NOSWORTHY (Stephen)** Bapt. Manaton, Devon 28/6/1773, s. Stephen Nosworthy [pleb] and Joan Ley. St Mary Hall, Oxford 1792, BA 1796, dn96 (Ely), p97 (Ely), MA1813. R. Brushford, Som. 1811 to death. Dom. Chap. to 2nd Earl of Carnarvon 1811. Died 8/1/1835 (CCEd says 26/1/1835) [C41681]

**NOTT (Edward)** Born Widham, Cricklade, Wilts. 15/3/1774 (bapt. Bath), s. Capt. John Neale Pleydell Nott, *R.N.*, and Catherine Andrews. Oriel, Oxford 1793, dn98 (unspecified bishop for Win.), p98 (Chich. for Win.). R. Weeke (Wyke), Hants. 1816 to death 22/4/1842 [C82451] Married Hallow, Worcs. 10/4/1799 Mary Crane, with issue (incl. 2 generals). Port. miniature online.

**NOTT (George Frederick)** Bapt. Westminster, London 10/6/1768, s. Rev. Samuel Nott and Augusta Hawkins. Christ Church, Oxford 1784, BA1788, then All Souls, Fellow to 1814, dn91 (Ox.), MA1792, p92 (Ox.), BD1802, DD 1807. V. Upchurch, Kent 1798-9, R. Wistanstow, Shropshire 1799-1806, V. Broadwindsor, Dorset 1807-13, Fittleworth Prebend in Chichester Cathedral 1799-1802, then Colworth Prebend 1802-32, Canon of 12th Prebend in Winchester Cathedral 1810-41, R. Harrietsham, Kent 1813 and R. Woodchurch, Kent 1813 (w. Prebend of Torleton in Salisbury Cathedral 1814) to death 25/10/1841 [C37235. ODNB] *F.S.A.* On 6/1/1817, while supervising repairs to the cathedral, he fell thirty feet, sustaining severe injuries to the head and from which he never fully recovered. Susbsequently he spent much time in Italy, accumulating a major collection of paintings and books (12,500 volumes).

**NOTTIDGE (John)** Born Bocking, Essex 24/5/1764, s. Josias Nottidge and Margaretta Maria Block. St John's, Cambridge 1783, BA 1787, dn88 (London), p89 (London), MA1790. R. Ashingdon, Essex 1795 and R. East Hanningfield, Essex 1798 to death. Dom. Chap. to 9th Earl of Northampton 1798. Died 21/8/1846 aged 82 [C120784] Married Bocking 26/10/1790 Ann Frances Wakeham, and had clerical son of same name in same place. Doubtless related to the man below.

**NOTTIDGE (John Thomas)** Born Bocking, Essex 23/2/1776, s. Thomas Nottidge and Ann Wall. Trinity, Cambridge 1793 [adm. Lincoln's Inn 1794] BA1797, MA1800, dn11 (London), p12 (London). R. (and patron) of Ipswich St Helen w. St Clement, Suffolk 1821-47, V. Old Newton, Suffolk 1823. Died 21/1/1847 [C114295. *A selection from the correspondence of the Rev. J.T. Nottidge ...*, edited C. Bridges (1849 and sketch)] Married Chelsea, London 7/8/1810 Louisa Robinson. Doubtless related to the man above.

**NOURSE (William)** Bapt. Liverpool 25/5/1783, s. William Nourse and Margaret Walker. St Alban Hall, Oxford 1798, BA1802, MA1808, p09 (Win.). R. Clapham, Sussex 1821 to death (Brighton) 4/4/1871, leaving £9,000 [C7647] Married Carisbrooke, IoW 16/9/1817 Jane Cadogan Gill, with issue.

**NUCELLA (Thomas)** Born London 11/5/1772, s. Timothy Nucella (a merchant) and Isabella Bolwerk (of Dutch extraction). Magdalen, Oxford 1804, then Trinity Hall, Cambridge 1807, BA1809, dn09 (Win.), p10

(Salis. for Win.), MA1812. R. Glympton, Oxon. 1818 to death 5/2/1856 [C37238] Married Elizabeth before 1810, with issue. 'A worthy man - primitive simplicity' (Wilberforce).

**NUNNS (Thomas)** From Lancaster, s. Jackson Nunns and Elizabeth Stoddart. St John's, Cambridge 1819, BA1823, dn24 (C&L), p25 (C&L), MA1834. PC. Burslem St Paul 1828-32, Curate Birmingham St Bartholomew 1833/4/5-43, PC. Leeds St Paul 1844-5, V. Leeds Holy Trinity 1846 to death 27/12/1854 [C18413] Married Birmingham 18/3/1828 Anne Smith, with clerical sons Thomas Jackson Nunns, and Robert Augustine Luke Nunns.

**NUTTALL (William)** Bapt. Deane, Bolton, Lancs. 1/4/1763, s. William Nuttall [*pleb*]. BNC, Oxford 1783, BA1789, MA1789, dn91 (Chester), p91 (Chester). PC. Swinton, Eccles, Lancs. 1791 to (burial) 5/5/1833 (CCEd says 20/7/1833) [C170130] Married Blackburn, Lancs. 25/4/1791 Betty Whalley, with issue.

**OAKELEY (Herbert, Sir, 3rd Bart.)** Born Madras 19/2/1791, s. Sir Charles Oakeley, 1st Bart. and Helen Beatson. Christ Church, Oxford 1807, BA1811, MA1813, dn14 (Ox.), p15 (London). Prebend of Gaia Minor in Lichfield Cathedral 1816-32 (res.), Mapesbury Prebend in St Paul's Cathedral, London 1816-25 (then Wenlocksbarn Prebend 1825-45), Prebend of Worcester Cathedral 1817, V. Ealing, Middx. 1822-34, 'Dean and R'. of the Peculiar of Bocking, Essex 1834-45, Archdeacon of Colchester 1841 to death. Dom. Chap. to Bishop of Londo n/ Abp of Canterbury 1814-26. Died 27/3/1845 aged 54 [C18683] Married Westminster, London 5/6/1826 Atholl Keturah (dau. Very Rev. Lord Charles Murray-Aynsley), with issue. Assumed title 1829.

**OAKES (James)** Born Bury St Edmunds, Suffolk 24/9/1769, s. James Oakes (banker) and Elizabeth Adamson. Trinity, Cambridge 1786, BA1791, dn91 (Lin. for Nor.), p94 (Ely for Nor.), MA1795. V. Tostock, Suffolk 1796, R. Rattlesden, Suffolk 1808-61, V. (and patron) of Thurston, Suffolk 1812. Died 28/1/1861, leaving £50,000 [C71658] Married 16/10/1792 Elizabeth Tyrell (a clergy dau.), with issue.

**OAKLEY (Francis)** From Dorchester, Dorset, s. Francis and Mary Oakley. Magdalen Hall, Oxford 1818 (aged 30), dn19 (Salis. for Bristol), SCL, p21 (Salis. for Bristol). PC. Chaldon Herring, Dorset 1822, V. Bradpole, Dorset [C52146] 1835 to death 6/10/1843 [C53461] Married Owermoigne, Dorset 17/12/1809 Mary Ingram, with issue.

**OATES (John)** Literate: dn79 (York), p79 (York). PC. Winksley w. Grantley, Yorks. 1779 and PC. Sawley, Ripon 1783 to death 30/7/1836 aged 82 [C105797. YCO] Married (2) 1791 Mary Hodgson, with issue.

**OBINS (Archibald Eyre)** Born Castle Obins, Portadown, Co. Armagh 1776, s. Michael Obins and Hon. Nichola Acheson (dau. 1st Viscount Gosford). TCD1793, then Exeter, Oxford 1797, BA1799, MA1811. R. Hemingford Abbots, Hunts. 1811. Lived in Birkenhead, Cheshire. Died Bath 6/1/1868, leaving £14,000 [C71664. Al.Dub.] Had issue. Sold his Irish estates c.1814.

**OGILVIE (Charles Atmore)** Born Whitehaven, Cumberland 20/12/1793, s. John Ogilvie and Catharine Curwen. Balliol, Oxford 1811, BA1815, Fellow 1816-34, dn17 (Ox.), MA1818, p18 (Ox.), Tutor 1819-30, etc., (first) Regius Professor of Pastoral Theology, Oxford 1842. R. Wickford, Essex 1822-33, V. Abbotsley, Hunts. 1822-39, V. Dulow, Cornwall 1833-40, R. and V. Ross on Wye, Heref. 1839 [income in CR65 £1,100] and Canon of Christ Church Cathedral, Oxford 1849 to death. Dom. Chap. to Bishop of London / Archbishop of Canterbury 1834. Died 17/2/1873, leaving £6,000 [C37247. ODNB. Boase. In J.M. Chapman, *Reminiscences of three Oxford worthies* (1875)] Married Dinder, Som. 18/4/1838 Mary Anne Gurnell Armstrong, 2 dau.:
https://en.wikipedia.org/wiki/Charles_Atmore_Ogilvie

**OGLE (Edward Chaloner)** Born Kirkley Hall, Northumberland 7/8/1798, s. Rev. John Saville Ogle and Catherine Hannah Sneyd. Merton, Oxford 1816, BA1820, dn23 (Salis.), MA1823, p23 (Salis.). V. Sutton Benger, Wilts. 1824, Prebend of Gillingham Major in Salisbury Cathedral 1828 to death 7/11/1860 at Kirkley Hall, leaving £70,000 [C85946] Married Westminster, London 17/8/1830 Sophia Ogle [*thus*], with issue.

**OGLE (James)** Bapt. King's Worthy, Hants. 6/1/1778, s. Admiral Sir Chaloner Ogle, 1st Bart. and Hester Thomas (dau. of a Bishop of Winchester). Merton, Oxford 1794, BA1798, MA1801. R. Bishops Waltham, Hants. 1802, V. Crondall, Hants. 1811-33, V. Hartley Mauditt, Wilts. at death. Dom. Chap. to 3rd Earl of Abingdon 1803. Died 19/5/1833 (CCEd says 7/6/1833) [C82523] Married Farnham, Surrey 26/12/1807 Elizabeth Poulter, with issue.

**OKELL, O'KELL (George)** Bapt. Weaverham, Cheshire 29/11/1763, s. George Okell and Mary Barker. BNC, Oxford 1783, BA1787, dn87 (Chester), p90 (Chester), MA1815. PC. Witton, Northwich, Cheshire 1818 to death (Hartford, Cheshire) 6/3/1833 aged 69 (CCEd says 5/5/1833) [C170140]

**OKES (William)** Bapt. King's Lynn, Norfolk 9/6/1777, s. Thomas Okes (physician) and Rebecca Lydia Butcher. Caius, Cambridge 1797, BA1802, Fellow 1804-33, MA1806, dn07 (unspecified bishop for Nor.), p07 (Lin. for Ely), etc. R. Wheatacre w. Mutford and Barnby, Suffolk 1832 to death 12/7/1858, leaving £3,000 [C71809] Married Carshalton, Surrey 26/9/1833 Augusta Butcher (w).

**OLDACRES (Samuel)** Born South Wingfield, Derbys. 20/2/1763, s. Rev. Richard and Alice Oldacres. Emmanuel, Cambridge 1780, BA 1784, dn85 (York), MA1787, p87 (York). R. Gonalston, Notts. 1811-39. Died there 8/11/1842 [C121732. YCO] Married Gonalston 30/11/1807 Mary Lealand, with clerical son.

**OLDERSHAW (John)** Born Leicester 27/5/1754, s. James Oldershaw (an apothecary) and Elizabeth Wrightman. Emmanuel, Cambridge 1771, BA1776 [Senior Wrangler], Fellow 1778, MA1779, dn82 (Peterb.), p83 (Peterb.), Tutor 1783-93, BD1786. R. Ludham, Norfolk 1795-1833, R. Redenhall w. Harleston, Norfolk 1798-1847, V. Ranworth, Norfolk 1795-1842, Archdeacon of Norfolk (w. R. Coston, Norfolk appended) 1797 to death 31/1/1847 [C1099] Married Maddingley, Cambs. 23/10/1793 Anne Hinde Cotton. Note a contemporary namesake.

**OLDHAM (John)** Bapt. Shirland, Derbys. 19/5/1761, s. Thomas Oldham and Dorothy Johnston. Legal training - 'a clerical lawyer'. St John's, Cambridge 1780, BA1784, dn84 (C&L), p85 (C&L), MA1789. R. (and patron) of Stondon Massey, Essex 1791 and R. (and patron) of Aythorpe Roding >< Essex 1791 to death Dom. Chap. to 5th Duke of Argyll 1791. Died 21/1/1841 aged 79 [C18708] Married (1) Ormskirk, Lancs. 12/1/1785 Hannah Oldham [*thus*] (d.1792), w. issue (2) Ann --, and child. J.P. for Essex for 30 years. Capability Brown laid out the rectory garden. Online entry and port.

**OLIVE (John)** Born Frome, Som. 16/2/1800, s. Edward Olive and Betty Crabb. Wadham, Oxford, BA1819, BA1822, dn23 (Lin.), p24 (Lin.), MA1825. V. Hellingly, Sussex 1830 to death 27/2/1866, leaving £5,000 [C64723] Married Hellingly 6/5/1837 Emma Cumberbatch (w), with many ch.

**OLIVE (John)** Born Clifton, Bristol 4/4/1804, s. John Olive and Sarah Ames. Worcester, Oxford 1820, BA 1826, dn27 (Lin.), MA1829, p30 (Lin.). R. Ayot St Lawrence, Herts. 1830 to death (Wheathampstead House, Herts.) 3/1/1874, leaving £25,000 [C71897] Married Bath 18/8/1831 Ellen Brown (w), with issue.

**OLIVER (George)** Born Papplewick, Notts. 5/11/1782, s. Rev. Samuel Oliver (R. Lambley, Notts.) and Elizabeth Whitehead. Literate: dn13 (Lin.), p14 (Lin.), then Trinity, Cambridge 1814 (a Ten Year Man), DD1835 (Lambeth). S/M Caistor G/S, Lincs. 1803-9, then H/M King Edward's G/S Grimsby 1809-31; V. Clee, Lincs. 1815-35, V. Scopwick, Lincs. 1831-67, PC. Wolverhampton Collegiate Church 1834-46 (and Prebend there), R. South Hykeham, Lincs. 1847 to death. Dom. Chap. to 2nd Baron Kensington 1820. Died Lincoln 3/3/1867 aged 67, leaving £1,500 [C71837 says parentage wrong in Venn. ODNB. Boase. Kaye. R.S.E. Sandbach, *Priest and freemason: the life of George Oliver* (1988)] Married 1805 Mary Ann Beverley, 5 ch. Antiquarian; major masonic figure and writer. Photo. online: www.masonicdictionary.com/oliver.html

**OLIVER (Samuel)** Bapt. Gotham, Notts. 16/8/1801, s. Rev. Samuel, sen. ('one of the most distinguished and learned of English freemasons') and Elizabeth Oliver. Literate: dn25 (York), p26 (York). V. Calverton, Notts. 1827-74, V. Kneesall, Notts. 1827-30. Died Calverton 26/11/1874 aged 73, leaving £200 [C135666. YCO. Venn under his father. Austin 2] Married Radford, Notts. Frances Duke Holmes (w), with issue.

**OLIVER (William)** St John's, Cambridge 1820, re-adm. 1821 (a Ten Year Man), dn22 (Chester), p23 (Chester). PC. Fulford (in Stone), Staffs. 1824 and PC. Barlaston, Staffs. 1834 to death (Tittensor, Staffs.) 20/12/1870, leaving £600 [C18712] Had issue.

**OLIVIER (Daniel Josias)** Born Swainswick, Somerset 26/4/1789, s. Rev. Daniel Stephen Olivier (R. Clifton, Beds.) and Margaret Harriet Arnold (a clergy dau.). Clare, Cambridge 1809, BA1813, dn14 (Ely for Win.), p14 (London for Win.). R. Clifton 1827 to death (Moorcroft House, Hillingdon, Middx.) 12/2/1858, leaving £25,000 [C71902] Married St. Botolph without Bishopsgate, City of London 20/6/1815 Sarah Elizabeth Chambers (w) (of Newcastle upon Tyne), with issue.

**OMMANNEY (Edward Aislaby)** Born Mortlake, Surrey 13/9/1806, s. Sir Francis Molyneux Ommanney, *M.P.*, and Georgiana Frances Hawkes. Exeter, Oxford 1824, BA 1827, dn29 (London for Cant.), MA1830, p30 (Cant.). PC. Mortlake, Surrey 1832, V. Chew Magna, Som. 1841-78 (and RD of Chew 1850), Prebend of Combe V1 in Wells Cathedral 1848 to death (Bath) 21/1/1874, leaving £404-7s-8d. [C120804] Married Wandsworth, London 15/7/1841 Anna Catherine de Hochepied Larpent (w), (dau. of a baronet), with issue.

**ONSLOW (Arthur)** Born Ockham, Surrey 30/12/1773, s. Lt.-Col. George Onslow, *M.P.*, and Jane Thorp. Merton, Oxford 1791, BA 1795, dn97 (Ox.), MA1798, p98 (Ox.). R. Chevening, Kent 1803-13, R. Brook, Kent 1804, R. Merrow, Surrey 1812, R. Crayford, Kent (and Preacher throughout the Diocese of Canterbury) 1813 to death. Dom. Chap. to 5th Earl of Newburgh 1804. Died 29/11/1851 aged 77 [C37254] Married (1) Reigate, Surrey 25/8/1803 Marianna Campbell (d.1810), with issue (2) St James's, Piccadilly, London 17/6/1815 Caroline Mangles, w. clerical s. Henry John Onslow. Brother George Walton, below. Port. online.

**ONSLOW (Arthur Cyril)** Born Oxford 8/7/1788, s. Very Rev. Arthur Onslow (Dean of Worcester) and Frances Phipps. Christ Church, Oxford 1805, Student [Fellow] 1805-13, BA 1809, MA1811. R. Newington St Mary, Surrey [net income in CR65 £1,300] 1812 to death (Wantage, Berks.) 6/2/1869. No will traced [C158840] Married August 1812 Elizabeth Winnington (dau. of a baronet), with clerical son Thomas George. Brother Richard Francis, below.

**ONSLOW (George Walton)** Born Ockham, Surrey 25/6/1768, s. Lt.-Col. George Onslow and Jane Thorp. Christ Church, Oxford 1785, BA 1792, dn92 (Lin. for Win.), p92 (Ox.), MA 1793. V. Send and Ripley, Surrey 1792, V. Shalford, Surrey 1800, R. Wisley, Surrey 1806 and R. Pyrford, Surrey 1806 to death. Dom. Chap. to 7th Earl of Wemyss 1800-6. Died Ripley 13/2/1844 aged 75 [C37255] Married St Pancras, London 8/7/1800 Elizabeth Campbell, w. military issue. Brother Arthur, above.

**ONSLOW (Middleton)** Born 18/11/1774, s. Middleton Onslow, *M.P.*, and Anne Barrett. King's, Cambridge 1791, BA1799, dn06 (Win.), p06 (Win.). R. Bradford Peverell, Dorset 1814 to death 26/1/1837 aged 63 (influenza) [C53465] Married Hackney, London 16/7/1802 Matilda Boddington, with clerical son.

**ONSLOW (Richard Francis)** Born Reading, Berks. 16/1/1776, s. Very Rev. Arthur Onslow (Dean of Worcester) and Frances Phipps. Christ Church, Oxford 1793, BA1797, dn00 (Ox.), MA 1800, p00 (Ox.). R. Mordiford, Heref. 1801-4, V. Kidderminster, Worcs. 1801 [net income £1,107], Prebend of Beminster Prima in Salisbury Cathedral 1803-23, R. Newent, Glos. 1803 [net income £1,076] Prebend of Putson Minor in Hereford Cathedral 1804-8, Archdeacon of Worcester 1815-49, Prebend of Highworth in Salisbury Cathedral 1823 and R. Stoke Edith w. West Hide, Glos. 1834 to death. Dom. Chap. to Bishop of Lichfield, then Worcester 1801-4; to 5th Viscount Barrington 1816. Died 18/10/1849 [C37256] Married 7/7/1801 Harriet Mary Foley, with issue. Brother Arthur Cyril, above.

**ORCHARD (George Randall)** Bapt. Bath Abbey, Som. 11/4/1792, s. Abraham Orchard and Martha Bishop. Magdalen Hall, Oxford 1816, no degree, dn16 (Salis.), p17 (Salis.). PC. North Bradley (o/w Bradley Christ Church), Wilts. 1826 to death 21/6/1850 [C87208] Married Eliza Hooper, and issue (inc. dau. Xarifa Zara Orchard).

**ORD (Craven)** Born Holborn, London 16/3/1785, s. Craven Ord (antiquary, *q.v.* ODNB) and Mary Smith Redman. University, Oxford 1803, BA1807, dn08 (Win.), p09 (Win.), MA1811. V. Lincoln St Mary le Wigford (*sometimes* Wigtoft) 1809-46, V. Gretton, Northants. 1811-14 (res.), PC. Little Horkesley, Essex 1825-9 (res.). Dom. Chap. to 2nd Marquess Cornwallis 1811. Died (Clifton, Bristol) 14/12/1836 aged 50; living at Greenstead House, Essex (his mother's home) [C134463] Married Greenstead 29/12/1813 Margaret Blagrave, with issue. Doubtless related to the man below.

**ORD (Henry Craven)** Bapt. Fornham, Suffolk 9/9/1778, s. Rev. John Ord and Mary Norman. Trinity, Oxford 1800, BA1802, dn02 (Nor.), p03 (Nor.). V. Wheathampstead, Herts. (and Preacher throughout the Diocese of Lincoln) 1811-14, Prebend of Gretton in Lincoln Cathedral 1810-40, V. Gretton, Northants. 1814-19 (res.), V. Stratfield Mortimer, Berks. 1819 to death 1/8/1840 [C71907] Married Woodbridge, Suffolk 7/11/1805 Mary Anne Roper. Doubtless related to the man above.

**ORD (Ralph)** Bapt. Sunderland, Co. Durham 30/8/1762, s. of Ralph Ord and Mary Davison. Christ Church, Oxford 1788, BA1791, dn93 (Ox.), p94 (Ox.), MA1794, Student [Fellow] to 1813. PC. Tring, Herts. 1800-2 (res.), PC. Great Torrington, Devon 1806-12, PC. St Giles in the Wood Chapel, Devon 1806-17, PC. Hawkhurst, Kent/Sussex 1807-12, R. Semley, Wilts. 1812 to death. Dom. Chap. to 9th Baron Arundell 1820.

Died 15/9/1855 [C37258] Married Sunderland 13/8/1786 Ann Coulson, and had issue.

**ORD (Thomas Charles)** Bapt. Marylebone, London 24/6/1794, s. Rev. James Ord (Langton Hall, Leics.) and Barbara Brandling. University, Oxford 1812, BA1815, dn18 (Lin.), MA 1819, p19 (Lin.). V. King's Norton (o/w Norton by Gaulby), Leics. 1826 and R. Gaulby, Leics. 1826 to death (Boulogne) 6/10/1844 [C71910] Married Stainsby, Lincs. 21/12/1830 Elizabeth Penfold.

**ORDE (John)** Bapt. Whatton, Northumberland 28/10/1770, s. John Orde, *R.N.*, and Rosamond Dalgleish. Lincoln, Oxford 1788, BA1792, dn93 (Lin.), p94 (Lin.), MA1800. V. Kingsclere, Hants. 1796-1817 (and S/M 1797), R. Winslade, Hants. 1811-50, R. Itchen Stoke w. Abbotstone, Hants. 1817-29, V. Herriard, Hants. 1829-30, R. Wensley, Middleham, Yorks. [net income £1,337] 1829 to death (IoW) 13/1/1850 aged 79 [C71911] Married Kingsclere 24/8/1802 Hon. Frances Carleton, dau. 1st Lord Dorchester, with issue.

**ORGILL** see also under **LEMAN**

**ORLEBAR (Cuthbert)** Born 1808 Hinwick House, Podington, Beds., s. Richard Orlebar and Maria Longuet. Christ's, Cambridge 1826, dn30 (Lin.), BA1831, p32 (Lin.). V. Podington 1832 to death ('of fever, at his residence The Park, Nottingham') 1/8/1861, leaving under £600 [C71914] Married Marylebone, London 31/3/1838 Eleanor Kingston (w), with issue. Port. online.

**ORMAN (Charles [Joseph] Joshua)** Bapt. Mildenhall, Suffolk 25/6/1795, s. Rev. Nathan Orman and Elizabeth Andrews. Trinity, Cambridge 1812, then Sidney 1815, BA1818, dn18 (Ely), p19 (Nor.), MA1823. PC. Shouldham w. Shouldham Thorpe, Norfolk 1832 to death 5/9/1847 [C109346] Married Mildenhall 18/7/1826 Elizabeth Bucke, with issue.

**ORMANDY (John)** Possibly bapt. Aldingham, Cumberland 13/5/1792, s. Thomas Ormandy and Dorothy Bolton. Literate: dn15 (Car.), p16 (Car.). R. Greystoke, Cumberland 1815-22, PC. Thwaites, Millom, Cumberland 1822 (sequestrated) to death 16/5/1846 aged 54 [C5710] Married Greystoke 14/2/1819 Mary Wilkinson (an innkeeper's daughter?), with issue.

**ORME (Robert)** Born 20/10/1760, s. Capt. Robert Orme (of Devonshire and Bergham, North Brabant, Netherlands) and Hon. Audrey Townshend (dau. of 3rd Viscount Townshend). Trinity, Cambridge 1778, BA, MA1782, dn84 (Peterb.), p85 (Nor.). V. South Creake, Norfolk 1785-6, V. Toftrees, Norfolk 1785-8, V. Layston w. Buntingford. Herts. 1786-91, R. and V. Hertford All Saints w. St John, Herts. 1786-1843, R. Essendon, Herts. 1790 to death. Chap. in Ordinary 1790; Dom. Chap. to 2nd Marquess Townshend 1784. Died 23/10/1843 aged 83 [C71916] 'Note that he had a fear of being buried alive; therefore, he was buried with a key, and there is a keyhole on the West side of his tomb'.

**ORRETT (William Green)** Born Warrington, Lancs., s. (possibly foster son?) William Orrett and Ann Green. BNC, Oxford 1802 (aged 18), BA1805, dn12 (Chester), p13 (C&L), MA1815. R. (and patron) of Standish, Lancs. [net income £1,874] (and Preacher throughout the Diocese of Chester) 1826 to death (but sequestrated for debt 1834) 12/6/1841 aged 58 ('after a very long illness') [C18713] Married (1) Church Eaton, Staffs. 12/6/1809 Catharine Crockett (d.1829), w. issue (2) Farnworth, Prescot, Lancs. 17/5/1832 Mary Anne Crompton.

**ORTON (Francis)** Born Leicester 3/5/1797, s. Francis Orton and Maria Clayton. St Mary Hall, Oxford 1817, BA1821, dn21 (Lin.), p22 (Lin.), MA1824, BCL and DCL1833. V. Hope, Derbys. 1829, Incumbent Altrincham, Cheshire at death 4/2/1862, leaving £10,000 [C32589] Married Burton-on-Trent, Staffs. 12/8/1823 (Mary) Ann Teasdale (w), w. clerical s. Frederick Orton.

**OSBORNE (George, sen.)** Bapt. Godmanstone, Dorset 25/2/1765, s. Rev. George and Mary Osborne. Merton, Oxford 1782, BA1786, dn87 (Peterb.), p96 (Peterb.), then Clare, Cambridge, MA1799. V. Whissendine, Rutland 1802-3, R. Stainby w. Gunby, Lincs. 1803-25 (res.), V. Hungarton w. Twyford and Thorpe Satchville >< Leics. 1809-23, R. Haselbeach, Northants. 1822 to death. Dom. Chap. to Eleanor, Countess of Harborough 1809; to 6th Earl of Harborough 1818. Died 29/10/1839 [C110653. Bennett2] Married Eltham, Kent Mary Elizabeth Latham, with clerical son, below.

**OSBORNE (George, jun.)** Bapt. Teigh, Rutland 15/9/1801, s. Rev. George Osborne, sen. (above) and Mary Elizabeth Latham. St John's, Cambridge 1820, BA1824, dn24 (Lin.), p25 (Lin.), MA1828. R. Stainby w. Gunby, Lincs. 1825 (and Canon w. Prebend of Welton Rival in Lincoln Cathedral 1869) to death (London) 3/7/1871, leaving £30,000 [C71926. Bennett2] Married Stamford, Lincs. 18/2/1834 Frances Maurice (w) (a clergy dau.).

**OSBORNE (Sidney Godolphin, Lord)** Born Stapleford, Cambs. 5/2/1808, s. Francis, 1st Baron Godolphin and Hon. Elizabeth Charlotte Eden (dau. of 1st Baron Auckland). BNC, Oxford 1824, BA1830, dn31 (Lin.), p32 (Lin.). V. Stoke Poges, Bucks. 1832-41, R. Durweston w. Bryanston >< Dorset 1841-75. Died Pelham House, Lewes, Sussex 9/5/1889 aged 81, leaving £12,601-8s-10d. [C71958. ODNB. Boase] Married St George's Hanover Square, London 29/5/1834 Emily Charlotte Grenfell (Taplow Court, Bucks.), with clerical son Riversdale Brinsley Godolphin Osborne. His brother inheriting the Dukedom of Leeds, 'S.G.O.' (as he was known) was granted the rank of a Duke's son 1859. A letter-writer to *The Times* for forty years on such matters as free trade, education, women's rights, sanitation, cattle plague, and cholera. 'During the Crimean War, he made an unofficial inspection and aided the improvement of the hospitals under Florence Nightingale's care ... With respect to Ireland he was a Unionist, and in church matters an anticlerical. Agricultural labourers were a particular interest'. Photo. online. Excellent article at: www.dorsetlife.co.uk/2010/12/a-nobler-sense-of-duty/

**OSTREHAN (Joseph Duncan)** Born Barbados, West Indies, *c.*1801, s. Joseph Ostrehan. Worcester, Oxford 1818, dn21 (London), BA1822, p22 (London). PC. Sheepscombe, Glos. 1828, V. Creech St Michael, Som. 1851 to death (Teignmouth, Devon) 11/9/1870, leaving £4,000 [C114860. LBSO]) Married London 13/6/1822 Ann Withy, with issue.

**OTLEY (Charles Bethel)** From London, s. Richard Otley. Wadham, Oxford 1809 (aged 17), BA1813, dn14 (C&L for Win.), p16 (Ely for Chich.), MA1822. V. Tortington, Sussex 1817, R. Welby, Lincs. 1833 to death 11/7/1867, leaving £5,000 (left unadministered) [C18714] Married 7/9/1823 Maria Delafield (w).

**OTTER (Edward)** Born Cuckney, Notts. 15/4/1764, s. Rev. Edward Otter, sen. and Dorothy Wright. Jesus, Cambridge 1781, BA 1786, dn86 (Glos.), Fellow 1787-99, MA1789, p92 (Ely). V. All Saints, Cambridge 1797-8, V. Bolsover, Derbys. 1798-1818 (and Chap. to his patron the Duke of Portland), V. Elmstead, Essex 1798-1810, Chap. of the Donative of Cotham w. Sibthorp, Notts. 1806, Prebend of Ulleskelf in York Minster 1808-37, R. Bothal, Northumberland 1810 [income £1,484] to death (Sheepwash, Northumberland) 3/2/1837 [C18718] Married (1) Mansfield, Notts. 29/8/1799 Amelia Stanton, w. issue (2) Woodhorn, Northumberland 22/8/1811 Alice Gresswell, widow of Rev. George Smalbridge, of Bothal. J.P. Durham and Northumberland. Brother William, below.

**OTTER (John)** Bapt. Clayworth, Notts. 6/4/1767, s. John Otter (farmer) and Barbara Turner. Corpus Christi, Cambridge 1814, BA 1820, dn20 (Glos. for London), p21 (York), MA1843, V. Ranby, Lincs. 1824-41, V. Ludford Magna, Lincs. 1843 to death 2/5/1854, *s.p.* [C71928. YCO]

**OTTER (William, *later* Bishop of Chichester)** Born Cuckney, Notts. 23/10/1768, s. Rev. Edward Otter and Dorothy Wright. Jesus, Cambridge 1785, BA1790, dn91 (Glos. for York), MA1793, Fellow 1796-1804, p97 (Ely), Tutor. S/M Helston, Cornwall 1791-6; travelled with Malthus in Northern Europe 1799; R. Colmworth, Hunts. 1804-10, R. Sturmer, Essex 1799-1811, R. Chetwynd, Shropshire 1811, V. Alrewas, Staffs. 1811-18, V. Kinlet, Shropshire 1816, R. Kensington St Mark, London 1825, first Principal of King's College, London 1830-6, Bishop of Chichester 1836 to death. Dom Chap. to 4th Viscount Torrington 1804; to 4th Duke of Portland 1816. Died (Broadstairs, Kent) 20/8/1840 [C18719. ODNB. YCO] Married 3/7/1804 Mary Sadleir Bruère (dau. of a Governor of Bengal), with clerical son, below. One of the founders of Chichester Training College ('Bishop Otter College'). Brother Edward, above.

**OTTER (William Bruère)** Born 28/5/1805, s. William Otter (Bishop of Chichester, above) and Mary Sadleir Bruère. Peterhouse, Cambridge 1824, BA1828, dn28 (Peterb.), p29 (Win.), MA 1838. PC. Coverham w. Horsehouse, Yorks. 1830-2, V. Eyeworth, Beds. 1832-36, Chap. to the British Factory at Amsterdam 1833, V.

Kinlet, Salop 1837-47, V. Cowfold w. Horsham, Sussex 1839-76, Prebend of Somerley in Chichester Cathedral 1850 and Archdeacon of Lewes 1855 to death 25/6/1876 aged 71, leaving £4,000 [C71929. Boase] Married The Hague 18/5/1837 Elizabeth Melvil (w), dau. of the British Consul, Amsterdam, with issue.

**OUTRAM (Thomas Powys)** Born Cambridge 27/4/1802, s. Rev. Edmund Outram and Beatrice Postlethwaite. St John's, Cambridge 1820, BA1825, dn26 (Lin. for York), p27 (C&L for York), MA1830. R. Sturmer, Essex 1827-8, R. Redmile, Leics. 1828 to death 12/5/1853 [C18723. YCO] Married Worksop, Notts. 31/7/1827 Ann Hodgkinson, with issue.

**OVERTON (John, sen.)** Bapt. Monk Fryston, Yorks. 10/5/1763, s. George Overton. Magdalene, Cambridge 1785, BA1790, dn90 (Win. for York), p91 (York), MA1803. R. & V. York St Margaret Walmgate w. St Peter le Willows 1802 w. R. St Crux in Fossgate 1802 to death 17/7/1838 [C105808. ODNB. YCO] Married Reeth, Yorks. 1792 Elizabeth Stoddart, 12 ch. (his eight sons all being over six feet tall and some clerical, *q.v.* next two men).

**OVERTON (John, jun.)** Bapt. York 14/5/1795, s. Rev. John Overton, sen. (above) and Elizabeth Stoddart. S/M York Free School 1812; Trinity. Cambridge 1814, dn19 (Ex. for York), BA1820, p20 (York), MA1823. V. Elloughton w. Thormanby, Yorks. 1820-41, PC. Bilton in Holderness, 1824-36, R. Sessay, Yorks. 1836 to death 18/11/1879 aged 85, leaving £8,000 [C135669. YCO] Brother, below.

**OVERTON (William)** Bapt. York 30/1/1803, s. Rev. John Overton, sen. (above) and Elizabeth Stoddart. Trinity, Cambridge 1821, BA1826, dn26 (Lin. for York), p27 (York), MA1829. R. Full Sutton, Yorks. 1827 to death 1834 [C71932. YCO] Brother, above.

**OWEN (Charles Gustavus)** Born London 20/4/1801, s. Rev. Henry Butts Owen and Elizabeth Susanna Travers. Queen's, Oxford 1819, BA1823, dn24 (Ex.), p25 (Bristol), MA 1835. R. Dodbrooke, Devon 1828-37, R. Loddiswell, Devon 1837, R. Pinxton, Derbys. 1864 to death 18/9/1879 aged 73, leaving under £450. Dom. Chap. to Earl of Strafford [C140627] Married (1) St George's Hanover Square, London 21/5/1823 Elizabeth Sarah Hicks (d.1827), 1 dau. (2) Susannah Harrington Burnard, 2 ch.

**OWEN (Edward)** Born Montgomery 1/1/1783, s. David Owen and Mary Blayney. Trinity, Cambridge 1802, then Corpus Christi 1804, BA 1806, dn07 (B&W for Cant.), MA1809. PC. of the Donative of Aston Clinton St Leonard Bucks. 1811-63, Professor of Rhetoric, Gresham College, London 1817 to death (Sedlescombe, Sussex) 1/3/1863, leaving £5,000. Chap. to HRH Duke of York 1816 [C140627]] Married St Pancras, London 29/5/1817 Katherine Sutton, w. clerical son Edward Owen, jun.

**OWEN (Edward)** [MA but NiVoF - cannot disambiguate]. PC. Walmer, Sussex 1819-33, V. Chislet, Sussex 1819-33, Prebend of Llanwrthwl in Brecon Collegiate Church 1827-33, Archdeacon of St David's (w. Prebend of Meidrim) 1831 to death. Dom. Chap. to 2nd Earl of Liverpool 1819. Died 21/5/1833 (CCEd thus) [C132523]

**OWEN (Edward Henry [Mostyn])** Born Felton, Shropshire, s. Rev. William Mostyn Owen and Rebecca Dod. Christ Church, Oxford 1802 (aged 18), BA1806, then All Souls 1809-17, dn09 (Ox.), MA1810, p10 (Ox.). R. Cound, Shropshire 1816 to death 28/11/1838 [C18726] Married Bartholmey, Cheshire 8/1/1821 Elizabeth Sophia Hinchliffe, w. issue.

**OWEN (Edward Pryce)** Born Shropshire 3/3/1788, s. Rev. Hugh Owen and Harriet Jeffreys. St John's, Cambridge 1806, BA1810, dn11 (C&L), p12 (C&L), MA1816. R. and V. Wellington w. R. Eyton, Shropshire 1823-40. Lived for many years at Cheltenham, and latterly at Bettws Hall, Monmouth, dying 15/7/1863, leaving £180,000 [C18727. ODNB. Boase] Married Madeley, Shropshire 6//12/1825 Mary Darby Wright (of Colebrookdale, dau. of the artist Samuel Wright). An artist himself.

**OWEN (Henry)** Son of Rev. Hugh Owen, sen. (below) and Elizabeth Williams. Magdalene, Cambridge 1823 (aged 19), BA1827, dn27 (Nor.), p28 (Nor.), MA1830. R. (and patron) of Wilby, Suffolk 1831-8, R. Heveningham, Suffolk 1837 to death 1876. Will not traced. Dom. Chap. to Earl of Stradbroke [C114319] Married (1) Stoke Ash, Suffolk 5/2/1828 Louisa Long Stutter (2) 4/12/1851 Annie Gilbert (dau. of a

Cornish *M.P.*), with possible issue. *J.P.* Suffolk and Norfolk.

**OWEN (Henry Butts)** Born City of London 11/7/1763, s. Rev. Henry Owen (*M.D., F.R.S., q.v.* ODNB) and Mary Butts (dau. of a Bishop of Ely). St John's, Oxford 1780, Fellow 1783, BA1784, dn86 (Ox.), p07 (Ox.), MA1788, BD 1793, DD1805. (succ. his father as) R. St Olave Hart Street, City of London 1794 [net income £1,891] and R. Throcking, Herts. 1831 to death (Highgate, London) 29/11/1837 aged 75 [C37265] Married (2) City of London 18/10/1798 Elizabeth Susannah Travers, with issue. *J.P.* Middx. Described as this 'tithe scraper'.

**OWEN (Hugh)** From Soho, London, s. John Owen. Jesus, Cambridge, MA, migrated to Jesus, Oxford 1784 (aged 35?), BD and DD1790, p10 (S&M). S/M Stowmarket G/S, Suffolk 1806; S/M Beccles School, Suffolk 1813; PC. Stoven, Suffolk 1814, R. Beccles 1823 (w. PC. Great Redisham 1824-30 (res.)). Died 15/11/1854 [C7648. Not in Venn] Married Elizabeth Williams, w. clerical son Henry, above. Some dates wrong here.

**OWEN (John)** [BA by 1803 but unclear in V or F]. V. Milwich, Staffs. 1803-[49] ('resides Denbigh'). Died? [C18731]

**OWEN (Richard Evan)** From Churchstoke, Montgomery, s. Rev. Evan Owen. BNC, Oxford 1806 (aged 17), BA1810, MA1813, p13 (Heref.). PC. Hyssington, Shropshire 1822 and R. Snead, Shropshire 1834 to death 1/3/1870. Will not traced [C171307]

**OWEN (William)** From St James, London, s. William Owen. Christ Church, Oxford 1818 (aged 19), then St Alban Hall, BA1823. R. Stratton-on-the-Fosse, Som. 1823 to death 6/8/1858 aged 61. No will traced [C64452] Married Stowey, Somerset 21/5/1819 Sarah Raindle.

**OWSLEY, OUSLEY (John)** Born Hallaton, Leics. 29/5/1742, s. John Owsley (apothecary) and Ann Foxton. Queen's, Oxford 1761, then Merton, BA1765, dn65 (Lin.), p65 (Lin.). Chap. of the Donative of Blaston St Giles, Leics. 1767 to death there 26/7/1835 [C71971] Married (1) Kibworth Beauchamp, Leics. 14/11/1785 Elizabeth Wright (2) 4/4/1810 Catherine Mason Read, w. issue.

**OXENDEN (Montague)** Born Barham, Kent 4/5/1799, s. Sir Henry Oxenden, 7th Bart. and Mary Graham. Exeter, Oxford 1817, BA1821, dn22 (York), p23 (Lin. for Cant.), MA1824. R. Wingham, Kent 1825, R. Luddenham, Kent 1827-78, R. Eastwell, Kent 1837 to death 25/1/1880. No will traced [C124193. YCO] Married (1) Bildeston, Suffolk 26/2/1824 Elizabeth Wilson (d.1862), with issue (2) Westminster 3/8/1869 Elizabeth Goodyer.

**OXFORD (Bishop of)** see under **BAGOT Richard**

**OXNAM, OXENHAM (William)** Bapt. Madron, Cornwall 3/12/1770. Oriel, Oxford 1789, BA1794, dn94 (Ex.), p95 (Ex.), MA1798. Prebend in Exeter Cathedral 1803-44, R. (sequestrator) Exeter St Kerrian w. St Petrock 1803-44, R. Peter Tavy, Devon 1823 (and Preacher throughout the Diocese 1824) to 1844, V. Cornwood, Devon 1824. Died 23/2/1844. Dom. Chap. to Bishop of Exeter/St Asaph 1821 [C146029] Married Camborne, Cornwall 6/7/1805 Jane Michell, w. child.

www.ingramcontent.com/pod-product-compliance
Lightning Source LLC
Chambersburg PA
CBHW050717090526
44588CB00014B/2317